Shanshan Lü
A Reference Grammar of Caijia

Sinitic Languages of China

Typological Descriptions

Edited by
Hilary Chappell

Volume 8

Shanshan Lü
A Reference Grammar of Caijia

An Unclassified Language of Guizhou

DE GRUYTER
MOUTON

ISBN 978-3-11-163170-7
e-ISBN (PDF) 978-3-11-072480-6
e-ISBN (EPUB) 978-3-11-072488-2
ISSN 2365-8398

Library of Congress Control Number: 2022939098

Bibliographic information published by the Deutsche Nationalbibliothek
The Deutsche Nationalbibliothek lists this publication in the Deutsche Nationalbibliografie; detailed bibliographic data are available on the internet at http://dnb.dnb.de.

© 2024 Walter de Gruyter GmbH, Berlin/Boston
This volume is text- and page-identical with the hardback published in 2022.
Cover image: Waseda University Library, Tokyo, Japan
Typesetting: Integra Software Services Pvt. Ltd.

www.degruyter.com

The preface by the series editor

This impressive volume by Shanshan Lü 吕珊珊 represents the first major descriptive grammar of the endangered language, Caijia. Prior to this publication, only two or three sketches of Caijia phonology and lexicon were at hand, these being published in Chinese language journals. They already pointed to the fact that Caijia is an intriguingly conservative and archaic language. As Volume 8 in the series on *Sinitic languages of China*, the grammar illuminates the innumerable special features of this little-known language, spoken by a few small communities high up in the terraced mountains of Guizhou province in southwestern China.

Shanshan Lü became a member of my ERC SINOTYPE team from 2010-2013, and played an active role in this research project focusing on the typology of the languages of China and on diachronic change. In 2011, after successfully obtaining her Master's degree in *Sciences du langage* at the Université-Lumière in Lyon, she qualified to take up her doctoral studies at one of the *grands établissements* of France, the *Ecole des Hautes Etudes en Sciences Sociales* (EHESS Graduate School in Social Sciences) in Paris, gaining her PhD diploma in 2020.

The comprehensive description which she has undertaken has great significance not only for the typology of Sino-Tibetan and Southeast Asian languages in general, but also for determining the precise linguistic affiliation of Caijia within this family. Caijia is claimed to represent one of the first splits from the ancestral tree of Sino-Tibetan. The very topical issue of language contact also comes into play in her research, given that Caijia has been in close contact with the neighbouring Tibeto-Burman language, Yi.

For the research on Caijia, Dr. Lü carried out five extensive fieldwork trips to Guizhou province in China between 2012 and 2018, each of two months' duration, mainly working in the county seat of Hezhang 赫章 with funding from both the EHESS and the *Centre de recherches linguistiques sur l'Asie orientale* (CRLAO, Research Centre for East Asian Languages) in Paris. Her data include not only elicited material but also traditional stories, ballads and narratives about different customs and festivals, important for the preservation of Caijia culture. These include healing rituals and descriptions of traditional immunization methods for which the expertise of the Caijia became renowned in Guizhou and which serve as an important aspect of the intangible heritage of China's rich and diverse culture.

In 2020, Dr Lü took up the position of research professor in the newly established Institute of Corpus Studies and Applications at the Shanghai International Studies University 上海外国语大学 where she continues to work on both Caijia and Naxi, a Tibeto-Burman language.

Sinitic languages of China: Typological descriptions is a book series specializing in the description of the grammar of Sinitic languages, 'Sinitic' being the technical term for the Chinese branch of the Sino-Tibetan language family. As such, it includes the national language of China, *Pǔtōnghuà* 普通话, known as Standard Chinese or Mandarin in English, other well-known languages outside China such as Cantonese 广东话, Hokkien or Southern Min 闽南话, Shanghainese 上海话 and Hakka 客家话, as well as the lesser-known languages, including Hunanese Xiang 湘语, the Jin languages 晋语 of Shanxi, and Pinghua 平话 of Guangxi. Even Mandarin comes in many non-standardized forms including the Sichuanese variety of Southwestern Mandarin 西南官话 spoken in Chengdu, the Southern Jiang-Huai Mandarin 江淮官话 of Nanjing, the Central Plains Mandarin 中原官话 of Xi'an, not to overlook the typologically unusual varieties spoken in Gansu and Qinghai in northwestern China, such as Tangwang 唐汪话, Gangou 甘沟话 and Linxia 临夏话 which are case-marking languages with verb-final word order.

The primary goal of this series is to promote scientific knowledge of Sinitic languages and their typological characteristics through the publication of high calibre linguistic research, based on empirical fieldwork, detailed analysis of the data and solid, theoretical interpretations. The grammatical descriptions, written in a functionalist and descriptive framework, are illustrated by linguistic examples presented in a 'value-added' four-line format that includes romanization, glossing, the idiomatic English and Chinese translations, the latter useful for our sinophone readers.

The specific objective is to reveal the great structural diversity found in Sinitic languages and to dispel many recurrent clichés about Chinese. The authors involved in this series are all highly trained fieldwork linguists with a background in both typology and Chinese linguistics.

The series thus aims to reach an international readership for the first time, given that most literature available on Sinitic languages other than Mandarin, up until now, has been mainly written in the medium of Standard Written Chinese.

The large-scale research project, *The hybrid syntactic typology of Sinitic languages* (SINOTYPE), provided the initial impetus behind this series. SINOTYPE benefitted from funding in the form of an Advanced Grant (No. 230388) awarded by the European Research Council (ERC) for the period 2009 – 2013. The host institute, the Ecole des Hautes Etudes en Sciences Sociales (EHESS), graciously provided managerial support and accounting resources, not to mention spacious premises for the SINOTYPE research centre in inner-city Paris, at 2, rue Küss in the 13th arrondissement, for the entire period of the project. We take this opportunity to express our many thanks to both the ERC and the EHESS.

The other volumes planned for this series are:

Volume 2: *A grammar of Nanning Pinghua*, by Hilário de Sousa

Volume 4: *A grammar of Central Plains Mandarin*, by Yujie Chen

Volume 6: *A reference grammar of Jixi Hui*, by Wang Jian

Volume 7: *A grammar of Waxiang, a Sinitic language of northwestern Hunan*, by Hilary Chappell

H.M. Chappell
Series Editor
Paris, 2022

Acknowledgements

The present piece of work could not have been realized without the help of many people to whom I am indebted.

First and foremost, I would like to express my deep gratitude to my supervisor Professor Hilary M. Chappell, who has guided, encouraged and supported me, showing endless tolerance of my ignorance and limited knowledge in linguistics and without whom my research could never have progressed this far. It has been a great honor to be her PhD student. Her enthusiasm and joy for research on Sinitic languages has been inspiring and motivational for me. Even though my interest has always been endangered languages, thanks to her, I realized how fascinating and diverse Sinitic languages can be. It is also she who opened the door to a brand-new world of research for me and who led me towards a broader path in my studies.

I would also like to acknowledge Professor Alain Peyraube for his generous advice and support on my thesis, my research papers, and academic activities, as well as on my future career. He enriched my thoughts greatly with his expertise in Chinese diachronic syntax and semantics.

I would like to express my appreciation to my school, École des Hautes Études en Sciences Sociales (EHESS), and my affiliated research center, Centre de Recherches Linguitiques sur l'Asie Orientale (CRLAO), for sponsoring my field trips to Xingfa Township in Hezhang county of Guizhou Province in China, and my other academic activities all over the world. My gratitude also goes to Chiang Ching-Kuo Foundation for International Scholarly Exchange (CCKF) for granting me the Doctoral Dissertation Fellowship for the year 2015 (DD027-U-13). It was indeed a great honor. I am also profoundly grateful to the China Scholarship Council (CSC) for granting me the 2019 Chinese Government Award for Outstanding Self-Financed Students Abroad. I acknowledge the Xingfa Township government for their generous accommodation and reception when I was in my field trips. The finalization of this grammar is also financed by the project 'Caijiahua Yufahua Wenti Yanjiu' [Investigation on grammaticalization in Caijia] (project number: 41004525/001).

I would like to thank all my consultants, Mr. Li Wentai, Mr. Li Kaiju, Ms. Li Xingzhi, Mr. Chen Weixian and Ms. Zhao Guozhen as well as their lovely families, who kindly taught me the Caijia language and their culture with patience and shared with me their life experiences. Without these data the present grammar could have never been finished.

Living and studying in Paris was a fantastic experience in my life. I was lucky to have many friendly colleagues working together in a lovely office right on the famous rive gauche of Seine at Rue de Lille. I thank, in particular, HE Lisha, with whom I often share my moments of inspiration, for proofreading my draft papers. I also thank Sara Mortaji for her kind offer of polishing my French when I was still an M. A. student in Lyon. I am glad that she is on the path of becoming what she wants herself to be.

I would like to thank Ms. Kirstin Börgen at De Gruyter Mouton, Mr. GENG Mengzhe, Miss ZOU Yidan and Miss LIU Yichen for their editorial help.

A special thanks goes to the Waseda University Library for authorizing me to use the illustration of Caijia as the cover of this book.

Finally, I would like to thank my family for their unconditional support, love and encouragement. I am so lucky to have them.

Thank you all!

Preface

On the front cover of this book is an illustration of the Caijia people, an excerpt from *Mán Miáo Tú Shuō* 蛮苗图说 [A picture book of Hmong] compiled by Chen Hao during 1796-1820 in the Qing Dynasty of China. A brief description about Caijia customs is provided in this illustration.

蔡家苗在贵筑修文清镇威宁平远等州县，男子衣毡衣，女则制毡为髻，缘饰青布，高尺许，若牛角，以长簪绾之，翁媳不通言，居丧三月不食稻肉，惟饭稗粥，犹存古礼，夫死以妇殉，若外家抢去则免

Càijiā miáo zài guìzhù, xiūwén, qīngzhèn, wēiníng, píngyuǎn děng zhōu xiàn, nánzǐ yī zhānyī, nǚ zé zhì zhān wéi jì, yuán shì qīng bù, gāo chǐ xǔ, ruò niújiǎo, yǐ cháng zān wǎn zhī, wēng xí bù tōng yán, jū sāng sān yuè bù shí dào ròu, wéi fàn bàizhōu, yóu cún gǔ lǐ, fū sǐ yǐ fù xùn, ruò wàijiā qiǎngqù zé miǎn.

Hmong people of Caijia are distributed across Guizhu, Xiuwen, Qingzhen, Weining, Pingyuan. The Caijia men wear clothes made of felt. Each Caijia woman uses felt to make a bun several inches' high in the shape of horn on the top of her head, which is decorated with a blue cloth and is fixed by a long hairpin. Daughters-in-law and their fathers-in-law are not supposed to speak with each other. The people of Caijia follow ancient rituals. They do not eat rice or meat during the three months of mourning but are only allowed to have millet porridge. A Caijia woman is not supposed to live alone, once her husband dies. She should follow her husband in death, unless she is taken away by a member of her parents' family.

The original copy of *Mán Miáo Tú Shuō* is now archived in the Waseda University Library and the digital copy can be accessed in the Kotenseki Sogo Database (Japanese & Chinese Classics).

Contents

The preface by the series editor —— V

Acknowledgements —— IX

Preface —— XI

List of figures —— XXIII

List of tables —— XXV

Abbreviations —— XXVII

Chapter 1
Introduction —— 1
1.1 Background —— 1
1.2 Previous research —— 4
1.3 Data and methodology —— 4
1.4 Basic features —— 6
1.5 Organization of the grammar —— 12

Chapter 2
Sound system —— 14
2.1 Introduction —— 14
2.2 Onsets —— 14
2.2.1 Plosives —— 15
2.2.1.1 Bilabial plosives [p], [pʰ], and [b] —— 16
2.2.1.2 Alveolar plosives [t], [tʰ], and [d] —— 18
2.2.1.3 Retroflex plosives [ʈ], [ʈʰ], and [ɖ] —— 20
2.2.1.4 Velar plosives [k], [kʰ], and [g] —— 24
2.2.2 Affricates —— 25
2.2.2.1 Alveolar affricates [ts], [tsʰ], and [dz] —— 26
2.2.2.2 Alveolo-palatal affricates [tɕ], [tɕʰ], and [dʑ] —— 28
2.2.3 Other consonants —— 29
2.2.3.1 Nasals [m, n, ŋ] —— 29
2.2.3.2 Fricatives [s, z, ɕ, ʑ, f, v, x, ɣ, h] —— 30
2.2.3.3 Lateral approximant [l], lateral retroflex [l̠ɖ], and lateral fricative [ɬ] —— 31
2.2.4 Discussion —— 32

2.3	Rimes —— 33	
2.3.1	Monophthongs —— 33	
2.3.2	Diphthongs —— 34	
2.3.3	Rimes of nasal codas —— 35	
2.3.4	Syllabic consonants —— 36	
2.4	Tones —— 36	
2.5	Conclusion —— 44	

Chapter 3
Noun phrases —— 45

3.1	Introduction —— 45
3.2	Demonstratives —— 46
3.3	Nouns —— 49
3.3.1	Distributional features of Caijia nouns —— 50
3.3.2	Noun formations —— 53
3.3.2.1	Compounds —— 53
3.3.2.1.1	Modifier-head compounds —— 54
3.3.2.1.2	Head-modifier compounds —— 56
3.3.2.1.3	Conjunct compounds —— 56
3.3.2.1.4	(S)VO compounds —— 56
3.3.2.2	Suffixation —— 57
3.4	Pronouns —— 59
3.4.1	Personal pronouns —— 60
3.4.2	Possessives —— 62
3.4.2.1	Pronominal possessives —— 63
3.4.2.2	Adnominal possessives —— 64
3.4.3	Reflexive pronoun and reciprocal expressions —— 68
3.4.4	Indefinite pronouns —— 71
3.4.4.1	Q-ever —— 71
3.4.4.2	Negative 'any one', 'anything', and 'anybody' —— 74
3.4.4.3	'Some' —— 75
3.4.4.4	'All' —— 76
3.5	Numerals, classifiers, and measure words —— 76
3.5.1	Numerals —— 77
3.5.2	Classifiers and measure words —— 78
3.6	Place words, localizers, and time words —— 92
3.6.1	Place words and localizers —— 92
3.6.2	Time words —— 97
3.7	Headless noun phrase —— 100

Chapter 4
Verb phrases —— 104
4.1	Introduction —— 104
4.2	Verbs —— 104
4.2.1	Distributional features of verbs —— 105
4.2.1.1	Common features —— 105
4.2.1.2	Distinctive features of adjectives —— 108
4.2.1.2.1	Attributive adjectives —— 109
4.2.1.2.2	Vivid forms: A-BB —— 112
4.2.1.2.3	Derivational adverbs —— 116
4.2.2	Copular, locative and existential verbs —— 119
4.2.2.1	Copula —— 119
4.2.2.2	Locative verb —— 123
4.2.2.3	Existential and possessive verb —— 125
4.2.3	Resultative complements —— 127
4.2.3.1	General achievement complements —— 128
4.2.3.2	Directional complements —— 133
4.2.3.2.1	Type i: [V-V$_{PATH}$(-V$_{DEICTIC}$)] —— 134
4.2.3.2.2	Type ii: [V-V$_{DEICTIC}$] —— 137
4.2.3.2.3	Type iii: [V-xɯ^{55}] —— 138
4.2.3.2.4	Beyond directions —— 139
4.2.4	Extent and manner complementation —— 142
4.2.5	Quadrisyllabic descriptive phrases —— 145
4.3	Adverbs —— 151
4.3.1	Manner adverbs and adverbials —— 152
4.3.2	Degree adverbs —— 154
4.3.3	Adverbs of time —— 156
4.3.4	Scope adverbs —— 159
4.4	Verbal classifiers —— 160
4.4.1	Instrument verbal classifiers —— 162
4.4.2	Mensural verbal classifiers —— 165
4.4.3	Double classifiers —— 169
4.5	Prepositions —— 171
4.5.1	The preposition ta^{55} —— 173
4.5.2	The prepositions di^{33}, dza^{33}, and tsʰɔ^{21} —— 174
4.5.3	The preposition tsaŋ^{33} 'along' —— 176
4.5.4	The preposition a^{33} 'with' (instrumental)/OM —— 176
4.5.5	The preposition dʐ^{33} and a^{21}sɿ^{55} —— 177
4.5.6	The preposition tɯ^{21} 'at, to' —— 177
4.5.7	The preposition pie^{55} 'to' —— 178

4.5.8	The preposition $sɿ^{55}$ 'to' —— 180
4.6	Conclusion —— 181

Chapter 5
Ditransitive constructions —— 183

5.1	Definition and typology —— 183
5.2	Caijia ditransitive constructions —— 184
5.2.1	Double object construction [V + R + T] —— 185
5.2.2	Indirective construction [V + T + $sɿ^{55}_{DAT}$ + R] —— 187
5.2.3	Differential object marking constructions —— 193
5.2.4	Two other minor constructions —— 196
5.3	Conclusion —— 198

Chapter 6
Analytic causative constructions —— 200

6.1	Introduction —— 200
6.2	Overview of Caijia causation —— 201
6.3	Caijia analytic causative constructions —— 203
6.3.1	Type I extent complement causative —— 204
6.3.2	Type I pivot-causee causatives —— 207
6.3.2.1	Source constructions and the two causative verbs —— 207
6.3.2.2	Type IIa —— 211
6.3.2.3	Type IIb —— 216
6.4	Conclusion —— 218

Chapter 7
Passive constructions —— 219

7.1	Definition and Sinitic typology —— 219
7.2	Passives in Caijia —— 220
7.2.1	VPs in passives —— 222
7.2.2	Type I suffer: dy^{33} '(passively) receive, suffer, hit the target' —— 226
7.2.2.1	Source of dy^{33} —— 226
7.2.2.2	Part of speech and source construction of dy^{33} passives —— 233
7.2.3	Type II let: $a^{21}sɿ^{55}$ 'take-give ~ give/let' —— 237
7.2.4	Syntactic and semantic differences between dy^{33} and $a^{21}sɿ^{55}$ —— 240
7.3	Conclusion —— 241

Chapter 8
Differential object marking constructions —— 243
8.1 Definition and Sinitic typology —— 243
8.2 Caijia object marking constructions —— 245
8.2.1 Source of the object/cross-reference marker —— 246
8.2.2 Type 1 common disposal: (NP$_{SUBJECT}$) – MARKER$_{OM}$ – NP$_{OBJECT}$ – VP —— 247
8.2.3 Type 2 cross-reference marking: (NP$_{OBJECT}$) – (NP$_{SUBJECT}$) – MARKER$_{DCR}$ – VP —— 252
8.2.4 Type 3 double marked: (NP$_{OBJECT}$) – (NP$_{SUBJECT}$) – MARKER$_{DCR}$ – VP —— 259
8.3 Conclusion —— 262

Chapter 9
Constructions of comparison —— 263
9.1 Introduction —— 263
9.2 Parameter of comparison —— 264
9.3 Equative constructions —— 266
9.3.1 Types A and B: Equatives with conjoined referents and comitative equatives [CMP STM ST DEGR PARA] —— 269
9.3.2 Types C: Equatives with only a degree marker [CMP V ST DEGR PARA] —— 273
9.3.2.1 Degree marker $sɿ^{21}$ 'way' —— 274
9.3.2.2 Differences between 'reach'-type and 'resemble'-type —— 280
9.3.3 Conclusion —— 284
9.4 Inferior comparatives —— 285
9.5 Superior comparatives —— 288
9.5.1 Type A: Prepositional comparatives —— 290
9.5.2 Type B: Surpass comparatives —— 292
9.5.3 Type C: Zero-marked comparatives —— 295
9.5.4 Type C: Comparatives with the verbal classifier mi^{55} as a degree marker —— 296
9.5.5 Concluding remarks —— 299
9.6 Conclusion —— 300

Chapter 10
Aspect system —— 302
10.1 Introduction —— 302
10.2 Aspect in Caijia —— 304
10.2.1 Perfective (negated) [pɣ̍^{33}-tɣ̍^{33} VP] —— 306

10.2.2	Completive [VP ha⁵⁵] —— **311**	
10.2.3	Currently relevant state [VP o] —— **314**	
10.2.4	Inchoative [VP kʰɯ⁵⁵ɣɯ²¹ ~ xɯ⁵⁵ɣɯ²¹] —— **317**	
10.2.5	Experiential —— **322**	
10.2.5.1	*ja²¹* [VP ja²¹] —— **322**	
10.2.5.2	*gua³³* [VP gua³³] —— **326**	
10.2.6	Prospective [niɔ³³ VP] —— **327**	
10.2.7	Delimitative [VP mi⁵⁵] —— **330**	
10.2.8	Continuous [sɿ³³ VP sɿ²¹] —— **334**	
10.2.9	Continuous (manner) [VP lɛ⁵⁵] —— **340**	
10.2.10	Durative [VP-xɯ⁵⁵] —— **345**	
10.2.11	Frequentative [kʰā⁵⁵ VP] —— **349**	
10.3	Conclusion —— **352**	

Chapter 11
Modal system —— 354

11.1	Introduction —— **354**
11.2	Modal auxiliaries [AUX VP] —— **356**
11.2.1	*kʰā⁵⁵* 'be willing to' —— **358**
11.2.2	*ɕiaŋ⁵⁵* 'want' —— **359**
11.2.3	*niɔ³³* 'want, need' —— **360**
11.2.4	*niɔ³³dʐ³³* 'need' —— **366**
11.2.5	*tɕʰiɔ²¹* 'be necessary' —— **368**
11.2.6	*ti³³* 'know' —— **370**
11.3	Lexical epistemic possibility: *tsʰŋ³³* 'fear' and *dzɔ³³* 'resemble' —— **376**
11.3.1	*tsʰŋ³³* 'fear' —— **376**
11.3.2	*dzɔ³³* 'resemble' —— **381**
11.4	Post-VP 'can' modals —— **383**
11.4.1	*do³³* 'can' [VP do³³] and *tɣ³³ . . . do³³* 'can' [tɣ³³ VP do³³] —— **385**
11.4.1.1	*do³³* 'can' [VP do³³] —— **385**
11.4.1.2	*tɣ³³ . . . do³³* 'can' [tɣ³³ VP do³³] —— **391**
11.4.2	*tɣ³³* 'can' [VP tɣ³³] —— **393**
11.4.3	Conclusion —— **400**
11.5	Potential construction [V lɯ⁵⁵ VP] —— **403**
11.6	Modal adverbs —— **405**
11.7	Epistemic final particle: ɔ *pa* [S VP ɔ pa] —— **406**
11.8	Epistemic certainty: [S (sɿ³³) VP sɿ²¹] —— **407**
11.9	Reportative/quotative: *xa³³* < 'say' [(S) VP xa³³] —— **410**

11.10	Inferential certainty: Experiential *ja²¹* and *gua³³* [(S) VP ja²¹/gua³³] —— 412	
11.11	Conclusion —— 413	

Chapter 12
Negation —— 415

12.1	Introduction —— 415
12.2	Negation in Caijia —— 416
12.2.1	Negative existential and possessive verb —— 417
12.2.2	Standard negation —— 418
12.2.2.1	General and volitional negation: *pɣ³³* 'not' —— 418
12.2.2.2	Perfective negation: *pɣ³³-tɣ³³* 'not-obtain' —— 421
12.2.2.3	Post-VP negative possibility and negative potential —— 423
12.2.2.4	Negators in negative imperatives —— 424
12.2.2.4.1	General prohibitive: *piɔ²⁴ < pɣ³³ niɔ³³* 'not want' —— 424
12.2.2.4.2	Lack of necessity: *pɣ³³tɕʰiɔ²¹* 'not necessary' —— 425
12.3	Conclusion —— 426

Chapter 13
Interrogatives —— 427

13.1	Introduction —— 427
13.2	Alternative questions and the disjunction *lɔ²¹* 'or' —— 428
13.3	Polar questions —— 431
13.3.1	Alternative polar questions —— 431
13.3.1.1	Juxtaposition [VP (DISJ) NEG VP] —— 432
13.3.1.2	Reduced [VP (DISJ) NEG] —— 434
13.3.2	Particle polar questions [VP Q] —— 436
13.3.2.1	Particle *la²¹* [VP la²¹] —— 436
13.3.2.2	Particle *ɔ²¹sɛ⁵⁵* [VP ɔ²¹sɛ⁵⁵] —— 440
13.3.2.3	Particle *mo³³* [VP do³³/tɣ³³ mo³³] —— 440
13.4	Content questions —— 442
13.4.1	'Which' questions —— 443
13.4.2	'Who' questions —— 445
13.4.3	'Whose' questions —— 447
13.4.4	'What' questions —— 447
13.4.5	'Where' questions —— 449
13.4.6	'When' questions —— 450
13.4.7	'How (manner)' and 'why' questions —— 451
13.4.8	'How many/much' questions —— 455
13.5	Conclusion —— 457

Chapter 14
Relative clauses — 459

14.1 Definition and typology — 459
14.2 Relative clauses in Caijia — 461
14.2.1 Strategies of relativization in Caijia — 463
14.2.2 Types I and II headed relative clauses — 464
14.2.2.1 Heads of headed relative clauses and orders of modifiers — 464
14.2.2.2 Relativized subjects and direct objects — 467
14.2.2.3 Relativized genitives — 469
14.2.2.4 Relativized indirect objects and obliques — 470
14.2.3 Type III headless relative clauses — 475
14.2.4 Aspectual restrictions — 478
14.3 Conclusion — 479

Chapter 15
Clause linking: Complementation, coordination and adverbial subordination — 481

15.1 Introduction — 481
15.2 Complementation — 482
15.3 Coordination — 486
15.3.1 Conjunction — 487
15.3.1.1 Argument conjunction [CONJ ta⁵⁵ CONJ] — 487
15.3.1.2 Clause conjunction — 489
15.3.1.2.1 Emphatic conjunction — 490
15.3.1.2.2 Correlative simultaneous construction [NP ʑi²¹hɔ⁵⁵ VP$_1$ ʑi²¹hɔ⁵⁵ VP$_2$] — 497
15.3.1.2.3 Correlative comparative construction [NP$_1$ dzɔ³³ VP$_1$, NP$_2$ dzɔ³³ VP$_2$] — 499
15.3.1.3 Concluding remarks — 500
15.3.2 Disjunction — 501
15.3.2.1 Standard disjunction [[NP$_1$/VP$_1$] xuɔ²¹tsɛ⁵⁵ [NP$_2$/VP$_2$]] — 501
15.3.2.2 Interrogative disjunction [[NP$_1$/VP$_1$] lɔ²¹/(x)a²¹sɿ³³ [NP$_2$/VP$_2$]] — 503
15.3.2.3 Emphatic disjunction — 504
15.3.2.4 Concluding remarks — 506
15.3.3 Contrastive coordination — 507
15.4 Adverbial subordination — 511
15.4.1 Time clauses — 511
15.4.1.1 Temporal sequence — 512
15.4.1.2 Before and after — 516
15.4.1.3 S<small>INCE</small> — 519

15.4.1.4	When —— 520	
15.4.2	Consequence and cause —— 523	
15.4.2.1	Consequence —— 524	
15.4.2.1.1	$tɯ^{33}$-consequence —— 524	
15.4.2.1.2	$(lɛ^{21})tsʰɛ^{21}$-consequence —— 526	
15.4.2.2	Cause —— 527	
15.4.3	Conditional —— 529	
15.4.3.1	Sequence/effect: $tɯ^{33}$ and $(lɛ^{21})tsʰɛ^{21}$ —— 530	
15.4.3.1.1	$tɯ^{33}$-effect —— 530	
15.4.3.1.2	$(lɛ^{21})tsʰɛ^{21}$-effect —— 531	
15.4.3.2	$nɛ^{55}/\emptyset$-condition —— 532	
15.4.3.3	$kʰã^{55}$-condition —— 535	
15.4.3.4	$tsʰɛ^{21}niɔ^{33}$-condition —— 537	
15.4.3.5	$niɔ^{33}sɿ^{33}$-condition —— 538	
15.4.3.6	$niɔ^{33}pɣ^{33}sɿ^{33}$-condition —— 539	
15.4.3.7	$tɯ^{33}sa^{21}$-concessive condition —— 541	
15.4.3.8	$pɣ^{33}sɿ^{33}$-condition —— 541	
15.4.3.9	Summary —— 543	
15.4.4	Concession —— 544	
15.4.4.1	$pɣ^{21}kuɪŋ^{55}$-concessive —— 545	
15.4.4.1.1	No matter (Indefinite) —— 546	
15.4.4.1.2	Although —— 547	
15.4.4.2	$tɯ^{33}$-concessive —— 548	
15.4.5	Substitutive clauses (preferred option) —— 550	
15.4.6	Tail-head linkage —— 552	
15.5	Conclusion —— 554	

Chapter 16
Conclusion —— 556

Text 1 —— 559
The man and the tiger —— 559

Text 2 —— 568
The zombie wife —— 568

Bibliography —— 575

Index —— 593

List of figures

Map 1.1 Xingfa Caijia —— 5
Figure 10.1 Binary opposition of aspect (Comrie 1976: 25) —— **302**

List of tables

Table 1.1	Linguistic diversity in Bijie Prefecture —— 3	
Table 1.2	Percentage of cognates among Caijia and other languages —— 4	
Table 1.3	Caijia within the linguistic area of MESA (1) —— 11	
Table 1.4	Caijia within the linguistic area of MESA (2) —— 11	
Table 1.5	Sinitic languages —— 13	
Table 1.6	Periodization of Chinese —— 13	
Table 2.1	Inventory of Caijia onsets —— 14	
Table 2.2	Inventory of Caijia rimes —— 33	
Table 3.1	Caijia demonstratives —— 46	
Table 3.2	Caijia personal pronouns —— 60	
Table 3.3	Caijia possessive pronouns —— 63	
Table 3.4	Caijia indefinite pronouns —— 72	
Table 3.5	Caijia localizers —— 95	
Table 4.1	Path and deictic verbs in Caijia —— 134	
Table 4.2	Typology of verbal classifiers in East and Southeast Asian languages —— 161	
Table 4.3	Verbs with sortal/instrument verbal classifiers in Caijia —— 165	
Table 4.4	Mensural verbal classifiers —— 167	
Table 4.5	Prepositions in Caijia —— 171	
Table 5.1	Typology of ditransitive alignments —— 183	
Table 5.2	Ditransitive constructions in Sinitic languages —— 184	
Table 5.3	Verbs in the Caijia ditransitive constructions —— 185	
Table 5.4	Ditransitives vs. verb types —— 198	
Table 6.1	Analytic causative constructions in Caijia —— 203	
Table 7.1	Sources of Sinitic passive agent markers —— 220	
Table 7.2	Caijia passives —— 221	
Table 7.3	ZHUO/ZHU in Caijia, Middle Chinese and Southwestern Mandarin —— 227	
Table 7.4	Polysemy of dy^{33} in Caijia —— 227	
Table 8.1	Three major sources for object markers in Sinitic —— 244	
Table 8.2	Five configuration types for Sinitic object marking constructions —— 244	
Table 8.3	Caijia object marking constructions —— 245	
Table 9.1	Typology of equatives —— 267	
Table 9.2	Equative types in Sinitic languages (Chappell 2017) —— 267	
Table 9.3	Caijia equatives —— 267	
Table 9.4	Equative constructions in Caijia —— 284	
Table 9.5	Caijia inferior comparatives —— 286	
Table 9.6	Cognitive schemata of superior comparatives —— 289	
Table 9.7	Sinitic superior comparatives —— 289	
Table 9.8	Caijia superior comparatives —— 289	
Table 9.9	Constructions of comparison in Caijia —— 300	
Table 10.1	Lexical aspect types and features —— 302	
Table 10.2	Aspect categories in Caijia —— 305	
Table 11.1	Semantic nuances of Modality —— 355	
Table 11.2	Modal elements in Caijia —— 355	
Table 11.3	Modal auxiliaries in Caijia —— 356	

https://doi.org/10.1515/9783110724806-207

Table 11.4	Post-VP 'can' modals in Caijia —— 383	
Table 12.1	Semantic typology of negation in Sinitic —— 416	
Table 13.1	Typology of Sinitic question forms —— 428	
Table 13.2	Caijia interrogatives —— 429	
Table 13.3	Caijia interrogative words —— 442	
Table 13.4	Caijia interrogatives (reproduced) —— 457	
Table 14.1	Typology of relative clauses —— 459	
Table 14.2	Strategies of relativization —— 460	
Table 14.3	Relative clauses and strategies of relativization in Caijia —— 462	
Table 15.1	Conjunctions in Caijia —— 500	
Table 15.2	Disjunctions in Caijia —— 506	
Table 15.3	Contrastive conjunctions in Caijia —— 511	
Table 15.4	Time clauses in Caijia —— 523	
Table 15.5	Consequence and cause clauses in Caijia —— 529	
Table 15.6	Conditionals in Caijia —— 544	
Table 15.7	Concessive clauses in Caijia —— 550	
Table 15.8	Substitutive clauses in Caijia —— 552	

Abbreviations

*	ungrammatical
<>	slip of the tongue
[]	unpacked fusion form
1	first person
2	second person
3	third person
A	agent
ADJ	adjective
ADV	adverbial
AFF	affirmative
AG	agent marker
AUX	auxiliary
CLF	classifier
CONT	continuous
COP	copula
CRS	currently relevant state
DEM	demonstrative
DCR	differential cross-reference marker
DOM	differential object marker
DUR	durative
EXP	experiential
FOC	focus
FP	final particle
FREP	frequentative
HON	honorific
IMP	imperative
INC	inchoative
INTJ	interjection
LOC	localizer
M	marker
MEAS	measure word
MOD	modifier linker
NEG	negator
NP	noun phrase
NUM	numeral
ONO	onomatopoeia
P	patient
PASS	passive marker
PFV	perfective
PL	plural
POSS	possessive
PROSP	prospective
PRT	clause/sentence final particle
PURP	purposive

https://doi.org/10.1515/9783110724806-208

Q	question marker
QUAN	quantifier
SAP	self-addressed pronoun
SG	singular
SW	Southwester Mandarin
REL	relativizer/relative
REP	reportative
SUF	suffix
TOP	topic marker
VCLF	verbal classifier
VP	verb phrase
VCOMP	verb complementizer

Chapter 1
Introduction

1.1 Background

Caijia 蔡家 or *meŋ²¹ni³³ŋoŋ³³* is an under-described and critically endangered language spoken by about 1,000 people in Bijie 毕节 Prefecture in the northwest of Guizhou 贵州 Province in southwestern China, as reported by the Language Team of the Bureau of Ethnic Identification in Bijie (hereafter LTBEIB 1982). The people of Caijia, numbering about 18,000, are distributed throughout Bijie, Dafang 大方, Qianxi 黔西, Zhijin 织金, Nayong 纳雍, Hezhang 赫章, and Weining 威宁 counties within Bijie Prefecture (LTBEIB 1982). See Map 1.1. In addition, they are also found in Liupanshui 六盘水 Prefecture of Guizhou as well as several neighboring counties in Yunnan 云南 Province (LTBEIB 1982).

The people of Caijia are recorded as the descendants of the State of Cai 蔡国 (11th–447 BC) and were more widely distributed than nowadays in the Ming and Qing Dynasties (1368–1912 AD). According to many local gazetteers or official historical documents, it is recorded that they were exiled to the border in the south after the State of Cai was destroyed by the State of Chu 楚国. Earlier official records can be dated back to the Ming Dynasty (1368–1644 AD). The *Dà Míng Yī Tǒng Zhì* 大明一统志 'Gazetteer of the Ming Dynasty' (Li and Peng 1461) records the following:

> 卢山长官司：......【风俗】种类非一，习俗各异。旧志本司所辖夷人类种非一曰罗罗，曰宋家，曰蔡家，......习俗各异。
>
> Lúshān zhǎngguānsī: . . . [fēngsú] zhǒnglèi fēi yī, xísú gè yì. Jiù zhì běn sī suǒxiá yírén zhǒnglèi fēi yī, yuē luóluó, yuē sòngjiā, yuē **càijiā**, . . . xísú gè yì.
>
> *Department of Lushan: . . . [Customs] Various ethnic groups with various customs. It is recorded in the former gazetteer(s) that inhabitants of different ethnic groups live in this area, such as the Lolo, Songjia, **Caijia** . . . They have different customs.*
>
> 《大明一统志·卷八十八》1461
> [Gazetteer of the Ming Dynasty, Vol. 88, 1461]

Still more records can be found in historical documents of the Qing Dynasty (1636–1912 AD), including

Qiánnán Shí Luè《黔南识略》'Local History and Gazetteer of the Qiannan Area' (Niohuru · Aibida[1] and Zhāng Fēngshēng, 1794);

---

[1] The names of the Manchu authors follow the Möllendorff transliteration system.

Guìzhōu Tōngzhì《贵州通志》'Gazetteer of Guizhou Province' (Jìng Dàomò and Sirin Gioro · Ortai, 1736–1795);
Huángqīng Zhígòng Tú《皇清职贡图》'Portraits of Periodical Offering of Qing' (Fuca · Fuheng, 1751–1805);
Qián Shū《黔书》'A Book of Guizhou' (Tián Wén 1796–1820);
Qiánnán Zhífāng Jìluè《黔南职方纪略》'A Sketch of the Local History in Qiannan' (Luó Ràodiǎn, 1847);
Píngyuǎnzhōu Zhì《平远州志》'Gazetteer of Pingyuan' by (Chén Hòuguāng and Xú Fēngyù, 1848).

The people of Caijia were often denoted as the *Càijiā Miáo* 蔡家苗 'Hmong of Caijia' in these documents, but in fact their customs are very different from the Hmong, as recorded in the *Portraits of Periodical Offering of Qing*. Some of the extracts are given below.

蔡家即蔡人，亦为楚子所俘，在贵筑，修文，清平，清镇，威宁，大定府，平远州皆有，男子制毡为衣，妇人以毡为髻，饰以青布，若牛角状，高尺许，用长簪绾之，短衣长裙，翁媳不通言，居丧三月不食米肉，惟饮稗粥，犹存古礼，杀牛宰牲聚亲属，吹笙跳舞名曰做戛，夫死将妇殉葬，妇家抢去乃免。

Càijiā jì càirén, yì wéi chǔzǐ suǒ fú, zài guìzhù, xiūwén, qīngpíng, qīngzhèn, wēiníng, dàdìngfǔ, píngyuǎnzhōu jiē yǒu, nánzǐ zhì zhān wéi yī, fùrén yǐ zhān wéi jì, shì yǐ qīng bù, ruò niújiǎo zhuàng, gāo chǐ xǔ, yòng cháng zān wǎn zhī, duǎn yī cháng qún, wēng xí bù tōng yán, jū sāng sān yuè bù shí mǐ ròu, wéi yǐn bàizhōu, yóu cún gǔ lǐ, shā niú zǎi shēng jù qīnshǔ, chuī shēng tiàowǔ míng yuè zuòjiá, fū sǐ jiāng fù xùnzàng, fù jiā qiǎngqù nǎi miǎn.

Caijia, i.e the people of Cai, their ancestors have been exiled too after the State of Cai was destroyed by the State of Chu. They are distributed across Guizhu, Xiuwen, Qingping, Qingzhen, Weining, Dading, and Pingyuan. The Caijia men wear clothes made of felt, while the Caijia women wear short jackets with long skirts. Each Caijia woman uses felt to make a bun several inches' high in the shape of horn on the top of her head, which is decorated with a blue cloth and is fixed by a long hairpin. Daughters-in-law and their fathers-in-law are not supposed to speak with each other. The people of Caijia follow ancient rituals. They do not eat rice or meat during the three months of mourning but are only allowed to have millet porridge. They kill cows and domestic animals to treat friends and relatives in funeral ceremonies. They play on pipe instruments and dance in funeral ceremonies. These funeral activities are labelled as zuòjiá (tɕie^{55}tɕi^{33}). A Caijia woman is not supposed to live alone once her husband dies. She should follow her husband in death, unless she is taken away by a member of her parents' family. 《贵州通志·卷七》1736–1795
[Gazetteer of Guizhou Province, Vol. 7, 1736–1795]

蔡家有二种，一名写果，一名阿乌纳，性淳谨，勤力作，男子衣装略同罗鬼，......近来苗民獠家蔡家衣食充裕者多习诗书，仿用汉人衣冠，耻沿旧俗......

Càijiā yǒu èr zhǒng, yī míng xiěguǒ, yī míng āwūnà, xìng chúnjǐn, qín lì zuò, nánzǐ yīzhuāng luè tóng luóguǐ, ... jìnlái miáomín nóngjiā càijiā yīshí chōngyù zhě duō xí shīshū, fǎng yòng hànrén yīguān, chǐ yàn jiù sú ...

There are two varieties of Caijia, the variety of Xiěguǒ and the variety of Āwūnà. They are characterized by their simple and hardworking personalities. The men dress themselves like the Lolo men ... Recently, the well-off Hmong people from Nongjia and Caijia usually attend school, dress themselves like the Han people and are not willing to follow their ancient rituals ...   《平远州志·卷十六》 1848
[Gazetteer of Pingyuan County, Vol. 16, 1848]

These customs recorded in these historical documents conform with what our consultants described (who are introduced below in §1.3). Almost 300 years ago, it was also reported that both the people of Songjia and Caijia had mastered the Chinese language since and that it was difficult to tell them apart from the Han Chinese (Niohuru and Zhang 1749: Vol. 1). This is essentially the current situation of the Caijia people as well. Portraits of Caijia can also be found in several different illustrated collections of Hmong people, as shown on the cover.

As recorded in these historical documents, Caijia has always been spoken in a multi-linguistic area. The three major languages in Xingfa township are Southwestern Mandarin (Sinitic), Hmong (Hmong-Mien), and Lolo (Lolo-Burmese), among which Southwestern Mandarin and Lolo are the two most important languages as far as language contact issues are concerned. In Dafang, in the neighboring county of Hezhang, there are also Longjia (probably extinct) and Gelao (Tai-Kadai). See the table below and Map 1.1 as well as Table 1.2.

Table 1.1: Linguistic diversity in Bijie Prefecture.

Southwestern Mandarin (Sinitic, Sino-Tibetan)
Hmong (Hmong-Mien)
Lolo (Lolo-Burmese, Tibeton-Burman, Sino-Tibetan)
Longjia (Unclassified)
Gelao (Tai-Kadai)

The genetic affiliation of Caijia remains unclear. Hu Hongyan (2013) considers it to be a Chinese dialect, i.e. Sinitic. It is true that Caijia is very close in many of its features to Sinitic. Our compilation of the Swadesh expanded list reveals that 54% of the 207 items are phonetically similar to Standard Mandarin. According to LTBEIB (1982: 24), 34.75% of 800 common words are phonetically related to the Hezhang dialect of Southwestern Mandarin, which bears many grammatical features distinct from Standard Mandarin, with the result that it is not immediately and fully intelligible to monolingual speakers of the latter variety. However, in the remaining 65.25% of items in the word list found to be different from Hezhang Southwestern Mandarin, there are also words that can be traced back to Middle or Old Chinese (Zhengzhang 2010). As pointed out by LTBEIB (1982: 21), 10.63% of these items are related to the Bijie variety of Lolo, i.e. Nisu. See Table 1.2 for more information. See Map 1.1 for the locations of Bijie and Dafang counties.

Table 1.2: Percentage of cognates among Caijia and other languages.

	LTBEIB (800 items)	Swadesh (207 items)
Standard Mandarin		54%
Longjia (Dafang)	35.75%	
Southwestern Mandarin (Hezhang)	34.75%	
Hmong (Bijie)	13.12%	
Nisu (Bijie)	10.63%	
Gelao (Dafang)	10.25%	

Zhengzhang (2010) proposes that Caijia may be related to the Bai language, of which the affiliation is also controversial within Sino-Tibetan. Sagart (2011) suggests that Caijia constitutes an early split from Old Chinese along with the Waxiang language of northwestern Hunan. LTBEIB (1982), Zhengzhang (2010), Sagart (2011), and Hu Hongyan (2013) all consider Caijia to be a language in the Sino-Tibetan family. Nevertheless, identifying the classification of Caijia is not the aim of this grammar. This topic should, undoubtedly, be addressed in depth in the future. Rather, the present work offers a synchronic description of the language's grammar and structures.

1.2 Previous research

There is very little literature to be found on Caijia. Previous research on this language includes two brief grammatical sketches of this language (LTBEIB 1982, Bo Wenze 2004), a paper on the lexicon of Caijia (Zhengzhang 2010) and a paper on the pronominal system (Hu Hongyan 2013). This work is the first comprehensive grammar of the language.

1.3 Data and methodology

The data presented in this work were collected in Xingfa Township 兴发乡 (26° 56′ 48.19″ N, 104° 48′ 55.91″ E) in Hezhang between 2012–2015 during nine months of fieldwork in total. See Map 1.1 below for the locations of Guizhou, Bijie Prefecture and Xingfa Township.

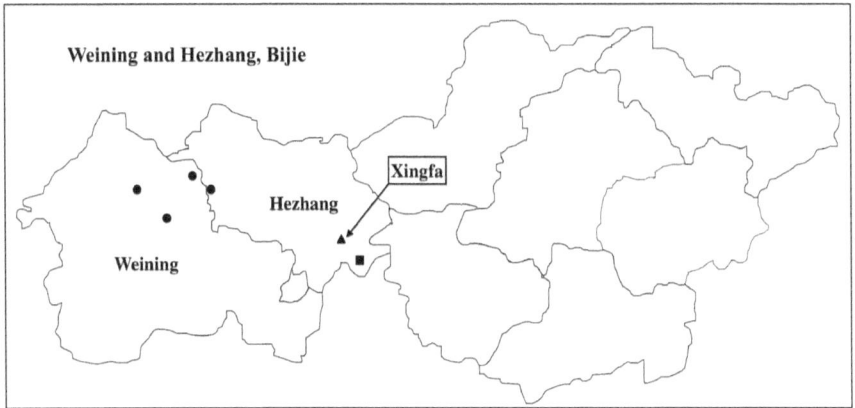

Legend: Spot: Weining variety of Caijia;
         Triangle: Xingfa variety of Caijia;
         Square: Songlin variety of Caijia

Map 1.1: Xingfa Caijia.

The data are composed of a list of high frequency lexical items, 147 spontaneous texts, including conversations, folk stories, ballads, poetic verses for drinking, and personal life experiences among other topics, and about 4000 elicited sentences concerning different grammatical features. Elicitation was realized either by sentence-by-sentence interpretations from Standard Mandarin to Caijia or by stimuli, such as videos and pictures. It should be mentioned that all of the data, including the elicited types, were non-intervened, meaning that our consultants were never interrupted, corrected, or oriented when producing data. Standard Mandarin is my working language, while our consultants speak Southwestern Mandarin.

The data used in this grammar are provided by three Caijia native speakers:

Mr. Li Wentai 李文太, from Cheluo Village 车落寨 of Xingfa Township, born in 1934, whose Caijia family name is $kɿ^{55}saŋ^{21}$ and who is our major consultant. Most of the data used in this grammar are provided by him. He speaks three languages: Caijia, Southwestern Mandarin, and Lolo.

Ms. $a^{33}mɛ^{21}je^{33}je^{33}$ 赵国珍 **Zhao Guozhen**, from Cheluo Village of Xingfa Township, born in 1957, one of the daughters-in-law of Mr. Li Wentai, is the daughter of a Lolo father and a Caijia mother. She speaks Caijia, Lolo, and Southwestern Mandarin.

Mr. Chen Weixian 陈卫贤, born in 1940, bears the Caijia family name $loŋ^{33}tʏ^{33}$. He is from Songlin 松林 Township, which is tagged by the square in Map 1.1. Despite the short distance between Xingfa and Songlin, Mr. Chen speaks a different variety of Caijia than the two consultants introduced above. For example, the retroflex stops /ʈʰ, ʈ, ɖ/ in the Xingfa variety are pronounced as /tʰ, t, d/ in the Songlin variety. These two varieties are entirely intelligible. Together with Mr. Li Wentai, he provided conversational data. He speaks Caijia and Southwestern Mandarin.

Mr. Li Kaiju 李开举, born in 1948, bears the Caijia family name $tɕi^{33}je^{21}$, and Ms. Lü Xingzhi 吕兴芝, born in 1932, whose family name is $kɿ^{55}saŋ^{21}$, also provided me with both spontaneous and elicited data in 2013. However, both of them speak the Weining variety of Caijia, tagged by spots in Map 1.1, which will not be presented in this work.

Audio data were recorded using a Zoom Handy 4 recorder and transcribed in IPA by following the Leipzig Glossing Rules, with modifications made to suit the specific features of Caijia grammar. In this grammar, data are presented in a four-line format with both English and Standard Mandarin translations.

1.4 Basic features

This section will introduce several basic features of the Caijia language, knowledge of which will help one to understand the language more easily. These features will appear intermittently but will not be addressed in detail in the main body of the grammar.

First, lacking inflections and with a small inventory of derivational types of morphology, Caijia is a typical analytic, tonal language. Compounding is the major strategy of word formation. Grammatical relations are realized by independent prepositions. Nevertheless, there are still some phenomena that can be considered derivational morphology. For example, tone change is used on a small number of words to derive plural of pronouns and diminutives of nouns (see Chapter 2 §2.4). Compared with Sinitic languages, Caijia is isolating to a higher degree. Most of the words in Caijia are monosyllabic and affixation is limited, while noun-forming suffixes are widely observed in Sinitic languages. For example, the suffix *-zi* 子 is a noun marker in many Standard Mandarin words such as *tù-zi* 兔子 [tʰu⁵¹-tsɿ] 'rabbit' and does not bear any lexical meaning. Rather, it is *tù* which is the root denoting 'rabbit', not *-zi*. The counterpart in Caijia is simply *tʰγ²⁴* 'rabbit'. Nonetheless, Caijia may adopt the loaned suffix *-xɯ⁵⁵* to derive plural personal pronouns and a native optional suffix, *-sui⁵⁵*, to derive plural nouns (see Chapter 3 §3.3.2 2.2.). The classifier *bo⁵⁵* can also serve as a suffix-like nominalizer. Reduplication is adopted to derive adverbs from adjectives. In an adjectival vivid form, A-BB, -BB is a suffix-like morpheme (Chapter 4 §4.2.1.1.2.2). Moreover, several other types of morphological processes can also be perceived. Fusion words can be observed in Caijia. For example, *mɔ²¹* 'which' + *ha⁵⁵* 'place' → *ma²⁴* 'there'. Resultative complements, including both achievement and directional complements, are used to realize lexical aspect. Using the marker *lɛ⁵⁵* to form manner adverbials is a very productive strategy, as is the complementizer *lɯ⁵⁵* for forming manner and extent complements.

Second, Caijia is basically an SVO language. However, two other word orders are also observed. They are: the object-topicalized construction OSV, in which the object is morphologically unmarked, and the object marking construction S[OM O]V, within which the object is marked by a preposition. Let us give some examples to illustrate these three word orders in Caijia. Example (1.1), a serial verb construction with two clauses sharing a common subject ($SV_1O_1V_2O_2$), illustrates the canonical VO order in Caijia, while example (1.2) shows the order OSV with the topicalized object *mɛ²⁴* 'frog' occupying the sentence initial position without any morphological marking.

(1.1)   S V_1 O_1 V_2 O_2
ni²⁴   a³³   ã²¹ã⁵⁵   ɣɯ²¹   lɯ²¹   mi³³.
3   take   jar   PURP   exchange   rice
'Someone took a jar to exchange for some rice.'
人家拿罐子来换米。
(*Exchange of product*, texts)

(1.2)   O   S   VP
mɛ²⁴   nɯ³³   a²¹   pie⁵⁵   la²⁴   kuɛ²¹   o?
frog   2SG   DCR   toss   where   go   CRS
'The frog, where did you put (it)?'
青蛙，你放哪儿了？
(*The frog*, texts)

In fact, the order OSV is very common in our spontaneous data and it is even usual in certain cases, as shown in (1.3). Our consultant claimed that the order OSV is the most usual way to express the meaning 'I've eaten strawberries (before)'.

(1.3) O   S   V
       tɔ²⁴mɔ²¹   ŋo³³   zγ³³   ja²¹.
       strawberry   1SG   eat   EXP
       'Strawberries, I've eaten (them before).'
       草莓我吃过。

However, the order SVO is still treated as the canonical order in Caijia because the VO order is the only possible order in a relative clause with the subject relativized. The sentence in (1.4a) is a case with a topicalized object, that is, $mɔ^{21}\ mɛ^{24}\ k^wɔ^{21}$ 'that frog'. When the subject je^{33} 'he' is relativized, the object $mɔ^{21}\ mɛ^{24}\ k^wɔ^{21}$ 'that frog' cannot be in the clause-initial position anymore. That is, the OV order is ungrammatical, as in (1.4b), meaning that the only possible order is VO, as shown in (1.4c), that is, the object $mɔ^{21}\ mɛ^{24}\ k^wɔ^{21}$ 'that frog' is in the post-verbal position.

(1.4) a. **mɔ²¹   mɛ²⁴   kʷɔ²¹**   je³³   pγ²¹   pie⁵⁵
          that   frog   CLF   3SG   put   to
          tʰγ⁵⁵po²¹   tγ³³   o.
          stove   upside   CRS
          'The frog, he put (it) on the stove.'
          那个青蛙，他放到炉子上去了。

     b.   O   V
          ***mɔ²¹   mɛ²⁴   kʷɔ²¹**   pγ²¹   pie⁵⁵
          that   frog   CLF   put   to
          tʰγ⁵⁵po²¹   tγ³³   mɔ²⁴   ni³³.
          stove   upside   that   CLF
          'the one who put the frog on the stove'
          把青蛙放到炉子上的那人

     c.   V   O
          pγ²¹   mɔ²¹   mɛ²⁴   kʷɔ²¹   pie⁵⁵
          put   that   frog   CLF   to
          tʰγ⁵⁵po²¹   tγ³³   mɔ²⁴   ni³³.
          stove   upside   that   CLF
          'the one who put the frog on the stove'
          把青蛙放到炉子上的那人

The next example below illustrates the object marking construction, S[OM O]V.

(1.5) S [OM O]
lɔ²⁴ni³³ lɛ²¹tsʰɛ²¹ a³³ mɔ²¹ u²¹tsʰo²¹ ni²¹ hm̩⁵⁵ ɯ³³
who on.earth OM that person CLF POSS clothes
VP
tʰɣ²¹-kuɛ²¹.
take.off-go
'(They made a bet to see) who on earth could take off that man's coat.'
（他们打赌看）谁才能把那人的衣服脱掉。
(*The north wind and the sun*, texts)

Third, Caijia is a pro-drop (pronoun dropping) language, that is, a language with zero anaphora. To be more precise, pronouns, which serve as subjects or objects in Caijia, can be omitted once they can be pragmatically inferred from the context. This phenomenon is also commonly observed in many East and Southeast Asian languages, as pointed out by Wiedenhof (2015: 122–123), Matisoff (2019: XII), and Vittrant and Watkins (2019: 6). It is very often observed, especially in our spontaneous data, that a sentence is formed only by a verb or a VP with neither subject nor object. One can easily perceive this phenomenon, while examining the data presented in this grammar.

Let us see an example below, which is a complex sequential sentence with the event in CLAUSE₂ following the event in CLAUSE₁. In CLAUSE₁, the subject 'someone, one' of the intransitive VP *kʰɯ⁵⁵ ɣɯ²¹* 'get up' is omitted, while both the subject, co-referential with the subject of *kʰɯ⁵⁵ɣɯ²¹* 'get up', and the object of the verb *kʰŋ⁵⁵* 'pull', which is 'cow', are omitted in CLAUSE₂. One should note that oblique arguments are not omitted in Caijia. For instance, as in (1.6) below, the allative argument *sɿ⁵⁵kʰa³³ mo³³* 'the side of the well' is marked by the preposition *pie⁵⁵* 'to'.

(1.6) (S₁) VP₁ (S₂) V₂
CLAUSE1[tɔ²¹kʰɯ⁵⁵ ∅S1 kʰɯ⁵⁵-ɣɯ²¹] tɯ³³ CLAUSE2[∅S2 kʰɪŋ⁵⁵
morning rise-come then pull
(O₂)
∅O2 **pie⁵⁵**, mɔ²¹kʷɔ²¹, sɿ⁵⁵kʰa³³ mo³³].
to INTJ well inside
'Once (one) gets up in the morning, (he/she) then brings (the cow) to, eh, the well.'
早上起来就牵到，嗯，水井边。
(*Cows' birthday*, texts)

Fourth, interpreting a sentence in Caijia relies, to a large extent, on the context it exists in. From examples (1.1)-(1.6), one may have already observed that verbs in Caijia are not indexed by person or number. If context is not taken into consideration, the referent would be unclear for the subject and the object. For instance, the subject of the verb $k^h\eta^{55}$ 'pull' in CLAUSE$_2$ in (1.6) above can be singular or plural; it can also be the first, the second, or the third person. The unclear referent in example (1.6) is due to the zero anaphora, while the example below is a different case of ambiguity caused by the multifaceted functional word ta^{55} 'with, for, and'.

The sentence $\eta o^{21}\ ta^{55}\ nu\mtext^{21}\ li^{21}\ \eta a^{55}$ can be interpreted in three ways as 'I take care of the child(ren) for you', 'I take care of the child(ren) with you' or 'You and I take care of the child(ren)' in (1.7a), while the same sentence can only be interpreted as 'I take care of the child(ren) for you' in the context of (1.7b), since the participant $nu\mtext^{33}$ 'you' will be freed from taking care of the child(ren) by ηo^{33} 'I' so as to be able to look for the mother. But note also that, given that plurality is not overtly marked in Caijia, the word ηa^{55} can be either singular or plural denoting 'child' or 'children' in both the sentences in (1.7).

(1.7) a. ŋo²¹   ta⁵⁵   nuɯ²¹   li²¹   ŋa⁵⁵.
         1SG   for/with/and   2SG   take.care   child
         'I take care of the child(ren) for you.'
         'I take care of the child(ren) with you.'
         'You and I take care of the child(ren).'
         我给你带孩子。
         我跟你（一起）带孩子。

     b. ŋo²¹   ta⁵⁵   nuɯ²¹   li²¹   ŋa⁵⁵.   nuɯ³³
         1SG   for   2SG   take.care   child   2SG
         tsʰe⁵⁵-kuɛ²¹   ko²¹   nɛ²¹   ʑi³³   mẽ!
         go.out-go   look.for   your.family   mother   PRT
         'I take care of the child(ren) for you and you go to look for your mother.'
         我给你带孩子。你出去找你妈吧！

From an areal perspective, i.e. within the linguistic area of Mainland East and Southeast Asia (MESA), Caijia possesses many common features with the languages of different families, including Mon-Khmer, Tai-Kadai, Hmong-Mien, Sinitic, and Tibeto-Burman. Most of these languages are tonal; except for some Tibeto-Burman languages they usually lack inflected case-marking or cross-referencing; many possess numeral classifier systems for enumeration or individualization; and serial verb constructions are very common (Enfield 2003: 50–51).

Caijia is very similar to these languages from many perspectives. Table 1.3, based on a modified version of Enfield's (2003: 51) summary of the areal features of languages in East and Southeast Asia, shows the common morphological features Caijia shares with other languages located in MESA (cf. shared features are discussed in detail in Bisang 1996, 2006, Matisoff 1991, 2019, and Vittrant and Watkins 2019: 653–680).

Table 1.3: Caijia within the linguistic area of MESA (1).

	Mon-Khmer	Tai-Kadai	Hmong-Mien	Sinitic	Tibeto-Burman	Caijia
Inflected case-marking	–	–	–	–	±	–
Cross-referencing	–	–	–	–	±	–
Fusional-affixing	–	–	–	–	–	–
Num. class. constructions	+	+	+	+	+	+
Verb serialization	+	+	+	+	+	+
Lexical tone	±	+	+	+	±	+

Furthermore, there are common semantic features, or "universal patterns of verbleaching" (Matisoff 1991: 414), found in the languages in the MESA area as well. For example, the verbs 'get, obtain, acquire' often develop into modal auxiliaries denoting 'be able, have to, must'; verbs of giving are a common source of causatives, datives or benefactives; 'come' verbs extend to denote purpose; 'finish' verbs become perfective markers; and verbs of saying develop into quotative markers. Some of these are also attested in Caijia, as shown in Table 1.4.

Table 1.4: Caijia within the linguistic area of MESA (2).

		Caijia
i.	'dwell, be at' > progressive	–
ii.	'get, obtain' > MANAGE/GET TO, HAVE TO/MUST, ABLE TO	+
iii.	'give' > causative/benefactive	+
iv.	'finish' > perfective	+
v.	'come' > purposive	+
vi.	'come/go' > toward/away from the deictic center	+
vii.	'say' > quotative/topicalizer/conditional	+

It is necessary to mention that we will argue in Chapter 8 that the verbal marker a^{33} (< 'take') functions as a cross-reference marker signaling that a certain direct object has already been mentioned in the previous context. However, this cross-reference marker is only used in two differential object constructions, while cross-referencing on verbs is not overtly marked in general in Caijia. Therefore, Caijia is not regarded as a cross-referencing language, as demonstrated in Table 1.3.

1.5 Organization of the grammar

On the basis of general linguistic theories, this work aims to create the first reference grammar of the language of Caijia – the Xingfa variety in a typological perspective. It is organized as follows.

Chapter 2	Sound system
Chapter 3	Noun phrases
Chapter 4	Verb phrases
Chapter 5	Ditransitive constructions
Chapter 6	Causative constructions
Chapter 7	Passive constructions
Chapter 8	Differential object marking constructions
Chapter 9	Constructions of comparison
Chapter 10	Aspect system
Chapter 11	Modal system
Chapter 12	Negation
Chapter 13	Interrogatives
Chapter 14	Relativization
Chapter 15	Clause linking
Chapter 16	Conclusion

Given that the analysis of Caijia found in the present grammar is discussed within a typological perspective, certain comparisons between Caijia and Sinitic languages will also be considered, and accordingly terminology on 'Chinese' needs to be clarified.

The term 'Sinitic languages' refers to contemporary Chinese dialects, which include ten branches (Wurm et al. 1987) and Standard Mandarin. Standard Mandarin is the lingua franca in China. Its pronunciation is based on Beijing Mandarin. Its vocabulary is based on the Mandarin dialects and its grammar is based on Written Vernacular Chinese, also known as *báihuà* 白话, the standard written style since 1920s. Note that the Mandarin branch is subdivided into eight groups with Southwestern Mandarin being the major Sinitic language spoken in the Caijia area. See Table 1.5 for a list of Sinitic languages.

Table 1.5: Sinitic languages.

	Standard Mandarin 普通话	
I.	Mandarin 官话	Northeastern 东北官话
		Beijing 北京官话
		Jilu 冀鲁官话
		Jiaoliao 胶辽官话
		Jianghuai 江淮官话
		Central Plains 中原官话
		Lanyin 兰银官话
		Southwestern 西南官话
II.	Jin 晋	
III.	Xiang 湘	
IV.	Gan 赣	
V.	Hui 徽	
VI.	Wu 吴	
VII.	Min 闽	
VIII.	Hakka 客家	
IX.	Yue (Cantonese) 粤	
X.	Pinghua 平话	

Two types of periodization of Chinese can be found in this work: one based on the rhyming and phonetic series and one based on grammatical features. See Table 1.6 below.

Table 1.6: Periodization of Chinese.

I.	**Periodization based on rhyming**
	Old Chinese (1200 BC – 221 BC) (Baxter and Sagart 2014)
	Middle Chinese (Chinese recorded in *Qieyun* rime dictionary, 6th century – 12th century AD)
II.	**Periodization based on grammatical features (Peyraube 1988)**
	Early Archaic Chinese (11th century – 6th century BC)
	Late Archaic Chinese (5th century – 3rd century BC)
	Pre-Medieval Chinese (206 BC – 220 AD)
	Early Medieval Chinese (3rd century – 6th century)
	Late Medieval Chinese (6th century – 1250)
	Pre-Modern Chinese (1250 – 1400)
	Modern Chinese (15th century – 18th century)

Chapter 2
Sound system

2.1 Introduction

This chapter aims at giving a brief description of the sound system of the Caijia language, but will not explore its phonological system in depth. On the one hand, this work mainly focuses on the grammatical system, morphology and syntactic structures of the language. On the other hand, many factors make it hard to systematize the organization of the Caijia sound inventory. For example, it is hard to find minimal pairs for several consonants. Several voiced consonants can surface in both voiced and unaspirated voiceless iterations. Although the tones of several words in their citation forms are high (or even extra high) level, in compounds, these same tones surface as mid-level or with a low falling contour, likely due to tone sandhi rules. These seemingly non-standard features will be identified along with our description, which is divided into a first section on onsets, or initials, and a second section on rimes.

2.2 Onsets

There are 33 onset consonants observed in Caijia, as shown in Table 2.1.

Table 2.1: Inventory of Caijia onsets.

	BILABIAL			LAB.-DEN.		ALVEOLAR			RETROFLEX			ALV.-PAL			VELAR			GLOTTAL
PLOSIVE	p	pʰ	b			t	tʰ	d	ʈ	ʈʰ	ɖ				k	kʰ	g	
AFFRICATE						ts	tsʰ	dz				tɕ	tɕʰ	dʑ				
NASAL				m			n										ŋ	
FRICATIVE				f	v	s	z					ɕ	ʑ		x	ɣ	h	
LAT.-APP						l			ɭ									
LAT.-FRI.						ɬ												

Among these consonants, the consonants [v] and [m̩] are syllabic consonants which also serve as rimes. The labial-velar nasal [m͡ŋ] which is not included in the table of onsets above is syllabic as well. Only the nasals [n] and [ŋ] are observed in coda position. See §2.3 further below for details and also LTBEIB (1982) and Bo Wenze (2004) for two other versions of the Caijia onsets inventory. The one presented by

Bo Wenze is actually a mixed version of two different varieties, the Xingfa and the Songlin varieties, whose locations are given on Map 1.1 in Chapter 1.

Next, the onsets will be elaborated with examples.

2.2.1 Plosives

We count in total 12 plosives in Caijia, which can be divided into four groups:
i. bilabial [p, pʰ, b],
ii. alveolar [t, tʰ, d],
iii. retroflex [ʈ, ʈʰ, ɖ],
iv. alveolo-palatal [k, kʰ, g].

The Caijia plosives, or stops, appear to have a three-way contrast: unaspirated voiceless, aspirated voiceless, versus unaspirated voiced, as shown in Table 2.1 above. The phonemic value for voiced consonants can indeed be established, as pointed out by Bo Wenze (2004). However, the contrast between voiceless and the voiced consonants is not entirely salient, since pronouncing the voiced plosives as voiceless will, in many cases, not affect one's understanding. However, some contrastive minimal pairs do exist. These will be shown in the following sections. Unlike the voiced series of plosives, it should be noted that the voiceless consonants do not have allophones in the form of their voiced counterparts. This means that the voiced plosives can surface as voiceless, but not vice versa. This labile feature of voiced consonants creates the biggest obstacle in establishing the Caijia phonological system.

In spite of this, it is still necessary to point out the possible existence of voiced consonants, because some of them may signal their lexical sources or a connection with Middle Chinese (the 6th century – 12th century AD). In fact, there is a portion of lexical items from which one can easily observe the connection between Caijia and Middle Chinese (see LTBEIB 1982). This connection is important for determining the genetic affiliation of Caijia. However, it is still too early to identify these words as being either loans or cognates. Given that most of our data are texts and sentences, the list of voiced consonants given here is not exhaustive. To be specific, there are some lexical items whose citation forms were not collected, especially those appearing in spontaneous texts. We have mentioned that the underlyingly voiced consonants can surface as voiceless consonants. This means that the voiced consonants can only be identified by judging citation forms. In the following sections, we will give examples of each group of plosives with minimal sets (as found in the data).

2.2.1.1 Bilabial plosives [p], [pʰ], and [b]

Below is a list of the Caijia bilabial plosives. Minimal sets, attesting to the phonemes [p, pʰ, b], are observed with the rimes [a, e, o, i, ia, iɔ, ie, oŋ, ɣ].

[p]: pa³³mi²¹ 左面 'left side'   pa⁵⁵ 爸爸 'father'
pa³³ 爷爷 'grandfather'
pe⁵⁵ 头发 'hair'   pe²¹ 热 'be hot'
po²¹ 皮肤 'skin'   po⁵⁵ 斧 'axe'
poŋ²¹ 根 CLF for hair, grass
pi²¹ 嘴 'mouth'
pia³³ 问、娶 'ask, marry (a woman)'   pia³³ 缺 'wane, be incomplete'
piɔ³³ 跑 'run'
pie⁵⁵ 丢 'toss, throw'
pɣ³³ 不 'not'   pɣ³³ 飞 'fly'

[pʰ]: pʰa³³ 拍 'pat'
to²¹pʰa³³ 从前 'once upon a time'   pʰa²⁴ 帕 'towel'
to²¹pʰe³³ 从前 'once upon a time'   pʰe³³ 翻 'turn over'
pʰo²¹ 肺 'lung'   pʰo²¹ 盖子 'lid'
pʰoŋ³³ 纺 'spin'
pʰi²¹ 慢 'be slow'
pʰia⁵⁵ 魂 'spirit'
pʰiɔ³³ 烧 'burn'   pʰia³³ 煮 'cook (in water)'
pʰie⁵⁵ 簸箕 'dustpan'
pʰɣ²¹ 铺 'cover'

[b]: ba³³mi³³ 旁边 'side'   ɛ³³ba³³ 伙伴 'friend'
ko²¹ba³³ 红稗 'barnyard millet'
be³³ 烧/焚 'burn'
bo⁵⁵ 果 'fruit'/CLF   bo²¹ 孵 'hatch'
bo²¹ 备 'prepare'   so⁵⁵bo³³ 妻子 'wife'
boŋ²¹ 逢 'meet'
bi⁵⁵ 变 'turn into, become'   bi³³ 矮 'be short'
bi²¹ 麻/痹 'be numb'   bi²¹kɪ⁵⁵ 鼻子 'nose'
bia³³ 白 'be white'   bia²⁴ 菠萝 'pineapple'
biɔ³³ 小锄头 'hoe'
la²¹bie³³ 大腿 'thigh'
bɣ²¹ 背/负 'carry/owe'   bɣ³³ 薄 'be thin'

The voiced plosive [b] can surface as its unaspirated voiceless counterpart [p], just as shown below in the phrase *pe²¹ tsɿ⁵⁵ pe²¹ ɕiaŋ³³* 'burn paper money and burn incense' in (2.1a). Two spectra of [be³³] 'burn' in its citation form and [pe²¹] 'burn', extracted from the phrase 'burn paper money' are given in (2.1b). One can immediately observe the difference between them.

The two spectra illustrate two completely different patterns of voice onset time (VOT), which can distinguish the different types of plosives, since they feature distinct VOTs. For example, an aspirated voiceless plosive shows a long lag for its positive pattern of VOT; an unaspirated voiceless plosive features a short lag for its VOT; and a voiced one shows, instead, a negative pattern of VOT. The spectrum of [be^{33}] 'burn' is the negative one, with a VOT of -195 milliseconds, that is, the vibration of vocal cords begins long before the burst or release of the voiced plosive [b]. At the same time, one can observe the voicing bar at low frequencies for the duration measured as the VOT of [b], as signaled by the rectangle. By comparison, the spectrum of [pe^{21}] shows the short lag positive pattern with only 31 milliseconds of VOT. That is, the release of the voiceless plosive [p] begins almost at the same time as the vowel [e]. In (2.1), apart from the devocalization of [be^{33}], the mid-level tone surfaces as the low falling contour since it precedes a word of the high-level tone, which is a tone sandhi rule in Caijia (see §2.4).

(2.1) a. pe^{21} tsʅ^{55} pe^{21} ɕiaŋ^{33}
burn paper burn incense
'burn paper money and burn incense'
烧纸烧香

b. be^{33} VOT [b]: -195 ms   pe^{21} VOT [p]: 31 ms

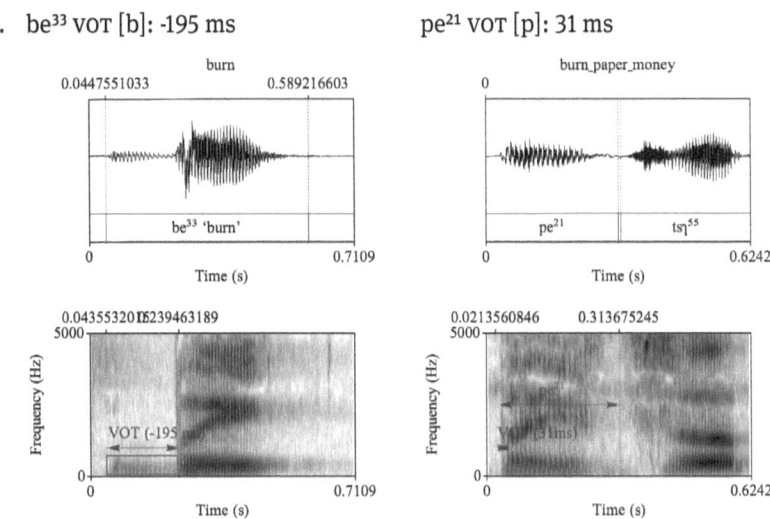

Even though the three-way contrast of voiceless unaspirated, voiceless aspirated, and voiced plosives at the bilabial place of articulation are only observed with the rimes [a, e, o, i, ia, iɔ, ie, ɣ], the data is sufficient to attest to a contrast. We would like to reiterate that there is no free variation for the voiceless consonants which are usually not realized as voiced. In other words, the voiced plosives may be realized as voiceless, but not vice versa. Thus voiceless [p] does not surface as voiced [b].

2.2.1.2 Alveolar plosives [t], [tʰ], and [d]

Minimal pairs for the alveolar plosives [t] and [tʰ] are abundant in our data, while those for the plosives [t], [tʰ], and [d] are few since there are only a handful of words commencing with the voiced [d] (see also Bo Wenze [2004]). Only the vowels [ɯ], [o], and [i], and the syllabic [v] are observed with all of the three alveolar plosives in our data, which, nevertheless, still attests to a three-way contrast in this group of alveolar plosives. Words commencing with the voiced alveolar plosive [d] in our data are all listed below.

[t]: to³³ 笼子 'cage'
     tɔ²¹ 像 'resemble'
     tɯ²¹ 住 'live'　　　　　　tɯ³³ 戴 'put on'
     ti²¹ 山 'hill'
     tv̩³³ 得 'obtain'

[tʰ]: tʰo³³ 钻 'get into/out'
     tʰɔ²⁴ 时候 'moment'
     tʰɯ²⁴ 瞬间 'a short moment'
     tʰi⁵⁵ 听 'listen'
     tʰv̩³³ 烫 'be hot, burn'

[d]: do²⁴ 豆子 'bean'　　　　　　tʰɯ³³do³³ 笨蛋 'idiot'
     dɔ³³ （雨）停 '(rain) stop'
     dɯ⁵⁵ 坏/歹 'bad'　　　　　　dɯ³³ 思考 'think about'
     dɯ²¹ 浅 'shallow'
     to⁵⁵di²¹ 舂碓 'pestle'　　　　di²⁴ 笛、唢呐 'flute'
     dv̩³³mi²¹ 上面 'upside'　　　　dv̩³³ 过 'pass by'

By observing the spectra of the consonants [t] and [d] in the words [tɯ²¹] 'live' and [dɯ³³] 'think about' presented in example (2.2), one can easily notice a difference and contrast similar to the case of [b] and [p] illustrated in (2.1b). The spectrum for *tɯ²¹* 'live', with a VOT of 17 milliseconds, demonstrates a short lag positive pattern characteristic of unaspirated voiceless pattern. The spectrum for *dɯ³³* 'think about', with a VOT of -151 milliseconds, demonstrates a negative pattern characteristic of voiced. The bar before the burst also indicates voicing. This is an obvious illustration of the contrast between the unaspirated voiceless alveolar [t] and the voiced alveolar [d].

(2.2)   a. tɯ²¹ 住 'live'   b. dɯ³³ 思考 'think about'
            VOT [t]: 17 ms   VOT [d]: -151 ms

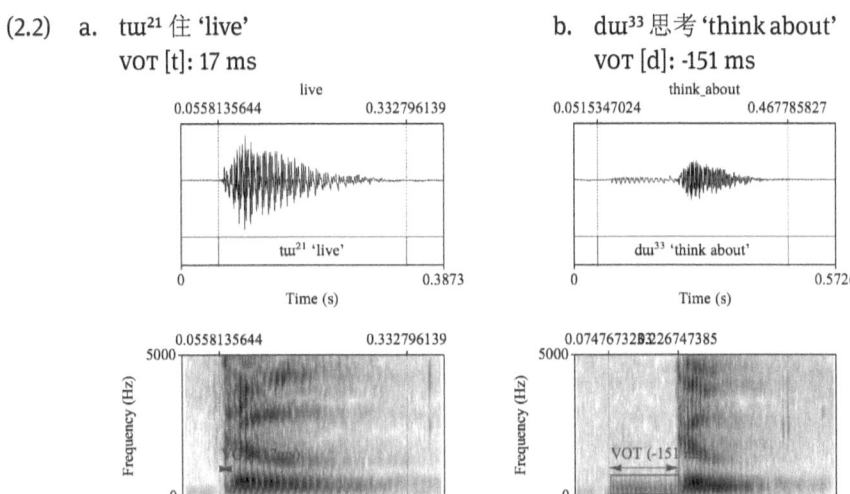

Just as observed for the group of bilabial plosives, it has also been noted that the voiced alveolar positive [d] may be pronounced as the unaspirated voiceless [t]. As illustrated in (2.3), both the voiced and voiceless forms of the word [dɯ³³] 'think about' are observed in speech sequences in our data. In (2.3a), it is the voiced [dɯ²¹] that is used, while the voiceless form [tɯ²¹] is used in the clause in (2.3b), the spectrum of which looks very much like the one of the word *tɯ²¹* 'live' illustrated in (2.2a). Note that each bears relevant sandhi tone.

(2.3)   a. ŋo³³   ji³³   **dɯ²¹**...   b. **tɯ²¹**-pγ³³-ha⁵¹   o.
            1SG   one   think.about   think.about-NEG-finish   CRS
            'As soon as I think of (it)...'   '(I) can't stop think about (it).'
            我一想（到）......   想不完了。

            VOT [d]: -110 ms   VOT [t]: 21 ms

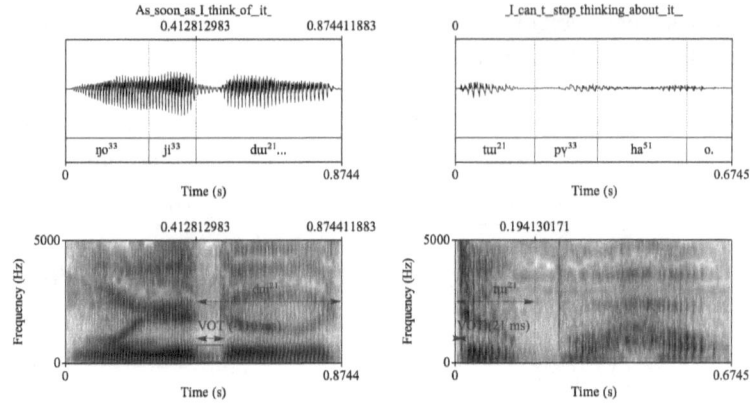

2.2.1.3 Retroflex plosives [ʈ], [ʈʰ], and [ɖ]

For this group, we only observe the co-occurrence of the vowels [ɛ], [ɔ], and [a], the syllabic [v], and the rime [oŋ], with the series of retroflex plosives as initial consonants. Minimal sets for the three retroflex plosives [ʈ, ʈʰ, ɖ] listed below are boldfaced. The vowel [l̩] is observed with the voiceless [ʈ] and the aspirated [ʈʰ]; the rime [aŋ] appears with [ʈʰ] and [ɖ]; the rime [ɪŋ] appears with [ʈ] and [ɖ]; the vowel [o] is observed with [ʈ] and [ɖ]; the vowel [ɯ] only appears with the aspirated [ʈʰ].

[ʈ]: ʈa²¹ 拄 'prop up (with a stick)'   ʈa²¹ʈo³³ 蜘蛛 'spider'
      ʈo³³ʈo³³ 秧 'seedling'   ʈo²¹ 踩 'step on'
      ʈo⁵⁵ 碰触 'touch'   ʈo⁵⁵ 筑 'build'
      ʈɔ⁵⁵pa³³ 太爷爷 'great grandfather' **ʈɔ²¹kʰɯ⁵⁵ 早晨 'morning'**
      ʈɛ²¹sɿ⁵⁵ 露水 'dew'
      ʈv³³ 长 'grow'   **ʈv³³ 咒 'curse'**
      ʈv²¹ 锄 'hoe'   **ʈv²¹ 长 'be long'**
      ʈoŋ²¹ 摞 'pile up'
      ʈl̩²¹ 锤 'hammer'
      ʈɪŋ⁵⁵ 转 'turn around'   ʈɪŋ²¹ 圈 'circle, round'
      ʈɪŋ⁵⁵ʈɪŋ⁵⁵ 盏 'cup'
[ʈʰ]: ʈʰa²¹ 坏 'break down'
      ʈʰɔ⁵⁵ 当（兵）'serve (in military)'   **ʈʰɔ³³ 瘸 'limp'**
      ʈʰɯ³³ 蠢 'be stupid'
      ʈʰɛ³³（心里有）数 'ins and outs'
      ʈʰv⁵⁵ 脱/除 'take off'
      ʈʰoŋ³³ 塌 'collapse'
      ʈʰl̩²⁴ 刹那 'a short momen'   bv²¹ʈʰl̩²¹ʈʰl̩²⁴ 薄菲菲 'thin'
      ʈʰaŋ³³ 插 'insert'

Note that the retroflex plosive [ɖ] is not identified by Bo Wenze (2004), while it is clearly identifiable in our data.

[ɖ]: **ɖa**³³ 晴 'be sunny'   **ɖa**³³ 关 'close, shut'
     ɖo³³ 柱 'pillar'   **ɖo**³³ 贮（肥）'compost'
     ɖɔ²¹ 升 'liter'   **ɖɔ**³³ 浊 'muddy'
     ɖɛ³³ 柴刀 'firewood chopper'
     ɖʏ³³ ~ **ɖʏ**²¹ 筷子/箸 'chopstick'
     ɖʏ³³ 着 passive marker 'by'/'bear fruit'
     ɖoŋ³³ 重 'heavy'
     ɖɪŋ³³ 羞 'be shy'
     ɖaŋ³³ 站 'stand'   ɖaŋ³³ 嚣张 'naughty, rampant'
     ɖaŋ³³ 腿 'leg'

First of all, let us examine contrastive spectra for the retroflex plosives [ʈ, ɖ] attesting to these two consonants. Compare the spectrum for the word *ʈɪŋ*⁵⁵ 'turn around, spin' and the one for the word *ɖɪŋ*³³ 'be shy' in (2.4) below.

(2.4) a. ʈɪŋ⁵⁵ 'turn around, spin' 转   b. ɖɪŋ³³ 'be shy' 害羞
     VOT [ʈ]: 13 ms   VOT [ɖ]: -143 ms

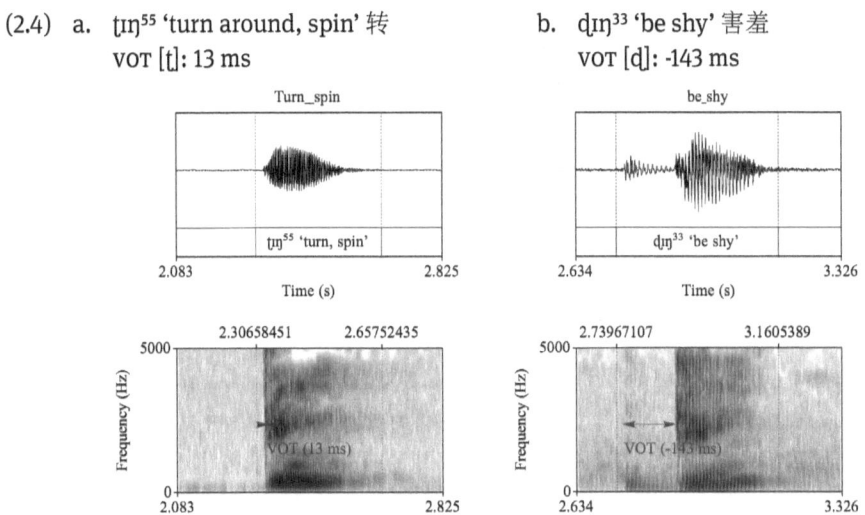

The following example of the passive marker [ɖʏ³³] clearly shows the instability of voiced plosives. Both [ʈʏ³³] and [ɖʏ³³] illustrated in (2.5) are citation forms from exactly the same recording with the voiced form following the voiceless form. The sharp contrast can easily be observed. We also need to mention that the consultant was not asked to articulate the two different forms on purpose. He was in fact not even aware he had given different pronunciations for the same word [dʝ³³]. The VOT for the voiceless [tʝ³³] is 8 milliseconds, while the VOT for the voiced [dʝ³³] is -143ms.

(2.5)   Passive marker 'by': VOT [t]: 8ms and VOT [d] -143 ms

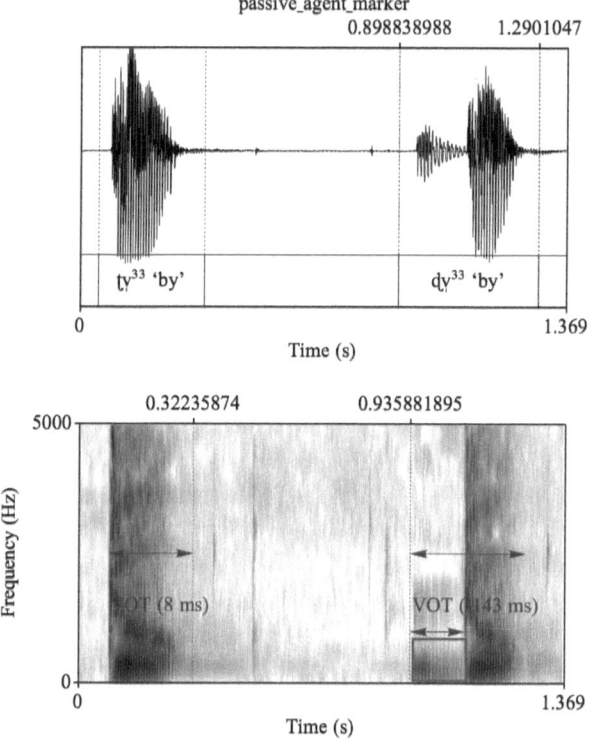

One more example of the word dʝ³³ ~ dʝ²¹ 'chopstick' surfacing as [tʝ²¹] is given below. In fact, two citation forms for the word 'chopstick', dʝ³³ with the mid-level tone and dʝ²¹ with the low-falling contour tone, were given by our consultants. The spectrum given in (2.6a) for the word 'chopstick' is the citation form with the mid-level tone, [dʝ³³]. It shows a negative pattern with a VOT of -222 milliseconds. The voicing bar clearly appears before the burst of sound. In contrast to this, the voiced word dʝ³³ 'chopstick' surfaces as [tʝ²¹] with a very short VOT of only 13 milliseconds in the phrase (2.6b) ŋo⁵⁵ɔ²¹ dan³³ tʝ²¹ 'as for the (process) of standing chopsticks on end (in) our (local place)' illustrated in (2.6d). This example is a dangling topic in a spontaneous narrative introducing how to practice the activity of standing chopsticks on end. Yet it remains as voiced in the sentence (2.6c) a³³ dʐ̝²¹ sa³³ pʰe³³ ɣɯ²¹ 'take three chopsticks', which is extracted from the same text as (2.6b). See the two spectra for (2.6b) and (2.6c) in (2.6d).

(2.6) a. dʐ̝³³ 'chopstick' 筷子   VOT [ɖ]: -222 ms

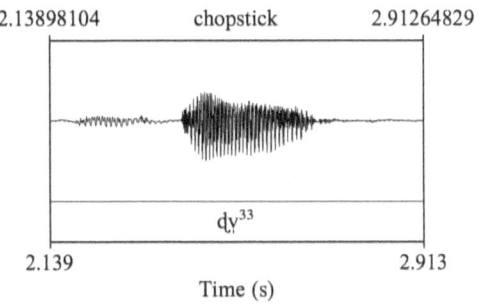

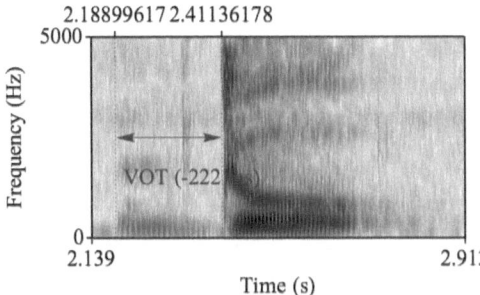

b. ŋo⁵⁵   ɔ²¹   daŋ³³   tʐ̝²¹...
   1PL   this   stand   chopstick
   'As for the (process) of standing chopsticks on end (in) our (local place)...'
   我们这站筷子……
   (*Standing chopsticks on end*, texts)

c. a³³   dʐ̝²¹   sa³³   pʰe³³   ɣɯ²¹.
   take   chopstick three   CLF   come
   'take three chopsticks.'
   拿三根筷子来。
   (*Standing chopsticks on end*, texts)

d. VOT [t̪] in (2.6b): 13 ms   VOT [d̪] in (2.6bc): -115 ms

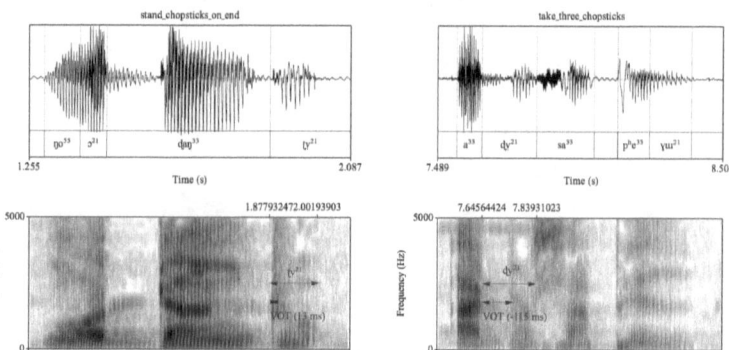

2.2.1.4 Velar plosives [k], [kʰ], and [g]

Within the velar plosives, the vowels [a], [ɯ], [o], [ui], [uɔ] ~ [ʷɔ], and the rime [ã] ~ [aŋ] can be combined with all three consonants, [k], [kʰ], and [g]. Note that the vowels [uɔ] and [ʷɔ] are free variants, as are the nasalized [ã] and the rime [aŋ]. Find a list of words below.

[k]: ka³³ 干 'be dry'   tsʰɿ³³ka³³ 干净 'clean'
      kɯ²¹ 骑 'ride (a horse)'   kɯ²⁴ 时候 'moment'
      kɛ²¹ 价 'price'   kɛ²¹ 嫁 'marry'
      ko⁵⁵ 挂 'hang'   ko³³ 冷 'be cold'
      kɿ⁵⁵ 系 'tie'   kɿ³³ 鸡 'chicken'
      ky³³ 脚 'foot'   ky²¹ 坐 'sit'
      kui⁵⁵ 断 'be broken'
      kʷɔ³³ 高 'tall, long'
      kua²¹ 国 'country'
      kã³³ 金 'gold'

[kʰ]: ma²¹kʰa³³ 门 'door'
      kʰɯ⁵⁵ 起 'rise'   kʰɯ³³ 开/启 'open'
      kʰɿ²¹kʰo²⁴ 斑鸠 'turtledove'
      kʰɛ³³ 脸颊 'cheek'
      kʰui⁵⁵ 狗 'dog'   kʰui²¹ 累 'be tired'
      kʰʷɔ³³ 放 'put, place'
      kʰua²¹ 好 'be good'
      kʰã⁵⁵ 肯 'be willing'

[g]: ga²¹ 勤快 'hardworking'   ga²⁴ 茄子 'eggplant'
       ga³³ 赶（集）'go (to market)'   ti²¹ga²⁴ 山谷 'valley'
       gɯ³³ 划（船）'row'   gɯ²¹ 冰 'ice'
       go³³ 厚 'thick'   go³³ 找 'look for'
       gui³³ 滑 'slippery'
       gʷɔ²¹ 桥 'bridge'
       gua³³ 过 'surpass, pass, live (a life)'
       gã²⁴ 勺子 'spoon'   gã³³ 衔/含 'hold in the mouth'

An example with a voiced velar surfacing as voiceless is given below. The spectrum for the citation form of the verb *go³³* 'look for' in (2.7a) has a long lag negative pattern with a VOT of -143 milliseconds, whereas *ko²¹* in (2.7b) demonstrates a positive (voiceless) pattern with a VOT of 25 milliseconds.

(2.7) a. go³³ 'look for' 找   b. ko²¹   tsʏ⁵⁵
                                              look.for   herb
                                              'look for herbs' 找药
       VOT [g]: -143 ms   VOT [k]: 25 ms

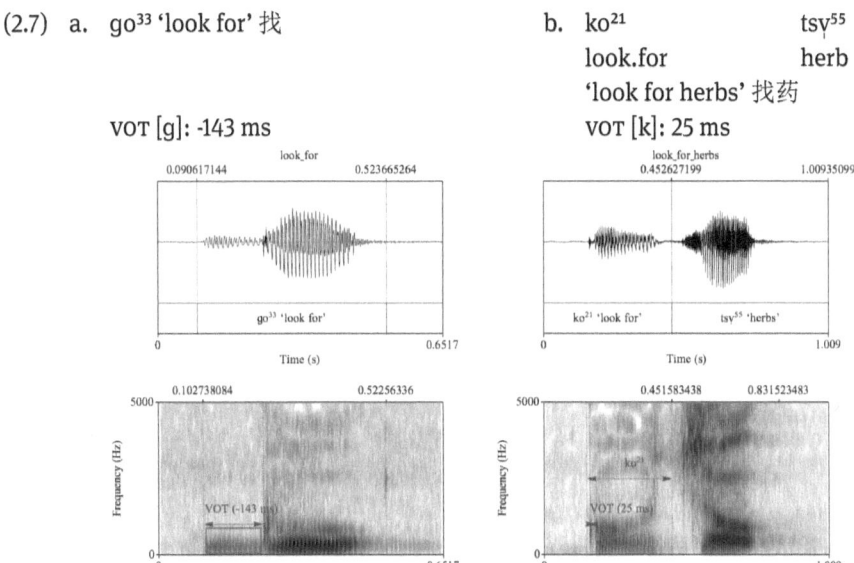

2.2.2 Affricates

Two groups of affricates are attested in Caijia. Each group contains a three-way contrast: three alveolar affricates [ts, tsʰ, dz] and three alveolo-palatal affricates [tɕ, tɕʰ, dʑ]. We will now examine these with examples.

2.2.2.1 Alveolar affricates [ts], [tsʰ], and [dz]

See the following list for some examples of the three alveolar affricates.

[ts]: tsa²¹ 借 'lend/borrow'
tso²¹ 照 'shed light'   tso⁵⁵ 哥哥 'elder brother'
tsɔ⁵⁵ 装 'put in'
tsɛ²¹ 苋菜 'pigweed'
tsɿ²¹tsɿ²⁴ 鸟 'bird'
tsɣ⁵⁵ 药 'herb/medicine'
tsaŋ³³ 看 'look'
tseŋ²¹kʰa⁵⁵ 亲戚 'relative'

[tsʰ]: tsʰa³³ta²¹ 厕所 'toilet'
tsʰo³³ 刺 'prickle'
tsʰɔ⁵⁵ 草 'grass'
tsʰɿ⁵⁵ 红/赤 'red'   tsʰɿ³³ 蓝/青 'blue'
tsʰɛ³³ 干 'be thin'
tsʰɣ³³ 搓 'twist'
tsʰaŋ³³ 挪 'move, approach'
tsʰeŋ³³ 咳嗽 'cough'

[dz]: dza³³to²¹ 石头 'stone'   dza²¹ 上/爬 'go up, climb (up)'
dzɛ²¹ 真 'real'
dzo³³ 丑 'be ugly'
dzɔ³³ 像 'resemble'   pa³³dzɔ³³ 男人 'man'
dzɿ³³ 睡/躺 'spleep/lie'   dzɿ³³da²¹ 舌头 'tongue'
dzɣ³³ 藏 'hide'   dzɣ³³ 还 'return'
dzaŋ³³ 十 'ten'

Admittedly, the pronouncing voiced alveolar affricates as voiceless is less frequent in comparison with the process as it is seen with plosives, but examples can still be found. Take the verb *dza²¹* 'go up, climb' as an example. As shown in (2.8), the voicing bar is signaled by a rectangle.

(2.8) [dza²¹] 'go up, climb' 上/爬

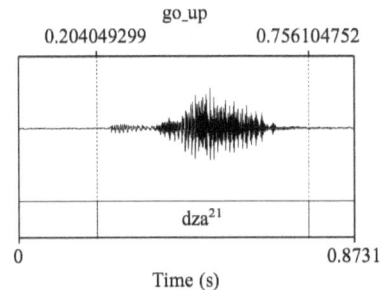

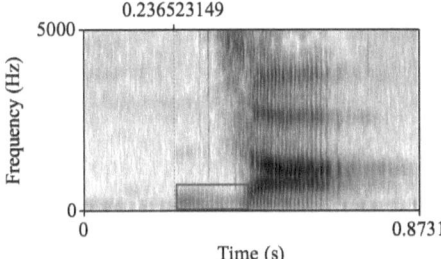

The verb *dza²¹* 'go up, climb' is voiceless in (2.9a) and voiced in (2.9b). It can be observed that the voicing bar does not appear in (2.9a) before the release of the vowel [a]. The word 'go up' in (2.9a) is, thus, clearly voiceless. By contrast, (2.9b) is a voiced form, determined by examining its spectrum. Signaling the vibration of vocal cords, the voicing bar appears before the release of the vowel, just as in its citation form [dza²¹].

(2.9) a. **tsa²¹**-xɯ⁵⁵ pio³³ nɛ³³ b. ŋo³³ tɯ³³ **dza²¹**-xɯ⁵⁵ pio³³ o.
      go.up-up run PRT   1SG then go.up-up run CRS
      '(I) ran away...'   'I ran away.'
      （我）跑了。   我就跑了。

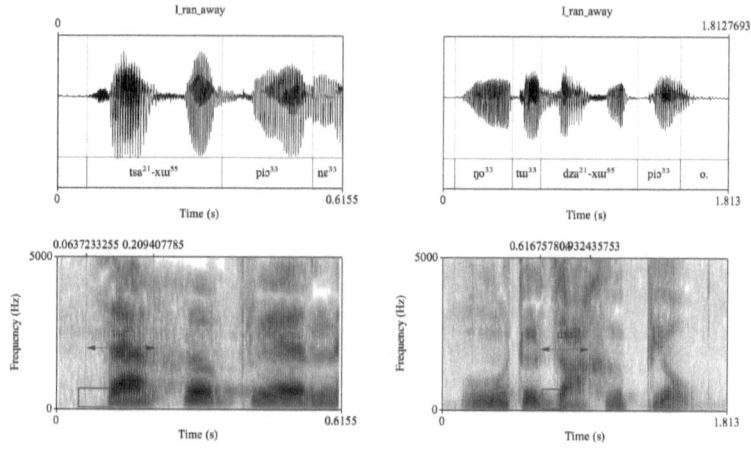

It is also worth mentioning that one of our consultants who comes from the same family as our primary consultant was never observed to pronounce the word 'go up, climb' as voiced, but that this does not cause any misunderstanding.

2.2.2.2 Alveolo-palatal affricates [tɕ], [tɕʰ], and [dʑ]

The three alveolo-palatal affricates in Caijia are illustrated below.

[tɕ]:	tɕi⁵⁵ (or tɕie⁵⁵) 姐姐 'elder sister'		
	tɕie⁵⁵ 做 'do'		
	tɕiu⁵⁵ 韭菜 'chive'	tɕiu²¹ 快 'fast'	
	tɕɪŋ²¹mi³³ 前面 'front'	tɕɪŋ²¹ 钱 'money'	
	tɕiɔ⁵⁵mɔ⁵⁵ 怎么 'why, how'		
[tɕʰ]:	tɕʰi³³kʰa³³ 喜欢 'like'	tɕʰi²¹tɕʰi²⁴ 蜻蜓 'dragonfly'	
	tɕʰie⁵⁵ 辈 'generation'	tɕʰiɔ²¹ 消 'be necessary'	
[dʑ]:	dʑi³³ 聪明/警惕 'be smart, vigilant'	dʑi³³ 犁 'plough'	
	dʑi²¹ 用 'use'		
	dʑie²¹ 喂 'feed'	dʑie³³ 下 'go down'	
	dʑiu⁵⁵m²¹ 过世 'die/pass away'	dʑiu⁵⁵ 到 'arrive'	
	dʑiɔ²¹ 跳 'jump'		

As with the passive marker [dʝ³³] above, two forms are given for the word 'be smart, be vigilant' in the recording by the same consultant, a voiceless version followed by a voiced version. See the spectrum in (2.10). Both of these forms can be freely detected in phrases, clauses, and sentences. Two of our consultants habitually pronounce the segment as voiceless.

(2.10) 'be smart, be vigilant' 聪明/警惕: [tɕi³³] vs. [dʑi³³]

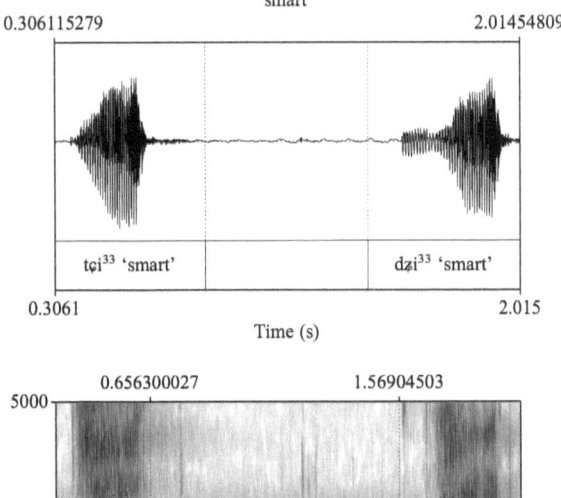

2.2.3 Other consonants

As discussed above, the Caijia plosive and affricate series present major obstacles to the classification of the Caijia phoneme inventory. Other consonant series are less problematic. It will be explained below that only the consonants [ɖ͡ʐ] and [ɬ] need additional elaboration.

2.2.3.1 Nasals [m, n, ŋ]
Some of examples of the Caijia nasals, [m], [n], [ŋ] are given below.

[m]: ma³³ 满 'be full'   mɔ²² 那 'that'
      mo³³ 丈夫 'husband'   mo²¹ 锅 'pot'
      mo³³lo³³ 肚子 'belly'
      mɛ³³ 马 'horse'   mɛ³³ 骂 'scold'

	me³³ 挖 'dig'	me³³ 袜 'sock'
	mi³³ 蜜蜂 'bee'	
	mɣ²¹ 结实 'durable'	
[n]:	na²¹ 打 'beat'	
	no³³ 揉 'rub'	
	nɛ²¹ 水牛 'buffalo'	
	ni²⁴ 时间/日子 'time'	ni³³ 人 CLF for persons
	ni³³dʐɿ³³ 眼睛 'eye'	
	nɣ²¹ 弩 'bow'	
[ŋ]:	ŋa⁵⁵ 孩子 'child'	ŋa³³ 瓦 'tile'
	ŋo²¹ 牛 'cow'	ŋo³³ 我 1SG
	ŋɣ²¹ 鹅 'goose'	

2.2.3.2 Fricatives [s, z, ɕ, ʑ, f, v, x, ɣ, h]

Four sibilant fricatives, [s, z, ɕ, ʑ], and five non-sibilant fricatives, [f, v, x, ɣ, h], have been identified in Caijia.

Sibilant fricatives

[s]:	sa³³ 酸 'be sour'	sa³³ 算 'calculate'
	so⁵⁵ 手 'hand'	
	sɔ⁵⁵ 树 'tree'	sɔ²¹ 笑 'laugh'
	sɛ²¹ 舍 'room'	
	se⁵⁵ 虱子 'louse'	
	sɿ⁵⁵ 水 'water'	
	sɣ²¹ 穷 'be poor'	sɣ⁵⁵ 绳子 'rope'
[z]:	zɛ²¹ 传染 'epidemical'	
	zɿ³³ 雨 'rain'	zɿ²¹ 加热 'to heat'
	zɣ²¹ 吃 'eat'	zɣ³³ 饭 'meal'
[ɕ]:	ŋo²¹ɕia²⁴ 未生育的母牛	
	'nonparous cow'	
	ɕie²¹ 小 'small'	ɕie³³ 哑 'be hoarse'
	ɕi³³ 杀 'kill'	ɕi⁵⁵ 铁 'iron'
[ʑ]:	ʑi³³ 一 'one'	ʑi³³ 妈妈 'mother'
	ʑi³³ 歪 'be crooked'	ʑi²¹ 剩 'be left, remain'
	ʑe²¹ 花 'flower'	

Note that it is observed that the numeral ʑi³³ 'one' often surfaces as [i] (usually transcribed as [ji] in this grammar) when it modifies an NP in its post-nominal position. See example (2.11) below.

Non-sibilant fricatives

[f]: fa³³ 捋/擦 'stroke (one's beard)/wipe'
fe⁵⁵ 蛇 'snake'
fɛ⁵⁵ 火 'fire'
fɣ³³ 墙 'wall'
[v]: va²¹ 地 'ground'
[x]: xɯ⁵⁵ 起 'up'   xɯ⁵⁵ 骗 'lie'
xɯ³³ 哭 'cry'
xa³³ 说 'say, speak'
xaŋ³³ 喊 'yell'
pʰɔ³³xu²⁴ 薄荷 'mint'   xu²¹ 和 'be harmonious/fit'
[h]: ha⁵⁵ 完 'finish'
hɔ⁵⁵ 路 'road'
hɛ⁵⁵ 弟弟 'younger brother'   hɛ⁵⁵ 梯子 'ladder'
hɛ⁵⁵ 家 'family'
hu⁵⁵ 线 'thread'
[ɣ]: ɣa²¹ 走 'walk'   ɣa³³ 落 'fall'
ɣa²¹ 蜡 'candle'   ɣa²¹ 林 'forest'
ɣɯ²¹ 来 'come'
ɣu²¹ 赶 'drive away, shoo off'
ɣã³³ 有 'have, there be'
ɣoŋ²¹ 龙 'dragon'   ɣoŋ²⁴ 鱼 'fish'

2.2.3.3 Lateral approximant [l], lateral retroflex [l͡ɖ], and lateral fricative [ɬ]

The lateral approximant [l] is exemplified below.

[l]: lɯ²¹ 换 'change, exchange'
la²¹ 大 'big'
lɔ²¹bo⁵⁵ 桃子 'peach'   lɔ²¹ 够 'be enough'
mo³³lo³³ 肚子 'belly'
lɛ²¹ 够 'reach out'
laŋ²¹ 凉 'be cool'
loŋ³³ 城 'city'

Only several rimes can combine with the lateral retroflex [l͡ɖ], as shown below. There are several minimal pairs which can be observed in Caijia for the lateral series: l͡ɖo²¹ 'gourd' and lo³³ in the word mo³³lo³³ 'belly', l͡ɖa²¹ 'peel off', and la²¹ 'big', and l͡ɖã²¹ 'sickle', and laŋ²¹ 'be cool'. Note that the rimes [ã] and [aŋ] are free variants. It should also be noted that the consonant [ɭɖ] is only found in the citation forms of the words below and that it is often reduced to the lateral retroflex [ɭ], which is chosen to represent [ɭɖ] in most transcriptions of the data, or the lateral approximant [l], as shown in (2.11). However, upon imitating these words with the consonant [l] as the initial, I was immediately corrected by my consultant.

[ɭɖ]:   ɭɖo²¹ 瓜 'gourd'   ɭɖo²¹ 推 'push'
        ɭɖy³³ 阴茎 'penis'   ɭɖa²¹ 剥 'peel off'
        ɭɖã²¹ 镰刀 'sickle'

(2.11) lo²¹   ji²¹   bo⁵⁵
        gourd   one   CLF
        'a gourd'
        一个瓜

Finally, the lateral fricative [ɬ] only collocates with the vowels [a] and [o]. The word ɬa⁵⁵ 'young, young people' is probably borrowed from Lolo (Yi). In the Weining variety of Caijia, the combination [ɬɛ³³] is found, denoting 'lie, cheat', but this word has not been observed in the Hezhang variety.

[ɬ]   ɬa⁵⁵ 年轻（人） 'young, young people' (Dafang Lolo: ɬa¹³ 'young' [Chen et al. 1985: 270])
        ɬo⁵⁵ 蛆 'maggot'

2.2.4 Discussion

We have shown is this section that examples of citation forms indeed create many minimal pairs attesting to sets of three-way contrast among both plosives and affricates. However, we have also shown the lability of both voiced plosives and affricates. The fact that pronouncing them as voiceless does not create problems of understanding should not be neglected.

Two hypotheses might explain this lability. First, Caijia is in the process of devocalization of voiced plosives and affricates and the contrast between these two types of consonants is losing dominance. The degree of devocalization varies according to different consultants of different ages and genders. Our major consultant, Mr. Li Wentai tends to contrast the voiced and the voiceless when producing citation forms of words, whereas his daughter-in-law, Ms. a³³mɛ²¹je³³je³³, tends not to make such a distinction. This phenomenon is very common in Sinitic languages, for example, Standard Mandarin is a perfect case of a language which has undergone the process of devocalization. Both voiced plosives and affricates have been reconstructed for Middle Chinese (Baxter 1992) but they have been lost in contemporary Standard Mandarin and in neighboring Southwestern Mandarin (see Ming Shengrong 2007 for Bijie Southwestern Mandarin), as well as in most other branches of Sinitic (Yuan et al. 2001: 23). Second, tones and pragmatic contexts can help to a great extent in distinguishing words more efficiently.

We will now consider Caijia rimes.

2.3 Rimes

In Caijia, 33 rimes are observed. See Table 2.2 for an inventory. Thirty are formed with vowels or nasal codas, while the remaining three are syllabic consonants, which were identified by neither LTBEIB (1982), nor by Bo Wenze (2004).

Table 2.2: Inventory of Caijia rimes.

Monophothongs	Diphthongs						Rimes of nasal coda			Syllabic consonants
i ɪ ɿ ʅ ɯ u	ie	iɔ	iɯ	iu	ia	in	iŋ	ian	m̩
e	o	ui	uɛ	uɔ ~ ʷɔ		ua	en			n̩
ɛ	ɔ						un	uiŋ	uaŋ	
a							yn			
							oŋ			
							aŋ ~ ã			

Most of the rimes were already listed in the previous section on onsets. In the following sections we will only elaborate upon a few rimes.

2.3.1 Monophthongs

Eleven monophthongs are observed in Caijia: [i, ɪ, ɿ, ʅ, ɯ, u, e, o, ɛ, ɔ, a]. The vowels [ɪ, ɿ, ʅ, e, o] usually do not form syllables, i.e. they always combine with consonant onsets.

[i, ɪ, ɿ, ʅ]: The vowels [i, ɪ, ɿ, ʅ] are, actually, in complementary distribution.

[i] appears after [p, pʰ, b, t, tʰ, d, m, n, l, ɕ, ʑ, tɕ, tɕʰ, dʑ]. Two examples of [li] are given below. See also examples of [i] combined with other onsets in §2.2 above.

li²¹ 猪 'pig'   li²¹ 进 'enter'

[ɪ] occurs after [k, kʰ, ∅] or before [n, ŋ]: [k, kʰ]___, ___[n, ŋ]. See also §2.2.1.4 for the combinations [kɪ] and [kʰɪ].

ɪ⁵⁵ 屎 'feces'   ɪ⁵⁵ 压 'press'
ŋ⁵⁵soŋ³³ 太阳 'sun'   ɱ²¹ 回 'be back'

The two apical vowels [ɿ] and [ʅ] collocate with alveolar affricates [ts, tsʰ, dz] and retroflex plosives [ʈ, ʈʰ], respectively. See §2.2.2.1 and §2.2.1.3 for some examples.

[ɯ]:   ɯ³³ 衣服 'clothes'   ɯ²¹ 穿 'wear'
       lɯ²¹ 换 'change, exchange'   nɯ²¹ 潮湿 'be damp'
       tʰɯ³³do³³ 笨蛋 'idiot'

[u, o]: The vowels [u] and [o] are also in complementary distribution. The vowel [u] appears after [x, ɣ, h, ∅] (see also §2.2.3.2), while the vowel [o] occurs after all other consonants except [z, ɕ, ʑ, tɕ, tɕʰ, dʑ]. See §2.2 for more examples of [o].

           u⁵⁵ 瘦 'be thin'   u³³ 碗 'bowl'
           ɣu²¹ 漏 'leak'
           tso⁵⁵ 酒 'alcohol'
           to²¹pʰe³³ 从前 'once upon a time'
[e]:   tsʰe³³pe³³ 牙齿 'tooth'   me³³ 蔓 'vine'
           be³³ 午饭 'lunch'   ʈ͡ʂ²¹pa²¹fe⁵⁵ 蜈蚣 'centipede'
[ɔ]:   ɔ⁵⁵ 屋 'house'   pɔ³³ 蹲 'squat'
           sa³³lɔ²¹pie²⁴ 蝴蝶 'butterfly' nɔ²¹ 毒 'be poisonous, poison'
[ɛ]:   ɛ³³ 布依族 'the Bouyei'
           bɛ²¹ 挠/挖 'scratch, dig'   ʈ͡ʂ⁵⁵pʰɛ³³ 惊慌 'stunned'
           lɛ²¹lɛ²⁴ 汉族人 'people of Han'
[a]:   a⁵⁵ 鸭 'duck'   a³³ 拿 'take'
           pa²¹bo²⁴ 蚂蚁 'ant'   la²¹la²⁴ 茧 'cocoon'
           na²¹ 打 'beat'

2.3.2 Diphthongs

We count a total of nine diphthongs in Caijia. They are [ie, iɔ, iɯ, ia, iu, ui, uɛ, uɔ, ua]. Only the vowels [ie, iɔ, iɯ, ia, uɛ, ua] can form independent syllables or words. The vowels [ie, iɔ, ia] are transcribed as [je, jɔ, ja] when forming independent syllables in this grammar.

[ie]:	je³³ 他 3SG 'he, she, it'		pie⁵⁵ 丢 'toss, throw'
	pʰie⁵⁵ 簸箕 'dustpan'		
[iɔ]:	jɔ²¹ 动 'move'		niɔ³³ 要 'want'
[iɯ]:	jɯ²¹sɿ²¹ta³³laŋ³³ 游手好闲 'idle about'		tɕiɯ³³ 撸 'roll up'
[iu]:	niu²¹ 软 'be soft'		niu³³ 等 'wait'
[ui]:	ŋui⁵⁵ 月 'month'		sui⁵⁵ 些 'some'
[uɛ]:	suan³³uɛ³³ 威宁 PLACENAME		kuɛ³³ 去 'go'
	kʰuɛ³³ 拱、挑拨 'stir up'		

[uɔ ~ ʷɔ]: The diphthong [uɔ] can labialize the preceding consonants and often surfaces as [ʷɔ].

        kʷɔ³³sɣ³³pa³³ 老师/医生 'teacher/doctor'
        ŋɔ²¹ ~ ŋʷɔ²¹ 炒 'stir and fry'   ɣuɔ²¹ 圈 'pen'

[ua]:   ua³³lɛ²¹ 外面 'outside'   kʰua²¹ 好 'be good'
        kua³³ 花 'spotted, blurred'

2.3.3 Rimes of nasal codas

We observe ten rimes for nasal codas: [ɪn, ɪŋ, ian, en, un, uɪŋ, uaŋ, oŋ, yn, aŋ]. As can be seen, only nasals [n] and [ŋ] can occupy the coda position. Examples are given below.

[ɪn]:	ɪn²⁴ 燕子 'swallow'		
[ɪŋ]:	pʰɪŋ²¹ 只 CLF		pɪŋ³³ 边 'side'
[ioŋ]:	nioŋ²⁴ 女孩 'girl'		
[ian]:	jan²¹tɕi²¹ 求 'beg'		ta³³bian²¹ko³³ 葡萄 'grape'
	nian²¹kɿ⁵⁵ 饼 'pancake'		
[en]:	men²¹ni³³ 蔡家 'Caijia'		pen⁵⁵ 分 'divide, share'

[un]: The rime [un] is only found with the onset [s] in our data.
        sun³³ 帮 'help'

[uɪŋ]: The rime [uɪŋ] is only observed with the onset consonant [k] in our data.
        kuɪŋ³³ 卷 'curl'   kuɪŋ²¹ 裙 'skirt'
        kuɪŋ³³ 军人 'military'   kuɪŋ²¹ 下（蛋）'lay eggs'

[uan]:   ŋa²¹kuan³³kuan³³ 硬邦邦 'hard'
(NB: *kuan³³* does not possess lexical meaning [see Chapter 4 §4.2.1.2.2], while *ŋa²¹* denotes 'hard'.)

[oŋ]:   noŋ³³ 生气 'be angry'   poŋ²¹ 根 CLF
        pʰoŋ⁵⁵ 纺 'spin'

[yn]: The rime [yn] is only found with the onset [tɕ].

    tɕyn⁵⁵ 骂 'scold'

[aŋ ~ ã]: The rime [aŋ] often surfaces as [ã]. They are free variants.

    aŋ³³ ~ ã³³ 喝 'drink'   aŋ³³ 答应 'answer, promise'
    saŋ³³ 盐 'salt'

2.3.4 Syllabic consonants

Three syllabic consonants are found in Caijia. They are [ɣ, m͡ŋ, h͡m].

[ɣ]:   ɣ²¹ 肠子 'intestine'   bɣ³³ 晚饭 'supper'
        tɣ²¹pi²⁴ 苍蝇 'fly'   kʰɣ⁵⁵pa³³ 老虎 'tiger'
        kʰɣ⁵⁵ 熊 'bear'

[m͡ŋ]: The place of articulation of this syllable is velar with the back of the tongue at the soft palate but with the mouth closed. This syllabic consonant is only found in the Hezhang variety of Caijia and only two words make use of it; the verbs 'swell' and 'wrap', as shown below. Both of these are pronounced as [oŋ³³] in the Weining variety.

    m͡ŋ³³ 肿 'swell'   m͡ŋ³³ 包 'wrap'

[h͡m̥]: The syllabic consonant [h͡m̥] is also only attested in the Hezhang variety. This sound is pronounced as [m], with an airstream coming from the nose. We only find one single word formed by it, i.e. the possessive marker. In the Weining variety, it is pronounced as [ɣoŋ⁵⁵].

    h͡m̥⁵⁵ 的 POSS

2.4 Tones

Both LTBEIB (1982) and Bo Wenze (2004) identify just four tones in Caijia:

    High-level: 55
    Mid-level: 33
    Low-falling: 21
    Low-rising: 24

LTBEIB (1982) further point out that another representation of the contour tone /21/ is the low-level tone [22] which they treat as the allotone of the contour /21/.

Here we have decided to treat the low-level tone [22] as an independent tone, because it is found on several citation forms. Therefore, we suggest five tones in Caijia.

Five citation tones:
High-level (H):   55   ɔ⁵⁵ 屋 'house'
Mid-level (M):   33   mɛ³³ 马 'horse'
Low-level (L):   22   ɔ²² 这 'this'
Low-falling (LF):   21   ɔ²¹ 留 'stay'
High-rising (HR):   24   mɛ²⁴ 蛙 'frog'

However, it is necessary to mention that there is also an instability among the tones. As mentioned earlier, two citation tones were given for the word 'chopstick' by the same consultant, *dy³³* and *dy²¹*. The citation tone given by Mr. Li Wentai for the word 'vine' is the mid level tone /33/, i.e. *mɛ³³*, while Ms. a³³mɛ²¹je³³je³³ pronounced it as *mɛ²¹*, the contour /21/, even though they speak the same variety.

Both tone sandhi and tone change exist in Caijia. **Tone sandhi** refers to a process whereby a tone is affected by an adjacent tone or tones. Tone sandhi is often observed within compounds and syntactic phrases (such as NP, VP) in Caijia. We have listed above five different citation tones, but generally only four surface tones can be detected. They are:

Four surface tones:
H: 55
M: 33
LF: 21
HR: 24

Several rules governing tone have been observed. **Rule 1**, the high-rising tone remains unchanged in many cases, except for on plural pronouns, which will be shown below. See example (2.12) with the word *mɛ²⁴* 'frog' adjacent to different tone patterns.

(2.12)   a.   mɛ²⁴ 'frog' 蛙

       b.   tsʰɿ³³bie³³mɛ²⁴ 'frog with green legs' 青腿蛙

       c.   mɛ²⁴toŋ³³toŋ³³ 'bullfrog' 牛蛙

       d.   mɛ²⁴-sui⁵⁵ 青蛙 'frogs'

Rule 2, the low-level tone often surfaces as low-falling. The example below shows the surface tone for the distal demonstrative *mɔ²²* 'that' in a sentence.

(2.13) **mɔ²¹** pa³³tsɔ³³ ni³³ kuɛ³³ tɔ²¹ mɔ²¹ ky³³ja²⁴ ni³³.
that man CLF go kiss that woman CLF
'The man went to kiss the woman.'
那个男的去亲那个女的。

Rule 3, the mid-level tone becomes low-falling when it precedes the high-level tone. This rule can be formulated as **/M 33/ → [LF 21]/__/H 55/**. This is a compulsory sandhi rule. In (2.14), the citation form of the word 'chicken' is [kɪ³³], as shown in (2.14a). It remains unchanged in the compound *kɪ³³bo³³* 'rooster' in (2.14b), while it surfaces as [kɪ²¹] in the compound *kɪ²¹tɕie⁵⁵* 'hen', as shown in (2.14c).

(2.14) a. kɪ³³ 'chicken' 鸡

b. kɪ³³bo³³ 'rooster' 公鸡

c. kɪ²¹tɕie⁵⁵ 'hen' 母鸡

In the following example, the verb *ɣa³³* 'fall' surfaces as [ɣa²¹] when it is compounded with the resultative complement *-tsʰe⁵⁵yɯ²¹* 'come out', as in (2.15a). Yet it remains unchanged when it is compounded with the complement *-tɕie²¹yɯ²¹* 'come down' in (2.15b).

(2.15) a. pʰa⁵⁵ je²¹ ji²¹ sɯ⁵⁵ je³³ tɯ³³ **ɣa²¹**-tsʰe⁵⁵yɯ²¹ o.
pat 3SG one VCLF:palm 3SG then fall-be.out.come CRS
'(You) give it a pat and it'll fall out.'
拍它一掌，它就掉下来了。

b. pʰa⁵⁵ je²¹ ji²¹ sɯ⁵⁵ je³³ tɯ³³ **ɣa³³**-tɕie²¹yɯ²¹ o.
pat 3SG one VCLF:palm 3SG then fall-be.down.come CRS
'(You) give it a pat and it'll fall down.'
拍它一掌，它就掉下来了。

Two more examples, concerning the verbs *ã³³* 'drink' and *ɖaŋ³³* 'stand', are given below.

(2.16) a. ã³³ 'drink' 喝

b. ã²¹ sɿ⁵⁵
drink water
'drink water'
喝水

c. ã³³   sɿ²¹   sɿ⁵⁵
   drink   NMLZ   water
   'the water for drinking'
   喝的水

(2.17) a. ɖaŋ³³ 'stand' 站

   b. ɖaŋ²¹-xɯ⁵⁵
      stand-up/DUR
      'stand up' 站起来
      'in the posture of standing' 站着

Rule 4 involves free alternation. When a mid-level tone follows a high-level tone, it can either remain unchanged or surface as a low-falling tone. This rule can be formulated as /M 33/ → [M33]//H 55/___; or /M 33/ → [LF 21]//H 55/___. It is not possible to predict which of the two tone sandhi patterns will apply. Examples (2.18) and (2.19) illustrate two compounds, each of which is formed by a word with a high-level tone and the word kʰa³³ 'hole, pit', which has mid-level tone. Both the patterns [H M] and [H LF] can be found. As for the word 'sun' in (2.20), even though it is unclear whether the disyllabic word 'sun' is a compound or not, given that the two morphemes are no longer analyzable, both ɿŋ⁵⁵soŋ³³ and ɿŋ⁵⁵soŋ²¹ can be observed in our data.

(2.18) a. sɿ⁵⁵ 'water' 水

   b. kʰa³³ 'hole' 洞

   c. sɿ⁵⁵kʰa³³ 'well' 水井

   d. sɿ⁵⁵kʰa²¹ 'well' 水井

(2.19) a. fɛ⁵⁵ 'fire' 火

   b. fɛ⁵⁵kʰa³³ 'fire pit' 火塘

   c. fɛ⁵⁵kʰa²¹ 'fire pit' 火塘

(2.20) a. ŋ⁵⁵soŋ³³ 'sun' 太阳

   b. ɿŋ⁵⁵soŋ²¹ 'sun' 太阳

Rule 5 also relates to free alternation. When a low-falling tone precedes another low-falling tone, the preceding tone can either surface as a mid-level tone or else it remains as low-falling. This rule can be formulated as /LF 21/ → [M33]/ __/LF 21/; or /LF 21/ → [LF 21]/ __/LF 21/. As with Rule 4, predicting which pattern will be adopted is not possible. Compare the several compounds given in (2.21). By compounding with the word $kʰua^{21}$ 'be good', several new words can be formed. In (2.21a), the citation forms for the words $kʰua^{21}$ 'good', $zγ^{21}$ 'eat', $tɯ^{21}$ 'live', and $dɯ^{55}$ 'bad' are illustrated. The new word 'delicious', composed of $kʰua^{21}$ 'good' and $zγ^{21}$ 'eat', can be either $kʰua^{33}zγ^{21}$ or $kʰua^{21}zγ^{21}$. Another similar case is found with the word 'comfortable' in (2.21d). By contrast, the word $kʰua^{21}dɯ^{55}$ 'anyhow' does not show any tone sandhi.

(2.21) a. kʰua²¹ 'good' 好
zγ²¹ 'eat' 吃
tɯ²¹ 'live' 住
dɯ⁵⁵ 'bad' 坏

b. **kʰua³³**zγ²¹ 'delicious' 好吃;   **kʰua²¹**zγ²¹ 'delicious' 好吃

c. **kʰua²¹**tɯ²¹ 'comfortable' 舒服;   **kʰua³³**tɯ²¹ 'comfortable' 舒服

d. kʰua²¹dɯ⁵⁵ 'anyhow' 好歹

The word $tγ^{21}$ 'hoe' is often compounded with the adjective la^{21} 'big' to denote 'hoe'. Both the forms $la^{33}tγ^{21}$ and $la^{21}tγ^{21}$ can be observed, as shown in (2.22).

(2.22) a. la²¹ 'big' 大
tγ²¹ 'hoe' 锄

b. la³³tγ²¹ 'hoe'

c. la²¹tγ²¹ ʑi²¹   kʰo⁵⁵
hoe   one   CLF
'a hoe'
一把锄头

For **Rule 6**, we observe that there is free alternation for the combination of syllables with tone values of [33 33] which may either remain the same or change to [55 55] or vice versa. We take the word $kɿ^{33}bo^{33}$ 'rooster' as an example again, which can also surface as $kɿ^{55}bo^{55}$.

Similarly, in many cases combinations of syllables with the tone values [21 33] are in free alternation with the combination [21 55]. Example (2.23) shows that when the two verbs $zγ^{21}$ 'eat' and $zγ^{33}$ 'itch' are modified by the degree adverb $xɪŋ^{55}$ 'very', both of the two phrases can surface either as [$zγ^{21}$ $xɪŋ^{55}$] or [$zγ^{21}$ $xɪŋ^{33}$].

(2.23) a. zɣ²¹ 'eat' 吃
zɣ³³ 'itch' 痒

b. zɣ²¹   xɪŋ⁵⁵
eat/itch   very
'eat (food) frequently' 总在吃
'very itchy' 很痒

c. zɣ²¹   xɪŋ³³
eat/itch   very
'eat (food) frequently' 总在吃
'very itchy' 很痒

The rules summarized above are only a few of the regular rules and do not cover all the sandhi patterns found in Caijia. Quite a number of unpredictable patterns are also observed. Example (2.24a) shows the citation form of the word *tɕɪŋ²¹* 'bottle'. In the compound *sɿ⁵⁵tɕɪŋ²¹* 'water bottle' in (2.24b), 'bottle' remains unchanged, but surfaces as [tɕɪŋ³³] in the compound *tɕɪŋ³³tsʰɯ³³* 'bottle stopper' in (2.24c).

(2.24) a. tɕɪŋ²¹ 'bottle' 瓶子

b. sɿ⁵⁵tɕɪŋ²¹ 'water bottle' 水瓶

c. tɕɪŋ³³tsʰɯ³³ 'bottle stopper' 瓶塞

The demonstratives, bearing the low-level tone in Caijia (see Rule 2), usually surface as the contour [21], as in (2.25a), but can also surface with other tone patterns, as shown in (2.25b) and (2.25c). The conditioning factor remains a mystery.

(2.25) a. **mɔ²¹**   kʷɔ⁵⁵pe⁵⁵ja²¹   bo⁵⁵
that   moon   CLF
'that moon'
那个月亮 (*Three thieves*, texts)

b. ɕie²¹   **mɔ²⁴**   ni³³   lo³³   mɔ²¹   la²¹   **mɔ²⁴**   ni³³.
small   that   CLF   push   that   big   that   CLF
'The short person pushed that tall person.'
小的那个推大的那个。

c. **mɔ³³**   u²¹tsʰo²⁴   ni³³
that   person   CLF
'that person'
那个人

Compare the verb *ɣã³³* 'have, there be' in the three examples below. Instances of the verb surfacing as [21] and [24] are unpredictable patterns. Furthermore, the word *neŋ²¹* 'year' is low-falling in its citation form but it surfaces as [33] in examples (2.27) and (2.28).

(2.26) **ɣã³³** pa³³dzɔ³³ ni³³ tɯ²¹ ma²⁴ lo²¹ mɔ²¹ kɣ²¹ja²⁴ ni³³.
there.be man CLF at there push that woman CLF
'There's a man pushing that woman.'
有一个男人在那儿推那个女人。

(2.27) **ɣã²¹** ji³³ **neŋ³³**.
there.be one year
'There was once a year.'
有一年。
(*The crow and the jar*, texts)

(2.28) **ɣã²⁴** ji³³ **neŋ³³**, ŋo²⁴ ma⁵⁵ ɣã²¹ kʰʏ⁵⁵pa²¹ kʷɔ²¹ e²¹...
there.be one year 1PL there there.be tiger CLF PRT
'One year, there was a tiger in out place...'
有一年，我们那儿有只老虎。……
(*Two little tigers*, texts)

Apart from unpredictable patterns, prosodic factors such as intonation and stress can definitely affect the surface tone of a morpheme. As shown in the example below, two tonal forms are observed for the word 'pat'. Even though its citation tone of this word is unclear due to the lack of the word's citation form in our data, two possible explanations related to intonation and stress can be provided. The first *pʰa³³* 'pat' may have a lower pitch than the second one because it is situated in the sentence final position of a declarative. Alternatively, the higher second *pʰa⁵⁵* may be due to stress.

(2.29) mɛ³³ɣoŋ²⁴ tɕʰɪn³³-tʏ³³ niɔ³³ a³³ so⁵⁵ **pʰa³³**. **pʰa⁵⁵**
leech bite-obtain need with hand pat pat
je²¹ ji²¹ sɯ⁵⁵ je³³ tɯ³³ ɣa²¹-tsʰe⁵⁵ɣɯ²¹ o.
3SG one VCLF:palm 3SG then fall-be.out.come CRS
'(You) should pat (it) with your hand when you're bitten by a leech. (You) give it a pat and it'll fall out.'
蚂蝗咬到要用手拍。拍它一掌，它就掉出来了。

Tone change which is not caused by adjacent tones but should be regarded as a derivational strategy (Downer 1959, Kam 1977), and is observed in two cases: (i) deriving plural pronouns and (ii) deriving diminutive nouns. The singular personal pronouns in Caijia bear the mid-level tone /33/. The plural forms are derived by changing the mid-level tone /33/ into the high-rising tone [24], as shown in (2.30).

(2.30)　　　SG　　　　　　PL
　　1　　ŋo³³ 'I'　　　　ŋo²⁴ 'we'
　　2　　nɯ³³ 'you'　　nɯ²⁴ 'you'
　　3　　je³³ 'he/she'　je²⁴ 'they'

Plural pronouns can surface as the high-level tone [55], which is often observed in sentences but is unpredictable, as shown below.

(2.31) a. mɔ²¹　kɯ⁵⁵　a,　**ŋo²⁴**　tsʰɿ⁵⁵　mo³³　sɿ²¹　hɔ⁵⁵...
　　　　　that　moment　PRT　1PL　village　inside　MOD　road
　　　　　'In those days, the road to our village...'
　　　　　以前，我们村子里的路......
　　　　　(*The road to our village*, texts)

　　　b. mɔ²¹　kɯ⁵⁵　**ŋo⁵⁵**　tɯ²¹　ɔ²¹kʷɔ²¹　pi²¹tɕia²⁴sã³³
　　　　　that　moment　1PL　at　INTJ　Bijiashan_PLACENAME
　　　　　ɔ²¹　ha⁵⁵　sɿ²¹　ɕiu²¹　sɿ³³ta²¹　bo⁵⁵.
　　　　　this　place　COP　build　pond　CLF
　　　　　'At that time, it is when we were, eh..., building a reservoir.'
　　　　　以前，我们在这个......毕家山这儿是修一个水库。
　　　　　(*Building the reservoir*, texts)

The high-rising tone /24/ can also be used to create the diminutive form of a noun, as shown in (2.32)-(2.34).

(2.32) a. ŋo²¹ 'cow' 牛

　　　　b. ŋo²⁴ 'calf' 小牛
　　　　　COW.DIM

(2.33) a. ã²¹ 'jar' 罐子

　　　　b. ã²⁴ 'little jar' 小罐子
　　　　　jar.DIM

(2.34) a. la²¹ ɯ³³**bi³³**
big front.piece.of.a.garment
'the big front piece of a shirt (with buttons on the side)'
衣大襟

b. (ɕie²¹) ɯ³³**bi²⁴**
small front.piece.of.a.garment.DIM
'the small front piece of a shirt (with buttons on the side)'
衣小襟

In this section, we presented two types of tone change and several rules of tone sandhi in Caija, but these only give us a glimpse of the Caijia sandhi patterns. More work needs to be done to elaborate the language's complete sandhi system in the future.

2.5 Conclusion

This chapter has given a brief description of the sound system in Caijia. Our observations on the voiced plosives [b, d, g] and the voiced alveolar affricate [dz] are consistent with Bo Wenze's (2004) observations. In addition, we also proposed the voiced retroflex plosive [ɖ] and the voiced alveolo-palatal affricate [dʑ]. However, in plosives and affricates onsets, we also show that the contrast between the voiced and the voiceless series is not primary, since devocalization often occurs in fluent speech. Given that much of our data are composed of sentences and long texts, in a large part of the data presented in the following chapters, the voiced plosives and affricates are transcribed as their voiceless counterparts. As for the Caijia rimes, we found three extra syllabic consonants, [v̩, m̩n̩, hm̩], that are not included in Bo Wenze (2004).

Five citation tones were observed, but only four surface tones. Examples have been given to show that tone sandhi certainly exists in Caijia, but only those sandhi rules which can be clearly stated at present are given. There are still sandhi patterns which remains a mystery barring further research. Throughout the grammar, data will be presented with surface tones unless the citation forms of words are given.

Chapter 3
Noun phrases

3.1 Introduction

In a very broad sense, noun phrases perform the same grammatical function as nouns, such as arguments of verbs or objects of prepositions. Noun phrases can be divided into simple phrases, complex phrases and those without a head noun, i.e. headless phrases (Dryer 2007: 151). Simple noun phrases may be formed only by demonstratives, pronouns, or nouns; complex noun phrases may contain clausal modifiers, such as relative clauses; while headless noun phrases are similar to English headless relatives, such as *what I need*. Examples of each type will be given in the following discussion.

In the most expanded noun phrase in Caijia, two orders of constituents can be observed:
i. [POSS [$_{REL}$CLAUSE] (REL) DEM ADJ [N] [(NUM) CLF]]
ii. [POSS DEM [$_{REL}$CLAUSE] REL ADJ [N] [(NUM) CLF]]

The two complex NPs presented below show variation in word order. In each, the head noun *nioŋ²⁴* 'daughter' is highlighted. In the Type i order, the relativizer *sɿ²¹* is optional, as shown in (3.1a), while it is obligatory in the Type ii order.

(3.1) a. je³³   kʷɔ³³   la²¹ɕyɔ²¹   pe⁵⁵-ɣɯ²¹   (sɿ²¹)
         3SG   learn   university   return-come   REL
         mɔ²¹   ɕie²¹   **nioŋ²⁴**   ni³³
         that   little   girl   CLF
         'his little daughter that came back from college'
         他读大学回来（的）那个小女儿

   b. je³³   mɔ²¹   kʷɔ³³   la²¹ɕyɔ²¹   pe⁵⁵-ɣɯ²¹   sɿ²¹
       3SG   that   learn   university   return-com   REL
       ɕie²¹   **nioŋ²⁴**   ni³³
       little   girl   CLF
       'his little daughter that came back from college'
       他那个读大学回来的小女儿

In this chapter, we will present the major elements that can form noun phrases in Caijia as well as their distributional features, including demonstratives, nouns, pronouns, numerals, classifiers and headless noun phrases realized via nominalization.

3.2 Demonstratives

Demonstratives, often possessing a distance feature in Sinitic languages (q.v. Chen Yujie 2010), refer to deictic words or morphemes which function to refer to and to distinguish entities from each other. Broadly speaking, there are pronominal demonstratives, adnominal demonstratives, as well as adverbial demonstratives (q.v. Diessel 1999).

Caijia makes a simple two-way distinction between demonstratives: i.e. proximal and distal demonstratives. These can be further semantically divided into four types: (i) basic, (ii) place, (iii) time, and (iv) manner/degree demonstratives. The last three types are all formed by compounding with the basic singular demonstratives, i.e. $ɔ^{22}$ 'this' and $mɔ^{22}$ 'that', specifically. Only the basic demonstratives possess plural forms, which are realized by suffixing or compounding the plural marker sui^{55}, derived from the pronoun 'some'. Place, time, and manner/degree demonstratives are formed by compounding the aforementioned basic demonstratives with the words ha^{55} 'place', $kɯ^{24}$ 'moment', and $sĩ^{55}$ 'way', respectively. It should be mentioned that ua^{24} 'here' and ma^{24} 'there' are the fused forms of $ɔ^{21}ha^{55}$ and $mɔ^{21}ha^{55}$, respectively. See Table 3.1.

Table 3.1: Caijia demonstratives.

	Basic	Place	Time	Manner/Degree
Proximal	$ɔ^{22}$ 'this'	'this' + 'place'	'this' + 'moment'	'this' + 'way'
	$ɔ^{21}sui^{55}$ 'these'	$ɔ^{21}ha^{55}$ > ua^{24} 'here'	$ɔ^{21}kɯ^{24/55}$ 'now'	$ɔ^{21}sĩ^{55}$ 'so'
Distal	$mɔ^{22}$ 'that'	'that' + 'place'	'that' + 'moment'	'that' + 'way'
	$mɔ^{21}sui^{55}$ 'those'	$mɔ^{21}ha^{55}$ > ma^{24} 'there'	$mɔ^{21}kɯ^{24/55}$ 'then'	$mɔ^{21}sĩ^{55}$ 'so'

In their singular forms, Caijia **basic demonstratives** can be both pronominal and adnominal, as is the case in most languages of the world (Diessel 2013). Basic plural forms are mainly pronominal in our data. Examples (3.2)-(3.4) show the pronominal uses of singular basic demonstratives, while (3.5) and (3.6) show the pronominal uses of plural basic demonstratives. The demonstratives $ɔ^{21}$ 'this' and $mɔ^{21}$ 'that' are copular subjects in (3.2) and (3.3), while $mɔ^{21}$ 'that' is a dangling topic in (3.4).

Pronominal
(3.2) $ɔ^{21}$ $sĩ^{33}$ $mɔ^{21}$ ta^{55} ni^{33}.
       this   COP   that   two   CLF
       'This is (about) those two (persons).'
       这是那两个人（的事）。
       (*The drowning persons*, texts)

(3.3) "aijəu! **mɔ²¹** tsʰɛ²¹ sɿ³³ ji²¹mi⁵⁵mi⁵⁵. [...]"
    INTJ   that   only   COP   little.thing
    ' "My! That is almost nothing!..." '
    "哎呦！那就只是一点点。......"
    (*The man and the tiger*, texts)

(3.4) **mɔ²¹** nɛ⁵⁵, je³³   sɿ²¹   ta⁵⁵   kʰɣ⁵⁵pa²¹ pi²¹   mo³³   kuɛ³³
    that   PRT   3SG   AFF   from   tiger   mouth inside   PURP
    ə   ti³³-ɣɯ²¹   sɿ³³   a³³.
    INTJ   snatch-come   AFF   PRT
    '(It turns out that) that, it is from the tiger's mouth that he snatched (her life).'
    （原来）那个呢，他是从老虎嘴里抢来的啊。
    (*The man and the tiger*, texts)

In (3.5) and (3.6), the pronominal uses of *ɔ²¹sui⁵⁵* 'these' and *mɔ²¹sui⁵⁵* 'those' are illustrated. Being the subject, *ɔ²¹sui⁵⁵* in (3.5) refers to 'these places like Magu'; while *mɔ²¹sui⁵⁵* refers to 'those persons' and is the object of the VP 'see'.

(3.5) ma³³kɣ³³   **ɔ²¹sui⁵⁵**   la³³   tʰoŋ²¹   ha⁵¹   o.
    Magu_PLACENAME these   all   collapse COMPL   CRS
    'The places like Magu all collapsed.'
    妈姑这些（地方）都塌了。

(3.6) tsaŋ³³-kɪŋ²¹   **mɔ²⁴sui⁵⁵** e,   tɯ²¹   tɣ²⁴   tɣ³³   na²¹   tsoŋ²¹.
    look-see   those   PRT   at   yard   upside beat   wheat
    '(I) saw those people threshing wheat in the yard.'
    看见那些（人），在院坝上打麦子。
    (*Wheat-threshing*, texts)

Both the demonstratives *ɔ²²* 'this' and *mɔ²²* 'that' can be adnominal, accompanying or modifying nouns. See the example below, as well as (3.2), for the adnominal use of *mɔ²²*.

Adnominal
(3.7) ɔ²¹   la²¹   tso⁵⁵   ni³³
    this   big   brother   CLF
    'this big brother'
    这个大哥
    (*The man and the tiger*, texts)

The plural forms ɔ²¹sui⁵⁵ 'these' and mɔ²¹sui⁵⁵ 'those' are rarely used to modify nouns or other elements. Very few examples of their adnominal uses are found in our data. One such use, extracted from a spontaneous narrative, can be seen in (3.8a). Yet it is the form illustrated in (3.8b) that is most commonly used, schematized as [ɔ²¹/mɔ²¹ + N + sui⁵⁵].

(3.8) a. **ɔ²¹sui⁵⁵**   u²¹tsʰo²¹
       these   person
       'these persons'
       这些人
       (*The drowning persons*, texts)

   b. ɔ²¹   u²¹tsʰo²¹   **sui⁵⁵**
      this   person   PL/some
      'these persons'
      这些人

Place, time, and **manner/degree** demonstratives are often classified as adverbial demonstratives, i.e. demonstrative adverbs (Diessel 1999: 4). Despite this classification, they are nominal in nature in Caijia. Even though it is not common to find them in core argument positions, that is, as subject and object, time demonstratives present a special case and can be prepositional objects. Let us see some examples which show their nominal features.

The fused forms of place demonstratives are given in (3.9). The place distal demonstrative *ma²⁴* 'there' is the object of the verb *tɯ²¹* 'live, be at' in (3.9a), while the proximal *ua²⁴* 'here' is the object of the preposition *tɯ²¹* 'at' in (3.9b).

(3.9) a. je³³   tɯ²¹   **ma²⁴**.
       3SG   live/be.at   there
       'He lives/is there.'
       他住/在那儿。

   b. nɯ³³   tɯ²¹   **ua²⁴**   tɕie⁵⁵   mɔ⁵⁵?
      2SG   at   here   do   what
      'What're you doing here?'
      你在这儿干嘛？

The proximal time demonstrative ɔ²¹kɯ²⁴ 'now' serves as the object of the preposition *tɕiu⁵⁵* 'to' in the following example.

(3.10) tɕiu⁵⁵ ɔ²¹kɯ²⁴ ŋo³³ la²¹ pɣ³³ tiu³³u³³ se²¹.
to now 1SG even NEG know AFF.PRT
'I didn't even know until now.'
到现在我都不知道。

The proximal manner demonstrative ɔ²¹sʅ⁵⁵ 'this way' is the object of the verb 'resemble, be like' in (3.11a), while the distal mɔ²¹sʅ⁵⁵ 'that way' is a prepositional object in (3.11b). Note that mɔ²¹sʅ⁵⁵ can be analyzed as an adverb when tsɔ²¹ 'as' is not used, as in the case of (3.11b).

(3.11) a. nɯ³³ piɔ²⁴ tsɔ²¹ **ɔ²¹sʅ⁵⁵**.
2SG NEG.IMP resemble this.way
'Don't be like this.'
你别像这样。

b. (tsɔ²¹) **mɔ²¹sʅ⁵⁵** tɕie⁵⁵ pɣ³³ kʰua²¹.
as that.way do NEG good
'It's not good to do like that.'
（像）那样做不好。

3.3 Nouns

Nouns can be understood as "the class of words in which occur the names of most persons, places and things" (Schachter and Shopen 2007: 5, cf. Creissels 2006a: 37). They designate "a region in some domain" (Langacker 1987: 58). In Caijia, monosyllabic nouns make up a big portion of the noun class. Morphology alone does almost nothing to differentiate them from other parts of speech. Compare the nouns and verbs listed below. One can observe that there are no morphological devices which can help to tell verbs and nouns apart. This phenomenon exists in many isolating languages.

(3.12) Noun Verb
a. dʐ³³ 'chopstick' 筷子 dʐ³³ 'bear (fruit)' 着/结（果）
b. kʐ³³ 'foot' 脚 kʐ²¹ 'sit' 坐
c. lɛ²¹ 'land' 地 lɛ²¹ 'reach out' 够

The only way to identify nouns is to examine their meanings, distributional features and syntactic behaviors.

3.3.1 Distributional features of Caijia nouns

In Caijia, common nouns possess the following features. They serve as:
i. core and oblique arguments, i.e. subject, object, and prepositional object.

They can be restricted or modified by:
ii. classifiers or measure words;
iii. demonstratives;
iv. nouns, adjectives, or relative clauses;
v. possessive pronouns;
vi. postpositioned quantifiers;
vii. plural marker(s).

See example (3.1) above where the noun *nioŋ²⁴* 'daughter' is modified by several modifiers including classifier, demonstrative, possessive pronoun, and relative clause. Note that some nouns only possess some of features (ii – vii), while the distributional feature (i) is a common feature for all nouns. Let us consider some more examples. In (3.13a) and (3.13b) the noun *sɿ⁵⁵* 'water, river' is restricted by a numeral-measure phrase [NUM MEAS] and a numeral-classifier phrase [NUM CLF], respectively.

(3.13)　Measure word　　　　　　　　　Classifier
　　　a.　sɿ⁵⁵　　ji³³　　tɕɯŋ²¹　　b.　sɿ⁵⁵　　ji²¹　　tsɿ⁵⁵
　　　　　water　one　　bottle　　　　　river　one　　CLF
　　　　　'a bottle of water'　　　　　　'a river'
　　　　　一瓶水　　　　　　　　　　　　一条河

In (3.14), it is the phrase [DEM N CLF] that serves as the subject.

(3.14)　[mɔ²¹　tʰɣ⁵⁵po²¹　po⁵⁵]　a²¹tsɛ⁵⁵　tʰa³³　　　　　　　sɿ²¹.
　　　　that　oven　　　　CLF　　still　　be.out.of.order　CONT
　　　　'That oven still doesn't work.'
　　　　那个炉子还坏着。

The example below shows a case where the plural noun *ŋa⁵⁵sui⁵⁵* 'children' is modified by a relative clause and the third person singular pronoun to indicate a possessive relation.

(3.15) [je³³ ᵣₑₗ[nian²¹tɕi³³ tsʰɿ⁵⁵] sɿ²¹ ₙ[ŋa⁵⁵-sui⁵⁵]]]
   3SG   age   light   REL   child-PL
   'her children of younger age'
   她年纪小的孩子们
   (*Exchange of product*, texts)

However, not all Caijia nouns interact with classifiers or measure words. The word *kɛ²¹* 'price' in (3.16) and the word *ja²¹pa²¹* 'crops, farming, work' in (3.17) are examples of such nouns, although they can still be restricted by other elements. In (3.16), the word *kɛ²¹* 'price' is modified by the noun *li²¹* 'pig' and *li²¹ kɛ²¹* is modified by the proximal demonstrative. Alternatively, *li²¹ kɛ²¹* 'price of pork' can also be analyzed as a compound word, which will be discussed in §3.3.2.1. Note that the adjective *la²¹to⁵⁵* 'old' is used to denote 'expensive' in this context.

(3.16) [ɔ²¹ [li²¹ kɛ²¹]] la²¹to⁵⁵ xɪŋ⁵⁵ ɔ mẽ!
   this pig   price   old   very   PRT PRT
   'The price of pork is very high.'
   这猪肉价高得很。

In (3.17a), the word *ja²¹pa²¹* 'crops, farming, work', serving as the object in an object marking construction, is modified by *ɔ²¹* 'this'. In (3.17b), *ja²¹pa²¹* is modified by the locational phrase *so³³ mo³³* 'in the hand', as well as by the postpositioned quantifier *mi⁵⁵* 'a little'.

(3.17) a. a³³ [ɔ²¹ ja²¹pa²¹] niɔ²¹tɕɪŋ⁵⁵ xɪŋ⁵⁵.
       OM this farming   prioritize   very
       'Prioritize the farming.'
       把活儿抓紧。

   b. ɔ²¹ sɿ³³ [[so³³ mo³³] sɿ²¹ ₙ[ja²¹pa²¹] mi⁵⁵]].
      this COP hand   inside MOD   work   a.little
      'This is what I'm good at (LIT: This is a little work in my hand).'
      这是我擅长的（LIT:这是我手里的一点活儿）。

Unlike the common nouns, proper nouns tend not to be modified and they can usually be observed as either core or oblique arguments, as shown in (3.18) and (3.19).

(3.18) je³³   ɣa²¹   **loŋ⁵⁵kɯ²¹**   kuɛ²¹   o.
3SG   walk   Bijie_PLACENAME   go   CRS
'He went to Bijie.'
他去毕节了。

(3.19) lɔ²⁴ni³³   sɿ³³   **li²¹kʰɛ⁵⁵tɕy³³**?
who   COP   NAME
'Who is Li Kaiju?'
谁是李开举？

Where this is not the case, demonstratives are the most common modifiers, as shown in (3.20) and (3.21).

(3.20) je³³   sɿ³³   niɔ³³   tɯ²¹   [mɔ³³   tsʰui³³tɕia³³ja⁵⁵kʰɯ²¹]
3SG   COP   PROSP   at   that   bealock.of.the.Family.Cui_PLACENAME
ma²⁴   pɔ²¹-xɯ⁵⁵   e,   niɔ³³   ɕi³³   u²¹tsʰo²⁴   xa³³.
there   squat-DUR   PRT   PROSP   kill   person   REP
'(He) said that he would squat at the bealock of the Family Cui (to wait for the person) and kill him.'
说他是要在那崔家垭口那儿，蹲着（堵他们），要杀人。
(*The two families*, texts)

(3.21) mɔ²¹kɯ²⁴   [mɔ²¹   ɪn³³ɕyɔ²¹tsʰaŋ³³]   sɿ³³   tɯ²¹
that.time   that   NAME   COP   be.at
ɔ²¹   koŋ⁵⁵ɕiɔ³³sɛ²⁴   mo³³.
this   supply.and.marketing.agency   inside
'At that time, that Yin Xuechang was working in the supply and marketing agency.'
那时候印学昌是在供销社（工作）。

The following example is the only case in our data where a proper noun is modified by both the distal demonstrative and an adjective. Denoting 'far', *po⁵⁵* is only used to modify place words in the form illustrated below. Hu Hongyan (2013) treats *po⁵⁵* as a 'yonder' locational demonstrative. However, given that *po⁵⁵* 'far' and *mɔ²¹* 'that' are used in adjacent positions in the example below, it is hardly plausible to analyze *po⁵⁵* as a demonstrative.

(3.22) je³³   ɣa²¹   [po⁵⁵   mɔ²¹   suaŋ⁵⁵uɛ⁵⁵]   kuɛ²¹   o.
       3SG   walk   far   that   Weining_PLACENAME   go   CRS
       'He went to the faraway Weining.'
       他去那个在很远的威宁了。

3.3.2 Noun formations

In Caijia, two strategies of noun formation are observed: compounding and suffixation. Compounding is much more common than suffixation, which codes plurality.

3.3.2.1 Compounds

The definition of the morpheme as the smallest unit of meaning is well-known. In contrast, the word can be composed of either a single morpheme or multiple morphemes. Words made up of a single morpheme in Caijia are usually also monosyllabic, as shown in (3.12), but they can be polysyllabic as well. For example, the two nouns in (3.23) are disyllabic. Neither of their component syllables are analyzable as a morpheme, which means that the internal structure for each of these two words is monomorphemic.

(3.23) a.   ta²¹to³³   'spider' 蜘蛛

       b   u³³tsʰo³³   'person' 人

Caijia words with multiple morphemes are composed of two or more syllables, each of them being analyzable. This kind of word formation is often described as 'compounding' in the literature on Chinese linguistics (Chao 1968: 552–563, Li and Thompson 1981: Chapter 6, 45–81) and it is a commonly attested and very productive process in analytic languages. Compounding is also the major word formation strategy in Caijia. None of the other common strategies of word formation in Sinitic, such as suffixation (see §3.3.2.2), prefixation or reduplication (Chao 1968: Chapter 4, Li and Thompson 1981: 28–44) are systematically attested in Caijia.

However, difficulties do indeed exist when distinguishing compound words from words of a single morpheme in Caijia. Sometimes, even though a word appears to contain multiple morphemes in its composition, consultants may not be able to explain each morpheme. Therefore, what is presented in this section are those words for which it is certain that they are veritable compounds, some of which are composed themselves of disyllabic monomorphemic constituents,

such as (3.25) and (3.7). On the basis of our data, the following types of nominal compounds can be identified:
i. Modifier-head compounds,
ii. Head-modifier compounds,
iii. Conjunct compounds,
iv. (S)VO compounds.

3.3.2.1.1 Modifier-head compounds

The modifier-head compounds are the most common type found in the formation of nouns. The following four examples illustrate different modifiers that modify their respective right-positioned heads.

(3.24) ni²¹-sʅ⁵⁵
eye-water
'tear'
眼泪

(3.25) [tɔ³³   sɔ³³]-tsʅ²¹tsʅ²⁴
[peck   tree]-bird
'woodpecker'
啄木鸟

(3.26) la²¹to⁵⁵-u²¹tsʰo²¹
old-person
'dead person'
过世的人

(3.27) [kua²¹   soŋ³³koŋ²¹]-u³³pa³³
[spotted   neck]-crow
'white-collared crow'
白颈鸦

(3.28) nioŋ²¹-hɛ⁵⁵
girl-younger.brother
'younger sister'
妹妹

(3.29) tɛ²¹sʅ⁵⁵-hɔ⁵⁵
dew-road
'the Milky Way'
银河

In Sinitic languages, gender affixes for animals are used as one of the criteria for grouping northern and southern dialects (Hashimoto 1976, Norman 1988). The form [prefix-N] is considered as the northern pattern, while the form [N-suffix] is treated as the southern pattern. Caijia seemingly adopts the southern pattern. It uses *bo³³* to denote 'male' and *tɕie⁵⁵* to denote 'female', as shown below. The morpheme *tɕie⁵⁵* is probably derived from the word 'sister'.

(3.30) a. kɪ³³-bo³³
chicken-male
'rooster'
公鸡

b. kɪ²¹-tɕie⁵⁵
chicken-female
'hen'
母鸡

(3.31) a. ŋɔ²¹-bo³³   b. ŋɔ²¹-tɕie⁵⁵
            cow-male   cow-female
            'bull'   'cow'
            公牛   母牛

However, we treat this kind of word formation in Caijia as a modifier-head compound, since both *bo³³* 'male', which also surfaces as *po³³*, and *tɕie⁵⁵* 'female', function as independent nouns. Examples (3.32a) and (3.32b) are answers to the question 'Is that rabbit female or male?'. Both *bo³³* and *tɕie⁵⁵* are modified by the classifier *kʷɔ²¹* used for animal terms serving as copular complements. This means that these two morphemes are independent nouns according to the determining criteria for nouns listed in §3.3.1.

(3.32) -   mɔ²¹   tʰɣ²⁴   kʷɔ²¹   sɿ²¹   tɕie⁵⁵   lɔ²¹   sɿ²¹   bo²⁴?
            that   rabbit CLF   COP   female   or   COP   male
            'Is that rabbit male or female?'
            那只兔子是公是母？

        a- sɿ²¹   tɕie⁵⁵   **kʷɔ²¹**.   b- sɿ²¹   bo²⁴   **kʷɔ²¹**.
            COP   female   CLF   COP   male   CLF
            'It's female.'   'It's male.'
            是母的。   是公的。

The morpheme *tɕie⁵⁵* is stably used to denote the female gender of animals, while *bo³³* is commonly but not exclusively used to signal the male gender. The morphemes *pa²⁴*, *kʰa²⁴*, and *peŋ²⁴* possess the same meaning: *kʰa²⁴* is exclusively used for horses and *peŋ²⁴* is particularly employed for pigs, while *pa²⁴* is probably derived from *pa³³* 'grandfather'. On the basis of its sound and meaning, *peŋ²⁴* is probably cognate with *fén* 豶 [fən²⁴] 'boar' in Sinitic.

(3.33) a. kʰui³³-pa²⁴   b. kʰɣ⁵⁵-pa³³
            dog-male   tiger-male
            'male dog'   'tiger/male tiger'
            公狗   老虎/公老虎

        c. li²¹-peŋ²⁴   d. mɛ²¹-kʰa²⁴
            pig-male   horse-male
            'boar'   'male horse'
            公猪   公马

3.3.2.1.2 Head-modifier compounds

Nouns composed of a head-modifier compound make up an extremely small fraction of the noun inventory. This strategy is mainly observed in the formation of terms for castrated domestic animals. The word $kɿ^{33}ti^{33}$ 'capon' in (3.34) is composed of the word $kɿ^{33}$ 'chicken' and the verb ti^{33} 'sew' and it can thus be literally interpreted as 'sewn chicken'. The term $li^{21}kɿ^{55}$ 'castrated pig' in (3.35) is formed in the same fashion and can be interpreted as 'tied pig'. In contrast to the gender compounds, both ti^{33} 'sew' and $kɿ^{55}$ 'tie' follow their respective heads.

(3.34) $kɿ^{33}$-ti^{33}
  chicken-sew
  'capon'
  阉鸡

(3.35) li^{21}-$kɿ^{55}$
  pig-tie
  'hog'
  阉猪

3.3.2.1.3 Conjunct compounds

Conjunct compounds are usually composed of two morphemes of the same category. The two morphemes in a conjunct compound do not show modifier-modified relation. Instead, they are more like NP coordination with zero marking. When compounded together, a new word is produced. Examples (3.36) and (3.37) are the cases of two verbs and two adjectives combined together, respectively, while (3.38) and (3.39) are cases of two nouns.

(3.36) $soŋ^{21}$-$zɤ^{33}$
  hurt-itch
  'symptom'
  病症

(3.37) $tɤ^{21}$-$tsʰo^{33}$
  be.long-be.short
  'gossip'
  闲话

(3.38) $tsɤ^{33}$-kui^{33}
  root-bone
  'family background'
  家世背景

(3.39) $sɿ^{55}$-$lɛ^{21}$
  water-field
  'place', 'wealth'
  地方，财产

3.3.2.1.4 (S)VO compounds

(S)VO compounds are the nouns whose internal structures are either VPs or full clauses, out of which new meanings are reanalyzed. Take (3.40) as an example. As a noun, $sɿ^{21}kʰɯ^{55}$ denotes 'knowledge'. As a VP, $sɿ^{21}\ kʰɯ^{55}$ denotes '(can) read, be literate'. Compare (3.40b) and (3.40c).

(3.40) a. sɿ²¹-kʰɯ⁵⁵
            recognize-word
            'knowledge'
            学问

        b. ŋo³³ pɣ³³ sɿ²¹ kʰɯ⁵⁵.
            1SG   NEG   recognize word
            'I'm illiterate', 'I can't read.'
            我不识字。

        c. je³³ sɿ²¹kʰɯ⁵⁵ la²¹.
            3SG   knowledge   big
            'He's learned.'
            他学问大。

Several more examples are given below. The VP 'find the road' is reanalyzed as the noun 'idea' in (3.41); the VP 'prick person', as in (3.42), is actually the physical property of a kind of nettle known for its soft burrs.

(3.41) go²¹-hɔ⁵⁵   (3.42) tsʰa³³-ni²¹
        find-road   prick-3
        'idea'   'nettle'
        主意   禾麻

In (3.43), the full clause 'dragon drinks water', inside which the word ɣoŋ²¹ 'dragon' is the subject, is used to refer to a 'rainbow'. One can observe from the example that it is modified by the classifier ʈa⁵⁵ or hɔ⁵⁵ which reveals clearly its nature of being a noun.

(3.43) ɣoŋ²¹-ã²¹-sɿ⁵⁵   ji²¹   ʈa⁵⁵/hɔ⁵⁵
        dragon-drink-water   one   CLF
        'a rainbow'
        一道彩虹

3.3.2.2 Suffixation

Even though it is very rare, suffixation is also observed in Caijia. (See also §3.7 for the nominalizer bo⁵⁵.) Two markers are used to code plurality. They are:
i.   -sui⁵⁵
ii. -xɯ⁵⁵

The suffix -*sui*^{55} is derived from its lexical form 'some', while -*xɯ*^{55} is a loan morpheme from Lolo and is used as a plural suffix. This function can be observed in several Lolo varieties, for example, -*xɯ*^{33} in Nisu (Zhai Huifeng 2011: 40) and -*yo*^{44} in Nuosu (Gerner 2013: 124). The two plural markers behave differently. The morpheme -*sui*^{55} is suffixed to common nouns, whereas -*xɯ*^{55} can be suffixed to both common nouns and pronouns (see §3.4 for more details), even though the suffix -*sui*^{55} is overwhelmingly preferred. Examples are given below to illustrate both their uses. Examples (3.44) and (3.45) are extracted from spontaneous narratives. Example (3.46) shows the inanimate plural noun *tɔ*^{21}*p*^{h}*a*^{24} 'history'. Consultants confirmed that in the following three examples -*xɯ*^{55} can be substituted for -*sui*^{55}.

(3.44) je^{21} ta^{55} mɔ^{21} ŋa^{55}-**sui**^{55} xa^{33}: "ŋa^{55}-**sui**^{55}, tsʰ₁^{33} sɔ^{21}mɔ^{55}! ..."
3SG with that child-PL say child-PL fear what
'She said to her children: "My kids, don't worry! [...]"'
她跟那些孩子们说："孩子们，怕什么！......"
(*Exchange of product*, texts)

(3.45) ŋo^{33} kuɛ^{33} xaŋ^{33} je^{33} tsa^{21}-**sui**^{55} ɣɯ^{21} [...]
1SG go call 3SG uncle-PL come
'I went to ask his uncles to come.'
我去喊他叔叔们来。
(*The life of Zhao Guozhen*, texts)

(3.46) ŋo^{55} meŋ^{21}ni^{33} tsɔ^{21} mɔ^{21} tɔ^{21}pʰa^{24}-**sui**^{55},
1PL Caijia people that history-PL
xuɔ^{21} ŋo^{21} tɔ^{55}pa^{33} la^{33} pɣ^{33} tiu^{33}u^{33} nɛ^{33},
even 1SG great.grandfather also NEG know PRT
piɔ^{24} xa^{21} ŋo^{21} pa^{55} o.
NEG.IMP say 1SG father CRS
'As for the history of us Caijia people, even my great grandfather doesn't know (anything about it), let alone my father.'
我们蔡家人那些历史，连我祖爷都不知道的话，别说我爸了。

Examples (3.47) and (3.48) are extracted from traditional Caijia drinking verses, which are chanted when drinking and in which there are often uncommonly used expressions or terms from daily life.

(3.47) tsʰʅ⁵⁵ pɪŋ⁵⁵ tsʰʅ⁵⁵ u³³ mɤ²¹tɕiaŋ²¹-**xɯ⁵⁵** a,
village side village back aromatic.litsea-PL PRT
tɯ²¹ sɣ̩³³ pɣ³³ ni³³ kʰɯ³³.
at snow put sun open
'The aromatic litsea trees blossom when the sunny days come after the snow.'
寨边寨后的木姜啊，在雪后放晴时绽放。
(*Drinking verses*, texts)

(3.48) tʰã²¹luɔ²¹ ã²¹ kʰuɔ³³ nɛ³³,
basket jar put.in PRT
sʅ³³ sʅ²¹tsʰuã²¹ jɔ²¹-**xɯ⁵⁵** tsɯ²⁴.
COP Sichuan_PLACENAME Hmong-PL fabric
'What the baskets and jars hold is the fabric made by the Hmong people of Sichuan.'
筐里罐里装的是四川苗人织的布。
(*Drinking verses*, texts)

There is a common rule for both -*sui*⁵⁵ and -*xɯ*⁵⁵: they do not interact with classifiers or measure words, as shown below.

(3.49) a. nioŋ²⁴-*sui⁵⁵/*xɯ⁵⁵ ta⁵⁵ ni²¹   b. nioŋ²⁴ ta⁵⁵ ni²¹
girl-PL two CLF   girl two CLF
'two girls'   'two girls'
两个女孩   两个女孩

This feature can be explained by the principle of economy in linguistics, since it might be redundant to have both the numeral classifier phrase and the plural marking. As noted by Greenberg, "Numeral classifier languages generally do not have compulsory expression of nominal plurality, but at most facultative expression" (1974: 25).

3.4 Pronouns

Pronouns substitute for nouns and form a limited closed class of words. They thus can function as core and oblique arguments, and modifiers. Yet they differ from nouns in several respects. For example, they usually are not modified by demonstratives, adjectives or [NUM CLF] phrases. The structure [PRO NUM CLF] indeed exists, but the pronoun and the [NUM CLF] phrase are not in a head-modified relation. Instead, they show a relation of apposition: [PRO] [NUM CLF].

(3.50) a. *mɔ²¹ je³³
          that   3SG
          (Attempted: '*two he')
          *那他

b. nɯ²⁴ sa²¹ lɛ²⁴
   2PL   three CLF
   'the three of you'
   她们三个
   (*Three daughters-in-law*, texts)

3.4.1 Personal pronouns

The Caijia personal pronouns are listed in Table 3.2.

Table 3.2: Caijia personal pronouns.

	SG HON	SG	PL	
1		ŋo³³	ŋo²⁴	ŋo²⁴-xɯ⁵⁵
2	nɯ³³la²¹to⁵⁵/nɯ³³la²¹tiŋ⁵⁵	nɯ³³	nɯ²⁴	nɯ²⁴-xɯ⁵⁵
3	je³³la²¹to⁵⁵/je³³la²¹tiŋ⁵⁵	je³³	je²⁴	je²¹-xɯ⁵⁵
			ni³³	

One can observe from Table 3.2 that there are two types of plural pronouns. One type is realized by a change of tone, from the mid-level [33] to the high-rising contour [24]. It has also been observed that the monosyllabic forms of the plural personal pronouns sometimes surface as the high-level tone [55] in fluent speech. Compare the two sentences in (3.51).

(3.51) a. **ŋo²⁴** ji²¹ la²¹ tsʰo²¹ tɯ²¹ ma²⁴ na³³xa²¹lɛ²¹.
          1PL   one big group at   there cultivate.virgin.land
          'The big group of us were cultivating the virgin land there.'
          我们一大帮在那儿开荒。
          (*Two little tigers*, texts)

b. mɔ²¹kɯ⁵⁵ a,   **ŋo⁵⁵** ɣã²¹ la²¹tо⁵⁵ u²¹tsʰo²⁴ ni⁵⁵.
   that.time PRT 1PL   have old   person   CLF
   'At that time, there was an old person (in our place) (LIT: we had an old person).'
   以前，我们（那儿）有个老人。
   (*Exchange of product*, texts)

The other type is formed via suffixation with the loan suffix *-xɯ⁵⁵* from Lolo, as mentioned earlier above. Compare the forms given above with the plural pronouns in Nisu, a Lolo language spoken in the same area as Caijia.

(3.52) Nisu plural pronouns (Zhai Huifeng 2011: 40)
   1PL   ŋʊ²¹-xɯ³³
   2PL   na²¹-xɯ³³
   3PL   thi²¹-xɯ³³

(3.53) kʰɪŋ⁵⁵mi²¹sa³³ je²¹-xɯ⁵⁵ tɯ²¹ tsʰe⁵⁵-kuɛ²¹ tɔ²¹ ni³³.
   evening   3-PL   then go.out-go   steal 3
   'They go out to steal people in the evening.'
   晚上他们就出去偷人家。
   (*Three thieves*, texts)

Below is an example with the first and the second person singular pronouns serving in different syntactic positions, i.e. subject, pivotal object-subject, object.

(3.54) "**nɯ²¹** koŋ⁵⁵koŋ⁵⁵ la²¹ soŋ²¹ zɣ⁵⁵ sɿ⁵⁵   **ŋo²¹** zɣ²¹
   2SG   every.day   all   send   meal give/let 1SG   eat
   se³³,   **ŋo³³** tʰai²⁴ tɔ²¹ **nɯ³³** xɪŋ⁵⁵ ɔ   lɔ. [...]"
   CONT.PRT 1SG   too   miss 2SG   very   PRT PRT
   'You've been bringing my meals every day to give me to eat and I long for you so much.'
   你天天都送饭给我吃，我太喜欢你了。
   (*The man and the stone*, texts)

Honorific forms are used for the second- and third-person singular pronouns when addressing people of advanced age. The morpheme *la²¹tо⁵⁵* serves also as an adjective denoting 'old', while *la²¹tɪŋ⁵⁵* is exclusively used to form honorific pronouns.

(3.55) **[nɯ³³la²¹to⁵⁵]/[nɯ³³la²¹tɪŋ⁵⁵]**, nian²¹tɕi²⁴ la²¹ xɪŋ⁵⁵ o.
2SG.HON age big very CRS
'You (reached) a very high age.'
您老人家，年纪很大了。

The third person pronoun *ni³³* 'people, other, someone (else)', which can also be used as a classifier for human nouns, can be used in either the singular or plural. Furthermore, it can be either indefinite or definite in reference. Its exact meaning depends entirely on its context. As illustrated in (3.56), the first *ni³³* is indefinite, for it is the first time the referent is mentioned in the narrative. On the contrary, the second and the third *ni³³* are both definite, since these two refer to the person that wanted to exchange the jar for some rice. Both of the latter *ni³³* can be replaced by the third person singular *je³³* without any change of meaning.

(3.56) **ni²⁴** a⁵⁵ ã²¹ã⁵⁵ ɣɯ²¹ lɯ²¹ mi⁵⁵. **ni³³** xa²¹ tsʰɛ²¹ niɔ²¹
3 take jar PURP exchange rice 3 say only want
pa³³ seŋ³³ a, je³³ a²¹ pe⁵⁵ seŋ²¹ sɿ⁵⁵ **ni³³**.
half UNIT PRT 3SG take eight UNIT to 3
'Someone took a jar to exchange for some rice. He said he just wanted one kilo (of rice), but she gave him eight kilos.'
人拿罐子换米。人说才要半升（米），她给人八升。
(*Exchange of product*, texts)

The pronoun *ni³³* in (3.57), by contrast, denotes a plural referent because it is usually a group of people that go to greet a bride. See also *ni³³* in (3.53).

(3.57) lɔ²⁴koŋ⁵⁵ **ni³³** niu²¹ so⁵⁵po²⁴ ta⁵⁵ ma²⁴ kua²¹ nɛ⁵⁵ [...]
when 3 greet wife from there pass.by PRT
'When people greeting bride pass by, ...'
哪天人家接亲从那儿过呢，......
(*The man and the tiger*, texts)

3.4.2 Possessives

The Caijia pronominal and adnominal possessives can both be formed via the marker *hm̩⁵⁵* of which the source is unclear. Importantly, the marker *hm̩⁵⁵* is obligatory when it is used to form pronominal possessives, while it is optional when forming adnominal possessives. These points will be examined in detail in the following sections.

3.4.2.1 Pronominal possessives

Possessive pronouns substitute nouns for possessum nouns, that is, a possessed object or person, equivalent to 'mine', 'yours', 'his', etc. in English. The Caijia possessive pronouns are listed in Table 3.3 below.

Table 3.3: Caijia possessive pronouns.

	SG	PL
1	ŋo^{21} hm̩^{55} 'mine'	ŋo^{24} hm̩^{55} 'ours'
2	nɯ^{21} hm̩^{55} 'yours'	nɯ^{24} hm̩^{55} 'yours'
3	je^{21} hm̩^{55} 'his'	je^{24} hm̩^{55} 'theirs'
	ni^{21} hm̩^{55} 'someone's, people's, his, theirs'	

One can immediately perceive that the marker hm̩^{55} follows the pronoun, representing the most common order of possessive and possessive marker in the languages of the world (Dryer 2013a). Let us see some examples.

Serving as the object of the negated verb pγ^{33} lɛ^{21} 'not reach' in (3.58), the pronoun nɯ^{21} hm̩^{55} 'yours' stands for the whole NP, 'your hand writing', after omission of the possessum noun. In (3.59), being a copular subject, nɯ^{21} hm̩^{55} 'yours' in boldface stands in for 'what you have', while ŋo^{21} hm̩^{55} in boldface refers to 'what I have'.

(3.58) je^{33} je^{21} sɿ^{21} kʰɯ^{55} pγ^{33} lɛ^{21} **nɯ^{21} hm̩^{55}**.
    3SG   write   REL   word   NEG   reach   2SG   POSS
    'The characters written by him aren't as good as yours'
    他写的字不如你的。

(3.59) **nɯ^{21} hm̩^{55}** sɿ^{21} nɯ^{21} hm̩^{55}, **ŋo^{21} hm̩^{55}** sɿ^{21} ŋo^{21} hm̩^{55}.
    2SG   POSS   COP   2SG   POSS   1SG   POSS   COP   1SG   POSS
    tɯ^{33}sɿ^{33} tɕʰiŋ^{21} tso^{55}hɛ^{55},   la^{21} niɔ^{21} peŋ^{55}-kʰɯ^{33}.
    Even   blood   sibling   all   should   divide-open
    'Yours is yours and mine is mine. Even though (we're) blood brothers, (we) need to do accounts correctly.'
    你的是你的，我的是我的。就是亲兄弟，也要分开。

Referring to 'the money he has', the pronoun *je²¹ hm̥⁵⁵* 'his' in (3.60) is the marked direct object of an object marking construction.

(3.60) ŋuɛ²¹   hɛ⁵⁵   kʰã⁵⁵   tv̩²¹   tɕiŋ²¹   xiŋ⁵⁵.
my.family younger.brother be.willing.to gamble money   very
je³³   a³³   **je²¹ hm̥⁵⁵** tv̩³³-sv̩²¹   ha⁵⁵   la²¹   pv̩³³
3SG OM   3SG POSS   gamble-lose   COMPL all   NEG
xa³³,   xuɔ²¹   ŋo³³ a²¹   sɿ⁵⁵   je²¹   sɿ²¹   la²¹   sv̩²¹
say   even   1SG take give 3SG   NMLZ   all   lose
lɯ⁵⁵   ji²¹   pʰe⁵⁵   la²¹   pv̩³³   ʑi²¹   o.
VCOMP one   UNIT   all   NEG   be.left CRS
'My younger brother often gambles. He lost not only his, but also lost all (the money) I gave him, so that there's not even a penny left.'
我弟弟爱赌钱得很。他不仅把他的输了，连我给他的都输得一分不剩。

One should be aware that suffixed plural pronouns are not typically used to form possessive pronouns. One must use the set which has undergone a tone changed. As in (3.61a), the plural pronoun *je²⁴* 'they', whose singular form is *je³³* 'he, she, it', is used along with *hm̥⁵⁵* to form the possessive pronoun, whereas using the suffixed form *je²¹-xɯ⁵⁵* 'they' is ungrammatical, as in (3.61b).

(3.61) a. ɔ²¹   sɿ³³   je²⁴   hm̥⁵⁵.
this   COP   3PL   POSS
'This is theirs.'
这是他们的。

b. *ɔ²¹   sɿ³³   je²¹-xɯ⁵⁵   hm̥⁵⁵.
this   COP   3-PL   POSS
(Attempted: 'This is theirs.')
这是他们的。

3.4.2.2 Adnominal possessives

When serving to form adnominal possessives, *hm̥⁵⁵* marks the possessor and the phrase [POSSESSOR hm̥⁵⁵] precedes the possessum. This order can be schematized as [POSSESSOR hm̥⁵⁵ POSSESSUM], which also represents the most common order of possessive and noun in the languages of the world (Dryer 2013b). See the following examples.

(3.62) [ni²¹ hm̥⁵⁵ ɔ²¹ kʷɔ²¹] kʰɯ²¹ kɿ⁵⁵kɿ⁵⁵ na²¹-pγ³³-tɕie⁵⁵
3   POSS this CLF   several   lump   beat-NEG-do
kɿ⁵⁵kɿ⁵⁵ mɔ²¹ o.
lump   that CRS
'(This jar) of his, several lumps (of clay) can't even be kneaded into that lump (of jar).'
人家这个，几坨坨（泥）也做不出那（个罐子）。
(*Exchange of product*, texts)

(3.63) mɔ²¹ u²¹tsʰo²⁴ ni³³ sɿ³³ [ŋuɛ²¹ pa⁵⁵ hm̥⁵⁵ ɛ³³tɯ³³].
that person   CLF COP my.famliy father POSS friend
'That person is my father's friend.'
那个人是我爸爸的朋友。

(3.64) je³³ tɯ³³ a²¹ [ti⁵⁵tɕɩŋ²¹ ɔ²⁴ ni²¹ hm̥⁵⁵ tɕɩŋ²¹] tɯ³³ a³³
3SG then OM front   this CLF POSS money   then DCR
kɿ⁵⁵ pie⁵⁵ je²¹ pe⁵⁵ tγ³³.   [. . .]
tie to   3SG hair upside
'He tied the money of this person in front to his (=the money owner's) hair.'
他就把前面这人的钱就系到他头发上。
(*Coins*, texts)

It is quite interesting that the ligature *sɿ²¹* can be used to link the phrase [POSSESSOR hm̥⁵⁵] and the possessum, which can be schematized as [[POSSESSOR hm̥⁵⁵] sɿ²¹ [POSSESSUM]], as demonstrated below. However, this phenomenon is not frequently observed in our data.

(3.65) tɯ²¹   ji³³kʰa³³ ni²⁴ tγ²¹ko⁵⁵ o, li²¹li²⁴ lɛ⁵⁵   tɯ³³ ji³³
be.at   together time long   CRS slowly   ADV   then one
ni³³ tiu³³u³³ ji³³ ni²¹ hm̥⁵⁵ sɿ²¹ saŋ³³ o.
CLF know   one CLF POSS MOD heart CRS
'(People) begin to know more about each other's personality (LIT: they begin to know **each other's** heart) when they spend a lot of time together.'
在一起时间久了，慢慢地，一个就了解一个的性情了。

In fact, personal pronouns can and indeed do tend to directly modify nouns to express a possessive relation. Inalienability and alienability are conceptual domains which often motivate different coding of possessive noun phrases in the languages of the world (Creissels 2006a: 152, Stassen 2013a), but these do not appear to affect this usage of personal pronouns in Caijia. If a possessum is obligatorily possessed by its possessor, this type of possession is identified as inalienable possession. Inalienable possession usually includes body parts, kinship terms, and part-whole relations. The phrase $je^{21}\ pe^{55}$ 'his hair' in (3.64) illustrates how the third person singular pronoun directly modifies the body-part term pe^{55} 'hair', which typically demonstrates the set of semantic categories recognized for inalienable possession. In spite of this, the two examples below show that personal pronouns can also directly modify what are typically considered to be alienable nouns, that is, without hm^{55} marking to express ownership.

(3.66) a³³ **nɯ²¹ pio⁵⁵** tsa⁵⁵ ŋo²¹ tɕi²¹ ji³³ xa²⁴ lɛ⁵⁵
      OM 2SG hoe lend 1SG use one VCLF PRT
      ŋo²¹ hm̩⁵⁵ tʰa²¹ kʷɔ²¹ o.
      1SG POSS be.broken go.CRS CRS
      'Could you lend me your hoe to use for a while? Mine is broken.'
      把你的锄头借我用一下。我的坏了。

(3.67) ŋo³³ tɯ³³sɿ³³ tsaŋ²¹ **nɯ⁵⁵ sʏ²¹** mi⁵⁵.
      1SG just look 2SG book a.little
      'I just took a look at your book.'
      我就是看了一下你的书。

It is worth mentioning that singular personal pronouns are often fused with the morpheme $hɛ^{21}$ 'family' to modify kinship terms and entities belonging to the whole family.

(3.68) ŋo³³ + hɛ²¹ → ŋuɛ²¹ 'my family' 我家
      nɯ³³ + hɛ²¹ → nɛ²¹ 'your family' 你家
      je³³ + hɛ²¹ → je²¹ 'his family' 他家

Example (3.69) is an extract from a speech addressed to all the dead family members of the speaker on the Ghost Festival on the 13th day of the seventh month of the Chinese Lunar Year. $tsɿ^{21}sa^{33}$ 'thirteen' in the example refers to the Ghost Festival.

(3.69) tɔ⁵⁵pa³³, tɔ⁵⁵ja³³, **ŋuɛ²¹** pa³³,
      great.grandfather great.grandmother my.family grandfather
      ŋuɛ²¹ ja³³, […], nɯ⁵⁵ tɛ²¹tɕʰi²⁴
      my.family grandmother   2PL everyone

ɣɯ²¹ kua³³ tsɿ²¹sa³³ la³³.
come celebrate thirteen PRT
'Great Grandfather, Great Grandmother, my Grandfather, my Grandmother, ... all of you, come to celebrate the Ghost Festival.'
祖爷，祖奶，我家爷爷，我家奶奶，......你们大家来过中元啊。

An example of *nɛ²¹* 'your family' is given below. Unfortunately, it is hard to find an example of *je²¹* denoting only 'his family' due to its form. Given that changes in tone commonly occurs in sequences of words or sentences, the phrase [je²¹ POSSESSUM] can be interpreted either as 'his possessum' or 'the possessum of his family's'.

(3.70) **nɛ²¹** ŋo²¹
your.family cow
'the cow of your family's'
'your cow'
你（家的）牛

A similar phenomenon is also observed in other Sinitic languages and the morpheme 'family' has further developed into a possessive marker in both Medieval Chinese (the 3rd century AD – 1250) and contemporary Sinitic languages (Wang Miao 2015). See the example from Shexian Hui below.

(3.71) Shexian Hui 歙县徽语
阿家家里
A **ka³³** JIALI
1SG POSS house
'(in) my house'
'(in) my family'
(Wang Miao 2015: 33, cited from Huang Borong 1996: 546)

However, *hɛ²¹* 'family' has not grammaticalized to this extent in Xingfa Caijia.[2]

---

[2] In the Weining Niuchishui variety of Caijia, the equivalent counterpart *xɛ²¹* 'family' has not only developed into a possessive marker, but has also developed into a nominalizer or modifier linker.

3.4.3 Reflexive pronoun and reciprocal expressions

The Caijia **reflexive pronoun** tsʅ²¹tɕia²⁴ is borrowed from the local Mandarin dialect *zìjiā* 自家 'oneself'. It can be used along with pronouns in the form of [PRO tsʅ²¹tɕia²⁴] and can also be used alone. The phrase [PRO tsʅ²¹tɕia²⁴] always denotes a definite reference, while whether *tsʅ²¹tɕia²⁴* alone denotes definiteness or not depends on its context.

König and Gast (2002) point out that *self*-forms in English can be divided into anaphoric reflexives and emphatic reflexives. These two types possess different distributional features. For example, the English pronoun *herself* in the sentence *She kept some flowers for herself* is an anaphoric reflexive, while *herself* in the sentence *Olivia herself put out the fire in the kitchen* is an emphatic reflexive. This functional contrast is also observed in Caijia and both of the two forms, that is, the bare form *tsʅ²¹tɕia²⁴* and the compound form [PRO tsʅ²¹tɕia²⁴] can be used to denote both types of reflexive. However, anaphoric and emphatic reflexives can still be distinguished in Caijia.

An **anaphoric reflexive** in a predicate is usually co-referent with the subject of the same predicate. See the following two examples. The compound reflexive pronoun *nɯ³³tsʅ²¹tɕia²⁴* 'yourself' in (3.72) is the object of the verb *pia³³* 'ask' and is co-referent with the subject *nɯ³³* 'you'. Example (3.73) contains two pivotal clauses. The reflexive *je³³tsʅ²¹tɕia²⁴* 'himself' is the object of *sʅ⁵⁵* 'give, let' and is co-referent with the subject *je³³* 'he', which is also the object of the causative verb *sʅ⁵⁵* 'let' in the sentence initial position.

(3.72) [nɯ³³]ᵢ pia³³ [(**nɯ³³**) **tsʅ²¹tɕia²⁴**]ᵢ mi⁵⁵ nɯ³³ xa²¹ pia³³ŋoŋ³³
      2SG   ask   2SG   oneself   a.little 2SG say lie
      lɔ²¹   pỵ³³-tỵ³³!
      or   NEG-PFV
      'You ask yourself if you lied (to me)!'
      你问问（你）自己你说谎了没！

(3.73) sʅ⁵⁵ [je²¹]ᵢ ɔ²¹ mi⁵⁵ sʅ⁵⁵ [(je²¹) **tsʅ²¹tɕia²⁴**]ᵢ zy²¹ mɛ̃²¹.
      let 3SG keep some give/let 3SG   oneself   eat PRT
      'Ask him to keep some for himself to eat.'
      让他留点给自己吃嘛。

By contrast, an **emphatic reflexive** is not co-referent with another argument within the same predicate and can be replaced by a personal pronoun. In (3.74), the reflexive *je³³tsʅ²¹tɕia²⁴* 'himself' is the subject of the adjective *tɕʰi³³kʰa³³* 'be happy'. Within the bracketed clause, *je³³tsʅ²¹tɕia²⁴* 'himself' is the only argument and therefore it can be co-referential with another argument. Furthermore, it can be unproblematically replaced by the third person pronoun *je³³* 'he, she'. By comparison, if the anaphoric reflexive *je³³tsʅ²¹tɕia²⁴* 'himself' is replaced by *je³³* 'he' in (3.73), the sentence will be ungrammatical.

(3.74) niɔ²¹   sʅ⁵⁵   [**je²¹ tsʅ²¹tɕia²⁴**   tɕʰi³³kʰa³³]   tsʰɛ³³   niɔ²¹tɣ³³
should   let   3SG   oneself   be.happy   only.then be.all.right
              je³³ 'he, she'
'It's feasible only if she agrees herself.'
她自己同意才行。

In a similar fashion, *tsʅ²¹tɕia²⁴* in (3.75ii) functions as the subject and can be replaced by the first-person pronoun *ŋo³³* 'I'.

(3.75) i) ni²⁴   mɔ²¹-sui⁵⁵   nɛ⁵⁵   ɣã³³tɕiŋ²¹ɣã³³ma³³   lɛ³³,
3   that-PL   PRT   rich   CONT
niɔ³³   sʅ²¹mɔ⁵⁵   la³³   a²¹   lɯ⁵⁵   tsʰe⁵⁵-ɣɯ²¹.
need   what   all   take   VCOMP   be.out-come
ii) **tsʅ²¹tɕia⁵⁵**   nɛ⁵⁵   ka⁵⁵tʰɣ²¹tʰɣ²⁴   lɛ⁵⁵,
oneself   PRT   poor   CONT
ŋo³³ 'I'
ji²¹tsoŋ⁵⁵   la²¹   pɣ³³   ɣã²¹.
anything   even   NEG   have
'For those that are rich, whatever is needed, they can afford. As for myself, I'm poor and have nothing.'
人家那些呢，有钱有财的，要什么都拿得出来。自己呢，穷兮兮的，什么都没有。

It was mentioned above that the reflexive *tsʅ²¹tɕia²⁴* can denote either definiteness or indefiniteness. To be specific, it is actually the emphatic *tsʅ²¹tɕia²⁴* that can be ambiguous, while the anaphoric form always denotes definiteness. For example, the sentence in (3.76) is addressed to a person who lost her husband and was uttered in order to soothe her. In such a context, the emphatic *tsʅ²¹tɕia²⁴* refers to 'yourself'. Otherwise, it would refer to 'oneself' outside of this context.

(3.76) tsʅ²¹tɕia²⁴   niɔ³³   pɣ²¹   kʰua²¹saŋ²¹kʰua²¹sʅ²⁴   mi⁵⁵.
oneself   should   put   be.relax   a.little
'You must let (the sadness) go by yourself.'
'One must let (the sadness) go by oneself.'
自己要放宽心。

Caijia does not possess reciprocal pronouns, but the **reciprocal meaning** can be realized in a periphrastic way via pronominal phrases in the form of
i.   [2SG VP$_i$ 1SG, 1SG VP$_i$ 2SG] or
ii. [ʑi^{33} CLF VP$_i$ ʑi^{33} CLF VP$_{ii}$]

denoting 'do something with each other'. These two schemata are usually inter-transformable. One should note that in the first schema, the two VPs of the two clauses should be the same. Furthermore, the first and the second singular pronouns can no longer be literally interpreted. For example, (3.77) describes a reciprocal action between two little tigers from a third person perspective. The 'you' and 'I' in the bold clause apparently refer to the two little tigers.

(3.77) ɕie²¹   kʰɣ⁵⁵pa²⁴   ta⁵⁵   kʷɔ²¹   […]   tɯ²¹   mɔ³³   ti²¹   tɣ³³
        small   tiger.DIM   two   CLF   at   that   hill   upside
        ko²¹-pɣ³³-tɣ³³,   zɣ²¹   sɿ²¹,
        find-NEG-obtain   eat   NMLZ
        nɯ³³   na³³   ŋo³³   ŋo³³   na³³   nɯ³³   lɛ³³.
        2SG   beat   1SG   1SG   beat   2SG   CONT
        'The two little tigers up on the hill. . .couldn't find anything to eat and were playing around with each other.'
        两只小老虎在山上找不到吃的，你打我我打你地（玩）。
        (*Two little tigers*, texts)

The example below is extracted from a dialogue but in this case the 'you' and 'me' do not refer to the two participants involved in this dialogue. Instead, they are used to express a reciprocal meaning.

(3.78) niɔ³³   ɣã²¹   u²¹tsʰo²¹   ta⁵⁵   ni²¹   tɯ²¹   ji²¹kʰa⁵⁵,
        need   there.be   person   two   CLF   at   one.place
        nɯ³³   xa³³   ŋo²¹   tʰi⁵⁵   ŋo³³   xa³³   nɯ²¹   tʰi⁵⁵.
        2SG   say   1SG   listen   1SG   say   2SG   listen
        'There should be two persons together, talking with each other.'
        要两个人在一起，你说我听，我说你听。
        (*Chatting between Li and Chen*, dialogue)

As mentioned above, these two schemata are inter-transformable. Take (3.79) as an example. The clause *nɯ³³ xa³³ ŋo²¹tʰi⁵⁵, ŋo³³ xa³³ nɯ²¹ tʰi⁵⁵* 'they talk with each other' can be transformed into:

(3.79) ji³³   ni³³   xa³³   ji³³   ni²¹   tʰi⁵⁵.
one   CLF   say   one   CLF   listen
'(Two persons) talk with each other.'
一个说一个听。

Two more examples are given to illustrate the second reciprocal schema, [ʑi³³ CLF VP$_i$ ʑi³³ CLF VP$_{ii}$]. Note that the numeral ʑi³³ 'one' in this schema often surfaces as ji³³, as described in Chapter 2.

(3.80) ta⁵⁵   mɔ²¹ha⁵⁵   tɯ³³   **ji³³**   **kʷɔ²¹**   **lui⁵⁵**   **ji²¹**   **kʷɔ²¹**   […]
from   there   then   one   CLF   chase   one   CLF
ja²¹kʰa³³pa²¹sa³³,   tɯ³³   piɔ²¹-tsʰe⁵⁵kuɛ²¹.
the.middle.of.the.night   then   run-be.out.go
'(The two bulls) then chased each other and ran out of there in the middle of the night.'
从那儿，（那两头公牛）就一个撵一个，半夜三更跑出去了。
(*My two bulls*, texts)

(3.81) mɔ²¹   ta⁵⁵   lɛ²¹   **ji³³**   **ni³³**   **pɤ³³**   **tɤ²¹**   **ji³³**   **ni³³**.
that   two   CLF   one   CLF   NEG   like   one   CLF
'Those two (sisters), they don't like each other.'
那（姊妹）俩，一个不喜欢一个。

3.4.4 Indefinite pronouns

Four main types of indefinite pronouns are found in Caijia:
i.   Q-ever;
ii. Negative anyone, anything, anybody;
iii. Some;
iv. All.

These are synthesized in Table 3.4. See *ni³³* 'people, other, someone (else)' in §3.4.1 for description of its indefinite use.

3.4.4.1 Q-ever

The Caijia interrogatives form *wh-in-situ* questions and show a tendency towards formal regularity. Most of them are formed by the question morpheme *lɔ²¹* 'which' and all of them are analyzable. Furthermore, they can also be used as 'Q-ever'

Table 3.4: Caijia indefinite pronouns.

I. Q-EVER	
Which(ever)	lɔ²¹+CLF 'which+CLF' 哪+CLF
Who(ever)	lɔ²⁴ni⁵⁵ 'which CLF$_{PERSON}$/person' 谁
Whose(ever)	lɔ²¹ni⁵⁵ hm̩⁵⁵ 'which CLF$_{PERSON}$ POSS' 谁的
What(ever)	lɔ²⁴tsoŋ⁵⁵ 'which type' 什么
	sɿ²¹mɔ⁵⁵ 'what' 什么
Where(ver)	lɔ²⁴kʰa⁵⁵ or la²⁴ 'which place' 哪儿
When(ever)	lɔ²¹kɯ²⁴ 'which moment' 什么时候
How(ever)	tɔ²¹lɔ²⁴sɿ⁵⁵ 'be like which way' 怎么
	tɕie⁵⁵me⁵⁵ (tɕie⁵⁵) ~ tɕie⁵⁵mɔ⁵⁵(tɕie⁵⁵) 'do what do' 怎么
	tɕiɔ⁵⁵mɔ⁵⁵ 'do-what' 怎么
II. NEGATIVE ANYONE/ANYTHING/ANYBODY	
Anyone	ʑi³³ + CLF 'one + CLF' 一+CLF
Anything	ʑi²¹tsoŋ⁵⁵ 'one type' 一种
Anybody	ʑi³³ni³³ 'which CLF$_{PERSON}$' 一人
III. Some	
Some	ʑi²¹sui⁵⁵ 'one some' 一些
IV. ALL	
Everybody	tɛ²¹tɕʰi²⁴ <? 大家
	hu⁵⁵ni³³ 'all CLF$_{PERSON}$' 所有人
Everything	hu⁵⁵tsoŋ⁵⁵ 'all types' 所有东西
Everywhere	hu⁵⁵kʰa⁵⁵ 'all places' 所有地方

indefinite pronouns. It should be mentioned that Caijia actually distinguishes nine types of interrogatives. These will be separately discussed in Chapter 8. However, the 'why' type and the 'how' type are not listed in Table 3.4 above, since they cannot be used as indefinite pronouns. To be more accurate, the Caijia question word 'how(ever)' is actually not a pronoun but an adverb.

An example of the Caijia 'what' pronouns *lɔ²⁴tsoŋ⁵⁵* and *sɿ²¹mɔ⁵⁵* is given below to simply illustrate how a *wh-in-situ* question is formed in Caijia. When denoting 'what', they are interchangeable. As can be observed, *lɔ²⁴tsoŋ⁵⁵* or *sɿ²¹mɔ⁵⁵* occupy the same position as *kua³³se³³* 'fern' does, serving as the copular complement. For more details, see Chapter 13 on interrogatives.

(3.82) ɔ²¹   sɿ³³   **lɔ²⁴tsoŋ⁵⁵/sɿ²¹mɔ⁵⁵**?
       this COP   what
       'What's this?'
       这是什么？

- ɔ²¹   sɿ³³   kua³³se³³.
  this   COP   fern
  'This is a fern.'
  这是蕨草。

We will mainly present the indefinite use of interrogative pronouns in this section. When denoting indefiniteness, the Caijia interrogative pronouns often co-occur with the scope adverb *la³³* 'all', which aids to code an indefinite meaning and which will be exemplified below.

Unlike the other indefinite pronouns listed in Table 3.4, Caijia 'whichever' is not an invariable form. Given that it is formed by [lɔ²¹ + CLF], the classifier varies according to the noun it modifies or refers to. The classifier for the noun *kʰa²⁴* 'box' is *bo⁵⁵*. Therefore, 'which' in (3.83) is formed by *lɔ²¹* and *po⁵⁵*.

'Whichever'
(3.83) mɔ²¹   kʰa²⁴-sui⁵⁵   nɯ³³   a³³   **lɔ²⁴po⁵⁵**   la²¹   niɔ²¹tγ̩³³.
       that   box-PL   2SG   take which.one   all   be.all.right
       'You can take whichever box among those.'
       那些盒子，你拿哪个都可以。

The following six examples illustrate the indefinite uses of the other indefinite pronouns.

'Whoever'
(3.84) **lɔ²¹ni⁵⁵**   **la³³**   γã²¹   tsʰγ⁵⁵   tsʰɿ⁵⁵kʰa³³.
       who   big   have   mistake   place
       'Whoever can have drawbacks.'
       谁都有错的地方。

'Whosever'
(3.85) pγ²¹kuɪŋ⁵⁵   je³³   sɿ²¹   **lɔ²⁴ni⁵⁵**   **hm̩⁵⁵**
       no.matter   3SG   COP   who   POSS
       la²¹   piɔ²⁴   pγ²¹   pie⁵⁵   ɔ²¹ha⁵⁵.
       all   NEG.IMP   put   to   here
       'Whosever it is, don't put it here.'
       不管它是谁的，都别放到这儿。

'Whatever'

(3.86) mɔ²¹ u²¹tsʰo²⁴ ni³³ ta³³ la²¹ xɪŋ⁵⁵,
that person CLF courage big very
lɔ²⁴tsoŋ⁵⁵/sɿ²¹mɔ⁵⁵ je³³ **la³³** pɣ³³ tsʰɿ³³.
what 3SG all NEG fear
'That person is really courageous and he doesn't fear anything.'
那个人胆大的很，什么他都不怕。

'Wherever'

(3.87) **lɔ²⁴kʰa³³ la²¹** pɣ³³ lɛ²¹ ŋuɛ²¹ mo³³.
where all NEG reach my.family inside
'Nowhere can be compared to my home.'
哪儿都不如我家。

'Whenever'

(3.88) tɕiu⁵⁵ **lɔ²¹kɯ²⁴** ŋo³³ **la²¹** pɣ³³ ti³³ tɕʰi³³kʰa³³ je³³.
to when 1SG all NEG know like 3SG
'No matter when, I will never like him.'
（不管）到什么时候，我都不会喜欢他。

'However'

(3.89) nɯ²¹ **tɕie⁵⁵me⁵⁵/tɔ²¹lɔ²⁴sɿ⁵⁵** tɕie⁵⁵ **la²¹** je³³
2SG how do all 3SG
pɣ³³ ti³³ pɣ²¹ nɯ³³ tɕiaŋ²¹tsɯ²¹.
NEG know carry.on.the.back 2SG kindness
'However you act, he won't even remember your kindness.'
无论你怎么做，他都不会领你人情。

3.4.4.2 Negative 'any one', 'anything', and 'anybody'

The indefinite pronouns [ʐi³³ CLF] 'any one', ʐi²¹tsoŋ⁵⁵ 'anything' and ʐi³³ni³³ 'anybody' usually interact with negation and the use of the scope adverb *la³³* 'all'. As for the pronoun 'which(ever)', the classifier in the pronominal expression [ʐi³³

CLF] 'any one' varies according to the noun it replaces [ʑi³³ CLF]. For example, in (3.90), the classifier ka²¹ is chosen to substitute for either of the two keys.

(3.90) mɔ²¹   sɔ³³nioŋ²¹   sɿ³³   ɣã²¹   ta⁵⁵   ka²¹   sɿ²¹.
        that   key   AFF   have   two   CLF   AFF
        ɔ²¹kɯ²⁴   **ji³³**   **ka²¹**   la²¹   pɣ³³   kɪŋ³³   o.
        now   one   CLF   all   NEG   see   CRS
        'It is two keys that (we) had. Now, neither of them can be found.'
        那钥匙是有两把的。现在一把都不见了。

Examples of ʑi²¹tsoŋ⁵⁵ 'anything' and ʑi³³ni³³ 'anybody' are given below. Both of these are used in negated sentences as [ʑi³³ CLF] 'any one'.

(3.91) ɔ⁵⁵   ʑi²¹   sɣ²¹   xɪŋ⁵⁵   **ji²¹tson⁵⁵**   la²¹   pɣ²¹   ɣã²¹.
        house inside poor very   anything   all   NEG   have
        'My family was very poor and (we) didn't have anything (valuable).'
        家里很穷，什么都没有。

(3.92) pe³³   kɯ²¹   o,   **ji³³ni³³**   la²¹   pɣ³³-tɣ³³   pe⁵⁵-ɣɯ²¹.
        eight hour   CRS anybody   all   NEG-PFV   return-come
        'It's eight o'clock (in the evening), but no one come back.'
        八点了，一个都没回来。

3.4.4.3 'Some'
The pronoun ʑi²¹sui⁵⁵ is a plural indefinite pronoun which can substitute for either animate or inanimate nouns denoting 'some'. For example, ji²¹sui⁵⁵ 'some' refers to 'some people' in (3.93), whereas it refers to 'some mushrooms' in (3.94).

(3.93) ɣã²¹   **ji²¹sui⁵⁵**   nɛ⁵⁵   ã²¹   tso⁵⁵   po³³   to³³.
        there.be   some   PRT   drink alcohol   NEG   can
        'There're some (people) that can't drink alcohol.'
        有一些呢，不能喝酒。

(3.94) zɣ²¹   san³³   nɛ⁵⁵,   niɔ³³   ɕie²¹san²⁴.
        eat   mushroom   PRT   should   be.careful
        ɣã²¹   **ji²¹sui⁵⁵**   ti³³   nɔ²¹   u²¹tsʰo²¹   se²¹.
        there.be   some   know   poison   person   AFF.PRT
        'You should be careful when eating mushrooms. Some can be poisonous.'
        吃蘑菇呢，要小心。有一些会有毒的。

3.4.4.4 'All'

The morpheme hu^{55} 'all, whole' is used to form several pronouns related to the meaning 'all': $hu^{55}ni^{33}$ 'all people, everybody', $hu^{55}tsoŋ^{55}$ 'all things, everything' and $hu^{55}kʰa^{55}$ 'all places, everywhere'. Note that the pronoun $tɛ^{21}tɕʰi^{24}$ can also be used to denote 'all people, everybody'. Consider the following examples.

(3.95) kʰɪŋ⁵⁵mia⁵⁵   kʰɪŋ⁵⁵mi²¹   la²¹   py²¹   peŋ⁵⁵   o. [...]
day   night   all   NEG   distinguish CRS
ɔ²¹   sɿ⁵⁵   **tɛ²¹tɕʰi²⁴/hu⁵⁵ni³³**   la²¹   tɕʰi³³kʰa³³   xɪŋ⁵⁵   o.
this let   everybody   all   be.happy   very   CRS
'There's no day and night.... This made everybody very happy.'
不分白天黑夜了。......这让大家都很高兴。
(*Three thieves*, texts)

(3.96) tɯ²¹   loŋ³³   mo³³   nɛ³³,   **hu⁵⁵tsoŋ⁵⁵**   la²¹   yã²¹.
at   city   inside PRT   everything   all   there.be
'There's everything in town.'
在城里呢，什么都有。

(3.97) u²¹tsʰo²⁴-sui⁵⁵   ta⁵⁵   **hu⁵⁵kʰa⁵⁵**   piɔ³³-ɣɯ²¹   tsaŋ²¹
person-PL   from   everywhere   run-come   see
sɔ⁵⁵   ty³³   sɿ²¹   mɔ²¹   kʷɔ⁵⁵pe⁵⁵ja²¹   po⁵⁵
tree   upside MOD   that   moon   CLF
'People came from everywhere to see the moon on the tree.'
人们从四面八方跑来看树上的月亮。
(*Three thieves*, texts)

3.5 Numerals, classifiers, and measure words

Numeral classifiers are a representative feature of East and Southeast Asian languages (Bisang 1993, 1999). Numeral classifiers are best described among other types of classifiers (Grinevald 2000). Caijia is also a language of this kind. As with many languages of the East and Southeast Asian area, numerals cannot modify nouns alone, but can only modify nouns that have been classified. This section presents Caijia numerals and classifiers as well as measure or mensural words that are similar to classifiers.

3.5.1 Numerals

Caijia uses a decimal system as is generally the case for Sinitic. In Standard Mandarin, the numerals from eleven to ninety-nine are predictable, if one knows the numerals from one to ten, the numerals from eleven to ninety-nine are predictable, since different numerals within one hundred can be compounded on the basis of these ten numerals (see Chao 1968: 566–573). However, the Caijia numerals are not as predictable as the ones in Standard Mandarin, especially 'two', 'ten', 'twelve', and 'twenty', which are *ta^{55}* 'two', *dzaŋ^{33}* 'ten', and *nĩ^{21}tɕi^{33}* 'twenty'. The cardinal numerals are listed below. Both 'thousand' and 'ten thousand' are loanwords from the local Southwestern Mandarin.

ʑi^{33} 'one' 一   tsɿ^{21}ʑi^{33} 'eleven' 十一
ta^{55} 'two' 二   **tsɿ^{33}ni^{33}** 'twelve' 十二
sa^{33} 'three' 三   tsɿ^{21}sa^{33} 'thirteen' 十三
sɿ^{21} 'four' 四   tsɿ^{33}sɿ^{21} 'fourteen' 十四
ŋoŋ^{33} 'five' 五   tsɿ^{21}ŋoŋ^{33} 'fifteen' 十五
fɣ^{33} 'six' 六   tsɿ^{21}fɣ^{33} 'sixteen' 十六
tɕʰi^{33} 'seven' 七   tsɿ^{21}tɕʰi^{33} 'seventeen' 十七
pe^{33} 'eight' 八   tsɿ^{21}pe^{33} 'eighteen' 十八
ko^{33} 'nine' 九   tsɿ^{21}ko^{33} 'nineteen' 十九
dzaŋ^{33} 'ten' 十   **nĩ^{21}tɕi^{33}** 'twenty' 二十

nĩ^{21}tɕi^{33}ʑi^{33} 'twenty-one' 二十一
nĩ^{21}tɕi^{33}ni^{33} 'twenty-two' 二十二
sa^{33}tsɿ^{33} 'thirty' 三十
sa^{33}tsɿ^{33}ni^{33} 'thirty-two' 三十二
sɿ^{21}tsɿ^{33} 'forty' 四十
sɿ^{21}tsɿ^{33}ni^{33} 'forty-two' 四十二
ʑi^{21}pia^{55} 'one hundred' 一百
ʑi^{21}pia^{55}ta^{21}ta^{55} 'one hundred and two' 一百零二
ʑi^{21}pia^{55}nĩ^{21}tɕi^{33} 'one hundred and twenty' 一百二
ta^{55}pia^{55} 'two hundred' 两百
ta^{55}pia^{55}ta^{21}ta^{55} 'two hundred and two' 两百零二
ʑi^{21}tɕʰɩŋ^{55} 'one thousand' 一千
ʑi^{21}tɕʰɩŋ^{55}ta^{21}ta^{55}pia^{55} 'one thousand and two hundred' 一千零二百
ji^{21}tɕʰɩŋ^{55}ta^{55} 'one thousand and two hundred' 一千二
ʑi^{21}tɕʰɩŋ^{55}ni^{21} 'one thousand and two hundred' 一千二
ta^{55}tɕʰɩŋ^{55} 'two thousand' 两千
ʑi^{21}wɛ̃^{24} 'ten thousand' 一万

As for **ordinal numerals,** Caijia mirrors the Chinese pattern by using the morpheme ti^{21} for each numeral. This is probably cognate with dì 第 [ti^{51}] in Standard Mandarin. Once again, in the numeral 'second', it is ni^{33} that is used instead of ta^{55}.

ti^{21}ʑi^{33} 'first' 第一
ti^{21}**ni^{33}** 'second' 第二
ti^{21}sa^{33} 'third' 第三
ti^{21}sɿ^{21} 'fourth' 第四
ti^{21}ŋoŋ^{33} 'fifth' 第五
...

Many examples have already shown that the cardinal numerals are postnominal, but the ordinal numerals are observed in both postnominal and prenominal positions, as shown below. Furthermore, the cardinal numerals do not interact with classifiers.

(3.98) a. sɿ^{55}pie^{21} hɛ^{55} **ti^{21}ni^{21}**   tso^{55}
Wang$_{\text{SURNAME}}$ family second elder.brother
'the second elder brother of Wang's family'
王家二哥

b. ŋa^{55} ti^{21}ni^{24}
child   second
'the second child'
二胎

3.5.2 Classifiers and measure words

Enumeration of nouns is regarded as the major function of **numeral classifiers** along with semantic categorization. As mentioned at the beginning of this section, numerals can only modify nouns when used along with classifiers. This is also the reason why this kind of classifier system is labelled as 'numeral classifier' (Keith 1977). There are four attested orders demonstrating the paradigm of how numeral, classifier and noun are arranged in a noun phrase among languages of the world (Allan 1977, Bisang 1999).

(3.99) i.   [NUM CLF] N
       ii. N [NUM CLF]
       iii. [CLF NUM] N
       iv. N [CLF NUM]

Caijia features the order of [N NUM CLF], which is quite different from the common Sinitic order [NUM CLF N]. As demonstrated below in (3.100), the phrase ji^{33} ni^{33} 'one CLF: person' follows the head noun. In this example the absence of ni^{33}, the classifier for persons, would ostensibly be ungrammatical. On the contrary, it is actually the numeral ji^{33} 'one' that is optional, i.e. $nioŋ^{24}$ ni^{33} 'one girl'. Note that 'one' is the only numeral which can be omitted. See also (3.101).

(3.100)   nioŋ²⁴   (ji³³)   *(ni³³)
        girl   one   CLF
        'one girl'
        一个女孩

(3.101)   kɿ²¹   tsʅ⁵⁵   sʅ²¹   o.
        chicken   CLF   die   CRS
        'A chicken died.'
        一只鸡死了。

The Caijia classifiers and classifier phrases possess the following features:
i. they make nouns enumerable;
ii. they are sortal i.e. different semantic categories of nouns are classified by different classifiers (see the list further below) commonly on the basis of animacy and the physical parameters of entities;
iii. the numeral 'one' is optional (as in example [3.101]) and is the only optional numeral;
iv. a minimal classifier phrase can be [DEM CLF], [N CLF] or [NUM CLF] with the first two being singular (as in example [3.101]);
v. the phrases [NUM CLF] and [DEM (NUM) CLF] are anaphors equivalent to pronouns.

The features (iii) and (iv) are already shown in (3.100) and (3.101). Both of them show the form [N CLF], which is recognized as a 'bare classifier phrase' (Li and Bisang 2011, Wang 2015). Given that only the numeral 'one' can be omitted in Caijia, it is not surprising that the phrase types [N CLF] and [DEM CLF] denote singular. This is because these two patterns can always be interpreted as [N one CLF] and [DEM one CLF]. It has been reported that the preverbal bare classifier phrases in some languages in China, including both Sinitic and non-Sinitic languages, are related to definiteness (Bisang 2012, de Sousa 2015, Wang 2015). However, this is not the case for [N CLF] in Caijia. The bare classifier phrase in (3.101), $kɿ^{21}$ $tsʅ^{55}$, denotes 'one chicken' or 'a chicken' instead of 'the chicken'. The rest of the features listed above will be discussed below.

The following example demonstrates several of the features listed above. When the phrase 'three daughters-in-law' is first mentioned in (3.102i), it is in the form of [N NUM CLF], indicating three persons are involved, which represents the function of enumeration of a classifier phrase, i.e. feature (i). Composed of a numeral and a classifier, [NUM CLF], the phrase *sa²¹ lɛ²¹* 'three ones' in (3.102ii) illustrates the pronominal feature of classifier phrases, i.e. feature (v). It functions as the anaphor of 'three daughters-in-law' in (3.102i). The classifier *lɛ²¹* is the particular classifier for siblings, cousins, and sisters and brothers-in-law, and illustrates the sortal feature of numeral classifiers, i.e. feature (ii). Similarly, the three minimal classifier phrases *ji³³ ni³³* 'one' in the following sequence of speeches (3.102iii, iv, and v) are also anaphors referring to each one of the three daughters-in-law, respectively.

(3.102) mɔ²¹kɯ²⁴   yã²¹   u²¹tsʰo²⁴   ji²¹   fɛ⁵¹hɛ²¹.
         that.time there.be   person   one   family
   i)   pia⁵⁵   **tsɿ⁵⁵so³³po²¹**   **sa³³**   **ni³³**. [...]
         marry   daughter-in-law   three   CLF
   ii)   "nɯ²⁴   **sa²¹**   **lɛ²¹**   ɣɯ²¹,   ŋo²¹   ta⁵⁵   nɯ²⁴   xa²¹.
         2PL   three   CLF   come   1SG   with   2PL   say
         ɕiaŋ⁵⁵   pe⁵⁵ɪn²¹   kuɛ³³   kua³³   neŋ²¹   nɛ⁵⁵,
         want   return.home   PURP   celebrate   year   PRT
   iii) **ji³³**   **ni³³**   kuɛ³³   sa³³   ŋon³³   koŋ³³,
         one   CLF   go   three   five   day
   iv)   **ji³³**   **ni³³**   nɛ³³   kuɛ³³   tɕʰi³³   pe³³   koŋ³³,
         one   CLF   PRT   go   seven   eight   day
   v)   **ji³³**   **ni³³**   kuɛ³³   pa³³   kʷɔ²¹   ɲui⁵⁵   nɛ⁵⁵,
         one   CLF   go   half   CLF   month   PRT
   vi)   nɯ²⁴   **sa²¹**   **lɛ³³**   niɔ³³   ji²¹hɔ⁵⁵
         2PL   three   CLF   need   together
         kuɛ²¹   ji²¹hɔ⁵⁵   yɯ²¹."
         go   together   come

'Once upon a time, there was a family with three daughters-in-law. . . . "Come, the three of you and I'll tell you (something). (If) you want to go back home to celebrate the New Year, one of you goes for three to five days, one of you goes for seven to eight days, and one of you goes for half a month. The three of you must depart and come back on the same day".'

以前，有一家人。娶了三个儿媳妇。......"你们三个来，我跟你们说。想回家过年呢，一个去三五天，一个去七八天，一个去半个月。你们三个要一起出发一起回来。"

(*Three daughters-in-law*, texts)

The sortal feature of classifiers, feature (ii), can be demonstrated by polysemous and homophonic nouns. For example, the word $k^wɔ^{55}pe^{55}ja^{33}$ in Caijia can denote 'sunflower' or 'moon'. With different classifiers, one can easily tell these meanings apart, as in (3.103). The classifier $tɔ^{55}$ is commonly used for flowers, while the classifier bo^{55} is the most frequently used for covering a large range of entities. See a list below for the classifier bo^{55}.

(3.103) a. $k^wɔ^{55}pe^{55}ja^{33}$ ji^{21} **$tɔ^{55}$**
        sunflower   one   CLF
        'a sunflower'
        一朵向日葵

     b. $k^wɔ^{55}pe^{55}ja^{33}$ ji^{21} **bo^{55}**
        moon   one   CLF
        'a moon'
        一个月亮

In a similar fashion, the word $k^hɪŋ^{24}pa^{33}mi^{33}$ 'corn' can denote different things, along with different classifiers, as in (3.104). When classified by bo^{55} the phrase refers to a corn on the cob. The classifier p^he^{55} is used to classify tiny things, while dzo^{21} is used for certain kinds of plants.

(3.104) a. $k^hɪŋ^{24}pa^{33}mi^{33}$ ji^{21} **bo^{55}**
        corn   one   CLF
        'a corn on the cob'
        一穗玉米

     b. $k^hɪŋ^{24}pa^{33}mi^{33}$ ji^{21} **p^he^{55}**
        corn   one   CLF
        'a kernel of corn'
        一粒玉米

     c. $k^hɪŋ^{24}pa^{33}mi^{33}$ ji^{33} **dzo^{21}**
        corn   one   CLF
        'a corn plant'
        一株玉米

Let us examine the list of Caijia classifiers below with the representative nouns they may co-occur with. In general, the classification system in Caijia is based on several major semantic factors: animacy and physical parameters (cf. Adams and Conklin 1973), as well as the functions and nature of entities. We will try to point out common semantic similarities for each group of nouns grouped together by the same classifier. However, it is not easy to discover similarities for each group. This is because some groups only consist of one member, or there are not enough members to work out their semantic relations, or the semantic relations among these members are opaque. For most of the classifiers, their sources are no longer traceable. Possible sources of several classifiers will be mentioned below.

ni³³: for persons; < 3; cognate with *rén* 人 'person' (< Middle Chinese *nyin* [Baxter 1992: 784]) in Standard Mandarin.

u³³tsʰo³³ 'person' 人　　　　　　　　pa³³dzɔ³³ 'man' 男人
ɬa⁵⁵ 'young person' 年轻人　　　　　kɣ²¹ja²⁴ 'woman' 女人
pa³³ 'grandfather' 爷爷　　　　　　ja³³ 'grandmother' 奶奶
pa⁵⁵ 'father' 爸爸　　　　　　　　ʑi³³ 'mother' 妈妈
tsɿ⁵⁵ŋa⁵⁵ 'son, boy' 男孩　儿子　　nioŋ²⁴ 'daughter, girl' 女孩　女儿
ŋa⁵⁵ 'child' 孩子　　　　　　　　　tso⁵⁵ 'elder brother' 哥哥
hɛ⁵⁵ 'younger brother' 弟弟　　　　nioŋ²¹hɛ⁵⁵ 'yonger sister' 妹妹
go²¹go²⁴ 'uncle (= mother's younger brother)' 舅舅
kʰa⁵⁵pa³³ 'uncle (= mother's elder brother)' 舅舅
pa³³pa³³ 'uncle (= father's elder brother)' 大伯
tsa²¹tsa²⁴ 'uncle (= father's younger brother)' 叔叔
xɯ³³pa³³ 'Taoist priest' 道士　　　kʷɔ³³sɣ²¹ŋa⁵⁵ 'student' 学生
kʷɔ³³sɣ³³pa³³ 'teacher, doctor' 老师　医生
tɔ²⁴ 'thief' 小偷
…

There are several classifiers that are used particularly for terms that relate to pairs of kin, that is, in the plural: *lɛ³³*, *tɕie⁵⁵*, *bo²⁴*, *kʰo⁵⁵*.

lɛ³³: for plural siblings(-in-law) and cousins. See example (3.102).
tɕie⁵⁵: < 'sister'; for mothers and daughters or mothers and sons.

(3.105)　ʑi²¹　　　nioŋ²⁴　　　ta⁵⁵　　tɕie⁵⁵
　　　　mother　daughter　two　　CLF
　　　　'the mother and the daughter'
　　　　两母女

bo²⁴: for fathers and sons.

(3.106) tsɿ⁵⁵ pa⁵⁵ ta⁵⁵ bo²⁴
son father two CLF
'the son and the father'
两父子

kʰo⁵⁵: for couples.

(3.107) ta⁵⁵ kʰo⁵⁵
two CLF
'a couple'
两口子

bo⁵⁵: is the most common classifier in Caijia and is probably derived from the word *bo⁵⁵* 'fruit',[3] as in (3.108).

(3.108) sɔ⁵⁵ tʏ²¹ dʏ²¹ **bo⁵⁵** o.
tree upside bear fruit CRS
'The tree is bearing fruit.'
树上结果了。

Interestingly, the classifier *bo⁵⁵* has undergone similar semantic extensions as its counterpart in Standard Mandarin, the general classifier *gè* 个 [kʏ⁵¹]. Like the Standard Mandarin *gè*, Caijia *bo⁵⁵* can be used to denote 'height', yet these two forms have undergone different processes. Compare the two examples in (3.109). In Caijia, as shown in (3.109a), the new word *bo⁵⁵bo⁵⁵* 'height' is formed via reduplication of the classifier *bo⁵⁵*. But note that reduplication is not a common or systematic process deriving new words in Caijia. By comparison, in (3.109b) the Standard Mandarin nominal counterpart *gèr* 'height' is realized by rhotacizing the classifier *gè*. Small and round things constitute a large portion of the entities that can be classified by *bo⁵⁵*, and this is probably related to the fact that the source of *bo⁵⁵* is the word 'fruit'. However, *bo⁵⁵* may also classify many objects with different physical features, such as containers, planets, and tableware, as can be perceived below in the list.

---

3 The phenomenon of the noun 'fruit' developing into a classifier classifying round objects is not only attested in Caijia. This phenomenon is also attested in Naxi, a Tibeto-Burman language spoken in Yunnan, the neighboring province of Guizhou, according to Lü Shanshan and Mu Yanjuan's field notes. The noun *ly³³* 'fruit' in Naxi is used to classify round objects and also extends to classify a large range of objects in the same way as the classifier *bo⁵⁵* does in Caijia.

(3.109) Caijia
    a. je²¹ **bo⁵⁵bo⁵⁵** la²¹.
       3SG height big
       'He is tall in height.'
       他个儿高。

Standard Mandarin
    b. 他个儿高。
       tā gèr gāo.
       3SG height tall
       'He is tall in height.'

See below a list of nouns that can be classified by bo⁵⁵.

lɔ²¹bo⁵⁵ 'peach' 桃子
xɯ⁵⁵tsɿ⁵⁵ 'pear' 梨
tsʰɿ⁵⁵po⁵⁵ 'potato' 土豆
tsʰo²¹to²¹ 'radish' 萝卜
zɿ³³ 'kernel' 核
pe³³sɔ²¹ 'hot pepper' 辣椒
xeŋ²⁴ 'apricot' 杏
saŋ³³ 'heart' 心
ni³³tsɿ³³ 'eye' 眼睛
loŋ³³ 'city' 城市
sɿ⁵⁵kʰa³³ 'well' 井
ã³³ 'jar' 罐子
ɪŋ⁵⁵soŋ³³ 'sun' 太阳
ɕie³³so²¹ 'star' 星星
dza³³to²¹ 'stone' 石头
ti²¹ 'hill' 山
tsɿ²⁴ 'basin' 盆
kʰa²⁴ 'box' 盒子
li²¹ 'bag' 包
tsɿ³³kɿ³³ '(hair) bun' 发髻
do³³ 'pillar' 柱子
kã²¹ 'tomb' 坟
tsʰa³³ta²¹ 'toilet' 厕所
hm̩⁵⁵lo⁵⁵ 'package' 包袱
kã²⁴ 'spoon' 勺子

ʑi³³tsɿ³³ 'chestnut' 栗子
kʷɔ⁵⁵tsɿ³³ 'walnut' 核桃
ɖo²¹ 'gourd' 瓜
bia²⁴ 'pineapple' 菠萝
kʰɪŋ²⁴pa³³mi³³ 'corn' 玉米
ga²⁴ 'eggplant' 茄子
pi²¹kɪ⁵⁵ 'nose' 鼻子
to²¹to⁵⁵ 'head' 头
mo³³lo³³ 'belly' 肚子
mi³³tsʰo²² 'honeycomb' 蜂窝
tʏ²¹tʏ²⁴ 'stool' 凳子
pʰo²⁴ 'fermented soybean' 豆豉
kʷɔ⁵⁵pe⁵⁵ja³³ 'moon' 月亮
ta²¹ 'pond' 水塘
tɪŋ²¹ 'pagoda' 塔
to²⁴ 'cupboard' 柜子
ma²¹ka³³tʃ²¹ 'laundry stick' 洗衣棒
sɔ⁵⁵tʰoŋ²¹ 'padlock' 锁
tɕɪŋ²¹ 'bottle' 瓶子
kʰa³³ 'hole' 洞
kʷɔ²¹to²⁴ 'pillow' 枕头
pia²¹ 'ladle' 瓢
la²¹la²⁴ 'cocoon' 茧
po²⁴ 'package' 包袱
ɬo⁵⁵ 'maggot' 蛆

so⁵⁵nioŋ²¹ 'ring' 戒指
pʰi²¹lɔ²⁴ 'pack basket' 背篓
...

lɛ²¹po²¹ 'world' 世界
tɕia²¹tɯ²⁴ 'pack basket' 背篓

(3.110) loŋ³³ ji²¹ bo⁵⁵
       city one CLF
       'a city'
       一座城

pʰe⁵⁵: for tiny entities often in granular or droplet form.
    niaŋ²¹bo⁵⁵ 'sesame' 芝麻   zɿ³³ 'rain' 雨
    mi²¹ 'rice' 米   tsʰe³³pe³³ 'tooth' 牙齿
    tsɿ²¹ 'mole' 痣   kʰɯ⁵⁵ 'character' 字
    dʑ²¹ 'chopstick' 筷子   mi³³ 'bee' 蜜蜂
    lʷɔ²¹sɿ⁵⁵ 'screw' 螺丝   tsɔ²¹tsɔ²⁴ 'bead' 珠子
    tsoŋ²¹ 'wheat grain' 麦子   tsoŋ³³ 'seed' 种子
    ɕiaŋ³³tsaŋ²¹po²⁴ 'aromatic litsea' 木姜
...

tsɿ⁵⁵: The classifier tsɿ⁵⁵ is probably derived from the word tsɿ²¹tsɿ²⁴ 'bird' and is quite possibly related to *zhī* 只 [tʂɿ⁵⁵] in Standard Mandarin, the core use of which happens to be the classifier for birds. Like *zhī* in Standard Mandarin, the classifier tsɿ⁵⁵ can be used, but not exclusively, to classify birds. In Caijia, it can classify other entities as shown below, including 'field', 'bowl', 'stool', and 'needle', items between which the semantic connection is opaque.
    kɪ³³ 'chicken' 鸡   hu³³lo³³do³³ 'owl' 猫头鹰
    bo³³bo³³ja²⁴ 'bat' 蝙蝠   li²⁴u³³pa³³ 'eagle' 老鹰
    sa³³lɔ²¹pie²⁴ 'butterfly' 蝴蝶   kʰa²¹la²¹tɕie³³ 'magpie' 喜鹊
    ŋʑ²¹ 'goose' 鹅   a⁵⁵ 'duck' 鸭子
    tʑ²¹pi²⁴ 'fly/mosquito' 苍蝇/蚊子   kʷɔ³³kʷɔ³³ 'corner' 角落
    tɪŋ⁵⁵ 'cup' 杯子   sɿ⁵⁵ 'river' 河
    leŋ²¹ 'field' 田   tsaŋ²⁴ 'needle' 针
    ɕi³³ 'knife' 刀   u³³ 'bowl' 碗
    tʑ²¹ 'table' 桌子   tʑ²¹tʑ²⁴ 'stool' 凳子

kʷɔ²¹: commonly used for animals that do not fly. This classifier is also the default one in situations where the speaker does not know which classifier should be used for certain objects. It is cognate with the general classifier *gè* 个 [kɤ⁵¹] in Standard Mandarin.

ɣoŋ²⁴ 'fish' 鱼
ŋo²¹ 'cow' 牛
li²¹ 'pig' 猪
nɛ²¹ 'buffalo' 水牛
pa²¹po²⁴ 'ant' 蚂蚁
tʂ̩²¹pa²¹fe⁵⁵ 'centipede' 蜈蚣
ta²¹to³³ 'spider' 蜘蛛
tsʰɣ³³pa²¹ 'corpse' 尸体
kui⁵⁵ 'ghost' 鬼
...

mɛ³³ 'horse' 马
tsʰɿ³³ 'goat' 羊
kʰui³³ 'dog' 狗
kʰɣ³³pa³³ 'tiger' 老虎
mɛ³³ɣoŋ²⁴ 'leech' 蚂蟥
ŋo²⁴pʰia³³ 'mantis' 螳螂
tɣ²¹pi²⁴ 'fly, mosquito' 苍蝇 蚊子
lɛ²¹po²¹ 'world' 世界
sɿ⁵⁵lɛ²¹ 'place' 地方

go²¹: mainly for things with seats or some kind of support.

gʷɔ²¹ 'bridge' 桥
tseŋ²¹ 'boat' 船
tɕʰiɔ³³ 'litter' 轿子
tʰa³³ 'bed' 床
sɯ³³kɯ²⁴ 'saw' 锯子
hɛ⁵⁵ 'ladder' 梯子
ɔ⁵⁵ta²¹ 'foundation' 地基
ja²⁴ 'garden' 园子

leŋ²¹ 'boat' 船
tsʰɛ³³ 'car' 车
ŋuɛ³³ 'saddle' 马鞍
ji²⁴ 'chair' 椅子
sɯ³³kɯ³³ 'loom' 织布机
tie²¹ 'steamer' 笼屉
miɔ²⁴ 'temple' 庙
tsʰɿ³³ 'village' 村庄

The following three classifiers are commonly used for long objects.

tsɿ²¹:

fe⁵⁵ 'snake' 蛇
tsoŋ²¹tsoŋ²⁴ 'wrinkle' 皱纹
ja³³mĩ²¹kʰɔ⁵⁵pa²⁴ 'towel' 毛巾

sɣ⁵⁵ 'rope' 绳子
ɣ²¹ 'intestine' 肠子

poŋ²¹:

tsʰɔ⁵⁵ 'grass' 草
pe⁵⁵ 'hair' 头发

ta²¹ 'leek' 葱
tɕiŋ³³ 'tendon' 筋

to⁵⁵:

ɣa²¹tsɔ⁵⁵ 'candle' 蜡烛
sɔ⁵⁵ 'tree' 树
sɯ²¹kɯ⁵⁵ 'thorn' 刺
sɔ⁵⁵tsɣ²¹ 'root' 根
to⁵⁵to⁵⁵ 'seedling' 秧苗

poŋ²⁴ 'stick' 棍子
bia²¹ka³³tsʰɯ²¹ 'cabbage' 白菜
pʰie⁵⁵ 'dustpan' 簸箕
pi²¹ 'pen' 笔
kʰɪŋ⁵⁵ 'sky' 天

ko⁵⁵: < 'hang'; for things that can be suspended.
          saŋ³³ 'umbrella' 伞   sɯ²¹kɯ⁵⁵ 'thorn' 刺
          ɕi⁵⁵pɪŋ²⁴ 'whip' 鞭   ɣoŋ²¹ta²⁴ 'fishing net' 渔网

va²¹: for string-shaped things.
          hu⁵⁵ 'thread' 线   nɣ²¹hu⁵⁵ 'bowstring' 弓弦

The classifiers *pie⁵⁵* and *tsa⁵⁵* are for houses and rooms.

pie⁵⁵: ɔ⁵⁵ 'house' 房   li²¹ɣuɔ²⁴ 'pig pen' 猪圈

tsa⁵⁵: ɔ⁵⁵ 'room' 屋   li²¹ɣuɔ²⁴ 'pig pen' 猪圈

tsoŋ⁵⁵: < 'seed' 种.
           nia²¹nia²¹ 'thing' 东西   sɿ²¹ 'thing' 事情

ka²¹: for lumps or two-dimensional flat things.
          pɣ²¹ 'cloth' 布   sɔ³³nioŋ²¹ 'key' 钥匙
          pia²¹kʰɔ³³ 'cake' 蛋糕   ɕi⁵⁵ 'iron' 铁
          to²¹nian²⁴ 'beancurd' 豆腐   tɕɪŋ²⁴ 'mirror' 镜子
          ŋa³³ 'tile' 瓦

tɔ⁵⁵: for flowers and flower-shaped entities.
          je²¹ 'flower' 花   saŋ³³ 'mushroom' 蘑菇
          tɪŋ⁵⁵ 'cloud' 云   kʷɔ⁵⁵pe³³ja²¹ 'sunflower' 向日葵

ɣa³³: for clothes.
          ɯ³³ 'clothes' 衣服   kʰɣ²¹ 'trousers' 裤子

kʰo⁵⁵: for tools that can be grasped by a handle (or handles).
          la²¹tɣ²¹ 'hoe' 大锄头   piɔ³³ 'hoe' 小锄头
          tɕɪŋ⁵⁵ 'sissors' 剪子   po⁵⁵ 'axe' 斧头

dʑie³³: big farming or hunting tools that come in sets.
           ɣoŋ²¹ 'plough' 犁   fɛ³³ 'shotgun' 枪
           ɕi⁵⁵kɣ³³ 'flail' 连枷

dɔ³³: for excreta.
          ʐi³³ 'feces' 屎   niɔ²¹ 'urine' 尿

ta⁵⁵: for road-shaped entities, but also extends to classify certain abstract nouns.
hɔ⁵⁵ 'road' 路 γoŋ²¹ã²¹sɿ⁵⁵ 'rainbow' 彩虹
tɕʰi³³kʰa³³ 'brook' 小溪 tsʰɿ²¹po⁵⁵ 'sound' 声音
mia²¹ 'life' 命

biaŋ³³: for entities that form a bunch.
ta⁵⁵biaŋ²¹ko³³ 'grape' 葡萄 tsɿ⁵⁵niaŋ²⁴ 'firecracker' 鞭炮

so⁵⁵: for household items made of fabric.
pʰe⁵⁵ 'quilt' 被子 tseŋ²¹piaŋ²⁴ 'felt cloak' 披毡
po²¹tʰɯ²⁴ 'piece of felt for carrying a baby on one's back' 背小孩的毡子

pʰɪŋ²¹: the singular form for entities that are usually found in pairs.
tã²¹tʰoŋ³³ 'bucket' 桶 loŋ²¹koŋ³³ 'bracelet' 手镯
kγ³³ 'foot' 脚 so⁵⁵ 'hand' 手
pi²¹po²¹ 'lip' 嘴唇 ni³³tsɿ³³ 'eye' 眼睛

(3.111) ni³³tsɿ³³   ji³³   pʰɪŋ²¹
  eye   one   CLF
  'one eye'
  一只眼睛

tie²¹: 'pair' for certain entities that form pairs.
ni³³tsɿ³³ '(a pair of) eyes' （一对）眼睛
suaŋ³³tʰɛ³³ 'twins' （一对）双胞胎
dγ²¹ '(a pair of) chopsticks' （一双）筷子

dγ²¹: 'pair' for certain entities that come in pairs.
ʑi²¹ '(a pair of) shoes' （一双）鞋   me³³ '(a pair of) socks' （一双）袜子

tɭ⁵⁵: < 'flow, shed (tears)', for droplets of liquid.
ni²¹sɿ⁵⁵ 'tear' 眼泪 sɿ⁵⁵ 'water' 水

ti⁵⁵: for thin flat objects.
se⁵⁵ti⁵⁵ 'leaf' 叶子 la²¹pa²⁴ 'chopping board' 案板
pʰaŋ²¹zγ²¹peŋ⁵⁵ 'spatula' 馈饭板

hɔ⁵⁵: < 'road'; for road-shaped things.
γoŋ²¹ã²¹sɿ⁵⁵ 'rainbow' 彩虹 lɛ²¹ 'field' 田

dzo²¹: for a certain type of plant, but also extending to classify mosquito nets.

    sa²¹ 'garlic plant' 大蒜   kʰɪŋ²⁴pa³³mi³³ 'corn plant' 玉米
    tsaŋ²⁴ 'mosquito net' 蚊帐

The following group of nouns illustrates a case in which the semantic relations among a commonly classified group are opaque.

kɣ³³:

    kuɪŋ²¹ 'skirt' 裙子   tɣ²⁴ 'yard' 院坝
    sɔ⁵⁵tsʰɣ²¹ 'broom' 扫帚   sɔ⁵⁵zɣ²⁴ 'brush' 刷子
    kʰɯ³³sɛ²¹ 'smell' 气味

Below are some classifiers that appear to modify only one object in our data.

tɕie⁵⁵: ŋoŋ³³ 'speech' 话
tɣ³³: dza²¹ 'felt' 毡子
doŋ³³: fɛ⁵⁵ɪŋ³³ 'tobacco' 烟
ka³³: sɿ²¹ 'letter' 信
ɣ²¹: kʰɯ³³ta³³ 'crack' 裂缝
peŋ²¹: cognate with the classifier *běn* 本 [pən²¹⁴] 'volume' in Standard Mandarin, which is also used to classify books.
    sɣ³³ 'book' 书
seŋ²¹: cognate with the classifier *shàn* 扇 [ʂan⁵¹] 'fan' in Standard Mandarin, which is also used to classify doors.
    ma²¹kʰa³³ 'door' 门
tsaŋ⁵⁵: do²⁴ 'bean' 豆角
naŋ³³: sɔ³³ 'coffin' 棺材
fɛ⁵⁵(hɛ²¹): < 'family'.
    kua²¹ 'country' 国家

In conclusion, Caijia is a language possessing abundant numeral classifiers. Similar to many languages with numeral classifiers (see Grinevald 2000), classification in Caijia is based on animacy, physical properties, and functions, as well as the nature of entities. These features conforms to the early observations of Adams and Conklin's (1973). See also Gerner and Bisang (2008) for a very special classification system based on definiteness, speaker role (gender and age), and size (augmentative, medial, diminutive) as well as plurality in Weining Ahmao, a Hmong language spoken in the same area as Caijia. According to Grinevald (2000: 72–73), languages with numeral classifiers tends to follow the principle of physical quality, including shape, size, and consistency to classify nouns (see also Croft 1994). Caijia uses different classifiers to classify nouns for humans, birds, and non-flying animals, a system which seems to be based on animacy. It adopts different classifiers to categorize human nouns on the basis of kinship. As can be found in the description above, a large portion of nouns are categorized according to their physical properties. For example, ti^{55} is for thin and flat objects, p^he^{55} is for tiny granular entities, and bo^{55} is for round objects, but has also extended to classify a broader range of entities.

Compared with Chinese classifiers, sources for the Caijia classifiers are not readily transparent, probably due to its situation of language endangerment. Only a handful of classifiers appear to have clear sources, as signaled above. Nonetheless, certain semantic similarities and divergences can still be observed. For example, both Chinese and Caijia use classifiers derived from the verbs meaning 'hang' to classify 'fishing net' and 'thorn'; both the Chinese and Caijia classifiers for 'water' and 'tear' are derived from the verbs denoting 'flow'. As for divergences, the loan classifier $k^wɔ^{21}$ for animals that do not fly in Caijia is used to classify entities from different lexical fields in Chinese.

Classifiers are apparently not a universal category, but every language possesses **measure words** or mensural classifiers which are similar to classifiers, such as the word 'cup' in the English example *a cup of tea* or the word 'verre' in the French example *un verre d'eau* 'a glass of water' (Grinevald 2004: 1020). Measure words are excluded from classifier systems, since they are not sortal (Greenberg 1974, Becker 1975, Adams 1989). In Caijia, measure word phrases function similarly to classifier phrases. As shown above, measure words occupy the same position as classifiers. Measure word phrases can also be anaphors, functioning like pronouns.

(3.112) xa^{21} tɕiu^{55} **ã^{21}**   **tso^{55}**,   mɔ^{21}kɯ^{24} ŋo^{33} ã^{21}
speak   to   drink   alcohol   that.time   1SG   drink
to^{21} xɪŋ^{55}.   **ta^{55}**   **la^{21}**   **tɪŋ^{55}**   la^{21} pγ^{33} lɔ^{21}
can   very   two   big   cup   all   NEG   be.sufficient
ŋo^{33} ã^{21}.   ɔ^{21}kɯ^{24} **ã^{21}**   **ji^{21}**   **tɪŋ^{55}**   tɯ^{33}
1SG   drink   this.time   drink   one   cup   then
ã^{21}-tsɿ^{33} kuɛ^{21} o.
drink-be.drunk   go   CRS
'Speaking of drinking, I used to drink a lot before. Two big glasses (of alcohol) weren't sufficient for me. Now, I get drunk even drinking one glass (of alcohol).'
以前我能喝得很。两大杯都不够我喝。现在喝一杯就喝醉了。

However, several features of measure words can distinguish them from classifiers in Caijia.

First, the most important difference between classifiers and measure words is that classifiers are sortal but measure words are not. Compare (3.113) and (3.114). Obviously, the measure word $\tilde{a}^{21}$ 'jar' is not sortal, since it can quantify everything that can be put into it, for instance, $niaŋ^{21}bo^{55}$ 'sesame' and $dza^{33}to^{21}$ 'stone' in (3.113). $niaŋ^{21}bo^{55}$ 'sesame' and $dza^{33}to^{21}$ 'stone' also interact with different classifiers, as in (3.114).

Measure word

(3.113) a. niaŋ²¹bo⁵⁵ ji²¹   **ã²¹**
           sesame   one   jar
           'a jar of sesame seeds'
           一罐芝麻

  b. dza³³to²¹ ji²¹   **ã²¹**
     stone   one   jar
     'a jar of pebbles'
     一罐石头

Classifier

(3.114) a. niaŋ²¹bo⁵⁵ ji²¹   **pʰe⁵⁵**
           sesame   one   CLF
           'a sesame seed'
           一粒芝麻

  b. dza³³to²¹ ji²¹   **bo⁵⁵**
     stone   one   CLF
     'a stone'
     一块石头

Second, the numeral 'one' cannot be omitted in a measure word phrase. Revisiting (3.112), if the numeral ji^{33} 'one' in $tso^{55}\,ji^{21}\,tŋ^{55}$ 'a glass of alcohol' is omitted, the meaning of the utterance will change. The phrase $tso^{55}\,tŋ^{55}$ no longer denotes 'a glass of alcohol', but 'a glass for alcohol'. See also the following example.

(3.115) a. sɔ²¹   ji³³   li²¹
           Sichuan.pepper   one   bag
           'a bag of Sichuan pepper'
           一袋花椒

b. sɔ²¹   li²¹
Sichuan.pepper   bag
'the bag for Sichuan pepper'
花椒袋

Finally, adjectives can modify measure words when immediately preceding them in a measure word phrase, as in (3.116). However, this operation cannot be realized in a classifier phrase. As already shown at the very beginning of this chapter, the adjective precedes the noun in the most highly expanded NP.

(3.116) a. ti⁵⁵m²¹kɯ²⁴   ɣɯ²¹   zɿ⁵⁵   ji³³   **la²¹**   pʰo²¹.
just.now   come   rain   one   big   fall
'It was a heavy fall of rain just now.'
刚才下了一场大雨。

b. *zɿ⁵⁵   ji³³   **la²¹**   pʰe⁵⁵
rain   one   big   CLF
(Attempted: 'a big drop of rain')
一大滴雨

3.6 Place words, localizers, and time words

In Chinese, place words, localizers and time words are three sub-categories of substantives, which also include nouns, demonstratives, pronouns, and classifiers (Chao 1968: Chapter 7). These three types of words are also attested in Caijia. They are actually nominals but differ from nouns. For example, they are usually not modified by numerals, classifiers, or adjectives. Place and time words often function as adverbials. However, they can function as subjects, objects of certain verbs, or objects of certain prepositions. Let us see how they function as nominals in detail.

3.6.1 Place words and localizers

As in Chinese, Caijia place words can be direct objects of verbs of existence, movement, and direction (Chao 1968: 519, Chappell and Peyraube 2008), including *ɣã³³* 'have, there be', *tɯ²¹* 'live, be at', *ɣa²¹* 'walk', *tɕiu⁵⁵* 'arrive', *kuɛ³³* 'go', *ɣɯ²¹* 'come', or the objects of locative prepositions, including *ta⁵⁵* 'from', *pie⁵⁵* 'to', and *tɯ²¹* 'at'. Otherwise, they would not be place words. Unlike many languages of the world, these verbs listed above are syntactically transitive in Caijia. Even so, similar phenomena can be observed in some better-known languages. Take the verb *habiter* 'live, dwell' in French as an example to better understand such verbs in Chinese. The verb *habiter* can be used both transitively and intransitively. To express 'I live in Paris', one can either use the transitive *habiter*, as in *J'habite Paris*, or the intransitive *habiter*, as in *J'habite à Paris*. Verbs of existence, movement, and direction in Caijia function just like the transitive *habiter* in French.

Compare the transitive verb zy^{21} 'eat' and the verb of existence $tuɯ^{21}$ 'live, be at' in the following examples. One can observe that 'live, be at' functions just like transitive verbs, e.g. 'eat', taking the place word/placename $la^{21}sɿ^{55}$ 'Guiyang' as its direct object.

(3.117) a. ŋo³³ **zɣ²¹** zɣ³³ ha⁵¹ o.
1SG eat meal COMPL CRS
'I've had my meal.'
我吃完饭了。

b. ŋo³³ **tuɯ²¹** **la²¹sɿ⁵⁵** sɿ²¹.
1SG live/be.at Guiyang_{PLACENAME} CONT
'I live in Guiyang/I'm in Guiyang.'
我住/在贵阳。

Examples are given below with a verb of movement or direction and with a locative preposition. The word ti^{21} 'hill' is the object of the movement or direction verb tsa^{33} 'go up' in (3.118), while the prepositional object $tsʰɿ^{55}kʰa^{33}$ 'place' is modified by a relative clause in (3.119). Both ti^{21} and $tsʰɿ^{55}kʰa^{33}$ are thus place words according to the definition given above.

(3.118) je³³ **tsa³³** **ti²¹** tɕie⁵⁵ ja²¹pa²¹ kuɛ²¹ o.
3SG go.up hill do farming go CRS
'He went up the hill to do farming.'
他上山干活去了。

(3.119) a³³ mɔ²¹ kʷɔ²¹ a²¹-tsʰe⁵⁵kuɛ²¹ pie⁵⁵-kuɛ²¹. pie⁵⁵ **pie⁵⁵**
OM that CLF take-be.out.go throw-go throw to
[[mɔ²¹ ni²⁴ pɣ³³ tsaŋ³³-kɪŋ³³] sɿ²¹ [**tsʰɿ⁵⁵kʰa³³**]].
that 3 NEG look-see REL place
'Take that thing out and throw it away. Throw it into some place out of sight.'
把那个拿出去扔掉。扔到别人看不见的地方。

Localizers indicate a relative spatial relation between two entities (see also Peyraube 1980: 16). They form a closed category in Caijia. The function of localizers is to turn ordinary nouns into place words, or to derive place words from nouns by way of compounding in the forme of [NP LOC]. As demonstrated in (3.120), the absence of *tγ³³* 'upside' is ungrammatical.

(3.120) nɛ⁵⁵, lɔ²⁴koŋ³³   pγ²¹   yɯ²¹ la²¹
         INTJ   whenever   carry.on.the.back come   all
         tɯ²¹ [mɔ²¹ tsa³³to²¹ po⁵⁵ *(tγ²¹)]   sɯ⁵⁵.
         at   that   stone   CLF   upside   rest
         'Whenever (he) carried (grass) back, he rested himself on that stone.'
         每天（他）背（草）回来都在那块石头上休息。
         (*The man and the stone*, texts)

Localizers in Caijia can be divided into pairs of monosyllabic and disyllabic types. Generally speaking, monosyllabic localizers (except *tɕiŋ²¹* 'front') cannot be used alone, as exemplified in (3.121a), under the condition that pragmatic contexts are not taken into account. On the contrary, disyllabic localizers are typically found used alone, indicating a vague and larger spatial area, as shown in (3.121b). Consequently, according to the definition given above disyllabic localizers themselves are also place words. See Table 3.5 for an inventory of Caijia localizers.

(3.121) a. ta⁵⁵   *(tγ²¹)   tγ³³   lɯŋ³³-tɕie²¹yɯ²¹   tɕiŋ²¹   ta⁵⁵   tsʅ⁵⁵.
             from   table   upside   roll-be.down.come   bottle   two   CLF
             'Two bottles rolled off the table.'
             从桌子上滚下来两个瓶子。

         b. ta⁵⁵   **ʑi³³mo³³**   pγ²¹-tsʰe⁵⁵   hu³³lo³³to²⁴   tsʅ⁵⁵.
             from   inside   fly-be.out   owl   CLF
             'An owl flew out of the hollow.'
             从树里面飞出一只猫头鹰。

Some of the localizers listed in Table 3.5 deserve more elaboration. The disyllabic localizer *ʑi³³mo³³* 'inside' is composed of two monosyllabic localizers, both of which denote the meaning 'inside'. However, compared with the monosyllabic localizer *mo³³*, the usage of *ʑi³³*, whose source is not clear, is extremely limited. It is only used when the reference entity is *ɔ⁵⁵* 'house' or *sɛ²¹* 'room', while the usage of *mo³³* is quite generalized. The localizer *ta²¹tɯŋ⁵⁵* 'beside', whose source meaning is 'pediment (triangular upper side wall)', is also only found occuring

Table 3.5: Caijia localizers.

Spatial relation	Localizers	
	Monosyllabic	Disyllabic
in front of	tɕɪŋ²¹ 'front' 前	tɕɪŋ²¹mi³³ ~ tɕɪŋ²¹mĩ³³ 前面
		tɕɪŋ²¹lɛ²¹
on	dɣ̩³³ 'upside' 上	
above		dɣ̩³³mi²¹ ~ dɣ̩³³mĩ²¹ 上面
		dɣ̩³³lɛ²¹
in	ʑi³³ 'inside' 里	ʑi³³mo³³ 'inside' 里面
	mo³³ 'inside' 里 (< mo³³lo³³ 'belly')	tu³³lɛ²¹ 'inside'
in the middle of		ta²¹fa⁵⁵ 'middle' 中间
under (vertical)	tie⁵⁵ 'bottom' 底	tie⁵⁵mi²¹ ~ tie⁵⁵mĩ²¹ 底下
		tie⁵⁵lɛ²¹
under (non-vertical)	kɣ̩³³ 'under' 下 (< kɣ̩³³ 'foot')	
at the foot of	kɣ̩³³ 'under' 下	
behind	u³³ 'backside' 后	u³³mi²¹ ~ u³³mĩ²¹ 后面
		u³³lɛ²¹
		kɪŋ²¹u³³ 'backside'
beside	pɪŋ⁵⁵ 'beside' 边	ba³³mi³³ ~ ba³³mĩ³³ 'beside' 旁边
		ta²¹tɪŋ⁵⁵ 'beside' 山花 (< mã³³tɪŋ³³ 'buttock')
side, end	mi²¹/mĩ²¹ 'side' 面 (< mĩ²¹kʰɔ⁵⁵ 'face')	
at the head of	to²¹ 'head' 头 (< to²¹to⁵⁵ 'head')	
at the end of	mã³³ 'tail' 尾 (< mã³³ta²¹ 'tail')	
left		pa³³mi²¹ ~ pa³³mĩ²¹ 'left' 左面
right		tsɿ³³mi³³ ~ mĩ³³ 'right' 右面
outside		ua³³lɛ³³ 'outside' 外面
in the face of		ti(e)²¹mi²¹ ~ ti(e)²¹mĩ²¹ 'opposite' 对面

with 'house'. kɪŋ²¹u³³ 'behind' is limited to ma²¹kʰa³³ 'door'. In addition, the localizers to²¹ 'head/at the head of' and mã³³ 'tail/at the back of' are limited to 'house', 'boat', 'queue', 'bridge', 'bed' and like words, all of which metaphorically possess a 'head (front)' and a 'tail (end)' in Caijia culture.

The localizer *mi²¹ ~ mĩ²¹* is not used in the same way as the other monosyllabic localizers. This is mainly because of its meaning 'side, end'. One object may have two, or more than two, ends or sides. For example, a stick has two ends and a cube has six sides. This localizer is mainly used with deictic words, such as the demonstratives *ɔ²²* 'this' and *mɔ²²* 'that' or the morphemes *ʑi³³* 'one' and *pa³³* 'other'. See example (3.122). The context is carrying water on the shoulder with a carrying-pole.

(3.122) **ji³³ mi²¹** tsʰɿ³³ **ji³³ mi²¹** toŋ³³, ta⁵⁵ po³³ to³³.
one side be.light one side be.heavy lift NEG can
'(If) one side of (the pole) is light and the other side is heavy, it's impossible to carry (the water).'
（扁担）一面轻一面重，抬不了。

Given that disyllabic localizers are place words in nature, they are undoubtedly nominal, as example (3.121b) above has demonstrated. By contrast, monosyllabic localizers are less independent in their syntactic distribution. Nonetheless, it can be argued that the Caijia monosyllabic localizers are still nominal. This is because (i) they can be modified by demonstratives and (ii) they can stand alone when the NP they interact with is mentioned in the previous context. For example, in (3.123) it is the boiling water that the mushrooms should be put into. Since *sɿ⁵⁵* 'water' is already mentioned in the first clause (3.123i), it is not necessary for it to be repeated in the immediate sequence of clauses. Furthermore, *mo³³* in (3.123ii) can either stand alone or be modified by the demonstrative *mɔ²¹*, which precisely illustrates the nominal nature of *mo³³* 'inside'

(3.123) i) tɕʰiŋ²¹ a²¹ **sɿ⁵⁵** zɿ³³-piɔ³³, ii) lɛ³³tsʰɛ²¹ pɣ²¹
first OM water boil-be.boiling only.then put
saŋ²¹ pie⁵⁵ (**mɔ²¹**) **mo³³** tsɣ²¹.
mushroom to that inside cook
'(You) first boil some water and after the water boils (you) put the mushrooms into (it).'
先把水烧开，才把蘑菇放进（水里）煮。

One more example is given below in which the localizer *dɣ³³* 'upside' is used alone. The context of this example is that one needs to burn some ghost money for the dead family members, whose names should be written onto the money bills.

(3.124) tɕʰi³³ ŋui³³ nɛ⁵⁵, niɔ³³ pe²¹ **tsɿ⁵⁵** [...] tɯ²¹ ha⁵⁵ nɛ⁵⁵,
seven   month   PRT   need   burn   paper   at   here PRT
niɔ³³ a³³ je²¹ pie⁵⁵, je²¹ pie⁵⁵ **tɣ³³**.
need   DCR write to   write to   upside
'One needs to burn some ghost money (for the dead) in July. . . . Right here, one must write (the names of dead persons) to, write (the names) onto (the ghost money bills).'
在这儿呢，要把（死人的名字）写到，写到上面。
(*Funeral custom*, texts)

In conclusion, a Caijia positional phrase [NP LOC] is actually a complex nominal phrase with the localizer as its head synchronically. The localizer indicates a spatial region, while the NP in this positional phrase narrows this region down to a relevant surface or part of the object it denotes. Reconsidering (3.124) as an example in which the localizer *tɣ³³* denotes the top of something: in using the noun *tsɿ⁵⁵* 'paper, ghost money' to modify *tɣ³³* its spatial area is further specified as the top of the ghost money bills.

3.6.2 Time words

Time words refers to those denoting temporal concepts. They are often observed as temporal adverbials in sentences, like *mɔ²¹kɯ²⁴* 'at that time, before' in (3.112). Though quite limited, the nominal uses of time words are still observed:
i. they can usually be the objects of the preposition *ta⁵⁵* 'from', verbs/prepositions *tɯ²¹* '(be) at', and *dʑiu⁵⁵* 'arrive/to';
ii. some of them can be modified by numerals, [NUM CLF], demonstratives, or relative clauses (see also Chapter 15 §15.6.1 on time clauses).

Consider the following examples. The phrase *mɔ²¹ kɯ²⁴* in (3.125) is the object of the verb *tɕiu⁵⁵* 'arrive'. Unlike *mɔ²¹kɯ²⁴* 'before' in (3.112), this phrase refers to some moment in the future.

(3.125) tsɛ²¹tsɛ²⁴ **tɕiu⁵⁵ mɔ²¹ kɯ²⁴**   nɯ³³ tɯ³³ tɯ²¹-pɣ²¹-ha⁵⁵   o.
really   arrive   that   moment   2SG   then   think-NEG-finish   CRS
'You'll regret it when that moment really comes.'
真到那时候你就后悔了。

Even though the boldface phrases in (3.126)-(3.128) function as adverbials, their internal structures reflect the nominal nature of time words. Example (3.126) shows ɣa²¹ji³³ 'the first day (of every month)' being the object of the preposition ta⁵⁵ 'from' and tsɿ²¹ŋoŋ³³ 'the fifteenth day (of every month)' being the object of the preposition tɕiu⁵⁵ 'to'.

(3.126) ta⁵⁵   ɣa²¹ji³³   tɕiu⁵⁵   tsɿ²¹ŋoŋ³³   ŋo⁵⁵
        from   the.first.day to   the.fifteenth.day   1PL
        la²¹   na²¹kɿ³³   sɔ²¹kʷɔ⁵⁵.
        all   play.ball.of.chicken.feather   have.fun
        'From the first day to the fifteenth day of the New Year, we all play the game with a ball of chicken feather for fun.'
        从初一到十五，我们都打鸡毛球玩。

It is, by contrast, a relative clause that modifies the time word in (3.127).

(3.127) tsʰɿ³³   ŋo²¹   tsʰɿ⁵⁵-kuɛ³³   mɔ²¹   kɯ²⁴
        fear   1SG   rot-go   that   moment
        tsʰɔ²¹-tɣ³³   nɯ³³   e.
        stink-obtain   2SG   PRT
        '(I'm) afraid at the moment when I will have rotted away, I'll stink so much that you'll sense the smell.'
        怕我烂掉那时候臭到你。
        (*The corn and the grass*, texts)

In (3.128), the object of tɯ²¹ 'at' is a complex phrase composed of the time word ɲui⁵⁵ 'month' and the localizer mo³³ 'inside'. The time word ɲui⁵⁵ is, in turn, modified by the classifier phrase ji³³ kʷɔ²¹ 'one CLF' and the proximal demonstrative ɔ⁵⁵.

(3.128) tɯ²¹   ɔ⁵⁵   ji³³   kʷɔ²¹   ɲui⁵⁵   mo³³   nɛ⁵⁵, tɯ³³   niɔ³³
        at   this   one   CLF   month   inside PRT   then   need
        piɔ²⁴   zɣ²¹   pe³³sɔ²¹,   piɔ²⁴   zɣ²¹   sa²¹,   ɛ,
        NEG.IMP   eat   hot.pepper   NEG.IMP   eat   garlic   INTJ
        tsɿ⁵⁵tsɿ⁵⁵ zɣ²¹   tsʰɿ³³tsʰɯ²¹.
        only   eat   leafy.vegetable
        'During this month, one can't eat hot peppers or garlic and one can only eat leafy vegetables.'
        这个月里，就不要吃辣椒，不要吃蒜，只吃青菜。
        (*Funeral customs*, texts)

Example (3.129) reflects a special feature of time words: numerals can directly precede time words, which means that time words function like measure words. See also (3.102).

(3.129) tɕʰi³³ koŋ³³ xuɔ²¹tsɛ⁵⁵ sa³³ koŋ³³
seven   day   or   three day
'seven days or three days'
七天或者三天
(*Funeral customs*, texts)

(3.130) sa³³ neŋ³³
three   year
'three years'
三年
(*Funeral customs*, texts)

(3.131) ŋoŋ³³ kɯ²¹
five   hour
'five hours/five o'clock'
五个小时/五点

It should be mentioned that *ŋui⁵⁵* or *ŋoŋ⁵⁵* 'month', as found in our fieldwork material, is the only time word that can be modified by a classifier. As shown in (3.128), the classifier phrase [ji³³ kʷɔ²¹] 'one' precedes *ŋui⁵⁵*. See also (3.102).

The time words *koŋ⁵⁵* 'day', *ŋui⁵⁵* 'month', and *neŋ²¹* 'year' can be reduplicated to denote 'every day', 'every month', and 'every year', as shown below.

(3.132) a. koŋ⁵⁵koŋ⁵⁵ 'every day' 每天
             (*The man and the stone*, texts)

         b. ŋui⁵⁵ŋui⁵⁵ 'every month' 每月

         c. neŋ²¹neŋ⁵⁵ 'every year' 每年
             (*The New Year's visit*, texts)

This is a feature exclusive to the three time words illustrated above, i.e. *koŋ⁵⁵* 'day', *ŋui⁵⁵* 'month', and *neŋ²¹* 'year'. The other time words cannot be reduplicated. Although this feature can be adopted as a diagnosis to distinguish time words from nouns, it is still different from nominal reduplication. We remarked earlier that reduplication for nouns is rather limited and unsystematic. Some nouns can indeed be reduplicated without any semantic change involved, as illustrated in the following example.

(3.133) a. tɿŋ⁵⁵ 'cup' 杯子 → tɿŋ⁵⁵tɿŋ⁵⁵ 'cup' 杯子
b. kʰui⁵⁵ 'dog' 狗 → kʰui⁵⁵kʰui⁵⁵ 'dog' 狗

3.7 Headless noun phrase

As mentioned at the beginning of this chapter, some noun phrases do not have a head noun. This section will introduce the category of headless noun phrases in Caijia. Headless noun phrases are usually formed by two nominalizers:
i. sɿ²¹ (which is also a relativizer and modifier marker)
ii. and bo⁵⁵ (< classifier bo⁵⁵).

The nominalizer sɿ²¹ is the one used to form relative clauses (see Chapter 14 on relativization for more details). The headless noun phrases formed by sɿ²¹ can be actually regarded as headless relative clauses standing alone as noun phrases in the form of [VP sɿ²¹]. The gapped or relativized positions usually represent the slot where the noun or nominal has been omitted and to which this kind of headless noun phrase refers. For example, in (3.134), the headless noun phrase niɔ³³ kɛ²¹ sɿ²¹, serving as the subject, and the empty position ∅ are co-referential. Here they refer to the one(s) collecting the debts.

(3.134) [∅ᵢ **niɔ³³ kɛ²¹ sɿ²¹**]ᵢ la²¹ piɔ⁵⁵ tɕiu⁵⁵ je²¹ ɔ⁵⁵ ʑi²¹
       ask.for debt NMLZ all run to 3SG house inside
ɣɯ²¹ ta⁵⁵ je²¹ niɔ³³ kɛ²¹ o.
PURP from 3SG ask.for debt CRS
'Those who were collecting their debts all rushed into his house and asked for money from him.'
要债的都跑到他家来跟他要债了。

Similarly, in (3.135) the headless noun phrase nɯ³³ tɕʰɿŋ²¹ tsɿ²¹ sɿ³³ refers to 'the person that you raised by yourself'. The empty position inside this phrase is marked by ∅. This phrase serves as the copular complement.

(3.135) je³³ pɣ³³ sɿ³³ [nɯ³³ tɕʰɪŋ²¹ tsɿ²¹ ∅ᵢ sɿ³³]ᵢ la²¹?!
3SG NEG COP 2SG   by.oneself raise   NMLZ PRT
'Isn't he your own kid?! (LIT: Isn't he the one that you raised by yourself?!)'
他不是你亲生的啊！

The second type of headless noun phrases is only used in certain specific contexts and is less productive than the *sɿ²¹* headless phrases. It is a special expanded use of the classifier *bo⁵⁵*. Being a nominalizer, *bo⁵⁵* follows bare verbs in the form of [V-bo⁵⁵]. This kind of nominalization is often observed in two contexts.

First, *bo⁵⁵*, often surfacing as *po⁵⁵*, commonly turns emotion verbs and adjectives into noun phrases to express the feeling of a certain emotion. They commonly interact with the verb *ɣɯ²¹* 'come' to express that someone, the undergoer, is overcome with a specific feeling. As shown in (3.136), the nominalizer *bo⁵⁵* turns the verb *tsʰɿ³³* 'fear, be afraid' into a noun phrase denoting 'the feeling of fear' by marking it in the following position. It should be mentioned that the nominalizer *kʰɔ²¹* is a nominalizer in the local Southwestern Mandarin which is not commonly used in Caijia. The *kʰɔ²¹* in (3.136) is the only example in our data. *kʰɔ²¹* is not used elsewhere in our 147 texts.

(3.136) a. piɔ²⁴   **tsʰɿ³³**.
            NEG.IMP   fear
            'Don't be afraid.'
            别怕。

       b. i) je³³   kʰɔ²¹   tɕie⁵⁵ sɿ²¹   nɛ⁵⁵,
              3SG   NMLZ   do   NMLZ   PRT
          ii) ŋo³³   la³³   **tsʰɿ²¹bo⁵⁵**   ɣɯ²¹   o.
              1SG   all   fear.NMLZ   come   CRS
          'What he did, (makes) me overcome with fear.'
          他所做的，我都害怕起来了。

Examples with the verbs *sɔ²¹* 'laugh', *xɯ³³* 'cry', and *dɿŋ³³* 'shy' are given below.

(3.137) **sɔ²¹bo⁵⁵**   ɣɯ²¹   lɯ⁵⁵   mɔ⁵⁵sɿ⁵⁵, ŋo³³   la²¹   pɣ²¹   kã⁵⁵   **sɔ²¹**.
        laugh.NMLZ   come   VCOM   very   1SG   all   NEG   dare   laugh
        '(I was) overcome with excitement, (but) I didn't dare to laugh.'
        我想笑得不行，（但）我也不敢笑。

(3.138) xɯ³³ 'cry' 哭   **xɯ²¹bo⁵⁵** 'the feeling of weepiness, sadness' 哭意
         dʑɪŋ³³ 'shy' 害羞   **dʑɪŋ²¹bo⁵⁵** 'the feeling of being ill at ease' 羞意

Second, the headless noun phrases formed by *bo⁵⁵* are often observed as objects of the verb *ɣã²¹* 'have, there be' along with the post-VP 'can' modal *to³³* in the form of [ɣã²¹ [V-bo⁵⁵] to³³] to express certain negative meanings, such as 'something isn't worth being done', or 'there is no necessity to do something'. This structure seems to be a fossilized pattern based on *bo⁵⁵* nominalization. The sentence *ɣã²¹ sɿ²¹mɔ⁵⁵ ã²¹bo⁵⁵ to³³* '(it) isn't worth drinking' in (3.139a) is used to comment on alcohol of low quality. In fact, *sɿ²¹* can also nominalize bare verbs but it semantically contrasts with *bo⁵⁵*. As shown in (3.139b), *ã²¹ sɿ²¹* refers to anything that can be drunk, that is drink(s), so *ã²¹bo⁵⁵* cannot be used in this context. By contrast, *ã²¹bo⁵⁵* emphasizes the intrinsic value or quality of certain drinks.

(3.139) a. mɔ²¹   tsɔ⁵⁵   tsɔ²¹   mɔ²¹   ã²¹   sɿ⁵⁵   sɿ²¹.
             that   alcohol   be.like   that   drink water   way
             tsɔ⁵⁵   kʰɯ³³sɛ²¹ la³³   pɣ³³   tsʰɔ²¹.
             alcohol smell   all   NEG   thick
             ɣã²¹   sɿ²¹mɔ⁵⁵   **ã²¹bo⁵⁵**   to³³.
             there.be what   drink.NMLZ   can
             'That alcohol tastes just like water. It doesn't smell like alcohol. It isn't worth drinking.'
             那酒就像喝水一样。酒气也不浓。有什么可喝的。

         b. ɣã²¹   sɿ²¹mɔ⁵⁵   [ã²¹   sɿ²¹]/*ã²¹bo⁵⁵
             there.be what   drink   NMLZ/drink.NMLZ
             lɔ³³   pɣ³³   ɣã²¹?
             or   NEG   there.be
             'Is there anything to drink?'
             有什么喝的没有？

The sentence in (3.140a-iii) expresses the lack of necessity to go to the hospital and can be replaced by the alternative sentence given in (3.140b) with the nominalized *kuɛ²¹* 'go', *kuɛ²¹po⁵⁵*.

(3.140) a. i)   pɣ³³   sɿ³³   sɿ²¹mɔ⁵⁵   la²¹   soŋ²¹.
                  NEG   COP   what   big   sickness
             ii) kʰua²¹   la³³   kʰua²¹   ha⁵¹   o.
                  be.good all   be.good   COMPL CRS

iii) pɣ³³ tɕʰiɔ²¹ tsa²¹ ji²¹jyɛn²⁴ lɛ³³.
        NEG need   go.up   hospital   PRT
   'It's not a serious sickness. I'm recovered. It's not necessary to go to the hospital.
   不是什么大病。好都好了。不需要去医院了。

b. pɣ³³ ɣã²¹ **kuɛ²¹po⁵⁵** to³³ o.
   NEG there.be go.NMLZ   can CRS
   'It's not necessary to go (to the hospital).'
   没必要去了。

One more example is given below.

(3.141) nɯ³³ la³³ tiu³³u³³ ha⁵¹ o.
        2SG   all   know   COMPL CRS
        ŋo³³ pɣ³³ ɣã²¹ **xa²¹po⁵⁵** to³³ o.
        1SG NEG have say.NMLZ   can CRS
        'You've already known (about it). It's not necessary for me to say (it again).'
        你都知道了。我就没有可说的了。

This chapter has introduced Caijia noun phrases. Unlike many Sinitic languages, suffixation is mainly used for plurality and one type of nominalization, that is nominalization with *bo⁵⁵*. We have shown the distributional features and syntactic behaviors of nouns by using several important diagnostics in order to distinguish them from other parts of speech. Caijia adopts a two-term demonstrative system, contrasting proximal and distal, for categories of basic, place, time, and manner and extent demonstratives. Two strategies have been observed for deriving plural pronouns in Caijia: tone change and suffixation. The suffixation strategy is borrowed from Lolo. Caijia is a language with a numeral classifier system so that most of the nouns can only be modified by numerals along with proper classifiers. The Caijia word order for combining demonstrative, numeral, classifier and noun in a noun phrase shows some turbulence. The phrase [NUM CLF] follows the noun, while the demonstrative precedes the noun, i.e. [DEM N NUM CLF]. While the general Sinitic order is prenominal modification, verb-medial languages of [N NUM CLF] in the East and Southeast Asian area often possess postnominal demonstratives, such as Bai, Thai, and Khmer. Monosyllabic localizers in many Sinitic languages are regarded as postpositions, but Caijia localizers remain nominal since they can stand alone as objects of locative verbs and prepositions. We have also presented two strategies used to form headless noun phrases in Caijia: the relativizer *sɿ²¹* and the classifier *bo⁵⁵*.

Chapter 4
Verb phrases

4.1 Introduction

A verb phrase is a syntactic unit that contains at least a verb. It can also contain other dependent elements of the verb, such as object(s), complement(s) or modifier(s). For example, in the English sentence *John sent me the sample immediately*, one can observe two objects (indirect and direct) as well as an adverbial modifier. A verb phrase can also be generally understood as a predicate, which can sometimes can be non-verbal. In English and French, verb phrases can be further divided into finite or infinite phrases. However, this contrast is not a feature of Caijia, due to its analytic nature. This chapter will focus on some major constituents that may appear in verb phrases: verbs (including adjectives), verbal classifiers, adverbs, and prepositions which form prepositional or adjunct phrases and are an integral part of the predicate.

4.2 Verbs

"*Verb* is the name given to the parts-of-speech class in which occur most of the words that express actions, processes, and the like" (Schachter and Shopen 2007: 9). Caijia verbs can be roughly divided into three broad categories:
i. intransitive verbs,
ii. transitive verbs
iii. adjectives.

See Chapter 11 for Caijia auxiliary verbs.
    Yet this is not a perfect sub-classification of Caijia verbs. For example, when serving as predicates, adjectives cannot be easily distinguished from intransitive verbs. At the same time, certain adjectives can directly modify nouns, which is the canonical feature of the classical understanding of adjectives. Quite a number of adjectives also possess vivid A-BB forms (see §4.2.1.1.2 for more details). Here the term 'adjective' is adopted to distinguish this class of word from intransitive verbs. Given that *pro-drop* is overwhelmingly used in Caijia, transitive verbs often appear to surface intransitively, i.e. objects are usually absent. Labile verbs also exist in Caijia, and unlike the *pro-drop* cases, they possess both a transitive valency and an intransitive valency. There are also copular, locative, and existential verbs that will be discussed separately.

4.2.1 Distributional features of verbs

Similar to Standard Mandarin, which is an adjectival-verb language (Schachter and Shopen 2007: 18), the Caijia adjectives function just like verbs when forming predicates. Though Caijia adjectives do share many common features with canonical verbs, they also possess distinctive features.

4.2.1.1 Common features
In Caijia, verbs, including intransitive verbs, transitive verbs and adjectives, possess the following features. They can:
i.   form independent predicates;
ii. be negated;
iii. be marked by aspectual markers;
iv. be transformed into polar questions via the V-N-V strategy;
v.   stand alone as positive answers to polar questions;
vi. interact with post-VP 'can' modals;
vii. be modified by adverbs.

Some of them can:
viii. take resultative complements (see §4.2.3 for more details) or complement clauses;
ix.   or be modified by verbal classifiers (see §4.4).

In Sinitic languages, reduplication is a common method for deriving tentative verb forms (Chao 1968: 204, Norman 1988: 156, Chappell 2001b, Arcodia et al. 2015). Caijia does not adopt this strategy to code the tentative aspect (see Chapter 10 §10.2.7).

Below are some examples of the Caijia verb features mentioned above. Example (4.1) includes the three major types of verbs in Caijia. The sentences (4.1i)-(4.1iii) are all simple sentences, in which each predicate is formed by a single VP, showing verbs forming independent predicates. The predicate in (4.1i) is formed by the intransitive verb $xã^{33}$ 'yell, crow' along with the currently relevant state marker o. In the same prospective context marked by $niɔ^{33}$, mia^{21} and $tsʰo^{55}$ in (4.1ii) and (4.1iii) semantically correspond respectively to the adjectives 'bright' and 'busy' in English, respectively, but they function just as $xã^{33}$ 'yell, crow' in (4.1i). The adjective $tsʰo^{55}$ is marked by the inchoative marker $kʰɯ^{55}yɯ^{21}$ ~ $xɯ^{55}yɯ^{21}$. In (4.1iv), two transitive VPs are chained together in the prospective context. Note that some Caijia transitive verbs may be intransitive in other languages, for example, the verb $kuɛ^{33}$ 'go' in (4.1iv) can take place words as its objects (see also Chapter 3 §3.4.1).

(4.1) i) kɪ³³ **xã³³** o.
chicken yell CRS

ii) kʰɪŋ⁵⁵ niɔ³³ **mia²¹** o.
sky PROSP be.bright CRS

iii) je³³ niɔ²¹ **tsʰo⁵⁵** kʰɯ⁵⁵ɣɯ²¹ o.
3SG PROSP be.busy INC CRS

iv) niɔ³³ **kuɛ²¹** xɯ⁵⁵tsɿ⁵⁵ya²¹ mo³³ **li³³** xɯ³³tsɿ³³ o.
PROSP go pear.orchard inside pick pear CRS

'The rooster crowed. The sky's going to brighten up. He's going to begin to be busy. (He)'s going to the pear orchard to pick pears.'
鸡叫了。天要亮了。他要忙起来了。要去梨子林里摘梨子了。
(*Pear story*, texts)

In example (4.2), the intransitive verb *tsʰe⁵⁵* 'exit, be out' takes the complement *ɣɯ²¹* 'come'. Modified by the post-VP adverb *xɪŋ⁵⁵* 'very', *mia²¹* 'be bright' is stative in this sentence, which is different from the dynamic form seen in (4.1ii).

(4.2) i) kʷɔ⁵⁵pe⁵⁵ja²¹ **tsʰe⁵⁵-ɣɯ²¹** o. ii) **mia²¹** xɪŋ⁵⁵.
moon be.out-come CRS be.bright very.

'The moon came out. It was very bright.'
月亮出来了。很亮。

Example (4.3) shows two V-N-V polar questions with the adjective *tsʰo⁵⁵* 'be busy' and the transitive verb *ã³³* 'drink' alongside positive answers. The sentence in (4.3b) also provides the negative answer to the polar question of *ã³³* 'drink'.

(4.3) a. A- nɯ²¹ **tsʰo⁵⁵** (lɔ²¹) pɣ²¹ **tsʰo⁵⁵**?
2SG be.busy or NEG be.busy
'Are you busy?'
你忙不忙？

B- ɣã²¹mi⁵⁵ **tsʰo⁵⁵** e. ŋo³³ ji²¹xa²⁴ kuɛ³³ ko²¹ nɯ³³.
a.little be.busy PRT 1SG a.moment go look.for 2SG
'I'm a little busy (right now). I'll go to look for you in a moment.'
有点忙。我一会儿去找你。

b. A- je³³   ã³³   ɪŋ³³   **pɣ³³** ã³³?
        3SG   drink tobacco NEG   drink
        'Does he smoke?'
        他抽烟吗？

    B₁- ã³³   se²¹.
        drink AFF.PRT
        '(Yes, he) does.'
        抽的。

    B₂- pɣ³³   ã³³.
        NEG   drink
        '(No, he) doesn't.'
        不抽。

Example (4.4) shows both the adjective *tsʰo⁵⁵* 'be busy' taking a complement via the complementizer *lɯ⁵⁵*, and the verb *kɪŋ³³* 'see' in its negated form. Example (4.5a) presents a case with the verbal classifier *mi⁵⁵* 'a little' modifying the intransitive verb *sɯ⁵⁵* 'rest'. Note that when the verbal classifier *mi⁵⁵* 'a little' modifies VPs of degree, most of which are adjectives, it denotes intensification, as in (4.5b) (see also Chapter 9 on constructions of comparison for more details).

(4.4) i) ŋo²¹ ha⁵⁵   **tsʰo⁵⁵** lɯ⁵⁵   pɣ³³sɿ³³. ii) nɯ³³ pɣ³³ **kɪŋ³³** la²¹.
          1SG   place be.busy   VCOMP very   2SG   NEG   see   PRT
      'I'm extremely busy here. Don't you see?'
      我这儿忙得不行。你没见啊！

(4.5) a. sɿ⁵⁵ je²¹   **sɯ⁵⁵** mi⁵⁵   lɛ²¹.
          let   3SG   rest   a.little PRT
      'Let him have a rest.'
      让他歇一下。

     b.   je³³ pi²¹   mi⁵⁵.
          3SG   short a.little
      'He's shorter.'
      他矮一点。

It should be mentioned that some time words can stand alone as predicates. For example, the NP [tsʰa³³ kɯ²¹] 'lunch hour' in (4.6).

(4.6) tsʰa³³ kɯ²¹ o.
lunch hour CRS
'It's lunch time.'
午饭时间了。

This means that serving as an independent predicate cannot be the sole criterion used to identify verbs. One must consider all the other features listed above. For instance, example (4.6) cannot be negated. If negation is needed, it must be realized via a verb. As shown below, using the perfective negator *pɣ³³tɣ³³* without the verb *tɕiu⁵⁵* 'arrive' is ungrammatical.

(4.7) (xa²¹) pɣ³³-tɣ³³ *****(tɕiu⁵⁵)** tsʰa³³ kɯ²¹.
yet NEG-PFV arrive lunch time
'It's not lunch time yet.'
（还）没到午饭时间。

4.2.1.2 Distinctive features of adjectives
According to Dixon (2004) the two basic cross-linguistic features of adjectives are:
i. they are the class of words denoting qualities, properties or attributes;
ii. they modify nouns.

Adjectives in some languages can also:
iii. form comparative constructions,
iv. or modify verbs.

Similar to Sinitic verbs, Sinitic adjectives can also be reduplicated in the form of AA or ABAB, to realize vivid adjectival forms (Chappell 2001b). However, only a very limited number of adjectives can be reduplicated without change to their adjectival nature in Caijia. Reduplication is only systematically used to derive adverbs from adjectives. See §4.3 for more on Caijia adverbs.

In Caijia, one can observe from some of the examples above that adjectives functions as verbs. They can certainly form comparative constructions but they are not the only predicate type found in comparisons (see Chapter 9 for more details). It is thus not easy to distinguish Caijia adjectives from verbs. However, they do indeed differ from verbs in several aspects:
i. they can usually be modified by degree adverbs, due to their semantic properties (e.g. *xiŋ⁵⁵* 'very' [< 'fierce']);
ii. a limited number of adjectives can modify nouns directly without a linker;

iii. quite a number of Caijia adjectives (and a few emotional verbs as 'laugh' and 'cry') possess trisyllabic vivid forms, which can be roughly schematized as the form A-BB, in which A is the adjective head;
iv. some adverbs are derived from adjectives.

None of these features apply to Caijia verbs. Caijia adjectives therefore possess the same distributional features as verbs in addition to features distinct from verbs.

4.2.1.2.1 Attributive adjectives

Some of the Caijia adjectives directly modify bare nouns in the form of [ADJ N]. Though attributive adjectives are infrequent in our spontaneous data when compared to predicative adjectives, it is the attributive function which distinguishes adjectives from other verbs. Attributive adjectives in Caijia are mainly (but not exclusively) distributed across five favored semantic fields (q.v. Dixon 2004: 3–4) which are:
i. dimension;
ii. age;
iii. value;
iv. color;
v. physical property.

Let us examine these five semantic types of adjectives in Caijia with lists and examples.

i. Dimension:
la²¹ 'big' 大   *ɕie³³* 'small' 小
kʷɔ³³ 'tall, long' 高、长   *tγ²¹* 'long' 长
tsʰo³³ 'short' 短、矮   *kʰua³³* 'wide' 宽
ta³³ 'narrow' 窄
. . .

(4.8) niɔ³³ ɣɯ²¹ na³³ **la²¹** niaŋ²¹. ε²¹ **ɕie²¹** niaŋ²⁴
need come make big cake INTJ small bread.DIM
lε⁵⁵ na²¹-xɯ⁵⁵ nε⁵⁵...
PRT make-up PRT
'(That day we) need to make big cakes. Eh, small cakes are (also) made.'
（那天我们）要来做大饼。诶，小饼（也）做起来呢......
(*Cows' birthday*, texts)

(4.9) kɣ²¹ja²⁴   nɛ⁵⁵   ɯ³³   sɿ²¹...   kuŋ²¹   sɿ³³   **kʷɔ³³**   kuŋ²¹,   **tsʰo³³**   ɯ³³.
woman   PRT   wear   REL   skirt   COP   long   skirt   short   clothes
'(As for) women, they wear long skirts and short jackets.'
女人呢，穿的......裙子是长裙，短衫。
(*Life in old days*, texts)

    ii. Age:
        la²¹to⁵⁵ 'old' 老   ɬa⁵⁵ 'young' 年轻
        ɕɪŋ³³ 'new' 新   kɣ²¹ 'old' 旧
        ...

(4.10) **ɬa⁵⁵**   nioŋ²⁴
young   girl
'young lady'
年轻女孩儿

(4.11) ti³³   **ɕɪŋ²¹**   sɿ⁵⁵
strive   new   water
'strive for (the first fetch of) water of the New Year'
抢新水
(*The water of the New Year*, texts)

    iii. Value:
        kʰua²¹ 'good' 好   du⁵⁵ 'bad' 坏
        tsʰɿ²¹ 'rotten' 烂   tʰa²¹ 'broken' 坏
        pɣ²¹ 'fat' 肥   ka³³ 'poor' 穷
        ...

(4.12) pɣ²¹   tsa²¹
fat   meat
'fat meat'
肥肉

    iv. Color
        kʰɯ³³ 'black' 黑   tsʰɿ⁵⁵ 'red' 红
        tsʰɿ³³ 'blue' 蓝   ɣoŋ²¹ 'yellow' 黄
        lɔ⁵⁵ 'green' 绿   bia³³ 'white' 白
        kua²¹ 'spotted' 花...

(4.13) **kʰɯ³³** ɯ³³
black clothes
'black clothes'
黑衣

(4.14) **kua²¹** kʰui³³
spotted dog
'spotted dog'
花狗

v. Physical property
xa³³ 'unripe, strange' 生   zɿ³³ 'warm' 暖
ka²¹ 'cold' 冷   ko³³ 'cold' 冷
pe²¹ 'hot' 热   tɕiaŋ²¹ 'sweet' 甜
sa³³ 'sour' 酸
…

(4.15) **zɿ²¹** tsʰɿ⁵⁵kʰa⁵⁵
warm place
'warm place'
暖和的地方
(*Three thieves*, texts)

(4.16) **tɕiaŋ²¹** tso⁵⁵
sweet alcohol
'sweet liquor'
甜酒

It is worth noting that only a small subset of adjectives can be reduplicated, including *kʰua²¹* 'be good', *la²¹* 'big', *ɕie³³* 'be small', *ɖoŋ³³* 'heavy', while other verbs or adjectives are not reduplicated. The reduplicated forms of these adjectives can be used in both attributive and predicative functions, as shown below.

(4.17) a. **kʰua²¹kʰua²⁴** sɿ²¹ sγ³³ ji²¹ peŋ²¹
good   MOD book one CLF
'a book in a good state'
好好的一本书

b. ɔ²¹   sɣ³³   ji²¹   peŋ²¹   **kʰua²¹kʰua²⁴**   lɛ⁵⁵.
   this   book   one   CLF   good   CONT
   nɯ²¹   tɕiɔ⁵⁵mɔ⁵⁵   tɯ²¹   a²¹   pie⁵⁵   kʷɔ²¹   o.
   2SG   why   then   DCR   toss   go.CRS CRS
   'The book is in a good state. Why did you throw it away?'
   这本书好好的。你怎么把（它）扔了？

4.2.1.2.2 Vivid forms: A-BB

The second distinctive feature of adjectives in Caijia is vivid forms. An adjective's vivid form can be schematized as A-BB, in which the A slot is filled by an adjective and the -BB slot is filled by a suffix-like morpheme of two identical syllables. The lexical sources of -BB morphemes are untraceable. The term 'vivid' was first used by Chao (1968: 199) to describe the same phenomenon of adjectives in Standard Mandarin. As is labelled, the A-BB form of an adjective is semantically more intense than its root. The term 'vivid adjectival form' can also refer to adjectival reduplication in Sinitic languages (Zhang Min 1997, Tsao 2001), where AA represents monosyllabic adjectives and ABAB disyllabic ones. Given that adjectival reduplication is neither productive nor systematic in Caijia, the term 'vivid adjectival form' is exclusively used for the A-BB form. In contrast to common adjectives, which can be both dynamic and stative, the vivid forms denote only the stative meaning and are often marked by the manner continuous marker *lɛ⁵⁵* (see Chapter 10 on aspect). Moreover, they are usually not modified by the adverb *xŋ⁵⁵* 'very' as common adjectives are. Functionally, the vivid adjectival forms usually serve as predicates, as shown below.

(4.18) nɯ³³   tsaŋ²¹   mɔ²¹   ɕie²¹   kʰui³³.   **ɕie²¹mi⁵⁵mi⁵⁵**   lɛ²⁴.
        2SG   look   that   small   dog   be.small   CONT
        'Look at that dog! (It's) so small.'
        你看那只小狗。小小的。

(4.19) mɔ³³,   kɣ²⁴   nɛ⁵⁵   ɣã²¹   u²¹tsʰo²¹   kʷɔ³³.   tsʰe⁵⁵   tsɿ²¹   ɣɯ²¹
        that   paddy.plant   TOP   have   person tall   be.out   ear   come
        nɛ⁵⁵,   pɣ³³   ti³³,   m̩,   pa²¹-tɕie³³ɣɯ²¹.   sɿ³³   **tɣ³³kuɛ²¹kuɛ²⁴**
        PRT   NEG   know   INTJ   bend-be.down.come   COP   be.erect
        lɛ⁵⁵   ...
        CONT
        'The paddy plants were as tall as a person. They (could) form tassels but couldn't bear grains (LIT: the ears didn't bend down). Instead, they were erect.'
        那谷啊，有一人高，抽穗了（穗也）不会弯下来。是直挺挺的。
        (*The trial of paddy planting*, texts)

(4.20) mɛ²⁴ kʷɔ²¹ **tsʰɛ³³lɛ³³lɛ³³**.
frog CLF be.skinny
'The frog was skinny.'
那个青蛙干瘪瘪的。
(*The frog*, texts)

Even though the vivid adjectival forms are rarely observed as attributives, exceptions exist.

(4.21) ŋo²¹ ta⁵⁵ nɯ²¹ xa²¹ **tsɿ²¹li³³li²⁴** ŋon²¹ ji²¹ tɕie⁵⁵
1SG with 2SG say straight speech one CLF
'I'll be honest with you.'
我跟你说句实话。

Below is a non-exhaustive list of Caijia vivid adjectival forms grouped according to their different -BB morphemes. Given that the tone of each -BB morpheme varies, depending on its adjectival root, the tone value of each citation form is not given in the heading for each group. Note that the Chinese characters beside the English translations represent Standard Mandarin and do not necessarily correspond morpheme-by-morpheme to the Caijia -BB morphemes.

-kɛkɛ
    la²¹to⁵⁵kɛ²¹kɛ²⁴ 'old' 老苍苍
    bi³³kɛ²¹kɛ²⁴ 'short' 矮墩墩
    sv²¹kɛ³³kɛ²⁴ 'poor' 穷兮兮
    ma³³kɛ³³kɛ³³ 'full' 满当当
    naŋ³³kɛ²¹kɛ⁵⁵ 'muddy' 稀乎乎
    dzo²¹kɛ²¹kɛ⁵⁵ 'ugly' 丑兮兮

-lolo
    pe²¹lo³³lo²⁴ 'hot' 热乎乎
    z̩³³lo²¹lo²⁴ 'warm' 暖洋洋
    tɕʰie²¹lo³³lo²⁴ 'neat' 利利索索
    tɪn²¹lo³³lo²⁴ 'round' 圆乎乎
    tso²¹lo³³lo²⁴ 'bright' 亮堂堂
    bi³³lo²¹lo²⁴ 'short' 矮墩墩

-sɿsɿ
    lã²¹sɿ³³sɿ²⁴ 'chill' 凉悠悠
    sɔ²¹sɿ³³sɿ²⁴ 'smiley' 笑嘻嘻
    pe³³sɿ²¹sɿ²⁴ 'reverse' 反着
    dã³³sɿ²¹sɿ²⁴ 'brave, active' 勇敢

-titi
    ka²¹ti³³ti²⁴ 'cold' 冷嗖嗖
    sa³³ti³³ti³³ 'sour' 酸溜溜
    tsʰɿ⁵⁵ti²¹ti²⁴ 'red' 红彤彤
    nia³³ti²¹ti²⁴ 'disordered' 乱哄哄

-tʏtʏ
    kʰua³³tʏ²¹tʏ²⁴ 'wide' 宽宽敞敞
    pʰaŋ³³tʏ²¹tʏ²⁴ 'fat' 胖嘟嘟
    tɕʰi²¹tʏ³³tʏ²⁴ 'neat' 齐
    kuɪŋ³³tʏ²¹tʏ²⁴ 'curly' 卷碌碌

-lili
    bia³³li²¹li²⁴ 'in vain' 白白   tsɿ²¹li³³li²⁴ 'straight' 直溜溜
    pɪŋ²¹li³³li²⁴ 'flat' 平坦坦

-tãtã/taŋtaŋ
    kʰɤ⁵⁵tã²¹tã³³ 'bitter' 苦兮兮   kʰoŋ³³tã³³tã³³ 'empty' 空荡荡
    mi²¹tã³³tã²⁴ 'dark' 暗

-kaka
    mɔ³³ka²¹ka²⁴ 'thin' 细   tsʰɿ⁵⁵ka²¹ka²⁴ 'naked' 赤条条
    xa³³ka²¹ka²⁴ 'unripe' 生碌碌

-kuɛkuɛ
    dɯ³³kuɛ²¹kuɛ²⁴ 'infertile' 贫瘠   tɣ³³kuɛ²¹kuɛ²⁴ 'erect' 直愣愣

-piepie
    niu²¹pie³³pie²⁴ 'soft' 软趴趴   tsɿ³³pie²¹pie⁵⁵ 'wet' 湿漉漉

-tʰɭtʰɭ
    ŋa²¹tʰɭ³³tʰɭ²⁴ 'tough, neat' 硬朗朗/利利索索
    bɤ³³tʰɭ²¹tʰɭ³³ 'thin' 薄菲菲
    mɔ³³tʰɭ²¹tʰɭ³³ 'thin' 细溜溜

-mãmã/maŋmaŋ
    kʰɤ³³mã²¹mã²⁴ 'fragrant, tasty' 香喷喷   tɕiaŋ²¹mã³³mã²⁴ 'sweet' 甜蜜蜜
    saŋ³³mã²¹mã²⁴ 'be at ease' 安逸

-pʰepʰe
    ka³³pʰe²¹pʰe²⁴ 'dry' 干   tsʰɿ²¹pʰe²¹pʰe²⁴ 'light' 轻飘飘

-nono
    u³³no²¹no²⁴ 'thin' 瘦兮兮   pɤ²¹no³³no²⁴ 'fat' 胖嘟嘟

-paŋpaŋ
    go³³paŋ²¹paŋ⁵⁵ 'thick' 厚   la³³paŋ³³paŋ³³ 'big' 大

Other -BB morphemes

There are still other -BB morphemes with only one example found in our data set.

    u³³to²¹to²⁴ 'thin' 瘦兮兮   ka³³ŋɔ²¹ŋɔ⁵⁵ 'thin' 瘦兮兮
    ka²¹sa³³sa²⁴ 'hardworking' 勤快   ka³³tʰɤ²¹tʰɤ²⁴ 'poor' 穷嗖嗖
    kʷɔ⁵⁵daŋ²¹daŋ³³ 'tall' 高   gui³³pia²¹pia²⁴ 'slippery' 滑溜溜
    kʰɯ³³pi³³pi³³ 'black' 黑漆漆   la²¹to⁵⁵ŋuɛ²¹ŋuɛ³³ 'old' 老苍苍
    lɔ³³ja²¹ja²⁴ 'green' 绿油油   ɬa⁵⁵dza²¹dza²¹ 'young' 年轻
    mia²¹kua³³kua²⁴ 'pretty' 水灵灵   ma³³ha²¹ha²⁴ 'blurred' 模糊
    niaŋ²¹tso³³tso²⁴ 'faithful' 讲义气   naŋ³³kɯ²¹kɯ⁵⁵ 'muddy' 稀乎乎
    noŋ³³dzɤ²¹dzɤ³³ 'angery' 气鼓鼓   nɯ²¹kɤ³³kɤ²⁴ 'damp' 潮乎乎
    ŋa²¹kuaŋ³³kuaŋ³³ 'hard' 硬邦邦   pi⁵⁵tʰa²¹tʰa²⁴ 'flat' 扁塌塌

bia³³kʰɔ²¹kʰɔ²⁴ 'white' 白花花
tie²¹pʰa³³pʰa²⁴ 'polite' 客气

toŋ³³tʰɔ²¹tʰɔ²⁴ 'heavy' 重
tsʰɣ³³poŋ²¹poŋ³³ 'thick' 粗
tsʰɔ³³xã²¹xã³³ 'smelly' 臭轰轰
tsaŋ³³tʃ³³tʃ³³ 'mean' 凶巴巴
tɕie²¹tʰaŋ³³tʰaŋ²⁴ 'clear' 清清楚楚
tɕɪŋ⁵⁵tɔ²¹tɔ²⁴ 'muscular' 精壮
ɣoŋ³³sɔ²¹sɔ³³ 'yellow' 黄灿灿
ʑi³³nɔ²¹nɔ²⁴ 'crooked' 歪拽拽

ta³³tsʰaŋ²¹tsʰaŋ⁵⁵ 'narrow' 窄兮兮
dɔ²¹naŋ³³naŋ⁵⁵ 'dirty' （衣物）脏兮兮
tsʰɛ³³lɛ³³lɛ³³ 'skinny' 干瘪瘪
tsʰɔ³³ko²¹ko²⁴ 'cowering' 瑟瑟缩缩
tsʰɔ³³pi²¹pi²⁴ 'smelly' 臭轰轰
ɕie²¹mi⁵⁵mi⁵⁵ 'small' 小
tɕiu²¹me⁵⁵me⁵⁵ 'quiet' 静悄悄
tɕʰi²¹sɣ³³sɣ²⁴ 'crisp' 脆生生
va²¹pʰi³³pʰi²⁴ 'arrogant' 牛轰轰

One can observe from the lists above that different adjectives interact with different -BB morphemes. In other words, the -BB morphemes can have a sortal function, just like numeral classifiers. We return to a few of the adjective vivid forms from above to elaborate their sortal feature. In (4.22), the morphemes -*kɛkɛ* and -*lolo* can further differentiate the 'ugly' *dzo²¹* and the 'bright' *tso²¹*, when the word *dzo²¹* 'ugly' surfaces as [tso²¹] (see Chapter 2 for more details on the devocalization). In (4.23), it is the -BB morphemes -*ko²¹ko²⁴* and -*xã²¹xã³³* that help to distinguish the two homophonic roots *tsʰɔ³³*.

(4.22) a. tso²¹kɛ³³kɛ⁵⁵ 'ugly' 丑兮兮

b. tso²¹lo³³lo²⁴ 'bright' 亮堂堂

(4.23) a. tsʰɔ³³xã²¹xã³³ 'smelly' 臭轰轰

b. tsʰɔ³³ko²¹ko²⁴ 'cowering' 瑟瑟缩缩

Examples (4.24) and (4.25) are cases of the same adjective root. The word *ka³³* in (4.24) denotes both 'dry' and 'thin', but 'dry' and 'thin' respectively go with different -BB morphemes. Sharing the same root *bia³³* in (4.25), *bia³³kʰɔ²¹kʰɔ²⁴* denotes 'white', while *bia³³li²¹li²⁴* denotes 'in vain'.

(4.24) a. ka³³pʰe²¹pʰe²⁴ 'dry' 干瘪瘪

b. ka³³ŋɔ²¹ŋɔ⁵⁵ 'thin' 瘦兮兮

(4.25) a. bia³³kʰɔ²¹kʰɔ²⁴ 'white' 白花花

b. bia³³li²¹li²⁴ 'in vain' 白白

Moreover, some adjectives can interact with more than one -BB morpheme. For instance, $la^{21}to^{55}$ can either associate with $-k\varepsilon^{21}k\varepsilon^{24}$ or $-\eta u\varepsilon^{21}\eta u\varepsilon^{33}$ denoting exactly the same meaning 'old'. The same goes for $u^{33}no^{21}no^{24}$ 'thin' and $u^{33}to^{21}to^{24}$ 'thin'.

4.2.1.2.3 Derivational adverbs

The third distinctive feature of Caijia adjectives is that some can serve as adverbs, whether alone or via a process of reduplication. In general, verbs are not able to perform this function in Caijia. Adjectives, as well as their vivid A-BB forms, are important sources of adverbs, which are usually preverbal. Semantic similarities exist between adjectives and adverbs. Adjectives describe properties of entities, while some members of the class of adverbs describe properties of actions, just as the English word 'fast' can be an adverb or an adjective. When modifying verbs, some adjectives may remain in their original forms. Most, however, need to be reduplicated. This means that a vivid adjectival form can appear in the form of [ABB-ABB] to modify a verb (see §4.3 for more details on adverbs). The reduplication strategy is optional for vivid adjectival A-BB forms.

Examples (4.26)-(4.28) show cases of adjectives modifying verbs in their original forms: $k^h ua^{21}$ 'be good', $t\varepsilon iu^{21}$ 'be quick, fast' and tie^{33} 'be many'. However, it is quite uncommon for non-reduplicated adjectives to directly modify verbs. It should be noted that the adverb marker $l\varepsilon^{55}$ cannot be used to link the adverb with the head in the following cases.

(4.26) **$k^h ua^{33}$** $z\gamma^{21}$
good eat
'delicious/taste good'
好吃

(4.27) nu^{33} **$t\varepsilon iu^{24}$** γa^{21} la^{21}!
2SG quick walk PRT
'You hurry up!'
你快走啦！

(4.28) nu^{33} $t\varepsilon^h in^{21} t\varepsilon^h in^{21} t\varepsilon i\eta^{55} t\varepsilon i\eta^{55}$ $l\varepsilon^{55}$ **tie^{33}** tu^{21} $k^h u^{33}$ nen^{24}.
2SG peacefully ADV long exist several year.
'(May) you live peacefully for many more years.'
你清清静静地多在几年。
(*The New Year's visit*, texts)

More commonly, it is the reduplicated adjectives that are used as adverbs and they optionally associate with the adverb marker *lɛ⁵⁵*. See the example below.

(4.29) nɯ³³ **kʰua²¹kʰua²⁴** (lɛ²¹) nian³³soŋ²¹.
 2SG well ADV recover
 'You take care of yourself and recover well.'
 你好好养病。

(4.30) ɕie²¹ kʰui³³ **tɕiu²¹tɕiu²⁴** lɛ²¹ tsa³³ tɕiŋ²¹ piɔ⁵⁵.
 small dog quickly ADV toward front run
 'The little dog ran quickly forward.'
 小狗快快地朝前跑。

Adverbs can also be stacked, as shown below.

(4.31) je³³ tɯ³³ **kʰua²¹kʰua²⁴** lɛ⁵⁵, **mã³³mã⁵⁵** lɛ²¹ tɯ²¹ mɔ²¹
 3SG then well ADV appetizingly ADV at that
 <sɿ⁵⁵kʰa³³>, tɕiŋ²¹ po⁵⁵ piŋ³³ **kʰua²¹kʰua²⁴**
 well bottle CLF side well
 ã³³ ji²¹ ti³³ kuɛ²¹ o.
 drink one VCLF go CRS
 'It then took a good and appetizing drink from the bottle.'
 它就好好地、香香地在瓶子边好好喝了一顿。
 (*The crow and the bottle*, texts)

Furthermore, adverbs formed by reduplicated adjectives can further be reduplicated to denote intensification in the form of [AA-AA].

(4.32) ŋo³³ **tɕiu²¹tɕiu²⁴~tɕiu²¹tɕiu²⁴** lɛ²¹ tγ³³ nɛ³³...
 1SG quickly~quickly ADV grow PRT
 'I'll (try to) grow up very quickly...'
 我快快快地长呢......
 (*The corn and the grass*, texts)

The following two examples show how the vivid adjectival forms modify verbs. Even though the adverb marker *lɛ⁵⁵* is all present in both these examples, it has been observed that *lɛ⁵⁵* can be absent in other cases.

(4.33) mɔ^{21} u^{21}tsʰo^{24} ni^{33} tɯ^{33} ka^{21}, **tsʰɔ^{33}ko^{21}ko^{24}** lɛ^{55} tɯ^{33}
that person CLF then be.cold flinchingly ADV then
a^{33} to^{21}to^{55} la^{21} tsʰɔ^{33}-tɕie^{21}ɣɯ^{21} o.
OM head all withdraw-be.down.come CRS
well bottle CLF side well
'That person then felt cold and tucked his head (into his clothes) in a flinching way.'
那个人就冷（起来），瑟瑟缩缩地把头缩下来了。
(*The north wind and the sun*, texts)

(4.34) mɔ^{21} u^{21}tsʰo^{24} ni^{33} **va^{21}pʰi^{33}pʰi^{24}** lɛ^{33} tsaŋ^{21} ni^{33}.
that person CLF arrogantly ADV look 3
'That person (often) looks at people arrogantly.'
那个人牛轰轰地看人。

The vivid adjectival A-BB forms can also be reduplicated when modifying verbs. Similar to example (4.32), the reduplication suggests semantic intensification, as illustrated in (4.35).

(4.35) [...] **tsɿ^{21}li^{33}li^{24}~tsɿ^{21}li^{33}li^{24}** lɛ^{21} tɯ^{21} ʈaŋ^{21}-kʰɯ^{55}ɣɯ^{21} o.
straightly~straightly ADV then stand-rise.come CRS
'He stood up (in the water), in a very upright manner.'
直挺挺直挺挺地就站起来了。
(*Drowning Persons*, texts)

All the derivational adverbs shown above in this section are preverbal. We also pointed out above that Caijia adverbs are typically preverbal. However, there is indeed one exception: the only post-VP degree adverb, *xɪŋ^{55}* 'very', which is derived from its related adjective form 'fierce, capable'. Unlike preverbal adverbs derived from adjectives, *xɪŋ^{55}* is never reduplicated. The two sentences in (4.36) respectively demonstrate the predicative and attributive uses of *xɪŋ^{55}* 'fierce, capable', while example (4.37) shows its use as a post-VP adverb, modifying the adjective *tso^{33}* 'be bright'.

Adjective

(4.36) a. tγ^{55}pi^{21} lɔ^{21}ni^{33} lɛ^{21}tsʰɛ^{21} **xɪŋ^{55}**.
bet who only capable
'(The tiger and the buffalo) made a bet to see who was more capable.'
老虎和水牛）打赌看（究竟）谁才厉害。

b. ŋo⁵⁵   ta⁵⁵   ni²¹   kʷɔ²¹   ɣã³³   kʷɔ²¹   hm̩⁵⁵   **xɪŋ⁵⁵**
1PL   two   CLF   oneself   have   oneself   POSS   capable
tsʰ₁⁵⁵kʰa³³   se²¹.
place   AFF.PRT
'Each of us has our own proper strength.'
我们两个各自有各自的强处。
(*The tiger and the buffalo*, texts)

Adverb
(4.37) "tso³³   nɛ³³   tso²¹   **xɪŋ⁵⁵**   ei   ..."
be.bright   PRT   be.bright   very   PRT
' "(As for the light), it is (indeed) very bright..." '
"（那灯）亮呢，很亮哦......"
(*Lightening up the cigarette*, texts)

4.2.2 Copular, locative and existential verbs

Copular, locative, existential, and possessive verbs are cross-linguistically attested to have unique semantic correlations (Meillet 1923, Clark 1978). In Tibeto-Burman languages, locative, existential and possessive verbs often share one form, while three distinct verbs are used to express these semantic domains in many Sinitic and Tai-Kadai languages (see Chappell and Lü 2022 for more information). In Caijia, these semantic domains are coded by three distinct verbs, as in many Sinitic languages. They are:

Copula: *sɿ³³* 'be' (cognate with copula *shì* 是 in Standard Mandarin)
Locative verb: *tɯ²¹* 'exist, be at' (< 'live, dwell')
Existential/possessive verb: *ɣã³³* 'have, there be'

4.2.2.1 Copula
Typologically a copula may cover the following semantic relations (Dixon 2010: 159):

			Caijia Copula
i.	Identity	My aunt is a lawyer.	√
ii.	Attribution	My niece is cute.	
iii.	Possession	This car is my father's.	√
iv.	Benefaction	This is for you.	
v.	Location	The key is in the drawer.	

The key identifying features of a copula as defined by Dixon (2010: 160) are that it must at least cover the feature (i) and/or the feature (ii), and that it always occurs with two arguments, i.e. the copular subject and the copular complement. In Caijia, the copula $sɿ^{33}$ covers the features (i) and (iii) listed above. In both cases, it forms a nominal predicate, as shown in (4.38). Note that the classifier $lɛ^{24}$ in (4.38) is a classifier for siblings, cousins, sisters and brothers-in-law (see the preceding Chapter §3.5 for some examples).

(4.38)   _{SUB}[ɔ²¹   ɪŋ⁵⁵soŋ²¹   ta⁵⁵   kʷɔ⁵⁵pe⁵⁵ja²¹]   **sɿ²¹**   _{COMPL}[ta⁵⁵   lɛ²⁴]   xa²¹.
         this   sun   and   moon   COP   two   CLF   REP
       'It's said that the sun and the moon are brother and sister.'
       说这太阳和月亮是两兄妹。
       (*The sun and the moon*, texts)

(4.39)   _{SUB}[ɔ²¹   sɣ³³   peŋ²¹]   **sɿ³³**   _{COMPL}[nɯ²¹   hm̩⁵⁵].
         this   book   CLF   COP   2SG   POSS
       'This book is yours.'
       这本书是你的。

Being a verb, the copula $sɿ^{33}$ can be negated and form a polar question via the V-NEG-V strategy, as shown in (4.40).

(4.40)   a.   ŋuɛ²¹   pa⁵⁵   pɣ³³   sɿ²¹   xɯ⁵⁵pa³³.
            my.family   father   NEG   COP   Taoist.priest
            'My father is not a Taoist priest.'
            我爸爸不是道士。

       b.   Q-   nɛ²¹   pa⁵⁵   sɿ²¹   xɯ⁵⁵pa³³   (lɔ²¹)   pɣ³³   sɿ³³?
                 your.family   father   COP   Taoist.priest   or   NEG   COP
                 'Is your father a Taoist priest?'
                 你爸爸是不是道士？

            A-   [sɿ³³   e.]   /[pɣ³³   sɿ³³].
                 COP   PRT   NEG   COP
                 'Yes.' / 'No.'
                 是啊。/不是。

However, unlike the definition of a copula given above, the copula $sɿ^{33}$ or its negated form $pɣ^{33}$ $sɿ^{33}$ without any argument can stand alone as the answer to a polar question, as do other non-copular verbs in Caijia. See the second response line of example (4.40b) illustrated above. Naturally, the arguments of the verb are understood from the context. Furthermore, the copula can also be used to answer polar questions formed by the particle *la²¹*, a particle which usually involve speakers' presuppositions. Take the question formed by the particle *la²¹* in (4.41) as an example. It suggests that the presupposition 'he isn't married yet' is considered true by the speaker asking this question. Unlike the positive answer in (4.40b), in which *sɿ³³* is interpreted as 'yes' or 'it's so', the *sɿ³³* in (4.41) should be interpreted as 'no'. In this example it is actually used to affirm the question asker's assumption, denoting 'it's indeed so'.

(4.41) Q- je³³ a²¹ pγ³³-tγ³³ tɕie⁵⁵ ɔ⁵⁵ la²¹?
       3SG still NEG-PFV do house Q
       'Isn't he married yet?'
       他还没结婚啊？

   A- sɿ³³ o.
       COP CRS
       'No, he isn't.'
       是啊。

The copula *sɿ³³* still behaves differently from other non-copular verbs. For example, it cannot be negated by the perfective negator *pγ³³tγ³³* and only interacts with aspectual markers in certain specific contexts. For example, the completive marker *ha⁵⁵* cannot be used in a positive context, but it can be used in a negative context to underline the meaning 'already'

(4.42) a. je³³ sɿ³³ kʷɔ³³sγ³³pa³³ *ha⁵¹ o.
         3SG COP teacher COMPL CRS
         'He became a teacher.'
         他当老师了。

    b. je³³ pγ³³ sɿ³³ kʷɔ³³sγ³³pa³³ **ha⁵¹** o.
         3SG NEG COP teacher COMPL CRS
         'He's not a teacher any more.'
         他不是老师了。

The copula can only be marked by the continuous aspect marker *sɿ³³ . . . sɿ²¹* in certain specific semantic and syntactic contexts (see also Chapter 10 on aspect). The copula cannot take any resultative complement. Moreover, it usually does not interact with post-VP 'can' modals (see also Chapter 11 on modality), nor can it be modified by degree or manner adverbs.

The copula sɿ³³ also possesses some other non-copular uses, which are quite similar to the copula *shì* 是 [ʂɿ⁵¹] in Standard Mandarin. For instance, it can denote 'correct', whose use can only be predicative and cannot be modified by degree adverbs.

(4.43) niɔ³³ je³³ xa³³ sɿ²¹ lɛ²¹tsʰɛ²¹ **sɿ³³**.
must 3SG say NMLZ only correct
'Only what he says is correct.'
要他说的才是。
(*Bullies*, texts)

Forming a kind of cleft construction, the copula sɿ³³ can either be used to emphasize the subject, the whole sentence, or to emphasize the predicate in a sentence. When emphasizing a subject, sɿ³³ precedes the subject, as in (4.44). This sentence can possess another interpretation, i.e. it is the whole sentence ŋo³³ ko²¹tɣ³³ je³³ 'I found him' that is emphasized.

(4.44) **sɿ³³** ŋo³³ ko²¹-tɣ³³ je³³.
COP 1SG look.for-obtain 3SG
'It's me who found him'
'It's the fact that I found him.'
是我找到他。

When emphasizing a predicate, sɿ³³ directly precedes the predicate. In (4.45), the fact that the cow was in its pen is underlined by the copula sɿ³³. In (4.46), the use of the copula suggests that it is a bet that was involved.

(4.45) kʰɯ⁵⁵-ɣɯ²¹ kuɛ³³ tsaŋ³³ ŋo²¹ nɛ⁵⁵, ŋo²¹ **sɿ³³** tɯ²¹ ɣuɔ²¹ mo³³.
rise-come PURP look cow PRT cow COP be.at pen inside
'(The child) got up to check the cow. It was indeed in the pen.'
起来去看牛呢，牛是在窝里。
(*The loss of the cow*, texts)

(4.46) to²¹pʰa³³ mɔ²¹ kʰɣ⁵⁵pa²¹ ta⁵⁵ nɛ²¹ **sɿ³³** tɣ⁵⁵pi²¹.
once that tiger and buffalo COP bet
'Once upon a time, the tiger and the buffalo made a bet.'
很久以前，那老虎和水牛是打赌。
(*The tiger and the buffalo*, texts)

One may question the nature of the copula in these cases, especially when $sı^{33}$ emphasizes predicates. That is, one may wonder whether $sı^{33}$ should be treated as an adverb of intensification. However, the fact that $sı^{33}$ can still be negated points to its verbal nature, as in (4.47b). The copula precedes a negated clause in (4.47a). We offer this example to avoid the possible conclusion that the negator used to negate $sı^{33}$ can be understood as the negator of the predicate γa^{21} $suaŋ^{55}u\varepsilon^{33}$ ja^{21} 'have been to Weining'.

(4.47) a. je³³ **sı³³** pɣ³³-tɣ³³   ɣa²¹   suaŋ⁵⁵uɛ³³   ja²¹.
           3SG   COP   NEG-PFV   walk   Weining_PLACENAME EXP
           'He definitely has (never) been to Weining.'
           他是没去过威宁。

b. je³³ la²¹   **pɣ³³** sı³³ pɣ³³-tɣ³³   ɣa²¹   suaŋ⁵⁵uɛ³³   ja²¹.
    3SG   also   NEG   COP   NEG-PFV   walk   Weining_PLACENAME EXP
    'It's not that he has (never) been to Weining.'
    他也不是没去过威宁。

See also Chapter 11 on modality for another type of cleft or affirmative construction formed with $sı^{33}$.

4.2.2.2 Locative verb

A locative verb is a verb used to form the locative construction like 'The book is on the table' in English. Derived from the verb 'live, dwell', $tuı^{21}$ is used as the locative verb in Caijia, and takes place words or locational phrases as its objects. In the example below, both the source meaning 'live', and the locative meaning, 'be at', are evident.

(4.48) ŋo⁵⁵   ta⁵⁵   ɕie²¹   tʰɔ⁵⁵   tuı³³   tsʰɛ²¹sı³³   ŋo⁵⁵   ta⁵⁵   fɛ⁵⁵hɛ²¹
        1PL   from   small   moment   then   only   1PL   two   family
        tuı²¹ ji²¹   kʰa³³.   je³³   la³³   sı³³   je³³   tɔ²¹   ni²⁴   **tuı²¹** ɔ⁵⁵
        live   one   place   3SG   also   COP   3SG   alone CLF   be.at   house
        ʑi²¹,   ŋo³³   la³³   sı³³   ŋo³³   tɔ²¹   ni²⁴.
        inside   1SG   also   COP   1SG   alone CLF
        'Since we were young, just our two families have been living in this place. He was at home all by himself and so was I.'
        自从我们小时候起，就只是我们两家住在一起。他是他一个人独自在家，我也是我一个。
        (*My friend and I*, texts)

Two more examples, with an animate subject and an inanimate subject respectively, are given below.

(4.49) mɔ²¹ kʰɪ²¹kʰo²⁴ nɛ⁵⁵ **tɯ²¹** mɔ²¹ sɔ⁵⁵ tsɤ²¹ tɤ³³.
that turtledove PRT be.at that tree CLF upside
'The turtledove was in the tree.'
那斑鸠呢，在那棵树上。
(*The man and the tiger*, texts)

(4.50) tsaŋ³³-kɪŋ³³ ŋo²⁴ mɔ²¹ kʰa²⁴ po⁵⁵ xa²¹tsɛ⁵⁵ **tɯ²¹** ma²⁴.
look-see 1PL that pit.DIM CLF still be.at there
'(I) saw our pit was still there.'
看见我们的坑还在那儿。
(*The darts game*, texts)

Verbs like *tɯ²¹* 'be at' may be treated as locative copulas in the literature, but we treat this particular Caijia instance as a true verb. First, *tɯ²¹* does not cover the identifying features of a copula outlined earlier in this chapter, denoting the relation of identity between the copular subject and its complement. As suggested by (Dixon 2010: 160), if a verb only occurs in the location relationship, it should not be regarded as a copula. As opposed to the copula *sɿ³³*, which only stands alone without any complement in answers or responses, *tɯ²¹* 'be at' can be used intransitively without an argument in common declarative sentences denoting 'be here or there, exist'. This is a further piece of evidence that *tɯ²¹* cannot be treated as a copula, as shown below.

(4.51) ɣã²¹ ŋo³³ **tɯ²¹**. nɯ³³ piɔ²⁴ tsʰ1³³.
there.be 1SG be.at 2SG NEG.IMP fear
'There's me being here. Don't be afraid.'
有我在。你别怕。

(4.52) ɔ²¹kɯ²⁴ mɔ²¹ kʰa²⁴ po⁵⁵ la²¹ a²¹tsɛ⁵⁵ **tɯ²¹**.
now that hole CLF even still be.at
'Even now the pit is still (there).'
现在那个坑还在。
(*The darts game*, texts)

Furthermore, it can also denote 'be alive', as illustrated below.

(4.53) "ŋo³³ pɣ³³-tɣ³³ sɿ⁵⁵ sɿ²¹ lo³³. e⁵⁵a, ŋo³³ sɿ³³ **tɯ²¹**
1SG NEG-PFV die AFF/CONT PRT INTJ 1SG AFF be.alive
sɿ³³ ma³³."
AFF PRT
' "I didn't die. I'm alive." '
"我没有死。我是活着的。"
(*The zombie wife*, texts)

4.2.2.3 Existential and possessive verb

The existential verbs refer to those forming constructions like 'There is a book on the table'. In Caijia the verb *ɣã³³* is used to form an existential construction, usually taking a place word or a locational phrase as optional theme or topic. In an existential construction, the existential argument is indefinite. Example (4.54) is a sentence with the locational phrase *mɔ²¹ ti²¹ka²⁴ mo³³* 'the inside of the valley' as the topic, while both (4.55) and (4.56) are impersonal. Both (4.54) and (4.55) contain simple predicates, while (4.56) contains a complex predicate.

(4.54) mɔ²¹ ti²¹ka²⁴ mo³³ tɯ³³ **ɣã³³** kʰa²¹ po⁵⁵.
that valley inside just there.be hole CLF
'There's a big hole in the valley.'
那山谷里就有个洞。
(*The dead tiger*, texts)

(4.55) mɔ²¹kɯ²⁴ **ɣã²¹** u²¹tsʰo²⁴ ji²¹ fɛ⁵¹hɛ²¹.
that.time there.be people one family
'There was once a family of people.'
以前，有一家人。
(*The zombie wife*, texts)

(4.56) **ɣã²¹** ji³³ ni³³ tɯ⁵⁵ ta⁵⁵ u²¹ ɣa²¹ o⁵⁵.
there.be one CLF then follow back walk PRT
'There was a person following behind.'
有一个（人）就跟在后面走哦！
(*Coins*, texts)

Not surprisingly, the existential verb *ɣã³³* 'there be' is also used for predicative possession in Caijia, denoting 'have, possess'. In the construction for predicative possession, which is transitive, the subject of *ɣã³³* is the possessor and the object of *ɣã³³* is the possessed entity. See the two examples below.

(4.57) ɕie²¹ kʰɣ⁵⁵pa²⁴ ta⁵⁵ kʷɔ²¹ tɯ³³ pɣ³³ **ɣã³³** ʑi³³ o.
small tiger.DIM two CLF then NEG have mother CRS
'The two little tigers then didn't have their mother (any more).'
两只小老虎就没有妈妈了。
(*Two little tigers*, texts)

(4.58) nɯ³³ la²¹ **ɣã²¹** zɣ²¹ sɿ²¹ mẽ!
2SG all have eat NMLZ PRT
'You all have something to eat!'
你都有吃的嘛！
(*Chatting between Li and Chen*, conversation)

In (4.59Q), the possessed NP ɔ²¹sɿ⁵⁵ tie³³ sɿ²¹ tɕiŋ²¹ 'so much money' is topicalized and moved to the sentence initial position. In the answer, the verb ɣã³³ is marked by the durative marker -xɯ⁵⁵.

(4.59) Q- ɔ²¹sɿ⁵⁵ tie³³ sɿ²¹ tɕiŋ²¹ je³³ **ɣã²¹** to³³ mo³³?
this.so much MOD money 3SG have can Q
'Is it possible for him to have so much money?'
这么多钱，他能有么？

A- je³³ **ɣã²¹-xɯ⁵⁵** se²¹.
3SG have-DUR AFF.PRT
'He definitely has.'
他有的。

In many Sinitic languages, the existential and possessive verb is negated by a distinct negator other than the general one. For example, negated existence and possession is realized via the negator *méi* 没 [me²⁴] 'not' in Standard Mandarin. The general negator is *bù* 不 [pu⁵¹], the cognate of the Caijia general negator *pɣ³³*. In contrast, the verb *ɣã³³* 'there be, have' in Caijia is negated by the general negator *pɣ³³* like other verbs, as shown in (4.57). One more example is also given below.

(4.60) ŋo³³ tsɛ²¹tsɛ²⁴ **pɣ³³** ɣã²¹ ko²¹hɔ⁵⁵ o.
1SG really NEG have idea CRS
'I really don't have any more solutions.'
我真的没有办法了。

4.2.3 Resultative complements

The term 'resultative' may refer to verbs "that express a state implying a previous event" (Nedjalkov and Jaxontov 1988: 6). For instance, *The picture is hung on the wall* denotes that the state of the picture's being on the wall is due to the action of hanging. However, resultative complements (RC) refer also to a type of verb compounding strategy widely attested in Sinitic languages and have been well-described in the literature on Chinese linguistics. It is a predicate type in many Southeast Asian languages as well and is treated as one of the common multi-verb constructions by Enfield (2018: 191–192).

By contrast, a resultative phrase is composed of a verb followed by a complement which denotes the result of its preceding verb. This relation is not encoded by any morphological device, which means that it is zero-marked in the form of [V-RC]. In Caijia, resultative complements can be, in general, divided in two semantic types:
i. general achievement complements;
ii. and directional complements.

In spite of these two different types, the [V-RC] phrases possess some common features.
i.   Semantically, resultative complement phrases are all telic usually involving change of state;
ii. they, thus, do not interact with durative and continuous aspects;
iii. similarly, they are not compatible with the delimitative aspect either.
iv. Except for the directional complement xu^{55} (< 'rise'), they can be negated in two ways: [NEG [V-RC]] and [V-NEG-RC]. The latter form can denote negative potential, and is an important identifying feature to justify the establishment of a category for resultative complements.
v.   Most of the resultative complements can stand alone as independent verbs.

The semantic features (i) and (iv) deserve more elaboration. The telic feature of a resultative phrase can be represented by semantic contrast with its bare verb form.

Take the verb go^{33} 'look for, search for' in (4.61) as an example. As for its counterpart in English, 'look for', the action of 'look for' is an activity which does not guarantee any result. But once compounded with the verb ty^{33} 'obtain', as in (4.61b), the new verb compound denotes 'find', i.e. discovery after the action of searching. In the same fashion, the directional complement $tsʰe^{55}yu^{21}$ 'come out' adds telic meaning to the verb go^{33} 'look for', that is, one looks for something and finally finds it among many other things.

(4.61) a. go³³ 'look for' 找

   b. go³³-tv̩³³　　　c. go²¹-tsʰe⁵⁵-ɣɯ²¹
      look.for-obtain　　look.for-be.out-come
      'find'　　　　　　　'find out (among other things)'
      找到　　　　　　　找出来

Given that Caijia is a pro-drop language, it often occurs that verb-derived aspectual markers may be confused with resultative complements in certain syntactic contexts. For example, ha⁵⁵ in the phrase [zv̩²¹ ha⁵⁵] 'eat-finish, have eaten' can be either analyzed as a resultative complement denoting 'finish' or a completive aspect marker. One criterion for distinguishing between the two is that only the resultative complement can be negated. Next, we discuss the different types of resultative verb complements. These are general achievement and directional complements.

4.2.3.1 General achievement complements

In a [V-RC] general achievement phrase, the RC slot is commonly filled by monosyllabic telic verbs (including adjectives), which denote that a certain result is attained by the action. For example, the action of pounding, to³³ in (4.62), can be performed without necessarily making any visible or palpable damage, while the complement tsa³³ 'be broken' turns the action of pounding into a telic action, denoting 'pound into pieces'. The phrase to³³pi³³ tɩŋ²¹tɩŋ²⁴ further specifies the result of pounding, i.e. 'into powder'.

(4.62) niɔ²¹　a³³　mɔ²¹　tsʰa²¹tsɤ³³,　ei,　tsʰa²¹tsɤ³³　**to³³-tsa³³**.
       need　OM　that　liquor.yeast　INTJ　liquor.yeast　pound-be.broken
       to³³-pi³³　tɩŋ²¹tɩŋ²⁴　nɛ⁵⁵　sa²¹　pie⁵⁵　ɔ²¹kʷɔ²¹
       pound-become　powder　PRT　scatter　to　INTJ
       zv̩³³　mo³³.
       rice　inside
       '(You) need to **pound** the liquor yeast **into** pieces. **Pound** it **into** powder and then scatter it into the (steamed) rice.'
       要把那酒曲，嗯，酒曲舂碎。舂成粉呢，撒到这个饭里。
       (*Making sweet liquor of rice*, texts)

More examples are given below, including different types of verbs serving as resultative complements, such as transitive and intransitive verbs, as well as adjectives.

(4.63) je³³ tɯ³³ a²¹ **pie⁵⁵-kʰɯ³³** o.
3SG then DCR toss-open CRS
'It (= the tiger) then **let go hold of** (our pony).'
它（=老虎）就把（小马驹）放开了。
(*Our pony*, texts)

(4.64) ŋoŋ²¹ po⁵⁵ **sɔ³³-kuɛ²¹** sa²¹ po⁵⁵ tsʰɛ²¹ ʑi²¹ ta⁵⁵ po⁵⁵.
five CLF be.few-go three CLF only leave two CLF
'Five minus three leaves two.'
五个减去三个剩两个。

(4.65) mɔ²¹ lɔ²¹po⁵⁵ niɔ³³ tɣ²¹ ɪŋ⁵⁵soŋ²¹ **tsa⁵⁵-tɣ³³**
that peach should PASS sun shine-hit.(the target)
lɛ²¹tsʰɛ²¹ tsʰɿ⁵⁵ to³³.
only.then be.red can
'Peaches can only turn red after being **shone upon**.'
桃子要被太阳晒到才能红。

(4.66) na²¹ tɕiu⁵⁵ la³³ zɣ³³ zɣ³³ kɯ²⁴ la³³ pɣ³³-tɣ³³
hit to even eat meal moment even NEG-PFV
ka³³-tɣ³³ kuɛ³³ nɛ⁵⁵. [. . .] **xa³³-tɣ³³** tɕɪŋ²¹ tsɿ²¹pe³³ pʰe³³.
catch-obtain go PRT say-obtain money eighteen UNIT
tɕɪŋ²¹ tsɿ²¹pe³³ pʰe³³ nɛ⁵⁵, tsʰɛ²¹ **xa³³-kʰua²¹**.
money eighteen UNIT PRT only say-be.good
'(They kept) pounding on our door until meal time, but still didn't **take** (my younger brother) **away**. [. . .] (My grandmother) **negotiated** the price **down to** eighteen silver coins (with the official). They only **reached an agreement** after (paying) eighteen silver coins.'
打到吃饭的时候也没抓走。......（我奶奶找人）说到18大洋。18大洋才说好。
(*Exempt from military service*, texts)

General achievement phrases of [V-RC] are often observed negated by the perfective negator *pɣ³³tɣ³³* in the form of [pɣ³³tɣ³³ [V-RC]]. This is not difficult to explain, since it is very much related to the semantic function of resultative complements. When an action or a situation reaches a certain result state, it implies completion. For this reason, the perfective negative is compatible with the negation of resultative complements but not usually the general negator *pɣ³³*. See the following example as well as (4.66) above.

(4.67) nɯ³³ a²¹ **pɣ³³-tɣ³³** kʷɔ³-tso²¹.
2SG still neg-pfv learn-be.ripe
'You haven't mastered (it).'
你还没学好。

The general negator *pɣ³³* used to negate the [V-RC] phrases with the structure [pɣ³³ [V-RC]], can also be observed in certain contexts. For example, in conditional clauses, the pattern [V-pɣ³³-RC] is also used to denote the meaning as the pattern [pɣ³³ [V-RC]]. See examples (4.68) an (4.69). In these two sentences, the conditional clauses cannot stand alone as independent sentences when using the pattern [pɣ³³ [V-RC]], as respectively illustrated in (4.68b) and (4.69b). By contrast, when using the pattern [V-pɣ³³-RC] in independent sentences, a change of meaning will occur in each of the clauses, as in (4.68c) and (4.69c).

(4.68) a. nɯ³³ **[pɣ³³** zɣ²¹-ha⁵⁵]/[zɣ²¹-pɣ²¹-ha⁵⁵] tɯ⁵⁵
2SG NEG eat- finish/eat-NEG-finish then
piɔ²⁴ tsʰe⁵⁵-kuɛ²¹ sɔ²¹kʷɔ⁵⁵.
NEG.IMP be.oout-go play
'If you don't finish your meal, then you won't go out to hang out (with your friends).'
你[不吃完]/[吃不完]就别出去玩。

b. *nɯ³³ **pɣ³³** zɣ²¹-ha⁵⁵.
2SG NEG eat-finish
(Attempted: 'You don't finish (your meal).')
*你不吃完。

c. nɯ³³ zɣ²¹-pɣ²¹-ha⁵⁵.
2SG eat-NEG-finish
'You're not capable of finishing (the meal).'
你吃不完。

(4.69) a. ŋo³³ **[pɣ³³ ko³³-tɣ³³]/[ko³³-pɣ³³-tɣ³³]** ɔ²¹ ŋo²¹
1SG NEG look.for-obtain/look.for-NEG-obtain this cow
tɯ³³ pɣ²¹ pe⁵⁵-ɣɯ²¹.
then NEG return-come
'I won't come back if I don't find the cow.'
我[不找到]/[找不到]这牛就不回来。

b. *ŋo³³   **pɣ³³**   **ko³³-tɣ³³**.
   1SG   NEG   look.for-obtain
   (Attempted: 'I don't find it.')
   *我不找到。

c. ŋo³³   **ko³³-pɣ³³-tɣ³³**
   1SG   look.for-NEG-obtain
   'I can't find it.'
   我找不到。

In the previous example we have shown how negation is performed on [V-RC] phrases in Caijia. One should note that only the general negator *pɣ³³* can negate resultative complements in the form of [V-pɣ³³-RC], while the perfective negator *pɣ³³tɣ³³* can never appear in this post-verbal pre-RC position. In this role, *pɣ³³* denotes negative potential, as in (4.68b) and (4.69b). Two more examples are given below. See also Chapter 11 for more details.

(4.70)   mɔ²⁴   mi²¹   sɿ²¹   lɔ²¹po⁵⁵   ɪŋ⁵⁵soŋ²¹   **tsa⁵⁵-pɣ³³-tɣ³³**.
         that   side   MOD   peach   sun   shine.upon-NEG-hit.(the target)
         'The peaches on that side can't be shone upon.'
         那面的桃子太阳晒不到。

(4.71)   nɯ³³   **ɣã²¹-pɣ³³-tsʰe⁵⁵**   tie²¹to²¹   nɯ³³   piɔ²⁴   nen²¹na³³   xa³³.
         2SG   have-NEG-be.out   evidence   2SG   NEG.IMP   gratuitously   say
         'If you can't provide evidence, don't fabricate stories.'
         你拿不出证据，你别乱说。

In certain negated resultative phrases, we observe a special word order: [V-O-pɣ³³-RC]. Even though this order is not very common, it still deserves to be mentioned. This pattern is also found in Sinitic languages where it appears to be the more archaic form, such as in Cantonese (see Yue-Hashimoto 2001). The following two examples are both extracted from spontaneous data. The sentence in (4.72) is extracted from a narrative, while example (4.73) is extracted from a ballad, in which rhyming is often used.

(4.72)   koŋ⁵⁵koŋ⁵⁵   a²¹   **tsaŋ²¹**   nɯ³³   pɣ³³   kɪŋ³³.
         every.day   PRT   look.forward   2SG   NEG   see
         'I never have you here (LIT: Every day I can't see you).'
         天天啊盼不到你。
         (*Looking forward to your visit*, texts)

(4.73) **tɕie⁵⁵ zɤ²¹ pɤ³³ m²¹** pʰia³³ lɔ²¹pie²⁴.
do meal NEG win cook porridge
'(If you) don't have enough time to make a meal, make some porridge then.'
来不及做饭就煮粥
(*Ballad*, texts)

To the extent of the coverage of our data being representative, only a few resultative complements can barely serve as independent verbs. Two of these can be classified as achievement complements: *ha⁵⁵* and *m²¹*. The morpheme *ha⁵⁵* is most commonly used as a resultative complement denoting 'finish' or as the completive marker. However, its verbal use can still be detected in some rare cases.

(4.74) a. je²¹-xɯ⁵⁵ xa²¹ pɤ³³ tiu³³u³³ kʰua²¹ ni²⁴ tɯ³³
3-PL still NEG know good life then
niɔ³³ **ha⁵¹** o.
PROSP finish CRS
'They didn't know their good life would come to an end.'
他们还不知道好日子就要结束了。

b. bo²¹-xɯ⁵⁵ pɔ²¹kɤ²¹ pie⁵⁵ lɛ²¹ mo³³.
break.off-down corn throw field inside
pɤ²¹-pɤ²¹-**ha⁵⁵**.
carry.on.the.back-NEG-finish
'(We) picked corn cobs and threw them in the field. (There were too many corn cobs so that we) couldn't carry them all.'
掰下苞谷扔地里。背不完。
(*Encountering the ghost*, texts)

The complement *m²¹*, whose lexical meaning is discussed just below, is much less frequent than other resultative complements. It is often the verb *pe⁵⁵* 'return' and *dʑiu⁵⁵* 'arrive' that associate with *m²¹*.[4] The phrase *pe⁵⁵m²¹* particularly denotes 'come back home', while *dʑiu⁵⁵m²¹* metaphorically denotes 'die'. In contrast to *ha⁵⁵* 'finish' for which the verbal use can still be occasionally observed, *m²¹* is not

---

4 There is another homophonic *m²¹* that also functions as a resultative complement but usually appears in its negated form, denoting 'too late to do'. Its source form is probably the verb *yín* 赢 'win' in the local Southwestern Mandarin, since the same complement use is attested in the latter as well. See the example (4.73).
  Given that the semantic connection between 'be back' and 'win, too late to do' is extremely weak, we, thus, do not consider these two *m²¹*s share the same lexical source.

used as a verb at all in the daily language of Caijia. Fortunately, its possible source is found in some texts regarding the ritual practice of 'spirit-retrieving', which is often performed to call back the spirit of a sick person. Apparently, its source meaning is very much related to its meaning as a complement, that is, 'be back, come back'. Compare the two sentences in (4.75).

(4.75) a. ji³³   neŋ³³   tie³³   o,   ɕiaŋ⁵⁵   **pe⁵⁵-ɪn²¹**
one   year   bottom CRS want   return.be.back
kuɛ³³ kua³³   neŋ²¹   xɪŋ⁵⁵.
go   celebrate year very
'It was the end of a year. (They) wanted go back home very much to celebrate the New Year.'
一年年底了，想回（娘）家过年得很。
(*Three daughters-in-law*, texts)

b. pʰia³³   **ɪn²⁴**   uən²¹tʰai²⁴. [...]
spirit   come.back   NAME
nɯ³³   **ɪn²¹**   nɛ²¹   tɕi⁵⁵   mo³³.
2SG   come.back   your.family elder.sister inside
ɪn²¹   nɯ²¹   hɛ⁵⁵   mo³³.
come.back   2SG   younger.brother inside
'Come back, the spirit of Wentai. . . . You come back to your elder sister's house. Come back to your younger brother's house.'
魂归，文太。……你回你姐家。回你弟家。
(*Spirit-retrieving*, texts)

Next, we will present the second type of resultative complement found in Caijia.

4.2.3.2 Directional complements

In general, it is usually motion verbs that take directional complements. The Caijia directional complement phrases are more complicated than those for general achievement. Three types are observed in our data:
i.   V-V$_{PATH}$(-V$_{DEICTIC}$)
ii. V-V$_{DEICTIC}$
iii. V-xɯ⁵⁵

Both Types (i) and (ii) contain path verbs and deictic verbs. These two types are also attested in Standard Mandarin (Chao 1968, Lamarre 2003). A limited number of path and deictic verbs are given in Table 4.1. All of them can stand alone as independent verbs.

Table 4.1: Path and deictic verbs in Caijia.

V$_{PATH}$	V$_{DEICTIC}$
dza³³ 'go up' 上	kuɛ³³ 'go, thither' 去
dʑie³³ 'go down' 下	ɣɯ²¹ 'come, hither' 来
tsʰe⁵⁵ 'go out' 出	
li²¹ 'enter' 入	
dɤ³³ 'pass' 过	
kʰɯ⁵⁵ 'rise' 起	
pe⁵⁵ 'return' 返	
niaŋ²¹ 'approach' 靠	

The Type (iii) complement -xɯ⁵⁵ 'up, down' is actually more grammaticalized than other forms in Table 4.1 and usually associates with only a small number of verbs. However, this does not mean that these verbs are only restricted to this type. They can also enter into the verb slot of the Type (i) complement phrases.

Let us look at into each type in the following sections.

4.2.3.2.1 Type i: [V-V$_{PATH}$(-V$_{DEICTIC}$)]

A directional complement of Type (i) can be formed by one of two elements: a path verb followed by a deictic verb, or simply by a path verb. The pattern [V-V$_{PATH}$(-V$_{DEICTIC}$)] is often observed when the main verb is intransitive, or in certain cases when the object is not in its canonical post-verbal position, for example, when the main verb is transitive. Examples (4.76) and (4.77) are cases with intransitive verbs. Note that the phrase tsaŋ²¹-tɤ²¹-kuɛ²¹ 'look over' does not take any object even though the verb tsaŋ³³ 'look' is transitive.

(4.76) ɕie²¹   kʰui⁵⁵   ta⁵⁵   ɕie²¹   tsɿ⁵⁵ŋa⁵⁵   tsa²¹   tɯ²¹   sɔ⁵⁵tʰoŋ²¹
       small   dog   and   small   boy   climb   to   trunk
       tɤ³³   **tsaŋ²¹-tɤ²¹-kuɛ³³**.
       upside look-pass-go
       'The little dog and the little boy climbed up the trunk and looked through (there).'
       小狗和小男孩爬上树桩看过去。

(4.77) sɤ⁵⁵   ji²¹   kʷɔ²¹   ta⁵⁵   tʰɤ³³kʰa³³   mo³³   **tʰo⁵⁵-tsʰe⁵⁵-ɣɯ²¹**.
       rat   one   CLF   from   hole   inside   pop.out-exit-come
       'A rat popped out from the hole.'
       一只老鼠从洞里钻出来。

The examples below present two cases of transitive verbs. Neither of the objects are in the post-verbal position. Example (4.78) is a case of zero anaphora. The object 'frog' is mentioned in the preceding context. It is, thus, unnecessary to repeat it in this sentence.

Zero anaphora
(4.78) **a²¹-pe⁵⁵-ɣɯ²¹**   khɔ²¹   pie⁵⁵   je²¹   thɣ⁵⁵po²¹   tɣ³³.
       take-return-come   put   to   3SG   oven   upside
       '(They) took (the frog) back and put (it) on the oven.'
       把青蛙）拿回家放在炉子上。
       (*The frog*, texts)

Example (4.79) is a case of an object marking construction with a pre-positioned object.

Object marking
(4.79) ɣã²¹   nioŋ²⁴   ni³³   a³³   je²¹   ji²¹   tɔ⁵⁵   **tɣ³³-tɣ²¹-kuɛ³³**.
       there.be girl   CLF   OM   flower one   CLF   hand.over-pass-go
       'There was a girl who handed over a flower (to him).'
       有一个女孩儿把一朵花递过去了。

Two different orders are observed when the object is post-verbal. They are the patterns [V-V$_{PATH}$-O-V$_{DEICTIC}$] and [V-O-V$_{PATH}$-V$_{DEICTIC}$]. See the following examples.

[V-V$_{PATH}$-O-V$_{DEICTIC}$]:
(4.80) nɯ³³   **tshaŋ³³-niaŋ²¹**   ŋo³³   piŋ³³   **ɣɯ²¹**   nɛ⁵⁵
       2SG   move-approach   1SG   side   come   PRT
       sɿ⁵⁵   ŋo²¹   tɔ²¹   nɯ²¹   mi⁵⁵.
       let   1SG   kiss   2SG   a.little
       'You get closer to me to let me give you a little kiss.'
       你挪到我旁边来让我亲你一下。
       (*The man and the stone*, texts)

(4.81) **tɕi²¹-tshe⁵⁵**   mɛ²⁴   kwɔ²¹   **ɣɯ²¹**.
       plough-be.out   frog   CLF   come
       '(They) ploughed out a frog.'
       犁出一只青蛙来。
       (*The frog*, texts)

[V-O-V$_{PATH}$-V$_{DEICTIC}$]:

(4.82) nɯ³³ li²¹li²⁴ lɛ⁵⁵ **tʏ²¹** so⁵⁵ pʰɪŋ²¹ **li³³-ɣɯ²¹** nɛ⁵⁵
2SG slowly ADV stretch.out hand CLF enter-come PRT
'You gently extend your hand in (my tummy).'
你慢慢伸一只手进来呢。
(*The man and the stone*, texts)

(4.83) nɯ³³ **a³³** ɔ²⁴sui²¹ **tsʰe⁵⁵-ɣɯ²¹** tɕie⁵⁵mɔ⁵⁵?
2SG take these be.out-come do.what
'What do you take these out for?'
你拿这些出来干嘛？

Similar to complements of achievement, the pre-VP negation is often realized via the perfective negator *pɣ³³tʏ³³*, while pre-RC negation is basically a potential negation, as in (4.84a). However, in the context of (4.84a), the pre-VP negation of (4.84b) can also be used.

(4.84) a. ko²⁴ jɯ²⁴ ɣɯ²¹, ta⁵⁵ je²¹ kʰɪŋ⁵⁵.
monkey also come with 3SG pull
la²¹sɿ²¹ **kʰɪŋ⁵⁵-pɣ²¹-kʰɯ⁵⁵-ɣɯ²¹**.
still pull-NEG-rise-come
'The monkey came and helped him to tug at the radish. But they couldn't pull it out.'
猴子也来了，帮他拔。也是拔不起来。
(*Pulling out the radish*, texts)

b. **pɣ³³-tʏ³³** kʰɪŋ⁵⁵-kʰɯ⁵⁵-ɣɯ²¹.
NEG-PFV pull-rise-come
'(They) didn't pull it out.
没有拔出来。

The following example illustrates the [V-V$_{PATH}$] pattern with the object following. Note that the pattern [V-O-V$_{PATH}$] is not observed.

(4.85) **soŋ³³-tsa²¹** ta²¹ ha⁵⁵ nɛ⁵⁵...
send-go.up bamboo.forest COMPL PRT
'After sending (the coffin) up to the bamboo forest...'
送上箐林了呢......
(*Funeral customs*, text)

(4.86) je²¹ ta⁵⁵ li²¹ mo³³ **a²¹-tsʰe⁵⁵** lɔ²¹po⁵⁵ ji²¹ po⁵⁵.
3SG from bag inside take-exit peach one CLF
'He took out a peach from his bag.'
他从包里拿出一个桃子。

4.2.3.2.2 Type ii: [V-V_DEICTIC]

A directional complement phrase of Type (ii) [V-V_DEICTIC] is composed of either a motion or a path verb as the head verb, and a deictic verb as the complement. In our data, this pattern with path verbs is much more frequent than it is with motion verbs, as shown in (4.87) and (4.88).

(4.87) je³³ ji³³tɕiɔ²¹ji³³tɕiɔ²¹ lɛ³³ **tɤ²¹-kʷɔ²¹** o.
3SG keep.hopping ADV pass-go.CRS CRS
'She passed by in a manner of hopping.'
她一蹦一跳地过去了。

(4.88) ŋo⁵⁵ ta⁵⁵ ti⁵⁵mĩ²¹ **tsa²¹-kuɛ²¹**.
1PL from bottom go.up-go
'We went up from the bottom (of the valley).'
我们从（坡）下面上去。
(*Two little tigers*, texts)

Example (4.89) shows the case with the verb *a³³* 'take'.

(4.89) **a³³** kɪ³³mɔ²⁴ **ɤɯ²¹**.
take chicken.feather come
'(One) takes a feather.'
拿根鸡毛来。
(*Vaccination*, texts)

We have mentioned earlier above in §4.2.3.1 and §4.2.3.2.1 that pre-VP negation for complements of achievement and the Type (i) directional complements are usually realized with the perfective negator. However, both the general negator *pɤ³³* and the perfective negator *pɤ³³tɤ³³* can be used to negate Type (ii) directional complements. The use of *pɤ³³* denotes negative volition, as illustrated below.

(4.90) ŋo³³ tɕɪŋ²¹tɕɪŋ²⁴ tɯ³³ xã³³ je³³ o. je³³ tsɿ²¹tɕia²⁴ **pɣ²¹**
1SG early then call 3SG CRS 3SG oneself NEG
kʰɯ⁵⁵-ɣɯ²¹.
rise-come
'I (went to) wake him up very early. He didn't get up.'
我早早就叫他（起床）了。他自己不起来。

4.2.3.2.3 Type iii: [V-xɯ⁵⁵]

The pattern [V-xɯ⁵⁵] is a more grammaticalized pattern than Types (i) and (ii). First, only a small number of verbs that are conflated with directional meanings can appear in this pattern. For example, verbs as kɣ²¹ 'sit' can involve downward direction, while ɖaŋ³³ 'stand' can involve upward direction. Second, xɯ⁵⁵ cannot be negated in the same way as other resultative complements. Third, xɯ⁵⁵ cannot stand alone as an independent verb, even though it does possess a verb source, i.e. the verb kʰɯ⁵⁵ 'rise' (see also Chapter 10 on aspect), as in (4.90). The representation of its phonetic weakening also suggests that it is a grammaticalized morpheme (Heine, Claudi and Hünnemeyer 1991, Hopper 1991). Finally, despite its source meaning 'rise', denoting an upward motion, the meaning of xɯ⁵⁵ is generalized. It can denote either 'up' or 'down' depending on which verbs it is interacting with – further evidence of grammaticalization.

Example (4.91) shows that the morpheme xɯ⁵⁵ denotes 'down' along with the verb 'put'. Undoubtedly, the action of 'put' may involve an upward direction as well, for example, to place something up high. The context of this example is that a group of people were cultivating wasteland with hoes, then went after two little tigers, leaving their hoes in the field. In this instance, the morpheme xɯ⁵⁵ should be interpreted as 'down'.

(4.91) ŋo²⁴ tɯ²¹ **pɣ²¹-xɯ⁵⁵** la²¹ tɣ²¹ tɯ³³ kuɛ³³ ta²¹ u³³
1PL then put-down big hoe then go follow back
kuɛ²¹ ko³³.
go look.for
'We put down our hoes and followed behind to look for (the little tigers).'
我们放下锄头就跟着去找（小老虎）。
(*Two little tigers*, texts)

In a separate function, the morpheme xɯ⁵⁵ is commonly used as a durative marker (see Chapter 10). Postural verbs can be marked by the morpheme xɯ⁵⁵ to denote durative states. However, the use of the adverb ji²¹tʰɯ²⁴ 'suddenly' in the following example suggests a dynamic context. The phrase *taŋ²¹xɯ⁵⁵* should be, thus, interpreted as 'stand up'.

(4.92) je³³ ji²¹tʰɯ²⁴ **taŋ²¹-xɯ⁵⁵** piɔ⁵⁵-kuɛ²¹ o.
        3SG   suddenly   stand-up   run-go   CRS
        'He suddenly stood up and ran away.'
        他突然站起来跑掉了。

Example (4.93) is from video stimulus-based data. The same morpheme *xɯ⁵⁵* is used to denote the horizontal, anti-clockwise direction of turning off a tap, and the upward direction of picking up a pear.

(4.93) ja²¹-tsʰɿ⁵⁵ka³³ o.   je³³ tɯ³³ a²¹ sɿ⁵⁵ **taʔ²¹-xɯ⁵⁵** o.
        wash-be.clean   CRS 3SG   then OM   water close-off   CRS
        u²¹su³³ je³³ tɯ³³ **a²¹-xɯ⁵⁵** xɯ⁵⁵tsɿ⁵⁵ zv̩²¹ o.
        then   3SG   then take-up   pear   eat   CRS
        '(He) cleaned (the pear). He then turned off the water tap. He then picked up the pear and ate (it).'
        洗干净了。他就把水关上。然后，他就拿起梨吃了。

The generalized directional use of *xɯ⁵⁵* probably represents the intermediate stage of its lexical form *kʰɯ⁵⁵* 'rise' and its more grammaticalized durative use, for which the directional meaning is entirely absent. As it turns out, several directional complements have been expanded to other uses, as will be shown in the next section.

4.2.3.2.4 Beyond directions

Apart from -*xɯ⁵⁵*, the complements -*kʰɯ⁵⁵ɣɯ²¹* 'rise up', -*dʑie²¹kuɛ²¹* 'get down' and -*tsʰe⁵⁵ɣɯ²¹* 'come out' also possess non-directional uses. Among these, the markers -*xɯ⁵⁵* and -*kʰɯ⁵⁵ɣɯ²¹* are more grammaticalized than the others. They have not only undergone the process of change of meaning, but have also lost the feature of being resultative complements, i.e. they can no longer be negated any more, although each of them still occupies the same syntactic position as resultative complements. By contrast, -*dʑie³³kuɛ²¹* and -*tsʰe⁵⁵ɣɯ²¹* have only undergone semantic bleaching. Let us consider their non-directional uses with some examples.

First, along with locative phrases, the morpheme -*xɯ⁵⁵* is often used as the durative marker, as shown in (4.94). The postural verb *dzɿ²¹* 'lie, sleep' is marked by *xɯ⁵⁵*. The pre-VP locative phrase *tɯ²¹ tʲ³³mĩ²¹ kʰã⁵⁵ tʲ³³* 'on the ridge above' suggests it is a stative context. Therefore, the phrase *dzɿ²¹xɯ⁵⁵* cannot be interpreted as 'lie down'.

(4.94) mɔ²¹ kʰɣ⁵⁵pa²¹ tɯ³³ tɯ²¹ tɣ³³mĩ²¹ kʰã⁵⁵ tɣ³³ dzɿ²¹-**xɯ⁵⁵**.
that tiger then at upside ridge upside sleep-DUR
'The tiger was then lying on the ridge above.'
那老虎就在上面坎上睡着。
(*Our pony*, texts)

Second, both the morpheme -*xɯ⁵⁵* and the complement -*kʰɯ⁵⁵ɣɯ²¹* can be used to stativize verbs of perception so as to express that something is perceived to have a certain property, like 'it tastes good' in English. In Caijia, these verbs are not limited to typical verbs of perception such as *tʰi³³* 'listen', *tsaŋ³³* 'look' and *kʰɣ⁵⁵* 'smell', but include verbs of physical contact whereby one acquires sensory information about one's environment. For example, one can feel the weight of an entity by taking it in one's hand(s) or feel the surface of an entity by touching it. If a verb of this type is compounded with -*xɯ⁵⁵* or -*kʰɯ⁵⁵ɣɯ²¹*, it then takes a descriptive verbal complement instead of a nominal object. As illustrated in (4.95), both the verbs *tsaŋ³³* 'look' and *zɣ²¹* 'eat' take negated VPs as complements, after being compounded with -*xɯ⁵⁵* or -*kʰɯ⁵⁵ɣɯ²¹*.

(4.95) nɯ³³ ŋuɔ²¹ sɿ²¹ ɔ²¹ tsʰɯ²¹sɿ⁵⁵ **tsaŋ²¹-xɯ⁵⁵/-kʰɯ⁵⁵ɣɯ²¹**
2SG stir-fry REL this dish look-up
pɣ³³ tɔ²¹ lɔ²⁴sɿ⁵⁵, **zɣ²¹-xɯ⁵⁵/-kʰɯ⁵⁵ɣɯ²¹** xa²¹
NEG be.like which.way eat-up still
pɣ³³ tsʰɣ³³
NEG be.wrong
'The dish you made doesn't look good, (but) it doesn't taste bad.'
你炒的这菜看着不怎么样，吃着还不错。

One more example is given below. It is the verb *ya²¹* 'walk' interacting with -*xɯ⁵⁵* or -*kʰɯ⁵⁵ɣɯ²¹*. It is true that the verb *ya²¹* is not a verb of perception. However, as mentioned above, one can perceive the physical condition of a road by walking on it.

(4.96) mɔ²¹kɯ²⁴ ŋo²⁴ tsʰɿ⁵⁵ mo³³ sɿ²¹ hɔ⁵⁵ ta³³tsʰaŋ²¹tsʰa³³
that.moment 1PL village inside MOD road narrow
lɛ³³. **ya²¹-xɯ⁵⁵/-kʰɯ⁵⁵ɣɯ²¹** ni²¹kʰa³³ni²¹kʰoŋ³³.
CONT walk-up be.muddy
'At that time, the road to our village was very narrow. It was very muddy.'
以前，我们村里的路窄窄的，走起来泥泞不堪。
(*The road to our village*, texts)

4.2 Verbs — 141

Third, the directional complement -$k^hɯ^{55}yɯ^{21}$ 'rise up' further develops into an inchoative marker marking the beginning of an action with -$xɯ^{55}yɯ^{21}$ as its phonetically weakened form (see Chapter 10 for more details). In the example below, the marker -$k^hɯ^{55}yɯ^{21}$ is no longer semantically related with the meaning 'rise up'.

(4.97) $k^hɪŋ^{33}$ ka^{21}-**$k^hɯ^{55}yɯ^{21}$** o.
sky   be.cold-INC   CRS
'It begins to be cold.'
天冷起来了。

Fourth, the complement -$dʑie^{33}kuɛ^{21}$ 'get down' can denote 'keep doing, continue'. For example, the phrase xa^{33}-$tɕie^{21}kuɛ^{21}$ in (4.98) does not denote 'say downward'. Instead, it denotes 'continue to talk, keep talking'. By contrast, the phrase $ã^{33}$-$tɕie^{21}kuɛ^{21}$ can be ambiguous, either denoting 'drink something down' or 'keep drinking'. Apparently, in (4.99) it denotes 'keep drinking', according to the context.

(4.98) $sɿ^{55}$ je^{21} **xa^{33}-$tɕie^{21}kuɛ^{21}$**.
let   3SG   say-down
'Let him go on talking.'
让他说下去。

(4.99) $tsɔ^{21}$ $ɔ^{21}$ $sɿ^{55}$ **$ã^{33}$-$tɕie^{21}kuɛ^{21}$** $nɯ^{33}$ $saŋ^{33}ka^{33}$ ti^{33}
be.like   this   way   drink-down   2SG   liver   know
t^ha^{33}-$kuɛ^{21}$.
break.down-go
'If you keep drinking like this, your liver will be overloaded.'
像这样再喝下去，你的肝会坏掉。

Finally, interacting with typical verbs of perception ('see', 'notice', 'listen', etc.), the complement of -$tsʰe^{55}yɯ^{21}$ 'come out' is used to denote 'recognizable'.

(4.100) je^{21} $hm̥^{55}$ $tsʰɿ^{21}po^{55}$ $ŋo^{21}$ **$tʰi^{55}$-$tsʰe^{55}yɯ^{21}$** to^{33}.
3SG   POSS   sound   1SG   listen-out   can
'I can recognize his voice.'
他的声音我能听出来。

(4.101) $ɔ^{21}$ $loŋ^{33}$ mo^{33} pi^{33} $lɯ^{33}$ la^{21} **$sɿ^{21}$-py^{21}-$tsʰe^{55}yɯ^{21}$** o.
this   city   inside   change   VCOMP   all   identify-NEG-out   CRS
'The downtown has changed so much that (I) can't recognize (it).'
这城里变得都认不出来了。

In this section, we presented two types of resultative complements in Caijia: complements of general achievement and complements of direction. In Caijia, apart from aspect marking, the productive formation of resultative verb phrases with a closed set of resultative complements is a very important feature of verbs distinguishing them from nouns, another major category of the parts-of-speech found in the language. Most resultative complements can still stand alone as independent verbs. One can observe that resultative phrases also serve as an important syntactic environment in which several grammatical functions breed, as shown right above in §4.2.3.2. In contrast to the unmarked resultative complement, there is also, as it happens, a marked complement in Caijia, which will be presented below.

4.2.4 Extent and manner complementation

Extent and manner complementation is commonly known as *dé zì jiégòu* 得字结构 'the structure of DE (< 'obtain')' in Chinese linguistic literature. It is described as a 'complex stative construction' in Standard Mandarin by Li and Thompson (1981). It is also widely attested in mainland East and Southeast Asian (MESEA) languages and labelled as 'descriptive complementation' by Enfield (2003) (cf. Ke Lisi 2001, Wu Fuxiang 2001, 2002). The sources of complementizers in extent and manner complementation in the languages of MESEA tend to be *acquire* verbs (Enfield 2003).

Extent and manner complementation is quite different from typical core argument complementation. Although an extent and manner complement is also situated within a VP just as an object complement is, it does not function as a core argument of its higher clause. Instead, introduced by the complementizer, it serves as a post-verbal adverbial phrase and modifies its preceding verb in the form of [(NP) $_{VP}$[V VCOMP [(NP) VP]]], providing the meaning of either extent or manner to this verb. Extent refers to the degree reached by a state, while manner refers to the way in which an action is carried out. The syntactic status of an extent and manner complement is similar to a relative clause. Both of them are modifiers. The extent and manner complement modifies a verb, while the relative clause modifies a NP.

Unlike many languages in MESEA, the complementizer lw^{55} (< ?) in Caijia does not show any synchronic connection with the *acquire* verb ty^{33}:

[(NP) $_{VP}$[V lw^{55} [VP/DEGR]]].

The semantic and syntactic features of Caijia extent and manner complementation can be summarized as below:

i. It denotes a stative and descriptive meaning (See also Chapter 9 and Lü Shanshan 2017).
ii. It functions as an AdvP situated within a VP.
iii. The complementizer *lɯ⁵⁵* is obligatory.
iv. The *lɯ⁵⁵* complement either denotes extent or manner, i.e. to what extent an action denoted by the verb modified by the *lɯ⁵⁵* complement is attained or in which manner this action is realized.
v. The matrix verb should be in its bare form, as shown in the schema above.

Let us see some examples.

The manner complementation marked by *lɯ⁵⁵* can be interpreted as 'an action X is realized in the manner of Y'. Examples (4.102)-(4.104) illustrate the manner *lɯ⁵⁵* complementation in Caijia. The complement in (4.102) describes how gunshots sound, i.e. 'like breaking hemp stalks'.

Manner complementation
(4.102) [...] tsʰ₁²¹fɛ⁵⁵toŋ²¹ ᵥₚ[mia²¹   [lɯ⁵⁵,   a,   ᵥₚ[tsɔ³³ mɔ²¹
               gun   make.a.sound VCOMP INTJ   be.like that
        tsɿ⁵⁵   tsʰo²¹ka⁵⁵   sɿ²¹   kuɛ³³ o]]].
        break   hemp.stalk   way   go   CRS
        '(They) fired guns making some popping sounds like breaking hemp stalks.'
        枪响得像折麻秆一样。
        (*The family of Deng*, texts)

In (4.103), the verb *sɯ⁵⁵* 'rest' in the complement is in its negated form and expresses that the magpies are twittering incessantly.

(4.103) je²¹-xɯ⁵⁵ tɯ²¹ ma²⁴   kɿ⁵⁵kɿ⁵⁵kua⁵⁵kua⁵⁵ lɛ³³. xaŋ⁵⁵ **lɯ⁵⁵**
        3-PL   at   there ONO   ADV   yell   VCOMP
        [pɣ²¹ sɯ⁵⁵]
        NEG   rest
        'They (the magpies) kept twittering over there.'
        他们在那儿叽叽喳喳喊得不停。
        (*Three neighbors*, texts)

Along with the complement *tsʰ₁²¹pʰe²¹pʰe²⁴*, the vivid form of the adjective *tsʰ₁³³* 'be light', in the example below, the complex VP *xa²¹ lɯ⁵⁵ tsʰ₁²¹pʰe²¹pʰe²⁴* literally denotes 'say in an airy way' and is used here to refer to ignorant and irresponsible remarks.

(4.104) nɯ⁵⁵ xa²¹ lɯ⁵⁵   tsʰɿ²¹pʰe²¹pʰe²⁴ o!
         2SG   say   VCOMP   be.lightweight   PRT
         'It's easy for you to say (but hard to be realized)!'
         你说得轻巧！
         (*Three neighbors*, texts)

The extent complement, semantically distinct from the manner complement exemplified above, can be interpreted as 'an action X is attained to the extent of Y' or 'so… that, so… as to' (cf. Chao 1968: 354–355, see also Chapter 6 on causative constructions). Several examples are given in (4.105)-(4.109). In (4.105), the complement, a full clause, describes that how coldness reaches a point where one cannot fall asleep.

Extent complementation
(4.105) meŋ²¹sa³³   ka²¹   **lɯ⁵⁵**   [ŋo³³ tsɿ²¹ni²¹-pʏ³³-kuɛ²¹].
         yesterday.night   cold   VCOMP   1SG   sleep-NEG-go
         'It was so cold that I couldn't fall asleep.'
         昨天晚上冷得我睡不着。

The complement in the next example, (4.106), is the adjective *tie³³*, rendering the additional meaning of 'much', which modifies its higher predicate 'better', i.e. the complement intensifies the positive degree of 'being better'.

(4.106) ɣã³³   zɿ²¹   tsʰɿ⁵⁵ka⁵⁵ kʷɔ²¹   pi⁵⁵   tɯ²¹   kʷɔ²¹   tie⁵⁵   kʰua²¹
         have   warm   place   CLF   than   live   bridge   bottom   be.good
         lɯ⁵⁵   tie²¹   o.
         VCOMP   be.many   CRS
         'Having a warm place (to stay) is much better than living under the bridge.'
         有个暖和的地方比住桥底好得多了。
         (*Three thieves*, texts)

Two *lɯ⁵⁵* complements are chained together in (4.107) below. The adjective *tɕʰi³³kʰa³³* 'be happy' is the highest matrix verb taking a complement which itself also comprises a *lɯ⁵⁵* complement. Complement (I) denotes extent, while complement (II) denotes manner.

(4.107) je²⁴ ta⁵⁵ tɕie⁵⁵ tɕʰi³³kʰa²¹ ₍ᵢ₎[lɯ⁵⁵ ɣɯ²¹ ₍ᵢᵢ₎[lɯ⁵⁵ pɣ²¹ sɯ⁵⁵]].
3PL two CLF be.happy VCOMP cry VCOMP NEG rest
'The two of them were so happy that they kept crying.'
她们（母女）俩高兴得哭得不停。

The examples of the extent complement above have already demonstrated different types of verbs serving as complements. It is also observed that the complementizer *lɯ⁵⁵* may also simply introduce the degree marker *mɔ⁵⁵sɿ⁵⁵* 'very', probably derived from *mɔ²²* 'that' + *sɿ³³* 'copula' with tone sandhi, or similarly, the degree marker *pɣ⁵⁵sɿ⁵⁵* 'very' developed from *pɣ³³* 'negator' + *sɿ³³* 'copula'. Both of these two degree markers are more like VPs. Note that other non-VP derived degree markers are not observed in this construction and that the only post-VP adverb, *xɪŋ⁵⁵* 'very', cannot be introduced by the complementizer *lɯ⁵⁵*.

(4.108) kʰɪŋ⁵⁵tɔ²¹kʰɯ⁵⁵ ka²¹ **lɯ⁵⁵** **mɔ⁵⁵sɿ⁵⁵** e, a²¹ na²¹pʰɔ²¹sɣ²⁴ mi⁵⁵.
this.morning cold VCOMP very PRT also mist little
'It was very cold this morning and also misted a bit.'
今天早上冷得厉害诶，还下了些雾。
(*Drowning persons*, texts)

(4.109) ɔ⁵⁵ ʑi²¹ la²¹ nɯ²¹ lɯ⁵⁵ **mɔ⁵⁵sɿ⁵⁵/pɣ⁵⁵sɿ⁵⁵**.
house inside all humid VCOMP very
'It is extremely humid in the house.'
屋里潮得不行。

This section introduced a marked verb complement construction in Caijia, a construction type which is also widely attested in South East Asian languages. A VP is introduced by the complementizer *lɯ⁵⁵*, the source of which is unclear, and follows a bare verb as its extent or manner complement. Unlike its counterpart construction in Standard Mandarin or many other Sinitic languages, the potential meaning of this construction is not its primary use in Caijia. The potential interpretation is certainly possible, but Caijia usually adopts two post-VP 'can' modals to express possibility (see Chapter 11 on modality).

4.2.5 Quadrisyllabic descriptive phrases

Quite a number of quadrisyllabic idiomatic expressions or elaborate expressions, as labelled in Vittrant and Watkins (2019), are used in Caijia. They are very similar

to the quadrisyllabic idiomatic expressions known as *chéngyǔ* 成语, in Standard Mandarin. For most of the cases:
i. they are semantically descriptive capturing states of affairs and are often used metaphorically;
ii. each syllable of each quadrisyllabic phrase is, theoretically, analyzable;
iii. they can serve as independent predicates at the end of the phrase, commonly marked by the continuous marker $l\varepsilon^{55}$, but rarely interacting with other aspectual markers;
iv. they can be used as adverbial modifiers, modifying VPs.

Only a very small portion of quadrisyllabic idiomatic expressions found in our data can modify NPs. Let us see some examples.

As mentioned above, each syllable, or morpheme, in a quadrisyllabic idiomatic phrase is practically and theoretically analyzable. For example, the phrase $ta^{21}poŋ^{33}l\varepsilon^{21}k^hui^{21}$ literally denotes 'walk with a stick and walk by dragging one's legs', as in (4.110a). Definitely, it can be used literally to describe someone who walks with a stick, but it can also be used to describe someone, especially an aged person, in poor physical condition, as shown in (4.110b). The phrase $ta^{21}poŋ^{33}l\varepsilon^{21}k^hui^{21}$ serves as the predicate of the clause (4.110bi) marked by the manner continuous marker $l\varepsilon^{55}$. When serving as a predicate, a quadrisyllabic idiomatic phrase usually denotes that an entity, animate or inanimate, is in an enduring state (See also Chapter 10 on aspect).

(4.110) a. ta²¹ poŋ³³ lɛ²¹ kʰui²¹
lean.on stick drag kneel.down
'walk with a stick and walk by dragging one's legs'
步履蹒跚

b. ŋa⁵⁵-sui⁵⁵ nɛ⁵⁵ tsʰɿ²¹ka²⁴ la²¹ piɛ⁵⁵ sɿ⁵⁵ la²¹to⁵⁵ u²¹tsʰo²¹.
child-PL PRT clean all toss to old person
i) la²¹to⁵⁵ sɿ²¹ nɛ⁵⁵ ᵥₚ[ta²¹poŋ³³lɛ²¹kʰui²¹ lɛ³³], ii) la²¹
old NMLZ PRT totter CONT also
niɔ³³ tɯ²¹ ɔ⁵⁵ ʑi²¹ tsan²¹ ɔ⁵⁵ li²¹ ŋa⁵⁵.
need at house inside look house take.care child
'(Their) children are all left with the old persons. (Even though) they are weary and slow, the aged ones still need to take care of their families and grandchildren.'
孩子们呢，全部丢给老人。老的（这些）呢，颤颤巍巍地，也要在家看家带孩子。

Literally denoting 'ask for loans and get into debts', the phrase $k^hɪŋ^{33}kɛ^{21}a^{33}po^{21}$ in (4.111b) can be either interpreted literally or metaphorically as 'at any cost'. The clause (4.109bii) is a construction with subject complementation using the VP $(ŋo^{33})$ $k^hɪŋ^{33}kɛ^{21}a^{33}po^{21}$ 'I ask for loans and get into debt' as the subject and the phrase $k^hɪŋ^{33}kɛ^{21}a^{33}po^{21}$ as the predicate inside the complementation clause.

(4.111) a. $k^hɪŋ^{33}$ $kɛ^{21}$ a^{33} po^{21}
             pull   debt   take   burden
             'ask for loans and get into debt'
             借钱背债

         b. i) $tsʰɛ^{21}niɔ^{33}$ $ŋa^{55}$-sui^{55} $tsɔ^{21}$ $ɔ^{21}sɿ^{55}$ $ɣã^{21}$ $fɛ^{55}ka^{33}$
             only.if   child-PL   be.like   this.way   have   prospect
             $nɛ^{55}$, ii)$_{VP}[(ŋo^{33})$ $_{VP}[\mathbf{k^hɪŋ^{33}kɛ^{21}a^{33}po^{21}}]]$ la^{33} $tsɿ^{21}$-$tɣ^{33}$.
             PRT   1SG   get.into.debts   all   be.worth-obtain
             'As long as the children can succeed, it will be worth getting into debt.'
             'As long as the children can succeed, it will be worth supporting (them) at any cost.'
             只要孩子们有出息，借钱背债/不惜代价也值得。

However, our consultants provided only metaphoric meanings for some of the quadrisyllabic idiomatic phrases, as they probably learnt them this way or simply forgot the literal meanings due to their low frequency of use. The phrase $sa^{33}ti^{21}sɿ^{21}moŋ^{24}$ 'pretend, pose' is one such case. In the following example, it is used as a manner adverbial modifying the VP $tsaŋ^{21}$ $sɣ^{33}$ 'read a book' and is marked as an adverbial phrase by $lɛ^{55}$.

(4.112) $ti^{33}ɪn^{21}$ $kɯ^{24}$ je^{33} xa^{21} $tɯ^{21}$ ma^{24} $sɔ^{21}k^wɔ^{55}$, je^{21} $ʑi^{33}$
         just.now   moment   3SG   still   at   there   play   3SG   mother
         ji^{33} $ɣɯ^{21}$, je^{33} $tɯ^{33}$ $\mathbf{sa^{33}ti^{21}sɿ^{21}moŋ^{24}}$ $lɛ^{55}$ $tsaŋ^{21}$ $sɣ^{33}$.
         once   come   3SG   then   pose   ADV   look   book
         'He was playing around just now. Once his mother came, he pretended to read the book.'
         他刚才还在那儿玩儿，他妈一来，他就装模作样地看书。

Two more examples are given below, one with quadrisyllabic phrase as a predicate and the other as an adverbial. The phrase $tɕie^{55}kui^{55}tɕie^{55}pe^{33}$ 'disguise oneself as a ghost or a deity (to fool people), deliberately mystify things' is negated by the imperative negator $piɔ^{24}$ in (4.113).

(4.113) nɯ³³ piɔ²⁴ tɯ²¹ ma²⁴ **tɕie⁵⁵kui⁵⁵tɕie⁵⁵pe³³** la³³! ŋo³³ la²¹
2SG NEG.IMP at there deliberately.mystify PRT 1SG all
tiu³³u³³ sɿ²¹
know AFF
'Don't mystify things! I know (everything).'
你别在那儿装神弄鬼啊！我都知道的。

The phrase *ka⁵⁵paŋ²¹ka⁵⁵sɿ⁵⁵* 'catch wind catch water' is often used to describe a state of being in a flurry and is used as manner adverbial in (4.114).

(4.114) pʰaŋ²¹tsʰɔ⁵⁵ **ka⁵⁵paŋ²¹ka⁵⁵sɿ⁵⁵** lɛ²¹ ta⁵⁵-xɯ⁵⁵ taŋ³³lu³³ tɯ²¹
chubby.woman be.in.a.flurry ADV lift-up lantern then
tsʰe⁵⁵ ma²¹kʰa³³ kuɛ³³ ko²¹ je²¹ ŋa⁵⁵.
go.out door PURP look.for 3SG child
'The woman took up the lantern and hurried out to look for her child.'
胖嫂慌慌张张地打着灯笼就出门找她孩子去了。
(*The careless woman*, texts)

The examples above have demonstrated the two most common uses of quadrisyllabic idiomatic phrases, i.e. predicative and adverbial uses. The following two examples show two idiomatic phrases serving as adnominal modifiers, which are both connected to their respective head NPs with *sɿ²¹*.

(4.115) ŋo³³ sɿ³³ **ta³³seŋ³³ta²¹so⁵⁵** sɿ²¹ u²¹tsʰo²⁴ ni⁵⁵ nɛ⁵⁵. tɯ²¹
1SG COP lonely MOD person CLF PRT be.at
lɛ²¹po²¹ tv̩³³.
world upside
'I'm a lonely person. (I'm all alone) in this world.'
我是形单影只一个人。在这个世界上。
(*My loneliness*, texts)

(4.116) pe³³ ŋui²¹ tie⁵⁵ **ma²¹ti²¹ma²¹toŋ²¹** sɿ²¹
eight month bottom all.over.the.mountains MOD
tɕiu⁵⁵je²¹ la²¹ kʰɯ³³ o.
chive.flower all blossom CRS
'At the end of August, the chive flowers all over the mountains blossom.'
八月底，漫山遍野的韭菜花都开了。

The phrase *ma²¹ti²¹ma²¹toŋ²¹* 'all over the mountain', illustrated in (4.116) can even serve as copular subject, as shown in (4.117).

(4.117)　**ma²¹ti²¹ma²¹toŋ²¹**　　la²¹　sɿ²¹　tsʰɿ³³luɔ²¹　sɿ²¹　tɕiu⁵⁵je²¹.
　　　　all.over.the.mountains　all　COP　purple　　　　MOD　chive.flower
　　　　'Purple chive flowers will be all over the mountains.'
　　　　漫山遍野都是紫色的韭菜花。

In fact, the function of a quadrisyllabic idiomatic phrase depends on its meaning and its inner syntactic nature. The quadrisyllabic phrases in examples (4.110), (4.111), (4.113) and (4.114) are actually VPs in nature. For example, the phrases $kʰɪŋ³³kɛ²¹a³³po²¹$ 'ask for loans and get into debt ~ at any cost' and $ka³³paŋ²¹ka³³sɿ⁵⁵$ 'catch wind and catch water ~ in a flurry' share the same inner syntactic structure, i.e. [VOVO], while the syntactic structure of $ta²¹poŋ³³lɛ²¹kʰui²¹$ 'walk with a stick and walk by dragging ~ trudge, be in a weak physical condition' can be represented as [VOVV]. The phrases $ta³³seŋ³³ta²¹so⁵⁵$ 'single body and single hand ~ be all alone' and $ma²¹ti²¹ma²¹toŋ²¹$ 'all over the mountain' are nominal in nature. They can be represented as [Adj-N-Adj-N]. Furthermore, the phrase $ma²¹ti²¹ma²¹toŋ²¹$ is not extended to other metaphorical meanings and is actually equivalent to a place word. Due to its semantic and inner syntactic nature, $ma²¹ti²¹ma²¹toŋ²¹$ cannot serve as a predicate. By contrast, given that it has the common metaphorical meaning of $ta³³seŋ³³ta²¹so⁵⁵$, i.e. 'be all alone', this phrase can serve as a predicate, like other VP-natured quadrisyllabic phrases. Unfortunately, not all the internal structures of quadrisyllabic phrases are analyzable. As mentioned above, our consultants were not able to provide the exact meaning of each syllable for quite a number of quadrisyllabic phrases.

In the relevant literature (Sun Yan 2005, Gerner 2013: 51–54), quadrisyllabic phrases are often classified on the basis of their internal structure for the four syllables according to which components are reduplicated. Three different patterns are observed in our Caijia data: (i) AABB, (ii) ABAC, and (iii) ABCD, among which the second pattern is the most frequent. Note that the quadrisyllabic phrases listed below are definitely non-exhaustive.

AABB

pa²¹pa²¹tɪŋ³³tɪŋ³³ 'wander about' 转来转去
pʰɣ³³pʰɣ³³dzɣ³³dzɣ³³ 'cove and hide' 遮遮掩掩
tɣ²¹tɣ²¹mɛ³³mɛ³³ 'be foul-mouthed' 骂骂咧咧
mɣ²¹mɣ²¹fa³³fa³³ 'dillydally' 磨磨蹭蹭
na²¹na²¹ɕi³³ɕi³³ 'fight and kill ~ solve problems with violence' 打打杀杀
tɕʰi³³tɕʰi³³kʰa³³kʰa³³ 'happy' 高高兴兴
xɯ⁵⁵xɯ⁵⁵pʰɪŋ³³pʰɪŋ³³ 'weep and wail' 哭哭啼啼

ABAC

ka⁵⁵paŋ²¹ka⁵⁵sɿ⁵⁵ 'be in a flurry' 着急忙慌
kʰɯ³³mĩ²¹kʰɯ³³kʰɔ³³ 'draw a long face' 丧眉丧眼
lu³³li³³lu³³tã²¹ 'muddle-headed, lose one's head' 糊里糊涂
bia³³kʰɛ³³bia²¹kʰoŋ⁵⁵ 'talk nonsense' 胡言乱语
mo³³ja²¹mo³³sɿ³³ 'be mum' 不吭不哈
ma²¹ti²¹ma²¹toŋ²¹ 'all over the mountain' 漫山遍野
nia²¹tɣ²¹nia²¹ti³³ 'be in an awful mess' 乱七八糟
ni²¹kʰa³³ni²¹kʰoŋ³³ 'be muddy' 泥泞不堪
ta³³seŋ³³ta²¹so⁵⁵ 'be all alone' 形单影只
tɣ³³mɔ²¹tɣ²¹tsɣ⁵⁵ 'be a mess' 蓬头乱发
tʰɯ³³tɯ³³tʰɯ³³nɔ²¹ 'clumsy' 笨头笨脑
tsʰɿ³³ka³³tsʰɿ²¹ma²⁴ 'be in order' 井井有条
tsʰɿ²¹kɣ³³tsʰɿ²¹so⁵⁵ 'walk quietly, tiptoe' 轻手轻脚
tsʰo⁵⁵kɣ²¹tsʰo⁵⁵pia³³ 'be in a hurry, hustle and bustle' 匆匆忙忙
tsʰoŋ³³kʰɪŋ³³tsʰoŋ²¹tʰɣ⁵⁵ 'parade one's ability' 逞强好胜
tsʰoŋ³³pi⁵⁵tɔ²¹kɣ³³ 'parade one's ability' 逞强好胜
tɕie⁵⁵tɕʰi²¹tɕie⁵⁵noŋ²¹ 'furious, angry' 怒气冲冲
tɕie⁵⁵kui⁵⁵tɕie⁵⁵pe³³ 'disguise oneself to be a ghost or a deity (to fool people)' 装神弄鬼
ɕi³³ni²¹ɕi³³mo²¹ 'wink' 挤眉弄眼
ɕie³³kʰɯ³³ɕie³³sɛ²¹ 'hoarse' 哑声哑气
ɣ²¹kui⁵⁵ɣ²¹pe³³ 'act as a lunatic' 疯疯癫癫

ABCD

ga²¹zɣ²¹tsoŋ²¹tɕie⁵⁵ 'be gluttonous and lazy' 好吃懒做
kʰɪŋ³³kɛ²¹a³³po²¹ 'ask for loans and get into debts' 借钱背债
ʈa²¹poŋ³³lɛ²¹kʰui²¹ 'walk with a stick and walk by dragging one's legs' 步履蹒跚
tɕɪŋ²¹kʰɯ⁵⁵ja²¹ʑi³³ 'work from dawn to night' 起早贪黑
jɯ²¹sɿ²¹ta³³laŋ³³ 'idle about' 游手好闲
ɕi³³kʰɛ³³la²¹kʰoŋ³³ 'brag' 夸夸其谈
sa³³ti²¹sɿ²¹moŋ²⁴ 'pretend, pose' 装模作样

Quadrisyllabic idiomatic phrases are widely attested in East and Southeast Asian languages including Sinitic, Tibeto-Burman, Hmong-Mien, Tai-Kadai (Clark 1989, Sun Yan 2005, Vittrant and Watkins 2019), as well as in Austroasiatic (see Jenny 2014: 594–595 for Mon and Nguyen 1970 for Vietnamese). In Caijia, we have shown that three patterns of quadrisyllabic idiomatic phrases can be observed. They are commonly used as predicates describing states of affairs. We pointed out in §4.2.1.2

that manner adverbs can be derived from adjectives in Caijia, while the quadrisyllabic idiomatic phrases are also an important source for manner adverbs. Their marginal functions have been equally described, such as acting as adnominal modifiers or subjects. Basically, both the meaning and the internal syntactic structure of a quadrisyllabic idiomatic phrase both play key roles in determining its function.

4.3 Adverbs

The term 'adverb' may refer to different ranges of words in different languages. As shown in the English example below, all the bold words are classified as adverbs. 'Unfortunately' is a sentence-modifying adverb; 'home' and 'yesterday' are locative and time adverbs, respectively; 'very', in this case, is an adverb-modifying adverb of degree; and 'late' is also a degree adverb.

(4.118) *Unfortunately, I arrived **home very late yesterday**.*

One can thus observe that adverbs may cover a very large range of words. They are defined as "modifiers of constituents other than nouns" (Schachter and Shopen 2007: 20, see also Creissels 2006a: 253, 256).

In Caijia, sentence-modifying adverbs are uncommon. In general, adverbs are not easily classified due to their various sources, polysemy, different forms, and large semantic ranges. Only manner adverbs in Caijia can be easily identified. This is the only type possessing derivational morphology and an overt marker. Indeed the identification of manner adverbs is seemingly less problematic cross-linguistically than other types of adverbs, as pointed out by Dryer (2007: 81).

In this section, we will introduce several semantic types of adverbs that are commonly identified in the literature on Chinese linguistics (Chao 1968: 767–789, Zhu Dexi 1982: 192–201) but which may not cover all the adverbs in Caijia. They are manner adverbs, degree adverbs, adverbs of time and frequency, and scope adverbs. Moreover, negators are also regarded as adverbs in the literature of Chinese linguistics (Zhu Dexi 1982). One can find more details in Chapter 12 on negation.

In spite of the difficulties mentioned above, there is one common feature for all adverbs in Caijia: They precede the predicate in a sentence (except for the degree adverb $xiŋ^{55}$ 'very', the only post-VP adverb in this language) and the extent and manner complements introduced by lu^{55}, as presented in §4.2.4 above. Some of the adverbs, especially time adverbs, can be observed in sentence initial positions as well.

4.3.1 Manner adverbs and adverbials

Manner adverbs are used to describe how an action is performed. The Caijia manner adverbs possess the following features:

i. They are derived from four major sources: manner demonstratives, $ɔ^{21}sɿ^{55}$ 'this way' and $mɔ^{21}sɿ^{55}$ 'that way' (see Chapter 3 §3.2), adjectives, vivid adjectival A-BB forms, and quadrisyllabic expressions. The manner adverbs are derived from nominal forms, while the latter three are usually derived from verbal forms, as presented in §4.2.1.2 and §4.2.5 in this chapter.

ii. Adjective-derived manner adverbs are usually found in reduplicated forms, except for a very small number of adjectives that can either modify verbs directly or in their reduplicated forms, such as, k^hua^{21} 'good ~ well' and $tɕiu^{21}$ 'quick ~ quickly'. See examples (4.26), (4.27), (4.29) and (4.30).

iii. Except for non-reduplicated manner adverbs, other adverbs can be marked by the marker $lɛ^{55}$.

iv. This use of the marker $lɛ^{55}$ to form manner adverbials is highly productive. Various forms can be observed. For instance, measure and classifier phrases, [NUM MEAS/CLF], and VPs can be used to modify predicates, once they are semantically related to 'manner'.

Let us examine these features with examples.

We have shown in §4.2.1.2 and §4.2.5 how adverbs are derived from adjectives, vivid adjectival forms as well as quadrisyllabic expression. An example of a manner demonstrative serving as an adverb is given below. In this case, the adverbial marker $lɛ^{55}$ is optionally used.

(4.119) "pɔ²⁴ ɣɯ²¹ o. pɔ²⁴ ɣɯ²¹ o." je³³ ɔ²¹sɿ⁵⁵ **(lɛ²¹)** xaŋ⁵⁵.
leopard come CRS leopard come CRS 3SG this.way ADV yell
' "Leopard came! Leopard came!" He shouted like this (for help).'
"豹子来了！豹子来了！"他这样喊。
(*The boy who cried 'Leopard!'*, texts)

One more example of a vivid adjectival form is given below. As can be observed, if there is also a preverbal prepositional phrase, the adverb will precede the prepositional phrase.

(4.120) je³³ [ADV**tɕiɔ²¹mɛ³³mɛ³³ lɛ²¹**] [PrepP[ta⁵⁵ ma²⁴] VP[kua³³-kuɛ²¹ o]]].
3SG quietly ADV from there pass-go CRS
'He passed by quietly.'
他悄悄地从那儿过去了。

4.3 Adverbs

As shown in the example below, monosyllabic manner adverbs cannot be marked by *lɛ⁵⁵*.

(4.121) nɯ³³ **tɕiu²⁴** ***lɛ⁵⁵** ɣa²¹ la²¹!
2SG quick ADV walk PRT
'You hurry up!'
你快走啦！

In fact, the marker *lɛ⁵⁵* is optional for manner demonstratives, vivid adjectival A-BB forms, reduplicated adjectives, and quadrisyllabic expressions. However, among these derivational adverbs, those possessing more complicated internal structures tend to be marked by *lɛ⁵⁵*. Therefore, adverbs derived from quarisyllabic expressions appear to be more commonly marked by the adverbial marker. Furthermore, if the adverb does not immediately modify the verb in a sentence, it tends to be marked by *lɛ⁵⁵*, as shown in (4.120) above.

Apart from these derivational adverbs, different forms of manner adverbials marked by *lɛ⁵⁵* can also be observed. In (4.122), the two manner adverbials occur respectively in the forms of [NUM CLF NUM CLF] and [NUM MEAS NUM MEAS].

(4.122) mɔ²¹ xeŋ²⁴-sui⁵⁵ nɛ⁵⁵, nɯ³³ a³³ ₐDV[**tsaŋ²¹ po⁵⁵ tsaŋ²¹**
that apricot-PL PRT 2SG DCR ten CLF ten
po⁵⁵ lɛ⁵⁵] tsɔ⁵⁵-xɯ⁵⁵. ₐDV[**ji³³ li²¹ ji³³ li²¹ lɛ⁵⁵**] peŋ⁵⁵-kʰɯ⁵⁵.
CLF ADV put.into one bag one bag ADV divide-open
tsaŋ²¹ po⁵⁵ tsɔ⁵⁵ ji²¹li²¹. ji³³ ni²¹ peŋ⁵⁵ ji³³ li²¹.
ten CLF put.into one bag one CLF assign one bag
'Those apricots, you pack (them) in tens. Pack them separately in bags. Each bag contains ten pieces. Each person can be assigned one bag (of apricots).'
那些杏啊，你把（它们）十个十个地装起来。一包一包地分开。十个装一包。一人分一包。

In example (4.122), the classifier phrases *tsaŋ²¹ po⁵⁵* 'ten pieces' and *ji³³ li²¹* 'one bag' are reduplicated. In contrast, it is two different classifier phrases with different head nouns that function as the manner adverbial in (4.123). It should be noted that a single classifier or measure phrase, i.e. [NUM CLF] or [NUM MEAS], cannot serve as manner adverbials alone.

(4.123) ŋo³³ ADV[ɿ⁵⁵ ji³³ tɔ³³ niɔ²¹ ji³³ tɔ³³ lɛ³³] a³³ je³³ tsɿ²¹-la²¹.
1SG feces one CLF urine one CLF ADV OM 3SG raise-big
'I raised him laboriously.'
我一把屎一把尿把他养大。

The following two examples show VPs functioning as manner adverbials.

(4.124) mɔ²⁴-sui⁵⁵ tɯ³³ ADV[tɕiu²¹tɕiu²⁴] ADV[[ta⁵⁵(-xɯ⁵⁵) tɣ²¹
that-PL then quickly carry-DUR hoe
ta⁵⁵(-xɯ⁵⁵) piɔ³³] lɛ³³] tsa²¹ ti²¹ ɣɯ²¹ sɿ⁵⁵.
carry-DUR hoe ADV go.up hill come PRT
'Carrying along their hoes, those (people) then went quickly up the hill.'
那些（人）就赶紧扛着大锄小锄地上山来了。
(*The boy who cried 'Leopard!'*, texts).

(4.125) ɔ²¹ zɿ⁵⁵ pɣ²¹ sɯ⁵⁵ lɛ²¹ ɣɯ²¹.
this rain NEG rest ADV come
'It has been raining ceaselessly.'
这雨不停地下。

4.3.2 Degree adverbs

Degree adverbs usually modify adjectives and some transitive verbs or VPs possessing a similar semantic value that can be evaluated as to their degree, such as many emotion verbs. There are several degree adverbs that are frequently used in Caijia: *xɿŋ⁵⁵* 'very', *tʰɛ²⁴* 'too', *taŋ²⁴* 'very', *ɣã²¹mi⁵⁵* 'a little bit'.

The adverb *xɿŋ⁵⁵* 'very' is the most frequently used and the only post-verbal degree adverb in Caijia. We pointed out in §4.2.1.2.3 that this adverb is derived from the adjective 'fierce, capable'. One more example is given below, in which both the adjectival and adverbial uses are illustrated.

(4.126) je³³ tɯ³³ saŋ²¹ **xɿŋ⁵⁵** **xɿŋ⁵⁵** lɛ⁵⁵ tɯ³³ tɣ²¹ so⁵⁵
3SG then heart fierce very ADV then stretch hand
ta⁵⁵ pʰɿŋ²¹ piɛ⁵⁵ mo³³ kuɛ³³ ji³³ ma²¹.
two CLF to inside PURP one grasp
'He then stretched out greedily his two hands into (the tummy of the stone) to fetch (more money).'
他就心狠地伸两只手到里面一抓。
(*The man and the stone*, texts)

Judging by its tonal value, the adverb $t^h\varepsilon^{24}$ 'too, excessively' is a loan word from local Southwestern Mandarin, *tài* 太 [t^hai^{213}] 'too, excessively', which is [t^hai^{51}] in Standard Mandarin. It is possible for $t^h\varepsilon^{24}$ to modify adjectives or verbs alone, but it is more commonly used along with the post-verbal $xi\eta^{55}$, as shown below.

(4.127) ŋo³³ **$t^h\varepsilon^{24}$** kʰui²¹ (**xɪŋ⁵⁵**) o.
1SG too tired very CRS
'I'm extremely tired.'
我太累了。

The adverb $ta\eta^{24}$ 'very' is only used in negated contexts by following the negator.[5]

(4.128) je³³ pɣ²¹ **taŋ²⁴** tɕʰi³³kʰa³³ ŋo³³.
3SG NEG very like 1SG
'He doesn't like me very much.'
他不太喜欢我。

In comparison with $ta\eta^{24}$ 'very', the degree of $xi\eta^{55}$ in a negated context is more intense.

(4.129) je³³ pɣ³³ tɕʰi³³kʰa³³ ŋo²¹ xɪŋ⁵⁵.
3SG NEG like 1SG very
'He dislikes me very much.'
他很不喜欢我。

One can use the adverb $t^h\varepsilon^{24}$ 'too, excessively' along with $xi\eta^{55}$ 'very' to express further intensification. It should be noted that $t^h\varepsilon^{24}$ precedes the negator in a negated context, which is different from the adverb $ta\eta^{24}$ 'very'.

---

[5] In the Weining variety of Caijia, $ta\eta^{24}$ can be used as a manner demonstrative denoting 'so', as shown in example (i). Compare this with (4.119).

(i) je³³ taŋ²⁴ xa²¹.
3SG so say
'She said so'
她这么说。

However, this phenomenon is not observed in Hezhang Xingfa Caijia.

(4.130) je³³ **tʰɛ²⁴** pɣ³³ xa²¹ me²¹tsɿ⁵⁵ **xɪŋ⁵⁵**.
3SG too NEG say reason very
'He is extremely unreasonable.'
他太不讲道理了。

The preverbal adverb ɣã²¹mi⁵⁵ 'a little bit' is derived from the VP ɣã²¹ mi⁵⁵ denoting 'there is some'.

(4.131) ŋo³³ ɣã²¹mi⁵⁵ kʰui²¹.
1SG a.little.bit be.tired
'I'm a little bit tired.'
我有点累。

Apart from degree adverbs, the meaning of degree can also be expressed by the extent complementation formed by lɯ⁵⁵ (see §4.2.4) and the verbal classifier mi⁵⁵ 'a little' (see §4.4 and Chapter 9).

4.3.3 Adverbs of time

Time adverbs cover not only what we identified as time words in Chapter 3 §3.6.2, such as mɔ²¹kɯ²⁴ 'before, previously, at that time', ɔ²¹kɯ²⁴ 'now', kʰŋ⁵⁵koŋ⁵⁵ 'today', tʰɪŋ²¹koŋ⁵⁵ 'tomorrow', etc., but also a series of words relevant to the concept of time, including lɔ²¹kɯ²⁴ 'always' (< 'when, whenever'), tɯ³³ 'then', jɯ²⁴ 'again (realis)', xa²¹tsɛ⁵⁵ 'still', tɕʰin²¹ 'first', lɛ²¹tsʰɛ²¹ 'only then', ʑi³³ 'as soon as', ta³³la²¹ 'again', etc. (Zhu Dexi 1982: 198–200). Among these adverbs, time words can be observed either in sentence-initial or sentence-medial position. The rest are all observed in sentence-medial position, i.e. the common pre-predicate position for all adverbs.

In Chapter 3 §3.6.2 we have argued that time words are nouns in nature but can function as adverbials. The time word koŋ⁵⁵koŋ⁵⁵ 'every day' functions as an adverbial in both of the sentences in (4.132). It occupies the pre-predicate position in (4.132a), whereas it is in the sentence-initial position in (4.132b).

(4.132) a. je²¹ **koŋ⁵⁵koŋ⁵⁵** niɔ³³ piɔ³³ ya³³ ma²⁴ ya²¹ mɔ²¹
3SG every.day need run to there walk that
sɿ⁵⁵kʰa³³ pɪŋ³³ kuɛ²¹ ã²¹ sɿ⁵⁵.
well side PURP drink water
'It went to the well to drink water every day.'
它天天要跑到那儿去那口井边喝水。
(*Our pony*, texts)

b. **koŋ⁵⁵koŋ⁵⁵** je³³ kuɛ²¹ tɔ⁵⁵ sɔ⁵⁵.
every.day 3SG go chop wood
'He went to chop wood every day.'
每天他去砍柴。

The following examples show the uses of *tɯ³³* 'then', *tɕʰin²¹* 'first' and *lɛ²¹tsʰɛ²¹* 'only then'. The previous context of (4.133) is that the pony went to drink water one day. Modifying the predicate 'the tiger was lying on the ridge above', the adverb *tɯ³³* denotes 'at the moment when the pony was drinking water'.

(4.133) mɔ²¹ kʰɣ⁵⁵pa²¹ **tɯ³³** tɯ²¹ mɔ²¹ tɣ³³mĩ²¹ kʰã⁵⁵ tɣ³³ tsɿ²¹-xɯ⁵⁵.
that tiger then at that upside ridge upside lie-DUR
'The tiger was **then** lying on the ridge above.'
那老虎就在那上面的坎上睡着。
(*Our pony*, texts)

Marked by the adverb *tɕʰin²¹* 'first', the action 'scoop out some (food) to the dead person' in (4.134i) is prior to the action 'scoop out (some food) into one's own mouth' in (4.134ii). The adverb *lɛ²¹tsʰɛ²¹* in (4.134ii) denotes an emphatic meaning, i.e. the action in (4.134ii) can take place only after the action in (4.134i).

(4.134) i) **tɕʰin²¹** pa³³ mi⁵⁵ sɿ⁵⁵ la²¹to⁵⁵ u²¹tsʰo²¹, nɛ⁵⁵,
first scoop a.little to old person INTJ
ii) tsɿ²¹tɕia⁵⁵ **lɛ²¹tsʰɛ²¹** pa²¹ pie⁵⁵ pi²¹ mo³³.
oneself only.then scoop to mouth inside
'(One must) scoop out some (food) **first** for the dead person. Eh, **only then** one can scoop out (some food) to put into one's own mouth.'
先舀点给老人，嗯，自己才舀到嘴里。
(*Funeral customs*, texts)

Both the adverbs *tɯ³³* 'then' and *lɛ²¹tsʰɛ²¹* 'only then' are polysemous and can serve as intensifiers in various contexts. They may also possess different interpretations according to these different contexts. In (4.135), *tɯ³³* is used to underline the action of the dog's barking which had already occurred before the action of entering the house.

(4.135) ŋo³³ a²¹ pɣ²¹-tɣ³³ li²¹-ɣɯ²¹, kʰui⁵⁵ **tɯ³³** po²¹-xɯ⁵⁵ɣɯ²¹ o.
1SG still NEG-PFV enter-come dog then bark-INC CRS
'I still hadn't entered (the house) and the dog **already** began to bark.'
我还没进来，狗就叫起来了。

In (4.136), *lɛ²¹tsʰɛ²¹* underlines the final winner after the fight between the tiger and the buffalo.

(4.136) lɔ²¹ni³³ **lɛ²¹tsʰɛ²¹** xɪŋ⁵⁵.
who   only   capable
'(The tiger and the buffalo made a bet to see) who on earth would be the capable one.'
（老虎和水牛打赌看究竟）谁才厉害。
(*The tiger and the buffalo*, texts)

Moreover, both *tuɯ³³* 'then' and *lɛ²¹tsʰɛ²¹* 'only then' are important operators to form complex sentences in Caijia. See more details in Chapter 15 on clause linking.

Examples of *jɯ²⁴* 'again', which is borrowed from Standard Mandarin *yòu* 又 'again' [jəu⁵¹], and *ta³³la²¹* 'again' are given below. The adverb *jɯ²⁴* is used for repetition of an action already performed. Example (4.137) suggests that the person came at least twice. The adverb *jɯ²⁴* 'again' can form an emphatic conjunction in the form of [NP jɯ²⁴ VP₁, jɯ²⁴ VP₂] denoting 'both. . . and. . .'. See Chapter 15 §15.3.1.2.1 for more discussions.

(4.137) je³³ **jɯ²⁴** ɣɯ²¹ o.
3SG   again   come   CRS
'He came again.'
他又来了。

The adverb *ta³³la²¹* 'again' denotes the repetition of an action, but it can be used in either irrealis or realis contexts, as shown below.

(4.138) a. ŋo³³ ta³³la²¹ mã²¹ ɕɪŋ³³ sɿ²¹ ji³³ ɣa³³ sɿ⁵⁵ nɯ³³.
1SG   again   buy   new   MOD   one   CLF   to   2SG
'I'll buy you a new pair (of trousers) **again**.'
我另给你买条新的（裤子）给你。

b. **ta³³la²¹** pi²¹   kʰɪŋ⁵⁵   to⁵⁵   o.
again   change   sky   CLF   CRS
'The weather changed **again**.'
另变一个天了。

4.3.4 Scope adverbs

The Caijia adverbs of scope are used to indicate the range of an action including *la^{33}* 'all', *tseŋ^{21}mi^{55}* 'almost', *tɕiŋ^{33}* 'all', *tsʰɿ^{21}ka^{24}* 'all' (< 'be clean'), *tsʰɛ^{21}* 'only', etc. Some examples are given below.

(4.139) to^{21}kʰɯ^{55}neŋ^{21} ɔ^{21} kʰɯ^{21} kʰa^{55} nɛ^{55}, **tɕɪŋ^{33}** sɿ^{21} kʰɯ^{55}
years.ago this open relative TOP all COP open
la^{21}to^{55} kʰa^{55}.
old relative
'As for (Caijia) marriages in the olden days, they were **all** consanguineous marriages.'
头几年，这结亲啊，净是近亲结亲。
(*Caijia marriages*, texts)

(4.140) mɔ^{21} ni^{21}ta^{21} mo^{33} tie^{55}tie^{55} sɿ^{33}, **tsʰɿ^{21}ka^{24}** sɿ^{33} mɔ^{21}
that bog inside bottom COP all COP that
tsoŋ^{55} naŋ^{33} ni^{21}kʰa^{24}.
type sludgy mud
'It's **all** sludgy mud at the bottom of the bog.'
那泥潭里的底下是，全是那种稀泥。
(*Falling into bog*, texts)

(4.141) ŋo^{33} **tseŋ^{21}mi^{55}** lɪŋ^{33} kʷɔ^{21} o.
1SG almost fall.over go.CRS CRS
'I **almost** fell over.'
我差点摔一跤。

(4.142) nɯ^{55} nian^{21}tɕi^{55} tsʰɿ^{55} sɿ^{21} neŋ^{21}neŋ^{55} **la^{33}** niɔ^{33} ɣɯ^{21}
2PL age be.light MOD every.year all will come
tsaŋ^{21} ŋo^{33} mi^{55}.
look 1SG a.little
'You young people **all** come to pay me a visit every year.'
你们年轻人，每年都要来看我一下。
(*The New Year's visit*, texts)

It is worth mentioning that the adverb *la^{33}* 'all' is also polysemous like *tɯ^{33}* 'then' does. It can also denote 'also, too' or 'even'.

(4.143) je³³ la³³ tɕiu²¹ ha⁵⁵ o.
3SG also arrive COMPL CRS
'He has also arrived.'
他也到了。

Moreover, *la³³* can form an emphatic conjunction in the form of [NP₁ la³³ VP₁, NP₂ la³³ VP₂] as well, denoting 'both... and...' and it is used with indefinite pronouns in constructions which code the -EVER series (see Chapter 3 on NPs). See more details in Chapter 15.

This section has given a general introduction to Caijia adverbs. Almost all the adverbs occupy pre-predicate positions. Derivational adverbs are very common in Caijia. Adjectives, vivid adjectival A-BB forms, manner demonstratives as well as quadrisyllabic idiomatic expressions are four major sources. Most of the derivational adverbs are manner adverbs, which are often marked by *lɛ⁵⁵*. Adjectives are usually reduplicated when serving as adverbs. Reduplicated adjectives, vivid adjectival A-BB forms, and quadrisyllabic expressions can further be reduplicated, so as to express intensification. The marker *lɛ⁵⁵* can be used to form various manner adverbials with VPs. Several other semantic types of adverbs were also introduced, including degree adverbs, time adverbs and scope adverbs. Unlike the manner adverbs, these adverbs cannot be marked by *lɛ⁵⁵* and cannot be reduplicated. The degree adverb *xiŋ⁵⁵* 'very' is the only post-verbal adverb in Caijia. The adverbs *tɯ³³* 'then', *la³³* 'all', *lɛ²¹tsʰɛ²¹* 'only then', and *jɯ²⁴* 'again' are also used in clause linking, forming different types of complex sentences in Caijia.

4.4 Verbal classifiers

As a category, verbal classifiers are not commonly referenced in general linguistic literature. The term 'verbal classifier' may refer to a kind of noun categorization reflected on verbs, that is, the marking on the verb categorizes the associated nominal arguments, as in a number of North American and Australian languages (Aikhenvald 2000, Grinevald 2000). It may also concern a counting or quantifying system for verbs, that is, verbal classifiers, usually interacting with numerals, count the number of times an action or event takes place (Chao 1968: 615). This is especially the case in East and Southeast Asian languages (Gerner 2009, 2014, see Killingley 1983 for Cantonese, Paris 2013 for Standard Mandarin). This system is similar to the nominal classifier system which operates within the noun phrase (see Chapter 3). Let us first view an example of Standard Mandarin in (4.144). The action of pushing is quantified by the numeral *yī* 'one' and the verbal classifier *bǎ* which is particularly used for verbs performed by the hands, denoting 'push once'.

(4.144) 他推了我一把。
       tā   tuī   le   wǒ **yì** **bǎ**.
       3SG push PFV 1SG one VCLF:grasp
       'He gave me a push/he pushed me once.'

The Caijia verbal classifiers belong to the East and Southeast Asian type. As in Sinitic, Tai-Kadai, and Hmong-Mien (Gerner 2014), verbal classifier phrases follow VPs in Caijia. Two configurations are schematized as follows:
i. [V (O) [NUM/QUAN VCLF]]
ii. [V (O) [VCLF]]

In the first schema, QUAN refers to quantifiers other than numerals such as k^hw^{33} 'several, some', $tsı^{21}k^hw^{33}$ 'more than ten', while the second schema is only observed with the verbal classifier mi^{55} denoting a short duration of time.

As illustrated in (4.145), the verbal classifier phrase $ta^{55}\ sw^{55}$ 'two-VCLF' follows the object $mɔ^{21}\ ŋa^{55}\ ni^{21}$ 'that child', denoting that the action of beating takes place twice. The verbal classifier sw^{55} further specifies that the action of beating is realized by the person's hand(s).

[V ₒ[DEM N CLF] [NUM VCLF]]
(4.145) je³³ vP[na²¹ ₒ[mɔ²¹ ŋa⁵⁵ ni²¹] **[ta⁵⁵ sw⁵⁵]**].
       3SG   beat   that child CLF two VCLF:palm
       'He slapped that child twice.'
       他打了那个孩子两巴掌。

Gerner (2014) observes four types of verbal classifiers appearing in East and Southeast Asian languages, as summarized in Table 4.2 below.

Table 4.2: Typology of verbal classifiers in East and Southeast Asian languages.

I. Sortal	II. Mensural		III. Double	IV. Auto-classifiers
INSTRUMENT	COLLECTIVE	MEASURE	same NCLF for	Verb reduplication
hand	time	while	EVENT NOUNS	V NUM V
foot	quick time	instant	WEATHER NOUNS	
fist	path	hour	SOME COUNT/MASS NOUNS	
eye	turn	day		

Table 4.2 (continued)

I. Sortal	II. Mensural		III. Double	IV. Auto-classifiers
INSTRUMENT	COLLECTIVE	MEASURE	same NCLF for	Verb reduplication
hammer	process	evening		
needle	..	year		
...		...		

Most of the sortal classifiers are related to instruments with which actions are performed; mensural verbal classifiers create temporal boundaries for events; 'double verbal classifiers' refer to those that can function either as nominal classifiers or verbal classifiers; the category of verbal auto-classifiers refers to the case in which verbs themselves serve as verbal classifiers. In Caijia, only Types I, II, and III are attested, that is sortal or instrument, mensural, and double verbal classifiers. However, we only count two types: the instrument and the mensural types, the reasons for which will be given below. We begin by investigating each type in detail, on the basis of the typology proposed by Gerner.

4.4.1 Instrument verbal classifiers

As observed by Gerner (2009, 2014), instrument nouns constitute a type of sortal verbal classifier. Moreover, instrument verbal classifier phrases can be transformed into an overt instrument-marking construction, in which the instrument is overtly marked by the preposition a^{33} 'with' (< 'take') in Caijia, as shown in the examples below.

(4.146) a. a^{33} **ni^{33}tsɿ^{33}** tsaŋ^{33}
with eye look
'look with one's eyes'
用眼睛看

b. meŋ^{21}-xa^{33} je^{33} soŋ^{21} o. ŋo^{21} ɕiaŋ^{55} kuɛ^{21}
hear-say 3SG sick CRS 1SG want go
tsaŋ^{33} je^{33} **ji^{33}** ni^{33}tsɿ^{33}.
look 3SG one VCLF:eye
'(I) hear that he's sick. I'd like to pay him a visit.'
听说他病了。我想去看他一眼。

(4.147) a. a³³ **poŋ²⁴** na²¹ je³³.
with stick beat 3SG
'Beat him with a stick.'
用棍子打他。

b. na²¹ je³³ **ji²¹ poŋ²⁴**.
beat 3SG one VCLF:stick
'Give him a blow with the stick.'
打他一棍。

(4.148) a. **a²¹ sɿ⁵⁵** ja³³ ɯ³³.
with water wash clothes
'Wash clothes with water.'
用水洗衣服。

b. mɔ²¹ ɯ³³ ɣa³³... ŋo³³ a³³ ja²¹-kua³³ **ji²¹ sɿ⁵⁵**
that clothes CLF 1SG DCR wash-pass one VCLF:water
ha⁵⁵ tsʰɔ³³ kʷɔ²¹ o.
COMPL shrink go.CRS CRS
'That item of clothing, after I washed it once, it shrank.'
那件衣服，我洗过一水，缩了。

However, exceptions do exist. First, the classifier *sɯ⁵⁵* 'palm' cannot be transformed into an instrument-marking construction. Instead, it is typically used as a verbal classifier, denoting an action of hitting performed with one's palm. If the instrument needs to be overtly marked, it will be the noun *so⁵⁵* 'hand' that is marked by the preposition *a³³*. The words *so⁵⁵* 'hand' and *sɯ⁵⁵* 'palm' seem to function in a complementary fashion, as the noun *so⁵⁵* cannot serve as a verbal classifier. See the example below.

(4.149) mɛ³³ɣoŋ²⁴ tɕʰɪn³³-tv̩³³ niɔ³³ **a²¹** so⁵⁵ pʰa³³. pʰa⁵⁵ je²¹
leech bite-obtain need with hand pat pat 3SG
ji²¹ sɯ⁵⁵ je³³ tɯ³³ ɣa²¹-tsʰe⁵⁵ɣɯ²¹ o.
one VCLF:palm 3SG then fall-be.out.come CRS
'(You) should pat (it) with your hand when you're bitten by a leech. (You) give it a pat and it'll fall out.'
蚂蟥咬到要用手拍。拍它一掌，他就掉出来了。

Second, instrument nouns are not the only source in Caijia. The verbal classifier *ma²¹* is derived from its verb form 'grasp, grab', which can also be used as a measure word denoting 'a handful of'. Being a verbal classifier, it often collocates with the verbs $k^h\mathrm{ŋ}^{55}$ 'pull' and lo^{21} 'push'. Given that ma^{21} is derived from a verb, it cannot be transformed into the instrument marking construction either. Compare the three examples in (4.150), illustrating respectively the verb, measure word and verbal classifier uses of ma^{21}.

(4.150) a. je³³ jɯ²⁴ **ma²¹** tʰɣ⁵⁵ **ma³³** sɿ³³kʰa³³
  3SG again grab earth grab dirt
  niaŋ³³ tɯ²¹ ŋo³³ kɣ³³ tɣ³³.
  stick to 1SG foot upside
  'She grabbed some earth and dirt and put (it) on my foot.'
  她又抓土抓灰抹到我脚上。
  (*The nettle witch*, texts)

  b. tʰɣ⁵⁵ **ji²¹** **ma²¹**
  earth one grasp
  'a handful of earth'
  一把土

  c. u²¹tsʰo²¹ sɣ²¹ xıŋ⁵⁵ tʰɔ⁵⁵ niɔ³³ ɣã²¹ u²¹tsʰo²¹
  person poor very moment need there.be person
  kʰŋ⁵⁵ je²¹ **ji³³** **ma³³** tɯ⁵⁵ kʰɯ⁵⁵-ɣɯ²¹ o.
  pull 3SG one VCLF:grasp then rise-come CRS
  'When someone falls down, he will get back on his feet, if there's a person giving him a pull.'
  人潦倒的时候，要有人拉他一把就起来了。

From the examples above, one can observe that both the measure word ma^{21} and the verbal classifier ma^{21} are closely related to the lexical item 'hand'. The verb ma^{21} 'grasp' thus shares a certain semantic similarity with the verbal classifiers derived from instrument nouns. Even though the word ma^{21} itself is not the instrument, it implies an action that is performed with one's hands. It is, thus, reasonable to put ma^{21} into the instrument type.

Gerner (2014) also observes that the instrument verbal classifiers often interact with three types of verbs:
i. HIT verbs, i.e. hitting an object with a physical instrument (body parts, hammer, knife etc.).
ii. ATTACH verbs, i.e. attaching something with a physical medium (needle, pen, rope, etc.).
iii. TRANSMIT verbs, i.e. reaching out to an object through an intermediate channel (eye, voice, fan, gun, etc.).

These three types of verbs can be classified by sortal/instrument verbal classifiers in Caijia. See, for instance, the verb of TRANSMIT *tsaŋ³³* 'look' in (4.146b) and the HIT verb *na³³* 'hit' in (4.147b). The following example shows a verb of the ATTACH class, i.e. *ti³³* 'stitch'.

(4.151) ti²¹   ta⁵⁵   tsaŋ²¹
         stitch two   VCLF:needle
         'give two stitches'
         缝两针

Nonetheless, since we were not able to do an exhaustive survey, we are not able to guarantee whether or not a fourth type also exists. See Table 4.3 for verbs which often collocate with sortal or instrument verbal classifiers, keeping in mind that this is not an exhaustive list.

Table 4.3: Verbs with sortal/instrument verbal classifiers in Caijia.

Verbs	Classifiers
na³³ 'hit (with one's hands)' 打	sɯ⁵⁵ 'palm' 掌/手
	tʰɯ⁵⁵ 'fist' 拳
	poŋ²⁴ 'stick' 棍
	tl̩²¹ 'hammer' 锤, …
	any instrument manipulated by one's hands.
pʰa³³ 'pat' 拍	sɯ⁵⁵ 'palm' 掌/手
kʰɪŋ⁵⁵ 'pull' 拉	ma²¹ 'grasp, grab' 把/抓
ɖo²¹ 'push' 推	ma²¹ 'grasp, grab' 把/抓
tʰe⁵⁵ 'kick' 踢	kv⁵⁵ 'foot' 脚
tɕʰin³³ 'bite' 咬	pi²¹ 'mouth' 嘴
tsʰŋ³³ 'blow' 吹	pi²¹ 'mouth' 嘴
ɣɯ⁵⁵ 'cry' 哭	pi²¹ 'mouth' 嘴
sɔ⁵⁵ 'cut' 切	ɕi⁵⁵ 'knife' 刀
tsaŋ³³ 'look' 看	ni³³tsɿ³³ 'eye' 眼睛
tʰi³³ 'listen' 听	ni³³kʰa³³ 'ear' 耳朵
ti³³ 'stitch' 缝	tsaŋ³³ 'needle' 针
ja³³ 'wash' 洗	sɿ⁵⁵ 'water' 水

4.4.2 Mensural verbal classifiers

According to Gerner's (2014) typology, Caijia mensural verbal classifiers can be divided into those counting the number of times the action signified by a verb occurs, that is, frequency, and those expressing duration. These categories correspond to the collective verbal classifiers and the mensural verbal classifiers, respectively. The two examples below show these two types of mensural verbal classifiers in Caijia. In (4.152), the classifier *pe⁵⁵* 'time', derived from its verb form 'return' as in (4.152ii), denotes the number of occurrences of a certain event. In (4.153), the time phrase *ji²¹ tʰŋ²⁴* 'an instant' is used as verbal classifier denoting the feature of duration since the meal was prepared.

Number of times

(4.152) i) mɔ²⁴-sui⁵⁵   tɯ²¹   jɯ²⁴   tγ̍³³   je²¹   xɯ⁵⁵
            that-PL   then   again   PASS   3SG   cheat
            ji²¹   **pe⁵⁵**   nɛ⁵⁵,
            one   VCLF:time   PRT

     ii)   tɯ²¹   **pe⁵⁵**-ɪn²¹   kʷɔ²¹   o.
            then   return-back   go.CRS   CRS

     iii)   nɛ⁵⁵   tγ̍³³   je²¹   xɯ⁵⁵   ta⁵⁵   **pe⁵⁵**   o.
            INTJ   PASS   3SG   cheat   two   VCLF:time   CRS

'Those (persons) were fooled by him again. (They) then went back. Um, (they) were fooled by him twice.'
那些（人）就又被他骗一次。就回去了。嗯，被他骗两次了。
(*The boy who cried 'Leopard!'*, texts)

Duration

(4.153) ɔ²¹   zv̩²¹   la²¹   tɕie⁵⁵-kʰua²¹   **ji²¹**   **tʰŋ²⁴**   o.
        this   meal   all   do-be.good   one   VCLF:instant   CRS

'The meal has been ready for a while.'
饭都做好一会儿了。

Some mensural verbal classifiers observed in our data are listed in Table 4.4 below.

Table 4.4 needs further elaboration. First, the classifiers *tʰaŋ²⁴*, *xa²⁴*, and *tɕia²¹xuɔ²⁴* are all borrowed from the local Southwestern Mandarin. The Southwestern Mandarin *tɕia²¹xuɔ²¹³* originally denotes 'instrument, fellow' and it can also be used as an instrument verbal classifier in this variety. It signals that a certain action is performed by an instrument but without indicating the specific instrument and only collocates with the numeral *ʐi³³* 'one'.

Table 4.4: Mensural verbal classifiers.

Numbers of Time	Verbs	Duration of Time	Verbs
tɨŋ⁵⁵ 'time' < 'turn' 转	piɔ⁵⁵ 'run' 跑 ɣa²¹ 'walk' 走 pɣ³³ 'fly' 飞 motion verbs of round trip	mi⁵⁵ 'a while' < 'some, a little' 点	OPEN CLASS
tʰaŋ²⁴ 'time' < Chinese *tàng* 'path' 趟	piɔ⁵⁵ 'run' 跑 ɣa²¹ 'walk' 走 pɣ³³ 'fly' 飞 ɣɯ²¹ 'come' 来 kuɛ³³ 'go' 去 motion verbs	ʑi²¹tʰŋ²⁴ 'a while' 一会儿 NUM/QUAN + kɯ²¹ 'hour' 时 NUM/QUAN + koŋ⁵⁵ 'day' 天 NUM/QUAN + sa³³ 'night' 夜 NUM/QUAN + ŋui⁵⁵ 'month' 月 ... TIME WORDS	OPEN CLASS
ti⁵⁵ 'time' < classifier for 'meal' 顿	ā³³ 'drink' 喝 zɣ²¹ 'eat' 吃 mɛ³³ 'scold' 骂 na³³ 'beat' 打		
pe⁵⁵ 'time' < 'return' 返	OPEN CLASS		
xa²⁴ 'time' < *xià* 下 'go down' in SW	OPEN CLASS	ʑi²¹xa²⁴ 'a while' 一下	OPEN CLASS
ʑi³³ tɕia²¹xuɔ²⁴ 'once' < *yī jiāhuo* 一家伙 'an instrument, a fellow' in SW	OPEN CLASS		

(4.154) ka⁵⁵-tɣ³³   ji³³   kʷɔ²¹   nɛ⁵⁵   je³³   tɯ²¹   piɔ⁵⁵   **ji²¹**
catch-obtain one   CLF   PRT   3SG then run   one
tʰaŋ²⁴.   [...] je³³   jɯ²⁴   piɔ⁵⁵   **ji³³   tɕia²¹xuɔ²⁴**   nɛ⁵⁵.
VCLF:path   3SG again run   one   VCLF:short.path   PRT
'(The tiger) caught one sheep, it then made a run. . . . It then made another run.'
（老虎）抓住一只呢，它就跑一趟。......它又跑一下。
(*The stupid sheep*, texts)

Second, when *xa*²⁴ is used to denote a short duration of time, it only co-occurs with the numeral *ʑi*³³ 'one' as *tɕia*²¹*xuɔ*²¹³ does. Compare the following two sentences in (4.155).

(4.155) Number of times
a. je²¹ pʰa³³ mɔ²¹ kɣ²¹ja²⁴ ni²¹ hm̩⁵⁵ so⁵⁵kɪn²⁴ **ta⁵⁵ xa²⁴**.
    3SG pat that woman CLF POSS arm two VCLF:time
    'He patted that woman's arm twice.'
    他拍了那个女人的胳膊两下。

Duration
b. nɯ³³ niu²¹ ŋo³³ [**ji²¹xa²⁴**]/[**mi⁵⁵**].
    2SG wait 1SG a.while/a.little
    'Wait for me for a moment.'
    你等我一下。

Third, the classifier *mi⁵⁵* 'a while', derived from 'some, a little', is the only one that does not interact with any numeral. It serves as a delimitative marker (See Chapter 10). The classifier *ji²¹xa²⁴* in (4.155b) can be replaced by *mi⁵⁵*. See the example below.

(4.156) sɿ⁵⁵ je²¹ sɯ⁵⁵ **mi⁵⁵** lɛ²¹.
    let 3SG rest VCLF:a.little PRT
    'Let him have a rest.'
    让他休息一下。

Finally, as observed by Gerner (2014), some mensural verbal classifiers can also be sortal, as the instrument verbal classifiers are in Caijia. For example, the classifier *tɿŋ⁵⁵*, derived from its verb form 'return', only collocates with motion verbs whereby the meaning of a round trip can be expressed, for instance, *piɔ⁵⁵* 'run' in the example below, or *ɣa²¹* 'walk'.

(4.157) piɔ⁵⁵ **kʰɯ²¹ tɿŋ⁵⁵** ha⁵⁵ lɛ²¹tsʰɛ²¹ kuɛ³³ ja³³ mĩ²¹kʰɔ³³.
    run several VCLF:round COMPL only.then go wash face
    'I went to wash my face after (I) ran around (our site) for several times...'
    跑几圈了才去洗脸......
    (*Drowning persons*, texts)

However, verbs as *ɣɯ²¹* 'come' and *kuɛ³³* 'go' do not collocate with this classifier, because these two verbs denote unidirectionality. Sortal classifiers also include the loanword *tʰaŋ²⁴* that classifies motion involving a defined distance and *ti⁵⁵*, which usually measures actions of eating, drinking, scolding and spanking.

4.4.3 Double classifiers

Double classifiers refer to those that can function both as nominal and verbal classifiers. In fact, we do not treat double classifiers as an independent type of verbal classifier parallel to the instrument and mensural verbal classifiers. This is due to the fact that (i) the instrument and mensural verbal classifiers are classified on the basis of semantics, while the double classifiers are only defined in terms of their multi-functionality and polysemy. We should also note that some of the instrument verbal classifiers have developed other functions. For example, select body-part terms have evolved into localizers, but this does not mean that they form an independent type. It is also due to the fact that (ii) these so-called double classifiers either belong to the instrument type or to the mensural type and there is almost no exception. Nevertheless, the phenomenon that a morpheme may serve as both a numeral (or measure word) and a verbal classifier deserves mention.

In §4.4.1, we have illustrated with example (4.150) that the verb ma^{21} 'grasp, grab' can be a measure word as well as a verbal classifier. More examples are given below. As shown in (4.158), the word pi^{33} 'mouth' serves as a measure word modifying the noun $sɿ^{55}$ 'water' denoting 'a sip of water' in (4.158a), while, by contrast, it is an instrument verbal classifier signifying the number of times the wind blows when occurring in conjunction with the numeral ji^{33} 'one' in (4.158b).

(4.158) a. je²¹ ɕiaŋ⁵⁵ ɣa²¹ mɔ²¹ sɿ⁵⁵kʰa³³ mo³³ kuɛ³³
   3SG want walk that well   inside PURP
   ko²¹   sɿ⁵⁵   **pi²¹** ã³³.
   look.for water mouth   drink
   'It wanted to go to the well to find a sip of water to drink.'
   它想去那个水井里去找口水喝。
   (*The crow and the bottle*, texts)

b. lɔ²¹sɿ⁵⁵ ju̟²⁴ tsʰɿ³³ **ji³³** **pi³³**.
   hard   again blow one   VCLF:mouth
   '(The north wind) gave another hard blow.'
   （北风）又使劲吹了一下。
   (*The north wind and the sun*, texts)

The following two sentences show the classifier ti^{55}, source unclear, serving respectively as the numeral classifier for the noun $zɣ^{33}$ 'meal' and the verbal classifier for the verb $mɛ^{33}$ 'scold'.

(4.159) a. zɣ³³ **ji²¹** **ti⁵⁵**
             meal one CLF
             'a meal'
             一顿饭

         b. je³³   pɣ³³ na²¹zɿ⁵⁵ ŋo³³   mi⁵⁵
             3SG   NEG   thank   1SG   VCLF:a.little
             xa²¹   a³³   ŋo³³   mɛ³³   **ji²¹** **ti⁵⁵**.
             still OM   1SG   scold one   VCLF:time
             'He didn't thank me, but (instead) he gave me a scolding.'
             他不谢谢我，还把我骂了一顿。

Given that a numeral classifier phrase itself can serve as a pronoun (see Chapter 3 §3.5), when the phrase [NUM ti⁵⁵] interacts with the verb zɣ²¹ 'eat', the phrase [zɣ²¹ NUM ti⁵⁵] is indeed ambiguous. As shown in the example right below in (4.160), the phrase zɣ²¹ ji²¹ ti⁵⁵ possesses two interpretations. However, when it collocates with other verbs, the ambiguity disappears. Compare (4.160) and (4.161), the two phrases [zɣ²¹ ji²¹ ti⁵⁵] and [ã³³ ji²¹ ti⁵⁵] share entirely the same syntactic structure. Since the classifier ti⁵⁵ only interacts with the noun zɣ³³ 'meal' and the noun 'meal' cannot serve as the object of the verb ã³³ 'drink', the phrase [ã³³ ji²¹ ti⁵⁵] can only be interpreted as 'drink once'. See also (4.159b).

(4.160) zɣ²¹ **ji²¹** **ti⁵⁵**
         eat   one   CLF
         'have a meal'
         'have a meal once'
         吃一顿（饭）/吃一次饭

(4.161) kʰua²¹kʰua²¹ [ã³³   ji²¹   **ti⁵⁵**]   kuɛ²¹   o.
         well   drink one   CLF:time   go   CRS
         '(The crow finally) had a good drink (of water).'
         好好喝了一顿。
         (*The crow and the bottle*, texts)

In this section, we have presented the Caijia verbal classifiers, which usually count the number of occurrences of an action or event, or express duration. This kind of verbal classifiers is not well-known in the literature of general linguistics but is widely attested in East and Southeast Asian languages (Gerner 2014). Two types of verbal classifiers in Caijia are observed: (i) the instrument type and (ii) the mensural type. The mensural type can be further divided into those counting number of times and those expressing duration of time. The instrument verbal classifiers and some of the mensural verbal classifiers that count number of times are sortal in nature, that is, they indicate some salient semantic feature of the actions or events they modify.

4.5 Prepositions

Prepositions are the major device used to mark oblique arguments in Caijia. Prepositional phrases form part of the predicate. Omission of prepositional phrases may affect both the semantics and syntax of sentences. For example, ditransitive verbs are trivalent. The indirect object is marked by the preposition $sı^{55}$ 'to' in an indirective ditransitive construction, as shown in (4.162). The omission of the $sı^{55}$ phrase $sı^{55}$ $ŋo^{33}$ 'to me' will make the sentence ungrammatical.

(4.162) nɯ³³ a³³ kʰɯ²¹ koŋ⁵⁵ *(sı⁵⁵ ŋo³³).
2SG take several day to 1SG
'You give me several days.'
你给我几天时间。

As in many Sinitic languages, the Caijia prepositions are commonly derived from verbs. Prepositional phrases are observed both pre-VP and post-VP. The pre-VP prepositions include: benefactive, comitative, ablative, lative, instrument, locative, perlative as well as passive agent and object markers, whereas the post-VP prepositions usually mark goal, destination, and recipient arguments, i.e. allative and dative. See the following table for a synthesis of the Caijia prepositions.

Table 4.5: Prepositions in Caijia.

FORM	MEANING	POSITION	SOURCE
ta⁵⁵	ABLATIVE 'from'	PRE-VP	'follow'
	LATIVE 'toward'	PRE-VP	
	COMITATIVE 'with'	PRE-VP	
	BENEFACTIVE 'for'	PRE-VP	
	DATIVE 'to' (SAY verbs)	PRE-VP	
di³³	LATIVE 'toward'	PRE-VP	'face'
dza³³	LATIVE 'toward'	PRE-VP	'go up'
tsʰɔ²¹	LATIVE 'toward'	PRE-VP	< Mandarin *cháo* 'face'
tsan³³	PERLATIVE 'along'	PRE-VP	'pick up'
a³³	INSTRUMENTAL 'with'	PRE-VP	'take'
	OBJECT	PRE-VP	

Table 4.5 (continued)

FORM	MEANING	POSITION	SOURCE
dy³³	PASSIVE AGENT 'by'	PRE-VP	'suffer'
a²¹sɿ⁵⁵	PASSIVE AGENT 'by'	PRE-VP	'take + give/to'
tɯ²¹	LOCATIVE 'at'	PRE-VP/POST-VP	'live'
	ALLATIVE 'to'	POST-VP	
pie⁵⁵	ALLATIVE 'to'	POST-VP	'toss, throw'
sɿ⁵⁵	DATIVE 'to'	POST-VP	'give'

In Caijia, the prepositional use of a morpheme and the verbal use of the same morpheme often exist side by side. In other words, the verb forms of Caijia prepositions are still active and productive. However, the prepositions possess different distributional features, as listed below.

i. Prepositional phrases cannot serve as independent predicates;
ii. they cannot take aspectual markers or resultative complements;
iii. and prepositional objects cannot be omitted.[6]

Let us see these features with some examples of both prepositions and their counterpart verbs. The follow pair of contrastive examples show the case that prepositions cannot be marked by aspectual markers. The verb *ta⁵⁵* 'follow' is marked by the durative marker *-xɯ⁵⁵* in (4.163a), but it is ungrammatical to use it to mark the preposition *ta⁵⁵* 'with' in (4.163b).

(4.163) Verb *ta⁵⁵* 'follow'
    a. ŋo³³   tɯ²¹   u³³mĩ²¹   **ta⁵⁵-xɯ⁵⁵**.
        1SG   at   back   follow-DUR
       'I was following behind.'
       我在后面跟着。

     Preposition *ta⁵⁵* 'with'
    b. ŋo³³   **ta⁵⁵-(*xɯ⁵⁵)**   je²¹   na²¹pia²¹.
        1SG   with-DUR   3SG   chat
       'I chat with him.'

---

[6] Some of the prepositions, such as the morpheme *dy³³*, also forms agentless passive construction, as in the form [dy³³ VP]. In this case, *dy³³* is treated as an auxiliary-like functional word rather than a preposition. Similarly, in one of the differential object constructions, [a³³ VP], the morpheme *a³³* is treated as a verb marker but not as a preposition. See Chapters 7 and 8.

The following examples illustrate cases where a prepositional object cannot be omitted. Omitting the object 'there' in (4.164b) makes the sentence ungrammatical, while the object ɔ⁵⁵ ʑi²¹ 'home' of the verb tɯ²¹ 'live, be at' can be omitted, as shown in (4.164a).

(4.164) Verb *tɯ²¹* 'live, be at'
    a. je³³   pɣ³³-tɣ³³   **tɯ²¹**   (ɔ⁵⁵   ʑi²¹).
        3SG   NEG-PFV be.at   house inside
        'He wasn't at home.'
        他没在（家）。

    Preposition *tɯ²¹* 'at'
    b. je³³   pɣ³³-tɣ³³   **tɯ²¹**   *(ma²⁴)   tɕie⁵⁵ zɣ²¹.
        3SG   NEG-PFV at   there   do   meal
        'He wasn't cooking there.'
        他没在那儿做饭。

Now, let us examine the prepositions individually and in detail.

4.5.1 The preposition *ta⁵⁵*

The preposition *ta⁵⁵*, derived from its verb form 'follow', displays a high degree of polysemy. It is observed that the lexemes from the semantic field of 'follow' are characterized by multifunctionality in varying degrees in many Sinitic languages, for example in Standard Mandarin, Southwestern Mandarin (Li and Liu 2015), Waxiang (Chappell et al. 2011), and other languages (see also Cao et al. 2008 Vol. 3: Map 3). Example (4.163) illustrates the verb/lexical use of *ta⁵⁵* as well as its comitative use. Examples of other meanings are given below. Examples (4.165)-(4.167) give the ablative, lative, and benefactive uses of the preposition *ta⁵⁵*, respectively

Ablative 'from'
(4.165) ɣã³³   ʑi²¹tsʅ⁵⁵   po⁵⁵   **ta⁵⁵**   sɔ⁵⁵   tɣ³³   ɣa³³-tɕie²¹ɣɯ²¹.
         there.be chestnut   CLF   from   tree   upside fall-go.down.come
         'There's a chestnut that fell off the tree.'
         有一个栗子从树上掉下来了。

Lative 'toward'
(4.166) ŋo³³ tsʰuaŋ²⁴kʰa⁵⁵ **ta⁵⁵** naŋ²⁴ kʰɯ³³.
1SG window   toward south open
'My window opens to the south.'
我的窗户朝南开。

Benefactive 'for'
(4.167) pia²¹sɿ⁵⁵ **ta⁵⁵** sɿ⁵⁵lɛ²¹ɔ⁵⁵tso⁵⁵ tɕie⁵⁵ ja²¹pa²¹.
people   for   landlord   do   farming
'Peasants works for landlords.'
百姓给地主干活。

When denoting 'to', the preposition *ta⁵⁵* often interacts with verbs of saying. The dative 'to' marking the recipient in a ditransitive construction is realized by the preposition *sɿ⁵⁵*, which will be shown later below.

Dative 'to' (with verbs of saying)
(4.168) piɔ²⁴ ta⁵⁵ pʰa²¹sɿ²¹ xa²¹.
NEG.IMP to other   say
'Don't tell others.'
别跟别人说。

The preposition *ta⁵⁵*, the comitative *ta⁵⁵* to be specific, has further developed into the NP conjunction 'and' in Caijia. This is quite a common phenomenon attested not only in Sinitic languages (Cao et al. 2008 Vol. 3: Map 3) but also in many languages of the world (Kuteva et al. 2019: 108–111).

Conjunction 'and'
(4.169) ŋo³³ tɕʰi³³kʰa³³ zɣ²¹ [xɯ⁵⁵tsɿ⁵⁵ **ta⁵⁵** lɔ²¹po⁵⁵].
1SG like   eat pear   and   peach
'I like eating pears and peaches.'
我喜欢吃梨和桃子。

4.5.2 The prepositions *di³³*, *dza³³*, and *tsʰɔ²¹*

The prepositions *di³³*, *dza³³*, and *tsʰɔ²¹* all denote 'toward'. Both the prepositions *di³³* and *tsʰɔ²¹* are derived from verbs denoting 'face'. More specifically, *tsʰɔ²¹* is borrowed from the Mandarin *cháo* 朝 'face'. See the following examples for the verbal uses of these two verbs. The verb *ti³³* is marked by the durative marker, while the verb *tsʰɔ²¹* takes the complement *tɣ³³* 'obtain'.

(4.170) ɕie²¹ tsɿ³³ŋa⁵⁵ **ti²¹-xɯ⁵⁵** tʰɣ³³kʰa³³ xaŋ³³ mɛ²⁴toŋ³³toŋ³³.
        small boy   face-DUR   hole   yell   little.frog
        'The little boy called in the direction of a hole in the ground for the little frog.'
        小男孩对着洞喊小青蛙。

(4.171) ɔ²¹ ta²⁴ sɿ³³ **tsʰɔ²¹-tɣ³³** mɔ²⁴ mĩ²¹ sɿ²¹.
        this inn   AFF   face-obtain   that   side AFF
        'It is that side that the inn faces.'
        这旅馆是朝那面的。

The preposition *dza³³* is derived from the verb 'go up', as in (4.88). Compared with the other two prepositions coding lative 'toward', *tsʰɔ²¹* occurs the most frequently. See the following example for the prepositional use of *tsʰɔ²¹* 'toward'.

(4.172) nɛ⁵⁵, tiu³³ a²¹ sɿ³³ **tsʰɔ²¹**   ɔ²¹   sɿ⁵⁵tseŋ²¹
        INTJ   know   PRT COP   toward   this   Shuicheng ₚₗₐCENAME
        ɔ²⁴   mĩ²¹ kuɛ³³ lɔ⁵⁵   ei,   sɿ³³   **tsʰɔ²¹**   suaŋ³³uɛ³³
        this side   go   or   INTJ COP   toward   Weining ₚₗₐCENAME
        kuɛ³³ la³³ pɣ³³ tiu³³u³³.
        go   all   NEG   know
        'Well, (he) had no idea whether (the thieves) went toward Shuicheng or whether (they) went toward Weining.'
        嗯，谁知道（贼）是朝水城这边去了还是是朝威宁去了。
        (*The loss of the cow*, texts)

However, when used to denote a forward movement, it is either *di³³* or *dza³³* that is selected, as shown below. Additionally, it is observed in our data that *dza³³* only interacts with the localizer *tɕiŋ²¹* 'front'.

(4.173) ɕie²¹ kʰui³³ tɕiu²¹tɕiu²⁴ lɛ³³ **ti³³/tsa³³** tɕiŋ²¹ piɔ⁵⁵.
        small dog   quickly   ADV   toward   front   run
        'The dog ran quickly forward.'
        小狗快快地朝前跑。

The locative phrase *di³³ tɕiŋ²¹* 'toward front' has the extended meaning of 'just now, quite a while ago'.

(4.174) ŋo³³ **ti³³** tɕɪŋ²¹ tɯ²¹ ta⁵⁵ nɯ²¹ xa²¹ o.
1SG toward front then with 2SG say CRS
'I've told you long ago.'
我早就告诉你了。

4.5.3 The preposition *tsaŋ³³* 'along'

Denoting 'along', the preposition *tsaŋ³³* is derived from the verb 'pick up'.

(4.175) a³³ sʅ²¹ **tsaŋ²¹-kʰɯ⁵⁵ɣɯ²¹**.
OM letter pick-rise.come
'Pick up the letter.'
把信捡起来。

(4.176) **tsaŋ²¹** ɔ²⁴ sʅ⁵⁵ tsʅ⁵⁵ ɣa²¹ nɯ³³ tɯ²¹ tɕiu⁵⁵ ma²⁴ to³³ o.
along this water CLF walk 2SG then arrive there can CRS
'Walk along this river and you will arrive there then.'
沿这条河走，你就能到那儿。

4.5.4 The preposition *a³³* 'with' (instrumental)/OM

It is widely attested that verbs of taking develop into instrumental markers in many languages in the world (Kuteva et al. 2019: 418–420). The Caijia verb *a³³* 'take' is one such case, and it has further developed into an object marker. Both these uses are found in (4.177) below. Verbs of taking are the dominant source for object markers in Sinitic languages (Chappell 2015b).

(4.177) je²¹-xɯ⁵⁵ **a³³** sʏ³³ tsʅ²¹ **a²¹** kʷɔ⁵⁵pe⁵⁵ja²¹ kɪ⁵⁵-xɯ⁵⁵.
3-PL with rope CLF OM moon tie-up
'They tied the moon up with a rope.'
他们用绳子把月亮系起来。
(*Three thieves*, texts)

See also (4.146a) and (4.149) for more examples of the instrumental preposition and Chapter 8 for more details on the object marker *a³³*.

4.5.5 The preposition dy^{33} and $a^{21}sı^{55}$

Two passive agent prepositions are observed in Caijia. The first, dy^{33}, is derived from the verb 'suffer, hit (the target)', which is a common source for passive agent markers in Sinitic languages (Chappell 2015b). The second, $a^{21}sı^{55}$, is a compound of 'take + give/to' derived from the ditransitive construction a^{33}...$sı^{55}$. Even though the compound marker is not very common, it is semantically similar to verbs of giving, which are another frequent source for passive agent markers in Sinitic (Chappell 2015b).

(4.178) tsɛ²¹tsɛ²⁴ je²¹ tsʰɿ⁵⁵ tɯ³³ **tγ³³** pɔ²⁴ tɕʰɪn²¹-kʷɔ²¹ o mẽ.
really 3SG goat then PASS leopard bite-go.CRS CRS PRT
'His goat was really savaged and taken away by the leopard.'
真的他的羊就被豹子咬走了。
(*The boy who cried 'Leopard!'*, texts)

(4.179) ji²¹ koŋ⁵⁵ tsa²¹ ti²¹ nɛ⁵⁵ **a²¹sɿ⁵⁵** zɿ⁵⁵ lã²¹.
one day go.up hill PRT PASS rain drench
'One day, I went up the hill and got drenched by the rain.'
一天上山，被雨淋了。
(*The haystack*, texts)

See Chapter 7 on passive constructions for more details.

4.5.6 The preposition $tɯ^{21}$ 'at, to'

The preposition $tɯ^{21}$ 'at, to' is derived from its verb form 'live, be at'. See its verbal use in (4.164a) and §4.2.2.2.2. When denoting 'at', it is found either pre-VP or post-VP. See (4.164b) for the pre-VP position of the preposition $tɯ^{21}$ 'at'. Examples (4.180) and (4.181) below illustrate the post-VP $tɯ^{21}$ 'at'. In (4.181), the locative phrase $tɯ^{21}$ $tɕɪŋ^{21}$ 'in front' is used to express a temporal concept, i.e. 'first'.

(4.180) ŋo⁵⁵ peŋ⁵⁵ lɛ²¹ **tɯ²¹** xuɔ²¹tɕia²¹tsʰoŋ²⁴ mo³³.
1PL divide land at Hejiachong_PLACE inside
'We divided the lands (taken away from landlords) in the Village of the Family He.'
我们在何家冲分地。
(*Encountering the ghost*, texts)

(4.181) ŋo³³ tsʰɿ³³ **tɯ²¹** tɕiŋ²¹.
1SG blow at   front
'I blow first.'
我先吹。
(*The north wind and the sun*, texts)

When denoting 'to', the preposition *tɯ²¹* is always post-VP. Note that the post-VP *tɯ²¹* may be ambiguous in certain contexts, that is, it can denote 'at' and alternatively 'to'. One must judge the meaning by analyzing the context in which it is used. The preposition *tɯ²¹* in (4.182) is not ambiguous and only denotes 'to', because the deictic verb *kuɛ³³* 'go' signifies that a movement along a path is involved. The marker of currently relevant state *o* also guarantees this dynamic scenario.

(4.182) ɕie²¹ tsɿ⁵⁵ŋa⁵⁵ tsɤ²¹ **tɯ²¹** la²¹ tsa³³to²¹ u³³ kuɛ²¹ o.
small boy   hide   to   big stone   back go   CRS
'The little boy hid behind the big stone.'
小男孩躲到大石头后面去了。

By contrast, the following example is ambiguous.

(4.183) je³³ kɤ²¹ tɯ²¹ ma²⁴.
3SG sit at/to there
'He is sitting there'
'(Let) him sit there.'
他坐在那儿/他坐到那儿。

4.5.7 The preposition *pie⁵⁵* 'to'

The verb *pie⁵⁵* 'toss' is used as a preposition marking an entity's locative destination and denoting 'to'. A prepositional phrase formed with *pie⁵⁵* is always post-VP. The sentence in (4.184) shows both the verbal use and the prepositional use of the word *pie⁵⁵* in an object marking construction. The object *tsa³³to²¹* 'stone' of the verb *pie⁵⁵* 'toss' is preposed before the verb and the prepositional phrase *pie⁵⁵ mo³³* 'to the inside (of the hole)' follows the verb.

(4.184)   tɯ³³   a³³   mɔ²¹   tsa³³to²¹   **pie⁵⁵**   **pie⁵⁵**   mo³³.
          then   OM   that   stone   toss   to   inside
          '(I) then threw the stone into (the hole).'
          就把石头扔到（洞）里。
          (*The big hole*, texts)

Apart from the meaning of tossing, *pie⁵⁵* can also denote 'place, put'.

(4.185)   a. a³³   sɔ⁵⁵nioŋ²¹   **pie⁵⁵**   tv̩²¹   tv̩³³.
              OM   key   put   table   upside
              'Put the key on the table.'
              把钥匙扔桌儿上。

          b. pi²¹   tɯ²¹   sv̩³³tv̩²¹   tv̩³³   **pie⁵⁵**-xɯ⁵⁵.
              pen   at   desk   upside   put-DUR
              'The key is placed on the table.'
              笔在桌上放着。

Two more examples of the prepositional use of *pie⁵⁵* are given below. Example (4.186) involves a self-agentive motion, i.e. the son of the magpie itself flies to the balcony, while example (4.187) shows a caused motion, as in (4.184).

(4.186)   kʰa²¹la²¹tɕie³³   jɯ²¹   sɿ⁵⁵   je²¹   tsɿ⁵⁵   pv̩²¹   **pie⁵⁵**   ta²¹sv̩³³   hɛ²¹
          magpie   again let   3SG   son   fly   to   squirrel family
          ɔ⁵⁵tsaŋ²¹   tv̩³³   kuɛ³³.
          balcony   upside go
          'The magpie asked her son to fly to the balcony of the squirrel's house.'
          喜鹊又让她孩子飞到松鼠家阳台上去。
          (*Three neighbors*, texts)

(4.187)   sɿ³³   niɔ²¹   **pie⁵⁵**   tʰa³³   tv̩³³
          urinate   urine   to   bed   upside
          'wet the bed'
          尿床

The verbs of tossing or throwing are not a common source for allative markers and are less reported in the relevant literature. However, a similar source is found in Mediaeval Chinese, i.e. *tóu* 投 'toss, throw', of which the meaning 'to' was derived in early Mediaeval Chinese (Jiang Shaoyu 2006, Song and Peyraube 2019) before it finally developed into a preposition marking temporal destination, denoting 'until'. This use is retained in some Sinitic languages, such as the Yinchuan and the Baoding dialects of Mandarin (Li and Zhang 1996: 202, Song and Bei 2019).

Late Mediaeval Chinese
(4.188) 湖边得二友，夜语投三更。（唐庚 [1070–1120]·湖上诗）
hú biān dé èr yǒu, yè yǔ **tóu** sān gēng.
lake side obtain two friend night speak to three hour
'(I) made two friends by the lake and (we'd been) chatting until midnight.'
(*Poem on the lake*, by Tang Geng [1070–1120])
(Cited from Song and Bei 2019: 106)

4.5.8 The preposition *sɿ^{55}* 'to'

Also denoting 'to', the preposition *sɿ^{55}* is used to mark the dative recipient, i.e. the indirect object in a ditransitive construction. It occurs in post-verbal position.

(4.189) ŋo^{33} a^{33} tɕiŋ^{21} la^{33} sy^{21} **sɿ^{55}** je^{21} kuɛ^{21} o.
1SG OM money all lose to 3SG go CRS
'I lost all my money to him.'
我把钱都输给他了。

(4.190) ɔ^{21} zɣ^{21} mi^{55} **sɿ^{55}** nɛ^{21} pa^{33}.
leave meal a.little to your.family grandfather
'Leave some food to your grandfather.'
留点饭给你爷爷。

The preposition *sɿ^{55}* is derived from its verb form 'give', which has already lost its verbality and cannot stand alone forming an independent predicate. Its verbal use can only be observed in the following syntactic environment, that is, in a purposive serial verb construction. The use of the purposive marker *yɯ^{21}* 'come' in (4.191) allows us to analyze the word *sɿ^{55}* as a verb.

(4.191) soŋ^{21} zɣ^{33} yɯ^{21} **sɿ^{55}** je^{33}.
send meal PURP give 3SG
'(She) brought the meal to give (it to) him.'
送饭来给他。

See Chapter 5 on ditransitive constructions for more details.

This section introduced Caijia prepositions and their constructions. As in the majority of Sinitic languages, the Caijia prepositions are all derived from verbs. Their verb forms are still very active, except for the preposition $sๅ^{55}$ 'to'. Yet even the verbality of this form can be traced. Although the prepositions and their counterpart verb forms co-exist side by side, the prepositions behave differently. They cannot serve as independent predicates or be marked by any aspectual markers, nor can they take any resultative complements. They have also undergone semantic changes. For example, as an allative preposition, the word pie^{55} does not denote 'toss' or 'throw' any more. The action of taking is bleached when the preposition a^{33} (< 'take') marks a direct object. Furthermore, pronoun dropping is heavily employed in Caijia, but, in stark contrast, prepositional objects cannot be dropped. Although it is hard to tell apart prepositions and their corresponding verb forms on the basis of morphology, the distributional features mentioned above differentiate one part of speech from the other. In fact, the phenomenon in which the grammaticalization of verbs is not accompanied by the coevolution of their forms can be regarded as an areal feature in East and Southeast Asian languages (Bisang 2004).

4.6 Conclusion

In this chapter, we have given a general presentation of Caijia verb phrases. By following the criteria for identifying verbs proposed by Chao (1968: 664–670) on the basis of Standard Mandarin, we illustrated the distributional features of Caijia verbs. We introduced two types of Caijia resultative complements: the general achievement and directional complements, and the Caijia extent and manner complementation formed by lu^{55}, both of which are commonly attested in East and Southeast Asian languages (Ke Lisi 2001, Enfield 2003, 2018, Wu Fuxiang 2001, 2002). Caijia adjectives function as verbs but they differ from canonical verbs in several ways. For example, some can modify bare nouns, quite a number of them possess the A-BB vivid forms, in which the -BB morphemes are sortal to a certain extent, and they can derive manner adverbs via reduplication. Another areal feature of East and Southeast Asian languages is also observed in Caijia, i.e. the quadrisyllabic idiomatic expressions (Sun Yan 2005, Vittrant and Watkins 2019). Most of these are predicative in nature, functioning both as predicates or manner adverbials.

Caijia possesses derivational adverbs and non-derivational adverbs. Most of the derivational adverbs are manner adverbs derived from adjectives, vivid adjectival A-BB forms, manner demonstratives, and quadrisyllabic idiomatic expressions. Most of the preverbal manner adverbs and adverbials can be marked by the adverbial marker $l\varepsilon^{55}$. The non-derivational adverbs include several semantic types: degree, time, and scope adverbs.

We also introduced the verbal classifiers of the language, an uncommon category in languages of the world, but quite a common category in East and Southeast Asian languages. Similar to those found in Sinitic languages, the Caijia verbal classifiers count either the number of occurrences or the duration of actions and events. Following Gerner's (2014) typology, we have proposed that the Caijia verbal classifiers can be divided into two types: instrument and mensural verbal classifiers. The auto-classifier type, i.e. the case of verb reduplication, attested in many East and Southeast Asian languages, is absent in Caijia. All the instrument classifiers and some of the mensural classifiers are sortal.

Finally, we introduced Caijia prepositions, all of which are derived from verbs but clearly behave differently.

Chapter 5
Ditransitive constructions

5.1 Definition and typology

Ditransitive constructions are canonical constructions with three arguments. This construction type involves physical transfer and consists of a ditransitive verb, i.e. a trivalent verb, an agent argument (A) which is the subject, a recipient-like argument (R) which is usually the indirect object, and a theme argument (T) as the direct object (Malchukov et al. 2010: 1). For example, in the sentence *Mary gave John a book*, 'Mary' is the A argument; 'John' is the R argument (the indirect object); and 'book' is the T argument, i.e. the direct object. Typical ditransitive verbs involving physical transfer include 'give', 'lend', 'sell', and 'return'. Malchukov et al. (2010: 2) also consider 'tell', 'show', 'offer', 'bequeath', and 'promise' as belonging to this class.

By extending the approach of alignment, i.e. how arguments (A[gent], S[ubject], and P[atient]) are encoded in intransitive and transitive constructions, Malchukov et al. (2010: 3–5) study how T and R are encoded in ditransitive constructions in the world's languages and observe the three major alignments shown in Table 5.1.

Table 5.1: Typology of ditransitive alignments.

I Indirective alignment <T = P ≠ R>
II Secundative alignment <T ≠ P = R>
III Neutral alignment <T = P = R>

In a ditransitive construction with indirective alignment, the T argument is coded the same way as the P argument of a transitive construction, while the R argument is coded differently. In a secundative ditransitive construction, the T argument is marked differently from the P argument, while the P and R arguments are marked the same. In a ditransitive construction with neutral alignment, both the T and R arguments are encoded in the same way.

Six types of ditransitive constructions are attested in contemporary Sinitic languages (Chappell and Peyraube 2007), as shown in Table 5.2.

Table 5.2: Ditransitive constructions in Sinitic languages.

I Double object [V + R + T]
II Inverse double object [V + T + R]
III Indirective [V + T + DAT + R]
IV V-give [V-give + R + T]
V Object marking [DOM + T + V + DAT + R]
VI Benefactive [BEN + R + V + T]

Caijia ditransitive constructions are generally similar to those found in Sinitic, but only three major types of ditransitive constructions are observed. They are:
i.   the double object construction [V + R + T];
ii. the indirective construction [V + (T) + DAT + R];
iii. the differential object marking constructions:
 Object marking: [OM + T + V + (DAT) + R],
 Cross-reference marking: [DCR + V + (DAT) + R], and
 Double marked: [OM + T + DCR + V + (DAT) + R].

Two additional constructions are also observed: the V-give construction and the comitative construction. These are less frequent than the three major types. In the following sections, Caijia ditransitive constructions will be presented in detail.

5.2 Caijia ditransitive constructions

As mentioned above, typical ditransitive verbs are trivalent taking two objects. Representative verbs of this type include 'give', 'sell', 'lend' etc., among which 'give' is the most typical. In Caijia, there is a series of verbs of giving which form ditransitive constructions, for instance, $peŋ^{55}$ 'offer', tsa^{33} 'lend', $mã^{33}$ 'sell', etc. However, these specific trivalent verbs are not always observed in the Caijia ditransitive constructions. Caijia is a language in which the most common ditransitive construction is, by virtue of a seeming paradox, formed by the verb a^{33} 'take' (see below). The verb $sɿ^{55}$ 'give' has already lost its full verbality and usually serves as the dative preposition 'to' or the causative verb 'let' (see Chapter 6). Many other verbs of taking can be observed in ditransitive constructions, such as $mã^{33}$ 'buy' and li^{21} 'pick'. Furthermore, apart from verbs of taking, verbs of doing such as $tɕie^{55}$ 'do, make', be^{33} 'burn', and $ʑe^{21}$ 'write', can also be observed in ditransitive constructions. According to Leclère (1978), verbs of giving are lexical datives, while both verbs of taking and doing are extended dative verbs. Unlike the first group, the latter two types do not obligatorily require R arguments. See

Table 5.3 below for a list of the three types of verbs that can occur in ditransitive constructions.

Table 5.3: Verbs in the Caijia ditransitive constructions.

Verbs of giving	Verbs of taking	Verbs of doing
peŋ⁵⁵ 'offer'	a³³ 'take'	tɕie⁵⁵ 'do, make'
mã³³ 'sell'	mã³³ 'buy'	be³³ 'burn'
tsa³³ 'lend'	tsa³³ 'borrow'	ʐe²¹ 'write'
pe³³ 'return'	tɔ²¹ 'steal'	ɔ²¹ 'keep'
dzɣ³³ 'return'	li²¹ 'pick'	
ã⁵⁵sɿ²¹ 'promise'	tl̩²¹ 'take, hold'	
...	...	...

Both Zhu Dexi (1979) and Bei Luobei (1986) have observed that certain correlations exist between verb types and ditransitive construction types in Chinese. A similar phenomenon is also observed in Caijia. In a nutshell, each of the three types of verbs listed in Table 5.3 can be found in differential object marking constructions. Additionally, verbs of giving can form either double object or indirective constructions, while verbs of taking and doing are only observed in indirective constructions. We will examine these constructions in the following subsections.

5.2.1 Double object construction [V + R + T]

In a Caijia double object construction, schematized as [V + R + T], neither the R argument nor the T argument is marked or flagged by a preposition, i.e. they are encoded the same way as the P argument in a canonical transitive construction. Only verbs of giving, i.e. dative verbs, can be found in this type. Due to the limited number of verbs of giving, this type of ditransitive construction is actually less frequent than the other two types. It is not observed in our spontaneous data. The examples given in this subsection all come from elicited data. Examples (5.1) and (5.2) show double object constructions respectively with the verb *peŋ⁵⁵* 'share, divide, offer' and the verb *ã⁵⁵sɿ²¹* 'promise'.

(5.1) ʑi²¹   peŋ⁵⁵   ŋo²¹   ʐe²¹   ʑi²¹   tɔ⁵⁵.
       mother   offer   1SG   flower   one   CLF
                V   R   T
       'My mother offered me a flower.'
       妈妈送了我一朵花。

(5.2) ŋo³³   ã⁵⁵sɿ²¹   je³³   sɿ²¹   ʑi²¹   tsoŋ⁵⁵.
      1SG   promise   3SG   thing   one   CLF
      'I promised him one thing.'
      我答应了他一件事。

In Caijia, a number of verbs may be both verbs of giving and verbs of depriving, such as *tsa³³* 'lend, borrow', *mã³³* 'buy, sell', *kɣ³³* 'rent to, rent from'. As shown below, the sentence in (5.3) can be either interpreted as 'My mother lent me fifty yuan' or 'My mother borrowed fifty yuan from me'. When *tsa³³* denotes 'borrow', the semantic role of the indirect object *ŋo³³* 'I' is not the recipient argument any more but, instead, is the source argument.

(5.3) ʑi²¹   tsa³³   ŋo³³   tɕiŋ²¹   ŋoŋ³³tsɿ³³   pʰe³³.
      mother   lend/borrow   1SG   money   fifty   CURRENCY.UNIT
      'My mother lent me fifty yuan.'
      'My mother borrowed fifty yuan from me.'
      妈妈借给了我 50 块钱。
      妈妈找我借了 50 块钱。

In most cases, one can determine the meaning of a giving-depriving verb by judging its context. The only unambiguous context is when the source argument is overtly marked by the source marker or ablative preposition *ta⁵⁵* 'from'. However, the source argument has to form part of a locative phrase (see Chapter 4 §4.5 for more the multifunctionality of the preposition *ta⁵⁵*). As shown below, the source argument is formed by *ŋuɛ²¹ ʑi²¹* 'my mother' and the word *ha⁵⁵* 'place'. Given that the preposition is multi-functional, if only the phrase *ŋuɛ²¹ ʑi²¹* 'my mother' serves as the oblique argument, the sentence may also be interpreted as 'I borrowed ten thousand yuan (from elsewhere) for my mother'.

(5.4) ŋo²¹   [ta⁵⁵   [ŋuɛ²¹   ʑi²¹   ha⁵⁵]]   tsa³³   tɕiŋ²¹
      1SG   from   my.family   mother   place   borrow   money
      ʑi²¹   uã²⁴   pʰe³³.
      one   ten.thousand   CURRENCY.UNITY
      'I borrowed ten thousand yuan from my mother (LIT: I borrowed ten thousand yuan from my mother's place).'
      我跟我妈借了一万块钱 (LIT: 我从我妈那儿借了一万块)。

5.2.2 Indirective construction [V + T + sɿ⁵⁵_DAT + R]

In an indirective construction, schematized as [V + T + sɿ⁵⁵_DAT + R], the R argument is marked by the dative preposition *sɿ⁵⁵*, which is derived from the verb 'give'. All three types of verbs, verbs of giving, taking, and doing, can be used in indirective constructions, which are frequently observed in spontaneous data. Let us consider some examples of different types of verbs, i.e. both dative and extended dative verbs.

Two examples with **verbs of giving** are given below. Compare also example (5.6) with example (5.1) in the double object construction.

(5.5) niɔ³³   kuɛ³³   **fa²¹**   tsɣ⁵⁵   sɿ⁵⁵   ŋa⁵⁵ …
      PROSP   go   distribute   medicine   to   child
      '(Then the doctor) will distribute the medicine to the children…'
      要发药给孩子们……
      (*Vaccination*, texts)

(5.6) ʑi²¹   **peŋ⁵⁵**   ʑe²¹   ʑi²¹   tɔ⁵⁵   sɿ⁵⁵   ŋo²¹.
      mother offer   flower one   CLF   to   1SG
      'My mother gave a flower to me.'
      妈妈送了一朵花给我。

The examples below show **verbs of taking**, *li²¹* 'pick' and *ti²¹* 'rob, snatch'. Unlike verbs of giving, verbs of taking do not usually require an R argument when used in a bivalent clause. By way of contrast, in an indirective construction with verbs of taking, two actions are sequentially involved, i.e. an action of taking followed by an action of giving. It is the use of the dative preposition *sɿ⁵⁵* 'to' that signifies the physical transfer. As shown in example (5.7), before the physical transfer, the pear must first be picked. Similarly, in example (5.8), the action of snatching a wife is followed by the action of giving.

(5.7) nɯ³³   **li²¹**   ʑi²¹   bo⁵⁵   sɿ⁵⁵   ŋo²¹   mɛ̃!
      2SG   pick   one   CLF   to   1SG   PRT
      'You pick me a pear!'
      你摘一个给我嘛！

(5.8) ŋo³³   **ti²¹**   ʑi³³   ni²¹   sɿ⁵⁵   nɯ³³.
      1SG   snatch   one   CLF   to   2SG
      'I'll snatch you a (wife).'
      我抢一个给你。

It is necessary to draw special attention to **the verb a^{33} 'take'** in Caijia, since it is typically used in the indirective construction to denote the meaning of 'give' instead of its source meaning 'take'. By contrast, the verb $sɿ^{55}$ 'give' has already lost its verbality in Caijia and usually serves as a causative verb or a dative preposition. Actually, the absence of the verb 'give' is attested in many Sinitic languages (Zhang Min 2009). One should be aware that the meaning 'take' of the verb a^{33} is still very productive in Caijia, as shown in (5.9).

(5.9)   **a⁵⁵**   tsaŋ³³   ɣɯ²¹...
       take   needle   come
       '(You) take a needle...'
       拿（根）针来......
       (*Vaccination*, texts)

The particular construction shown in the two examples below with the verb a^{33} 'take' denotes 'give'. It is not difficult to explain this phenomenon, since if one transfers an object, one needs to first grasp it in one's hand. The sentence in (5.10) can still be interpreted as '(They) first took medicine and then gave it to people'. By contrast, the sentence in (5.11) is elicited in a scenario where the man already has the flower in his hand. Therefore, no action of taking is involved.

(5.10)   **a⁵⁵**   tsʏ⁵⁵   mi⁵⁵   **sɿ⁵⁵**   ni³³
        take   medicine   a.little   to   3
        '(They) gave medicine to people.'
        给人药。
        (*Life in the old days*, texts)

(5.11)   mɔ²¹   pa³³tsɔ³³   ni³³   **a³³**   ʑe²¹   ʑi²¹   tɔ⁵⁵   **sɿ⁵⁵**   mɔ²¹   so⁵⁵bo²⁴   ni³³.
        that   man   CLF   take   flower   one   CLF   to   that   woman   CLF
        'That man gave that woman a flower.'
        那个男人给了那个女人一朵花。

As shown in (5.12), one cannot hold an abstract notion such as time in one's hand, which illustrates very well the loss of the meaning of 'take' in this construction. Example (5.13) is used when praying to God to express one's wish to have a child, but it cannot be interpreted as 'God takes a child and gives him or her to me'.

(5.12) nɯ³³ a³³ kʰɯ²¹ koŋ⁵⁵ sɿ⁵⁵ ŋo³³.
2SG take several day to 1SG
'You give me several days.'
你给我几天时间。

(5.13) jaŋ²¹tɕi²¹ kʰɪŋ⁵⁵pa⁵⁵ a³³ ŋa⁵⁵ ni²¹ sɿ⁵⁵ ŋo³³.
beg god take child CLF to 1SG
'I beg you, God, to give me a child.'
求老天爷给我一个孩子。

Even though the verb *a³³* denotes 'take', for most cases where it forms an indirective ditransitive construction, no action of taking is involved, as shown in the examples directly above. This makes the verb *a³³* distinct from other verbs of taking observed in this type of ditransitive construction (which involve the action of taking) as illustrated in (5.7) and (5.8).

Another function of the verb *a³³* 'take' is as an object marker in Caijia, as presented in §5.2.3 further below. Compare the two sentences with the morpheme *a³³* in (5.14). One can observe that these two sentences share the same surface structure. However, in (5.14a) *a³³* is treated as the verb 'take' and *sɿ⁵⁵* is regarded as the dative preposition, while in (5.14b) *a³³* is treated as the object marker and *peŋ⁵⁵* 'share, offer' is the verb.

(5.14) a. nɯ³³ **a³³** kʰɯ²¹ koŋ⁵⁵ **sɿ⁵⁵** ŋo³³.
2SG take several day to 1SG
  V T   PREP_DAT R
'You give me several days.'
你给我几天时间。

b. je²¹ pa⁵⁵ʑi³³ pɣ³³-tɣ³³ **a³³** lɛ²¹ ɣoŋ²¹ ɔ²¹-sui⁵⁵
3SG parents NEG-PFV OM land plough this-PL
       PREP_OM T
peŋ⁵⁵ je³³.
offer 3SG
V R
'His parents didn't give him the land and the plough.'
他父母没把地、犁这些分他。
(*The kind younger brother*, texts)

The primary reason why we do not treat (5.14a) as an object marking-ditransitive construction is that *sɿ⁵⁵* cannot function as a dative verb. If we were to treat it as an object marking-ditransitive construction, i.e. regarding $sɿ^{55}$ as a verb, it would mean that $kʰɯ^{21}$ $koŋ^{33}$ 'several days' would be the direct object of $sɿ^{55}$. However, neither the construction [$sɿ^{55}$ + R + T] nor the construction [$sɿ^{55}$ + T + $sɿ^{55}$ + R] exist in Caijia, as shown below. Furthermore, the phrase [$sɿ^{55}$ + R] cannot stand alone as an independent predicate in any context.

(5.15) a. *$sɿ^{55}$ ŋo^{33} kʰɯ^{21} koŋ^{33}.
give 1SG several day
(Attempted: 'Give me several days.')
给我几天（时间）。

b. *$sɿ^{55}$ kʰɯ^{21} koŋ^{55} $sɿ^{55}$ ŋo^{33}.
give several day to 1SG
(Attempted: 'Give several days to me.')
给我几天（时间）。

c. *$sɿ^{55}$ ŋo^{33} .
give 1SG
(Attempted: 'Give (it to) me.')
给我。

It is true that in most cases there is no straightforward way to distinguish the ditransitive construction with a^{33} from the object marking construction formed by a^{33}. Only some semantic restrictions for the object marking construction in certain cases can help to distinguish these two constructions. In an object marking construction, the marked object is usually definite. In a ditransitive construction with a^{33}, if the semantic condition permits, i.e. the T argument is definite, then the ditransitive construction can be transformed into an object marking construction, as illustrated in (5.16).

(5.16) a. je^{33} **a^{33}** mɔ^{21} xeŋ^{24} ji^{33} li^{21} **sɿ^{55}** ŋo^{33} o.
3SG take that apricot one bag to 1SG CRS
'He gave the bag of apricots to me.'
他给了我那袋子杏儿。

b. je^{33} **a^{33}** mɔ^{21} xeŋ^{24} ji^{33} li^{21} **a^{21}** sɿ^{55} ŋo^{33} o.
3SG OM that apricot one bag take to 1SG CRS
'He gave the bag of apricots to me.'
他把那袋子杏儿拿给我了。

It should be mentioned that once transformed into the object marking construction, the action of taking is underlined. This means that if the T argument is an abstract entity, the transformation may not be appropriate or even acceptable. Furthermore, if the T argument is indefinite, transforming the ditransitive construction with a^{33} into an object marking construction is ungrammatical. We take up the sentence in (5.14a) again. Given that the T argument in (5.14a) $k^hɯ^{21} koŋ^{55}$ 'several days' is apparently indefinite as well as abstract, it is ungrammatical to transform it into an object marking construction, as shown in (5.17).

(5.17) *nɯ³³ **a³³** kʰɯ²¹ koŋ⁵⁵ **a²¹** **sɿ⁵⁵** ŋo³³.
　　　 2SG　OM　several　day　take　to　1SG
　　　 (Attempted: 'You give me several days.')
　　　 *你把几天给我。

This corroborative evidence indicates that the construction [a³³ + T + sɿ⁵⁵ + R] should not be regarded as an object marking construction.

Like the verbs of taking, an indirective construction with **verbs of doing** also involves two sequential actions, the action of doing and the action of giving. In example (5.18), a spell is first written and is then given to the recipient. In example (5.19), paper money must be first burnt so that it can be transferred to the dead.

(5.18) nɯ³³ pɣ³³ sa²¹ 　 nε⁵⁵, ŋo³³ **ʐe²¹**, tsɯ³³kə²¹te³³,
　　　 2SG　NEG　believe　PRT　1SG　write　INTJ
　　　 sɿ⁵⁵ ji²¹ kʷɔ²¹ **sɿ⁵⁵** nɯ³³ e.
　　　 spell　one　CLF　to　2SG　PRT
　　　 'If you don't trust (me), I'll write, eh, you a spell.'
　　　 你不信的话，我写，这个的，一道符给你。
　　　 (*The zombie wife*, texts)

(5.19) … **be³³** kʰua²¹tie³³ sɿ⁵⁵ je³³.
　　　　　 burn　how.many　to　3SG
　　　 '(According to how much paper money should be burnt for each of them), then one should burn that much for him (or her).'
　　　 （应该烧多少给谁），（就）烧多少给他/她。
　　　 (*Funeral customs*, texts)

It is mentioned above that the dative marker or preposition $sɿ^{55}$ 'to' is derived from its lexical form denoting 'give', which is a very common lexical source for dative prepositions in Sinitic languages (Chappell and Peyraube 2007). Moreover, the grammaticalization of GIVE verbs to dative markers is widespread in East and

Southeast Asian languages and is treated as one of 23 parameters investigated for establishing a mainland Southeast Asia linguistic area by Vittrant and Watkins (2019) with respect to the 13 languages studied in their volume. See also Chapters 6 and 7 respectively for the causative and the passive uses of $sɿ^{55}$ in Caijia.

The verb $sɿ^{55}$ is only used in either the second verb position of a serial verb construction to denote 'give (to R)', or as a causative verb. In both cases its syntactic behavior is restricted. Yet $sɿ^{55}$ cannot stand alone to form an independent predicate, as shown above in (5.15). Compare the two serial verb constructions in example (5.20). In each of them the second VP is chained to the first VP via the purposive marker $yɯ^{21}$ (< 'come') in (5.20a) and $kuɛ^{33}$ < 'go' in (5.20b). The use of the purposive marker in a serial verb construction can clearly attest the verbal nature of the word $sɿ^{55}$.

(5.20) a. je³³   a³³   ɯ³³   ʑi³³   ɣa³³   yɯ²¹   **sɿ⁵⁵**   ŋo³³.
       3SG take clothes one   CLF   PURP   give   1SG
       V₁   O₁   PURP   V₂   O₂
       'He took an item of clothes to give (it) to me.'
       他拿了一件衣服来给我。

   b. ŋo³³   kʰɯ⁵⁵ ma²¹kʰa³³   kuɛ²¹   tʰɔ⁵⁵   **sɿ⁵⁵**.
      1SG   open   door   PURP   pour   water
      V₁   O₁   PURP   V₂   O₂
      'I opened the door to pour the water.'
      我开门去倒水。

Example (5.21) shows an ambiguous context for a serial verb construction in which the word $sɿ^{55}$ can be interpreted as either 'give' or 'let', while example (5.22) illustrates its causative use 'let'.

(5.21) ŋo²⁴   **a²¹**   sɿ⁵⁵bo²¹zʋ²¹   mi⁵⁵   **sɿ⁵⁵**   nɯ³³   zʋ²¹.
       1PL   take   meal.for.ghosts   a.little   give/let   2SG   eat
       'We give you some food to you to eat.'
       我们拿些水饭给你吃。
       (*Standing chopsticks on end*, texts)

(5.22) **sɿ⁵⁵**   ŋo²¹   tɯ²¹   mi⁵⁵.
       let   1SG   think   a.little
       'Let me have a think.'
       让我想一下。

It is also worth mentioning that the ditransitive construction with the verb a^{33} 'take' as in example (5.21), is also the environment which leads to derivation of the compound causative verb $a^{21}sɿ^{55}$ 'let' and the passive agent marker $a^{21}sɿ^{55}$ 'by', as exemplified in (5.23). See also Chapters 6 and 7.

(5.23) piɔ²⁴   a²¹sɿ⁵⁵   ni³³   ɕie²¹tsaŋ³³.
       NEG.IMP let/PASS   3   look.down.upon
       'Don't let others look down upon you.'
       'Don't be looked down upon by others.'
       别让被人小看。
       别被别人小看。

From examples (5.20) and (5.21), one can observe that the Caijia indirective ditransitive construction is very much related to the serial verb construction. Malchukov et al. (2010: 13–14) consider serial verb constructions a strategy for forming ditransitive constructions. They also point out that it is not easy to distinguish between serial verbs and adpositions. This is, to a certain extent, also the case in Caijia, especially in the indirective construction with verbs of taking and doing in certain contexts, i.e. purposive markers $ɣɯ^{21}$ 'come' or $kuɛ^{33}$ 'go' can be inserted before the phrase [$sɿ^{55}$ + R], as shown in (5.20) and (5.21). However, we have shown that the verbality of $sɿ^{55}$ has been lost. Furthermore, purposive markers cannot be used in indirective constructions formed by verbs of giving and they are not always acceptable in ditransitive contexts with verbs of taking and doing, as in (5.24).

(5.24) ŋo³³ tsa³³ ŋuɛ²¹   piɔ³³ (*ɣɯ²¹) sɿ⁵⁵ je³³.
       1SG   lend   my.family   hoe   PURP   to   3SG
       'I lent my hoe to him.'
       我借给了他我的锄头。

5.2.3 Differential object marking constructions

As in many Sinitic languages (Chappell and Peyraube 2007), ditransitive constructions in Caijia can also be realized via the three Caijia differential object marking constructions, in which it is always the T argument, i.e. the direct object, that is marked or signaled by the object or cross-reference marker a^{33} (< 'take'). By contrast, whether the R argument is marked by the dative marker $sɿ^{55}$ 'to' or not depends on which type of verb is used. The R arguments of verbs of giving are optionally marked by $sɿ^{55}$, while the R arguments of verbs of taking and doing

are obligatorily marked. The three differential object marking constructions are listed below.
i.   Object (= T) marking: [a$^{33}_{DOM}$ + T + V + (s1$^{55}_{DAT}$) + R]
ii. Cross-reference marking [a$^{33}_{DCR}$ + V + (s1$^{55}_{DAT}$) + R]
iii. Double marked [a$^{33}_{DOM}$ + T + a$^{33}_{DCR}$ + V + (s1$^{55}_{DAT}$) + R]

One should be aware that the differential object marking constructions are not exclusively used to form ditransitive constructions but can be used with many kinds of direct objects that undergo explicit changes of state. Therefore, verbs of giving, taking, and doing, i.e. both dative and extended dative verbs, can all be observed in these constructions. Next, we will simply illustrate some examples of these differential object marking constructions with dative and extended dative verbs. See Chapter 8 for more details on these three constructions.

In an **object marking construction**, marked by the object marker *a^{33}*, the T argument precedes the verb with the R argument staying in its canonical post-verbal position. See the object marking construction in example (5.25) with the verb of giving *tsa^{33}* 'lend'. The object marker marks the T argument *nɯ^{21} piɔ^{33}* 'your hoe' with no marking of the R argument, while example (5.26) shows the case with the extended dative verb *ɔ^{21}* 'leave' in which the post-verbal R argument *ŋo^{33}* 'I' is marked obligatorily by the dative preposition *s1^{55}*.

(5.25) **a^{55}**   nɯ^{21} piɔ^{33} **tsa^{33}**   ŋo^{21} tɕi^{21} ji^{33} xa^{24} lɛ^{33}.
        OM   2SG   hoe   lend   1SG   use   one   VCLF   PRT
        'Lend me your hoe to have a use.'
        把你的锄头借我用一下。

(5.26) ŋuɛ^{21} ja^{33} **a^{33}**   je^{33} mɔ^{21} loŋ^{21}koŋ^{33}
        my.family   grandmother   OM   3SG   that   bracelet
        ɔ^{21} *(s1^{55})   ŋo^{33} o.
        leave   to   1SG   CRS
        'My grandmother left that bracelet to me.'
        我奶奶把她那镯子留给我了。

The **cross-reference marking construction** is often observed when the direct object is topicalized or dropped (i.e. zero anaphora), which means that the T argument is not always present. However, the cross-reference marker *a^{33}*, which is considered as a verbal marker (see Chapter 8), can always signal that there is a T argument somewhere in the context of a given utterance. In example (5.27), the T argument of the ditransitive construction (5.27iii) is *je^{33} mɔ^{21} nioŋ^{21}ni^{24}* 'his daughter', is mentioned in (5.27ii). Given that the verb *to^{33}* 'marry' is an extended dative verb in Caijia, the R argument je^{21} $me^{21}tsɿ^{55}$ $hɛ^{21}$ 'the Li family' is obligatorily marked by the dative $sɿ^{55}$.

(5.27) i) mɔ²¹kɯ²⁴ ŋo⁵⁵ ma⁵⁵ ɣã²¹ u²¹tsʰo²¹ ta⁵⁵ fɛ⁵¹hɛ²¹ sɿ⁵⁵.
that.time 1PL there there.be people two family CONT
ii) uən³³tɕʰi²¹ ᴛ[je³³ **mɔ²¹ nioŋ²¹** ni²⁴].
be.for 3SG that daughter CLF
iii) tɕiŋ²¹ tʰɔ⁵⁵ nɛ⁵⁵ sɿ³³ **a³³** **tɔ²¹**
front moment PRT COP DCR marry
sɿ⁵⁵ ʀ[**je²¹ me²¹tsɿ⁵⁵ hɛ²¹**] xa⁵⁵.
to 3SG Li_FAMILY NAME family REP
'At that time, there were two families at our place. It was because of the daughter from the family of Zhang. At the very beginning, (the Zhang family agreed to) marry their daughter to the Li family.'
那时候，我们这儿有两家人。(是)为了他那个女儿。之前呢，说是把 (她) 嫁给他李家。
(*Two families*, texts)

Example (5.28), presented below, illustrates the case of a topicalized object. The T argument $mɔ^{21}$ $sɿ^{21}$ $ʑi^{33}$ $foŋ^{21}$ 'the letter' is positioned in the sentence initial position. Like example (5.27), the R argument je^{33} 'he' is in its post-verbal position and is marked by the dative marker $sɿ^{55}$.

(5.28) ᴛ[**mɔ²¹ sɿ²¹ ʑi³³ foŋ²¹**] ŋo³³ **a³³** t͡ɬ²¹ sɿ⁵⁵ ʀ[je³³] ha²¹ o.
that letter one CLF 1SG DCR hold to 3SG COMPL CRS
'As for the letter, I've given (it) to him.'
那封信，我已经带给他了。

In a **double marked construction**, both the object marker and the cross-reference marker are used, as shown below.

(5.29) je³³ pɣ³³ **a³³** ᴛ[je³³ nioŋ²¹] **a⁵⁵** tɔ²¹ sɿ⁵⁵ ʀ[ŋuɛ²¹] xa⁵⁵nɛ⁵⁵…
3SG NEG OM 3SG daughter DCR marry to my.family REP.PRT
'He didn't marry his daughter to our family (any more).'
他不把他女儿嫁给我家了……
(*Two families*, texts)

Next, a short introduction to the two minor ditransitive constructions will be given.

5.2.4 Two other minor constructions

In Caijia, two more minor ditransitive constructions are also observed, as listed below.
i.   V-sɿ⁵⁵ construction: [V-sɿ⁵⁵ + R + T]
ii. Comitative construction: [ta⁵⁵_COM + R + V + T]

When used as ditransitive constructions, these two constructions are marginal.

The **V-sɿ⁵⁵ construction** is equivalent to the Sinitic V-give construction, as shown in Table 5.2 above. Compared with the three ditransitive constructions presented above, this type is much less frequent. Only a few examples are found in our elicited data but no cases are observed at all in the spontaneous data. In this construction, the R argument precedes the T argument and only a very small number of verbs of giving can be used, such as *tsa³³* 'lend' or *mã³³* 'sell'. It was pointed out above that *tsa³³* and *mã³³* are ambiguous, denoting both verbs of giving and taking. However, in this construction, this type of verbs can only be interpreted as verbs of giving, as shown in (5.30).

(5.30) ʑi³³   **tsa²¹ sɿ⁵⁵**   ᴿ[ŋo²¹]   ᴛ[tɕiŋ²¹   ŋoŋ³³tsɿ³³   pʰe³³].
        mother lend give   1SG   money   fifty   UNIT(for money)
        'My mother lent me fifty yuan.'
        妈妈借给我 50 块钱。

Example (5.31) shows that using the extended dative verb *to³³* 'marry' in the V-sɿ⁵⁵ construction is ungrammatical.

(5.31) *ŋo³³   to²¹   sɿ⁵⁵   je³³   ŋo³³   ɔ²¹   nioŋ²⁴   ni³³.
        1SG   marry   give/to 3SG   1SG   this   daughter   CLF
        (Attempted: 'I married my daughter to him').
        我把我的女儿嫁给他了。

The V-sɿ⁵⁵ construction raises some challenging theoretical issues. It is indeed hard to determine the nature of the word *sɿ⁵⁵* 'give, to', which can either be treated as a resultative complement or a dative preposition marking the R argument. If it is treated as a resultative complement, the compound V-sɿ⁵⁵ functions as a verb and this construction would thus be of neutral alignment with both the T and R arguments unmarked. By contrast, if the word *sɿ⁵⁵* is regarded as a preposition, this construction is of indirective alignment with the R argument marked. However, neither of these two analyses can be justified.

Benefactive and ditransitive constructions are not easily distinguished from each other (Malchukov et al. 2010: 2). For example, the sentence *John bought Mary a present* can either be interpreted as *John bought a present to (give to) Mary* or *John bought a present for Mary*. Many languages use benefactive constructions to express ditransitive meanings (Kittilä 2005) and this is exactly the case in certain Sinitic languages (Chappell and Peyraube 2007, Chin 2009: Chapter 3, 2011).

In Caijia, the benefactive preposition ta^{55} 'for' is observed with verbs of saying, or *verba dicendi*, which are also considered as ditransitive verbs by Malchukov et al. (2010), with which it forms ditransitive constructions. Given that the benefactive ta^{55} is probably derived from the comitative use of ta^{55} (Lü Shanshan 2021, see also §4.5.1 for more on the multi-functionality of ta^{55}), it is more appropriate to analyze ta^{55} as a comitative preposition when it is used with *verba dicendi*. See the sentences with the verb xa^{33} 'say, tell' in examples (5.32) and (5.33a). The R arguments in both of these two sentences are marked by the comitative preposition ta^{55} 'with' (< 'follow'). The verb xa^{33} 'say, tell' usually cannot be used in the double object or indirective construction. It can only collocate with the word $sɿ^{55}$ in a serial verb construction, as shown in (5.33b), where the omission of the verb $tʰi^{55}$ 'listen' is ungrammatical.

(5.32) ŋo²¹ **ta⁵⁵** nɯ²¹ xa²¹ sɿ²¹ ŋoŋ³³, nɯ³³ piɔ²⁴ **ta⁵⁵** je²¹ **xa²¹**.
1SG with 2SG say REL speech 2SG NEG.IMP with 3SG say
'Don't tell him what I told you.'
我跟你说的话你别跟他说。

(5.33) a. ŋuɛ²¹ pa³³ **ta⁵⁵** ŋo²¹ xa³³ to²¹pʰa³³.
my.family grandfather with 1SG say old.days
'My grandfather told me stories.'
我爷爷给我讲故事。

b. ŋuɛ²¹ pa³³ xa³³ to²¹pʰa³³ **sɿ⁵⁵** ŋo²¹ *(**tʰi⁵⁵**).
my.family grandfather say old.days to/let 1SG listen
'My grandfather told me stories to listen to.'
我爷爷讲故事给我听

One more example is given below. The verb $dzɣ^{33}$ 'return' is a verb of giving. When forming a ditransitive construction, it is either used in a double object construction or an indirective construction. The phrase $dzɣ^{21}$ $me^{21}tsɿ^{33}$ 'return an apology' is used to denote 'apologize'. Given that apologizing is often performed verbally, the phrase $dzɣ^{21}$ $me^{21}tsɿ^{33}$ can also be regarded as a VP of saying, just as the verb xa^{33} 'say, tell'.

(5.34) je²¹ **ta⁵⁵** ŋo²¹ **tsɣ²¹** me²¹tsɿ³³ ha⁵⁵ o.
        3SG   with   1SG   return   apology   COMPL CRS
        'He offered his apology to me.'
        他跟我道歉了。

In fact, pure benefactive contexts cannot be interpreted as ditransitive constructions. The sentence in (5.35a-i) is a case of a benefactive construction used in a context without any physical transfer involved. This information can be immediately obtained from the following sentence in (5.35a-ii), in which both the benefactive *ta⁵⁵* and the dative *sɿ⁵⁵* are included. By way of contrast, to express ditransitive, with the same VP *ti³³ sa²¹lo²⁴ po⁵⁵* 'stitch a sachet', one must use the indirective construction [V + T + sɿ⁵⁵ + R], as shown in (5.35b).

(5.35) a. i) ŋo²¹ **ta⁵⁵** je³³ ti³³   sa²¹lo²⁴ po⁵⁵.
                1SG   for   3SG   stitch   sachet   CLF
           ii) nɯ²¹ **ta⁵⁵** ŋo³³ tʂ̍²¹   **sɿ⁵⁵** je³³ niɔ²¹ tɣ³³   mo³³?
                2SG   for   1SG   take.along to   3SG   want   obtain Q
               'I made a sachet for her. Could you please bring it to her for me?'
               我给她缝了一个香包。你帮我带给她好吗？

       b. ŋo³³ ti³³   sa²¹lo²⁴ po⁵⁵ sɿ⁵⁵ je³³.
           1SG   stitch sachet   CLF   to   3SG
           'I made her a sachet.'
           我缝了一个香包给她。

5.3 Conclusion

In this chapter, we have presented three major ditransitive constructions in Caijia. Only dative verbs, i.e. verbs of giving, can be observed in the double object construction, while both dative and extended dative verbs can be observed in the indirective and differential object marking constructions, as summarized in Table 5.4.

Table 5.4: Ditransitives vs. verb types.

	Ditransitives	GIVE	TAKE	DO	Marked argument
i.	Double object	√			∅
ii.	Indirective	√	√	√	R
iii.	Differential object	√	√	√	T or T, R

In a double object construction, neither the T argument nor the R argument is marked, while it is the R argument that is marked by $s1^{55}$ in an indirective ditransitive construction. In a differential object marking construction, the T argument is always marked or signaled by the object/cross-reference marker a^{33}, whereas the marking on the R argument entirely depends on the type of verb. We reiterate here that differential object marking constructions are not exclusively used with ditransitives.

We have also presented two minor ditransitive constructions in Caijia: the V-$s1^{55}$ construction and the comitative construction. The V-$s1^{55}$ construction is restricted to use with a very limited number of dative verbs. Only with verbs of saying does the comitative construction with ta^{55} code ditransitive semantics. By way of contrast, the benefactive formed by ta^{55}, and the ditransitive are clearly distinct from each other in terms of constructional meaning.

Chapter 6
Analytic causative constructions

6.1 Introduction

A causative construction is a complex situation involving two events, i.e. the causing event and the caused event (Shibatani 1976: 1, Song 2001: 256–259) or the cause and its effect (Comrie 1989: 165). It is characterized by an additional argument, the causer (Dixon 2000: 30, Creissels 2006b: 59). Analytic or periphrastic causatives are one of the three major forms of causatives, while the others are morphological (e.g. by affixing, tone change, reduplication etc. [Dixon 2000]) and lexical causatives (e.g. *eat* vs. *feed*, *kill* vs. *die* in English). "The prototypical case of the analytic causative is where there are separate predicates expressing the notion of causation and the predicate of the effect" (Comrie 1989: 167). In other words, an analytic causative construction is biclausal, as pointed out by Song (2013), for example, *John made me go there* in English. A language may use more than one causative construction and how languages structure causatives may be related with different semantic parameters (Dixon 2000), for example, direct versus indirect causation.

In Sinitic languages, analytic causatives are derived from pivot constructions, $NP_{CAUSER} + V_1 + NP_{CAUSEE} + V_2$, in which the verbs in the V_1 position develop into causative verbs (Chappell and Peyraube 2006, see also Thepkanjana and Uehara [2008: 631–632] for a similar construction with 'give' in Thai). Major sources for the causative verbs in Sinitic are (Chappell 2015a):

I.   Speech act verbs
II. do, put
III. give
IV. wait
V.   contact

Some of these have grammaticalized into passive agent markers (Chappell 2015b: 32). Among these, the verbs of 'giving' are cross-linguistically attested as a common source for causatives verbs (Newman 1996: 171–200, Heine and Kuteva 2002: 152) and can be treated as an areal feature in East and Southeast Asian languages on the basis of the linguistic data available (Matisoff 1991, Heine and Kuteva 2002: 152, Lord et al. 2002, Yap and Iwasaki 2003, Chappell and Peyraube 2006, Chin 2011, Chappell 2015b, Lai 2015, Vittrant and Watkins 2019, inter alia).

Caijia analytic causative constructions are not only similar to Sinitic ones from a syntactic perspective, but in terms of the sources of causative verbs. For example, two verbs of doing can be used as causative verbs, while two causative verbs used to form Caijia analytic causative constructions are related with the meaning of giving. All of these will be discussed in the following sections.

6.2 Overview of Caijia causation

In Caijia, causation can be expressed in several ways.

First, a set of verbs exists that is lexically causative by nature in entailing a result state. Take for example ɕi³³ 'kill' vesus niaŋ³³ 'die' and the labile verb ɖaŋ³³ 'stand', which behaves just like its English counterpart 'stand', possessing both non-causative and causative meanings. The verb ɖaŋ³³ in ɖaŋ²¹-kʰɯ⁵⁵yɯ²¹ 'LIT: stand-rise.come ~ stand up' is non-causative, while it is causative in ɖaŋ³³ tʲ²¹ 'stand the chopsticks on end'.

Second, Caijia also uses a verb compounding strategy in the form of [V₁-V₂], i.e. a verb with its resultative complement (Chapter 4 §4.2.3), to realize causation. This type of causative is more compact than the biclausal analytic causative but less compact than the any morphological causative. This is due to the fact that though the phrase [V₁-V₂] is undoubtedly a complex VP, it nonetheless serves as a simple predicate. This type is equivalent to the causative of a serial verb construction proposed by Dixon (2000: 34–35). It can be further divided into two subtypes: (i) the one without a causative verb and (ii) the one with a causative verb occupying the V₁ position, which will be illustrated below.

In the first type, two verbs are compounded together forming a complex VP equivalent to a transitive verb with causative meaning. In (6.1), the phrase kʰui²¹-sʔ⁵⁵ is composed of the adjective kʰui²¹ 'be tired' in the V₁ position, which is not a causative verb, and the intransitive verb sʔ⁵⁵ 'die' in the V₂ position. One can observe immediately that the phrase kʰui²¹-sʔ⁵⁵, denoting 'exhaust', functions as a transitive verb with je³³ 'it' as its direct object. Change of valency is thus involved in the process of compounding.

(6.1) pɣ²¹   ɔ²¹-sʔ⁵⁵   tie⁵⁵   sʔ²¹   nia²¹nia²¹   tɯ²¹   nɯ³³   mɔ²¹
      put   this-so   many   MOD   thing   to   2SG   that
      mɛ²¹   tʲ³³,   nɯ³³   niɔ²¹   **kʰui²¹-sʔ⁵⁵**   je³³   la²¹!
      horse   upside   2SG   want   be.tired-die   3SG   PRT
      '(You) put so many things on your horse. You want to exhaust it?'
      放这么多东西在你那马上，你想累死它啊！

In the second type, the V₁ position of the VP [V₁-V₂] is occupied by a causative verb rendering causative meaning to the verb in the V₂ position. Two verbs can often be observed in the V₁ position, *tɕie⁵⁵* 'do' or *no²¹* 'rub, do', with *tɕie⁵⁵* being less productive than *no²¹*. In the V₂ position, it is either an intransitive verb or a verb of movement. Note that verbs of movement in Caijia function as transitive verbs, as do those in Standard Mandarin, taking place words or phrases denoting location as their direct objects. Example (6.2) shows the case of *tɕie⁵⁵* compounded with the verb of movement *ɣa³³* 'fall' as its resultative complement, while example (6.3) illustrates the case of *no²¹*, compounded with the verb of movement *tɕiu⁵⁵* 'arrive' and the intransitive verb *tʰa³³* 'be worn out'.

(6.2) ŋo³³ a²¹ sɔ⁵⁵nioŋ²¹ **tɕie⁵⁵-ɣa³³** o.
 1SG OM key do-fall CRS
 'I lost the key.'
 我把钥匙弄丢了。

(6.3) ɔ²¹ sı²¹ ji³³ foŋ²¹ ɣɯ²¹ tɕiŋ²¹ xıŋ⁵⁵ o. [...] ji²¹ kʰa⁵⁵
 this letter one CLF come early very CRS one place
 no²¹-tɕiu⁵⁵ ji²¹ kʰa⁵⁵ nɛ⁵⁵, a³³ **no²¹-tʰa³³** kuɛ²¹ o.
 rub-arrive one place PRT DCR rub-be.worn.out go CRS
 'This letter arrived quite a while ago. It's transferred from one place to the other, so that it is quite worn out.'
 这封信很早就到了。[...] 一处弄到一处，把（它）弄烂了。

Third, differential object marking constructions in Caijia can also express causative meanings. This mechanism works particularly for adjectives, rendering them as causative meanings as shown in (6.4). The adjective *kʰui²¹* 'be tired' does not take an object, functioning just like an intransitive verb in a non-differential object marking construction, as shown in (6.4b). Despite the same semantic role of *ŋo³³* '1SG', experiencer, in both (6.4a) and (6.4b), *ŋo³³* '1SG' is an overtly marked causee-object in (6.4a), as bracketed, but a subject in (6.4b). However, the italicized sentence in (6.4a) is still a mono-clausal construction, which is quite different from the canonical analytic causatives mentioned above. Furthermore, one should note that verbs or VPs which are causative by nature remain causative in differential object marking constructions (see also Chapter 8).

(6.4) a. ŋo³³   pɣ³³   nuɯ³³   ɣa²¹   ɔ²¹-sı⁵⁵ ti⁵⁵ sı²¹ hɔ⁵⁵,
         1SG   carry.on.the.back 2SG   walk   this-so   far   MOD   road
         a⁵⁵   CAUSEE-O[ŋo²¹]   kʰui²¹ xıŋ⁵⁵ o.
         OM   1SG   be.tired very CRS
         'I carried you on my back and walked for such a long way. (This/you) made me very tired.'
         我背你走这么远的路，把我累得不行。

     b. ŋo⁵⁵   kʰui²¹   xıŋ⁵⁵   o.
        1SG   be.tired very   CRS
        'I'm very tired.'
        我累得很。

Finally, three canonical analytic causative constructions are observed in Caijia, which are the focus of this chapter. More details are given in §6.3 below.

6.3 Caijia analytic causative constructions

The three analytic causative constructions can be divided into two types on the basis of their syntactic features: Type I Extent complement construction and Type II Pivot-causee constructions. These three constructions are summarized and schematized in Table 6.1.

Table 6.1: Analytic causative constructions in Caijia.

Type I	**Extent complement**
	$(NP_1) + \underbrace{V_1 + COMP_{lɯ⁵⁵}}_{CAUSE} + \underbrace{(NP_2) + VP_2}_{EFFECT}$
Type II	**Pivot-causee**
IIa.	$(NP_1) + \underbrace{V_{CAUS \sim sı⁵⁵/a²¹sı⁵⁵}}_{CAUSE} + \underbrace{NP_2 + VP_2}_{EFFECT}$
IIb.	$\underbrace{[(NP_1) + VP_1]}_{CAUSE} + sı⁵⁵ + \underbrace{[NP_2 + VP_2]}_{EFFECT}$

In all of these three constructions, the cause precedes the effect, and they can thus be considered sequential analytic causatives, and as such, a subtype of analytic causative (Song 2013). The major differences between the Type I and Type II constructions are that (i) the Type I construction does not require a causative verb, while the presence of a causative verb is obligatory in the two constructions of Type II; (ii) the effect clause in Type I is the complement of the verb in the causing event, instead of being the core argument (i.e. subject or object), while the causee NP is the object of the causative verb as well as being the subject of the verb in the effect event in the both constructions of Type II. In other words, the causee NP is a pivot NP.

6.3.1 Type I extent complement causative

An extent complement causative construction is schematized as below.

$$(NP_1) + \underline{V_1} + \quad COMP_{lui^{55}} + \underline{(NP_2)} + VP_2$$
$$\quad\quad\text{CAUSE} \quad\quad\quad\quad\quad \text{EFFECT}$$

The effect clause is introduced by the complementizer lui^{55} (see also Chapter 4 §4.2.4 on extent and manner complementation). As shown in (6.5), the effect clause $tsa^{21}\,la^{21}\,xa^{21}\,ɬo^{55}\,o$ 'the meat became maggoty' is the non-core complement of the adjective pe^{21} 'be hot', and acts as the extent complement of pe^{21}, denoting the consequences of the hot weather, that is, the extent to which a certain temperature has been reached.

(6.5) ɔ²¹ kʰɯŋ⁵⁵ ᵥₚ[**pe²¹** [lɯ⁵⁵ ᵥₚ[tsa²¹ la²¹ xa²¹ ɬo⁵⁵ o]]].
this sky   be.hot VCOMP   meat even be.born maggot CRS
                     CAUSE   EFFECT
'The weather is so hot that the meat became maggoty.'
这天热得肉都生蛆了。

This is quite different from complement clauses of core arguments. For example, the complement clauses that can serve as objects of verbs like *know, hear, think* in English, as in the clause *she's right*, is the object of the verb 'think' in the sentence *I think she's right*.

The verbs that can enter into the V_1 position of Type I can be both transitive and intransitive (including adjectives). It is unnecessary to point out that intransitive verbs and adjectives do not take object arguments. The adjective pe^{21} 'be hot' in example (6.5) is an adjective, while $tsʰɔ^{55}$ 'disturb (by making noise)' in example (6.6) is a transitive verb.

(6.6) ɣã²¹   ŋa⁵⁵   kʰɯ³³   ni²¹   tɯ²¹   ua³³lɛ²¹   na²¹xaŋ²¹na²¹sɔ²¹   lɛ⁵⁵,
      there.be child   several CLF   at   outside   fight.for.fun   CONT
      tsʰɔ⁵⁵   lɯ⁵⁵   ŋo³³   tsɿ²¹ni²¹-pɣ³³-kuɛ²¹.
      disturb.(by making noise)   VCOMP 1SG   sleep-NEG-go
      'There were several kids outside fighting for fun. (They) made so much
      noise that I couldn't fall asleep.'
      有几个孩子在外面打打闹闹的，吵得我睡不着。

The causative verb *no²¹* of very general meaning 'do' can also be used in this construction under the condition that the causing event or action has been mentioned earlier in the context of a given utterance. Note that the causative verbs *sɿ⁵⁵* 'let' and *a²¹sɿ⁵⁵* 'let' cannot be used in the Type I construction. In (6.7), the causing event is the bracketed clause *ɔ²¹ tsɔ²⁴ tsʰo⁵⁵ xɪŋ⁵⁵* '(I've) been very busy during these past days', preceding the causative clause. Instead of using the adjective *tsʰo⁵⁵* 'be busy', which is the actual causative action, as the head verb of the causative clause, i.e. V₁, the verb *no²¹* is used, anaphorically referring to the preceding CAUSE-clause in a more general way. It is the case that *tsʰo⁵⁵* can always be used to replace *no²¹* as in (6.7).

(6.7) [ɔ²¹   tsɔ²⁴   tsʰo⁵⁵   xɪŋ⁵⁵], **no²¹**   lɯ⁵⁵   ŋo³³   zɣ²¹   la²¹
      this   while   be.busy   very   make   VCOMP   1SG   eat   even
      zɣ²¹-pɣ³³-ɪn²¹.
      eat-NEG-catch.up
      '(I've) been so busy during these past days that I even don't have time to eat.'
      这阵子太忙，弄得我饭都来不及吃。

On the basis of the use of *no²¹* in the Type I construction, we can discern that the causative verb *no²¹* 'rub, do' can be used to replace *tsʰo⁵⁵* 'disturb (by making noise)' in (6.6), but it cannot be used to replace the adjective *pe²¹* 'be hot' in (6.5).

The examples above all illustrate the case in which the causee NP, i.e. NP₂, is present. However, it can be observed to be absent as well. The causee NP in (6.8) is *ŋo³³* 'I' and the causer and the causee is actually co-referential. The causee NP in (6.9) can be either 'I', the speaker, or 'people' in general.

(6.8) ŋo³³   ã²¹sɿ⁵⁵kʰa³³   soŋ²¹   lɯ⁵⁵   la²¹   ã²¹   sɿ⁵⁵   po³³   to³³.
      1SG   throat   hurt   VCOMP   even   drink   water   NEG   can
      'My throat hurts so much that I can't even drink.'
      我喉咙疼得都喝不了水。

(6.9) mɔ²¹ li²¹ kɛ²¹ la²¹to⁵⁵ lɯ⁵⁵ niɔ³³ mã²¹ po³³ to³³ o.
that pig price old VCOMP PROSP buy NEG can CRS
'The price of pork is so high that (I/people) won't afford it.'
那猪肉价贵得要买不起了。

The type presented in this section is labelled as the 'extent complement causative', because a verb complement overtly marked by *lɯ⁵⁵* can be semantically treated as a complement of extent or degree.⁷ It renders an additional meaning to its preceding verb, that is, what extent is reached, or what degree is attained by the action of the verb in terms of outcomes or consequences. As shown in (6.10a), *la²¹ xɪŋ⁵⁵* 'very heavily' indicates the extent of the action 'raining'. In fact, the effect complement clause in this type of causative is equivalent to the extent complement described in detail in Chapter 4 §4.2.4, since this construction can be interpreted as 'an action attains to a certain extent or degree so as to bring about certain consequences'. Therefore, (6.10b) can be interpreted as 'It rains to the extent that I'm upset'. The examples (6.5)-(6.9) can all be interpreted in the same way, i.e. effect equals extent.

(6.10) a. ɔ²¹ zɿ⁵⁵ ɣɯ²¹ **lɯ⁵⁵** la²¹ xɪŋ⁵⁵.
this rain come VCOMP big very
'It's raining heavily.'
这雨下得大得很。

b. ɔ²¹ zɿ⁵⁵ ɣɯ²¹ **lɯ⁵⁵** ŋo³³ saŋ³³ mo³³ nia²¹ xɪŋ⁵⁵.
this rain come VCOMP 1SG heart inside be.upset very
'The rain makes me very upset.'
这雨下得我心烦。

Caijia is not the only language using a verb complement construction to express causation. This construction resembles very much the complement construction with *dé* 得 [tə²⁴] (< 'obtain') in Standard Mandarin, which yields a causative reading and is also treated as a complement of extent by Chao (1968: 354–355).

(6.11) 你老叫，叫得我心慌。
nǐ lǎo jiào, jiào **de** wǒ xīn huāng.
2SG always call call VCOMP 1SG heart nervous
'You keep calling, it makes me nervous.' (Chao1968: 355, transcription in Pinyin and glossing are added by the author)

---

7 This construction sometimes also yields potential reading. See Chapter 11.

Similarly, Chao uses the pattern of 'so. . . as to' in English to interpret the complement of extent in Standard Mandarin. It is true that the complement constructions equivalent to the Caijia *luɯ⁵⁵* construction and the Standard Mandarin *dé* construction are widely attested in Sinitic languages (Ke Lisi 2001, Wu Fuxiang 2001, 2002), but that constructions have barely been studied from the perspective of causation. They are commonly treated as complements of state (Zhu Dexi 1982: 133–137, Ke Lisi 2001, Wu Fuxiang 2001, inter alia).

6.3.2 Type I pivot-causee causatives

In a nutshell, the two pivot-causee constructions are actually serial verb constructions. In Type IIa, the causer NP is the subject of the causative verb, while the causative verb in Type IIb serves rather like a linker connecting the cause clause and the effect clause. In Type IIb, it is understood that the causer is either the subject NP or the whole causing clause. Related to verbs of 'giving', both the causative verbs *sɿ⁵⁵* and *a²¹sɿ⁵⁵* can be used in the Type IIa construction, with *a²¹sɿ⁵⁵* being only restricted to transitive verbs under certain conditions; while only *sɿ⁵⁵* can be used in the Type IIb construction. This section presents the sources of the two causative verbs and the two constructions along with a description of the contrast of the two causative verbs.

6.3.2.1 Source constructions and the two causative verbs
In a Caijia serial verb construction, the chained VPs can share a common subject as illustrated in (6.12), or else the object of the first verb has a pivotal role serving simultaneously as the subject of the immediately following verb, as illustrated in (6.13).

(6.12) je³³ ᵥₚ₁[tsa²¹ ti²¹] ᵥₚ₂[se⁵⁵ tsʰɔ⁵⁵] kuɛ²¹ o.
3SG   go.up hill   cut grass   go   CRS
'He went up the hill to cut grass.'
他上山割草去了。

(6.13) je³³ [pγ³³ niɔ³³] [ŋo³³ tʰo²¹ mɛ³³] o.
3SG   NEG want   1SG   pull horse   CRS
'He doesn't want me to pull the horse (any more).'
他不要我拖马了。

It is from the second type that the pivot-causee causatives are derived. There is a series of verbs that can occupy the first verb position taking pivotal objects, for example, nio^{33} 'want'([6.13]), $jaŋ^{21}tɕi^{21}$ 'beg', $na^{33}je^{21}$ 'send (sb. on an errand)'(see [6.27] below), go^{33} 'look for', $xaŋ^{33}$ 'call, yell', $sı^{55}$ 'make, let', $a^{21}sı^{55}$ 'make, let'. Among these verbs, only $sı^{55}$ 'give, make, let' and $a^{21}sı^{55}$ 'give, make, let' develop into causative verbs. Compared with others verbs listed above, both of these verbs possess an abstract causative meaning and are related to the meaning of giving. We have mentioned earlier that verbs of giving are a cross-linguistically attested source of causative verbs. This is not coincidental, since the meaning of giving has connections with causation and enablement (Newman 1996: 171).

The **causative verb $sı^{55}$** is derived from the verb 'give'. However, its lexical use as 'give' is no longer active as it is only attested in serial verb constructions occupying the second verb position.[8] In the following example, the purposive marker $yɯ^{21}$ (< 'come') is used to link the two clauses, which enables us to determine that $sı^{55}$ is a verb. Making use of purposive markers is a common diagnostic test to differentiate a verb from a preposition in a serial verb construction in Chinese (Sun Chaofen 1996: 69–73) and also suits the Caijia cases.

(6.14) $tʰıŋ^{21}koŋ^{55}$ $ŋo^{33}$ li^{21} $xɯ^{55}tsı^{55}$ sui^{55} $yɯ^{21}$ **$sı^{55}$** $nɯ^{33}$.
tomorrow   1SG   pick   pear   some   PURP   give   2SG
'I'll pick some pears and give (them) to you.'
我明天摘些梨来给你。

The environment in which $sı^{55}$ likely developed into a causative verb from the lexical 'give' is shown in (6.15). The third person pronoun je^{33} in the boldface clause in (6.15ii) is the recipient of the verb 'give' as well as the agent of the verb 'drink', which follows in the verb chain. This is exactly the context in which a causative meaning can be reanalyzed. The verb $sı^{55}$ in this case can be either interpreted as 'give' or 'let'.

(6.15) i) $nɯ^{33}$ pio^{24} a^{33} $mı̃^{21}kʰɔ^{55}$ $sı^{55}$ je^{21}.
2SG   NEG.IMP   take   face   to   3SG

---

[8] The verb with the meaning of 'give' in Caijia cannot be used as the main verb of a canonical ditransitive construction of giving. Instead, the pattern 'take sth. to sb.' with the verb a^{33} 'take' is used to form the canonical Caijia ditransitive construction denoting giving, as show in (6.15). See also Chapter 5 on ditransitive constructions.

ii) niɔ³³ **a²¹** **pe⁵⁵sɔ²¹tʰɤ⁵⁵** **mi⁵⁵ sɿ⁵⁵** **je²¹ ã³³**, je³³
    must   take   hot.pepper.soup   little give/let   3SG   drink 3SG
    tsʰɛ²¹ tiu³³u³³.
    only   know
'Don't show him your respect (LIT: don't give him face). He'll understand only if you make him suffer (LIT: 'give him some hot pepper soup to let him to drink' or 'let him drink some hot pepper soup')'
你别给他脸。要拿点辣椒汤给/让他喝，他才知道。

The source of the other **causative verb** *a²¹sɿ⁵⁵* is more complicated than that of *sɿ⁵⁵*, but still related to the meaning 'give'. The verb *a²¹sɿ⁵⁵* is a compound form of two morphemes: *a³³* 'take' and *sɿ⁵⁵* 'give, to'. The source construction for *a²¹sɿ⁵⁵* is exactly the same as that of *sɿ⁵⁵*, as in (6.15ii), except that one more step is needed for *a²¹sɿ⁵⁵* to become a causative verb, i.e. the fusion of the two morphemes. The important triggering factor is the heavy use of pro-drop in Caijia. To be specific, it is the object of the verb *a³³* that is omitted in certain appropriate contexts, which allows *a³³* and *sɿ⁵⁵* to be syntactically adjacent. Consider the examples below. Example (6.16a) provides the syntactic context from which it is possible for *a²¹ sɿ⁵⁵* 'take to' to be reanalyzed as one single word denoting 'give'. One can treat either *a²¹ sɿ⁵⁵* as two individual morphemes with the object of *a³³* dropped, or treat *a²¹sɿ⁵⁵* as one word denoting 'give, let' as in (6.16b).

(6.16) a. mɔ²¹ sɿ²¹ ji³³ foŋ²¹ nɯ³³ piɔ²⁴ **[a²¹ sɿ⁵⁵]** je³³.
          that letter one   CLF   2SG   NEG.IMP take to   3SG
          'Don't give (it) to him.'
          那封信，你别拿给他。

      b. nɯ³³ **[a²¹ sɿ⁵⁵]** je³³ zɤ²¹.
         2SG take give   3SG   eat
         'You give (it) to him to eat.'
         'You let him eat.'
         你拿给他吃/你让他吃。

Actually, a similar compound form of 'take' and 'give' is also attested in the local Hezhang dialect of Southwestern Mandarin and neighboring Bijie Southwestern Mandarin,[9] in the form of *la²¹kən⁵⁵* 拿跟 'give, let' (Ming Shengrong 2007: 355–356, 417), as in (6.17).

---

[9] It should be mentioned that causative verbs derived from speech act verbs are used in both the Hezhang and Bijie dialects as well. For example, *xan⁴²* 'call for' and *tɕiau²¹³* 'call for' in the Bijie dialect (Ming Shengrong 2007).

(6.17) a. 拿跟老子遇屄倒这种事[...]
la²¹kən⁵⁵ lau⁴²tsɿ⁴² y²¹³-tɕʰiəu²¹-tau⁴² tsɿ⁵⁵ tsoŋ⁴² sɿ²¹³.
let   1SG   meet-fucking-achieve   this type   thing
'(If they) let me fucking encounter such kind of thing...'
(Ming Shengrong 2007: 417, glossed and translated by the author)

b. 他拿跟人打了。
la⁵⁵ **la²¹kən⁵⁵** zən²¹ ta⁴² ləu⁴².
3SG   PASS   person beat   PFV
'He was beaten by someone.'
(Ming Shengrong 2007: 373, glossed and translated by the author)

Furthermore, this phenomenon that 'take' and 'give' are fused as one single causative verb and its further passive use have been recorded in the Southwestern Mandarin as spoken in the late 19th century in the same area (DCF 1893), as shown in (6.18). Caijia *a²¹sɿ⁵⁵* is also used as an agent marker in passives (6.19) (see also Chapter 7 on passive constructions).

(6.18) a. 拿跟他喫，穿
lâ kēn tʼā   tchʼĕ, tchʼoūan
take give 3SG   eat   wear
'give him (things) to eat (and things) to wear'
'let him eat and wear'
(DCF 1893:302, glossed and translated by the author)

b. 我拿跟强盗偷了
Gò   **lâ kēn** kʼiâng táo tʼeōu lò
1SG   PASS   thief   steal   PFV
'I've been robbed by the thief.'
(DCF 1893: 302, glossed and translated by the author)

(6.19) [...] ji²¹ koŋ⁵⁵ tsa²¹ ti²¹ nɛ⁵⁵ **a²¹sɿ⁵⁵** zɿ⁵⁵ lã²¹.
        one   day   go.up hill PRT   PASS   rain pour
'One day, (I) went up the hill and was soaked by the rain.'
一天上山呢，被雨淋了。
(*The haystack*, texts)

In sum, the two causative verbs in Caijia not only reflect an areal feature of languages in East and Southeast Asia (Vittrant and Watkins 2019), but also demonstrate similarities to the local Southwestern Mandarin. In spite of their similar sources, the two causative verbs $sɿ^{55}$ and $a^{21}sɿ^{55}$ in Caijia behave differently. Compared with $sɿ^{55}$, the use of $a^{21}sɿ^{55}$ is relatively restricted. Its limited use represents, in fact, the persistence of its source use. We will now examine more details concerning these two causative constructions.

6.3.2.2 Type IIa

Schematized as:

$$(NP_1) + V_{CAUS\text{-}sɿ^{55}/a^{21}sɿ^{55}} + NP_2 + VP_2,$$

NP_1 is the causer NP, while NP_2 is the causee NP forming the caused event with VP_2. Both $sɿ^{55}$ and $a^{21}sɿ^{55}$ can be used in this construction, as shown below.

(6.20) piɔ²⁴   [sɿ⁵⁵]/[a²¹sɿ⁵⁵]   ni²¹   ko²¹saŋ³³   nɯ³³.
       NEG.IMP   let   3   hang:heart   2SG
       'Don't let/make others worry about you.'
       别让别人担心你。

(6.21) [sɿ⁵⁵]/[a²¹sɿ⁵⁵]   je²¹   taŋ³³   tsʰen³³tsan²¹,   tɛ²¹tɕʰi²¹   la²¹   tɕʰi³³kʰa³³.
       let   3SG   serve.as   village.chief   everyone   all   happy
       'Everyone'll be happy to let him be the village chief.'
       让他当村长，大家都开心。

Basically, a causative sentence formed by $a^{21}sɿ^{55}$ can also be formed by $sɿ^{55}$, under the condition that this sentence possesses an absolute causative reading, but not vice versa. By absolute causative reading, we refer to contexts without any ambiguity, given that it is very common that causative verbs can be reanalyzed as passive agent markers in Sinitic languages (Yue-Hashimoto 1993: 131, Chappell and Peyraube 2006, Chappell 2015a, 2015b inter alia). On the contrary, only $a^{21}sɿ^{55}$ can be used in causative-passive contexts.

In the **absolute causative contexts**, $[(NP_1) + V_{CAUS} + NP_2 + VP_2 + (NP_3)]$, the use of $a^{21}sɿ^{55}$ 'let' is restricted. In (6.16), we have shown a plausible syntactic context which could have given rise to $a^{21}sɿ^{55}$ 'let', i.e. a ditransitive serial verb construction with the object of a^{33} 'take' omitted. There exists a correlation between the $a^{21}sɿ^{55}$ causative construction and the ditransitive serial verb construction that can explain the restrictions on $a^{21}sɿ^{55}$ causatives. We consider the ditransitive serial verb as the underlying construction for the $a^{21}sɿ^{55}$ causatives:

$$[NP_{GIVER} + V_1 \sim a^{33} + NP_{THEME} + V_2 \sim sɿ^{55} + NP_{RECIPIENT/CAUSEE} + VP_3]$$

A causative sentence formed by $a^{21}sı^{55}$, [(NP$_1$) + **$a^{21}sı^{55}$** + NP$_2$ + VP$_2$], can be transformed into this serial verb underlying construction. This is to say, the object of the VP$_2$ in a Type IIa construction, overt or implied, is the object of a^{33}, i.e. NP$_{THEME}$, in the source construction. Where they are present, the correlation of each NP argument in the target and underlying constructions can be explained as: NP$_{CAUSER}$ = NP$_{GIVER}$; NP$_{CAUSEE}$ = NP$_{RECIPIENT}$; NP$_{OBJECT}$ (of the effect event) = NP$_{THEME}$. See (6.22).

(6.22) Target:

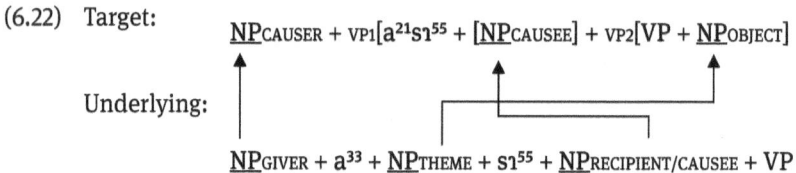

Underlying:

On the contrary, if the object of the VP$_2$ in the $a^{21}sı^{55}$ causative, i.e. NP$_{OBJECT}$ in (6.22), cannot be the object (NP$_{THEME}$) of a^{33} in its underlying (/source) construction, $a^{21}sı^{55}$ cannot be used.

One should note that this test only shows that there is a syntactic correlation between the $a^{21}sı^{55}$ causative and its source construction; but one should not expect these two constructions to have the same semantic value.

Now, let us implement this test with different types of verbs. According to what has been described above, there must be at least an implied object in the caused event in a causative with $a^{21}sı^{55}$. This means that $a^{21}sı^{55}$ cannot be used when verbs in the VP$_2$ slot are intransitive. Let us discuss some examples. In (6.23)-(6.25), the causative $a^{21}sı^{55}$ verb cannot be used, since the motion verb ya^{33} 'fall' in (6.23) itself is intransitive.

(6.23) ŋo²¹   ɕiaŋ⁵⁵   **[sı⁵⁵]/[*a²¹sı⁵⁵]**   ŋo⁵⁵   ɔ²¹   meŋ²¹ni³³ŋoŋ³³
        1SG   want   let   1PL   this Caijia.speech
        ji²¹   tɕʰie⁵⁵   ji²¹   tɕʰie⁵⁵   lɛ⁵⁵   **ya³³-tɕie²¹kuɛ²¹**.
        one   generation one   generation   ADV   fall-go.down
        'I want to have our language of Caijia passed down from generation to generation.
        我想让我们蔡家话一代一代传下去。

The verb xa^{33} 'speak, say' in (6.24) is transitive, as in xa^{33} $meŋ^{21}ni^{55}ŋoŋ^{55}$ 'speak Caijia', but the VP xa^{21}-$tɕie^{21}kuɛ^{21}$ 'go on speaking' is intransitive and not able to take any more object NPs after the resultative complement -$tɕie^{21}kuɛ^{21}$ 'go down' has compounded with xa^{33}.

(6.24) nɯ²¹ **[sɿ⁵⁵]/[*a²¹sɿ⁵⁵]** je²¹ **xa²¹-tɕie²¹kuɛ²¹**,
2SG let 3SG speak-go.down
nɯ³³ piɔ²⁴ pi²¹ tie³³.
2SG NEG.IMP mouth be.many
'Let him speak and don't interrupt.'
你让他说下去，你别多嘴

The VP *tsaŋ²¹mo⁵⁵sɿ⁵⁵ni⁵⁵* 'be astounded' in (6.25), which is a quadrisyllabic idiomatic expression in the form of VOVO, is used also intransitively.

(6.25) mɔ²¹ u²¹tsʰu²⁴-sui⁵⁵ ji²¹ xa³³ je³³ pɣ³³ mɔ²¹ po²¹ sɿ³³
that person-PL once say 3SG put that fart AFF
maŋ²¹ se²¹ ... **sɿ⁵⁵/*a²¹sɿ⁵⁵** u²¹tsʰo²¹ **tsaŋ²¹mo⁵⁵sɿ⁵⁵ni⁵⁵** lɛ⁵⁵.
fragrant AFF let person astounded PRT
'Once those people said that his fart smelt good, (it) made people astounded.'
那些人一说他放的那屁是香的，让人们瞠目结舌地。

The following case shows the situation of implied objects. The verb *tɯ²¹* 'think' possesses an implied object, i.e. *nɯ³³ xa²¹ sɿ²¹* 'what you said' in (6.26a). The causative can be transformed into its underlying construction *a³³*...*sɿ⁵⁵*... with 'what you said' as the object of the verb *a³³* 'take', as shown in (6.26b).

(6.26) a. nɯ³³ xa²¹ sɿ²¹ nɛ⁵⁵, nɯ²¹ **[sɿ⁵⁵]/[a²¹sɿ⁵⁵]** ŋo²¹ tɯ²¹
2SG say NMLZ TOP 2SG let 1SG think
mi⁵⁵.
a.little
'As for what you said, let me think (about it)'
你说的呢，你让我想一下。

b. nɯ³³ a³³ nɯ³³ xa³³ sɿ²¹ sɿ⁵⁵ ŋo²¹ tɯ²¹ mi⁵⁵.
2SG take 2SG say NLMZ give/let 1SG think VCLF
'LIT: You give what you said to me to think about.'
LIT: 你拿你说的给我想一下。

Compare (6.26a) with (6.27a). It can be immediately observed that the syntactic structures of these two sentences are exactly the same. There is also an implied object for the verb *niu³³* 'wait'. However, *a²¹sɿ⁵⁵* cannot be used in this case. The transformation into the underlying construction turns out to be a failure or ungrammatical, as shown in (6.27b). It is semantically impossible to form a sentence like (6.27b). This is because the meaning of 'wait' is not compatible with the meaning of physical transfer denoted by the ditransitive construction $a^{33}\ldots s\gamma^{55}$. One cannot wait for someone or something when it is implied that it has already come into one's possession by the use of a^{33}, which may explain why $a^{21}s\gamma^{55}$ cannot be used in the context of (6.27a).

(6.27) a. pɣ²¹ ɣɯ²¹ nɛ⁵⁵ na³³je²¹ ni²¹ ta⁵⁵ ŋo²¹ xa²¹ mi⁵⁵
NEG come PRT send 3 with 1SG say a.little
la²¹ niɔ²¹tɣ³³, **[sʏ⁵⁵]/[*a²¹sʏ⁵⁵]** ŋo²¹ tɯ²¹ ua²⁴
even be.all.right let 1SG at here
pia²¹li³³li³³ lɛ²¹ **niu³³.**
in.vain ADV wait
'If he couldn't come, it would've been OK to send someone to inform me (instead of) letting me wait here (for him) in vain.'
不来的话，打发人跟我说声也行，让我白白在这儿等。

b. *je³³ a³³ je²¹ sʏ⁵⁵ ŋo³³ niu³³.
3SG take 3SG give/let 1SG wait
(Attempted: *'LIT: He gave him(self) to me to wait for.')
*他拿他（自己）给我等。

Similar to the case where there is an overt object in VP₂, a test with the underlying construction [NP_GIVER + a^{33} + NP_THEME + $s\gamma^{55}$ + NP_RECIPIENT/CAUSEE + VP] is also tenable. As shown in (6.22), the NP_OBJECT of the effect event in the target construction, i.e. $a^{21}s\gamma^{55}$ causative, can be put back into the NP_THEME position following a^{33} in the underlying construction producing a grammatical sentence. See the examples in (6.28).

(6.28) a. piɔ²⁴ **[sʏ⁵⁵]/[a²¹sʏ⁵⁵]** ni²¹ ɕie²¹-tsaŋ³³ **nɯ³³.**
NEG.IMP let 3 small-look 2SG
'Don't let/make people look down upon you'
别让人小看你。

b. nɯ³³ piɔ²⁴ a³³ **nɯ²¹** sʏ⁵⁵ ni²¹ ɕie²¹-tsaŋ³³.
2SG NEG.IMP take 2SG give/let 3 small-look
'LIT: Don't give you(self) to people to look down upon.'
LIT: 你别拿你（自己）给人小看。

A pair of contrastive examples using the same verb *tɕie⁵⁵* 'do' in VP₂ in (6.29) can better illustrate the restricted use of $a^{21}s\gamma^{55}$. In (6.29a) $a^{21}s\gamma^{55}$ can be used, since the associated source or underlying construction 'whatever they give me to do' is grammatical. In contrast, (6.29b) is ungrammatical, for the underlying construction 'I give a cupboard to the carpenter to make (a cupboard)' does not make sense.

(6.29) a. ŋo⁵⁵ ɔ²¹   sı⁵⁵lɛ²¹mo³³ nɛ³³, kʰua²¹ sı²¹ ɕie²¹koŋ⁵⁵ naŋ²¹tv̩³³
       1PL   this place   TOP   good   MOD   odd.job   difficulty
       ko²¹ xıŋ⁵⁵. ni²⁴ **[sı⁵⁵]/[a²¹sı⁵⁵]** ŋo²¹ **tɕie⁵⁵** sı²¹mɔ⁵⁵ ŋo³³ la²¹
       find very   3   let   1SG   do   what   1SG   all
       tɕie⁵⁵.
       do

'It's difficult to find good odd jobs in our place. (Therefore,) I do whatever they (= those that offer jobs) ask me to do.'
我们这个地方呢，好的小工难找得很。人家让我干什么我就干。

b. ŋo³³ niɔŋ²¹hɛ⁵⁵   niɔ³³   kɛ²¹   ni²⁴   o.   ŋo²¹
   1SG   younger.sister   PROSP   marry   3   CRS   1SG
   [sı⁵⁵]/[*a²¹sı⁵⁵]   sɔ⁵⁵la²¹kɯ²⁴ ta⁵⁵ je²¹ **tɕie⁵⁵**   kʰua²¹
   let   carpenter   for   3SG   do   good
   to²⁴   po⁵⁵.
   cupboard   CLF

'My younger sister will get married. I asked the carpenter to make a good wardrobe for her.'
我妹妹要嫁人了。我让木匠给她做个好柜子。

It was mentioned earlier that, ambiguous **causative-passive contexts** also exist in Caijia. It is from these contexts that the agent marking use of $a^{21}sı^{55}$ is derived (see [6.19]). In such a context, the NP$_{CAUSER}$ is also the NP$_{PATIENT}$ and the implied NP$_{OBJECT}$ is co-referential with the NP$_{CAUSER}$. See the schema in (6.30) and the example in (6.31). Example (6.31) illustrates an imperative sentence in which the causer/patient NP 'you' is absent and only $a^{21}sı^{55}$ can be used.

(6.30) Causative/passive
       NP$_{CAUSER/PATIENT(i)}$ + a²¹sı⁵⁵ + NP$_{CAUSEE/AGENT}$ + $_{VP}$[VP + ∅$_{OBJECT(i)}$]

(6.31) piɔ²⁴   **[a²¹sı⁵⁵]/[*sı⁵⁵]**   ni²¹   na²¹.
       NEG.IMP   let/PASS   3   beat
       'Don't let others beat you/Don't be beaten by others.'
       别让/被别人打。

Actually, the semantic context of (6.31) is similar to the one in (6.28a), the NP$_{OBJECT}$ $nɯ^{33}$ 'you' in (6.28a) is co-referential with the NP$_{CAUSER}$ which is also a semantic patient. However, the syntactic structure is different, i.e. the NP$_{OBJECT}$ is not empty in (6.28a). The empty NP$_{OBJECT}$ is the key factor that gives rise to the development of $a^{21}sı^{55}$ from a causative verb to a passive agent marker, because this empty position allows the causative construction with $a^{21}sı^{55}$ to be syntactically identical to a passive construction. It is also the major reason why $sı^{55}$ cannot be used as a passive agent marker, since the NP$_{OBJECT}$, co-referential with the NP$_{CAUSER}$ in a $sı^{55}$ causative construction must not be empty. This means that the use of $sı^{55}$ will be ungrammatical, whenever the NP$_{OBJECT}$ is empty in (6.28a).

6.3.2.3 Type IIb

In a Type IIb causative construction, $sı^{55}$ is the only option. It functions as a linker or complementizer linking two clauses, with the first clause being the cause of the second:

$$[(NP_1) + VP_1] + sı^{55} + [NP_2 + VP_2]$$

The CAUSE-clause enables the EFFECT-clause. Semantically, $sı^{55}$ is thus more like its English counterpart 'so that, so as to', rather than 'let, make'.

Example (6.32) is extracted from a spontaneous narrative. One can observe that $sı^{55}$ links the cause 'he farted' and the effect 'the whole street became fragrant'. It should be mentioned that the italicized part je^{21} a... 'it euh...' is a speaker self-correction, since the speaker made an effort to explicitly state the referent instead of using the pronoun 'it'. Therefore, it should not be counted as one of the syntactic elements in the sentence.

(6.32) py^{21} po^{24} ji^{21} po^{55} tɯ^{21} kʰɯ^{33} tɣ^{33} **sı^{55}**   *je^{21} a...*
       put   fart   one   CLF   at   street   upside   so.that   3SG   INTJ
       ji^{21} kʰɯ^{55} la^{21} maŋ^{21}-kʰɯ^{55}ɣɯ^{21}.
       one   street   all   fragrant-INC
       '(He) farted so that the whole street then became fragrant.'
       放了一个屁让整条街都香起来了。
       (*The kind younger brother*, texts)

Another example extracted from a narrative is offered below.

(6.33) a^{33} nɯ^{21} mɔ^{21} ka^{55}pɣ^{21} pʰɣ^{55}-xɯ^{55} **sı^{55}**   ŋɔ^{21} tɕie^{21}-yɯ^{21}.
       OM   2SG   that   cloth   lay-rise   so.that   1SG   go.down-come
       'Lay your cloth (on the nettle) so as to let me get off (the tree).'
       把你的布铺起来让我下来。
       (*Nettle witch*, texts)

The phenomenon of a causative verb also being used as a causative linker or complementizer is reported in several Sinitic languages, for example, *khit⁴* 乞 'beg, give' in Early Southern Min (Chappell and Peyraube 2006), and *bun¹* 'share, give' in Hakka (Lai 2015). See the following example from Hakka.

(6.34) 捉魚仔賣，賺錢分吾老公讀書
       ngai⁵   zog⁴   ng⁵-e²   mai³   con³   qien⁵   **bun¹**
       1SG   catch   fish-SF   sell   make money BUN
       nga¹   lo²gung¹ tug⁸su¹.
       1SG:POSS husband   study
       'I caught fish to sell for money so as to support my husband to study.'
       (Lai 2015: 382)

We have explained in this section how the two causative verbs, $s1^{55}$ and $a^{21}s1^{55}$, are used in Caijia. They overlap as well as contrast with each other. As a causative verb, $a^{21}s1^{55}$ is used with more restrictions than $s1^{55}$. We have proposed using the underlying source construction for $a^{21}s1^{55}$ causatives to test their conditions of use, showing that the use of $a^{21}s1^{55}$ as a causative verb reflects to a great extent its source meaning and structure in an indirective ditransitive construction. The use of this causative can be explained by one of the five principles of grammaticalization proposed by Hopper (1991: 22), i.e. the principle of persistence, or the phenomenon that the meaning and function of a grammatical morpheme are related to its source lexical meaning and use. It can be observed that change of form, meaning, and syntactic behavior are also involved for $a^{21}s1^{55}$ 'let'. Given that a process of grammaticalization is a cline involving "a series of gradual transitions" instead of being an abrupt shift (Hopper and Traugott 1993: 6), the shift from a lexical verb to a causative verb represents a preliminary stage in $a^{21}s1^{55}$'s to development into a passive agent marker. Its status as a pure functional or grammatical word and the principle of persistence are, thus, suitable to explain its limited use. As for $s1^{55}$, its causative verb use is more generalized than that of $a^{21}s1^{55}$. Causative-passive contexts are the only cases in which it is cannot be used. The morpheme $s1^{55}$ can further be used as a linker or causative complementizer. The grammaticalization pathways for $s1^{55}$ and $a^{21}s1^{55}$ are summarized in (6.35).

(6.35) **$s1^{55}$:**
       'give' > $V_{CAUSATIVE}$ 'let' > $COMP_{CAUSATIVE}$ 'so that, so as to'
      $a^{21}s1^{55}$:
      Ditransitive [a^{33} T $s1^{55}$] > $a^{21}s1^{55}$ 'give' > $V_{CAUSATIVE}$ 'let' > PASS

6.4 Conclusion

In this chapter, we presented three analytic causative constructions in Caijia: one Type I Extent complement causative construction and two Type II Pivot-causee constructions. The Type I construction is commonly regarded as a type of the complement construction in Sinitic languages and does not require a causative verb, while a causative verb is obligatory in both the Type II constructions. The sources of Caijia causative verbs are also commonly attested among Sinitic languages: 'do' and 'give'. Only no^{21} 'rub, do' can be used in the Type I construction. Unlike in the local Hezhang Southwestern Mandarin, a speech act verb is not found evolving into a causative verb in Caijia. The general causative $s1^{55}$ is derived from the verb of giving. However, the other causative verb, $a^{21}s1^{55}$, with its limited use, exactly mirrors the local Mandarin strategy of forming a compound causative verb with 'take' and 'give'. It is common in Sinitic languages for causative verbs to be a source of passive agent markers. In Caijia, only $a^{21}s1^{55}$ has developed this function.

Chapter 7
Passive constructions

7.1 Definition and Sinitic typology

A construction can be identified as prototypical passive if it demonstrates the following features (Creissels 2006b: 19, Siewierska 2013):
i.   it contrasts with another construction, the active;
ii. the subject of the active corresponds to a non-obligatory oblique phrase of the passive or is not overtly expressed;
iii. the subject of the passive, if there is one, corresponds to the direct object of the active;
iv. the construction is pragmatically restricted relative to the active;
v.   the construction displays some special morphological marking on the verb.

Take for example, *Kim kicked Mary* vs. *Mary is kicked (by Kim)*, in which the agent-subject 'Kim' in the active becomes the non-obligatory agent-oblique in the passive. The patient-object 'Mary' becomes patient-subject in the passive and the verb 'kick' is in its participle form in the passive. Keenan and Dryer (2007: 329–330) consider the agentless passives to be basic passives, which are the most wide-spread type of passive across the languages of the world. A generalization can then be proposed: If a language has any passives, it has those which can be characterized as basic passives (i.e. the agentless passives). In addition, this language may have only basic passives (Keenan and Dryer 2007: 329). The basic passives are also known as 'short passives' in the literature, while those with agents are known as 'long passives'.

However, Sinitic passives are not prototypical and do not entirely conform to the generalization mentioned above (Chappell 2015b: 24).

First, the presence of an obligatory agent is attested in many Sinitic languages. Admittedly, we observe that agentless passives are also found in Sinitic, especially in the languages for which the passives belong to the SUFFER/CONTACT type (Table 7.1). For example, the passive auxiliary *bèi* 被 (< 'cover with quilt') in Standard Mandarin, *tuó* 驮 ('carry on the back (by pack animals)') in Nanchang Gan 南昌贛语 (Xiong Zhenghui 1995: 63), *ái* 捱 (< 'suffer') in Liuzhou Southwestern Mandarin 柳州西南官话 (Liu Cunhan 1995: 154), *zhuó* 着 ('< to be attached') in Dafang 大方 Southwestern Mandarin (Li Lan 2006: 198), and *zāo* 遭 (< 'suffer') in Chengdu 成都 Southwestern Mandarin (Liang and Huang 1998: 201).

Second, Sinitic passives with obligatory agents do not display special verbal morphology. Third, Sinitic passives tend to be used in events of adversity (Chappell

2015b: 24), which is also a common feature of Southeast Asian passives (Clark 1974, Li and Thompson 1981: 493). Fourth, verbs used in Sinitic passives often possess a strong meaning of affectedness, for example, lexical causative or disposal verbs. Yet not all active sentences in the form of [V O] can be transformed into passives (q.v. Shi Dingxu 1997).

Sinitic passive agent markers can be divided into three major types on the basis of their sources and grammaticalization pathways (Chappell 2015b: 27–34), as illustrated in Table 7.1.

Table 7.1: Sources of Sinitic passive agent markers.

Type	Markers
1. GIVE/TAKE	*pei²* 畀 'give', *khit⁴* 乞 'give', *hou⁷* 与 'give', *pun* 分 'share', *paʔ* 拨 'share', GEI 给 'give', *pa* 把 'take~give', *pa.ta⁴* 把得 'take~give', *ta⁴* 得 'obtain~give', NA 拿 'take', NUO 搦 'take' or 'give', LAU 捞 'dredge up'
2. SUFFER/CONTACT	BEI 被 'cover', ZHUO 着 'hit the target', AI 捱/挨 'suffer', ZAO 遭 'suffer', TUO 驮 'carry on the back (by a packanimal)'
3. CAUSATIVE VERBS	RANG 让 'let', JIAO 叫 'tell/ask', DENG 等 'wait', TINGREN 听任 'let it be', JIN 尽 'let'

The Sinitic languages typology for the passive agent markers suits Caijia, since its two passive agent markers, one of which can also be treated as passive auxiliary, can be found in this inventory.

7.2 Passives in Caijia

In general, Caijia passives also display the features of Sinitic passives, as mentioned above. The verbal uses of the markers which belong to the SUFFER and LET categories are still retained in Caijia. These are dy^{33} (< 'passively receive, suffer') and $a^{21}s1^{55}$ (< 'give, let'). Even though the Caijia passives are not particularly limited to adverse events, most of those in our data are related to adversity. It should be mentioned that transitivity is not the only condition for verbs to form passives in Caijia, since the verbs must also demonstrate affectedness. To code affectedness, Caijia makes use of resultative and other complements in what are essentially then non-canonical passive constructions (see Creissels 2006b: 48–49). This chapter will present two types of passive constructions with overt markers in Caijia, as summarized in Table 7.2, focusing on the VPs in these passives and describing the two different passive markers, the SUFFER type dy^{33} and the LET type $a^{21}s1^{55}$.

Table 7.2: Caijia passives.

I SUFFER	a.	NP$_P$ + **dɣ³³** + NP$_A$ + VP
	b.	NP$_P$ + **dɣ³³** + VP
II LET		NP$_P$ + **a²¹sɿ⁵⁵** + NP$_A$ + VP

Examples (7.1) and (7.2) demonstrate syntactic structures displaying these two markers. The NP$_A$s in the Type I passives are optional, while they are obligatory in Type II.

Type I SUFFER: (NP$_P$) + dɣ³³ + (NP$_A$) + VP

(7.1) meŋ²¹koŋ⁵⁵   ŋo³³   **tɣ²¹**   (zɿ⁵⁵)   lã²¹   o.
       yesterday   1SG   PASS   rain   water   CRS
                    NP$_P$ AUX$_{PASS}$/PREP$_{AG}$ NP$_A$ VP
       'I was caught in the rain yesterday.'
       昨天我被(雨)淋了。

Type II LET: (NP$_P$) + a²¹sɿ⁵⁵ + NP$_A$ + VP

(7.2) mɔ²¹   kʰui⁵⁵   kɔ²¹   mia²¹   la²¹   xıŋ⁵⁵.
       that   dog   CLF   life   big   very
       a²¹sɿ⁵⁵   tsʰɛ⁵⁵   ɿ⁵⁵-tɣ³³,   tsaŋ²¹-xɯ⁵⁵   niɔ²¹   sɿ⁵⁵   o.
       PASS   car   run.over-obtain look-up   PROSP   die   CRS
       PREP$_{AG}$ NP$_A$ VP
       jɯ²⁴   xa²¹-pe⁵⁵ɣɯ²¹.
       again   be.alive-come back
       'That dog was really lucky (LIT: That dog's life is very big). (It) was run over by a car. It seemed to be dying. (But it) came back to life again.'
       那条狗命大得很。被车撞，看着要死了。又活过来了。

Caijia Type I passives correspond to Chappell's (2015b) Type 2 SUFFER/CONTACT and Caijia Type II passives can be classified as Chappell's Type 3 CAUSATIVE VERBS.
Before dealing with the main target of this chapter, we need clarify:

(i) By using the term 'passive', we refer exclusively to the passiveconstructions with overt markers, i.e. Type I and Type II. We will not tackle semantic passives, which do not take any overt marking and can be treated as constructions with topicalized objects or patients (see LaPolla 1998 on the semantic passives in Standard Mandarin) or as *shòushì zhǔyǔ jù* 受事主语句 'patient-subject constructions' (Zhu Dexi 1982: 99–100). One can observe in (7.3) that the patient occupies the position of subject and there is no overt passive marker in each sentence.

(7.3) a. ɕie²¹ kɪ²⁴ po²¹-tsʰe⁵⁵ɣɯ²¹ o.
little chicken.DIM hatch-come out CRS
'The chicks are hatched out.'
小鸡孵出来了。

b. tsʰe⁵⁵ sɣ²¹ neŋ²¹ mo²¹ kɯ²⁴, pɣ³³ ɣã²¹ ma²¹sɿ⁵⁵.
be.out poor year that moment NEG there.be grain
zɣ²¹ tɣ³³ sɿ²¹ la²¹ zɣ²¹-ha²¹ o.
eat can NMLZ all eat-finish CRS
'During those years of famine, there was no food. Whatever could be eaten was all eaten up.'
出荒年的时候，能吃的都吃了。

(ii) It is also necessary to clarify that by the term 'actives' we refer to sentences with transitive verbs of which the objects are in their canonical positions, i.e. VO order, as in (7.4). Even though object marking constructions can also express active meanings, the objects are moved before the verbs. We do not, therefore, treat object marking constructions as actives.

(7.4) ta⁵⁵ ni²¹ ɣa²¹ ti²¹ tɣ³³ **tɕie⁵⁵ ja²¹pa²¹**.
two CLF walk hill upside do crops
tɕi²¹-tsʰe⁵⁵ mɛ²⁴ ko²¹ ɣɯ²¹.
plough-be.out frog CLF come
'Two people went up the hill to do farming. They ploughed out a frog.'
两人上山干活儿。犁出一只青蛙来。

(iii) We use the term 'passive marker' to refer to both passive auxiliary and passive agent marker *dʐ³³*.

7.2.1 VPs in passives

Given that both the two types of passives in Caijia demand a VP with a specific semantic feature, we introduce the VPs in Caijia passives before presenting the two markers. We have mentioned above that actives with transitive verbs cannot necessarily be transformed into passives in Caijia. Only those possessing a meaning of affectedness can form passives. In other words, the patient NP undergoes an explicit change of state in a passive construction in Caijia. Some verbs possess an inherent meaning of affectedness, while others can acquire such a meaning periphrastically, usually from different types of complements including the forms of V-V(ADJ), V-VCOMP-VP, V-NP, and V-PREP-NP. For convenience, we will use the passive constructions with *dy³³* 'by' to show the different ways that verbs to acquire the meaning of affectedness.

The verb *tɕʰɪŋ³³* 'bite' is a verb with an inherent meaning of affectedness, so it can be used directly in a passive and so is the verb *lã²¹* 'water' in example (7.1). As shown in (7.5), the resultative complement -*tγ³³* 'obtain, acquire', by means of which achievement of an action can be expressed, is not obligatory but it can be used to emphasize the accomplishment of the action 'bite'.

(7.5) kʰɯ³³   tγ³³   ɣã²¹   ɣ²¹   kʰui⁵⁵   kɔ²¹.   neŋ²¹na⁵⁵   lɛ²¹
      street upside   have   crazy   dog   CLF   randomly   ADV
      tɕʰɪŋ²¹ u³³tsʰo³³.   nɯ³³   ka²¹   kʰɯ³³   niɔ³³   ɕie²¹saŋ³³.
      bite   person   2SG   go   street must   be careful
      piɔ²⁴   tγ³³   je³³   **tɕʰɪŋ³³(-tγ³³)**   o.
      NEG.IMP   PASS   3SG   bite-obtain   CRS
      'There's a crazy dog in the street biting people randomly. You must be careful when you go to the market. Don't be bitten by it.'
      街上有条疯狗。乱咬人。你赶场要小心，别被它咬(到)了。

The resultative complement -*tγ³³* is a high-frequency morpheme which modifies verbs to realize the meaning of affectedness, but it is not the only marker which can achieve this result. See example (7.6).

(7.6) A₁- mɛ²⁴   tɯ²¹   la²⁴[lɔ²⁴+ha⁵⁵]?
           frog   be.at   where[which+place]
           'Where is the frog?'
           青蛙在哪儿？

      B₁- tγ³³   ŋo³³   **zγ²¹-kuɛ²¹**   o.
           PASS   1SG   eat-go   CRS
           'It is eaten up by me.'
           被我吃掉了。

The verb *kʰoŋ²¹* 'frighten' does not display the same level of affectedness as much as the verb 'bite', since the action of frightening can be performed without any frightening effect, as in (7.7a). The verb needs to acquire this meaning by different morphological means in order to form a passive. In (7.7b), the affectedness of the verb *kʰoŋ²¹* 'frighten' is realized by compounding with -*tγ³³* 'obtain, acquire', while *kʰoŋ²¹* takes a complement clause introduced by the complementizer *lɯ⁵⁵*, seen in (7.7c)

(7.7) a. nɯ³³ piɔ²⁴ **kʰoŋ²¹** je³³ la²¹!
 2SG NEG.IMP frighten 3SG PRT
 'Don't frighten him!'
 你别吓他！

b. nɯ³³ tɕiu²¹me⁵⁵me²⁴ lɛ⁵⁵! ŋa⁵⁵ la²¹ tʏ³³ nɯ³³
 2SG be.quiet PRT child then PASS 2SG
 kʰoŋ²¹*(-tʏ³³) o.
 frighten-obtain CRS
 'Be quiet! The child is frightened by you.'
 你静悄悄地。孩子都被你吓到了。

c. tl̩⁵⁵ na²¹ lɯ⁵⁵ la²¹ xɪŋ⁵⁵. tʰʏ²⁴ tʏ³³ **kʰoŋ²¹**
 thunder beat VCOMP big very rabbit PASS frighten
 *(lɯ⁵⁵ neŋ²¹na²⁴ lɛ²¹ tɕiɔ²¹).
 VCOMP aribitrarily ADV jump
 'It thundered terribly. The rabbit was so frightened that it jumped around insanely.'
 雷打得大得很。兔子都被吓得乱跳。

Some verbs can take nominal complements in order to express affectedness. Example (7.8b) shows such a case. The verb *tsʰɿ³³* 'blow' takes the nominal complement 'a crack', as the result of the action 'blow'. Deleting this complement would make the utterance ungrammatical. Compare the active use of 'blow' in (7.8a) with the use in a passive seen in (7.8b).

(7.8) a. **tsʰɿ³³** ɕiɔ³³toŋ²⁴
 blow vertical.bamboo.flute
 'play the flute'
 吹箫

b. tã²¹tʰoŋ⁵⁵ tʏ³³ pã²¹ **tsʰɿ³³** *(kʰɯ³³ta³³ ji³³ ʏ²¹).
 bucket PASS wind blow crack one CLF
 'the bucket was cracked by the wind'
 木桶被风吹裂一条缝。

One should note that affectedness is not an exclusive feature of passives. Verbs denoting affectedness can also form actives and other different constructions, such as object marking constructions and object topicalized constructions (see example [7.3]). Therefore, the verbal compounding strategy used to acquire the meaning of affectedness in passives cannot be treated as special passive morphology. Compare (7.9) with (7.7b) and (7.10) with (7.6).

(7.9) ɣa^{21} tɕiu^{55} kʰa^{33} pɪŋ^{21} kui^{55} tɯ^{21} tɯ^{21} ma^{24} xaŋ^{21}-xɯ^{55}ɣɯ^{21}.
walk to pit side ghost then at there yell-INC
kʰoŋ^{21}-tʏ^{33} ŋo^{24} tɯ^{55} pʏ^{21} kã^{55} kuɛ^{21} o.
frighten-obtain 1PL then NEG dare go CRS
'(We) walked to the pit and the ghost began to yell. (It) frightened us and then we didn't dare go any further.'
走到洞边，鬼就喊起来了。吓到我们，就不敢去了。
(*Encountering the ghost*, texts)

(7.10) je^{33} ji^{21} tɪŋ^{24} tɯ^{21} **zʏ^{21}-kuɛ^{21}** lɔ^{21}po^{55} fʏ^{55} po^{55}.
3SG one moment even eat-go peach six CLF
'He ate up six peaches at one go.'
他一会儿就吃掉六个桃子。

Examples (7.9) and (7.10) have illustrated that V-V compounds can be used to form active sentences. However, one should be aware that not all passives can be transformed into actives. For example, neither (7.7c) nor (7.8b) possess corresponding active forms, but can be transformed into object marking constructions. Transforming (7.8b) into an active construction results in an ungrammatical utterance, as in (7.11a). See also the examples contrasting for acceptability in (7.12).

(7.11) a. *pã^{33} tsʰɿ^{33} tã^{21}tʰoŋ^{55} kʰɯ^{33}ta^{33} ji^{33} ʏ^{21}.
wind blow bucket crack one CLF
(Attempted: 'The wind cracked the bucket.')
风把木桶吹裂了一条缝。

b. pã^{33} a^{33} tã^{21}tʰoŋ^{55} tsʰɿ^{33} kʰɯ^{33}ta^{33} ji^{33} ʏ^{21}.
wind OM bucket blow crack one CLF
'The wind cracked the bucket.'
风把木桶吹裂了一条缝。

(7.12) a. ɔ^{21} sɿ^{55} tʏ^{33} nɯ^{33} pʏ^{21}-tie^{55} xɪŋ^{55} o.
this water PASS 2SG put-much very CRS
pi^{55} lɔ^{21}pie^{55} kuɛ^{21} o.
become porridge go CRS
'Too much water has been added by you. It turned into porridge.'
?这水被你放太多了。变粥了。

b. *nɯ³³ pɣ²¹-tie⁵⁵ xɪŋ⁵⁵ ɔ²¹ sı⁵⁵ o.
   2SG put-much very this water CRS
   (Attempted: 'You put in too much water.')
   你把这水放太多了。

c. nɯ³³ a³³ ɔ²¹ sı⁵⁵ pɣ²¹-tie⁵⁵ xɪŋ⁵⁵ o.
   2SG OM this water put-much very CRS
   'You put in too much water.'
   你把这水放太多了。

In this section, we have presented the semantic feature of VPs in Caijia passive constructions. Not all transitive verbs used in active constructions can be used in passive constructions, nor can all active constructions be transformed into passive constructions and vice versa. However, it is observed that VPs in both passive and object marking constructions share similar semantic features, as shown in (7.11) and (7.12). In a passive construction, the verb or the VP must denote the affectedness of the patient NP. To be precise, the patient NP must undergoes an explicit affectedness or change of state. There are verbs which possess an inherent meaning of affectedness, such as *na²¹* 'beat', *tɕʰɪŋ³³* 'bite', *mɛ³³* 'scold', etc.; while *pɣ²¹* 'put', *tsʰʅ³³* 'blow', *kʰoŋ²¹* 'frighten', etc. are verbs lacking an inherent meaning of affectedness. For verbs lacking an inherent meaning of affectedness, acquiring the meaning of explicit affectedness can be realized in several ways, among which resultative complement compounding is the most common method.

7.2.2 Type I suffer: *dɣ³³* '(passively) receive, suffer, hit the target'

7.2.2.1 Source of *dɣ³³*

Forming both agentful and agentless passives in Caijia, the passive marker *dɣ³³* is derived from the lexical verb *dɣ³³* denoting '(passively) receive, suffer, hit the target'. We hypothesize that *dɣ³³* is the cognate of Chinese ZHUO/ZHU 着/著 'wear, place, attach, hit the target'. This hypothesis is proposed for two reasons: (i) phonetic similarity and (ii) semantic and functional similarities.

First, even though *dɣ³³* is phonetically quite different to the morpheme ZHUO/ZHU in the local Southwestern Mandarin, it is phonetically close to the reconstructed Middle Chinese form. As can be observed in Table 7.3, the onsets of Caijia *dɣ³³* and Middle Chinese ZHUO/ZHU (Baxter and Sagart 2014: 377–378)[10] are in the

---

[10] It should be mentioned that -r- in Baxter and Sagart's transcription represents a retroflex instead of a separate segment.

same coronal retroflex group, while the onset of ZHUO/ZHU in Dafang Southwestern Mandarin, a dialect geographically very close to the Caijia area, (Li Lan 2006: 199–200), is a coronal sibilant affricate.

Table 7.3: ZHUO/ZHU in Caijia, Middle Chinese and Southwestern Mandarin.

Caijia	Middle Chinese 著	Dafang Southwestern Mandarin 著
ʥɤ³³	trjoH	tso²¹
	drjak	tsao²¹
	trjak	tsʰo²¹

Second, *ʥɤ³³* in Caijia semantically and functionally overlaps with the uses of ZHUO/ZHU in the local Southwestern Mandarin, Standard Mandarin, Modern Chinese (15ᵗʰ–18ᵗʰ century), or even Late Medieval Chinese (7ᵗʰ century-1250). Let us compare the polysemy of the lexical *ʥɤ³³* in Caijia in comparison with ZHUO/ZHU in Southwestern Mandarin, Standard Mandarin as well as in Late Medieval and Modern Chinese. See Table 7.4.

Table 7.4: Polysemy of *ʥɤ³³* in Caijia.

	ʥɤ³³
I	receive passively
II	suffer
III	need, be worth
IV	hit the target
V	like
VI	grow, give birth, bear (fruit)

(I) As a lexical verb, *ʥɤ³³* can be used as a transitive verb denoting 'passively receive'. In (7.13a), *ʥɤ³³* takes *soŋ²¹* 'sickness' and is marked by the inchoative marker *kʰɯ⁵⁵ɣɯ²¹*, while it takes *saŋ³³ka³³* 'cold' as its object in (7.13b). Both bearing aspectual marking and serving as an independent predicate are determinant features of verbs. Similar uses like *tɤ³³ saŋ³³ka³³* 'catch cold' in (7.13b) and *ʥɤ²¹ fɛ⁵⁵* 'catch on fire' in (7.13c) can be found in Standard Mandarin as in (7.13d) and (7.13e).

(7.13) a. je³³ ji²¹tʰɯ²⁴ tɯ³³ **tɤ³³** soŋ²¹ kʰɯ⁵⁵ɣɯ²¹ o.
       3SG suddenly then get sickness INC CRS
       'He suddenly got ill.'
       他一下就病了。

b. a³³ ɯ³³ ɯ²¹-xɯ⁵⁵. tsʰɿ⁵⁵ **tɣ³³** san³³ka³³ kuɛ²¹.
   OM clothes wear-rise fear get cold go
   'Put on your clothes. (Or else) you'll catch cold.'
   把衣服穿上。怕着凉了。

c. **dɣ²¹** fɛ⁵⁵
   get fire
   'catch on fire'
   着火

Standard Mandarin
d. 着凉
   zháo liáng
   get cold
   'catch cold'

Standard Mandarin
e. 着火
   zháo huǒ
   get fire
   'catch on fire'

(II) The lexical word *dɣ³³* can also denote 'suffer', as illustrated in examples (7.14)-(7.16). The meaning 'suffer' is very much related to the meaning 'receive passively'. For example, the VP *tɣ²¹ tsɣ⁵⁵* 'suffer from medicine ~ be poisoned' in (7.14) can be interpreted as 'receive passively the effect of medicine'.

(7.14) mɔ²¹ u²¹tsʰo²⁴ ni³³ tsɔ²¹ mɔ²¹ **tɣ²¹** tsɣ⁵⁵ sɿ²¹.
       that people CLF resemble that suffer medicine way
       'That person seems to be poisoned.'
       那人好像中毒似的。

Several of the current expressions and uses of the Caijia *dɣ³³* can be correlated with those of Late Medieval Chinese. For example, *dɣ²¹ so⁵⁵* 'suffer hand ~ be tricked', as in (7.15a). The exact same expression *zhuó shǒu* 着手 'suffer hand ~ be tricked' is found in *Shuǐ Hǔ Zhuàn* 水浒传 [Water Margin] which was completed in the Ming dynasty (1368–1644). See (7.15b). The verb *tsau³¹* is attested in Guiyang Southwestern Mandarin with a similar meaning of 'suffer'. It is used intransitively denoting 'suffer from unlucky things', as in (7.15c). Compare it with the corresponding Caijia expression in (7.15d).

(7.15) a. ŋo³³ **tɣ²¹** so⁵⁵ o.
1SG suffer hand CRS
'I got tricked (LIT: I suffered hand).'
我上当了。

Modern Chinese
b. 又有若干菜蔬也把药来拌了。恐有不吃肉的，也教他着手。
yòu yǒu ruògān càishū yě bǎ yào lái
also there.be several vegetable also take medicine come
bàn le. kǒng yǒu bù chī ròu de,
mix PRT if:fear there.be NEG eat meat NMLZ
yě jiào tā **zhuó shǒu**.
also let 3SG suffer hand
'(We) also mix the poison with the vegetables. (In this way,) (we'll) have those who don't eat meat tricked.'
《水浒传》四十三回 [Water Margin Episode 43]
(quoted from Long Qian'an 1985: 860, glossed and translated by the author)

Guiyang Southwestern Mandarin
c. 我着了。
ŋo⁵³ tsau³¹ ou²⁴.
1SG suffer PFV
'Bad things occurred on me (LIT: I suffered).'
(Wang Ping 1994: 15, glossed and translated by the author)

d. ŋo³³ **tɣ³³** o.
1SG suffer CRS
'I got tricked (LIT: I suffered.).'
我上当了。

In addition, $dʐ^{33}$ in Caijia can be used as a trivalent verb when expressing 'suffer financial losses'. Specifically, it can form a double object construction with a human noun as an indirect object preceding the direct object 'money' in the form of [$dʐ^{33}$ IO$_{human}$ DO$_{money}$] denoting 'be defrauded of a certain amount of money by sb.', but this human indirect object is not obligatory, as illustrated in (7.16a). Li Lan (2006) reports a similar use of tso^{21} in Dafang Southwestern Mandarin, denoting 'suffer financial losses'.

(7.16) a. ŋo³³ **tɤ³³** (je³³) tɕɪŋ²¹ ta⁵⁵ pʰe⁵⁵.
　　　　 1SG　suffer.financial.loss　3SG　money　two　CURRENCY.UNIT
　　　　 'I was defrauded of two yuan (by him).'
　　　　 他坑了我两块钱/我亏了两块钱。

　　 Dafang Southwestern Mandarin
　　 b. 他之这一回才着三千块。
　　　　 TA　 ZHI　YI　 HUI　CAI　 tso²¹
　　　　 3SG　this　one　time　only　suffer.finacial.loss
　　　　 SAN　 QIAN　　 KUAI.
　　　　 three　thousand　CURRENCY.UNIT
　　　　 'He was only defrauded of 3000 yuan.'
　　　　 (Li Lan 2006: 199, glossed and translated by the author)

(III) To express 'need', the use of *dɤ³³* is very limited, but it is often used with *niɔ³³* 'want' to form a compound verb *niɔ³³dɤ³³* (see Chapter 11 on modality). The only case in our data in which *dɤ³³* is used alone as a verb denoting 'need, be worth' is exemplified below.

(7.17) - ɔ²¹ ã²¹ã⁵⁵ po⁵⁵ **tɤ³³** tɕɪŋ²¹ kʰua²¹ tie⁵⁵?
　　　　 this　jar　 CLF　need　money　how　much
　　　　 'How much is this jar?'
　　　　 这个罐子要多少钱?

　　 - **tɤ³³** tɕɪŋ²¹ tsaŋ⁵⁵ pʰe⁵⁵.
　　　　 need　money　ten　CURRENCY.UNIT
　　　　 '(It's) ten yuan.'
　　　　 要十块钱。

(IV) Denoting 'hit the target', *dɤ³³* is usually used as a verbal complement as in (7.18a), while the verbal use of this meaning has become obsolete and rare. The expression [dɤ³³ NP_HUMAN] in (7.18b) literally denotes 'hit someone', but is used metaphorically to express 'attract someone'. Interestingly, this use is also attested in Late Medieval Chinese, as can be seen in (7.18c).

(7.18) a. mɔ²¹ lɔ²¹po⁵⁵ niɔ³³ tɤ³³ ɪŋ⁵⁵soŋ²¹ tsa³³-**tɤ³³**
　　　　 that　peach　want　PASS　sun　shine.upon-hit.(the target)
　　　　 tsʰɛ²¹ tsʰɿ⁵⁵ to³³.
　　　　 so.that　red　can
　　　　 'The peaches can only turn red after being shone upon by the sun.'
　　　　 桃子要被太阳晒到才能红。

b. mɔ²⁴ ni³³ tʏ²¹ nɯ³³ lɔ³³ pʏ³³ tʏ³³?
   that CLF hit.(the target) 2SG or NEG hit.(the target)
   'Does that person attract you?'
   那个人中你的意吗？

Late Medieval Chinese
c. 我见你这小的，生的干净济楚，委的**着人**。
   wǒ jiàn nǐ   zhè xiǎo de,   shēng de   gānjìng
   1SG see 2SG this young NMLZ be.born VCOMP clean
   jǐchǔ, wěide **zhuó**   rén.
   neat   indeed hit.(the target) people
   'It seems to me that you look neat and clean and indeed attractive to people.'
   《挣报恩·楔子》 [Scrambling to requite favors · Prologue] (1271–1368)
   (quoted from Long Qianan 1985: 860, glossed and translated by the author)

(V) To express 'like', it is commonly the verb *tɕʰi³³kʰa³³* that is used in Caijia instead of *dʏ³³*, as in (7.19a). Even though 'like' is an obsolete use, the meaning 'like' of *dʏ³³* can still be observed, as in (7.19b) and (7.19c). Instances of the morpheme ZHUO/ZHU's denoting 'like' are rarely reported in contemporary Sinitic languages, but this use can be found in Late Medieval Chinese, as exemplified in (7.19d).

(7.19) a. ŋo³³ [tɕʰi³³kʰa³³]/[***tʏ²¹**] je³³ xɪŋ⁵⁵.
        1SG like/like   3SG very
        'I like him very much.'
        我很喜欢他。

    b. mɔ²¹ nioŋ²⁴ ni³³ tɯ²¹ ni³³ **tʏ²¹** xɪŋ⁵⁵.
       that girl CLF attract other like very
       'That girl is very attractive to people.'
       那个女孩儿很惹人爱。

    c. je²⁴ ta⁵⁵ fɛ²¹hɛ²¹ sʅ³³ ji³³ ni³³ pʏ³³ **tʏ²¹**
       3PL two family CONT one CLF NEG like
       ji³³ ni³³ sʅ²¹.
       one CLF CONT
       'These two families don't like each other.'
       他们两家人互相不喜欢。

Late Medieval Chinese
d. 吾老着读书，余事不挂眼
   wù   lǎo   **zhuó** dú   shū, yú   shì   bù   guà   yǎn
   1SG   old   like   read book other thing NEG   hang eye
   'I'm old and like reading; other things can't attract my attention.'
   韩愈《赠张籍》[For Zhang Ji] by Han Yu (768–824)
   (quoted from Jiang and Cao 1997:459, glossed and translated by the author)

(VI) Moreover, dy^{33} in Caijia also possesses the rare meaning of 'grow, give birth, bear (fruit)', as shown in (7.20a)-(7.20c). This meaning of ZHUO/ZHU for Early and Late Medieval Chinese is even rarer than 'like' in the literature, but can still be found. See the examples from Early and Late Medieval Chinese in (7.20d) and (7.20e).

(7.20) a. je^{33} **ty^{33}**-la^{21} tuu^{33} $tiu^{33}u^{33}$ o.
       3SG   grow-big   then   know   CRS
       'He'll know when he grows up.'
       他长大就知道了。

   b. je^{33} $mɔ^{21}$ $tsɿ^{55}$ $so^{55}po^{24}$ ni^{33} **ty^{33}** $ŋa^{55}$ o.
      3SG   that   son   wife   CLF   bear   child   CRS
      'His son's wife bore a child.'
      他那儿媳妇生孩子了。

   c. $lɔ^{21}po^{55}$ $sɔ^{55}$ **ty^{33}** $lɔ^{21}po^{55}$ o.
      peach tree   bear   peach   CRS
      'The peach tree bore peaches.'
      桃树结桃子了。

Early Medieval Chinese
d. 四岁，上下生成齿二；五岁，上下著成齿四
   sì   suì   shàng xià   **shēng**-chéng chǐ   èr;
   four year upside downside grow-become tooth two
   wǔ   suì   shàng xià   **zhuó**-chéng chǐ   sì;
   five year upside downside grow-become tooth four
   '(Cattles, mules and horses) grow two teeth respectively on their upper and lower (jaws) when they are four years old; (they) grow four teeth respectively on their upper and lower (jaws) when they are five years old.'
   贾思勰《齐民要术》[Essential techniques for the welfare of the people (533 – 544ad)] by Jia Sixie
   (quoted from Zhang Cheng 2000, glossed and translated by the author)

Late Medieval Chinese

e. 春根夏苗秋着子
chūn gēn xià miáo qiū **zhuó** zǐ
spring root summer seedling autumn bear seed
'The root of spring grows in summer and bears seeds in autumn.'
苏轼《周教授索枸杞因以诗赠》[For officer Zhou] by Su Shi
(1037–1101)

On the basis of both phonetic and semantic similarities, we can conclude that Caijia $dγ^{33}$ is probably cognate with ZHUO/ZHU 著/着 which is now a common passive marker in Sinitic languages (Li Lan 2006, Chappell 2015b).

In contemporary Sinitic languages, the passives with ZHUO/ZHU are mainly distributed in Southwestern Mandarin (Li Lan 2006). In comparison with *bèi* 被, whose passive use is already observed in Late Archaic Chinese (5th – 3rd B.C.) (Peyraube 1986), the passive use of ZHUO/ZHU is relatively recent. According to Tian Chunlai (2009), the passive use of ZHUO/ZHU began to appear in Early Medieval Chinese (3rd – 4th century) but only rose in frequency after the Song dynasty, i.e. during the periods of Pre-Modern (1250 – 14th century) and Modern Chinese (15th – 18th century). Tian Chunlai (2009) proposes that the agentful passives with ZHUO/ZHU are derived from its causative use of 'let', while the agentless ones developed from its lexical use of 'suffer'. By contrast, Wu Fuxiang (1996) considers the latter, i.e. 'suffer', as the source of the passives with ZHUO/ZHU. However, observing the examples used by Tian Chunlai (2009), we find that both agentful and agentless passives with ZHUO/ZHU have co-existed since the Tang dynasty. It would, however, be really difficult to explain how and why the passives with ZHUO/ZHU are derived from different functions. Therefore, we will not attempt this in the present chapter. In Caijia, $dγ^{33}$ cannot be used as a causative verb. Among all the lexical uses of $dγ^{33}$ 'passively receive, suffer', uses (I) and (II), seem to be the most plausible source for its current passive use.

7.2.2.2 Part of speech and source construction of $dγ^{33}$ passives

Like the passive marker *bèi* (< 'cover, suffer') in Standard Mandarin, it is also difficult to determine to which part of speech of the passive marker $dγ^{33}$ belongs due to the optional presence of NP$_P$, as in (7.1) and (7.7c). Recalling that the two subtypes of the SUFFER passives have the following forms:

Type I SUFFER: (NP$_P$) + **dγ^{33}** + NP$_A$ + VP
               (NP$_P$) + **dγ^{33}** + VP

Establishing the part of speech of *bèi* in Standard Mandarin is still controversial. It is treated as an auxiliary or verb in Hashimoto (1988), Yue-Hashimoto (1971), Chu (1973), and Tang (2001), or as a preposition in Chao (1968), Li and Thompson (1981), and Zhu Dexi (1982). Peyraube (1989) proposes that Standard Mandarin *bèi* in agentful passives can be treated as a preposition since it has undergone delexicalization, whereas its verbal status has been retained in many cases, such as in agentless passives. This can be explained by the divergence principle of grammaticalization (Hopper 1991). Lü Shuxiang (1999:67–68 [1980]) considers *bèi* as either a preposition or an auxiliary, depending on the different syntactic structures in which it appears. Shi Dingxu modifies Lü Shuxiang's analysis in proposing that there are actually two *bèi*'s and if "two beis occur in the same sentence, the second *bei* is deleted by the process of haplology" (1997: 49). The reason why the part of speech for *bèi*, especially the *bèi* of agentless passives, remains controversial is that prepositional objects cannot be omitted in Standard Chinese. This feature makes the agentless *bèi* distinct from other prepositions. By way of contrast, verbs can take verbs as objects or complements.

Considering languages as dynamic, we take the same stance as Peyraube (1989) for analyzing the passive $ɖʐ^{33}$ in Caijia. We treat $ɖʐ^{33}$ as a preposition in an agentful passive and as a passive auxiliary in an agentless passive.

The source constructions for Caijia passives can still be identified in certain cases in which the verb $ɖʐ^{33}$ 'receive, suffer' takes a clausal object, schematized as [NP$_1$ $_{VP}$[V$_{1(-}$ $ɖʐ^{33})$ $_O$[NP$_2$ VP$_2$ NP$_3$]]. One should not confuse the source construction with the agentful passive construction. Though the VP cannot take an object in the latter, this is not the case for the source construction.

Compare the source construction and the agentful passive construction in (7.21). In (7.21a), one can observe that the post-VP patient argument, NP$_P$, nu^{33} 'you', is co-referential with the omitted subject of the verb $tʂ^{33}$ 'receive, suffer', that is, the experiencer argument (NP$_E$); whereas in a common agentful passive construction, the post-VP position is empty, as shown in (7.21b). Given that a prepositional object cannot function as the subject of the clause chained after it, $ɖʐ^{33}$ must be analyzed as a verb in the case of (7.21a). This is similar to causative constructions, in which the causee is a pivotal argument, and the causative verb is usually not treated as a preposition. It is true that the morpheme ZHUO/ZHU in Medieval Chinese can be used as a causative verb and the causative ZHUO/ZHU is considered as the source for the passive marker in some Sinitic languages (Li Lan 2006, Tian Chuanlai 2009). Nonetheless, $ɖʐ^{33}$ in Caijia does not possess any causative interpretation or use at all.

7.2 Passives in Caijia — 235

(7.21) Source construction: [NP$_{E(i)}$ $_{VP}$[V$_1$(dʝ^{33}) $_O$[NP$_2$ VP$_2$ NP$_{3(i)}$]]

a. Ø$_i$ piɔ^{24} tʝ^{33} $_O$[ni^{21} ɕie^{21}-tsaŋ^{33} [**nɯ^{33}**]$_i$].
    NEG.IMP   receive   3   small-look   2SG
    (NP$_E$)   V$_1$ [NP$_A$ VP$_2$ NP$_P$]

'Don't let others look down upon you (LIT: Don't be looked down upon by others).'

别被人小看你。

Agentful passive construction: (NP$_P$) $_{PrepP}$[**dʝ^{33}** NP$_A$] VP

b. Ø$_i$ piɔ^{24} tʝ^{33} ni^{21} ɕie^{21}-tsaŋ^{33} Ø$_i$.
    NEG.IMP   PASS   3   small-look
    (NP$_P$)   PASS   NP$_A$ VP

'Don't let others look down upon you (LIT: Don't be looked down upon by others).'

别被人小看。

Two more examples of source constructions for passives are given below. Both can be schematized as [NP$_{E(i)}$ $_{VP}$[V$_{(\sim dʝ^{33})}$ $_O$[NP$_A$ [OM NP$_{P(i)}$] VP]]. Similarly, in both (7.22) and (7.23), *tʝ^{33}* takes a clausal object, which is at the same time an object marking construction. In (7.22), marked by the object marker *a^{33}*, the italicized *je^{33}* 'she', is co-referential with the omitted subject of the verb *tʝ^{33}*.

(7.22) je^{33} ji^{33}xa^{33} tɯ^{33} tsɔ^{21} ŋu^{21} sʅ^{21}.
       3SG   easily   then   resemble   ox   way

       Ø$_i$ **tʝ^{33}** $_O$[je^{21} pa^{55} a^{33} **je^{33}**$_i$ li^{21}-nia^{55} xɪŋ^{55} o].
                   receive   3SG   father   OM   3SG   lead-mess   very   CRS
       NP$_{E(i)}$ V $_O$[NP$_A$ OM   NP$_{P(i)}$ VP]

'She can easily lose her temper (LIT: She acts easily like an ox). (She) is led astray by her father.'

她动不动就使性子。被她爸把她带坏了。

The italicized marked object *je^{33}* 'it', in (7.23), is co-referential with the subject *mɔ^{21} ɔ^{55} ji^{21} tsa^{55}* 'that room'

(7.23) [mɔ^{21} ɔ^{55} ji^{21} tsa^{55}]$_i$ **tʝ^{33}** $_O$[nɛ^{21} ʑi^{33}
       that   room   one   CLF   receive   your.family   mother
       ta^{55} nɯ^{21} a^{33} (**je^{33}**$_i$)   pia^{33}-kʰɯ^{33} ha^{51} o].
       BEN   2SG   OM/DCR   3SG   move-open   COMPL   CRS

'That room is cleared out for you by your mother.'

那间房被你妈给你把(它)腾出来了。

Admittedly, even though dy^{33} is treated as a verb in (7.21a) as well as in (7.22) and (7.23) in terms of its certain syntactic behavior, its lexical meaning 'receive, suffer' has already been bleached, especially when compared with the lexical use of dy^{33} exemplified in (7.13)-(7.16). This is a common phenomenon when the process of grammaticalization takes place (Heine, Claudi and Hünnemeyer 1991: 40). In other words, although the source construction is syntactically distinct from the passives, it is semantically similar. What we have identified as source constructions for SUFFER passives is in the intermediate stage for dy^{33} situated between its lexical and grammatical forms.

We must emphasize that constructions like the one illustrated in (7.21a) are marginal. It is usually ungrammatical to repeat the patient argument in the post-VP position in a passive construction, as shown in (7.24).

(7.24) a. ŋo³³ tγ³³ je³³ mɛ³³ o.
       1SG   PASS 3SG   scold CRS
       NP$_P$ PASS NP$_A$ VP
       'I was scolded by him.'
       我被他骂了。

   b. *ŋo³³ tγ³³ je³³ mɛ³³ ŋo²¹ o.
       1SG   PASS 3SG   scold 1SG   CRS
       NP$_P$ PASS NP$_A$ VP   NP$_P$
       (Attempted: 'I was scolded by him (LIT: *I by him scolded me.).')
       *我被他骂我了。

The restriction on repetition is a solid piece of evidence that the agentful passive construction is more grammaticalized than the source construction. It shows a degree of conventionalization to which the patient argument can no longer appear in the post-VP position. This means that the syntactic ability of the VP in a passive construction has been reduced, that is, it is ungrammatical for it to take an object. As we have shown, this is quite different from the VP in the source construction. Therefore, dy^{33} can be treated as a more grammaticalized form of a preposition.

As for the dy^{33} in the agentless passive, its part of speech remains problematic. Treating it as an auxiliary is only an expedient solution or a compromise because it is less problematic than treating it as a preposition. Notably, prepositional objects usually cannot be omitted in Caijia, as in Standard Mandarin (see Chapter 4 §4.5 on Caijia prepositions). Note that the syntactic ability of the VP in a Caijia agentless passive is also reduced. Similar to the VP in an agentful passive, it cannot take an object, as shown in (7.25) below.

(7.25) *ŋo³³ tʏ³³ mɛ³³ ŋo²¹ o.
 1SG PASS scold 1SG CRS
 (Attempted: 'I was scolded by him (LIT: *I was scolded me).')
 *我被骂我了。

By way of contrast, the main verb in an auxiliary phrase functions as a common active verb. Compare (7.25) with the following example, in which ɕiaŋ⁵⁵ is an auxiliary.

(7.26) ŋo³³ la²¹ pʏ²¹ ɕiaŋ⁵⁵ mɛ³³ je³³ sɿ²¹.
 1SG also NEG want scold 3SG AFF
 'I certainly didn't want to scold him.'
 我也不想骂他的。

7.2.3 Type II let: *a²¹sɿ⁵⁵* 'take-give ~ give/let'

The second passive marker *a²¹sɿ⁵⁵*, specifically the passive agent marker, is also derived from a common Sinitic source, i.e. from causative verbs derived from verbs of 'giving'. It is a compound form composed of two analytical morphemes, the verb *a³³* 'take' and the verb *sɿ⁵⁵* 'give, let', as discussed in Chapter 6 on causative constructions. Example (7.27) below shows the lexical uses of these two morphemes, i.e. *a³³* as 'take' and *sɿ⁵⁵* as 'let' and 'give'. It should be mentioned that *sɿ⁵⁵* as 'give' in Caijia has already lost its full verbality (see also Chapter 5). It can only be used as the second verb in a serial verb construction but cannot be used to form an independent predicate, as shown in (7.28a). To form a ditransitive construction of giving, one must use the form 'take...to', as illustrated in (7.28b). One can observe that the purposive marker *ɣɯ²¹*, derived from 'come', is used to link two verb phrases 'take some peaches' and 'give you'. Therefore, we can judge that the second *sɿ⁵⁵* in (7.29) has to be a verb.

(7.27) ŋuɛ²¹ ʐi³³ **sɿ⁵⁵** ŋo²¹ **a³³** lɔ²¹po⁵⁵ sui⁵⁵
 my.family mother let 1SG take peach some
 (ɣɯ²¹) **sɿ⁵⁵** nɯ³³.
 PURP give 2SG
 'My mother asked me to take some peaches to give you to eat.'
 我妈让我拿些桃子给你。

(7.28) a. *je³³ **sɿ⁵⁵** ŋo²¹ ʑe²¹ ji²¹ tɔ⁵⁵.
3SG give 1SG flower one CLF
'He gave me a flower.'
他给了我一朵花。

b. je³³ **a³³** ʑe²¹ ji²¹ tɔ⁵⁵ **sɿ⁵⁵** ŋo²¹
3SG take flower one CLF to 1SG
'He gave me a flower (LIT: He took a flower to me).'
他给了我一朵花。

When $a^{21}sɿ^{55}$ is used as the passive agent marker, it must be treated as one word. However, its source form is actually a serial verb construction with the object NP of a^{33} 'take' dropped. Such syntactic environments make it possible to reanalyze a^{33} and $sɿ^{55}$ as one word denoting 'give, give/let', even though the empty object position of a^{33} can often be filled, as shown in (7.29) and (7.30).

(7.29) a. to²⁴ mo³³ ɣã²¹ kʰoŋ²¹ xu²⁴ po⁵⁵,
cupboard inside have empty box CLF
nɯ³³ [**a²¹** ∅ **sɿ⁵⁵**] ŋo³³.
2SG take to me
柜子里有个空盒子，拿给我。

b. a³³ mɔ²¹ kʰoŋ²¹ xu²⁴ po⁵⁵ sɿ⁵⁵ ŋo³³.
take that empty box CLF to 1SG
'Give me that empty box.'
给我那个空盒子。

(7.30) a. nɯ³³ tsaŋ²¹ sɿ²¹mɔ⁵⁵ sɿ²¹?
2SG look what CONT
[**a²¹** ∅ **sɿ⁵⁵**] ŋo²¹ tsaŋ²¹ mi⁵⁵.
[take give]/let 1SG look a.little
'What are you looking at? Give it to me to have a look/Let me have a look.'
你在看什么？拿给/让我看下。

b. **a³³** nɯ³³ tsaŋ²¹ sɿ²¹ **sɿ⁵⁵** ŋo²¹ tsaŋ²¹ mi⁵⁵.
take 2SG look NMLZ give/let 1SG look a.little
'Give the thing you're looking at to me to have a look.'
拿你看的给我看下。

Once the meaning 'give/let' is acquired, the context for reanalyzing $a^{21}sı^{55}$ as a passive agent marker is achieved. Example (7.31) shows an ambiguous context in which $a^{21}sı^{55}$ can be analyzed as a compound verb of 'giving', a causative verb or a passive agent marker; while (7.32) illustrates the overlap between 'let' and the passive agent marker. It should be mentioned that $sı^{55}$ 'let', $a^{21}sı^{55}$ 'let/PASS' and $dγ^{33}$ 'PASS' can all be used in the context of (7.32), but $a^{21}sı^{55}$ only can function in this particular context as a causative verb and a passive agent marker. If $sı^{55}$ is used, (7.32) can only be interpreted as belonging to a causative context. Similarly, if $dγ^{33}$ is used the sentence can only be treated as a passive. This neatly provides a piece of evidence that grammaticalization displays a certain degree of fortuity.

(7.31) mɔ²¹ sı⁵⁵   ji²¹   foŋ²¹   niɔ³³   **[a²¹   sı⁵⁵]**   ŋo²¹
       that   letter one   CLF   should [take   give]/[let]/[PASS] 1SG
       tsaŋ³³ ja²¹ nɛ⁵⁵, lɛ²¹tsʰɛ²¹ tl̩²¹ sı⁵⁵ je³³ tγ³³.
       look   EXP   PRT   so.that   send   to   3SG   can
       'You can send (it) to him only after
       (i) the letter is read by me.
       (ii) you give it to me to have a check.
       (iii) you let me read it.'
       那封信要让/给/?被我看过才能寄给他。

(7.32) piɔ²⁴   [sı⁵⁵]/[**a²¹sı⁵⁵**]/[tγ³³]   ni³³ tsaŋ²¹   pɪŋ²¹kɪ⁵⁵.
       NEG.IMP   [let]/[let/PASS]/[PASS]   3   pick.up advantage
       sı⁵⁵: 'Don't let others take advantage of (you).'
       a²¹sı⁵⁵: 'Don't let others take advantage of (you).'
                    'Don't be taken advantage of.'
       tγ³³: 'Don't be taken advantage of.'
       别让/给/被人占便宜。

Examples (7.30a)-(7.32) display different combinations of ambiguity of $a^{21}sı^{55}$: respectively <give, let> in (7.30a), <give, let, PASS> in (7.31), and <let, PASS> in (7.32). The combination <give, PASS> is not attested at all, which conforms to the universal (Chappell and Peyraube 2006: 985):

> If a language has a passive marker whose origin is a verb of giving, then it necessarily has a causative verb realized by the same form and having its source in a verb of giving.

In fact, the pathway: V [+ give] > V [+ causative] > passive agent marker is attested as a characteristic shared by some languages in East and Southeast Asia as pointed out by Yap and Iwasaki (2003) and Chappell and Peyraube (2006). Causative verbs as the source for passive agent markers, are particularly common in both contemporary Sinitic (see Chappell 2015b for the distribution of different passive markers) and diachronically in Chinese. For example, dating back to Late Medieval Chinese (6th century AD – 1250), *yǔ* 与 'give' is probably the first *give* verb to function as a passive agent marker attested in the literature of this period (see Feng Chuntian 1991: 14–17, Ma Beijia 2002: 223). The passive function of *yǔ* 'give' is also attested in Early Southern Min (late 16th – early 17th [Chappell and Peyraube 2006]). In addition, the compound form of 'take-give' functions as a passive agent marker in certain dialects of Southwestern Mandarin such as the Dafang dialect (Li Lan 2006), the Sichuan Yibin dialect (Su Ling 2013) and early Southwestern Mandarin (DCF 1893: 302).

7.2.4 Syntactic and semantic differences between dy^{33} and $a^{21}sɿ^{55}$

The syntactic difference between dy^{33} and $a^{21}sɿ^{55}$ is simple. The marker dy^{33} can be used to form both agentful and agentless passives, a common feature of SUFFER/CONTACT type of passives, while $a^{21}sɿ^{55}$ can only be used to form agentful passives. The passive markers *tso*^{21} 'suffer' and NA-GEI 'take-give' in Dafang show the same contrast (Li Lan 2006). To give a Caijia example:

(7.33) je³³ **tγ³³/*a²¹sɿ⁵⁵** mɛ³³ o.
      3SG PASS/PASS scold CRS
      'He was scolded.'
      他被骂了。

In general, dy^{33} and $a^{21}sɿ^{55}$ are inter-changeable in an agentful passive, as shown in (7.34).

(7.34) je²¹ kγ⁵⁵ **tγ³³/a²¹sɿ⁵⁵** ni³³ tɔ²¹-tsɿ⁵⁵ kʷɔ²¹[kuɛ²¹+o].
      3SG foot PASS/PASS 3 chop-break [go+CRS]
      'His foot was chopped and broken by someone.'
      他的脚被/让人砍断了。

The semantic difference between these two markers is actually motivated by their source meanings, i.e. 'passively receive, suffer' and 'let'. The causative meaning is more or less retained in passives formed by $a^{21}sɿ^{55}$, and is reflected in the limits of its usage. In (7.35), $a^{21}sɿ^{55}$ is not used because its use would lead to the interpretation that it was the speaker's willingness to have the alcohol watered-down.

However, the speaker is apparently not satisfied with the tasteless alcohol and $a^{21}sɿ^{55}$ thus cannot be used in this context.

(7.35) mɔ²¹ tso⁵⁵ **tɣ³³/*a²¹sɿ⁵⁵** je³³ tsʰoŋ²¹ sɿ⁵⁵ pie⁵⁵ mo³³ ja²¹.
that alcohol PASS/PASS 3SG add water to inside EXP
ta²¹ xɪŋ⁵⁵.
tasteless very
'That alcohol is watered-down by him. (It's) tasteless.'
那酒被他往里兑过水了。淡得很。

By contrast, the context of (7.36) permits the use of $a^{21}sɿ^{55}$, because the watered-down alcohol is particularly needed for someone who easily gets drunk to warm up.

(7.36) mɔ²¹ tso⁵⁵ **tɣ³³/a²¹sɿ⁵⁵** je³³ tsʰoŋ²¹ sɿ⁵⁵ pie⁵⁵ mo³³
that alcohol PASS/PASS 3SG add water to inside
ja²¹. nɯ³³ pɣ²¹ saŋ³³. tso⁵⁵tsɿ²¹ po³³ to³³ se²¹[sɿ²¹+e].
EXP 2SG put heart be.drunk NEG can [AFF+PRT]
nɯ³³ ã²¹ mi⁵⁵ tɯ³³ pe²¹-xɯ⁵⁵ɣɯ²¹ o.
2SG drink a bit then burn-INC CRS
'That alcohol is watered-down by him. Don't worry. You certainly can't get drunk. Drink some and you'll warm up.'
那酒被/拿给他兑过水。你放心。肯定不会醉的。你喝点就暖起来了。

7.3 Conclusion

This chapter has presented two passives in Caijia: (i) the SUFFER type and (ii) the LET (< 'take-give') type.

We have observed that verbs or VPs in both types of Caijia passives must possess the meaning of affectedness. Not all transitive verbs can be used in passives, nor can all active construction be transformed into passives, and vice versa. Interestingly, VPs in passives share semantic similarities with those in object marking constructions. We have introduced several periphrastic means which enable certain verbs to acquire the meaning of explicit affectedness, among which resultative complement compounding is the most common one.

Caijia passives are generally very similar to other Sinitic passives. The two Caijia types are not only attested in contemporary Sinitic languages, but also attested diachronically in Chinese. We have proposed that the passive marker $dʐ^{33}$ 'passively receive, suffer, hit the target' is cognate with ZHUO/ZHU 着/著 'suffer' in

Standard Mandarin. Both the phonetic form and several lexical uses of $d\underline{y}^{33}$ can be dated back to ZHUO/ZHU 着/著 in Middle and Medieval Chinese. The marker $d\underline{y}^{33}$ can form both agentful and agentless passives. Following the Sinitic grammaticalization pattern, $a^{21}s_1{}^{55}$ 'give' has developed into a passive agent marker via the causative stage. It can only form agentful passives, while its causative meaning is retained in many cases of ambiguous passives.

Chapter 8
Differential object marking constructions

8.1 Definition and Sinitic typology

> Differential object marking (DOM) and differential indexation (DOI) are a variation in the encoding of direct objects, whereby only a subset of direct objects receives overt coding (DOM), or is indexed on the verb (DOI), depending upon semantic or pragmatic features of the direct object, such as animacy, definiteness and specificity.
>
> (Iemmolo 2011: 2; see also Bossong 1985, Aissen 2003)

Also known as *chǔzhìshì* 处置式 'disposal constructions', which was first proposed and translated as "execution form" by Wang Li (1945 [1984]), object marking constructions can be regarded as a pan-Sinitic feature (Chappell 2013).[11] Take, for example, the famous *bǎ* 把 construction in Standard Mandarin. In a typical Sinitic object marking construction, the object precedes the verb or VP and is marked by a morphologically overt object marker. However, the canonical Sinitic word order is SVO with direct objects unmarked. Take the *bǎ* construction and the canonical VO construction in Standard Mandarin as examples in (8.1).

(8.1) Disposal/object marking
    a. 你先把水喝了吧。
        nǐ   xiān bǎ shuǐ hē   le   ba.
        2SG first OM water drink PFV PRT
        'You drink the water first.'

    VO
    b. 你先喝水吧。
        nǐ   xiān hē   shuǐ ba.
        2SG first drink water PRT
        'You drink (the) water first.'

It has been observed that the object in an object marking construction is usually definite (Lü Shuxiang 1948), or given information and "undergoes an explicit change of state" (Chappell 2013: 787). Explicit changes of state are usually realized

---

[11] Chappell (2015: 22) points out that an exception to the use of object marking constructions exists in the Far Southern area in China, i.e. the Yue, Hakka, and Pinghua area, where serial constructions with lexical 'take' are used instead of the object marking constructions. See also Cao et al. (2008: Map 92).

on verbs by various syntactic means to denote telic events, for example, resultative verbal complements, aspect marking, postposed locative phrases, or verbal classifiers, to name a few. Consequently, monosyllabic verbs usually cannot act as the VP (Zhu Dexi 1982: 185, Peyraube and Wiebusch 2020). Taiwanese Southern Min is an exception here since its object marking constructions may take monosyllabic verbs (Teng 1982).

Both Lü Shuxiang (1948) and Liu (1997) describe in detail different types of VPs in object marking constructions in Standard Mandarin. Admittedly, the strategies for forming telic events vary in different Sinitic languages. Moreover, different languages may use different object markers or different syntactic configurations. Three major sources of object markers and five construction types can be observed in Sinitic languages (Chappell 2013). See respectively Table 8.1 (Chappell 2013: 789–791) and Table 8.2 (Chappell 2013: 795). The verbs of taking and holding are both cross-linguistically (e.g. *bǎ*, *ná* 拿, *laq*[7] 搦 etc. [Chappell 2013: 789–790]) and diachronically (e.g. *bǎ*, *jiāng* 將, *zhuō* 捉 [Bei Luobei 1989]) attested as the commonest source of object markers in Sinitic.[12] Hence, the Type I construction in Table 8.2 is the most attested structure in all ten dialect groups. It is one in the same as the Standard Mandarin *bǎ* construction, and can be identified as the basic syntactic configuration for Sinitic object marking constructions.

Table 8.1: Three major sources for object markers in Sinitic.

I.	Verbs of taking and holding
II.	Verbs of giving and helping
III	Comitatives

Table 8.2: Five configuration types for Sinitic object marking constructions.

I.	Common disposal
	(NP$_{SUBJECT}$) – [MARKER$_{OM}$ + NP$_{DIRECT\ OBJECT}$] – VP
II.	"Medieval" disposal construction with a resumptive pronoun following verb
	(NP$_{SUBJECT}$) – [MARKER$_{OM}$ + NP$_{DIRECT\ OBJECT(I)}$] – VP$_1$ – (VP$_2$) – PRONOUN$_{(I)}$
III.	Disposal construction with clause-initial object and its resumptive pronouns introduced by the object marker
	NP$_{DIRECT\ OBJECT(I)}$ – [MARKER$_{OM}$ + PRONOUN$_{(I)}$] – VP

---

12 Verbs of taking are also attested as object markers in Kwa languages in West Africa (Lord 1993).

Table 8.2 (continued)

IV.	"Archaic Chinese" disposal construction with clause-initial object followed by the object marker with zero anaphor
	NP $_{\text{DIRECT OBJECT}}$ – [MARKER$_{\text{OM}}$ + ∅] – VP
V.	Hybrid disposal construction with two object markers
	(NP$_{\text{SUBJECT}}$) – [MARKER$_{\text{OM(I)}}$ + NP$_{\text{DIRECT OBJECT(I)}}$] – MARKER$_{\text{OM(II)}}$ – PRONOUN$_{\text{(I)}}$ – VP

Next, we will introduce object marking constructions in Caijia.

8.2 Caijia object marking constructions

The canonical word order of Caijia is SVO. As shown below, the respective objects of the verbs 'do', 'take care', and 'look after', are all post-verbal.

(8.2) VO

kɣ²¹ja²⁴	nɛ⁵⁵	[...]	sɿ³³	tɯ²¹	ɔ⁵⁵	ʑi²¹	**tɕie⁵⁵**	**ja²¹pa²⁴**,
woman	TOP		COP	at	house	inside	do	chore

tsɔ²¹fɣ²¹	ɔ⁵⁵	ʑi²¹,	li²¹	ŋa⁵⁵.				
take.care	house	inside	look.after	child				

'As for women, they do chores at home, take care of their homes and look after their children.'

女人呢，在家做活，照顾家里，带孩子。

(*Life in the old days*, texts)

Three object marking constructions are found in Caijia, as summarized in Table 8.3.

Table 8.3: Caijia object marking constructions.

1.	Object marking
	(NP$_{\text{SUBJECT}}$) – MARKER$_{\text{OM}}$ – NP$_{\text{OBJECT}}$ – VP
2.	Cross-reference marking
	(NP$_{\text{OBJECT}}$) – (NP$_{\text{SUBJECT}}$) – MARKER$_{\text{DCR}}$ – VP
3.	Double marked
	(NP$_{\text{SUBJECT}}$) – MARKER$_{\text{OM}}$ – NP$_{\text{OBJECT}}$ – MARKER$_{\text{DCR}}$ – VP

As schematized in Table 8.3, the objects are not in their canonical positions within these object marking constructions. The Type 1 Object marking construction perfectly mirrors the common disposal construction in Sinitic languages, i.e. Type I in Table 8.2. The Type 2 Cross-reference marking construction shares the same structure with the Sinitic Type IV, which is only attested in a handful of Sinitic languages (Chappell 2013). It can be observed that the Type 2 construction can appear only in the form of [MARKER$_{DCR}$ – VP], but the object marker can always signal an explicit direct object somewhere in the preceding context, which is also the reason this type is labelled as 'cross-reference marking'. The Type 3 Double marked construction looks similar to the Sinitic Type V. However, the second marker immediately precedes the VP, rather than an anaphoric pronoun, and this construction has not yet been found or reported among other Sinitic languages. In spite of having the same lexical source 'take', a^{33} is used to mark the object in Type 1; it is used to mark the VP in Type 2; and it appears twice in Type 3, marking both the object and the VP. Therefore, 'object marker (OM)' is used to refer to its NP marking function; while 'cross-reference marker (DCR)' is used to refer to its VP marking function.

In the following sections, we will present the object/cross-reference marker and the three object marking constructions.

8.2.1 Source of the object/cross-reference marker

The Caijia object marker a^{33} is derived from the verb 'take', the most common source of object markers in Sinitic. Unlike the object marker *bǎ* in Standard Mandarin, which has already lost its verbal features, a^{33} is still a very active verb in Caijia. See the following example for its lexical uses. The first a^{33} in (8.3) occupies the first verb position in a serial verb construction, which can be justified by the purposive marker $yɯ^{21}$ (< 'come') used between the two VPs. The second a^{33} is also used as a verb forming a ditransitive construction of giving in Caijia with the syntactic pattern of [a^{33} + NP$_{THEME}$ + sɿ^{55} + NP$_{RECIPIENT}$] (see also Chapter 5 on ditransitive constructions).

(8.3) ni²¹   **a⁵⁵**   ã²¹ã⁵⁵   yɯ²¹   lɯ²¹   mi³³.   ni³³   xa²¹   tsʰɛ³³
       3   take   jar   PURP   exchange   rice   3   say   just
       niɔ²¹   pa³³   seŋ³³   a,
       want   half   UNIT.OF.CAPACITY   PRT
       je³³   **a²¹**   pe⁵⁵   seŋ²¹   sɿ⁵⁵   ni²¹.
       3SG   take   eight   UNIT.OF.CAPACITY   to   3
       'Someone took a jar to exchange for some rice. He said he just wanted half *sheng* of rice. (But) he gave him eight *sheng*.'
       人家拿罐子来换米。人说才要半升。他给人八升。
       (*Exchange of product*, texts)

Chappell (2013: 791) hypothesizes that verbs of taking in Sinitic can grammaticalize in some cases into object markers via an instrumental stage, i.e. TAKE > instrumental > direct object. See also Kuteva et al. (2019: 419–420) for this pathway in different languages in the world as well as other pathways for patient markers. The object marker a^{33} can also be used as an instrumental marker or preposition. The sentences in (8.4) illustrate an ambiguous context for both 'take' and the instrumental preposition and an absolute context for the instrumental interpretation, respectively. Example (8.4a) was produced in a context where the speaker saw a person shaving someone else using a knife. The durative marker $-xɯ^{55}$ can even be added after a^{33}, i.e. a^{21}-$xɯ^{55}$, with a slight change of meaning. Both the instrumental and 'take' interpretations suit the context. In contrast, the 'take' interpretation is semantically singled out in (8.4b) because it is impossible for someone to play the drum by literally taking up one's own hands, even though the sentence 'The little elephant played the drum with his hands' superficially shares the same structure with (8.4a).

(8.4) a. je²¹   **a⁵⁵(-xɯ⁵⁵)**   ɕi⁵⁵   ta⁵⁵   je²¹   pɛ²¹   pi²¹mɔ²¹   sʅ²¹.
 3SG   with/take(-DUR)   knife   for   3SG   shave   beard   CONT
 'He was shaving the beard for him with a knife.'
 'He was holding a knife shaving for him.'
 他在用刀给他刮胡子。/他在拿着刀给他刮胡子。

b. pɤ³³   ɣã²¹   kɤ⁵⁵tʅ²¹   o.   ɕie²¹   ɕiaŋ²⁴   tɯ⁵⁵
 NEG   have   drumstick   CRS   little   elephant   then
 a⁵⁵   so⁵⁵   na²¹   kɤ⁵⁵.
 with   hand   beat   drum
 'There aren't any drumsticks. The little elephant played the drum with his hands then.'
 没有鼓槌了。小象就用手打鼓。

Given that a^{33} is a labile functional word in the three Caijia differential object marking constructions, i.e. object marker and cross-reference marker, the nature of a^{33} will be discussed in the following sections.

8.2.2 Type 1 common disposal: (NP$_{SUBJECT}$) – MARKER$_{OM}$ – NP$_{OBJECT}$ – VP

In this construction, the object immediately precedes the VP and is marked by the object marker a^{33}, schematized as

$$(\text{NP}_{\text{SUBJECT}}) - \textbf{MARKER}_{\text{OM}} - \text{NP}_{\text{OBJECT}} - \text{VP}.$$

In (8.5), being the object of the verb 'put', 'that vaccination' is marked by a^{33} and precedes the VP.

(8.5) ŋu²¹to³³   nɛ⁵⁵   sɿ²¹   ta⁵⁵   ta³³pɣ²¹   tɣ³³   ha⁵⁵,
      cowpox   TOP   COP   from   shoulder   upside   here
      a³³   tsaŋ³³   ɣɯ²¹   tiɔ²¹-tsʰe⁵⁵   tsʰɿ⁵⁵tsʰɿ⁵⁵   nɛ⁵⁵,   *a³³*
      take   needle   come   prick-be.out   blood   PRT   OM
      mɔ²¹   *to²¹tsoŋ⁵⁵*   *nɛ⁵⁵*   *pɣ²¹*   *pie⁵⁵*   ɔ²¹   ta³³pɣ²¹   tɣ³³.
      that   vaccine   PRT   put   to   this   shoulder   upside
      'For cowpox, in this case, one takes a needle to prick this (part of) shoulder so that it bleeds and then **injects the vaccine into this part**.'
      牛痘呢，是从肩膀这儿，拿针来挑出血呢，把痘种呢放到这肩膀上。
      (*Vaccination*, texts)

It has been widely accepted that object marking or disposal constructions are derived from serial verb constructions in Chinese of different periods (Zhu Minche 1957, Wang Li 1980[1957], Bei Luobei 1989, Wu Fuxiang 1997, inter alia) and Sinitic languages (Chappell 2013), which is also reflected in Caijia. However, it is difficult to distinguish an object marking construction from a serial verb construction if one only looks at the word order in these two constructions in certain cases, since no morphological indication can help to distinguish one from the other. Compare the serial verb construction of 'take' in (8.6) with the object marking part of the construction in italics in (8.5). In (8.6), the object of the verb 'take', i.e. 'fields', is also the object of the verb 'divide'. The major criterion to diagnose a^{33} as a verb and, subsequently, the sentence as a serial verb construction instead of an object marking construction, is the use of the purposive marker $ɣɯ^{21}$ derived from 'come', which can be used to connect the two VPs in a serial verb construction in order to express purposive meanings. In fact, one cannot literally take or fetch 'fields' with one's hands. However, it is reasonable in the context that the landlord class at that time was deprived of fields which were divided up by farmers, resulting in a change of ownership.

(8.6)   tɯ⁵⁵   **a⁵⁵**   ɔ²¹   lɛ²¹   sui⁵⁵   **ɣɯ²¹**   peŋ⁵⁵. [...]
      then   take   this   field   some   come   divide
      '(We) took these fields (of landlords) to divide.'
      就拿这些（地主的）土地来分。
      (*The Red Army*, texts)

8.2 Caijia object marking constructions — 249

There are further diagnostic approaches which can help to differentiate a Type 1 object marking construction from a serial verb construction, in other words, to justify the functional feature of a^{33}, as a preposition in the Type 1 construction.

(i) The first criterion is semantic bleaching, which involves the loss of lexical meaning or desemanticization (Heine and Reh 1982: 26), and can be observed as part of the process of grammaticalization. The serial verb construction superficially overlapping with the Type 1 object marking construction, [TAKE – NP_i – V – $Ø_i$], can be interpreted as 'take or get hold of X then act on X'. However, this pattern of interpretation cannot apply to the following example, (8.7). The interpretation 'you take or get hold of this tax and then pay it' does not make sense. Given that tax is a compulsory contribution levied by the government or an imposed duty, people do not take the initiative to 'get hold of it'. This implies that the lexical meaning of 'take' has already been bleached in this case.

(8.7) nɯ²¹   sun⁵⁵   koŋ⁵⁵   mã²¹   ni³³   [...]   lɛ²¹tsʰɛ²¹
       2SG   help   work   sell   labor   only.then
       a³³   ɔ²¹   ko²¹   tsa²¹-kuɛ³³   to³³.
       OM   this   tax   pay-go   can
       'You can **pay up this tax** only if you work for others and sell your labor.'
       你要帮工卖力才能把这税交上。
       (*Paying taxes*, texts)

It is similarly impossible to interpret a^{33} as 'take' in (8.8) as well. This sentence expresses a causative meaning and is most likely an extension in use of the object marking construction. The undergoer 'I' is made tired due to carrying 'you' on the back while walking so far. The VP is actually an adjectival predicate which does not take any object and the subject is a clause that cannot initiate the action of taking but rather represents the causing event. Note that the degree marker or adverb $xɪŋ^{55}$ 'very' is obligatory. Moreover, such VPs as 'very tired' in (8.8) are ungrammatical in the Standard Mandarin object marking construction.

(8.8) ŋo³³   py³³   nɯ³³   ya²¹   ɔ²¹sɿ⁵⁵   ti⁵⁵   sɿ²¹   hɔ⁵⁵
       1SG   carry.on.the.back   2SG   walk   this.way   far   MOD   road
       a³³   ŋo³³   la³³   kʰui²¹   xɪŋ⁵⁵   o.
       OM   1SG   all   be.tired very   CRS
       'Walking this far with you on my back **made me very tired**.'
       我背你走这么远的路把我都累得不行。

(ii) The second criterion concerns the **prepositional status** of object markers. In Sinitic common disposal constructions, equivalent to the Caijia Type 1 construction, object markers are usually treated as prepositions, such as *bǎ* in Standard Mandarin (Wang Li 1980: 410[1957], Lü Shuxiang 1999: 53[1980], Zhu Dexi 1982: 185 inter alia). The marker a^{33} in the Type 1 construction can be considered as a preposition. One could make use of the distributional features of prepositions to test which part of speech a^{33} corresponds to. For example, prepositions do not bear any aspectual marking, do not stand alone as predicates, and cannot take resultative complements, while prepositional objects cannot be omitted (see Chapter 4 §4.5), exactly as in Standard Mandarin (Chao 1968: 749–751). Take (8.9a) as an example. Let us use the resultative complement *-xɯ⁵⁵* 'rise, be up', which is also the durative marker, to run a diagnostic test. On the one hand, attaching *-xɯ⁵⁵* to the object-marking a^{33} in (8.9a) is ungrammatical, as shown in (8.9b). On the other hand, interpreting a^{33} in (8.9a) as the lexical verb 'take' does not work either, viz. 'I took up the hole and covered it up', since one cannot take up a hole by hand and then cover it up.

(8.9) a. nɛ⁵⁵, ŋo³³ tɯ³³ a³³ la²¹ tsa²¹peŋ⁵⁵ka²¹ ti⁵⁵ ɣɯ²¹
INTJ 1SG then take big stone.plank CLF come
a³³ je²¹ pʰɣ²¹-xɯ⁵⁵ o.
OM 3SG cover-up CRS
'I took a big flagstone and **covered it** (= the hole) up then.'
嗯。我就拿块大石板来把它（=洞）盖上了。
(*The big hole*, texts)

b. ***a²¹-xɯ⁵⁵** kʰa²⁴ pʰɣ²¹-xɯ⁵⁵.
take-up hole cover-rise
'(I) took up the hole and covered it up.'
（我）拿起来那个洞然后盖上。

(iii) The third criterion involves a syntactic test. Inserting a deictic verb *ɣɯ²¹* 'come' or *kuɛ²¹* 'go' between the a^{33} phrase and the following VP is also a diagnostic strategy. Sun Chaofen (1996: 69–73) uses *lái* 来 'come' and *qù* 去 'go' to diagnose the grammatical status of *bǎ* and *jiāng* as prepositions in Medieval Chinese. If one of the deictic verbs may be successfully inserted, it means that *bǎ* or *jiāng* is a verb. In an object marking construction, this test cannot be applied, as shown in (8.10). The context of (8.10a) is that the thief figured out within a few days how to steal a cow by observing how the family's daily routine and how they kept their cow. Apparently, it is the thief's observation that allowed him to accomplish this theft. Significantly, such mental work does not involve any physical manipulation.

Note that, in (8.10a), the construction [tiu³³ la²¹ + WH-QUESTION] 'even know + wh-question' denotes a negative meaning '(I) don't know...'.

(8.10) a. je³³ ɔ²¹ tɔ²¹ nɛ⁵⁵ tiu³³ la²¹ sɿ⁵⁵ lɔ²¹kɯ²⁴ ɣɯ²¹
　　　　3SG this thief TOP know even COP when come
　　　　a³³ ɔ²¹ ŋu²¹ tsaŋ²¹-ti²¹ kuɛ²¹. [...]
　　　　OM this cow see-clear go
　　　　'The thief, it is not clear when **he worked out the situation of the cow** (LIT: he saw clear the cow).'
　　　　他这贼呢，也不知道什么时候把牛（的情况）摸清了。
　　　　(*The loss of the cow*, texts)

b. *tɔ²¹ **a³³** ɔ²¹ ŋu²¹ **ɣɯ²¹** tsaŋ²¹-ti²¹ kuɛ²¹.
　　thief OM this cow come see-clear go
　　'The thief worked out the situation of the cow (LIT: saw clear the cow).'
　　贼把牛（的情况）摸清了。

Admittedly, a bridging context exists (Evans and Wilkins 2000, Heine 2002), linked with an intermediate stage of grammaticalization that gives rise to a possible new meaning. In this context, the diagnostic operations mentioned above can be applied, but will produce a different grammatical construction, in this case a serial verb construction. The object marking construction in (8.5) is on such bridging context. Both the resultative complement -*xɯ⁵⁵* 'up' and the deictic verb *ɣɯ²¹* 'come' can be used, as shown in (8.11). However, it should be noted that these particular operations can give rise to a change of meaning, i.e. the action of taking is involved. This is actually quite normal especially when the object marking *a³³* associates with verbs of manipulation. First, the verbal use of *a³³* 'take' is very active in meaning in Caijia, as mentioned earlier. Second, if one wants to manipulate or act on a concrete entity, one needs to first get hold of it. Therefore, in such cases, any change of meaning must be taken into consideration when differentiating object marking from serial verb constructions.

(8.11) **a²¹(-xɯ⁵⁵)** mɔ²¹ to²¹tsoŋ⁵⁵ **ɣɯ²¹**
　　　　take-rise that vaccination come
　　　　pɤ²¹ pie⁵⁵ ɔ²¹ ta⁵⁵pɤ²¹ tɤ⁵⁵.
　　　　put to this should upside
　　　　'(One) takes (up) the vaccine and then injects it into this (part of) shoulder.'
　　　　拿（起）那痘种来放到这肩膀上。

Like the *bǎ* construction in Standard Mandarin (see Lü Shuxiang 1948, Liu 1997), monosyllabic verbs cannot serve as VPs in Caijia Type 1 object marking constructions. The examples given above have already shown several VP patterns, including [V + resultative complement], [V + locative phrase], and [ADJ + degree marker]. Almost all the VP patterns found in the *bǎ* construction (Lü Shuxiang 1948, Liu 1997) can also be observed in Caijia. Let us see several more examples. The following examples illustrate [VP + VCLF], [one + V], and a ditransitive VP, respectively. Note that the patterns given here are not exhaustive.

(8.12) a³³   la²¹sa²¹   ja²¹   **mi⁵⁵**.
      OM   garlic   wash   a.little
      'Wash the garlic.'
      把大蒜洗一下。

(8.13) ŋo³³   a³³   mɔ²¹   tsʰo³³to²¹   po⁵⁵   **ji²¹**   **kʰɪŋ⁵⁵**
      1SG   OM   that   radish   CLF   one   pull
      tɯ⁵⁵   kʰɪŋ⁵⁵-tsʰe⁵⁵ɣɯ²¹   o.
      then   pull-come.out   CRS
      'I gave that radish a pull and then it was pulled out.'
      我把那萝卜一拔就拔出来了。

(8.14) ŋo³³   a³³   ɔ²¹   sɔ²¹   sui⁵⁵   peŋ⁵⁵
      1SG   OM   this   Sichuan.pepper   some   offer
      ji²¹sui⁵⁵   sɿ⁵⁵   nɯ³³   mẽ!
      some   to   2SG   PRT
      'I'll save you some of these Sichuan peppers.'
      我把这些花椒分你一些嘛。

8.2.3 Type 2 cross-reference marking: (NP$_{OBJECT}$) – (NP$_{SUBJECT}$) – MARKER$_{DCR}$ – VP

The Type 2 cross-reference marking construction in Caijia appears to be similar to the strategy of differential object indexation, since a cross-reference marker a^{33} on VPs has been identified in the form of [a^{33} + VP] and occurs frequently in the data. However, the marker a^{33} does not reflect any person agreement but rather denotes explicit affectedness of an entity, specifically the direct object. If the marker is used, it inherently implies the existence of a direct object, no matter whether it is present or not. It can be schematized as

$$(NP_{OBJECT}) - (NP_{SBUJECT}) - \textbf{MARKER}_{DCR} - VP$$

Example (8.15) shows the case of a topicalized object. The object 'the front and back of the house' is situated in the sentence initial position and the marker a^{33} stays with the VP.

(8.15)   ɔ⁵⁵   tɕɪŋ²¹   ɔ⁵⁵   u³³   (nɯ³³)   la²¹
         house   front   house   back   2SG   all
         a³³   sɔ²¹-tsʰʅ⁵⁵ka⁵⁵   mi⁵⁵.
         DCR   sweep-clean   a.little
         'Sweep it clean all around the house (LIT: The front and back of the house, sweep clean).'
         把房前屋后都扫干净点。

The following example illustrates a case of zero anaphora. Given that both the object $mɔ^{21}\ kʰa^{33}$ 'that hole' and the subject $mɔ^{21}\ kua^{33}se^{33}$ 'those ferns' are mentioned previously, this object marking construction is only composed of a marked VP.

(8.16)   mɔ²¹   kʰa³³   tɯ³³   tγ³³   mɔ²¹   kua³³se³³   tγ³³-ɣɯ²¹.
         that   hole   then   PASS   that   fern   block-come
         tsʰʅ²¹ka⁵⁵ **a³³**   pʰɣ²¹-xɯ⁵⁵. [...]
         all   DCR   cover-rise.
         'That hole was blocked up by the ferns. (The ferns) all covered up (the hole).'
         那洞就被那蕨草堵住。（蕨草）全把（洞）盖住了。
         (*The dead tiger*, texts)

The use of a^{33} on the VP causes the verb and its complements to acquire a connotation of having been manipulated, coding explicit affectedness of undergoers. Let us examine a pair of contrastive examples for the verb of placement pie^{55} 'throw, toss, put (with carelessness)', which is often used along with the durative marker -$xɯ^{55}$ to indicate in this context that inanimate entities are in an idle state. In the dialogue in (8.17), both the speakers A and B had reached their late 70s. Speaker A had not done farm work for quite a long time, while speaker B still was still farming at the time. Speaker A would like to persuade speaker B to quit farming. Even though letting the farming lands to lie idle is not Speaker A's main intention, it would be a chain consequence of quitting farming. Therefore, a^{33} is used in speech turn B₁ to mark pie^{55}-$xɯ^{55}$. In speech turn A₂, the speaker encouraged this change of state by repeating the cross-reference marking construction. By contrast, speaker A's farmland is in already an idle state as he was not farming, so when he describes the situation of his own land, the cross-reference marker a^{33} is expressly not used, as shown in the speech turn A₃.

(8.17) [...]

A₁- o!   la²¹to⁵⁵   o.   tɕie⁵⁵-tɣ²¹   kʰua²¹tie⁵⁵
     INTJ   old   CRS   do-obtain   how.many
     sa²¹   kʰua²¹tie⁵⁵   o   mẽ!
     count   how.many   CRS   PRT
     '(You're) old. Do as you please.'
     哦！老了。做多少算多少嘛！

B₁- pɣ²¹   tɕie⁵⁵,   mɔ²¹   lɛ²⁴...   mɔ²¹   lɛ²⁴-sui⁵⁵
     NEG   do   that   field   that   field-PL
     a²¹   pie⁵⁵-xɯ⁵⁵   nɛ⁵⁵   ...
     DCR   throw-rise   PRT
     'If I don't work, those fields..., if (I let) those fields lie idle....'
     不做，那地……把那些地放着呢……

A₂- **a²¹**   pie⁵⁵-xɯ⁵⁵   ma   jo!
     DCR   throw-rise   PRT   PRT
     'Let them lie idle then.'
     把（它们）放着吧。
     [...]

B₂- ......   **a²¹**   pie⁵⁵-xɯ⁵⁵   tɕie⁵⁵   la²¹fe³³?
                 DCR   throw-up   breed   snake
     'Let (it) lie idle to breed snakes?'
     把（地）放着养老蛇？

A₃- tɕie⁵⁵   la²¹fe⁵⁵   je²¹   tɕie⁵⁵   je²¹   hm̩⁵⁵   mẽ!
     breed   snake   3SG   breed   3SG   POSS   PRT
     ŋo²¹   hm̩⁵⁵   xa²¹pɣ³³sɿ³³   hu⁵⁵kʰa³³   la²¹
     1SG   POSS   also   everywhere   all
     pie⁵⁵-xɯ⁵⁵   tɕie⁵⁵ la²¹fe⁵⁵   e.
     throw-rise   breed   snake   PRT
     '(Let it) breed its snakes! Mine have also lain idle breeding snakes.'
     养老蛇，它养它的。我的还不是到处都放着养老蛇。
     [...]

We hypothesize that this type of construction is also derived from a serial verb construction but specifically under the syntactic environment of zero anaphora in the form of [V1ø$_i$V2ø$_i$...] with the verb a^{33} occupying the position of the first verb and the two co-referential objects omitted. This is the context for reanalyzing the verb a^{33} as a verb-marking functional word. Here we have argued that the Caijia Type 1 object marking construction and Type 2 cross-reference marking construction are derived from two different serial verb constructions undergoing two different pathways of grammaticalization. This hypothesis is made on the

8.2 Caijia object marking constructions

basis of the fact that (i) different VP patterns are observed in these two types (see below) and (ii) a specific syntactic bridging context for the verbal marking by a^{33} can be observed.

Most of the VP patterns in Type 1 can also be used in Type 2. Nevertheless, there are some differences: VPs composed of adjectival phrases are restricted to the Type 1 construction (see [8.8]), while monosyllabic verbs can only be used in the Type 2 construction. In (8.18), the monosyllabic verb $l\varepsilon^{21}$ 'sue' serves as the VP. The phrase $p\gamma^{21}\ po^{24}$ 'carry bundle on the back' in this example is metaphorically used to express 'be responsible, take responsibility'.

(8.18) nɯ³³ niɔ³³ xa²¹ tsɛ³³ ŋoŋ²¹ o⁵⁵. ni²⁴ niɔ³³ **a³³** lɛ²¹
2SG need say real speech PRT other want DCR sue
nɛ⁵⁵, nɯ³³ niɔ³³ pɣ²¹ po²⁴ sɛ²¹.
PRT 2SG will carry.on.the.back bundle AFF.PRT
'You must tell the truth. If he/she sues (you), it's you who will take the load.'
你要说真话啊。人要把（你）告（了）呢，你要负责任的。
(*Two families*, texts)

Furthermore, we also observe certain VPs composed of transitive verbs in the form of VO occuring exclusively in Type 2. However, these post-verbal objects are not co-referential with topicalized objects or objects which are represented by zero anaphora, in other words, omitted. This kind of VP often refers to one step in an activity or event which consists of a series of actions. Example (8.19) is extracted from a narrative about Caijia funeral customs. The phrase $p\gamma^{21}\ t^h\gamma^{55}$, literally denoting 'carry the ground on the back', refers to the ritual of laying the departed on a bamboo mat or plank which is placed on the ground for several hours before the departed is put into the coffin. Note that the VP $p\gamma^{21}\ t^h\gamma^{55}$ cannot function as a transitive verb taking an object in a sentence with canonical VO order.

(8.19) ŋo⁵⁵ la²¹to⁵⁵ u⁵⁵tsʰo³³ pɣ³³ tɯ²¹ ha⁵⁵ nɛ⁵⁵,
1PL old person NEG exist COMPL PRT
tɯ³³ niɔ³³ **a³³** tsɔ²¹ piɛ⁵⁵ peŋ⁵⁵ mo³³.
then need DCR put.in to coffin inside
a³³ tsɔ²¹ piɛ⁵⁵ peŋ⁵⁵ mo³³ nɛ⁵⁵, niɔ³³
DCR put.in to coffin inside PRT need
a³³ pɣ²¹ tʰɣ⁵⁵. pɣ²¹ tʰɣ⁵⁵
DCR carry.on.the.back ground carry.on.the.back ground

ha⁵⁵	nɛ⁵⁵	lɛ²¹tsʰɛ²¹	tsɔ²¹	peŋ⁵⁵	mo³³.
COMPL	PRT	only.then	put.in	coffin	inside

'In our place, when an old person passes away, (he/she) should be put into a coffin. Before doing this, (he or she) needs undergo the step of 'carrying the ground on the back'. Only after doing this, is he or she put into the coffin.'

我们老人过世以后呢，就要把（他/她）装进棺材。要背土。背土以后才装进棺材。

(*Funeral customs*, texts)

Literally denoting 'put down the cage', *tɕie²¹ to⁵⁵*, i.e. setting up a cage, in (8.20) is one of the steps to make a new place for hens and their new-born chicks to sleep. Both *pɤ²¹ tʰɤ⁵⁵* and *tɕie²¹ to⁵⁵* are procedures to follow or be experienced in order to achieve the final goals. In these two VPs, *tʰɤ⁵⁵* 'ground' is the object of *pɤ²¹*, 'carry on the back', while *to⁵⁵*, 'cage', is the object of *tɕie²¹* 'put down'. Like the VP *pɤ²¹ tʰɤ⁵⁵* in (8.19), *tɕie²¹ to⁵⁵* cannot take an object in a sentence with canonical VO order.

(8.20)
tsʰe⁵⁵	ɕie²¹	kɿ²⁴	ɤɯ²¹	nɛ⁵⁵,
hatch.out	small	chicken.DIM	come	PRT

niɔ³³	a³³	tɕie²¹	to⁵⁵.
need	DCR	put.down	cage

'(After) the chicks are hatched (from eggs), they need to undergo the step of 'putting down the cage'.'

出小鸡来呢，要下笼。

(*Hatching chicks*, texts)

It has been proposed above that the necessary syntactic environment for the lexical *a³³* to grammaticalize into a verbal marker is that two or more chained bare verbs, i.e. [V1∅ᵢV2∅ᵢ...], with *a³³* occupying the first verbal position, V1, and each verb sharing the same object. The heavy use of zero anaphora in Caijia makes this syntactic context possible.

In certain contexts, the morpheme *a³³* in the phrase [a³³ V] can be either interpreted as the cross-reference marker or as the verb 'take'. Analyzed as the verb 'take', the phrase [a³³ V] can be interpreted as 'take sth. to do' and one can insert *ɤɯ²¹* 'come' or *kuɛ²¹* 'go' between, i.e. [a³³ ɤɯ²¹/kuɛ²¹ V]. Similar to the Type 1 bridging context in (8.11), it is with verbs of manipulation that ambiguity often occurs.

Example (8.21) illustrates such a case. The bolded phrase *a²¹ tsʰaŋ⁵⁵* in sentence (8.21ii) can be interpreted both as 'weigh' with a meaning of affectedness and as 'take to weigh'. On the one hand, if the meaning of affectedness is not involved, one can just use the bare verb *tsʰaŋ³³* 'weigh', which is also grammatical. On the other hand, the serial verb construction a^{33} $ɣɯ^{21}$ $tsʰaŋ^{55}$ 'take to weigh' in sentence (8.21iii) can also reflect, to a certain degree, the meaning of a^{21} $tsʰaŋ^{55}$. This is because, in Caijia narratives, tail-head constructions are often used to advance the narrative, as in (8.19) above, i.e. a VP or part of the VP is repeated in its following sentence. As shown in (8.21), the VP ti^{33} $ɕiŋ^{21}$ $sɿ^{55}$ 'vie to fetch the water of the New Year' in sentence (8.21i) is repeated in sentence (8.21ii). Due to this feature, we can judge that the phrases a^{21} $tsʰaŋ^{55}$ '(take to) weigh' and a^{33} $ɣɯ^{21}$ $tsʰaŋ^{55}$ 'take to weigh' are semantically related. Besides, when weighing something, the action of seizing or taking is usually involved. Therefore, a^{21} $tsʰaŋ^{55}$ can also be treated as a serial verb construction with the direct object 'water' omitted. It should be mentioned that this example is extracted from a narrative which is about a New Year tradition for the people of Caijia. People from different families need to get up early on the first day of the Lunar Year in order to vie to fetch the first bucket of water. After coming back home, one should weigh a cup of the new water and a cup of the stored water. If the new water is heavier, it is a sign that there will be good harvests in the coming year.

(8.21) i) niɔ³³ tɕiŋ²¹tɕiŋ²⁴ lɛ²¹ kʰɯ⁵⁵-ɣɯ²¹ nɛ⁵⁵ kuɛ⁵⁵
        need   early   ADV   rise-come   PRT   go
        tsɯ³³kɯ²¹   ti³³ ɕiŋ²¹   sɿ⁵⁵.
        INTJ   vie   new   water
   ii) ti³³   ɕiŋ²¹ sɿ⁵⁵   pe⁵⁵-ɣɯ²¹   nɛ⁵⁵,
        vie   new   water return-come   PRT
        niɔ³³ ***a²¹***   ***tsʰaŋ⁵⁵***. […]
        need   take/DCR   weigh
   iii) ***a³³*** ***ɣɯ²¹*** ***tsʰaŋ⁵⁵*** nɛ⁵⁵, tsan³³ sɿ³³ ɕiŋ²¹
        take   come   weigh   PRT   see   COP   new
        sɿ⁵⁵   toŋ³³   lɔ³³   ko²¹   sɿ⁵⁵   toŋ³³.
        water   heavy   or   old   water   heavy

'(Everyone) should get up very early to vie to fetch the water of the New Year. After one vies to fetch the water of the New Year and comes back, **[one needs to weigh (it)]/[one needs to take (it) to weigh]**. One takes it to weigh in order to see if it is the water of the New Year that is heavy or it is the water of the last year that is heavy.'
要早早地起来呢去抢新水。抢新水回来呢，要称。拿来称呢看是新水重还是旧水重。
(*Fetching the water of the New Year*, texts)

One more example is given below. In exactly the same context concerning how to dispose of the skin and the bones after slaughtering of a tiger, both [a³³ V] and [a³³ ɣɯ²¹/kuɛ²¹ V] can be used.

(8.22) la²¹   po²¹   ha⁵⁵   nɛ⁵⁵,   po²¹   nɛ⁵⁵,   **a³³**   **mã²¹**,
       peel.off skin   COMPL   PRT   skin   PRT   take/DCR   sell
       kui⁵⁵to²¹ la²¹   **a³³**   kuɛ²¹   mã²¹.   [...]
       bone   also   take   go   sell
       'After peeling off the skin (of the tiger), **[we sold it]/[we took it to sell]**.
       As for the (tiger) bones, (we) also took them to sell.'
       剥完皮呢，皮呢，就卖/就拿（虎皮）去卖。骨头呢，也拿去卖。
       (*The dead tiger*, texts)

As pointed out by Chappell (2013: 798), a similar object marking construction is attested in Dongkou Xiang and can be expanded into a serial verb construction just like the Caijia case illustrated above.

It is indeed extremely hard to identify the part of speech of the cross-reference marker *a³³* in Caijia. It seemingly occupies the same syntactic position as auxiliaries or adverbs do, but no efficient tests can be done to ascertain its grammatical category. The status of a prefix might be proposed on the basis of the four given examples above. However, the following example can help exclude this possibility, since the adverb *li²¹li²⁴* 'gently' immediately precedes the VP *tsʰa²¹kʰɯ³³* 'open up'. The context of the example is about a fragile letter that has been transferred between many people.

(8.23) ɔ²¹kɯ²⁴   niɔ³³   **a³³**   li²¹li²⁴   lɛ²¹   tsʰa²¹-kʰɯ³³   nɛ³³   lɛ²¹tsʰɛ²¹
       now   need   DCR   slow   ADV   unpack-open   PRT   only.then
       tsaŋ³³-kɪŋ³³   to³³.
       look-see   can
       'One can look at (the letter) now, but only if one opens (it) up gently.'
       现在要把（信）轻轻地拆开才能看见。

In spite of the difficulty in determining its status, it is certain that a tendency for *a³³* to develop into a functional morpheme has arisen. Both loss of verbal features and semantic bleaching can be observed. Distinct from the *a³³* in (8.21) and (8.22), it would be implausible to understand the one in (8.24) as 'take' because a speech act such as 'to denounce someone' does not involve the action of taking.

(8.24) wən²¹xua²¹ta⁵⁵ke²¹mɪŋ³³   ɣɯ²¹   mɔ²⁴   neŋ³³, [...]   niɔ³³   xã³³
       Cultural.Revolution   come   that   year   want   call
       taŋ²¹   kua³³   sɿ²¹   ɣɯ²¹   pʰe³³pʰã²⁴,   **a³³**   tɯ²¹.
       do   official NMLZ   come   judge   DCR   denounce
       'The year when the Cultural Revolution came, [...], (the rebels) assembled those officials (in order to) judge (them) and denounce (them in public).'
       文化大革命来那年，[...]，要喊当官的来批判，斗。
       (*The Cultural Revolution*, texts)

The *a³³* in (8.25) cannot be regarded as 'take' either. The verb 'pick up' in (8.25) is actually already conflated with the meaning 'take'. One cannot take the eggs first then pick them up. Moreover, inserting *ɣɯ²¹* 'come' or *kuɛ²¹* 'go' between the cross-reference marker *a³³* and the verb *tsaŋ²¹* 'pick up' is ungrammatical.

(8.25) mɔ²¹   kɪ²¹tɕie⁵⁵   kuɪŋ²¹   pia³³kʰɔ²¹   ha⁵⁵   nɛ⁵⁵,
       that   hen   lay   egg   COMPL   PRT
       niɔ³³   **a³³**   tsaŋ²¹   sɿ⁵⁵   je²¹   po²¹.
       need   DCR   pick.up   let   3SG   hatch
       'After the hen lays eggs, one needs to gather the eggs to let them hatch.'
       那母鸡下完蛋呢，要把（蛋）捡给它孵。

Likewise, *a³³* in (8.26) has to be analyzed as a cross-reference marker instead of a verb, since it is impossible for a person to first take his or her own eyes and then make them go blurry.

(8.26) ŋo³³   tsaŋ²¹   lɯ⁵⁵   ni²¹tsɿ²¹   **a³³**   tsaŋ³³-kua³³   o.
       1SG   see   VCOMP   eye   DCR   see-blurred   CRS
       'I looked so hard that my vision became blurred'
       我看得把眼睛都看花了。

Next, the Type 3 differential object marking construction in Caijia will be discussed. Importantly, this type can show a further generalized use of the cross-reference marker *a³³*.

8.2.4 Type 3 double marked: (NP_{OBJECT}) – (NP_{SUBJECT}) – MARKER_{DCR} – VP

The double-marked construction in Cajia is a combination of Types 1 and 2. Both the object marking and the verbal marking *a³³* are used. The configuration is schematized as:

$$(NP_{SUBJECT}) - MARKER_{OM} - NP_{OBJECT} - MARKER_{DCR} - VP$$

as shown in (8.27). Note that *la²¹pia⁵⁵* is a form of self-address used especially when someone is angry.

(8.27) je³³ pɣ³³ **a³³** je³³ nioŋ²¹ **a³³** to²¹
      3SG NEG OM 3SG daughter DCR marry
      sɿ⁵⁵ ȵuɛ²¹ xa⁵⁵nɛ⁵⁵, la²¹pia⁵⁵ lɛ²¹tsʰɛ²¹
      to my.family REP.PRT 1SG only.then
      neŋ²¹na⁵⁵ xa²¹ je³³ kʰɯ²¹ tɕie⁵⁵ se²¹.
      indiscreetly say 3SG several CLF AFF.PRT
      'He (from the family of Zhang) didn't want to marry his daughter (any more) to our family (of Li), so I cursed him.'
      他（张家）不把他女儿嫁给我（李）家呢，老子才乱讲他几句。
      (*Two families*, texts)

In comparison with Types 1 and 2, the double-marked construction is much less frequently used. We observe that this construction signifies the greater affectedness of the same undergoer as a consequence of the given event. In other words, when expressing a series of affectedness events on the same undergoer via differential object marking constructions, the double marked one often follows, although not necessarily, the previous actions and events involving affectedness which have either been realized by the object marking construction or the cross-reference marking construction. The previous context for example (8.27) is that the family of Zhang agreed to marry the daughter to the family of Li, as shown below. One can see that the Type 2 construction is used to express this original deal between the two families.

(8.28) tɕiŋ²¹tʰɔ²⁴ nɛ⁵⁵ sɿ³³ **a³³** to²¹ sɿ⁵⁵
      previously PRT COP DCR marry to
      je²¹ me²¹tsɿ⁵⁵ hɛ²¹ xa⁵⁵.
      3SG Li_FAMILY NAME family REP
      'It is said that the daughter (of the family of Zhang) was originally to be married to the family of Li.'
      说是开始呢是把（女儿）嫁给他张家的。
      (*Two families*, texts)

Two more examples are given below. In (8.29), the first action on the copper coins is to string them together, realized by the cross-reference marking construction; a further action carried out on them, the sentence in italics, is to tie the string to the hair (so as to prevent them from being stolen), which is in sharp contrast to what people usually did at the time, i.e. simply carrying strings of coins on their shoulders.

(8.29) a³³ ji³³ piaŋ³³ ji³³ piaŋ³³ lɛ²¹ tsʰeŋ⁵⁵-xɯ⁵⁵ nɛ⁵⁵
DCR one string one string ADV string-rise PRT
taɪ⁵⁵ pie⁵⁵ ta³³pɣ³³ tɣ²¹.
hang.over to shoulder upside
ɣã²¹ ji³³ ni³³ tɯ³³ ta⁵⁵ u²¹ ya²¹ o⁵⁵.
there.be one CLF then follow back walk PRT
[...] je³³ tɯ³³ a³³ ti⁵⁵tɕɩŋ²¹ ɔ²⁴ ni²¹ hm̩⁵⁵
3SG then OM front this CLF POSS
tɕɩŋ²¹ tɯ³³ a²¹ kɪ⁵⁵ pie⁵⁵ je²¹ pe⁵⁵ tɣ³³.
money then DCR tie to 3SG hair upside

'(One) threaded (the copper coins) in the manner of a string and then hung (the strings) on his shoulder. There was a person walking behind (him). He tied this person's money to his (=the money owner's) hair.'

（一个人）把（铜钱）一串一串地穿起来呢搭在肩膀上。有一个人跟在后面走。他就把前面这人的钱就系到他头发上。

(*Coins*, texts)

The context of example (8.30), is the same as that in example (8.16), i.e. a tiger fell from a cliff into a big hole and died, after which the villagers gathered to get the tiger out. To winch the tiger out, for which the narrator chooses the double marked construction, the tiger needs, first of all, to be tied up. This action of tying up the tiger is expressed by the common object marking construction.

(8.30) a³³ kʰɣ³³pa²¹ kɪ⁵⁵-xɯ⁵⁵. kɪ⁵⁵-xɯ⁵⁵ nɛ⁵⁵,
OM tiger tie-rise tie-rise PRT
u²¹tsʰo²⁴ jɯ²⁴ tsa²¹ tɯ²¹ mɔ²¹ kʰɣ³³pa²¹ tɣ³³
people then go.up to that tiger upside
tã²¹-xɯ⁵⁵ nɛ⁵⁵, jɯ⁵⁵ li²¹li²⁴li²¹li²⁴ lɛ⁵⁵
stand-DUR PRT then slowly ADV
tsʰɛ²¹ a³³ mɔ²¹ kʰɣ³³pa³³ a²¹ zi⁵⁵-tsʰe⁵⁵ɣɯ²¹.
only.then OM that tiger DCR winch-come.out

'(They) tied up the tiger. After tying (it) up, people then climbed on the tiger standing (there). Only then, (they) winched the tiger slowly out (of the hole).'

把老虎捆住。捆住呢，人又上到老虎上站着，又慢慢慢慢才把那老虎绞出来。

(*The dead tiger*, texts)

It is true that this construction is rarely reported as a differential object marking construction in the existing literature in Sinitic. However, it is not surprising in the case of Caijia, since the verbal marking function of a^{33} to denote explicit affectedness has already evolved, as argued in §8.2.3. The double-marked construction can be treated as generalization of the verbal marking function of a^{33}, for it is no longer just limited to contexts of zero anaphora and topicalized objects.

8.3 Conclusion

This chapter has introduced three different types of differential object marking constructions in Caijia: Type 1 Object marking, Type 2 Cross-reference marking and Type 3 Double marked constructions, among which Type 3 is the least frequent in our sample of data. Derived from the lexical source 'take', a^{33} serves as an NP marker in Type 1, but as a VP marker in Type 2.

Given that different VP patterns are observed, we have argued that Types 1 and 2 are derived from two different serial verb constructions:

SOURCE		TARGET
$V_1 \sim a^{33} N_{1(i)} V_2 N_{2(i)}$	>	DOM a^{33}
$V_1 \sim a^{33} \emptyset_{1(i)} V_2 \emptyset_{2(i)}$	>	DCR a^{33}

Both Types 2 and 3 show irregular development pathways for differential object marking constructions, i.e. the lexical 'take' > cross-reference VP marker. Type 3 in Caijia contributes a new type to the current typology not included in the one outlined by Chappell (2013).

Chapter 9
Constructions of comparison

9.1 Introduction

Constructions of comparison usually involve at least two entities or referents which are compared with respect to a gradable property, such as degree, quantity or quality. Three primary constructions of comparison are identified (Ultan 1972):
i. Equative constructions (or comparative constructions of equality)
ii. Comparative constructions of inequality
    a. superior comparatives
    b. inferior comparatives
iii. Relative superlative constructions.

Some English examples are given below.

(9.1) Equative
    a. Olivia is as tall as Emma.

Superior comparative
    b. Olivia is taller than Emma.

Inferior comparative
    c. Olivia is less tall than Emma

Relative superlative
    d. Olivia is the tallest in the class.

Equatives are similar to comparatives of inequality in many ways. Five common components can be observed:
    Comparee (CMP): usually the subject in a construction of comparison in Caijia.
    Standard (ST): entity acting as the benchmark.
    Standard marker (STM): marker on the standard.
    Parameter (PARA): verb phrase denoting property, degree or quality.
    Degree marker (DEGR): modifier of the VP

In an equative construction, the comparee possesses a gradable property to the same degree with the standard, while the comparee in a comparative construction of inequality has a gradable property superior or inferior to the standard. See example (9.2) below.

(9.2) Equative
a. CMP   DEGR PARA STM ST
   Olivia is   as   tall   as   Emma.

Superior comparative
b. CMP   PARA-DEGR STM ST
   Olivia is   tall-er   than Emma.

Inferior comparative
c. CMP   DEGR PARA STM ST
   Olivia is   less   tall   than Emma.

This chapter will introduce equatives, related similatives and comparatives of inequality (superior and inferior comparatives) in Caijia. It should be mentioned that relative superlatives, as in (9.1d), are not our concern in this chapter, for Caijia does not particularly code the superlatives. As shown in (9.3), the superlative meaning is expressed by the absolute clause 'he runs fast' with the range of comparison designated in the dangling topic 'the three of them'.

(9.3) **je²¹-xɯ⁵⁵ u³³tsʰo²¹ sa³³ ni³³**, je³³ (tsʰɛ²¹) piɔ²¹ lɯ⁵⁵ tɕiu²¹.
     3SG-PL   person three CLF   3SG only   run VCOMP fast
     '(Among) the three of them, he runs the fastest.'
     他们三个人，他跑得（才）快。

The loan adverb *tsui³³* 'most' from the adverb *zuì* 最 [tsui⁵¹] 'most' used in many Sinitic languages can also be used.

(9.4) ŋo³³ sɿ²¹ ɔ⁵⁵ ʑi²¹ sɿ²¹ **tsui³³** ɕie²¹ sɿ²¹
     1SG COP house inside MOD most small NMLZ
     'I'm the youngest one in our family.'
     我是家里最小的。

9.2 Parameter of comparison

Before dealing with the equative constructions, it is necessary to briefly introduce the Caijia parameter of comparison, i.e. VPs in constructions of comparison. This is because, on the one hand, the parameter of comparison is characterized by various syntactic forms that are attested in all kinds of expressions of comparison, including superiority, inferiority and equality.

The parameter of comparison in Caijia can be realized by any form possessing a gradable property, such as adjectives (which are in fact a canonical parameter in constructions of comparison), stative verbs, auxiliary phrases, and phrases in the form of subject-predicate (S-P) compounds as in Standard Mandarin (see Chao 1968: 368–371 for more details of the functions of S-P compounds), as well as predicates with post-verbal modal elements. The following examples shown an S-P compound, a stative *have* phrase [have + NP], and an auxiliary phrase.

Subject-predicate
(9.5) ŋo²¹ ta⁵⁵ je²¹ ji²¹jaŋ²⁴ la²¹ **saŋ³³ pɣ³³ lɔ²¹**.
 1SG and/with 3SG equally also heart NEG be.sufficient
 'I'm as discontent as her.'
 我跟她一样不甘心。

Stative verb: *have* phrase [have + NP]
(9.6) je²¹ pi⁵⁵ je²¹ tɕi⁵⁵ **ɣã²¹ fɛ⁵⁵ka²¹**.
 3SG than 3SG elder sister have courage
 'She's braver than her elder sister.'
 她比她姐勇敢。

Auxiliary phrase
(9.7) la²¹sɿ⁵⁵ pɣ³³ ɣã²¹ kʰɯ⁵⁵loŋ²¹
 Guiyang_PLACENAME NEG have Hezhang_PLACENAME
 kʰã⁵⁵ ɣɯ²¹ zɿ⁵⁵.
 be.willing.to come rain
 'It rains less often in Guiyang than in Hezhang.'
 贵阳没有赫章常下雨。

In many languages, adverbs of degree can also serve as parameters in constructions of comparison. For example, in the English sentence *He runs faster than me*, the adverb 'fast' is in its comparative forms. However, Caijia adverbs of degree do not possess comparative forms. As shown in (9.8b), the preverbal adverb *tɕi-u²¹tɕiu²⁴* 'quickly, fast' cannot be used in a construction of comparison, nor in the comparative of inequality or the equative.

(9.8) a. nɯ³³ tɕiu²¹tɕiu²⁴ ya²¹!
  2SG quickly walk
  'Walk quickly!'
  你快走！

b. *nɯ²¹ pi⁵⁵ ŋo³³ tɕiu²¹tɕiu²⁴ ɣa²¹.
   2SG than 1SG quickly walk
   (Attempted: 'You walk faster than me.')
   你比我走得快。

Instead, equivalent meanings, i.e. gradable properties of actions, must be realized via an extent or manner complementation construction in which the complementizer introduces a VP or a full clause (see also Chapter 4 §4.2.4). This means that the word *tɕiu²¹* 'quick, fast' is not an adverb but an adjective. Note that the derivational adverb *tɕiu²¹tɕiu²⁴* 'quickly, fast' cannot be used to replace *tɕiu²¹* in (9.9).

(9.9) nɯ²¹ pi⁵⁵ ŋo³³ ɣa²¹ lɯ⁵⁵ tɕiu²¹.
      2SG than 1SG walk VCOMP be.quick
      'You walk faster than me.'
      你比我走得快。

Due to this feature, we consider Caijia a language that does not possess comparative adverbs. See Lü Shanshan (2017) for more discussion.

9.3 Equative constructions

A comparison of equality involves two entities that possess a certain gradable property to the same degree. Compared with comparatives of superiority, cross-linguistic studies on equative constructions have not attracted much attention in the past decades. As Haspelmath et al. pointed out, "equative constructions are rather difficult to compare in world-wide perspective, not only because there is even more variation than with comparative constructions, but also because they tend not to be thoroughly described in grammars, and because many languages apparently do not have strongly grammaticalized ways of expressing the relevant meanings" (2017: 28). On the basis of 119 languages of the world, Haspelmath et al. (2017) put forward a typology of equative constructions with six types, as shown in Table 9.1.

As for equatives in Sinitic languages, Chappell's (2017) typological studies reveal three major types of equatives: conjoined equatives, 'have' and 'resemble'-equatives (see Table 9.2). Among these the conjoined equative is equivalent to Type 3 in the typology of Haspelmath et al. (2017), i.e. degree marker unified, and the 'have'-equative semantically belongs to the 'reach'-equative. Chappell also points out that the 'resemble'-equative can be considered as the representative type for Southeast Asian languages (see also Bisang 1998).

9.3 Equative constructions

Table 9.1: Typology of equatives.

Equative type		Schema
1	Only standard marker	Kim is tall **like** + Pat.
2	Degree marker and standard marker	Kim is **equally** + tall **as** + Pat.
3	Degree marker unified	[Kim and Pat] are **equally** + tall.
4	Primary reach equative	Kim **reaches/equals** Pat in height.
5	Primary reach equative unified	[Kim and Pat] **are equal** in height.
6	Secondary reach equative	Kim is tall **reaching/equaling** + Pat.

Table 9.2: Equative types in Sinitic languages (Chappell 2017).

Equative type	Construction				
I	CONJOINED	[CMP	STM	ST	DEGR	PARA]
		tā	gēn	wǒ	yíyàng	gāo.
		3SG	and/with	1SG	equally	tall
		'He's as tall as me.'				
II	HAVE	[CMP	STM	ST	DEGR	PARA]
		tā	yǒu	wǒ	zhème	gāo.
		3SG	have	1SG	so	tall
		'He's as tall as me'				
III	RESEMBLE	tā	xiàng	wǒ	zhème	gāo.
		3SG	resemble	1SG	so	tall
		'He's as tall as me'				

Based on these two typologies, our study on the equative constructions in Caijia shows that equative patterns in Caijia are very similar to Sinitic ones. All of the three types of equatives in Sinitic languages illustrated in the table above are attested in Caijia as well. From the perspective of syntactic structure, we propose classifying the Caijia equatives into three types (Table 9.3).

Table 9.3: Caijia equatives.

Type A	Equative with conjoined referents
Type B	Comitative equative
Type C	Equative with only a degree marker
	C_1 *Reach* type ('have' and 'reach')
	C_2 *Resemble* type

Type A and Type B are two constructions with exactly the same constituents and the same constituent order. They share the same standard marker, *ta^{55}* 'and/with'.

The difference between them is that in Type A, *ta*^{55} is treated as a conjunction, but in Type B it is a comitative preposition (see §9.3.1 for detailed argumentation).

Caijia Type A corresponds to Haspelmath et al.'s (2017) Type 3 ("degree marker unified") and Chappell's (2017) Type I.

Caijia Type B is similar to Haspelmath's Type 2 ("degree marker and standard marker"), but the Caijia type should be interpreted as 'Kim is equally tall with Pat'.

Caijia Type C can be further subdivided into the 'reach'-type and the 'resemble'-type. There are two candidates for the verb slot in Type C$_1$: 'have' and 'reach', equivalent to Chappell's Types II. However, this Caijia type is a construction with only a degree marker, which can be claimed a "missing pattern" as defined by Haspelmath et al. (2017).

Type A Equative with conjoined referents

(9.10)　　CMP　　STM　　ST　　　DEGR　　　　PARA
　　　　　[ŋo²¹　ta⁵⁵　　je²¹]　ji²¹jaŋ²⁴　la²¹.
　　　　　1SG　　and　　3SG　　equally　　　big
　　　　　'He and I are the same age.'
　　　　　我跟他一样大。

Type B Comitative equative

(9.11)　　CMP　　　　　　　　　STM　　ST　　　DEGR　　　　PARA
　　　　　ŋo³³　mɔ²¹kɯ²⁴　　[ta⁵⁵　je²¹]　ji²¹jaŋ²⁴　saŋ³³　tɣ²¹
　　　　　1SG　　that.time　　with　　3SG　　equally　　　heart　　be.long
　　　　　'I was equally patient with him before.'
　　　　　我以前跟他一样有耐心。

Type C Equative with only a degree marker

(9.12)　　CMP　　HAVE/RESEMBLE/REACH　　　　　　ST　　　　　　　　DEGR　　PARA
　　　　　je³³　　ɣã²¹/lɛ²¹/tsɔ²¹　　　　　　　　je²¹　tɕi⁵⁵　　　sɿ²¹　　kʷɔ³³.
　　　　　3SG　　have/reach/resemble　　　　　　3SG　　elder.sister　way　　tall
　　　　　'He's as tall as his elder sister.'
　　　　　他有他姐姐那么高了。

Elaborated descriptions of the three constructions are given in the following sections.

9.3.1 Types A and B: Equatives with conjoined referents and comitative equatives [CMP STM ST DEGR PARA]

Types A and B are actually two different ways of analyzing one sentence, as illustrated in (9.13). In Type A, the subject refers to both a comparee and a standard that are unified by a conjunction into the one NP, while in Type B it is the comparee that is the subject, and the standard is found as an oblique, that is, the peripheral constituent of the predicate. According to Henkelmann (2006) and Haspelmath et al. (2017), the referents, i.e. comparee and standard, are unified in Type A and separated in Type B.

(9.13) je²¹   ta⁵⁵   ŋo³³   ji²¹jaŋ²⁴   toŋ³³.
       3SG   and/with   1SG   equally   heavy

Type A CONJOINED:
    ₙₚ[CMP   STM   ST]   ᵥₚ[DEGR   PARA]
             Subject
    LIT: 'He and I are equally heavy.'

Type B COMITATIVE:
    ₙₚ[CMP]   ₚᵣₑₚ[STM   ST]   ᵥₚ[DEGR   PARA]
    Subject   Oblique
    LIT: 'He with me is equally heavy.'

In each construction, the parameter is a predicate marked obligatorily by the preverbal degree marker *ji²¹jaŋ²⁴* 'equally, the same'. Like the corresponding Sinitic equative construction (Table 9.2), the Caijia degree marker is also obligatory. The word *ji²¹jaŋ²⁴* literally means 'one manner' and the morpheme *jaŋ²⁴* 'manner', judging from its tone value, is a loanword from the local Southwestern Mandarin *jaŋ²¹³* 样 'manner', which bears the departing tone.

The standard marker *ta⁵⁵* is derived from the verb 'follow', which is a common source of equative standard markers in Sinitic and is attested in many Mandarin dialects, in the Gan and Xiang groups and in Xianghua 乡话 (an unclassified Sinitic language), according to Chappell (2017). The verbal and the grammatical uses of *ta⁵⁵* exist synchronically side by side. When *ta⁵⁵* is a verb, it can be used both transitively and intransitively, as in (9.14). In addition, it can be followed by the durative aspectual marker *-xɯ⁵⁵*, one of the important syntactic features of Caijia verbs (Chapter 4 §4.5). In contrast, when *ta⁵⁵* is a grammatical word, in (9.15), that is a preposition or conjunction, it cannot be followed by *-xɯ⁵⁵*.

Verb *ta⁵⁵* 'follow'
(9.14) je³³ ɣa²¹ lɯ⁵⁵ tɕiu²¹ xɪŋ⁵⁵. ŋo³³ lɛ²¹   po³³ to³³.
      3SG walk VCOMP fast   very   1SG   reach NEG   can
      tsʰɛ²⁴ɣã²¹ tɯ²¹ u³³mi²¹ **ta⁵⁵-xɯ⁵⁵**.
      only   at   back   follow-DUR
      'He walked so fast that I couldn't catch up with him. I had to be following behind.'
      他走得快得很。我赶不上。只有在后面跟着。

Grammatical function word *ta⁵⁵* 'with/and'
(9.15) je²¹ ta⁵⁵-*****xɯ⁵⁵** je²¹ tɕi⁵⁵   ji²¹jaŋ²⁴ tsɛ²⁴kʰã²¹.
      3SG with/and-DUR   3SG   elder.sister equally   well-behaved
      'He is equally well-behaved with his elder sister.'
      'He and his elder sister are equally well-behaved.'
      他跟他姐一样乖。

The reason the *ta⁵⁵* equatives are analyzed two ways, i.e. *ta⁵⁵* as a comitative preposition or as a conjunction, is that some of the *ta⁵⁵* equatives belong to ambiguous contexts in which both the comitative *ta⁵⁵* and the conjunction *ta⁵⁵* are possible. We can test the ambiguity in two ways, using (i) relativization and (ii) plural NPs, designed on the basis of the syntactic and semantic behavior of comitative and coordinate phrases. The comitative *ta⁵⁵* serves to introduce oblique arguments. Since Caijia arguments can usually be relativized, relativization can be employed to judge whether a constituent is an argument or not. Caijia uses two strategies to form relative clauses, i.e. gaps and resumptive pronouns (see Chapter 14). The gap strategy is used to relativize subjects and direct objects, while the resumptive pronoun strategy is used to relativize indirect or prepositional objects. In contrast, the conjunction *ta⁵⁵* connects two nouns or NPs forming a complex NP denoting a plural. Therefore, the coordinate phrases can be replaced by plural pronouns or NPs.

Let us, first, perform these two tests on some unambiguous examples. In (9.16a), the use of the prospective marker *niɔ³³* before *ta⁵⁵* already suggests that it is impossible to analyze *ta⁵⁵* as a conjunction, while the *ta⁵⁵* phrase in (9.16b), on the other hand, suggests that *ta⁵⁵* is a conjunction connecting two nouns. The object of the comitative preposition can be relativized, as in (9.17a), but neither of the conjuncts can be relativized alone as in (9.17b).

(9.16) Comitative *ta⁵⁵* 'with'
a. tʰɪŋ²¹koŋ⁵⁵   ŋo³³   niɔ²¹   ₚᵣₑₚ[ta⁵⁵   je²¹]
   tomorrow   1SG   PROSP   with   3SG
   ji²¹hɔ⁵⁵   kuɛ²¹ ka²¹ kʰɯ³³.
   together   go   go   fair
   'I'll go to the fair with him tomorrow.'
   明天我要跟他一起去赶场。

Conjunction *ta⁵⁵* 'and'
b. ŋo³³ tɕʰi³³kʰa³³ zy̠²¹ ₙₚ[xɯ⁵⁵tsɿ⁵⁵ **ta⁵⁵** lɔ²¹po⁵⁵].
   1SG   like   eat   pear   and   peach
   'I like eating pears and peaches.'
   我喜欢吃梨和桃子。

(9.17) Relativized comitative object: resumptive pronoun
a. tʰɪŋ²¹koŋ⁵⁵   ŋo³³   niɔ²¹   ta⁵⁵   **je²¹**   ji²¹hɔ⁵⁵
   tomorrow   1SG   PROSP   with   3SG   together
   kuɛ²¹ ka²¹ kʰɯ³³ mɔ²¹   u²¹tsʰo²⁴ ni³³
   go   go   fair   that   person   CLF
   'the person with whom I'll go to the market'
   明天我要跟他一起去赶场的那个人

b. *ŋo³³ tɕʰi³³kʰa³³ zy̠²¹ xɯ⁵⁵tsɿ⁵⁵ ta⁵⁵
    1SG   like   eat   pear   and
    je²¹ mɔ²¹   tsɿ⁵⁵tsɿ⁵⁵po²¹po²⁴
    3SG   that   fruit
    (Attempted: '*the fruit that I like eating pears and')
    *我喜欢吃梨和它的那种水果

Instead, only the whole coordinate phrase can be relativized, since the coordinate phrase composed of two conjuncts should be treated as one syntactic unit functionally equivalent to a NP. In contrast, the coordinate phrase can be replaced by plural pronouns or NPs. In (9.17b), the coordinate phrase 'pears and peaches' is replaced by the plural NP 'those two kinds' in (9.18a). However, this test does not suit comitative phrases. If the comitative phrase in (9.17a) is replaced by a plural NP or pronoun, the meaning of the sentence will change, as in (9.18b).

(9.18) Plural NP
a. ŋo³³ tɕʰi³³kʰa³³ zɣ²¹ ₙₚ[mɔ²¹ **ta⁵⁵** tsoŋ⁵⁵].
1SG like eat that two kind
'I like eating those two kinds.'
我喜欢吃那两种。

b. tʰɪŋ²¹koŋ⁵⁵ ŋo³³ niɔ²¹ **je²¹-xɯ⁵⁵** ji²¹hɔ⁵⁵ kuɛ²¹ ka²¹ kʰɯ³³.
tomorrow 1SG PROSP 3SG-PL together go go fair
'I want them to go to the fair together tomorrow.'
明天我要他们一起去赶场。

The equative with *ta⁵⁵* is a context in which both tests of relativization and plural NPs can be realized, underlining the ambiguity. The comitative object 'this spotted dog' in (9.19) is relativized by the resumptive pronoun strategy in (9.20a); while the plural NP 'those two dogs' is used to replace the NP 'that white dog and this spotted dog' in (9.20b). Note that when the plural NP is used instead of the coordinate NP, there is no standard marker present, as pointed out by Haspelmath et al. (2017: 14).

(9.19) mɔ²¹ pia²¹ kʰui⁵⁵ kʷɔ²¹ ta⁵⁵ ɔ²¹ kua²¹ kʰui⁵⁵ kʷɔ²¹
that white dog CLF and/with this spotted dog CLF
ji²¹jaŋ²⁴ la²¹.
equally big
'That white dog and this spotted dog are equally big.'
LIT: 'That white dog is equally big with this spotted dog.'
那白狗和花狗一样大。

(9.20) Relativization
a. mɔ²¹ pia²¹ kʰui⁵⁵ kʷɔ²¹ ta⁵⁵ je²¹ ji²¹jaŋ²⁴ la²¹
that white dog CLF and 3SG equally big
mɔ²¹ kʰui⁵⁵ kʷɔ²¹
that dog CLF
LIT: 'the dog with which that white dog is equally big'
那只白狗跟它一样大的那只狗

Plural NP
b. mɔ²¹ kʰui⁵⁵ ta⁵⁵ kʷɔ²¹ ji²¹jaŋ²⁴ la²¹.
that dog two CLF equally big
'Those two dogs are equally big.'
那两只狗一样大。

Therefore, we believe that we have sound reasons to classify these equatives into two different construction types, i.e. [Kim and Pat are equally tall] and [Kim is equally tall with Pat] due to the multi-functionality of the standard marker ta^{55}. See Chao (1968: 681) and Bisang (1998: 709) who argue that there are two ways to analyze the standard marker *gēn* 'with/and' in Standard Mandarin.

9.3.2 Types C: Equatives with only a degree marker [CMP V ST DEGR PARA]

Caijia Type C equative constructions are a pattern in which a degree marker occurs without a standard marker. The two referents of comparison, comparee and standard, are separated rather than being unified in the same NP as in Type A. The examples in §9.3.1 have illustrated that the parameters in Types A and B function as core predicative verbs or VPs. However, in Type C, the parameter is only the complement of the main verb, or acts as a secondary predicate. In addition, the standard in this construction forms an adverbial, along with the degree marker modifying the parameter. The comparee is the subject and the standard modifies the parameter along with the compulsory degree marker s_1^{21} 'like this'. This pattern is paraphrasable as [Kim is tall in the manner of Pat] with the phrase [ST DEGR] functionally equivalent to manner demonstratives, as in (9.21). See §9.3.2.1 for details.

(9.21) je³³   ɣã²¹/lɛ²¹/tsɔ²¹   [[je²¹   tɕi⁵⁵   sı²¹]   kʷɔ³³].
      3SG   have/reach/resemble   3SG   elder.sister   way   tall
      CMP   ᵥₚ[V   ᵥₚ[[ST   DEGR]   [PARA]]]
      Subject   Adverbial   Complement
      'She's as tall as her elder sister.'
      她有她姐那么高。

As exemplified above, three verbs can be used in the verb slot of this construction: $ɣã^{33}$ 'have', $lɛ^{21}$ 'reach' and $dzɔ^{33}$ 'resemble'. Equatives with $ɣã^{33}$ and $lɛ^{21}$ are semantically similar and classified as the same subtype, the Type C_1 'reach'-type, whereas those with $dzɔ^{33}$ are semantically distinct from the 'reach'-type and are classified as the Type C_2 'resemble'-type.

In the following section, we will introduce the degree marker s_1^{21}, which possesses some unique features when compared with those in Sinitic and plays an important role in identifying $ɣã^{33}$, $lɛ^{21}$ and $dzɔ^{33}$ as verbs.

9.3.2.1 Degree marker sɿ²¹ 'way'

Example (9.19) demonstrates that the Type C equative construction shares syntactic similarity with the 'have'- and 'resemble'-equatives in Sinitic (see Table 9.2 for examples in Standard Mandarin). Given that Sinitic prepositions are often derived from verbs (Wang Li 1958, Li and Thompson 1974, Xing 2003), there have been debates as to the nature of Standard Mandarin *yǒu* 有 [jəu²¹⁴] 'have' in the 'have'-type equative, especially about whether *yǒu* should be treated as a preposition (Lin Tai'an 1986 1993, Song Yuzhu 1987) or as a verb (e.g. Zhu Dexi 1982, Cao Wei 1987, Ding Shengshu 1999, Lü Shuxiang 1999). It is true that the usual verb tests, for example, using aspectual markers or verbal classifiers (cf. Chao 1968: 664–665), do not work well for *yǒu* 'have' in equative constructions. Instead, its syntactic behavior is much closer to that of a preposition (see Chao 1968: 749–750).

The Caijia verbs *yã³³* 'have', *lɛ²¹* 'reach', and *dzɔ³³* 'resemble' face the same problem. Just like Standard Mandarin *yǒu* 'have', there is no way of testing their verbal nature in the equative, making it difficult to identify them as parts of speech. Are they verbs or prepositions – other possibilities having already been excluded? We need to recall that Caijia prepositions developed from verbs as well (see Chapter 4 §4.5). Nevertheless, it is important to identify the nature of *yã³³*, *lɛ²¹*, and *dzɔ³³* in the equative, because how these three words are analyzed directly determines how the Type C equative is classified. If *yã³³*, *lɛ²¹*, and *dzɔ³³* are treated as prepositions, the Type C equative is an equative with both a standard marker and a degree marker, or Haspelmath's Type 2. On the other hand, if these three words are treated as verbs, Type C should be classified as an equative with only a degree marker. We will therefore propose, on the basis of arguments to follow, that *yã³³* 'have', *lɛ²¹* 'reach', and *dzɔ³³* 'resemble' in equatives are verbs taking equative parameters as their complements with [ST DEGR] as adverbials. This seems likely for three reasons: (i) the degree marker *sɿ²¹* is a dependent morpheme; (ii) the phrase [ST DEGR] can be transformed into a How-question using *kʰua²¹*; (iii) when a Type C equative is transformed into a polar question, the verbal traces of these three words, *yã³³*, *lɛ²¹*, and *dzɔ³³*, can still be observed. We will now investigate these propositions in turn.

(i) The Type C equative appears to have the same surface structure as Sinitic 'have'- or 'resemble'-equatives. Compare the Caijia Type C equative with the one in Rucheng 汝城 (unclassified) in (9.22).

9.3 Equative constructions

(9.22) Caijia

	CMP	HAVE	ST		DEGR	PARA	
a.	je³³	ɣã³³	je²¹	pa⁵⁵	**sɿ²¹**	kʷɔ³³.	
	3SG	have	3SG	father	way	tall	

'He's as tall as his father.'
他有他爸那么高。

Rucheng (He Lisha 2017 p. c.)

	CMP	HAVE	ST		DEGR	PARA	
b.	tɕi³³	jou³³	tɕjou³³	pa³³pa³³	**koŋ³⁴**	kau³³	tɕi⁴³.
	3SG	have	3SG.KIN	father	so	tall	PRT

'He's as tall as his father.'
他有他爸那么高。

However, in spite of structural similarities, the Caijia degree marker *sɿ²¹* is different from those found in Sinitic languages. First, unlike many Sinitic languages, in which their degree markers in 'have'- or 'resemble'-equatives are manner demonstratives, e.g. *zhème* 这么 [tʂə⁵¹mə] 'this way' and *nàme* 那么 [na⁵¹mə] 'that way' in Standard Mandarin, *ka³³* 'so' in the Shaoxing Keqiao 绍兴柯桥 dialect of Wu (Sheng 2014: 100, 435), *gam* 'so' in Hongkong Cantonese of Yue (Matthews and Yip 2011: 193, 195), *an³* in Meixian 梅县 Hakka (Hashimoto 1973), and *koŋ³⁴* in the Rucheng dialect (He Lisha 2017 p. c.). All of these Sinitic degree markers can also be used to modify adjectives in contexts of non-comparison, whereas Caijia *sɿ²¹* cannot because it is not a manner demonstrative, as in (9.23a). Second, *sɿ²¹* is not an independent morpheme and can never stand alone to modify adjectives. A bare *sɿ²¹* modifying the adjective *la²¹* 'big' is ungrammatical (9.23a); it is the manner demonstratives, ɔ²¹sɿ⁵⁵ 'this way' or mɔ²¹sɿ⁵⁵ 'that way', that should be used in this case.

(9.23) Caijia

a.	ɔ²¹sɿ⁵⁵/***sɿ²¹**	la²¹	sɿ²¹	lɔ²¹po⁵⁵,	nɯ³³	zɣ²¹-ha⁵⁵	to³³	mo³³?
	this/way	big	MOD	peach	2SG	eat-finish	can	Q

'Can you eat up the peach (that is as) big as this?'
这么大的桃子你能吃完吗？

Rucheng (He Lisha 2017 p. c.)

b.	**koŋ³⁴**	ta⁴³	ki⁴³	piŋ⁵⁵ku²¹,	n̩³³	sɿ⁴³	tæ²¹	ɥya⁵⁵ ma³³?
	so	big	MOD	apple	2SG	eat	POT	finish Q

'Can you eat up the peach (that is as) big as this?'
这么大的桃子你能吃完吗？

Note that the manner demonstratives $mɔ^{21}sɿ^{55}$ 'that way' and $ɔ^{21}sɿ^{55}$ 'this way' cannot be used as degree markers in Caijia Type C equatives. As shown in the example below, using the demonstrative $ɔ^{21}sɿ^{55}$ 'this way' to replace $sɿ^{21}$ is ungrammatical.

(9.24) je³³   mɔ²¹   po⁵⁵po⁵⁵   nɛ⁵⁵   ɕie²¹mi⁵⁵mi⁵⁵   lɛ²¹,   tsʰɛ²¹   tsɔ²¹
       3SG   that   fruit   PRT   small   CONT   only   resemble
       mɔ²¹   tsʰɯ²⁴po⁵⁵   sɿ²¹/*ɔ²¹sɿ⁵⁵   la²¹.
       that   vegetable.seed   way/this.way   be.big
       'The fruit of a roadweed is very small. It's as small as a vegetable seed.'
       它那果实呢，小小的。才像菜籽那么大。
       (*Roadweed*, texts)

This dependent feature of the degree marker $sɿ^{21}$ determines that $ɣã^{33}$ 'have', $lɛ^{21}$ 'reach' and $dzɔ^{33}$ 'resemble' cannot be treated as prepositions. If they were, the standard NP 'her mother' would have to be bracketed into the PP as a prepositional object, while the degree marker $sɿ^{21}$ would have to be bracketed into the VP modifying the parameter alone, as example (9.25) illustrates with $ɣã^{33}$, $lɛ^{21}$ and $dzɔ^{33}$. This would violate the rule that $sɿ^{21}$ can never modifies verbs or adjectives alone, as has been shown in (9.23a). Therefore, $ɣã^{33}$, $lɛ^{21}$ and $dzɔ^{33}$ must be verbs (9.26).

(9.25) *je³³   ₚₚ[ɣã³³/lɛ²¹/tsɔ³³   ₙₚ[je²¹ ʑi⁵⁵]]   ᵥₚ[ADV[sɿ²¹]   ADJ[mia²¹]].

(9.26) je³³   ᵥₚ[ɣã³³/lɛ²¹/tsɔ³³   ᵥₚ[ADV[je²¹ ʑi⁵⁵]]   sɿ²¹   ADJ[mia²¹]].
       3SG   have/reach/resemble   3SG   mother   way   pretty
       'She's as pretty as her mother.'
       她有/像他妈那么好看。

(ii) In Caijia Type C equatives, the parameter is the complement of $ɣã^{33}$ 'have', $lɛ^{21}$ 'reach' or $dzɔ^{33}$ 'resemble'. The phrase [ST DEGR] is an adverbial marking the parameter as a whole. Treating *yǒu* 'have' in the Standard Mandarin equative as a verb, Cao Wei (1987) holds a similar point of view that the standard and the manner demonstrative together modify the parameter. Matthews and Yip (2011: 193) also treat the word *hóuchíh* 'resemble' in Cantonese equatives as a verb. Moreover, it is not rare for verbs to take complements rather than objects, e.g. English 'grow tall', 'seem right' and 'look delicious'. Caijia $ɣã^{33}$, $lɛ^{21}$, and $dzɔ^{33}$ are such verbs. Further proof is found in the fact that the phrase [ST DEGR] can be replaced by the question word $kʰua^{21}$, derived from 'good', to form a *how* question indicating that the standard in Type C equatives is not an argument marked by $ɣã^{33}$, $lɛ^{21}$, or $dzɔ^{33}$ but an adverbial of degree. This suggests that they are verbs rather than prepositions.

As in (9.27), the *how* question formed by k^hua^{21} in boldface in (9.27-B$_1$) is used to ask the degree of the girl's prettiness. The Type C equative in boldface in (9.27-A$_2$) is used to answer the question. This also suggests that the phrase je^{21} $ʑi^{55}$ $sɿ^{21}$ 'in the manner of her mother' is functionally equivalent to the question word k^hua^{21} 'how', that is, it is acting as an adverbial. In other words, the standard je^{21} $ʑi^{55}$ 'her mother' forms an adverbial phrase along with the degree marker $sɿ^{21}$ 'like this'.

(9.27) A$_1$- loŋ⁵⁵tɤ⁵⁵　　　　hɛ⁵⁵　mɔ²¹　ɕie²¹　nioŋ²⁴　ni³³
　　　　　Chen$_{FAMILY\ NAME}$ family that small daughter CLF
　　　　　mia²¹　xiŋ⁵⁵.
　　　　　pretty　very
　　　　　'Chen's little daughter is very pretty.'
　　　　　陈家那小女儿漂亮得很。

　　B$_1$- nɯ³³　piɔ²⁴　　　xa²¹　piã³³ŋoŋ³³　o²⁴!
　　　　　2SG　NEG.IMP　say　lie　　　　　PRT
　　　　　je³³　ɣã³³/lɛ²¹　　kʰua²¹　mia²¹?
　　　　　3SG　have/reach　how　pretty
　　　　　je³³　ɕie²¹　tʰɔ⁵⁵　　ŋo³³　kɪŋ³³　je³³　ja²¹.
　　　　　3SG　small　moment　1SG　see　3SG　EXP
　　　　　ji²¹　mi⁵⁵　la²¹　pɤ³³　mia²¹.
　　　　　one　bit　even　NEG　pretty
　　　　　'Don't lie! How pretty is she? I met her when she was little. She wasn't pretty at all.'
　　　　　你别说瞎话啊！她有多好看？她小时候我见过她。一点都不好看。

　　A$_2$- je³³　tɤ³³-la²¹　o　mẽ!
　　　　　3SG　grow-big　CRS　PRT
　　　　　ɣã²¹/lɛ²¹　[je²¹　ʑi⁵⁵　　sɿ²¹]　mia²¹　o.
　　　　　have/reach　3SG　mother　way　pretty　CRS
　　　　　tsɔ³³　　mɔ²¹　mo²¹nioŋ²⁴　pi³³　　sa³³lɔ²¹pie²⁴　sɿ²¹.
　　　　　resemble that　caterpillar　turn.into　butterfly　way
　　　　　'She's grown up and is as pretty as her mother. Just like a caterpillar becoming a butterfly.'
　　　　　她长大了。有她妈妈那么漂亮了。像毛毛虫变蝴蝶那样。

We have mentioned in §9.3.1 that arguments (core or non-core) can be relativized. However, the standard in Type C equatives cannot be relativized, as shown in (9.28). Even if this test cannot reflect the exact syntactic role of the standard in Type C equatives, it at least proves that it is not an argument.

(9.28) *$_{REL}$[mɔ²¹   nioŋ²⁴   ni³³   ɣã³³/lɛ²¹/tsɔ³³   je³³   sɿ²¹   mia²¹]
         that   girl   CLF   have/reach/resemble   3SG   way   pretty
         $_{NP}$[mɔ²¹   kɣ²¹ja²⁴   ni³³]
         that   woman   CLF
         (Attempted: '*the woman which the girl is as pretty as')
         *那个女孩有她那么漂亮的那个女人

(iii) Furthermore, *ɣã³³* 'have', *lɛ²¹* 'reach', and *dzɔ³³* 'resemble' retain verbal traces because they can all be used in a V…NEG V construction to form a polar question on the basis of the Type C equative. Unlike prepositions, they can be used alone in an affirmative response to such a question. In (9.29) and (9.30-B$_i$), *ɣã³³* 'have' in the equative is used in exactly the same way as the verb *ã³³* 'drink' when forming a polar question and its affirmative response. However, the benefactive preposition *ta⁵⁵* does not function in this way (9.30B$_{ii}$).

(9.29) A$_1$- nɛ²¹   nioŋ²⁴   ɣã²¹   je²¹   ʑi⁵⁵   sɿ²¹   kʷɔ³³
                your.family   daughter   have   3SG   mother   way   tall
                lɔ²¹   pɣ³³   ɣã²¹?
                or   NEG   have
                'Is your daughter as tall as her mother (or not)?'
                你家女儿有她妈高了没有？

         B$_2$- ɣã³³   sɿ²¹   o²⁴.
                have   AFF   PRT
                'Yes, she is.'
                有的哦！

(9.30) A$_1$- je³³   kʰɔ²¹-tɣ³³   ta²⁴ɕyɔ²¹,   ŋo²⁴   ta⁵⁵   je²¹
                3SG   take.(exam)-hit.(target)   university   1PL   for   3SG
                kuɛ³³   tɕiŋ²¹   lɔ²¹   pɣ³³   kuɛ²¹?
                give.(money as gift)   money   or   NEG   give.(money as gift)
                'She's got a place at the university. Are we going to offer her some money or not?'
                她考上大学了，咱们给他上钱还是不上？

         B$_i$- kuɛ³³   sɿ²¹.
                give.(money as gift)   AFF
                'Yes, we are.'
                上的。

B_{ii}- ***ta⁵⁵** sɿ²¹.
for AFF
(Attempted: 'Yes, we are.')
*给的。

On the basis of the evidence above, *ɣã³³* 'have', *lɛ²¹* 'reach' and *dzɔ³³* 'resemble' in Type C equatives should be treated as verbs; the Type C is, therefore, a construction with only a degree marker.

In fact, the phrase [ST sɿ²¹] in Type C equatives is equivalent in value to the manner demonstratives, as also illustrated in (9.27). We recall that manner demonstratives cannot be used to replace *sɿ²¹*, as shown in (9.24), a feature distinct from the relevant Sinitic pattern. Rather, it is the whole phrase **[ST sɿ²¹]** which is replaced by manner demonstratives to modify the parameter in Type C equatives in Caijia. Example (9.31a) is a degree question formed with *kʰua²¹* 'how'. Two responses are possible, both containing *ɣã²¹* 'have' in (9.31b) and (9.31c).

(9.31) a. mɔ²¹   saŋ⁵⁵   tɔ⁵⁵   ɣã²¹   **kʰua²¹**   la²¹?
            that   mushroom   CLF   have   how   big
            'How big is that mushroom?'
            那朵蘑菇有多大？

   b. mɔ²¹   saŋ⁵⁵   tɔ⁵⁵   ɣã²¹   [**tsɿ²⁴**   **po⁵⁵**   **sɿ²¹**]   la²¹.
       that   mushroom   CLF   have   basin   CLF   way   big
       'That mushroom is (as) big as a basin.'
       那朵蘑菇有个盆那么大。

   c. mɔ²¹   saŋ⁵⁵   tɔ⁵⁵   ɣã²¹   [**ɔ²¹sɿ⁵⁵**]   la²¹.
       that   mushroom   CLF   have   this.way   big
       'That mushroom is (as) big as this.'
       那朵蘑菇有这么大。

Given that the manner demonstratives *ɔ²¹sɿ⁵⁵* and *mɔ²¹sɿ⁵⁵* can be interpreted as 'in the manner of this/that', the phrase [ST sɿ²¹] can be interpreted as 'in the manner of ST' and treated as a manner phrase. As pointed out by Creissels (2014: 625) "noun phrases in similative role can usually be analyzed as a particular type of manner adjunct". Modeled on this statement, Caijia Type C equatives should be interpreted as following the model ***Kim [reaches/resembles [in the manner of Pat]] tall***.

9.3.2.2 Differences between 'reach'-type and 'resemble'-type

Type C equatives can be subdivided into a 'reach'-type and a 'resemble'-type on a semantic basis. The verb $lɛ^{21}$ originally denotes 'reach for (something), catch up', while 'resemble' is also the source meaning of the verb $dzɔ^{33}$. In contrast, $yã^{33}$ is a verb of existence/possession denoting 'have, possess, there be. . .'. However, when $yã^{33}$ is used in the equative construction, it denotes 'attain a certain extent' and is thus classified as a 'reach'-type. This is exactly the same as the verb *yǒu* 'have' in Standard Mandarin equatives, which according to Chao (1968: 681–682), denotes the "equaling degree" (i.e. "X approaches Y from below and equals it on the scale of A"). Chao points out that the equaling degree is similar to but still different from the equal degree construction (i.e. the one expressed by the *conjoined* type in Table 9.2). Lü Shuxiang (1999: 631), concurring with this position, considers that the verb *yǒu* 'have' in Standard Mandarin can be used to express 'attain a certain extent'.

The semantic difference between these two subtypes of equative is quite transparent. The verbs $yã^{33}$ and $lɛ^{21}$ express that the comparee attains a standard on the scale of a certain property, while $dzɔ^{33}$ denotes that the comparee merely resembles it. The context in example (9.32) is that the boy's beloved dog was accidentally poisoned to death and the boy was really sad. The speaker uses a rhetorical WH-question, to express the meaning 'No one can attain the boy's sadness'. The negative meaning introduces an absolute value which is incompatible with the more approximate meaning $dzɔ^{33}$ 'resemble'.

(9.32) i) mɔ²¹ kʰui⁵⁵ kʷɔ²¹ sɿ²¹ ta⁵⁵ je²¹ ji²¹hɔ⁵⁵ tγ³³-la²¹ sɿ²¹.
  that dog CLF AFF with 3SG together grow-big AFF
 ii) koŋ⁵⁵koŋ⁵⁵ ta⁵⁵ je²¹ sɔ²¹kʷɔ⁵⁵.
  every.day with 3SG play
 iii) je²¹ tɕie⁵⁵ sɿ²¹mɔ⁵⁵ mɔ²¹ kʰui⁵⁵ la²¹ tɯ²¹
  3SG do what that dog all at
  je³³ pin³³ pa²¹pa²¹tɪŋ⁵⁵tɪn⁵⁵ lɛ⁵⁵.
  3SG side wander round CONT
 iv) ɔ²¹kɯ²⁴ tγ³³ nɔ²¹-sɿ⁵⁵ kuɛ²¹ o.
  now PASS poison-die go CRS
 v) **lɔ²⁴-ni⁵⁵ yã²¹/lɛ²¹/*tsɔ²¹** je³³ sɿ²¹ nã²¹tγ³³kua³³ mẽ!
  who have/reach/resemble 3SG way sad PRT

'That dog grew up together with him. It always played with him. Whatever he did, the dog followed him around. Now it is poisoned to death. No one is as sad as him!'

那条狗跟他一起长大的。天天跟他玩。他做什么那狗都在他旁边转转悠悠的。现在被毒死了。谁能有他难过？

9.3 Equative constructions — **281**

Admittedly, there are contexts where both 'attain a certain extent' and 'resemble a certain extent' are acceptable interpretations, as shown below.

(9.33) ŋo³³   mɔ²¹   ɕie²¹   nioŋ²⁴   ni³³   pʰaŋ²¹   xɪŋ⁵⁵.
      1SG   that   little   daughter   CLF   fat   very
      tsʰɛ²¹   fɤ³³   nen²¹   tɯ³³   **ɣã²¹/lɛ²¹/tsɔ²¹**
      only   six   year   even   have/reach/resemble
      je²¹   tɕi⁵⁵   sɿ²¹   toŋ³³   o.
      3SG   elder sister   way   heavy   CRS
      'My little daughter is very fat. She's only six years old, but is (already) as heavy as her elder sister.'
      我那小女儿胖得很。才六岁就有她姐姐那么重了。

The verbs *ɣã³³* 'have' and *lɛ²¹* 'reach' are in the main interchangeable, but when the parameter is in the form of ᵥₚ[ɣã³³ NP], for example, *ɣã³³ tɕɪŋ²¹* 'have money ~ rich', *ɣã²¹fɛ⁵⁵ka²¹* 'have courage ~ brave', *ɣã²¹ laŋ²¹saŋ³³* 'have conscience ~ grateful', etc., speakers will avoid using *ɣã³³*.

(9.34) niɔ³³sɿ³³   je³³   **lɛ²¹/tsɔ²¹**   je²¹   pa⁵⁵   sɿ²¹
      if   3SG   reach/resemble   3SG   father   way
      ɣã²¹   fɛ⁵⁵ka²¹   tɯ³³   kʰua³³   o.
      have   courage   then   good   CRS
      'If he was as brave as his father, it would be great.'
      要是他像他爸那么有出息就好了。

Another important difference between the 'reach'-type and the 'resemble'-type is that the latter, with the verb *dzɔ³³* 'resemble', can be used in the negative imperative. In such cases, the parameter often concerns controllable qualities, such as, weight, temper, or attitude. See example (9.35). Note that the expression *pɣ³³ ɣã²¹ la²¹ɕie²¹*, literally denoting 'not having the big and small', is used to express that someone is not polite or does not show respect to others. Neither *ɣã³³* 'have' nor *lɛ²¹* 'reach' is grammatical in this case.

(9.35) (nɯ³³)   piɔ²⁴   **tsɔ²¹/*ɣã²¹/*lɛ²¹**   je³³   sɿ²¹
      2SG   NEG.IMP   resemble/have/reach   3SG   way
      pɣ³³   ɣã²¹   la²¹ɕie²¹.
      NEG   have   big.small
      'Don't be so impolite as him.'
      别像他这么没大没小。

The verb $dz\mathfrak{o}^{33}$ 'resemble' also forms two similative constructions in Caijia. Haspelmath and Buchholz's (1998) cross-linguistic study has already shown that similative constructions are formally analogous to equative constructions in many European languages. This similarity is also attested in Caijia. The 'resemble'-type equative shares the same structure with one of the similative constructions. The only difference between them is that the complement of $dz\mathfrak{o}^{21}$ 'resemble' in the equative is restricted to verbs or VPs possessing a gradable property, while the complement of $dz\mathfrak{o}^{21}$ 'resemble' in the similative is not always a VP. From a semantic perspective, as Haspelmath and Buchholz (1998: 313) point out, "similatives express identity of manner, whereas equatives express identity of degree or extent, or in other words, similatives express quality while equatives express quantity". Therefore, it is more appropriate to treat $s\mathfrak{1}^{21}$ as a manner marker in similative constructions, instead of as a degree marker, as in the equative construction.

The Type (i) similative construction can be schematized as *X resembles Y's manner*, as shown in (9.36). Note that when expressing X resembles Y in physical appearance, $s\mathfrak{1}^{21}$ forms an NP with an animate standard NP and together they appear to serve as the object of the verb $dz\mathfrak{o}^{33}$ 'resemble', which surfaces in its voiceless form $ts\mathfrak{o}^{33}$ in (9.36). In this case, the standard noun or NP cannot directly serve as the object of $dz\mathfrak{o}^{33}$. Rather, $s\mathfrak{1}^{21}$ must be used along with the standard NP [ɲuɛ²¹ pa⁵⁵ s1²¹], denoting 'like the way my father looks'.

Type i: **RESEMBLE (THAT)**   **ST**   **MAN**

(9.36)   ŋo²¹   tɕi⁵⁵   tsɔ³³   ₙₚ[ɲuɛ²¹   pa⁵⁵   *(s1²¹)].
          1SG   elder.sister   resemble   my.family   father   way
          'My sister looks like my father.'
          我姐像我爸。

If the similarity is 'cross-species', that is, made between different kinds, the manner phrase [ST s1²¹] is often observed modified by a demonstrative, $m\mathfrak{o}^{21}$ or $\mathfrak{o}^{21}$. In this case, semantic change is not a result of whether or not the manner phrase is modified by the demonstrative. For example, even if $m\mathfrak{o}^{21}$ is used in (9.37) similarity is not restricted to a specific standard, i.e. to a female bee. Instead, it still denotes generic similarity. Nonetheless, using $m\mathfrak{o}^{21}$ in (9.37) designates a specific manner 'the way a female bee behaves'. In other words, the distal demonstrative $m\mathfrak{o}^{21}$ modifies the phrase [ST s1²¹].

(9.37)   je³³   noŋ²¹-xɯ⁵⁵ɣɯ²¹   nɛ⁵⁵,   tsɔ²¹   (mɔ²¹)   mi²¹-tɕie⁵⁵   s1²¹.
         3SG   be.angry-INC   PRT   resemble   that   bee-female   way
         'When she gets angry, she is just like a female bee.'
         她生起气来，像个母蜂子一样。

The standards in both (9.36) and (9.37) are NPs. In fact, VPs or clauses are also observed in the position of the standard. In this case, the distal demonstrative *mɔ²¹* is compulsory. The VP [kʰɪŋ⁵⁵ pã⁵⁵] 'LIT: pull wind' occupies the position of similative standard in (9.38), referring to someone's crazy behavior in the culture of Caijia; while it is a clause that is the standard in (9.39).

(9.38) mɔ²¹   u²¹tsʰo²⁴   ni³³   ɣ²¹-kuɛ²¹   sɿ²¹   ɔ   pa!
        that   person   CLF   be.mad-go   AFF   PRT   PRT
        ji²¹   xa²⁴   xɯ³³   ji²¹   xa²⁴   sɔ²¹   lɛ⁵⁵.
        one   moment   cry   one   moment   laugh CONT
        tsɔ²¹   mɔ²¹   kʰɪŋ⁵⁵   pã⁵⁵   sɿ²¹.
        resemble   that   pull   wind   way
        'That person is probably crazy. He's been crying one moment and laughing the next like a gust of wind.'
        那个人疯了吧！一下哭一下笑的。像抽风一样。

(9.39) je³³   koŋ³³koŋ³³   la²¹   kʰɯ⁵⁵mĩ²¹kʰɯ⁵⁵kʰɔ⁵⁵   lɛ⁵⁵.
        3SG   every.day   all   sour-faced   CONT
        tsɔ²¹   mɔ²¹   ni²⁴   pɣ²¹   je³³   tɕɪŋ²¹   sɿ²¹.
        resemble   that   3   owe   3SG   money   way
        'He's sour-faced every day like someone owes him money.'
        他天天都黑着一张脸，像人家欠他钱一样。

The following example shows the second type of similative in Caijia, which is a serial verb construction with a verb or VP chained after the manner marker *sɿ²¹*.

Type ii: RESEMBLE ST   MAN   V
(9.40) ŋo³³   ɕiaŋ³³   tsɔ²¹   tsɿ²¹tsɿ²⁴   sɿ²¹   pɣ²¹.
        1SG   want   resemble bird   way   fly
        'I want to fly like a bird.'
        我想像鸟儿一样飞。

To make a final observation, in example (9.41) *dzɔ²¹ mɔ²¹. . .sɿ²¹* has already developed into an impersonal construction denoting 'it seems that way. . .'. Unlike (9.38) and (9.39), in which the subject can be added before *tsɔ²¹* 'resemble', the position of subject is empty in the impersonal construction formed by *dzɔ³³*. One should pay attention to the fact that *mɔ²¹* 'that' in this construction is not a complementizer but a determiner modifying the manner phrase [ST sɿ²¹], denoting 'the way of ST', for *mɔ²¹* does not function as a complementizer in Caijia. See also (9.37). It is evident that this is definitely a ripe syntactic environment for the occurrence of a complementizer, for which demonstratives are a common source. However, Caijia is a language that has not yet developed a complementizer viewed from any synchronic perspective.

(9.41) tsɔ²¹ [mɔ²¹ [ₛₜ[nɯ³³ ɣã²¹mi⁵⁵ pγ²¹ taŋ²⁴
resemble that 2SG a.little NEG much
tɕʰi³³kʰa³³ je³³] sɿ²¹]].
like 3SG way
'It seems that you don't like him very much.'
看起来你不太喜欢他似的。

9.3.3 Conclusion

In this section, we presented three equative constructions in Caijia, which can be summarized in Table 9.4. In general, equative constructions in Caijia possess many similarities with those found in Sinitic languages. Type A equative constructions in Caijia are equivalent to Type I *conjoined* equatives in Sinitic *as per* the typology set up by Chappell (2017). Like many Sinitic languages, the Caijia standard marker *ta⁵⁵* in Types A and B is derived from the verb 'follow'. Type C in Caijia is similar to Types II and III 'have' and 'resemble'-equatives in Sinitic. Both the verbs 'have' and 'resemble' are used in the Type C equatives in Caijia as well.

Table 9.4: Equative constructions in Caijia.

Type		STM	DEGR
A	Equative with conjoined referents	+	+
	Kim and Pat are equally tall.		
B	Comitative equative	+	+
	Kim is equally tall with Pat.		
C	Equative with only a degree marker	–	+
	Kim reaches/resembles tall in the manner of Pat.		
	C₁ REACH		
	C₂ RESEMBLE		

We have shown that the standard marker *ta⁵⁵* in Types A and B can be analyzed either as a conjunction 'and' or a comitative preposition 'with'. This ambiguity fully explains the entirely different classifications.

The Type C equative can be understood as a construction with only a degree marker, if we accept that the verbs *lɛ²¹* 'reach', *ɣã³³* 'have' and *dzɔ³³* 'resemble' only lexically code the meaning of equality. We have argued that the standard functions as an adverbial modifying the parameter together with the degree marker $s1^{21}$, which cannot modify the parameter alone. This type of degree marker in Caijia is relatively uncommon in comparison with those in Sinitic languages. It is a widespread phenomenon for the degree markers of corresponding equatives in Sinitic languages to be manner demonstratives. However, the Caijia marker does not function in this way.

Semantically, both $yã^{33}$ and $lɛ^{21}$ used in the Type C equatives denote 'attain to certain degree or level'. The 'resemble'-type is modeled on one of the similative constructions and provides a piece of good supporting evidence for Haspelmath and Buchholz's (1998) observation that there is generally a close connection between the equative and the similative. Creissels (2014) and König (2017) have also explored the diachronic and syntactic relationships between manner demonstratives, secondary predication, and these construction types.

9.4 Inferior comparatives

Inferior comparatives are a subtype of comparatives of inequality. In an inferior comparative, the comparee is lower in rank than the standard with respect to a certain gradable property. In some languages, inferior and superior comparatives share the same structure with different adverbs used to express superiority or a greater quantity, or inferiority or a smaller quantity. Both French and English are such languages, as shown in the following example.

(9.42) English
    a. Buying stamp duty online is **more** convenient **than** doing it in offline physical smoke shops.
    b. Buying stamp duty in offline physical smoke shops is **less** convenient **than** doing it online.

    French
    c. Acheter le timbre fiscal en ligne est **plus** pratique **que** l'acheter dans un tabac.
    d. Acheter le timbre fiscal dans un tabac est **moins** pratique **que** l'acheter en ligne.

In Caijia, adverbs like English 'less' and French 'moins' do not exist. Instead, the Caijia inferior comparatives are very much related to the Type C 'reach'-equatives, since they are, to a certain extent, the negated forms of the equatives with $yã^{33}$ 'have' or $lɛ^{21}$ 'reach'. Note that the verb $dzɔ^{33}$ 'resemble' is rarely used to form inferior comparatives. These two types of inferior comparative in Caijia are illustrated below in Table 9.5.

Table 9.5: Caijia inferior comparatives.

Type A NOT-HAVE	CMP NEG HAVE ST (DEGR) PARA
Type B NOT-REACH	1. CMP NEG REACH ST (DEGR) PARA
	2. CMP NEG REACH ST

Even though the connection between inferior comparatives and Type C equatives is indeed transparent, they are not merely the negated forms of equatives with *ɣã³³* 'have' or *lɛ²¹* 'reach'. As illustrated in the schemata in Table 9.5, the degree marker *sɿ²¹* is optional in inferior comparatives, as shown in (9.43), while it is obligatory in Type C equatives.

(9.43)   CMP   NEG   HAVE/REACH   ST   DEGR   PARA
         ŋo³³   **pɤ³³**   **ɣã²¹/lɛ²¹**   ŋuɛ²¹   tɕi⁵⁵   (sɿ²¹)   mia²¹.
         1SG   NEG   have/reach   my.family   elder.sister   way   pretty
         'I'm not as pretty as my elder sister.'
         我没有我姐漂亮

The NOT-HAVE inferior comparative shares more or less the same syntactic structure with one of the NOT-REACH comparatives. Consider the three examples below.

(9.44)   ŋo³³   **pɤ³³**   **ɣã²¹/lɛ²¹**   je³³   sɿ²¹   tsʰɿ⁵⁵   sɤ⁵⁵.
         1SG   NEG   have/reach   3SG   way   fear   mouse
         'I don't fear mice as she does.'
         我没有她那么怕老鼠。

(9.45)   ɔ²¹   men²¹ni³³ŋoŋ³³   ŋuɛ²¹   ʑi³³   **pɤ³³**   **ɣã²¹/lɛ²¹**
         this   Caijia   my.family   mother   NEG   have/reach
         ŋuɛ²¹   pa⁵⁵   ti³³   xa³³.
         my.family   father   know   say
         'As for the language of Caijia, my mother doesn't speak it as well as my father.'
         这蔡家话，我妈没有我爸会说。

(9.46)   nɯ³³   kuɛ³³   pɤ³³   **ɣã²¹/lɛ²¹**   ŋo³³   kuɛ³³   kʰua²¹
         2SG   go   NEG   have/reach   1SG   go   be.good
         'Your going is not as good as my going.'
         你去没有我去好。

9.4 Inferior comparatives

Given that the verb *lɛ²¹* 'reach' can also denote 'rival, be matched evenly', as in (9.47), its negated form by itself can denote 'be inferior to'.

(9.47) piɔ²⁴   xa³³   ŋo³³   u³³to²¹   la²¹.   nɯ³³   la³³   lɛ²¹   ŋo³³   sɿ²¹.
NEG.IMP   say   1SG   strength   big   2SG   also   reach   1SG   AFF
'Don't say that I'm strong. You also rival me (in this respect).'
别说我力气大。咱俩差不多的。

In this type, the negated *lɛ²¹* 'reach' forms a transitive construction with the comparee as its subject and the standard as its object. This type of inferior comparative, in fact, uses a lexical means to code comparison, as in (9.48).

(9.48)   CMP   NEG   REACH   ST
mɔ²¹   kɯ²⁴   ₛ[kua²¹   sɿ²¹   ni²⁴]   **pɤ³³**   **lɛ²¹**   ₒ[ni³³].
that   moment   live   REL   life   NEG   reach   3
'My life was not so good as other people's before.'
以前，过的日子不如人。

However, due to the lack of a parameter, this type of inferior comparative usually cannot denote inferiority with respect to a very specific gradable property. Example (9.48) can denote 'every aspect of my life wasn't so good as others' lives' or 'a certain respect of my life wasn't so good as other people's lives'. Similarly, if example (9.49) is in a context related to transportation, it may denote that taking a boat is less quick, less convenient, or less economical than riding a horse, while if it is in a context related to recreation, it may denote boating is less fun than riding a horse.

(9.49)   gɯ³³   tseŋ²¹   pɤ³³   lɛ²¹   kɯ²¹   mɛ³³.
row   boat   NEG   reach   ride   horse
'Boating is not so good as riding.'
划船不如骑马。

Once the gradable property needs to be specified in a context, this property or the range of comparison is introduced into the sentence by means of a dangling topic. In (9.50), the comparee 'the third child' is inferior to the standard 'the second child' with respect to thoughtfulness, whereas the comparee 'she' is inferior to the standard 'my elder sister' in terms of physical appearance in (9.51).

(9.50) **niɔ³³ xa²¹ tɕi³³pia³³,**   ti²¹sa²⁴   tɯ³³ pɣ³³ lɛ²¹   ti²¹ni²⁴.
        if   say   be.thoughtful   the.third then NEG   reach the.second
        'As for being thoughtful, (his) third child is inferior to (his) second one.'
        要说懂事，老三就不如老二了。

(9.51) **xa³³fa²¹   nɛ³³,** je³³ pɣ³³ lɛ²¹ ŋo²¹ tɕi⁵⁵.
        appearance PRT   3SG   NEG   reach 1SG   elder.sister
        'As for their appearance, she can't rival my elder sister.'
        论相貌呢，她不如我姐。

To summarize, the Caijia inferior comparatives show a close connection with the Caijia equatives. One of the constructions can almost be regarded as the negated form of Type C equatives with *yã³³* 'have' or *lɛ²¹* 'reach', except that the degree marker *sɿ²¹* is optional. In addition, the negated *lɛ²¹* forms an inferior comparative construction, which is transitive in nature, with the comparee as the subject and the standard as the object, but without any parameter within the predicate. Cross-linguistically, inferior comparatives are much less studied than equatives and superior comparatives, which will be discussed in the following section. Regardless, Caijia strategies for producing inferior comparatives are attested in various Sinitic languages.

9.5 Superior comparatives

In a superior comparative, the comparee is higher in rank than the standard with respect to a certain gradable property. Superior comparatives have been very well studied cross-linguistically in recent decades. Nine major types of superior comparatives are found in the languages of the world. Their cognitive schemata are summarized in Table 9.6 (Heine 1997: 112). In these schemata, X = comparee (CMP), Y = parameter (PARA, i.e. VP), and Z = standard (ST). Types 2, 3, 4, 6, 7, and 9 include a standard marker. Types 2, 3, and 4 are also labelled as locational comparatives by Stassen (2013), as the standard markers used in these types are derived from relevant locational case markers. Locational comparatives are the most common type in the languages of the world and are attested in 78/167 languages examined by Stassen (2013).

Despite their proliferation, superior comparatives in Sinitic languages are not characterized by the locational type. Rather, it is the compare schema and the action schema, which includes several subtypes, that are overwhelmingly observed in Sinitic. The topic and polarity types are also attested in Sinitic lan-

9.5 Superior comparatives

Table 9.6: Cognitive schemata of superior comparatives.

Type	Cognitive schema	Label of schema
1	X is Y surpasses Z	Action
2	X is Y **at** Z	Location
3	X is Y **from** Z	Source
4	X is Y **to** Z	Goal
5	X is Y, Z is not Y	Polarity
6	X is Y, **then** Z	Sequence
7	X is Y **like** Z	Similarity
8	X and Z, X is Y	Topic
9	X is Y **compared to** Z	Compare

guages. These three schemata are represented by seven different syntactic configurations (Chappell 2015b: 37), as illustrated in Table 9.7.

Table 9.7: Sinitic superior comparatives.

	Type	Configuration	Cognitive schema
I.	**Prepositional**	CMP [STM ST] PARA	Compare
II.	**Transitive**	CMP PARA-surpass ST	Action$_{(I)}$ (Surpass)
III.	**Zero-marked**	CMP PARA ST	Action$_{(II)}$
IV.	Adverbial	CMP DEGR$_{MORE}$ PARA ST	Action$_{(III)}$
V.	Hybridized	CMP [STM ST] DEGR$_{MORE}$ PARA	Compare + Action$_{(III)}$
VI.	Topic-comment	ST // *copula* CMP PARA	Topic
VII.	**Contrastive conjoined clauses**	CMP PARA$_X$ CL, ST PARA$_{-X}$ CL	Polarity

Four of the Sinitic patterns are also attested in Caijia. See Table 9.8 below.

Table 9.8: Caijia superior comparatives.

	Type		Configuration	Cognitive schema
A.	Prepositional		CMP [STM ST] PARA	Compare
B.	Surpass		CMP PARA-*surpass* ST	Action$_{(I)}$
C.	Zero-marked		CMP PARA ST (MEAS)	Action$_{(II)}$
D.	Degree adjunct	(i)	CMP PARA DEGR	Polarity
		(ii)	CMP PARA$_X$ DEGR, ST PARA$_{-X}$ DEGR	Polarity
		(ii)	TOP // CMP PARA DEGR	Topic
		(iii)	CLAUSE$_{DEPENDENT}$, CMP PARA DEGR	

We will now examine the Caijia superior comparatives one by one in the following sections.

9.5.1 Type A: Prepositional comparatives

In a prepositional comparative in Caijia, the standard is overtly coded by the standard marker *pi*^{55} 'compared to', which is identified as a preposition. The marked standard precedes the parameter, i.e. the VP. This syntactic configuration can be schematized as: [CMP $_{PrepP}$[STM ST] PARA]. Example (9.52) shows the canonical comparative in Caijia which is the prepositional comparative that has both the comparee and the standard as NPs and the parameter as an adjective.

(9.52)   CMP   STM   ST   PARA
         ɔ^{21} hɔ^{55} ta^{55} [pi^{55} mɔ^{21} hɔ^{55} ta^{55}]   tɣ^{21}.
         this   road   CLF   than   that   road   CLF   be.long
         'This road is longer that that one.'
         这条路比那条路长。

NPs and pronouns are common elements forming comparees and standards, but these can also be formed by other elements. The sentences in (9.53i) and (9.53ii) are formed with comparees and standards that have more complicated structures. Both the comparee 'I go' and the standard 'you go' are clauses in (9.53i), while both of them are in the form of [NP [Prep NP]] in (9.53ii). The sentence in (9.53iii) is formed with a pronominal comparee, a pronominal standard, and a parameter of the stative verb.

(9.53)   i)   [ŋo^{33} kuɛ^{21}]   **pi^{55}**   [nɯ^{33} kuɛ^{33}]   kʰua^{21}.
              1SG   go   than   2SG   go   be.good
       ii)   [ŋo^{21} [ta^{55} je^{21}]]   **pi^{55}**   [nɯ^{21} [(ta^{55} je^{33})]]   tso^{21}.
              1SG   with   3SG   than   2SG   with   3SG   be.familiar
      iii)   je^{21} hm^{55} tie^{55} ŋo^{21} **pi^{55}**   nɯ^{33}
              3SG   POSS   bottom   1SG   than   2SG
              tiu^{21}u^{21} lɯ^{55} tie^{21}.
              know   VCOMP   be.many
              'It's better that I go than you go. I'm more familiar with him than you. I know better what he really is like than you.'
              我去比你去好。我跟他比你跟他熟。他的底我比你清楚。

The following example illustrates the comparison of two actions, which is realized via the extent and manner complementation construction. Note that $ma^{21}k^ha^{33}$ mo^{33} 'LIT: door inside' in (9.54) is used to express 'outside' in Caijia.

(9.54) a^{33}　$ɯ^{33}$　ko^{21}　pie^{55}　$ma^{21}k^ha^{33}$　mo^{33}　pi^{55}　$tɯ^{21}$
OM　clothes　hang　to　door　inside　than　at
$ɔ^{55}$　$ʐi^{21}$　ka^{55}　$lɯ^{55}$　$tɕiu^{21}$.
house　inside　be.dry　VCOMP　quick
'Drying clothes outside is faster than inside.'
把衣服挂到外面比在屋里干得快。

Two more examples are given below.

(9.55) $nɯ^{21}$　$tsʰɿ^{55}$　$sɣ^{55}$,　$ŋo^{21}$　pi^{55}　$nɯ^{21}$　xa^{21}　$tsʰɿ^{55}$.
2SG　fear　mouse　1SG　than　2SG　even　fear
'You fear mice and I fear them even more.'
你怕老鼠，我比你还怕。

(9.56) $ɣã^{21}$　$zɿ^{21}$　$tsʰɿ^{55}ka^{55}$　$k^wɔ^{21}$　pi^{55}　$tɯ^{21}$　$k^wɔ^{21}$　tie^{55}
have　warm　place　CLF　than　live　bridge　bottom
k^hua^{21}　$lɯ^{55}$　tie^{21}　o.
good　VCOMP　many　CRS
'It's much better to have a warm place (to stay) than living under the bridge.'
有个暖和的地方比住在桥底好多了。
(*Two moons*, texts)

The prepositional type is currently the predominant comparative construction in Caijia. However, it is not a native construction, since the standard marker pi^{55} is borrowed from the Mandarin standard marker *bǐ* 比 [pi^{214}], derived from its verbal form *bǐ* denoting 'compare, stand close to, compete with'. An important piece of evidence supporting this conclusion is the fact that the source of the standard marker pi^{55} cannot be traced within the language of Caijia. We have shown in Chapter 4 §4.5 that Caijia prepositions are derived from verbs. The morpheme pi^{55} can only be used as the standard marker but does not possess any other lexical uses. The counterpart of the Chinese verbal *bǐ* 'compare' in Caijia is the verb dza^{33} 'compare, measure' which has not developed the function of a standard marker. See the two examples below for the lexical use of dza^{33} 'compare, measure'.

(9.57) zɣ²¹ sʅ²¹ ã³³   sʅ²¹   a³³   mɔ²¹ kɯ²⁴   yɯ²¹ **tsa³³**,
       eat NMLZ drink NMLZ   take that   moment PURP   compare
       pʰe⁵⁵   kʰɯ²¹   pʰe⁵⁵.
       multiply several multiple
       'Compared with those years, the food supplies have been multiplied now.'
       吃的喝的，跟那时候比，翻了几番。

(9.58) ɯ³³   ti³³-kʰua²¹   o.   a³³   ɣɯ²¹   ta⁵⁵
       clothes stich-good   CRS   take PURP   with
       ŋa⁵⁵   **tsa²¹**   mi⁵⁵.
       child   compare   a.little
       'The cloak is done. (She) took (the cloak) to compare the size with her baby.'
       衣服缝好了。拿来给孩子比了比。

Mandarin comparatives with *bǐ* have had a huge influence on different languages in China. According to Yuan Haixia (2010), the marker *bǐ* is attested in Tai-Kadai, Hmong-Mien, and Tibeto-Burman, as well as Austroasiatic languages. Moreover, this marker is also used in the local Southwestern Mandarin, i.e. the Hezhang dialect. The standard marker *bǐ* can be traced back to Early Medieval Chinese (3ʳᵈ – 4ᵗʰ century AD). It flourished in Modern Chinese (16ᵗʰ – 19ᵗʰ century AD) (Zhang Cheng 2010, Chappell and Peyraube 2015). Therefore, it is hard to determine whether the Caijia standard marker *pi⁵⁵* was borrowed from Early Medieval or Pre-Modern Chinese (1250–1400 AD) or it is borrowed from the local Southwestern Mandarin, which began to develop no earlier than the Ming Dynasty (1368 – 1644 AD) (Cui Rongchang 1985). It should be mentioned that, apart from *pi³¹*, a disyllabic standard marker *kən³¹pi³¹* is also used in Hezhang Southwestern Mandarin. However, this one has not been borrowed into Caijia.

9.5.2 Type B: Surpass comparatives

Surpass comparatives in Caijia correspond to the action schema in Heine's (1997) typology. The *surpass* comparatives are attested mainly in Southern Sinitic languages and are predominant in Southeast Asian languages (Chappell and Peyraube 2015: 146–148). In the Sinitic *surpass* pattern, the parameter usually takes a resultative complement denoting 'surpass'. In a similar fashion, it is the verb *gua³³* 'pass, surpass, live (a life)' that is used as the resultative complement of the parameter in a Caijia surpass comparative. See the example below for the verbal use of *gua³³*.

9.5 Superior comparatives — 293

(9.59) a. **gua³³** gʷɔ²¹
pass bridge
'cross the bridge'
过桥

b. ŋo²⁴ ɔ²¹-sui⁵⁵ sɿ³³ **gua³³** dzaŋ³³ ŋui³³ ɣa²¹ji³³ nɛ⁵⁵.
1PL this-PL COP pass ten month the.first.day PRT
'In our place, (we) celebrate the first day of the 10th lunar month.'
我们这些是过十月初一。
(*Cow's birthday*, text)

This Caijia pattern can be schematized as [CMP PARA-gua³³ ST] with the comparee as the subject and the standard as the object. See examples (9.60)-(9.62).

(9.60) CMP PARA-*surpass* ST
ŋo³³ kʷɔ³³-**kua³³** nɯ³³.
1SG be.tall-pass 2SG
'I'm taller than you.'
我比你高。

(9.61) ŋo³³ bi³³-**gua³³** nɯ³³.
1SG be.short-pass 2SG
'I'm shorter than you.'
我比你矮。

(9.62) je³³ mia²¹-**kua³³** ŋo³³.
3SG be.pretty-pass 1SG
'She is prettier than me.'
她比我好看。

The main reason that -*gua³³* is treated as a resultative complement instead of being a standard marker is that -*gua³³* can be negated in the same way as all the resultative complements. This suggests that the main verb and the complement -*gua³³* constitute a VP functioning as a compound verb. The complement -*gua³³* is a marker on the verb but not a marker on the standard. Compare the two lines in (9.63).

(9.63) a. ŋo³³ **dʑi³³-pɣ³³-kua³³** nɯ³³ la²¹!
1SG be.clever-NEG-pass 2SG PRT
'I can't be cleverer than you!'
我聪明不过你啦！

b. ŋo³³ **tsaŋ³³-pɣ³³-ti²¹** mɔ²¹ kʰɯ⁵⁵-sui⁵⁵.
   1SG look-NEG-be.clear that word-PL
   'I can't see clear those words clearly.'
   我看不清那些字。

By contrast, a post-VP prepositional phrase cannot be negated when the preposition occurs directly following the main verb, as illustrated below.

(9.64) a. je³³ pɣ²¹ ŋa⁵⁵ **pie⁵⁵** tʰa⁵⁵ tɣ³³.
        3SG put child to bed upside
        'She put the baby on the bed.'
        她把孩子放在床上。

     b. *je³³ pɣ²¹ ŋa⁵⁵ **pɣ²¹** **pie⁵⁵** tʰa⁵⁵ tɣ³³.
        3SG put child NEG to bed upside
        (Attempted: 'She can't put the baby on the bed.')
        *她把孩子放不在床上。

Unlike the prepositional type, in which any form of VP involving a meaning of gradable property can serve as the parameter, only adjectives can serve as parameter in *surpass* comparatives. The following two examples involve respectively a HAVE phrase, *yã²¹ tɕiŋ²¹* 'have money ~ rich', and a modal auxiliary phrase, *kʰã⁵⁵ yɯ²¹ zɿ⁵⁵* 'often rain'. Neither of them can serve as the parameter in the *surpass* comparative.

(9.65) a. *mɔ²¹ u²¹tsʰo²⁴ ni³³ ₚₐᵣₐ[yã²¹ tɕiŋ²¹] kua³³ ŋo³³.
        that person CLF have money pass 1SG
        (Attempted: 'That person is richer than me.')
        那人比我有钱。

     b. mɔ²¹ u²¹tsʰo²⁴ ni²¹ pi⁵⁵ ŋo³³ ₚₐᵣₐ[yã²¹ tɕiŋ²¹].
        that person CLF than 1SG have money
        'That person is richer than me.'
        那人比我有钱。

(9.66) a. *la²¹sɿ⁵⁵ ₚₐᵣₐ[kʰã⁵⁵ yɯ²¹ zɿ⁵⁵] kua³³
        Guiyang_PLACENAME be.willing.to come rain pass
        kã³³loŋ³³.
        Beijing_PLACENAME
        (Attempted: 'It rains more often in Guiyang than in Beijing.')
        贵阳比北京常下雨。

b. la²¹sʅ⁵⁵   pi⁵⁵   kã³³loŋ³³
   Guiyang_PLACENAME than Beijing_PLACENAME
   _PARA[kʰã⁵⁵   yɯ²¹   zʅ⁵⁵].
   be.willing.to come rain
   'It rains more often in Guiyang than in Beijing.'
   贵阳比北京常下雨。

Another Sinitic action schema attested in Caijia is discussed in the next section.

9.5.3 Type C: Zero-marked comparatives

Zero-marked comparatives are also transitive constructions, like the *surpass* comparatives, except that parameters are formed by bare verbs without taking any resultative complement. In this type, only several adjectives that involve measurable properties can serve as parameters, and they are often related with age, size, weight, height, and length, such as *la²¹* 'be big', *ɕie²¹* 'be small', *ɖoŋ³³* 'be heavy', *tsʰʅ³³* 'be light', *kʷɔ³³* 'be tall', and *bi³³* 'be short'. Due to this feature, in this type one can also observe a complement of measurement or quantification after the standard noun in this type for certain cases: [CMP PARA ST (MEAS)].

(9.67) CMP   PARA   ST   (MEAS)
        tɕi⁵⁵   la²¹   ŋo²¹   (ta⁵⁵   neŋ²¹).
        elder.sister be.big 1SG   two   year
        'My elder sister is two years older than me.'
        姐姐大我（两岁）。

(9.68) je³³   xa²¹ toŋ³³   ŋo³³ (kʰɯ³³   je²¹)
        3SG   even be.heavy   1SG   several catty
        'He's even several catties heavier than me.'
        他还重我几斤。

(9.69) piɔ²⁴   tsaŋ²¹ je³³ po⁵⁵po⁵⁵ la²¹   je³³ xa²¹ tsʰʅ³³   ŋo³³
        NEG.IMP look   3SG   height   be.big 3SG   even be.light 1SG
        (tsʅ²¹   kʰɯ³³   je²¹).
        ten   several catty
        'Don't just notice that he's tall. He's even a dozen catties lighter than me.'
        别看他个子大，他还比我轻十几斤。

By contrast, beauty and light intensity are usually not measured. The adjective 'be bright' and 'be pretty' cannot be used in this type of comparative construction. See the following two examples.

(9.70) *mɔ²¹ tã²¹ po⁵⁵ tso³³ ɔ²¹ po⁵⁵.
that bulb CLF be.brighter this CLF
(Attempted: 'That bulb is brighter that this one.')
那个灯比这个亮。

(9.71) *je³³ mia²¹ je²¹ tɕi⁵⁵.
3SG be.pretty 3SG elder.sister
(Attempted: 'She's prettier than her elder sister.')
她比她姐好看。

9.5.4 Type C: Comparatives with the verbal classifier *mi⁵⁵* as a degree marker

Type D comparatives can be divided into four types: (i) basic, (ii) polarity, (iii) topic, and (iv) dependent clause. The last three types are all formed on the basis of the **basic** comparative construction, which is that of the degree adjunct [CMP PARA DEGR] in which the standard is absent and the verbal classifier *mi⁵⁵* 'a bit' serves as the degree marker (see also Chapter 4 §4.4). Semantically, it is equivalent to the English degree adverbial comparatives, for example, *Working from home is more convenient*, in which the overt standard is implied. This type of comparative is often called the 'absolute comparative' in the relevant literature. See the Caijia pattern below.

(9.72) CMP PARA VCLF
mɔ²¹ ta²⁴ po⁵⁵ la²¹ mi⁵⁵.
that pool CLF big a.little
'That pool is larger.'
那个凼大点。

The basic pattern is often used when the standard in a comparison is not necessary, for example, if it has already been mentioned in preceding context or the comparee is superior to all of the possible standards. Furthermore, this pattern is preferred when the comparee exhibits complicated structure other than a simple NP. Example (9.73) illustrates a case with the standard *la²¹tɕi⁵⁵* 'elder sister' mentioned in the speech turn A_1 and the basic pattern of the degree adjunct following in turn B_2.

(9.73) A₁- tɔ⁵⁵pa³³,   nɯ³³ tsaŋ²¹ ŋo³³ kʷɔ³³ lɔ²¹
           great.grandpa 2SG   look   1SG   be.tall or
           la²¹ tɕi⁵⁵   kʷɔ³³?
           big   elder.sister be.tall
           'Great grandpa, who's taller according to you, me or my elder sister?'
           老祖，你看我高还是我姐高？

      B₂- ŋo³³ tsaŋ²¹ nɛ⁵⁵ **nɛ²¹**   tɕi⁵⁵   **kʷɔ²¹** **mi⁵⁵**.
           1SG   look   PRT   your.family   elder.sister be.tall   a.little
           'Well, your elder sister is taller.'
           我看啊，你姐高些。

Without further context, example (9.74) denotes that hanging clothes outside is a better way to dry them more quickly than other possible methods.

(9.74) ka⁵⁵ ɯ³³   nɛ⁵⁵, ko²¹ pie⁵⁵ ma²¹kʰa³³ mo³³
       dry   clothes PRT   hang to   door   inside
       ka⁵⁵   lɯ⁵⁵   tɕiu²¹ **mi⁵⁵**.
       be.dry VCOMP quick   a.little
       'As for drying clothes, it's faster to hang (them) outside.'
       把衣服挂到外面比在屋里干得快。

As can be observed in examples (9.72)-(9.74), the standard is absent in the basic pattern for a comparative with a degree adjunct. To designate the standard, one could adopt one of the other three patterns mentioned above.

A comparative of **polarity schema** is composed of two conjoined clauses; each of the clauses can stand alone as an independent clause. There are two sub-schemas in which different forms of the parameter are used (Heine 1997: 117):

(9.75) Antonymy:
       X has property *p* while Z has the opposite property *q*.
       Negative-positive polarity:
       X has property *p* while Z lacks *p*.

Caijia uses the antonymy strategy to form polarity comparatives. It is can be schematized as [CMP$_A$/(ST$_B$) PARA$_X$ mi⁵⁵, CMP$_B$/(ST$_A$) PARA $_{-X}$ mi⁵⁵]. It should also be mentioned that there is no syntactic standard noun possible in this construction. Both subjects of the two clauses are comparees within each clause and they are also the standards for each other. As shown in (9.76), the comparee mɔ²¹ ta²⁴ po⁵⁵ 'that pool' is larger when compared to ɔ²¹ ta²⁴ po⁵⁵ 'this pool', which is smaller with respect to 'that pool'.

(9.76) CMP_A/(ST_B)   PARA_X   VCLF   CMP_B/(ST_A)   PARA_X   VCLF
      mɔ²¹ ta²⁴ po⁵⁵   la²¹   mi⁵⁵,   ɔ²¹ ta²⁴ po⁵⁵   ɕie²¹   mi⁵⁵.
      that pool CLF   big   a.little this pool CLF   small   a.little
      'That pool is larger; this pool is smaller.'
      那个凼大点，这个凼小点。

(9.77) ɔ²¹   ta⁵⁵   ta²¹   mi⁵⁵,   mɔ²¹ ta⁵⁵ kʰua²¹   mi⁵⁵.
      this CLF   be.narrow a.little that CLF   be.wide   a.little
      'This road is narrower; that one is wider.'
      这条（路）窄点，那条（路）宽点。

In a comparative of the **topic schema**, i.e. *X and Z, X is Y*, the comparee and the standard appear in the dangling topic: [TOP//CMP PARA DEGR]. In (9.76), the comparee and the standard appear in a plural NP. Note that the auxiliary *niɔ³³* used in this sentence does not denote its lexical meaning 'want' or 'need'. It is used euphemistically to express one's opinion while avoiding being straightforwardness.

(9.78) _TOP_[tsen²¹   hɛ⁵⁵   ta⁵⁵   tɕi⁵⁵hɛ⁵⁵],
      Chen_FAMILY.NAME   family two   sister.and.brother
      ti²¹ni²⁴   niɔ³³   tɕi³³pia³³   mi²⁴.
      the.second   want   be.thoughtful   a.little
      'In the two sisters of Chen's, the second one is more thoughtful.'
      陈家两姐妹，老二要懂事点。

In (9.79), the comparee and the standard are simply juxtaposed without any linker.

(9.79) _TOP_[ta⁵⁵   ŋuɛ²¹   mo³³   tɕiu⁵⁵   je²¹   mo³³,
      from   my.family   inside to   3SG   inside
      ta⁵⁵   nɛ²¹   mo³³   tɕiu⁵⁵   je²¹   mo³³],
      from   your.family   inside to   3SG   inside
      ŋuɛ²¹   niɔ³³   tɕɪŋ²¹   mi⁵⁵.
      my.family   want   be.near   a.little
      'From my house to his house (and) from your house to his house, it's nearer from mine.'
      从我家到他家，从你家到他家，我家要近些。

Finally, a preceding dependent clause formed by the verb *dza³³* 'compare' can also be used to introduce or designate the standard noun for a basic comparative pattern with a degree adjunct: [Clause_DEPENDENT, CMP PARA DEGR], as shown in (9.80) and (9.81).

(9.80) [ta⁵⁵ jɛ²¹ hɛ⁵⁵ tsa²¹-xɯ⁵⁵ɣɯ²¹],
with 3SG younger.brother compare-INC
jɛ³³ niɔ³³ saŋ³³ tɣ²¹ mi⁵⁵.
3SG want heart be.long a.little
'Compared with his younger brother, he's more patient.'
跟他弟弟比起来，他要耐心些。

(9.81) [kɯ²¹ mɛ³³ ta⁵⁵ kʰɯ³³ tsʰɛ³³ tsa³³],
ride horse with drive car compare
xa²¹sɿ³³ kʰɯ³³ tsʰɛ³³ tɕiu²¹ mi⁵⁵.
still drive car fast a.little
'To compare riding and driving, driving is still faster.'
骑马和开车比，还是开车快点。

9.5.5 Concluding remarks

In Caijia, superior comparison is realized by several different constructions. Two canonical Sinitic patterns are attested in Caijia: the compare schema of Northern Sinitic and the action (surpass) schema of Southern Sinitic. The compare schema is the predominant pattern in Caijia and is the only pattern with a standard marker. It adopts the loan marker *pi⁵⁵* (< Chinese *bǐ*) to mark standard nouns or phrases. Various types of parameters can serve as predicative VPs in this schema, including any form of VP involving the meaning of a gradable property (degree, quality, or quantity). In a surpass schema, the verb *gua³³* 'pass, surpass', which is from the same lexical field as Sinitic *guò* and its cognates in the surpass schema, functions as a resultative verbal complement. Only adjectives can serve as parameters in this type. Apart from the surpass schema, there is a second type of action schema in Caijia, i.e. the zero-marked comparatives, which are restricted to a very limited number of adjectives related to size, length, weight and height. Finally, comparatives using the verbal classifier *mi⁵⁵* 'a little' as a degree adjunt also form a very commonly used type of comparison, consisting of four sub-patterns. The last three of these, i.e. patterns of polarity, topic and dependent clause, are all formed on the basis of the basic pattern. In the basic pattern, there is no standard noun, while the standard noun can be designated via any of the other three patterns.

9.6 Conclusion

This chapter has presented three types of constructions of comparison in Caijia: equatives, inferior comparatives, and superior comparatives. The Caijia constructions of comparison are similar to the general Sinitic patterns, in that they are all attested in other Sinitic languages.

Three types of equatives are observed in Caijia. Those derived from the verb 'follow', ta^{55} 'and' or 'with' are used as the standard markers in Types A and B equatives. The marker ta^{55} can be regarded as a conjunction in Type A, while it is treated as a comitative preposition in Type B. Type C equatives are a type with only a degree marker, i.e. $sı^{21}$ 'like this'. Unlike its Sinitic counterpart, $sı^{21}$ 'like this' is a dependent morpheme forming an adverbial along with the standard in a Type C equative. Three verbs can be used in Type C equatives. They are $y\tilde{a}^{33}$ 'have', $l\varepsilon^{21}$ 'reach', and $dz\mathfrak{o}^{33}$ 'resemble'.

The Caijia inferior comparatives show a close connection with Type C equatives. They can be regarded as the negated forms of Type C equatives using $y\tilde{a}^{33}$ 'have' and $l\varepsilon^{21}$ 'reach'. However, unlike Type C equatives, the degree marker $sı^{21}$ 'like this' is optional in inferior comparatives.

The Sinitic compare pattern has had a huge impact on Caijia. We have argued that the standard marker pi^{55} 'than' is borrowed from the Mandarin standard marker $bǐ$ 'than (< 'compare')', since the source is not found within Caijia. The native verb dza^{33} 'compare, measure' from the same lexical field with Mandarin $bǐ$ has not grammaticalized into a standard marker.

Table 9.9 synthesizes all the constructions introduced in this chapter.

Table 9.9: Constructions of comparison in Caijia.

Equatives	
Type A	Equative with conjoined referents
	$_{NP}$[CMP ta^{55}$_{STM}$ ST] DEGR PARA
Type B	Comitative equative
	CMP $_{PREPP}$[ta^{55}$_{STM}$ ST] DEGR PARA
Type C	Equative with only a degree marker
	C$_1$ *Reach* type ('have' and 'reach')
	CMP yã^{33}$_{HAVE\ AdvP}$[ST DEGR] PARA
	CMP lɛ^{21}$_{REACH\ AdvP}$[ST DEGR] PARA
	C$_2$ *Resemble* type
	CMP dzɔ^{33}$_{RESEMBLE\ AdvP}$[ST DEGR] PARA

Table 9.9 (continued)

Inferior comparatives	
Type A	NOT-HAVE
	CMP NEG ɣã³³$_{HAVE}$ ST (DEGR) PARA
Type B	NOT-REACH
	CMP NEG lɛ²¹$_{REACH}$ ST (DEGR) PARA
	CMP NEG lɛ²¹$_{REACH}$ ST
Superior comparatives	
Type A	Prepositional
	CMP $_{PREPP}$[pi⁵⁵$_{STM}$ ST] PARA
Type B	Surpass
	CMP $_{VP}$[PARA-gua³³] ST
Type C	Zero-marked
	CMP PARA ST (MEAS)
Type D	Degree adjunct
	D₁ Basic
	CMP PARA mi⁵⁵$_{DEGR}$
	D₂ Polarity
	CMP$_A$ PARA mi⁵⁵$_{DEGR}$, CMP$_B$ PARA mi⁵⁵$_{DEGR}$
	D₃ Topic
	TOP// CMP PARA mi⁵⁵$_{DEGR}$
	D₄ Dependent clause
	CLAUSE$_{DEPENDENT}$, CMP PARA mi⁵⁵$_{DEGR}$

Chapter 10
Aspect system

10.1 Introduction

Verbal aspect is defined as "different ways of viewing the internal temporal constituency of a situation" (Comrie 1976: 3) and is "not concerned with relating the time of the situation to any other time-point, but rather with the internal temporal constituency of the one situation" (1976: 5). Aspect can be generally regarded as the binary opposition between perfective and imperfective, or more straightforwardly, completion and non-completion. Sub-oppositions can be observed within the imperfective as well, as proposed by Comrie (1976: 25). See Figure 10.1.

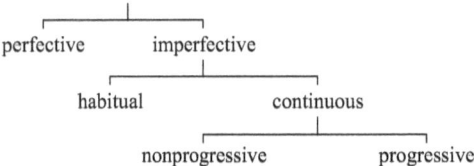

Figure 10.1: Binary opposition of aspect (Comrie 1976: 25).

Languages code aspect both grammatically and lexically. Grammatical aspect is usually manifested by inflectional and periphrastic distinctions (Croft 2012: 31), while lexical aspect, known also as Aktionsart, is related to the inherent properties of different classes of verbs and is commonly represented by the aspectual classification of Vendler (1967), i.e. verbs are classified into four categories: states, activities, achievements, and accomplishments. Smith (1994) adds a fifth category of verbs, semelfactives. Their semantic properties can be defined by three sets of binary features, stative vs. dynamic, durative vs. punctual, and bounded (telic) vs. unbounded (atelic), as synthesized by Croft (2012: 33, 35) on the basis of Mourelatos' (1978) analysis. See Table 10.1.

Table 10.1: Lexical aspect types and features.

States	Activities	Achievements	Semelfactives	Accomplishments
know	run	recognize	kick	paint a picture
believe	walk	spot	knock	make a chair
have	swim	find	cough	draw a circle
love	drive a car	die	jump	push a cart

https://doi.org/10.1515/9783110724806-010

Table 10.1 (continued)

	States	Activities	Achievements	Semelfactives	Accomplishments
Stative	✓				
Dynamic		✓	✓	✓	✓
Durative	✓	✓			✓
Punctual			✓	✓	
Bounded			✓		✓
Unbounded	✓	✓		✓	

Verbs of different properties may give rise to constraints on grammatical aspect marking. For example, progressiveness cannot be coded on the verb 'know' in English (e.g. *I'm knowing his teacher*), nor on verbs of achievement in Standard Mandarin, as shown in (10.1).

(10.1) a. 我在找钥匙。
    wǒ   zài   zhǎo   yàoshi.
    1SG   PROG   look.for   key
    'I'm looking for the key.'

b. *我在找到钥匙。
    wǒ   zài   zhǎo-dào   yàoshi.
    1SG   PROG   look.for-arrive   key
    '*I'm finding the key.'

A similar phenomenon is also observed in Caijia, i.e. grammatical aspect marking is also related to the lexical aspect of verbs. This is the reason the topic of lexical aspect has been introduced here.

Sinitic languages are often regarded primarily as aspectual (Norman 1988: 163), while the category of tense is absent. Suffixation is the most common strategy for coding aspect in Sinitic (see Chao 1968: 245-, Chappell 1992, Zhang Shuangqing 1996 for more Sinitic data), as illustrated in (10.2). Preverbal markers are also observed, especially in the case of progressive markers, as shown in (10.1).

Cantonese
(10.2) Gūngsī   gauhlín   jaahn-**jó**   msíu   chin.
    company   last-year   earn-PFV   not-little   money
    'The company made a good deal of money last year.'
    (Matthews and Yip 1994: 205)

Furthermore, Sinitic aspectual markers are usually derived from verbs (Mei Zulin 1981, Peyraube 1996, Chappell 1992; see also Bybee et al. 1994, in particular, Chapters 3 and 5 for the same phenomenon in many other languages).

Caijia is also an aspect language. Tense is not coded on verbs but only expressed by time words, usually serving as adverbials. The example below shows a future context. The completive marker ha^{51} denotes that the action of 'guests' arrival' is completed before the action 'your not yet getting up'.

(10.3) $t^h\mathrm{I}\eta^{21}\mathrm{ko}\eta^{33}$ nu^{21} $k^h\mathrm{u}^{55}\text{-}tɕ\mathrm{I}\eta^{21}$ mi^{55}. $\mathrm{pi}\mathrm{ɔ}^{24}$ $\mathrm{s}\mathrm{1}^{55}$
tomorrow 2SG rise-be.early bit neg.imp let
$\mathrm{mɔ}^{21}$ $k^h\mathrm{a}^{55}\text{-}\mathrm{sui}^{55}$ la^{21} yu^{21} ha^{51} o,
that guest-PL all come COMPL CRS
nu^{33} a^{21} $\mathrm{py}^{33}\text{-}\mathrm{ty}^{33}$ $k^h\mathrm{u}^{55}$.
2SG still NEG-PFV rise
'Get up earlier tomorrow. Don't let the guests arrive, when you're still in bed.'
明天你起早点。别让客人们都来了，你还没起。

Compare (10.3) with the following example of ha^{51} in a present context to better understand the absence of tense in Caijia. The use of the completive marker ha^{51} evidently does not concern the reference time.

(10.4) $\mathrm{ŋo}^{33}$ zy^{21} zy^{21} **ha^{51}** o. py^{33} zy^{21} o.
1SG eat meal COMPL CRS NEG eat CRS
'I've had a meal and won't eat any more.'
我吃了饭。不吃了。

This chapter will introduce how Caijia codes different types of aspect.

10.2 Aspect in Caijia

Caijia grammatically distinguishes eleven types of aspect in total. They can be divided into two major semantic groups: bounded (telic) vs. unbounded (atelic). A bounded event is usually interpreted as one which is attained to the terminal point of its situation, while an unbounded event does not have a built-in end point (Comrie 1976: 44–48). For example, *sing a song* is bounded but *sing* is unbounded. In Caijia, bounded types of aspect include currently relevant state (or change of state), perfective (negated), completive, experiential, inchoative, prospective, and tentative or delimitative. Unbounded types of aspect include continuous, continuous (manner), durative, and frequentative. Table 10.2 lists forms and syntactic strategies for different aspectual markers in Caijia.

Table 10.2: Aspect categories in Caijia.

Bounded (Telic)		Unbounded (Atelic)	
TYPE	FORM AND STRATEGY	TYPE	FORM AND STRATEGY
PERFECTIVE (ONLY IN NEGATED FORM)	pɣ³³-tɣ³³ 'NEG-obtain'	CONTINUOUS	<cir.cont.> sɿ³³ VP sɿ²¹ (< AFF/cleft)
COMPLETIVE	<POST-VP M> ha⁵⁵ (< 'finish')	CONTINUOUS (MANNER)	<FP> lɛ⁵⁵ (< ADV)
CURRENTLY RELEVANT STATE	<FP> o (< ?)	DURATIVE	<SUFF> -xɯ⁵⁵ (< kʰɯ⁵⁵ 'rise')
INCHOATIVE	<POST-VP M> kʰɯ⁵⁵ɣɯ²¹ ~ xɯ⁵⁵ɣɯ²¹ (< kʰɯ⁵⁵ɣɯ²¹ 'rise up')	FREQUENTATIVE	<AUX> kʰā⁵⁵ (< 'be willing to')
EXPERIENTIAL	<POST-VP M> ja²¹ (< gua³³ja²¹ 'experience') <SUFF> -gua³³ (< gua³³ja²¹ 'experience')		
PROSPECTIVE	<AUX> niɔ³³ (< 'want')		
DELIMITATIVE	<POST-VP M > mi⁵⁵ (< 'a little' or VCLF)		

AUX: auxiliary
cir.cont: circum-construction
FP: final particle
M: marker
SUFF: suffix

As shown above, and discussed below in more detail, verbs are also the major source of aspectual markers in Caijia. However, in comparison with Sinitic languages, the strategy of suffixation is not prominent. Only the experiential marker *-gua³³* and the durative marker *-xɯ⁵⁵* are suffixed to verbs. Most of them are post-VP morphemes or clitics, which means an aspectual marker is situated after the object (if there is one) in the form of [V O Marker$_{ASP}$].

In the following sections, the categories listed in Table 10.2 will be introduced in turn.

10.2.1 Perfective (negated) [pɣ³³-tɣ³³ VP]

Perfective signals "that the situation is viewed as bounded temporally" (Bybee et al. 1994: 54), denoting "a complete situation, with beginning, middle, and end" (Comrie 1976: 18). However, it "puts on no more emphasis, necessarily, on the end of a situation than on any other part of the situation, rather all parts of the situation are presented as a single whole" (Comrie 1976: 18).

While Caijia does not overtly code the perfective, the perfective can often be expressed by certain periphrastic means. The example below illustrates two different ways to add bounded meaning to the verb ɣa³³ 'fall': first, by compounding the directional complement tɕie²¹ɣɯ²¹ 'come down', and second, by adding the locational prepositional phrase tɯ²¹ la²¹ sɔ⁵⁵ tsɣ²¹ tɣ³³ 'onto a big tree'.

(10.5) o²¹,   sɿ³³   kɔ⁵⁵pe⁵⁵ja²¹   po⁵⁵   ɣa³³-tɕie²¹ɣɯ²¹,
       oh   COP   moon   CLF   fall-come.down
       ɣa³³   tɯ²¹   la²¹   sɔ⁵⁵   tsɣ²¹   tɣ³³.
       fall   to   big   tree   CLF   upside
       'Oh, it is the moon that fell down and (it) fell onto a big tree.'
       哦，是个月亮掉了下来，掉到了棵大树上。
       (*Two Moons*, texts)

Sometimes the perfective meaning can only be understood by judging its context. The context of the example below is that the narrator's younger brother is finally exempted from military service by paying money. Without this context, this sentence can also be interpreted as 'Only after making a deal, will they let my younger brother off'.

(10.6) xa³³-kʰua²¹   lɛ²¹tsʰɛ²¹   **pɣ²¹**   ŋuɛ²¹   hɛ³³.
       say-be.good   only   let.off   my.family   younger.brother
       'Only after making a deal, did (they) let my younger brother off.'
       说好以后才放了我弟弟。
       (*Exempt from military service*, texts)

The negated perfective is overtly marked by using the specific negator *pɣ³³-tɣ³³*, formed by the general/volitional negator *pɣ³³* and the verb *tɣ³³* 'obtain' (see also Chapter 12 on negation). The negator *pɣ³³-tɣ³³* serves to negate the presupposition of the completion of an event or action. In other words, the negated perfective denotes an event or an action is not yet performed or completed (see also [10.3]). The contrast between perfective negation and non-perfective negation is demonstrated by two sentences with the same verb *dza³³* 'pay (taxes)' in (10.7). In (10.7a), it is the action of *paying taxes* which is not completed in the present context while it is the generic action of *paying taxes* that is negated, i.e. *not paying taxes*, in a past context in (10.7b).

(10.7) a. kʰɪŋ³³neŋ²¹ sɿ²¹ ko²¹ xa²¹ **pɣ³³-tɣ³³** tsa³³.
this.year MOD tax still NEG-PFV pay
'The taxes for this year haven't been paid yet.'
今年的税还没上。

b. mɔ²¹kɯ²⁴ ko²¹ la²¹ tie⁵⁵ xɪŋ⁵⁵. tsoŋ⁵⁵ ma²¹sɿ⁵⁵ nɛ⁵⁵,
that.time tax all many very plant grain PRT
nɛ⁵⁵, niɔ³³ tsa³³ ko²¹, tɯ²¹ ua²⁴ tɯ²¹ nɛ⁵⁵, la²¹ niɔ³³
PRT must pay tax at here live prt also must
tsa³³ ko²¹. **pɣ³³** tsa³³ ko²¹ pɣ³³ tɣ³³.
pay tax NEG pay tax NEG be.all.right
'At that time, there were so many taxes. One must pay a tax for farming and even pay a tax for living here. Not paying taxes was out of the question.'
以前税多得很。种粮食呢，要上税，在这儿住呢，也要上税。不上税不行。

The negated perfective can be basically coded on almost all the dynamic verbs, as illustrated in (10.3) and (10.7a). More examples are given below with verbs of action, *ɣɯ²¹* 'come' in (10.8) and *tsaŋ³³* 'see' in (10.9). Note that adjectives in Caijia can be both dynamic and stative. Being dynamic, they usually involve a process of change of state, as shown in (10.10).

(10.8) ɔ²¹kɯ²⁴ xa²¹tsɛ⁵⁵ pɣ³³-tɣ³³ **ɣɯ²¹** zɿ⁵⁵. niɔ³³ ɣɯ²¹ sɿ²¹ xa²¹.
now still NEG-PFV come rain PROSP come AFF REP
'It hasn't rained yet. (But) it's said that it will rain.'
现在还没下雨。说是要下。

(10.9) ɔ²¹ u²¹tsʰo²⁴ ni³³ ŋo³³ la²¹ pɣ³³-tɣ³³ **kɪŋ³³** je³³ ja²¹.
this person CLF 1SG also NEG-PFV see 3SG EXP
'This person, I have never seen him.'
这个人，我没见过他。

(10.10) ɔ²¹ xeŋ²⁴-sui⁵⁵ a²¹ pɣ³³-tɣ³³ **tso³³**.
this apricot-PL still NEG-PFV ripe
'These apricots aren't yet ripe.'
这些杏还没熟。

However, using *pɣ³³-tɣ³³* to negate most of the stative verbs is ungrammatical. For example, the verb *ɣã³³* 'have' in (10.11), the verb *ti³³* 'know' in (10.12) or the copula *sɿ³³* in (10.13) cannot be negated by *pɣ³³-tɣ³³* but only by the general negator *pɣ³³*.

(10.11) mɔ²¹ kɯ²⁴ ŋo³³ ɕie²¹ tʰɔ⁵⁵,
that moment 1SG little moment
ɔ⁵⁵ ʑi²¹ **pɣ³³/*pɣ³³-tɣ³³** ɣã²¹ sɿ²¹mɔ⁵⁵ nε⁵⁵.
house inside NEG/NEG-PFV have what PRT
'When I was young, my family didn't have much.'
以前我小的时候，家里没有什么呢。
(*Haystack*, texts)

(10.12) mɔ²¹kɯ²⁴ ŋo³³ **pɣ³³/*pɣ³³-tɣ³³** ti³³ xa³³ men²¹ni³³ŋoŋ³³.
that.moment 1SG NEG/NEG-PFV know speak Caijia
'I couldn't speak Caijia before.'
以前我不会说蔡家话。

(10.13) je³³ **pɣ³³/*pɣ³³-tɣ³³** sɿ³³ xɯ³³pa³³.
3SG NEG/NEG-PFV COP religious.ritual.performer
'He's not a ritual performer.'
他不是念经先生。

We do observe that certain stative verbs can be negated by *pɣ³³-tɣ³³*, such as the verb *tɯ²¹* 'live, be at' and the verb *sa²¹* 'believe', as in the following two examples.

(10.14) je³³ ɣɯ²¹ tʰɔ⁵⁵ nɯ³³ pɣ³³-tɣ³³ **tɯ²¹** ɔ⁵⁵ ʑi²¹.
3SG come moment 2SG NEG-PFV be.at house inside
'When he came, you were not at home.'
他来的时候，你没在家。

(10.15) je²¹ ta⁵⁵ ŋo³³ xa³³ ja²¹, ŋo³³ pɣ³³-tɣ³³ **sa²¹**.
3SG with 1SG say EXP 1SG NEG-PFV believe
'He said (it) to me, (but) I didn't believe (him).'
他跟我说过，我没信。

Nevertheless, such cases as those in (10.14) and (10.15) are not very common. It is more common that *pɣ³³-tɣ³³* co-occurs with the experiential marker *ja²¹* when negating stative verbs, as illustrated in (10.16) with the stative verb *tɕʰi³³kʰa³³* 'like' (see also §10.2.5). Certainly, both *tɯ²¹* 'live, be at' and *sa²¹* 'believe' can also be used in the same structure with the experiential, whereas the three verbs in (10.11)-(10.13) cannot.

(10.16) ŋo³³   mɔ²¹   nioŋ²⁴   ni³³   tɯ⁵⁵   pɣ³³-tɣ³³   tɕʰi³³kʰa³³   je³³   ja²¹.
         1SG   that   daughter   CLF   exactly NEG-PFV   like   3SG   EXP
         'My daughter has never liked him.'
         我女儿就没喜欢过他。

As mentioned above, the perfective negator $pɣ^{33}$-$tɣ^{33}$ is formed by two morphemes with $tɣ^{33}$ being derived from its related verb form 'obtain'. One may be curious as to whether or not $tɣ^{33}$ should be treated as a preverbal perfective marker rather than treating $pɣ^{55}$-$tɣ^{55}$ as a negator. It is true that the preverbal perfective use of morphemes derived from similar lexical sources of 'obtain' or 'acquire' is attested in quite a number of languages in Southeast Asia, denoting "result of prior event", such as *daj* in Lao, or equivalent verbs in Khmer, Kmhmu Cwang, Hmong, and Vietnamese (Enfield 2003: 140, 292) as well as in Nanning Yue and Nanning Zhuang (Kwok, Chin and Tsou 2011). For example:

(10.17) Lao (Enfield 2003: 141)
         luuk⁴   qeej⁴   tang⁴.tèè¹   nii⁴   mùa¹-naa⁵   caw⁴   daj⁰
         child   VOC   since   this   time-front   2   RSLT.PRR.EVNT
         pên³   kamphaa⁵.
         be   orphan
         'Child – from now on after, you'll (have) become an orphan.' (848.5)

The word $tɣ^{33}$ in Caijia does not present exactly the same case. The [$tɣ^{33}$ V] construction is observed in very limited conditions and its lexical meaning still persists, especially when it precedes a transitive verb. The following example is a case with the intransitive word $sɔ^{21}k^wɔ^{55}$ 'play'. The preverbal $tɣ^{33}$ is far from expressing 'result of a prior event, since there is no prior event in the context. Instead, it is closer to the meaning of 'can', even though it should be interpreted as 'obtain opportunities to play' in (10.18) according to the consultant. Preverbal $tɣ^{33}$ is not productive in expressing possibility at all. See also Chapter 11 for the construction [$tɣ^{33}$ VP to³³].

(10.18) ɔ²¹kɯ²⁴   ɔ²¹   ŋa⁵⁵-sui⁵⁵   tsʰɛ²¹niɔ³³   je²¹   **tɣ³³**
         now   this   child-PL   as.long.as   3SG   obtain
         sɔ²¹kʷɔ⁵⁵,   pɣ³³   zɣ²¹   la²¹   je²¹   kʰã⁵⁵   o.
         play   NEG   eat   even   3SG   be.willing.to   CRS
         'The children of nowadays, as long as they can play, they don't even want to eat.'
         现在的这些孩子，只要他有得玩，不吃他也愿意。

The [tɣ³³ V] construction can be the result of a prior event in some contexts, as shown in (10.19a). '(It) would get (some water) to drink' is the result of 'the crow breaks the bottle'. However, *tɣ³³* in the [tɣ³³ V] construction can still be treated as a verb. First, the meaning of 'obtain, acquire' is not bleached at all in the case below, since one must obtain the water before drinking it. Second, the object 'water' can be added back after *tɣ³³*, i.e. *tɣ²¹ sɿ⁵⁵ ã²¹* as shown in (10.19b), while the order *tɣ³³ ã²¹ sɿ⁵⁵* 'obtain-drink-water' in (10.19c), as the case of Lao in (10.17), is not acceptable.

(10.19) a. ɕiaŋ⁵⁵ a³³ mɔ²¹ tɕiŋ²¹ na²¹-pʰɔ⁵⁵ kuɛ⁵⁵ nɛ⁵⁵, sɿ⁵⁵
want OM that bottle beat-be.broken go PRT water
tsʰe⁵⁵-ɣɯ²¹ je²¹ tɯ⁵⁵ tɣ³³ ã²¹ o.
be.out-go 3SG then obtain drink CRS
'(The crow) wanted to break the bottle so that the water could flow out and it would get (some water) to drink.'
想把那瓶子打破呢，水出去它就能喝了。
(*The crow and the bottle*, texts)

b. je²¹ tɯ⁵⁵ **tɣ²¹** **sɿ⁵⁵** **ã²¹** o.
1SG then obtain water drink CRS
'It would get some water to drink.'
它就得水喝了。

c. *tɣ³³ ã²¹ sɿ⁵⁵
obtain drink water
(Attempted: 'get some water to drink')
*得喝水了

Another similar example is given in (10.20). The object of *tɣ³³* 'obtain', *ʑi³³tsɿ³³* 'chestnut', can be dropped due to its presence in the previous sentence. With the dropped object, [**tɣ³³** zɣ²¹] then forms a structure seemingly identical to preverbal *daj* in Lao.

(10.20) ʑi³³tsɿ³³ ɣa³³-tɕie²¹ɣɯ²¹ tɯ²¹ a³³ kʰɔ³³kʰɔ³³ na²¹-pie⁵⁵
chestnut fall-come.down then OM shell beat-throw
kuɛ²¹ o. ɕie²¹ sɣ⁵⁵ tɯ²¹ **tɣ³³** (ʑi³³tsɿ³³) zɣ²¹ o.
go CRS little mouse then obtain chestnut eat CRS
'The chestnut fell down and the shell was broken. The little mouse then got (the chestnut) to eat.'
栗子掉下来就把壳摔丢了。小老鼠就有（栗子）吃了。

From the examples above, it can be observed that the lexical meaning 'obtain, acquire' for *tɣ³³* in [tɣ³³ V] still persists and that *tɣ³³* is still a verb, especially when it precedes a transitive verb. This preverbal *tɣ³³* is very different from the one in the perfective negator, which has already undergone both semantic change and shift of category and has formed a new negative morpheme coalescing with the general negator *pɣ³³-*. It is, thus, impossible to treat *tɣ³³* as the preverbal perfective marker.

10.2.2 Completive [VP ha⁵⁵]

Completive means "to do something thoroughly and to completion" (Bybee et al. 1994: 54). A completive action or event is terminated or finished in the same way as a perfective situation is, but it bears additional semantic value. That is to say there is an emphasis on thorough completion.

Derived from the verb *ha⁵⁵* 'finish, come to an end', *ha⁵⁵* marks the completive by following a VP in Caijia. It should be mentioned that *ha⁵⁵* is often stressed in a sentence and the tone value is often [51] when it is stressed. The lexical uses of *ha⁵⁵* are given below. It is used as a verb in (10.21) denoting 'come to an end'.

(10.21) je²¹-xɯ⁵⁵ xa²¹ pɣ³³ tiu³³u³³ kʰua²¹ ni²⁴ tɯ³³ niɔ³³ **ha⁵¹** o.
3SG-PL still NEG know good life then PROSP finish CRS
'They still didn't know their good life would come to an end.'
他们还不知道好日子就要完了。
(*Two Moons*, texts)

Serving as the resultative verbal complement of the verb *pɣ²¹* 'carry on the back' in (10.22), *ha⁵⁵* contributes the meaning of 'finish' to the verb 'carry'. The words *pɣ²¹* and *ha⁵⁵* form a complex VP. It can be observed that the resultative *ha⁵⁵* is negated by the general negator *pɣ³³*. This is a very important feature for distinguishing the resultative *ha⁵⁵* from the completive *ha⁵⁵*. The latter cannot be negated.

(10.22) bo²¹-xɯ⁵⁵ pɔ²¹kɣ²¹ pie⁵⁵ lɛ²¹ mo³³
break.off-down corn toss field inside
pɣ²¹-pɣ³³-**ha⁵⁵**.
carry.on.the.back-NEG-finish
'(We) broke off the corns, tossed (them) in the field but couldn't carry all (of them).'
掰下玉米扔地里背不完。
(*Encountering the ghost*, texts)

Almost all types of verbs can be marked by the completive, examples for which will be shown along with discussion below. In Caijia, the completive is often overtly coded in two situations.

First, it tends to be overtly coded when the completion of an action or event needs to be emphasized. Compare the two conversations in (10.23). In (10.23a), speaker A is not aware of the target person's presence and shows impatience for his lateness. Speaker B tries to clear up the misunderstanding by offering a response overtly marked by *ha⁵⁵* to emphasize the completion of the target person's arrival. By contrast, in (10.23b), the question in speech turn A₁ is neutral and the marked answer is thus optional.

(10.23) a. A₁- na²¹ xiŋ⁵⁵ o ma, ɔ²¹kɯ²⁴.
late very CRS PRT now
je³³ xa²¹ pγ³³-tγ³³ ɣɯ²¹ la²¹?!
3SG still NEG-PFV come PRT
'It's very late now. Hasn't he arrived yet?!'
晚得很了嘛，现在。他还没来啊？！

B₁- ɣɯ²¹ **ha⁵¹** o. tɯ²¹ u³³mĩ²¹ me²¹ tsʰɿ⁵⁵po⁵⁵ sɿ²¹.
come COMPL CRS at back dig potato CONT
'(He) has already arrived and is digging potatoes behind (the house).'
来了。在后面挖土豆呢。

b. A₁- je³³ ɣɯ²¹ lɔ²¹ pγ³³-tγ³³?
3SG come or NEG-PFV
'Has he arrived?'
他来了没？

B₁- ɣɯ²¹ (**ha⁵¹**) o.
come COMPL CRS
'(Yes, he's) arrived.'
来了。

It should be mentioned that *ha⁵⁵* co-occurs with the marker of currently relevant state *o* (§10.2.3) in an independent sentence as shown above and also in (10.24) and (10.25) below. The use of *o* is obligatory. Note that once there is an object, the completive marker *ha⁵⁵* follows it instead of immediately following the verb, as shown in (10.25).

(10.24) pe⁵⁵ la²¹ pia⁵⁵ ha⁵¹ *(o).
hair all be.white COMPL CRS
'My hair all turned white.'
我头发都白了。

(10.25) je²¹ tɕiu⁵⁵ suaŋ³³uɛ³³ ha⁵¹ *(o).
3SG arrive Weining_PLACENAME COMPL CRS
nɯ³³ kuɛ²¹ ko²¹ je⁵⁵ sɔ²¹kʷɔ⁵⁵ mɛ̃!
2SG go find 3SG play PRT
'He has arrived in Weining. Go hang out with him.'
他到威宁了。你去找他玩嘛。

Second, when there is a sequence of two events, EVENT₁-EVENT₂, and EVENT₂ can only be realized on the basis of the completion of EVENT₁, EVENT₁ is often marked by the completive *ha⁵⁵*. EVENT₁ and EVENT₂ form a complex sentence. Being a dependent clause, EVENT₁ is not marked by the currently relevant state aspect. Instead, it can be optionally marked by the particle *nɛ⁵⁵*, indicating a dependent clause. Compare (10.26) with (10.24) and (10.25). In (10.26), three sequences of events are illustrated. All the EVENTS₁ are marked by *ha⁵⁵*.

(10.26) i) niɔ³³ ta⁵⁵ fɛ⁵¹hɛ²¹ tɕʰi³³kʰa³³.
should two family like
ii) tɕʰi³³kʰa³³ **ha⁵¹** nɛ⁵⁵, tɯ³³sɿ³³
like COMPL PRT then
EVENT₁
niɔ³³ ã²¹ tɕʰi⁵⁵kʰa⁵⁵tso⁵⁵. [...]
should drink alcohol.of.joy
EVENT₂
iii) ŋa⁵⁵-sui⁵⁵ tγ³³-la²¹ **ha⁵¹** nɛ⁵⁵, tsɿ²¹kʰɯ³³neŋ²¹
child-PL grow-big COMPL PRT teenage
EVENT₁
nɛ⁵⁵ lɛ⁵⁵tsʰɛ²¹ ɣɯ²¹ na³³ tsɯ²¹.
PRT until.then come offer bride-price
EVENT₂
iv) na³³ tsɯ²¹ **ha⁵⁵** nɛ⁵⁵,
offer bride-price COMPL PRT
EVENT₁

tsʰɛ²¹   niu³³.
until.then greet
EVENT₂

'It should be that two families agree (with each other). After they agree, then (they) drink the alcohol of joy. [. . .] When the children grow up to their teens, (the family of the groom) comes to offer the bride-price. Only after offering the bride-price, the family of the groom can greet (the bride).'

要两家都高兴。高兴了呢，就是要喝喜酒。[...]孩子们长大了呢，十几岁呢，才来下聘。下聘了呢，才娶。

(*Tradition of marriage*, texts)

10.2.3 Currently relevant state [VP o]

The term 'currently relevant state' is used to describe the sentence final particle *le* 了 [lə] in Standard Mandarin (Li and Thompson 1981). It is also known as '*le*₂' or '*le*-two' in Chinese linguistics, as opposed to '*le*-one' which serves as a perfective marker, modifying a main verb post-verbally. It is defined as a state of affairs that has "special current relevance with respect to some particular situation" or the given reference time (Li and Thompson 1981: 240) and usually involves a change of state reporting progress towards completion (Li and Thompson 1981: 244, Zhu Dexi 1982: 209–210, Lü Shuxiang 1999: 351). The clause-final particle *le* in Standard Mandarin emphasizes change, denoting that the current state is different from the state prior to the given reference time. For example:

Standard Mandarin
(10.27)   饭好了。
          fàn   hǎo   le.
          meal good CRS.
          'The meal is ready (but it wasn't just before now).'

The equivalent function in Caijia is realized by the sentence final particle *o*, the source of which is untraceable. In general, the particle *o* appears in the sentence final position. It is not restricted to a specific type or certain types of verbs, which is probably related to the fact that *o* is a sentential marker instead of a verbal marker. The particle *o* can co-occur with other aspectual markers when required in a given context. However, it is observed that *o* cannot co-occur with the continuous marker $sı^{33}$... $sı^{21}$ (see §10.2.8), which is easy to explain, since continuity and change of states are semantically contradictory.

Let us now consider some examples of the particle *o* in Caijia. Even though it is labelled as 'currently relevant state', the particle *o* is not necessarily related to the present. Instead, it is related to the given reference time of the context. It denotes that the state at the given reference time holds and is different from the given anterior state. Example (10.28) belongs to a past context. The time boundary of the change of state occurs at the moment when the mother tiger fell into the hole, after which the two little tigers entered into the state of not having a mother. The VP 'didn't have a mother' in (10.28) is of stative nature.

(10.28) je⁵⁵ mɔ²¹ ʑi³³ ni³³ tɯ³³ ɣa³³ kʰa³³ mo³³ kuɛ³³,
3PL that mother CLF then fall hole inside go
ɕie²¹ kʰɣ⁵⁵pa²⁴ ta⁵⁵ kʷɔ²¹ tɯ³³ pɣ³³ ɣã³³ ʑi³³ o.
little tiger.DIM two CLF then NEG have mother CRS
'Their mother fell into the hole. The two little tigers didn't have a mother then.'
它们妈妈掉进洞里了，两只小老虎就没有妈了。
(*Two little tigers*, texts)

Example (10.29) illustrates an irrealis context with the speaker narrating how to cure ulcers with a special herb. The change of state 'be cured' occurs after baking in the sun with the herb applied on the ulcer(s). The reference time in this case is not related to the past, the present, or the future.

(10.29) nɯ³³ ɣa³³ ma²¹kʰa³³ mo³³ kuɛ³³ tsa⁵⁵ iŋ³³soŋ³³ nɛ⁵⁵,
2SG go door inside go expose sun PRT
tɯ³³ **kʰua²¹ o.**
then be.good CRS
'(After applying the herb on your ulcer,) you go outside and bake in the sun. Then the ulcer will be cured.'
(把药涂上以后，) 你去外面晒太阳，就好了。
(*The cure for ulcers*, texts)

In example (10.30), one can observe a series of changes of state with different types of VPs. Each particle *o* signals a new situation. In (10.30i), *o* co-occurs with the adjective *ka²¹* 'be cold' and is marked by the inchoative. It co-occurs with the VP of achievement *pɔ²¹-xɯ⁵⁵* 'hold up' marked by the prospective in (10.30ii). In (10.30iii) *o* is highly compatible in marking an object marking construction, which already involves the meaning of change of state (see also Chapter 8).

(10.30) lɔ²¹sɿ⁵⁵   jɯ²⁴   tsʰɿ⁵⁵   ji³³   pi³³.   e²⁴!
       hard   again blow   one   mouth INTJ
  i)   lɔ²¹sɿ⁵⁵   je³³   jɯ²⁴   **ka²¹-xɯ⁵⁵ɣɯ²¹**   o.
       hard   3SG   again be.cold-INC   CRS
  ii) tɯ³³   **niɔ³³**   a²¹   **so⁵⁵**   pɔ²¹-xɯ⁵⁵   o.   [...]
       then   PROS   with hand   hold-rise   CRS
  iii) tsʰɔ³³kɔ²¹ko²⁴   lɛ⁵⁵   tɯ³³   a³³   to²¹to⁵⁵   la²¹
       shrinking   ADV   then   OM   head   all
       tsʰɔ⁵⁵-tɕie²¹ɣɯ²¹   o.
       shrink-come.down   CRS

'(The North Wind) blows harder. He begins to feel colder. Next, he hugs (himself). [...] (He) then shrinkingly pulls in his head.'
(北风）使劲又吹一口。诶！他更是冷起来了。就要用手（把自己）抱住了。[...] 缩手缩脚地就把头都缩下来了。
(*The North Wind and the Sun*, texts)

In example (10.31), the verb *ɖaŋ³³* 'stand' is marked by the durative marker *-xɯ⁵⁵* (see also §10.2.10). Marked by the particle *o*, the sentence denotes that the man entered into a state of standing beside the stone from a prior state.

(10.31) kʰɪŋ⁵⁵-pɣ²¹-tsʰe⁵⁵ɣɯ²¹   sɿ³³,   koŋ⁵⁵koŋ⁵⁵   a   tɯ²¹
         pull-NEG-come.out   PRT   every.day   INTJ at
         mɔ²¹   tsa³³to²¹   pɪŋ³³   **ɖaŋ²¹-xɯ⁵⁵**   o.
         that   stone   side   stand-DUR   CRS

'(Because) he couldn't pull out (his hand from the mouth of the stone), (the man) was standing beside the stone every day.'
(手）抽不出来,（那人）天天啊在那石头边站着了。
(*The man and the stone*, texts)

It is often observed that the sentence final particle *o* is fused with the deictic verb *kuɛ³³* 'go', i.e. *kʷɔ²¹*, occupying the sentence final position, as shown in (10.32). Compare it also with the deictic 'go' in both (10.19) and (10.20).

(10.32) mɔ²¹   kʰɣ⁵⁵pa³³   tɯ²¹   ta⁵⁵   mɔ²¹   kʰã⁵⁵   tɣ³³
         that   tiger   then   from   that   ridge   upside
         ji³³   pɣ²¹   tɕiɔ³¹-tɕie²¹ɣɯ²¹   e.   tɯ²¹
         one   fly   jump-come.down   PRT then

a³³ ŋo³³ ɔ²¹ kʰui⁵⁵ ka²¹-xɯ⁵⁵ **kʷɔ²¹**.
OM 1SG this dog catch-up go.CRS
'The tiger suddenly jumped off the ridge and snatched my dog away.'
那老虎从断坡上一下子跳下来了，把我的狗抓走了。
(*My loyal dog*, texts)

An additional *o* has even been observed, used right after the fused form *kʷɔ²¹*. See the example below.

(10.33) tɯ³³ tsɔ²¹ ɔ²¹ sɿ⁵⁵ sɿ⁵⁵ kʷɔ²¹ **o**.
then be.like this way die go.CRS CRS
'Then (he) died like this.'
就像这样死掉了。
(*Drowning persons*, texts)

Moreover, different from other verbal aspectual markers, *o* can be used to mark time words in Caijia forming independent sentences, which is similar to the sentential *le*, i.e. *le₂*, in Standard Mandarin (Lü Shuxiang 1999: 355–356). A time word marked by *o* denotes that one enters into a certain moment or a period of time. See the two examples below.

(10.34) **ji³³ nen³³ tie³³ o.** ɕian⁵⁵ pe⁵⁵-ɪn²¹ kuɛ³³
one year bottom CRS want return-back PURP
kua³³ nen²¹ xɪŋ⁵⁵.
celebrate year very
'It was the end of a year. (The three daughters-in-law) wanted to go back home to celebrate the Spring Festival.'
一年年底了。（三个儿媳妇）实在想回（娘）家过年得很。
(*Three daughters-in-law*, texts)

(10.35) tsʰa³³ kɯ²¹ **o.**
lunch moment CRS
'It's noon.'
中午了。

10.2.4 Inchoative [VP kʰɯ⁵⁵ɣɯ²¹ ~ xɯ⁵⁵ɣɯ²¹]

Like the currently relevant state, the inchoative also involves change of state. It codes and emphasizes the commencement of a state or an action and is also known as the inceptive or ingressive (Bybee et al. 1994). It can be paraphrased as 'it begins to do' in English.

In Sinitic languages, the inchoative is often coded via the directional verbal complement derived from 'rise, arise, get up' (Chappell 1992), for example, *qǐlái* 起来 [tɕʰi²¹⁴lai¹⁵] 'rise, arise, get up' in Standard Mandarin. The Caijia inchoative mirrors the Sinitic pathway, the marker *kʰɯ⁵⁵ɣɯ²¹* or its reduced form *xɯ⁵⁵ɣɯ²¹* is derived from exactly the same semantic field, i.e. 'rise, arise, get up'. The morphemes *kʰɯ⁵⁵* and *ɣɯ²¹* are respectively derived from the verb 'rise' and the verb 'come'. The verbal use of *kʰɯ⁵⁵* 'rise, arise' is given in (10.36). See (10.23) for the verbal use of *ɣɯ²¹* 'come'. *kʰɯ⁵⁵ɣɯ²¹* 'rise, arise' serves as the predicate VP in (10.37) with *ɣɯ²¹* as the complement of *kʰɯ⁵⁵*. It should be noted that the reduced form *xɯ⁵⁵ɣɯ²¹* cannot serve as a VP.

(10.36) ɣã²¹ ji³³ tɔ²¹kʰɯ⁵⁵ ŋo³³ tɕɪŋ²¹tɕɪŋ²⁴ lɛ²¹ **kʰɯ⁵⁵**.
there.be one morning 1SG early ADV rise
'There was one morning and I got up very early.'
有一个早上我早早地起了。
(*Drowning Persons*, texts)

(10.37) ŋo⁵⁵ tɛ²¹tɕʰi²⁴ pɣ²¹ **kʰɯ⁵⁵-ɣɯ²¹** ta⁵⁵ je²¹
1PL everyone NEG rise-come with 3PL
ti²¹ nɛ⁵⁵, kua³³-pɣ³³-tɣ³³ ɔ²¹ ni²⁴.
resist PRT live-NEG-obtain this life
'If we hadn't arisen to resist them, (we) wouldn't have managed to live our lives.'
我们大家不起来跟他们抵抗呢，过不了这日子。
(*Anti-Japanese*, texts)

As *qǐlái* in Standard Mandarin, both *kʰɯ⁵⁵ɣɯ²¹* and its reduced form *xɯ⁵⁵ɣɯ²¹* can also be used as a directional verbal complement denoting an upward movement. Both the verbs *ɖaŋ³³* 'stand' and *ma³³* 'be full' can involve upward movement. For example, the action of standing up is upward. As for the verb *ma³³* 'be full', if a container is full or filled, it can be understood that the volume of its content increases from zero to the capacity of the container and this increase occurs in a visually upward direction.

(10.38) tsɿ²¹li²¹li²⁴ tsɿ²¹li²¹li²⁴ lɛ²¹ tɯ²¹ taŋ²¹-**kʰɯ⁵⁵ɣɯ²¹** o.
straight straight ADV then stand-rise.come CRS
'He stood up (in the water), in an upright manner.'
直挺挺直挺挺地就站起来了。
(*Drowning persons*, texts)

(10.39) ɔ²¹   sɿ⁵⁵   tɯ³³   tsa²¹-ɣɯ²¹   o,   ma²¹-**xɯ⁵⁵ɣɯ²¹**   o.
this   water   then   go.up-come   CRS   be.full-up   CRS
'The water then rose and (bottle) was filled up.'
这水就上来，满起来了。
(*The crow and the bottle*, texts)

Marking the inchoative, $k^hɯ^{55}ɣɯ^{21}$ ~ $xɯ^{55}ɣɯ^{21}$ follows the VP in a sentence and can be interpreted as 'begin to do' as mentioned above. This means that $k^hɯ^{55}ɣɯ^{21}$ ~ $xɯ^{55}ɣɯ^{21}$ follows the object, if there is one. Furthermore, $k^hɯ^{55}ɣɯ^{21}$ and $xɯ^{55}ɣɯ^{21}$ function as a pair of free variants. Both of them can be observed in similar contexts and no particular semantic difference between them has been detected. This will be illustrated with examples below.

When marking an adjective or an intransitive verb, there is no syntactic difference between the directional $k^hɯ^{55}ɣɯ^{21}$ ~ $xɯ^{55}ɣɯ^{21}$ and the inchoative $k^hɯ^{55}ɣɯ^{21}$ ~ $xɯ^{55}ɣɯ^{21}$. Compare $taŋ^{21}$-$k^hɯ^{55}ɣɯ^{21}$ 'stand up' in (10.38) with mia^{21} $k^hɯ^{55}ɣɯ^{21}$ 'began to make a sound' in (10.40) and tso^{21} $xɯ^{55}ɣɯ^{21}$ 'began to be familiar' in (10.41). However, the inchoative $k^hɯ^{55}ɣɯ^{21}$ ~ $xɯ^{55}ɣɯ^{21}$ is semantically very different from the directional $k^hɯ^{55}ɣɯ^{21}$ ~ $xɯ^{55}ɣɯ^{21}$. Neither the verb mia^{21} 'resound, make a sound' nor the adjective dzo^{33} 'be familiar' implies an upward movement, as 'stand' or 'be full' does. It is, thus, impossible to analyze $k^hɯ^{55}ɣɯ^{21}$ ~ $xɯ^{55}ɣɯ^{21}$ in the following two cases as the directional complement use. Instead, it is the commencement of each action which is marked by $k^hɯ^{55}ɣɯ^{21}$ ~ $xɯ^{55}ɣɯ^{21}$ expressing, respectively, 'the stone began to make a sound' in (10.40), and 'they' who 'began to be familiar and began to like each other' in (10.41).

(10.40) pie⁵⁵   pie⁵⁵   mo³³   kuɛ²¹   tɯ⁵⁵   tsɔ²¹   mɔ²¹   na³³
toss   to   inside   go   then   be.like   that   beat
lo²¹   na²¹   kɤ⁵⁵   sɿ²¹   mia²¹   **kʰɯ⁵⁵ɣɯ²¹**.
gong   beat   drum   so   resound   INC
'(I) tossed (the stone) into the hole and it began to make a loud sound like playing the drum and the gong.'
丢进去就像敲锣打鼓这样响起来了。
(*The big hole*, texts)

(10.41) ni²⁴   tɤ²¹ko⁵⁵   nɛ⁵⁵,   tɯ³³   tsɔ²¹   **xɯ⁵⁵ɣɯ²¹**,   tɯ³³
time   long   PRT   then   be.familiar   INC   then
ji³³   ni³³   tɕʰi³³kʰa³³   ji³³   ni²¹   **kʰɯ⁵⁵ɣɯ²¹**   o.
one   CLF   like   one   CLF   INC   CRS
'(They) began to be familiar with each other and to like each other over time.'
时间久了，就熟起来，就彼此喜欢起来了。

Examples (10.42) and (10.43) illustrate two cases with objects. One can observe that *kʰɯ⁵⁵ɣɯ²¹ ~ xɯ⁵⁵ɣɯ²¹* follows the object in each case. Similar to (10.40) and (10.41), in neither of the two cases below is there an additional meaning of upward movement for *kʰɯ⁵⁵ɣɯ²¹ ~ xɯ⁵⁵ɣɯ²¹* within the VP. Only the inchoative interpretation is possible. The falling of rain in (10.42) is downward and the directional meaning of *kʰɯ⁵⁵ɣɯ²¹ ~ xɯ⁵⁵ɣɯ²¹*, 'rise up', would thus be contradictory with such a predicate. As for (10.43), the action of uttering itself does not imply any upward movement.

(10.42) ɣɯ²¹   zɿ⁵⁵   **kʰɯ⁵⁵ɣɯ²¹**   o.
come   rain   INC   CRS
'It began to rain.'
下起雨来了。

(10.43) ɣã²¹   ji²¹   koŋ⁵⁵,   mɔ²¹   tsa³³toʔ²¹   po⁵⁵   tɯ⁵⁵   ta⁵⁵   je²¹
there.be one   day   that   stone   CLF   then   with   3SG
xa²¹   ŋoŋ³³   **xɯ⁵⁵ɣɯ²¹**   o.
speak speech   INC   CRS
'One day, the stone began to speak with him.'
有一天，那块石头就跟他说起话来了。
(*The man and the stone*, texts)

The inchoative is also described as involving a 'state that commences', and is often restricted to stative verbs (Bybee et al. 1994: 318). However, the examples listed above have already shown that the inchoative is not restricted to just stative verbs in Caijia. It can be used with speech act and event verbs as well. Even though we have not done an exhaustive survey, it is evident that the inchoative cannot be marked on verbs or VPs of achievement. Compare two pairs of contrastive examples in (10.44) and (10.45). In (10.44), both the verb *piɔ³³* 'run' and *tɕiu⁵⁵* 'arrive, achieve' are motion verbs. It is ungrammatical to mark *tɕiu⁵⁵* with the inchoative.

(10.44) a. ti⁵⁵ɪn²¹kɯ²⁴   je⁵⁵   xa²¹   tɯ²¹   ma²⁴   taŋ²¹-xɯ⁵⁵
just.now   3SG   still   at   there stand-DUR
ta⁵⁵   ni³³   na³³pia³³.
with   3   chat
tɕie⁵⁵me⁵⁵   ji²¹tʰɯ²⁴   tɯ³³   **piɔ²¹**   xɯ⁵⁵ɣɯ²¹   o!
how   suddenly   then   run   INC   CRS
'He was chatting with someone just now. How come he suddenly began to run!'
刚才他还在那儿和人聊天。怎么突然就跑起来了。

b. *je²¹ **tɕiu⁵⁵** xɯ⁵⁵ɣɯ²¹ o.
   3SG arrive INC   CRS
   (Attempted: '*He began to arrive.')
   *他到起来了。

In (10.45), the verb $zɣ^{21}$ 'eat' is the main verb in both examples. In (10.45a), the inchoative is acceptable with the verb $zɣ^{21}$ 'eat' as a pure activity verb. However, in (10.45b), $zɣ^{21}$ acquires the meaning of achievement by compounding the adjective $kʰua^{21}$ '(be) good' as its complement, denoting 'have eaten, feel unnecessary to eat more'. Similar to (10.44b), the inchoative cannot be used either, due to the fact that the VP possesses the meaning of achievement.

(10.45) a. ɔ²¹kɯ²⁴   xa²¹tsɛ⁵⁵   tɕiŋ²¹   xiŋ⁵⁵   a   mẽ.
            now   still   early   very   PRT   PRT
            nɯ³³   tɯ³³   **zɣ²¹**   pɣ²¹   kʰɯ⁵⁵ɣɯ²¹   o.
            2SG   then   eat   supper INC   CRS
            'It's still very early now. You've even begun to have your supper.'
            现在还早得很嘛。你就开始吃晚饭了。

       b. *je³³   **zɣ²¹**-kʰua²¹   kʰɯ⁵⁵ɣɯ²¹   o.
          3SG   eat-good   INC   CRS
          '?He began to finish eating.'
          *他吃好起来了。

It is not difficult to explain why the inchoative cannot associate with the verbs of achievement. The inchoative marks the beginning of an action or a state, whereas verbs of achievement are supposed to focus on accomplishment of actions or states, i.e. their endpoint. These two focuses are semantically incompatible in the same sentence.

It should be mentioned that, apart from $kʰɯ^{55}ɣɯ^{21}$ ~ $xɯ^{55}ɣɯ^{21}$, we also observe that the morpheme $xɯ^{55}$ marks the inchoative alone. As shown in the example below, $xɯ^{55}$ follows the VP $ã^{21} ɩŋ^{21}$ 'smoke (LIT: drink tobacco)' denoting 'began to smoke'.

(10.46) ŋo²¹   ta⁵⁵   tsʅ²¹ŋoŋ⁵⁵   fɣ⁵⁵   neŋ²¹
        1SG   from   fifteen   six   year
        tɯ⁵⁵   ã²¹   ɩŋ²¹   **xɯ⁵⁵**   o.
        then   drink   tobacco INC   CRS
        'I began to smoke from fifteen or sixteen years old.'
        我从十五六岁就开始抽烟了。

Although there are not many examples of this phenomenon in our database, it deserves further research.

10.2.5 Experiential

The experiential, also known as experiential perfect in the literature, is not a widely attested aspectual category in the languages of the world (Dahl 1985: 139), but it is one that commonly exists in the majority of Sinitic languages (Chappell 2001c). It denotes that "a given situation has held at least once during some time in the past" (Comrie 1976: 58; see also Dahl 1985: 141), emphasizing one's ([+ human]) gain of experience or knowledge.

The verb *guò* 过 [kuɔ^{51}] 'pass by' in Standard Mandarin is probably the most well-known lexical source for the experiential. Its cognate forms are also attested as the experiential marker in many other Sinitic languages (Chappell 2001c) (see also the entry CROSS in Kuteva et al. 2019). Caijia uses two markers to mark the experiential: *ja*^{21} and *gua*^{33}. In a nutshell, the lexical sources of these two markers are both related to the meaning 'experience'. *gua*^{33}, probably cognate with *guò* in Standard Mandarin, can also denote 'pass by'. *ja*^{21} is more frequently used to mark the experiential, while *gua*^{33} functions more like a resultative verbal complement or phase marker. Moreover, their syntactic positions are also different, i.e. [VP ja^{21}] and [V-gua^{33}]. A more detailed description is given below.

10.2.5.1 *ja*^{21} [VP ja^{21}]

The lexical uses of *ja*^{21} are not as numerous as those of *gua*^{33}. As a verb, *ja*^{21} is intransitive and denotes 'be used to', it is typically used in sentences with serial verb constructions. The sentence in (10.47a) is a case with two clauses in sequence and with *je*^{33} '3SG' as the shared subject and the verb *ja*^{21} occupying the position of the second VP. This is probably the only condition for *ja*^{21} to be used as a verb. The verbhood of *ja*^{21} has almost been lost in Caijia. It cannot form the major predicate in a sentence, as illustrated in (10.47b).

(10.47) a. je^{33} VP₁[koŋ^{33}koŋ^{33} la^{21} tsɔ^{21} mɔ^{21}sı^{55}
 3SG every.day all be.like that.way
 tɕɪŋ^{21}kʰɯ^{55}ja^{21}ʑi^{55} lɛ^{21}] VP₂[ja^{21}] o.
 work.from.dawn.to.night CONT be.used.to CRS
 'He works from dawn to night every day and he's used to it.'
 他天天都像那样起早贪黑地惯了。

b. *je³³ ja²¹   o.
   3SG   be.used.to CRS
   'He's used to (it).'
   他习惯了。

By contrast, *ja²¹* is very commonly used as a verbal complement denoting 'be used to' as well, as illustrated in (10.48).

(10.48) ŋo³³ zɣ²¹-**ja³³**   ŋuɛ²¹   ʑi³³   tɕie⁵⁵   sʅ²¹ zɣ³³   o.
        1SG   eat-be.used.to   my.family mother do   REL   meal   CRS
        'I'm used to my mother's cooking.'
        我吃惯我妈做的饭了。

One should note that the verbal complement *ja²¹* does not indicate the completion of an action, as do the Standard Mandarin *guò* or the Caijia *gua³³*, a feature which will be discussed below. It thus cannot be treated as a phase marker. 'Be used to' is the only interpretation for the verbal complement *ja²¹*.

When compounded together, *gua³³* and *ja²¹* form the disyllabic verb *gua³³ja²¹*, which denotes 'experience' and is semantically closely related to the experiential aspect. See the following two examples.

(10.49) ŋo⁵⁵ ta⁵⁵ ni²¹ ji²¹hɔ⁵⁵   **kua³³ja²¹** xa²¹sʅ⁵⁵   sʅ²¹ mẽ!
        1PL   two   CLF   together   experience   life.and.death   AFF   PRT
        'The two of us certainly have gone through tests of life and death.'
        我们俩是一起经历了生死的嘛。

(10.50) je³³ **kua³³ja²¹**   mɔ²⁴   sui⁵⁵ ha⁵⁵   nɛ⁵⁵, tsɔ²¹   mɔ²¹
        3SG   experience   that   some   COMPL PRT   resemble   that
        ta⁵⁵la²¹   pi³³   u²¹tsʰo²⁴   ni³³   sʅ²¹.
        afresh   turn.into   person   CLF   way
        'After he experienced all those things, he seems to be a different person.'
        他经历了那些以后呢，像是变了一个人似的。

One might rightly doubt whether or not the *ja²¹* in *gua³³ja²¹* can still be analyzed as a verbal complement, as in (10.48). The answer is negative. First, *ja²¹* cannot be negated in *gua³³ja²¹*, while verbal complements can be negated, as is shown in (10.56) further below. Second, given that *ja²¹* usually denotes 'be used to' as a verbal complement, this interpretation suits neither the context of (10.49) nor the context of (10.50). Besides, other meanings apart from 'be used to', have not yet been observed.

As mentioned above, *ja²¹* follows the VP in a sentence when serving as the experiential marker. Examples (10.51)–(10.54) illustrate different types of VPs. In (10.51), *ja²¹* follows the VP *kuɛ²¹ kʰɔ²¹ kʰɯ²¹ pe⁵⁵* 'go to attend the exams several times', in which *kʰɯ²¹ pe⁵⁵* 'several times' is a postpositioned verbal classifier denoting the frequency of the action it modifies. The sentence denotes '(The student) has attended the exams several times'.

(10.51) mɔ²¹ kʷɔ³³sɣ²¹ŋa⁵⁵ ni³³ jɯ²⁴ kuɛ³³ ka³³tɕi³³ o.
that student CLF again go attend.exams CRS
la²¹ kuɛ²¹ kʰɔ²¹ kʰɯ²¹ pe⁵⁵ **ja²¹** o.
all go attend.exams several time EXP CRS
'That student went to attend the exams again. (He) has already attended several times.'
那个学生又去考试了。都考过几回了。

In (10.52), *ja²¹* follows the intransitive verb *kua³³* 'pass by'. Apparently, *kua⁵⁵ ja²¹* in (10.52) cannot be analyzed as the verb *gua³³ja²¹* 'experience' in the given context. Preceded by the locative phrase *ta⁵⁵ tɣ³³* 'from the upside (of the water behind the back)', *kua³³* is the motion verb 'pass by'. Besides, the verb *gua³³ja²¹* 'experience' usually takes an animate subject, but it is the fart that passes over the water in (10.52).

(10.52) sɿ⁵⁵ tɯ²¹ hɔ⁵⁵ mo³³ e, mɔ²¹ u³³mĩ²¹ mɔ²⁴ pʰɪŋ²¹
water be.at road inside PRT that back that CLF
sɿ³³ pɣ²¹ pe²¹ ta⁵⁵ tɣ³³ kua³³ **ja²¹** se²¹.
AFF fart flatus from upside pass EXP AFF.
[...] pɣ³³ tsʰɿ³³ka³³.
NEG be.clean
'As for the water behind one's back, (when) the water is on the way (back home), the flatus passes over it. Consequently, (it) isn't clean.'
水在路上啊，后面那水，放的屁从上面过过。[......]不干净。
(*The water behind one's back*, texts)

The example below illustrates a case in which *ja²¹* follows the adjective *pe²¹* 'be hot' and associates with the perfective negator *pɣ³³tɣ³³*. The tone value of *ja²¹* changes from [21] to [24] for expressing an exclamation.

(10.53) ɔ²¹ sɿ⁵⁵lɛ²¹mo³³ xa²¹ pɣ³³-tɣ³³ tsɔ²¹ ɔ²¹ sɿ⁵⁵ pe²¹ **ja²⁴**.
this place even NEG-PFV be.like this way be.hot EXP
'It has never been hot like this in this place.'
这个地方还没像这么热过。

Example (10.54) shows that *ja²¹* follows the object of a sentence, when there is one.

(10.54) je³³ tsa³³ ta²⁴ɕyɔ²¹ **ja²¹**, sɿ²¹kʰɯ⁵⁵ la²¹.
3SG attend university EXP knowledge big
'He went to college and is a person of knowledge.'
他上过大学，学问大。

In fact, if one compares the experiential *ja²¹* with the verb *ja²¹* in a serial verb construction, as in (10.55), or the complement in a pro-drop construction, as in (10.56), one will find it very difficult to differentiate them by judging their syntactic positions. Diagnostic tests can be adopted to differentiate the experiential from the meaning of 'be used to'. For example, the experiential *ja²¹* often marks completed actions in the past, or at least anterior to the given reference time, but it cannot be used in irrealis contexts. Given that *ja²¹* in (10.55i) is used in a negated imperative context, it cannot be the experiential marker. Note that the expression 'lift one's head' in Caijia in (10.55) is metaphorically used to express 'encourage someone'.

(10.55) i) piɔ²⁴ ta⁵⁵ je²¹ to²¹ **ja³³**.
NEG.IMP lift 3SG head be.used.to
ii) ta⁵⁵ je²¹ to²¹ **ja²¹** ha⁵⁵ nɛ⁵⁵, tɯ³³ pi³³
lift 3SG head be.used.to COMPL PRT then turn.into
pʰi²¹tɕʰi²⁴ o.
temper CRS
'Don't get used to encouraging him. If you get used to do so, his temper will be spoiled.'
别纵容他惯了。纵容惯了以后呢，就变成脾气了。

If we do not consider (10.56ii), (10.56i) can be analyzed either as a verb or as a verbal complement, both denoting 'be used to', because the experiential *ja²¹* usually does not co-occur with the currently relevant state marker *o*. However, it is analyzed as the verbal complement due to the fact that it can be negated, as in (10.56ii), while both the verb *ja²¹* in a serial verb construction and the experiential *ja²¹* are not usually negated.

(10.56) i) nɯ⁵⁵ tɯ²¹ loŋ³³ mo³³ tɯ²¹-**ja³³** o.
2SG at city inside live-be.used.to CRS

ii) tsʰɿ⁵⁵ nɯ²¹ tɯ²¹ ha⁵⁵ tɯ²¹-pɤ³³-**ja²¹**   o.
    fear 2SG   at   here live-NEG-be.used.to CRS
'You're used to the urban life. I'm afraid that you won't be used to living here.'
你在城里住惯了。怕你在这儿住不惯。

10.2.5.2 *gua³³* [VP gua³³]

The second experiential marker in Caijia is -*gua³³*, for which the lexical source is 'pass by, pass through, spend (time), live (a life)'. Its lexical use is illustrated below. See also example (10.34) for the meaning 'spend (time)' and example (10.37) for the meaning of 'live (a life)'.

(10.57) mɔ²¹ kʷɔ²⁴ ko²¹ tsʰɛ⁵⁵ ta⁵⁵ ma²⁴ **kua³³** pɤ³³ tɤ³³.
         that bridge CLF   car   from there pass   NEG   can
'As for that bridge, cars cannot pass through there.'
那座桥，车不能从那儿过。

Serving as the experiential marker, -*gua³³* immediately follows the verb in a sentence, which is different from the post-VP *ja²¹*. Compare the two sentences in (10.58).

(10.58) a. ŋo³³ zɤ²¹-**kua³³** mɔ²⁴ tsoŋ⁵⁵ saŋ⁵⁵.
            1SG   eat-EXP   that   type   mushroom
'I've eaten that type of mushroom.'
我吃过那种蘑菇。

        b. ŋo³³ zɤ²¹ mɔ²⁴ tsoŋ⁵⁵ saŋ⁵⁵   **ja²¹**.
            1SG   eat   that type   mushroom EXP
'I've eaten that type of mushroom.'
我吃过那种蘑菇。

The markers *ja²¹* and -*gua³³* denote exactly the same meaning when coding the experiential. However, it is *ja²¹* that is usually preferred. Even though -*gua³³* is claimed to be totally acceptable and very natural by different consultants, we only observe *ja²¹* in spontaneous texts. On the contrary, -*gua³³* is more commonly used as a phase complement, which is defined as expressing "the phase of an action in the first verb rather than some result in the action or goal" (Chao 1968: 446). As shown in (10.59), one can find that the complement -*kua³³* 'pass by' can be replaced by the complement -*ha⁵¹* 'finish' with the meaning unchanged, indicating the completion of the action *ja²¹* 'wash'. Neither the complement -*ja²¹* 'be used to' or the experiential *ja²¹* can be accepted in this sentence.

(10.59) ɔ²⁴   mĩ²¹   sɿ²¹   u³³   tɣ³³   ŋo³³   ja²¹-**kua³³**/-ha⁵¹/*ja²¹   o.
       this   side   MOD   bowl   PASS   1SG   wash-pass.by/finish/EXP   CRS
       'I've washed the bowls on this side.'
       这边的碗被我洗过/完了。

Certainly, it cannot be denied that -*gua³³* does more than indicate the completion of an action in certain contexts. In (10.60), -*kua³³* not only indicates the completion of 'stir-fry', but also emphasizes that the salt should undergo the procedure of 'stir-fry' before a breastfeeding mother eats it. In this context, the meaning of -*kua³³* is very close to the experiential and the complement -*ha⁵⁵* 'finish' is not appropriate to replace it at all.

(10.60) ɔ²¹   saŋ³³   niɔ³³   a³³   ŋʷɔ³³-**kua³³**   ɣɯ²¹   zɿ²¹.
       this   salt   should DCR   stir-fry-pass   PURP   eat
       pɤ³³   a³³   ŋʷɔ³³-**kua³³**   nɛ³³,
       NEG   DCR   stir-fry-pass   PRT
       zɿ²¹   ha⁵⁵   ɔ²¹   ŋa⁵⁵   ti³³   ɣã²¹   xɯ³³pɔ³³.
       eat   COMPL   this   child   know   have   asthma
       'The salt should be fried. Otherwise, (if the breastfeeding mother feeds her baby) after eating it, (the baby) may suffer from asthma.'
       这盐要把（它）炒过。不把（它）炒过呢，（哺乳的妈妈）吃了后（再喂奶），孩子会得哮喘。
       (*Post-delivery care*, texts)

In (10.61), apart from the meaning of completion, the meaning of 'gain the experience of reading' can be interpreted from this context as well.

(10.61) mɔ²¹   sɤ³³   mo³³   je³³   kʷɔ³³-**kua³³**   sɿ²¹   sɿ³³   lɔ²⁴-sui⁵⁵.
       that   book   inside   3SG   learn-pass   NMLZ   COP   Q-PL
       'Which books among those has he read?'
       那些书里他看过的是哪些？

10.2.6 Prospective [niɔ³³ VP]

The prospective can be regarded as a relational future. The future codes the situation occurring after the moment of speech (Bybee et al. 1994: 244), while the prospective codes the situation subsequent to the given reference time, which is not necessarily after the moment of speech. Comrie (1976: 64–65) treats the expressions 'be about to', 'be going to', and 'be on the point of' as typical prospectives in English.

Caijia uses the auxiliary niɔ³³, of which the lexical source is the verb niɔ³³ 'ask for, want, need, must', to code the prospective. See examples (10.62)-(10.64) for the meanings 'ask for', 'want', and 'must', respectively. See also Chapter 11 for the further detail on the modal use of niɔ³³.

(10.62) ɣa³³ mɔ²⁴ fɛ⁵⁵hɛ²¹ mo³³ kuɛ³³ **niɔ³³** sa²¹tsʰɯ²¹ mi⁵⁵
walk that family inside PURP ask.for pickle a.little
ɣɯ²¹ tɕie⁵⁵ tsʰɯ²¹sı⁵⁵.
PURP do soup
'(We) went to that family to ask for some pickles to make soup.'
走到那家去要点酸菜来做汤。
(*Paving the road*, texts)

(10.63) ŋo²⁴ pɣ³³ **niɔ³³** ni²¹ hm̥⁵⁵ sı²¹mɔ⁵⁵.
1PL NEG want 3 POSS what
'We don't want anything from others.'
我们不要人家的什么。

(10.64) nɯ²⁴ sa²¹ lɛ³³ **niɔ³³** ji²¹hɔ⁵⁵ kuɛ²¹ ji²¹hɔ⁵⁵ ɣɯ²¹.
2PL three CLF must together go together come
'The three of you must depart on the same day and come back on the same day.'
你们三姊妹要一起去一起去回。
(*Three daughters-in-law*, texts)

Marking the prospective, niɔ³³ precedes the VP in a sentence. As illustrated in (10.65), the given reference time is the moment the speaker entered and niɔ³³ marks the event 'finish eating' subsequent to this moment. Apparently, the reference time is a certain moment in the past; the marked event also took place in the past and has nothing to do with the speech moment. Furthermore, compared with (10.62)-(10.64), the lexical meanings of niɔ³³ in (10.65) have been entirely bleached.

(10.65) ŋo³³ li²¹-ɣɯ²¹ tʰɔ²⁴, je²⁴ la²¹ **niɔ³³** zɣ²¹-ha⁵¹ o.
1SG enter-come moment 3PL even PROSP eat-finish CRS
'The moment I entered, they were about to finish eating.'
我进来的时候，他们都要吃完了。

Another example is given in (10.66). It is an irrealis context in the past. The narrator is recalling his personal experience of driving a horse to plough when he was only seven or eight years old. Again, the aspectually marked action of getting scolded would take place only after the speaker failed to pull the horse.

(10.66) kʰɪŋ⁵⁵ mɛ³³ kʷɔ²¹, kʰɪŋ⁵⁵ po³³ to³³, ni²⁴ **niɔ³³** mɛ³³.
pull horse CLF pull NEG can 3 PROSP scold
'To drive the horse (to plough), if (I) couldn't manage to drive the horse, (I) would get scolded.'
牵马（犁地）呢，牵不了，人家要骂。
(*Ploughing*, texts)

By comparing (10.66) and (10.64), one can observe that the prospective *niɔ³³* and the modal *niɔ³³* 'need, must' occupy exactly the same syntactic position. There is no diagnostic way to distinguish one from the other, except by judging the context where *niɔ³³* is used. The sentence in (10.64) is imperative and *niɔ³³* denotes the speaker's own desire, i.e. she obliges her daughters-in-law to come back on the same day. Therefore, *niɔ³³* in (10.64) cannot be analyzed as the prospective. By contrast, the conditional context in (10.66) does not allow *niɔ³³* to be analyzed as 'want', 'ask for', or 'need, must'.

The prospective marker *niɔ³³* can also be used in the context of the future, especially when there is no specific time reference. Examples (10.67) and (10.68) belong to future contexts. Each is related to a meteorological phenomenon and *niɔ³³* in these two cases must not be in its lexical form, since the verb *niɔ³³* 'ask for, want' requires an animate subject. In (10.67), it has not yet rained at the moment of speech; the prediction is made by the speaker on the basis of signs of rain at that moment. In (10.68), the sky's brightening up also takes place after the moment of speech. Both of the following cases are typical future events.

(10.67) **niɔ³³** ɣɯ²¹ zɿ⁵⁵ o.
PROSP come rain CRS
'It's about to rain.'
要下雨了。

(10.68) kɿ³³ xã³³ o. kʰɪŋ³³ **niɔ³³** mia²¹ o
chicken yell CRS sky PROSP be.bright CRS
'The rooster crowed. The sky is about to brighten up.'
鸡叫了。天要亮了。
(*Pear story*, texts)

However, once there is a specific future time indicator, such as 'tomorrow' or 'a while later', *niɔ³³* is no longer obligatory. As illustrated in (10.69), given that the specific future time indicator *kɔ⁵⁵mi⁵⁵* 'in a while' is used, *niɔ³³* can be omitted.

It should also be mentioned that *niɔ³³* is ambiguous in this context. It can also denote 'need'.

(10.69) ŋo²¹   kɔ⁵⁵mi⁵⁵   **(niɔ³³)**   kuɛ³³   nɛ²¹
         1SG   in.a.while PROSP/need   go   your.family
         la²¹pa³³   mo³³   ji²¹   tʰaŋ²⁴,   nɯ³³   kʰua²¹kʰua²⁴
         uncle   inside   one   VCLF   2SG   well
         tɯ²¹   ɔ⁵⁵   ʑi²¹   sɯ⁵⁵-xɯ⁵⁵.
         at   house   inside rest-DUR
         'I'm going to your uncle's in a second. You have a rest at home.'
         我一会儿（要）去一趟你大伯家，你在家好好歇着。

10.2.7 Delimitative [VP mi⁵⁵]

The delimitative, or delimited, aspect is used to mark an action that is performed only for a little while (Li and Thompson 1981: 232, Bybee et al. 1994: 318). This aspectual aspect is not widely attested in the languages of the world, but is well attested in Sinitic languages (Liu 2022), and serves to shorten the duration of an action.[13] The two forms [V (one) V] and [V a bit] are often adopted to code the delimitative in Sinitic. The component '(one) V' and 'a bit' are also known as verbal classifiers (Paris 2013), which express "the number of times an action takes place" (Chao 1968: 615). Note that the delimitative is one of the important functions of verbal classifiers. See also Chapter 4 §4.4.

Example (10.70) shows these two forms in Standard Mandarin and Yichun Gan with the same verb 'look'. Despite different strategies, the delimitative in these two languages shortens the duration of the action 'look', making it become bounded or telic. In Standard Mandarin, reduplication of the verb is used, and may have the numeral for 'one' inserted, whereas in Yichun Gan, an intervallic classifier is used which is modified by a diminutive suffix: *xa⁴²tsiʔ* is used (see Li Xuping 2018: 147 for details). Needless to say, a language may use both of these strategies to code the delimitative.

(10.70)   [V one V]: Standard Mandarin
     a.   让我看（一）看。
          ràng   wǒ   kàn   **(yí)**   **kàn.**
          let   1SG   look   one   look
          'Let me have a look.'

---

[13] See also Dickey (2007) for the term 'delimitative' for the Russian prefix *po-*.

[V a bit]: Yichun Gan

b. 你去商店看下仔，看得有卖么？
ȵi³⁴ tɕʰiɛ⁴⁴ ɕioŋ³⁴tien⁴⁴ kʰon⁴⁴-xa⁴²tsi?,
2SG go shop look-DELIM
kʰon⁴⁴tɛ? iu⁴² mai²¹³⁻²¹ mo?
look have sell Q
'Go to the shop to see whether they sell it.'
(Li Xuping 2018: 148)

Caijia only uses the form [VP a bit] to code the delimitative aspect with the delimitative marker *mi⁵⁵*, which is derived from the pronoun and quantifier marker *mi⁵⁵* 'some (of), a little bit'. Its lexical uses are illustrated below. It is a pronoun in (10.71) referring to some meat of the tiger as the object of the verb *peŋ⁵⁵* 'divide, get', while it is a post-nominal quantifier in (10.72), modifying the noun *saŋ³³* 'salt' and denoting 'some'. In this example, it occurs in the same position as a classifier.

Pronoun 'some (of)':
(10.71) mɔ³³ tsa²¹ nɛ⁵⁵, a²¹ peŋ⁵⁵ sı⁵⁵ hu⁵⁵ȵi²⁴.
that meat PRT DCR divide to everyone
hu⁵⁵fɛ⁵⁵ la²¹ ji²¹ fɛ⁵⁵ peŋ⁵⁵ **mi⁵⁵** kuɛ³³ . . .
every.family all one family get some go
'As for the meat (of the tiger), it was divided and distributed to everyone. Each family got a portion. . .'
那肉呢，把（它）分给了所有人。一家分了一点……
(*The dead tiger*, texts)

Post-nominal quantifier
(10.72) ɣa³³ saŋ²¹ kʰa⁵⁵ ma²⁴ kuɛ²¹ tsʰaŋ³³ saŋ²¹ **mi⁵⁵** pe⁵⁵-ɣɯ²¹.
go salt guest there PURP weigh salt some return-come
'Go to the salter's to buy some salt.'
去盐客那儿称点盐回来。

Serving as the delimitative marker, *mi⁵⁵* occupies the post-VP position. As mentioned above, the delimitative marker functions to shorten the duration of an action. Take the verb *tsaŋ³³* 'look, see, watch', which possesses a durative semantic feature, as an example. Compare the two sentences in (10.73). The VP *tsaŋ²¹ mi⁵⁵* in (10.73a) denotes 'a quick look at something', whereas the VP *tsaŋ²¹ sɣ³³* 'read a book' in (10.73b) is marked by the continuous marker denoting a relatively long-term action. Furthermore, *tsaŋ²¹ mi⁵⁵* 'have a look' is bounded or telic, whereas *tsaŋ²¹ sɣ³³* 'read a book' is unbounded or atelic.

(10.73) a. nɯ²¹ ta⁵⁵ ŋo²¹ **tsaŋ²¹ mi⁵⁵**, tsaŋ²¹ ɔ²¹ tv̩³³
2SG for 1SG look a.little look this upside
je²¹ sʅ²¹ sʅ³³ sʅ²¹mɔ⁵⁵.
write NMLZ COP what
'Please take a look at this for me and (tell me) what's written on it.'
帮我看下看这上面写的是什么。

b. je³³ **tsaŋ²¹** sv̩³³ sʅ²¹.
3SG look book CONT
'He's reading.'
她在看书。

In fact, regardless of the inherent semantic feature of a verb as bounded or unbounded, once marked by the delimitative *mi⁵⁵*, the meaning is unquestionably bounded. Several more examples are given below. In (10.74) and (10.75i), it is the bare verbs that are marked by *mi⁵⁵*, as in (10.73). Note that *mi⁵⁵* in (10.75) may possess a tentative interpretation. Some Sinitic languages contrast the delimitative and the tentative. Caijia, on the other hand, does not. Tentative meaning is interpreted according to different contexts.

(10.74) kʰɪŋ⁵⁵koŋ⁵⁵ ɪŋ⁵⁵soŋ²¹ kʰua²¹ xɪŋ⁵⁵. ŋo³³ a³³ nia²¹nia²¹
today sun be.good very 1SG OM thing
kʰɪŋ⁵⁵-tsʰe⁵⁵kuɛ²¹ ka⁵⁵ **mi⁵⁵**.
pull-be.out.go dry a.little
'It's very sunny today. I'll take these things out to dry them in the sun a bit.'
今天太阳好得很。我把东西拿出来晒一下。

(10.75) i) hu⁵⁵kʰa⁵⁵ ɣa²¹ mi⁵⁵ tsaŋ²¹ **mi⁵⁵**.
everywhere walk a.little look a.little
ii) tsaŋ²¹ mɔ²¹ la²¹ tsʰʅ⁵⁵kʰa⁵⁵ mɔ²¹-sui⁵⁵ **mi⁵⁵**.
look that big place that-PL a.little
'Go visit different places for a while. Take a visit to somewhere like those big cities.'
到处走走看看。看看那些大地方。

In (10.75ii)-(10.77), the VPs marked by *mi⁵⁵* all occur with objects. One can observe that *mi⁵⁵* is postposed to the object in each of the examples in the form of [V O mi⁵⁵].

(10.76) ɣã³³sɿ²¹xɯ²⁴   nɯ³³   la³³   niɔ²¹   ta⁵⁵   je²¹   to²¹   **mi⁵⁵**.
         sometimes   2SG   also   should lift   3SG   head   a.little
         'Sometimes, you should encourage him a little bit.'
         有时候你要鼓励他一下。

(10.77) mɔ²¹   ɕie²¹   ŋa⁵⁵   ni³³   tɯ²¹   ma²⁴   xɯ³³.   ŋo³³   tɯ³³
         that   little child   CLF   at   there cry   1SG   then
         xɯ³³   je²¹   **mi⁵⁵**.   je³³   tɯ³³   tɕʰi³³kʰa²¹   xɯ⁵⁵ɣɯ²¹   o.
         lull   3SG   a.little   3SG   then   be.happy   INC   CRS
         'That little child was crying over there. So, I lulled and soothed him a bit.
         He then began to cheer up.'
         那个小孩儿在那儿哭。我就哄了他一下。他就高兴起来了。

Apart from the post-nominal quantifier use, there are cases in which *mi⁵⁵* does not denote the delimitative. For most of the cases, when *mi⁵⁵* modifies VPs which possess a semantic feature of degree, quantity, quality, or frequency, as with all the adjectives and emotion verbs such as 'hate' and 'like', it functions as a degree marker denoting 'a little bit more', which is entirely opposite of a delimitative. Examples (10.78) and (10.79) show a case of an adjective and a case of a motion verb, respectively. The VP *tγ²¹ko⁵⁵ mi⁵⁵* in (10.78) does not denote 'a little while (LIT: a bit long)', but 'a little longer'. Similarly, instead of denoting 'like that item a little', the VP *tɕʰi³³kʰa³³ mɔ²¹ ɣa²¹ mi⁵⁵*, expresses 'like that item (of clothing) a little more'. There is an implied comparee in this context. More examples with *mi⁵⁵* as the degree marker 'a little more' can be found in Chapter 9 on constructions of comparison.

Post-VP degree marker
(10.78) niɔ³³   ni²⁴   **tγ²¹ko⁵⁵**   **mi⁵⁵**   lɛ²¹tsʰɛ²¹
         need   time   be.long   a.little.more only.if
         ti³³   tso²¹   xɯ⁵⁵ɣɯ²¹.
         know   be.familiar   INC
         'Only if a little more time passes by can (they) begin to be familiar (with each other).'
         要时间长些才会熟起来。

(10.79) ŋo³³   **tɕʰi³³kʰa³³**   mɔ²¹   ɣa²¹   **mi⁵⁵**.
         1SG   like   that   CLF   a.little.more
         'I like that item (of clothing) more.'
         我更喜欢那件（衣服）一些。

Sometimes, ambiguity can be observed between the post-nominal quantifier *mi⁵⁵* and the delimitative *mi⁵⁵*. The following example illustrates three types of *mi⁵⁵*. The first one in (10.80i) can either be analyzed as the post-nominal quantifier denoting 'a little grass' or the delimitative marker denoting 'make a quick cutting of grass'. Compare it also with the other uses of *mi⁵⁵* in the following sentences.

(10.80) i) ŋo³³ kuɛ²¹ se⁵⁵ tsʰɔ⁵⁵ **mi⁵⁵**.
    1SG go   cut   grass a.little

ii) ŋo³³ lã²¹ se⁵⁵-tɣ³³ ŋo²¹ so⁵⁵. kʰua²¹ la³³
    1SG sickle cut-obtain 1SG hand be.good all
    niɔ³³ kʰua²¹ **mi⁵⁵** o.
    PROSP be.good a.little CRS

iii) jɯ²⁴ tɣ³³ ŋo²¹ tɔ⁵⁵-tɣ²¹ **mi⁵⁵**.
    again PASS 1SG bump-hit.the.target a.little

iv) tɯ³³ fa²¹tsɔ²¹ xɯ⁵⁵ɣɯ²¹ o.
    then worsen INC CRS

'I went to cut some grass (or: I went to do a little grass-cutting). I got my hand cut by my sickle. (The wound) became somewhat better but I bumped it a little bit again. It then worsened.'
我去割了些/下草。我镰刀割到了手。好都要好点了。又被我碰了一下。就又严重起来了。

10.2.8 Continuous [sɿ³³ VP sɿ²¹]

Caijia is a language in which the continuous forms an aspectual category, which means Caijia does not make a contrast between non-progressive/stative and progressive. However, both Dahl (1985) and Bybee et al. (1994) do not treat the continuous as a cross-linguistic grammatical category. "Continuous views a situation, whether it be dynamic or stative, as on-going at reference time" (Bybee et al. 1994: 127). The continuous is subdivided into non-progressive and progressive under the framework of Comrie (1976). The non-progressive refers to continuous states, while the progressive refers to on-going actions. A prototypical progressive action can often be used to answer the question 'What is X doing' in which X is animate. The difference between the two is related to the involvement of change (Dahl 1985: 28).

The Caijia continuous aspect can be coded either by periphrasis or by a grammatical strategy. The periphrastic strategy usually combines inherent properties of verbs or predicates, i.e. lexical aspects, and other types of elements like locative phrases, adverbs, or modal words. Example (10.81) shows a pair of sentences for which the continuous meaning is realized via two stative locative phrases. In

(10.81a), the verb $t\tilde{a}^{33}$ 'stand' combines with the locative phrase $tu^{21}\ ma^{21}k^ha^{33}\ tcin^{21}$ 'in front of the door', denoting a continuous state. In (10.81b), the VP $tcie^{55}\ zy^{21}$ 'cook' associates with the locative phrase $tu^{21}\ ma^{24}$ 'over there' denoting an on-going action.

(10.81) Stative
 a. je³³ tã³³ tɯ²¹ ma²¹kʰa³³ tɕiŋ²¹.
  3SG stand at door front
  'He's standing in front of the door.'
  他站在门口。

 Progressive
 b. ŋo³³ ʑi²¹ tɯ²¹ ma²⁴ tɕie⁵⁵ zy²¹.
  1SG mother at there do meal
  'My mother is cooking over there.'
  我妈在那儿做饭。

In East and Southeast Asian languages, locative verbs are a major source of the progressive (Matisoff 1991). However, Caijia has developed a unique continuous marker, the construction *(sɿ³³) . . . sɿ²¹*, which is derived from the cleft or affirmative construction, as argued by Lü (2016). In this construction, the first *sɿ³³* is the copula, which is often omitted, and the second *sɿ²¹* is often used as the nominalizer or relativizer. The affirmative use is demonstrated below (see also Chapter 11 on modality). The post VP *se²¹* is actually the fused form of *sɿ²¹* and the final particle *e*.

(10.82) mɔ²¹ ny²¹hu⁵⁵ **sɿ³³** niɔ³³ a³³ ŋu²¹ kɯ⁵⁵
   that bowstring AFF need take cow leather
   ɣɯ²¹ ʑi⁵⁵ **se²¹**.
   PURP twist AFF.PRT
   'It is out of the cowhide that the bowstring is made.'
   那弓弦是拿牛皮来搓成的。

Marking the continuous, the construction *(sɿ³³) . . . sɿ²¹* sandwiches the VP that needs to be marked, as in the affirmative construction, i.e. [sɿ³³ VP sɿ²¹]. Morphologically, the construction *(sɿ³³) . . . sɿ²¹* demonstrates a strong tendency to be reduced to the form [VP sɿ²¹]. Both (10.83) and (10.84) are continuous states, since both the verb $y\tilde{a}^{33}$ 'have, there be' and ti^{21} 'face' possess a stative feature.

(10.83) ŋo⁵⁵ ha⁵⁵ ɣã³³ jɔ²¹ pa²⁴ ni³³ **sɿ³³**.
       1PL   place there.be Hmong old.man CLF CONT
       'The was an old Hmong man among us.'
       我们中间有一个苗族老头。
       (*Lightening up the Pipe*, texts)

(10.84) mɔ²⁴ xa⁵⁵ je³³ (**sɿ³³**) so²¹kui⁵⁵ ti²¹ ŋo³³ **sɿ²¹**,
       that moment 3SG   CONT   back   face 1SG   CONT
       ŋo³³ pɣ³³-tɤ³³ tsaŋ³³-ti²¹ je³³ mĩ²¹kʰɔ⁵⁵.
       1SG   NEG-PFV   see-be.clear 3SG   face
       'His back was facing me at that moment and I didn't see his face.'
       那会儿他背对着我，我没看清他的脸。

Examples (10.85) and (10.86) illustrate two on-going actions. The raining was on-going at the reference time 'when I was on my way (back)' in (10.85) and the owl was flying at the moment of speech in (10.86).

(10.85) ŋo³³ tɯ²¹ hɔ⁵⁵   mo²¹   tʰɔ⁵⁵,   tɯ³³ sɿ³³ **ɣɯ²¹** **zɿ⁵⁵** sɿ²¹.
       1SG   at   road   inside moment   then CONT come   rain   CONT
       'It was raining, when I was on my way (back).'
       我在路上的时候就在下雨。

(10.86) hu³³lo³³to³³ tɯ²¹ kʰɪŋ³³ tɤ³³   **pɣ²¹** sɿ²¹.
       owl   at   sky   upside fly   CONT
       'The owl is flying in the sky.'
       猫头鹰在天上飞。

We observe that the continuous marker cannot be used to mark the VP in a relative clause, which is probably because the post-VP *sɿ²¹* of the continuous itself has another function as a relativizer. As shown in (10.87), it is ungrammatical to mark the VP *zɣ²¹ zɣ³³* 'have meal' with the continuous in a relative clause.

(10.87) mɔ²¹ zɣ²¹ zɣ³³ *****sɿ²¹** sɿ²¹ u³³tsʰo³³
       that eat   meal CONT   REL   person
       'the person who is eating'
       那个吃饭的人

This restriction is not observed in other types of embedded clauses. In (10.88), the marked VP *xã³³ kɣ³³ mia³³* 'screaming for help' marked by the continuous is embedded in the existential construction ɣã²¹ u²¹tsʰo²⁴ ni³³ 'there's someone...', which is the object complement clause of the matrix verb tʰi⁵⁵-tɣ³³ 'hear'.

(10.88) ŋo²¹ tʰi⁵⁵-tɣ³³   [ɣã²¹   u²¹tsʰo²⁴ ni³³
         1SG   hear-obtain   there.be person   CLF
         [xã³³ kɣ³³   mia³³   sɿ²¹]].
         cry   rescue life   CONT
         'I heard someone screaming for help.'
         我听到有人在喊救命。

In (10.89), the marked VP is the object complement clause of the verb tsaŋ³³ 'see'. The expression 'fog lifts water up on the hill' denotes 'mist goes up', which suggests it is going to rain.

(10.89) kʰɿŋ⁵⁵ tɔ²¹kʰɯ⁵⁵ ŋo²¹   kʰɯ⁵⁵-yɯ²¹   sɿ³³,   tsaŋ²¹
         today   morning   1SG   rise-come   PRT   see
         [ti²¹mĩ²¹   ti²¹   tɣ³³   ɔ²¹   pʰɔ³³moŋ²¹   sɿ³³   ta²¹   sɿ⁵⁵
         opposite   hill   upside this   fog   CONT   lift   water
         tsa²¹   ti²¹   se²¹].
         go.up   hill   CONT.PRT
         'When I got up this morning, I saw the fog pushing moisture up (LIT: lift water up) on the opposite hill.'
         早上我起来的时候，看见对面山上这雾气在抬水上山。

In general, even though the continuous marker (sɿ³³)...sɿ²¹ tends to be reduced as sɿ²¹, the pre-VP sɿ³³ can often be re-added back. However, we do observe that the pre-VP sɿ³³ cannot be used in copular complement clauses. In the copular complement clause mo²¹tɬ²¹ja²⁴ tɯ²¹ je³³ sɔ²¹ sɿ²¹ 'the goddess of the bed is amusing him', the pre-VP sɿ³³ cannot be added to the position preceding tɯ²¹ 'amuse' in the example below.

(10.90) mɔ²¹   ɕie²¹   ŋa⁵⁵ŋa⁵⁵   tɯ²¹   tsɿ³³moŋ³³   kʷɔ²¹   mo³³
         that   small   baby   at   dream   CLF   inside
         ti³³   sɔ²¹   xɯ⁵⁵yɯ²¹.   mɔ²¹   sɿ³³   [mo²¹tɬ²¹ja²⁴
         can   laugh INC   that   COP   goddess.of.bed
         tɯ²¹   je³³   sɔ²¹   sɿ³³].
         amuse 3SG   laugh CONT
         'That baby can begin to giggle when sleeping. That's the goddess of the bed amusing him.'
         小婴儿在梦中会笑起来。那是床头婆在逗他笑。

Vendler's (1976) classification is more or less tenable for Caijia's continuous aspect. Verbs of durativity can be marked by the continuous marker $(s_1^{33})\ldots s_1^{21}$, i.e. verbs of state, activity, and accomplishment, which are respectively illustrated in (10.83), (10.86) and (10.89), while verbs of achievement cannot be marked by the continuous marker. Compare the two sentences in (10.91). In (10.91a), the phrase $tɕie^{55}\ to^{24}\ po^{55}$ 'make a cupboard' is a VP of accomplishment (see Table 10.1), which is a bounded but durative event and can be marked by the continuous marker $(s_1^{33})\ldots s_1^{21}$. However, by compounding the resultative complement $-k^hua^{21}$ 'be good', as shown in (10.91b), the event 'make a cupboard' is turned into a punctual event which is no longer compatible with the continuous meaning. However, the sentence in (10.91b) is still grammatical, except that the construction $(s_1^{33})\ldots s_1^{21}$ denotes affirmation/emphasis.

(10.91) a. je³³ s₁²¹ tɕie⁵⁵ to²⁴ po⁵⁵ s₁²¹.
3SG AFF do cupboard CLF AFF
'He's making a cupboard.'
他在做一个柜子。

b. je³³ s₁²¹ tɕie⁵⁵-kʰua²¹ to²⁴ po⁵⁵ s₁²¹,
3SG AFF do-good cupboard CLF AFF
tɯ³³s₁³³ py³³ s₁²¹ ta⁵⁵ nɯ²¹ tɕie⁵⁵ s₁²¹.
but NEG AFF for 2SG do AFF
'He indeed made a cupboard, but it's not for you'
他是做好了一个柜子，就是不是给你做的。

As it happens, semelfactive verbs, which are dynamic, unbounded, and punctual, can also be marked by $(s_1^{33})\ldots s_1^{21}$, denoting the repetition of an instantaneous action within the reference time. For example, the action of knocking once on a door is itself semelfactive. When it is marked by $(s_1^{33})\ldots s_1^{21}$, it denotes that repetitive 'knocking' is in progress, as shown in the example below. As pointed out by Smith (1994: 131), such cases should be treated as a derived multiple-event activity. This means that the lexical aspect type of 'knocking' shifts from semelfactive to activity. To be specific, 'knocking on a door' should be treated as an activity.

(10.92) ɣã²¹ u²¹tsʰo²⁴ ni³³ pʰa³³ ma²¹kʰa³³ s₁²¹.
have person CLF knock door CONT
'There's someone knocking on the door.'
有人在敲门。

Compared with dynamic verbs, **stative verbs** show complexity when the continuous marking is applied. Some restrictions are observed.

(i) The copular construction is usually not marked, except when durativity needs to be emphasized. Compare the two examples below. It is ungrammatical to mark the copular construction with the continuous, as in (10.93).

(10.93)　je³³　sɿ³³　kʷɔ³³sɣ²¹ŋa⁵⁵　*sɿ²¹.
　　　　　3SG　COP　student　　　　CONT
　　　　　'He's a student.'
　　　　　他是学生。

By contrast, since the durativity of his being a teacher is overtly expressed by the adverb lɔ²¹kɯ²¹ 'always, whenever', the marking is thus grammatical in (10.94). It should be noted that only the post-VP sɿ²¹ is used to mark the copular construction when required.

(10.94)　A-　je³³　sɿ³³　　　kʷɔ³³sɣ³³pa³³?
　　　　　　　3SG　COP　　　teacher
　　　　　　　ŋo²¹　tɕie⁵⁵me⁵⁵　pɣ³³　tiu³³u³³?
　　　　　　　1SG　how　　　　　NEG　know
　　　　　　　'He's a teacher? Why don't I know?'
　　　　　　　他是老师？我怎么不知道？

　　　　　B-　je³³　lɔ²¹kɯ²¹　la²¹　sɿ³³　kʷɔ³³sɣ³³pa³³　se²¹.
　　　　　　　3SG　always　　all　COP　teacher　　　　CONT
　　　　　　　'He's always been a teacher.'
　　　　　　　他一直是老师。

(ii) Adjectives are only marked by the continuous under the condition that durativity needs to be emphasized. Just as in (10.94), the adverb lɔ²¹kɯ²¹ 'always, whenever' is used to overtly mark durativity in (10.95), which makes the continuous marking possible. Otherwise, affirmation or emphasis is usually the primary interpretation of a marked adjective, denoting 'it is certain that.../certainly'. Compare the adjective kʰua²¹ 'be good' in (10.96) with the one in (10.95).

(10.95)　mɔ²¹　ta⁵⁵　kʰu⁵⁵　lɔ²¹kɯ²¹　la²¹　sɿ³³　kʰua²¹　se²¹.
　　　　　that　two　CLF　always　　all　CONT　good　CONT
　　　　　nɯ³³　piɔ²⁴　tɯ²¹　ta²¹fa⁵⁵　tʰa²¹fɛ⁵⁵kʷɔ²¹.
　　　　　2SG　NEG.IMP　at　middle　sow.discord
　　　　　'That couple has always been good. Don't sow discord between them.'
　　　　　那两口子一直好着呢。你别再中间挑拨离间。

(10.96) je³³ sɿ³³ kʰua²¹ se²¹, tɯ³³sɿ³³ ŋo³³ pɤ²¹ taŋ²⁴ tɕʰi⁵⁵kʰa⁵⁵.
3SG AFF good AFF.PRT but 1SG NEG so like
'He's certainly good, but I don't like him very much.'
他是好的，就是我不太喜欢。

(iii) It has been mentioned earlier above that the continuous in Caijia can be realized via periphrasis. When no periphrastic elements help to realize the continuous, intransitive stative verbs must be marked. A pair of contrastive examples are given in (10.97). The omission of *sɿ²¹* is ungrammatical in (10.97a), while *sɿ²¹* is optional in (10.97b) since the continuous meaning is coded both periphrastically and grammatically (by the durative marker *-xɯ⁵⁵*). See §10.2.10 below for more details. Similarly, *sɿ²¹* in (10.98) is also obligatory.

(10.97) a. je³³ kɤ²¹-(xɯ⁵⁵) *(**sɿ²¹**).
3SG sit-DUR CONT
'He's in the posture of sitting.'
他坐着呢。

b. je³³ tɯ²¹ tʰa⁵⁵ tɤ³³ kɤ²¹-xɯ⁵⁵ (**sɿ²¹**).
3SG at bed upside sit-DUR CONT
'He's sitting on the bed.'
他在床上坐着。

(10.98) ma²¹kʰa⁵⁵ kʰɯ⁵⁵-(xɯ⁵⁵) *(**sɿ²¹**).
door open-DUR CONT
'The door is open.'
门开着呢。

10.2.9 Continuous (manner) [VP lɛ⁵⁵]

'Manner continuous' is an aspect category not yet identified in the literature. It describes how an on-going situation exists, coded by the final particle *lɛ⁵⁵* in the form of [VP lɛ⁵⁵]. The marker *lɛ⁵⁵* can surface with different tone values, which can be perceived in the examples presented in this section. The manner continuous is different from the prototypical continuous coded by *(sɿ³³) . . . sɿ²¹* in Caijia. It cannot be used to answer the question 'What is X doing?', as it does not focus on an individual's, or an entity's (if inanimate) on-going action or state. Instead, it focuses on the on-going situation, as a whole, looking at how this individual or entity exists or behaves inside this situation. A sentence marked by the manner continuous can answer a ***how***-question in an appropriate context, which will be discussed later in this section. Even though it is not treated as an aspectual category, this type of aspect is common in Sinitic. For example, the morpheme *de* 的 [tə] in Standard Mandarin, as described by Lü Shuxiang (1999: 161–162, see also Chao 1968: 205–210).

(10.99)   大伙儿都有说有笑的。(Lü Shuxiang 1999: 162)
  dàhuǒer   dōu   yǒu   shuō   yǒu   xiào   **de**.
  everyone all   have say   have laugh CONT
  'Everyone is talking and laughing.'

The manner continuous *lɛ⁵⁵*, for which the lexical source is untraceable, is commonly used as adverb modifier marker connecting adverb and its modified head VP (see also Chapter 4 §4.3.1). In (10.100), the adverb 'quickly' modifying the verb *tɣ³³* 'grow' is marked by *lɛ²¹*, denoting how the action of growing will be performed. Clearly, this function is very much related with its function to mark the manner continuous aspect.

(10.100) nɯ³³   tsʰɿ²¹-kuɛ³³   tsʰɔ²¹-tɣ³³   ŋo³³   mɔ²¹   kɯ²⁴   nɛ⁵⁵,
          2SG   rot-go   stink-obtain   1SG   that   moment   PRT
          ŋo³³   [tɕiu²¹tɕiu²⁴tɕiu²¹tɕiu²⁴]   **lɛ²¹**   [tɣ³³]   nɛ³³,   […]
          1SG   quickly   ADV   grow   PRT
  'When you rot away and stink so much that I can sense the smell, I will grow up quickly...'
  你烂掉熏到我的时候呢，我就快快快快地长......
  (*The corn and the grass*, texts)

Serving as the manner continuous marker, *lɛ⁵⁵* follows the VP of a sentence in clause-final position. This shows it is not being used as the manner adverbial marker, as in (10.100) above. Just like the common continuous, the stative does not contrast with the progressive when expressing the manner continuous. Both (10.101) and (10.102) involve an on-going dynamic action. In (10.101), the VP *pa²¹pa²¹tɿŋ⁵⁵tɿŋ⁵⁵* 'move around', a quadrisyllabic rhyme form, is followed by *lɛ²¹*, denoting that the action 'move around' is on-going for quite a while. The omission of *lɛ²¹* will make this sentence ungrammatical.

(10.101) kʰɿŋ³³koŋ³³   ŋo³³   to²¹-tɣ³³   mo²¹pʰia⁵⁵tsʰɔ⁵⁵   o.
          today   1SG   step.on-obtain   grass.of.spirit.loss   CRS
          ji²¹   koŋ³³   [pa²¹pa²¹tɿŋ⁵⁵tɿŋ⁵⁵]   lɛ²¹,
          one   day   move.around   CONT

tsʰa²¹mi⁵⁵   ko²¹-pɣ³³-tɣ³³   hɔ⁵⁵   pe⁵⁵-yɯ²¹.
almost   find-NEG-obtain   road   return-back
'I (must) have stepped on the grass of the spirit of burial. I'd been walking around all day long and almost couldn't find my way back.'
我今天踩到埋魂草了，一天兜兜转转的，差点找不到路回来。

In (10.102), the complex VP *ji²¹ xa⁵⁵ ta²¹ ji²¹ xa⁵⁵ yɯ²¹* 'be sunny and rainy by turn' is marked by *lɛ⁵⁵* and expresses that the weather has been violently shifting during this period, in other words a continuous state with respect to manner.

(10.102) mɔ²¹   kʰɪŋ⁵⁵   to⁵⁵   [ji²¹   xa⁵⁵   ta²¹   ji²¹   xa⁵⁵
          that   sky   CLF   one   moment   be.sunny one   moment
          yɯ²¹]   lɛ⁵⁵   nɛ⁵⁵, ŋo³³   ɔ²¹   lɔ²¹   saŋ²⁴-sui⁵⁵
          come.(rain) CONT PRT   1SG   this   old   wound-PL
          a,   fa²¹   lɯ⁵⁵   mɔ⁵⁵sɿ⁵⁵.
          PRT   worsen VCOMP   very
          'The weather has kept changing and it makes my old illness flare up (again).'
          这天气一下晴一下雨的，我这老伤啊发作得不行。

Examples (10.103) and (10.104) show two cases of stative meaning. Even though the VP *kɣ⁵⁵ yɯ²¹ so⁵⁵ pɣ²¹ yɯ²¹* in (10.103), literally denoting 'the feet come but the hands don't come', is seemingly dynamic, it is actually metaphorically used to express 'be clumsy'. The marker *lɛ²¹* marks the currently continuous state of being clumsy. In (10.104), the VP is the adjective *ta³³* 'narrow' in its A-BB form, which is labelled as 'vivid reduplicate' by Chao (1968: 205-210), with *ta³³* in the A position (or root position). Marked by *lɛ²¹*, *ta³³tsʰaŋ²¹tsʰaŋ³³ lɛ²¹* denotes that the road is in the state of being narrow at the reference time and that this state endures.

(10.103) tsɿ²¹tɕia⁵⁵   a   la²¹to⁵⁵   a   tɕi⁵⁵   po²¹   to²¹   mẽ.
          onself   PRT   old   PRT   do   NEG   can   PRT
          [kɣ⁵⁵   yɯ²¹   so⁵⁵   pɣ²¹   yɯ²¹   **lɛ²¹**.
          foot   come   hand   NEG   come   CONT
          'Myself, I'm old and can't do anything. I've become clumsy now.'
          自己啊老了，（什么都）做不了了。笨手笨脚的。

(10.104) mɔ²¹kɯ⁵⁵ a, ŋo²⁴ tsʰ₁³³ mo³³ s₁²¹ hɔ⁵⁵
that.time PRT 1PL village inside MOD road
[ta³³tsʰaŋ²¹tsʰaŋ³³] **lɛ²¹**, ɣa²¹-xɯ⁵⁵ ni²¹kʰa³³ni²¹kʰoŋ⁵⁵.
narrow CONT walk-up be.muddy
'At that time, the road to our village was narrow. It (became) muddy, when people walked a lot.'
以前，我们村的路窄窄的，走起来泥泞不堪。
(*The road*, texts)

We observe that manner continuous marking is not just limited to the VP. For example, in (10.105), an NP of reduplication is formed by a reduplicated measure word phrase *ji³³ tsʰɔ²¹* 'one group' denoting that people are divided into many groups threshing wheat in the yard. In other words, it describes how people are doing the wheat threshing, that is, by being divided into many groups and this state lasts until the end of their wheat threshing.

(10.105) tsaŋ³³-kɪŋ²¹ mɔ²⁴-sui⁵⁵ e, tɯ²¹ tv̩²⁴ tv̩³³ na²¹
look-see that-PL PRT at yard upside beat
tsoŋ²¹. nɔ⁵⁵zɛ²¹ xɪŋ⁵⁵. [...] **ji³³ tsʰɔ²¹ ji³³ tsʰɔ³³ lɛ²¹**.
wheat lively very one group one group CONT
'(I) saw those people threshing wheat in the yard. (The scene) was busy and lively. [...] (There was) one group after the other.'
看见那些（人），在院坝上打麦子。热闹得很。[...]一帮一帮的。
(*Wheat-threshing*, texts)

The major reason to label the continuous marked by *lɛ⁵⁵* as a manner continuous is that a sentence in the manner continuous aspect can usually answer the question 'How is X?' or 'What is X like?'. Let us take the two sentences marked by *lɛ⁵⁵* in (10.102) and (10.104) as examples. The sentence *ji²¹ xa⁵⁵ ta²¹ ji²¹ xa⁵⁵ ɣɯ²¹ lɛ⁵⁵* '(The weather) keeps changing' can be used to answer the question 'How is the recent weather at your place?' in (10.106A).

(10.106) A- ɔ²¹tsɔ²⁴ nɯ²⁴ ha⁵⁵ mɔ²¹ kʰɪŋ⁵⁵ to⁵⁵
recently 2PL place that sky CLF
tɔ²¹ lɔ²⁴s₁⁵⁵?
be.like which.way
'How is the recent weather at your place?'
最近你们那儿天气怎么样？

B- ji²¹ xa⁵⁵ ta²¹ ji²¹ xa⁵⁵ ɣɯ²¹ lɛ⁵⁵.
one moment be.sunny one moment come.(rain) CONT
pɣ²¹ taŋ²⁴ kʰua²¹.
NEG so be.good
'It keeps changing. Not very good.'
一会儿晴一会儿雨的。不太好。

The sentence *ta³³tsʰaŋ²¹tsʰaŋ³³ lɛ³³* 'it was narrow' can be used to answer the question 'What was the road?' in (10.107A).

(10.107) A- mɔ²¹kɯ²⁴ ɔ²¹ hɔ⁵⁵ ta⁵⁵ sɿ³³ tɔ²¹ lɔ²⁴sɿ⁵⁵?
that.time this road CLF COP be.like which.way
'How was this road like at that time?'
那时候这条路是怎么样的？

B- ta³³tsʰaŋ²¹tsʰaŋ³³ lɛ³³,
narrow CONT
xa²¹ pɣ³³-tɣ³³ tʰɔ³³-kʰua²¹.
still NEG-PFV pave.(with concrete)-good
'It was narrow and not yet paved with concrete.'
窄窄的，还没有（用水泥）铺好。

It has been mentioned earlier above that the manner continuous is very much related to the manner adverbial formed by *lɛ⁵⁵*. We find that most of the predicative examples of [VP *lɛ⁵⁵*] can serve as adverbial modifiers of the verb, if the context permits. The sentence with the manner continuous aspect of *nɯ³³ na³³ ŋo³³ ŋo³³ na³³ nɯ³³ lɛ³³* 'they were fighting with each other' in (10.108a) can be used in a different syntactic frame as the adverbial modifier of the verb *sʷɔ²¹kʷɔ⁵⁵* 'play', as in (10.108b).

(10.108) a. tɯ²¹ mɔ²¹ ti²¹ tɣ³³ ko²¹-pɣ²¹-tɣ³³ zɣ²¹ sɿ²¹.
at that hill upside find-NEG-obtain eat NMLZ
nɯ³³ na³³ ŋo³³ ŋo³³ na³³ nɯ³³ lɛ³³.
2SG beat 1SG 1SG beat 2SG CONT
'(The two little tigers) couldn't find anything to eat on the hill. They were fighting with each other (for fun).'
(两只小老虎) 在山上找不到吃的。你打我我打你的。
(*Two little tigers*, texts)

b. ɕie²¹   kʰy⁵⁵pa²⁴   ta⁵⁵   kʷɔ²¹   tɯ²¹   ma²⁴
   small   tiger   two   CLF   at   there
   nɯ³³   na³³   ŋo³³   ŋo³³   na³³   nɯ³³   lɛ²¹   sʷɔ²¹kʷɔ⁵⁵.
   2SG   beat   1SG   1SG   beat   2SG   ADV   play
   'The two little tigers were playing in manner of fighting with each other.'
   两只小老虎在那儿你打我我打你地玩儿。

Similarly, the predicative NP marked by *lɛ⁵⁵, ji³³ tsʰɔ²¹ ji³³ tsʰɔ²¹* 'some groups' in (10.105), can also be used as an adverbial modifier, as shown in (10.109).

(10.109) mɔ²⁴-sui⁵⁵   ji³³   **tsʰɔ²¹   ji³³   tsʰɔ²¹   lɛ⁵⁵**   tɯ²¹   ty²⁴   ty³³
          that-PL   one   group   one   group   ADV   at   yard   upside
          na²¹   tsoŋ²¹.
          beat   wheat
          'They were threshing wheat in many groups.'
          他们一帮一帮地在院坝上打麦子。

From the examples above, one can see that the manner continuous and the prototypical continuous are functionally different from each other. These two types of continuous do not mark the same types of VP, which show a tendency towards complementary distribution. For example, the prototypical continuous marker *(sɿ³³)...sɿ²¹* only marks VPs, while *lɛ⁵⁵* can refer back to NPs ([10.105]). Bare verbs (including adjectives) and the form of VO cannot be marked by *lɛ⁵⁵* to express the manner continuous, but they can be marked by *(sɿ³³)...sɿ²¹*. The most common VP forms that can be marked by the manner continuous are quadrisyllabic rhyme forms and adjectives in the form of A-BB as in (10.101) and (10.104). However, neither of them can be marked by *(sɿ³³)...sɿ²¹* to express the prototypical continuous. Furthermore, it is demonstrated in both (10.108) and (10.109) that clauses in the manner continuous can serve as adverbial modifiers as well, while the VPs that can be marked by *(sɿ³³)...sɿ²¹* cannot.

10.2.10 Durative [VP-xɯ⁵⁵]

The durative in Caijia also serves to describe a continuous situation by using the suffix *-xɯ⁵⁵* that is derived from the verb *kʰɯ⁵⁵* 'rise', but remains distinct from both the prototypical and the manner continuous. See (10.36) and (10.37) for the lexical uses of *-xɯ⁵⁵*. One should be aware that *-xɯ⁵⁵* can also denote the directional 'up' ([10.22]) or act as a phase marker denoting an action achieved ([10.32]) and not just the durative.

For most of the cases marked by the durative -$xɯ^{55}$, change is not involved, which means the durative usually involves continuous states. The function of the Caijia -$xɯ^{55}$ is very similar to the Standard Mandarin *zhe* 着 [tʂə] (cf. Li and Thompson 1981: 217–226 for more details on *zhe*).

One can find barely any sentences in our sample of transcriptions which are only formed by [V-$xɯ^{55}$] when denoting the durative. A minimal sentence formed by [V-$xɯ^{55}$] should be marked by ($sɿ^{33}$) . . . $sɿ^{21}$, as shown in (10.110) and (10.111). See also (10.97). Both $tsɔ^{33}$ 'be with something inside, put into, install' and $m̃ŋ^{33}$ 'shroud' are used intransitively, describing the continuous unchanging state of the cup and the state of the fog, respectively.

(10.110) A- nɯ³³ mɔ²¹ tɪŋ⁵⁵tɪŋ⁵⁵ tsɿ⁵⁵ tsa⁵⁵ ŋo²¹ tɕi²¹ mi⁵⁵.
2SG that cup CLF borrow 1SG use a.little
'Lend me your cup for a bit to use.'
你那个杯子借我用一下。

B- pɣ²¹ tʰɔ⁵⁵ e. tsɔ²¹-**xɯ**⁵⁵ sɿ²¹.
NEG available PRT be.with.something.inside-DUR CONT
'It's not available. (There's) something inside it.'
不闲。装着东西的。

(10.111) ɔ⁵⁵ u³³ ti²¹ tɣ̩³³ pʰɔ³³mon²¹ m̃ŋ²¹-**xɯ**⁵⁵ se²¹.
house back hill upside fog shroud-DUR CONT.PRT
kʰɪŋ⁵⁵koŋ⁵⁵ ɣɯ²¹ zɿ⁵⁵ po³³ to³³.
today come rain NEG can
'On the hill behind the house, it's misting over. It won't rain today.'
对面山上雾气笼罩。今天不会下雨。

Examples (10.112) and (10.113) are two cases of transitive verbs. The sentence in (10.112) is a prototypical VO construction, while the one in (10.113) is a differential object marking construction and the object 'illness' is mentioned in the preceding context. Marked by -$xɯ^{55}$, neither pa^{21}-$xɯ^{55}$ 'cling to' nor $lɛ^{21}$-$xɯ^{55}$ 'ignore' involves change. It has been mentioned above that clauses only marked by -$xɯ^{55}$ are rarely used independently. The following two clauses marked by -$xɯ^{55}$ are not counterexamples, since they are actually dependent clauses; the one in (10.112) is followed by a clause of sequence and the one in (10.113) is an effect clause.

(10.112) sɔ⁵⁵ nɛ⁵⁵ pa²¹-**xɯ⁵⁵** mɔ²¹ sɔ⁵⁵ kɣ⁵⁵, tɯ⁵⁵ pɣ²¹
hand PRT cling.to-DUR that tree foot then NEG
kã⁵⁵ tɣ²¹ sɔ⁵⁵ tsa²¹ kuɛ²¹ ma³³ mɔ²¹ kʰɿ²¹kʰo²⁴.
dare stretch.out hand go.up PURP catch that turtledove
'The paws (of the tiger) were clinging to the tree trunk, but it didn't dare to stretch out to catch the turtledove.'
(老虎的) 手呢扒着那个树干, 就是不敢伸手上去抓那斑鸠。
(*The man and the tiger*, texts)

(10.113) nɯ³³ a³³ tsɔ²¹ ɔ²¹ sɿ⁵⁵ lɛ²¹-**xɯ⁵⁵** nɛ⁵⁵,
2SG DCR be.like this way ignore-DUR PRT
tsɔ²¹ lɛ²¹ tsɔ²¹ nan²¹tɣ³³ kʰɯ³³ o.
the.more drag the.more difficult cure CRS
'If you keep ignoring (your illness), it'll become more and more difficult to cure.'
你把（你的病）像这样拖着呢，越拖越难治了。
(*My sick cousin*, texts)

The suffix -*xɯ*⁵⁵ is very commonly observed marking positional verbs, such as postural verbs or verbs of placement, in locative or existential constructions denoting a continuous state resulting from the marked positional verb (see Lü 2018 for the list of Caijia positional verbs). Example (10.114) is the locative construction in which the positional verb, to be specific, the verb of placement *ko*⁵⁵ 'hang', is marked by -*xɯ*⁵⁵. The subject *tã*⁵⁵ 'lamp' is in a continuous unchanging state following the action of hanging. In other words, the state of the lamp is the caused state of hanging it there. See also example (10.32) for the postural verb *tã*³³ 'stand'.

(10.114) ɔ²¹kɔ²¹ tã⁵⁵ tɯ²¹ ma²⁴ **ko⁵⁵-xɯ⁵⁵**.
INTJ lamp at there hang-DUR
'The lamp was hanging there.'
这个，灯在那儿挂着。
(*Lightening up the pipe*, texts)

Examples (10.115) and (10.116) illustrate two types of existential constructions. The one in (10.115) is with the existential verb *yã*³³ 'there be, have', while the one in (10.116) is formed by the positional verb *kɣ*²¹ 'sit'. Unlike the caused state demonstrated in (10.114), the following cases present two self-agentive states. In (10.115), the person enters into the state of lying in the bed and maintains this state by himself or herself. Similarly, it is the dog itself that enters into the continuous state of sitting under the eaves.

(10.115) ɣã²¹   u²¹tsʰu²⁴   ni³³   tɯ²¹   tʰa³³   tɤ³³   **tsʅ²¹-xɯ⁵⁵**.
          there.be person   CLF   at   bed   upside sleep-DUR
          'There's a person lying in the bed.'
          有个人在床上躺着。

(10.116) ɔ⁵⁵tsaŋ²¹   kɤ⁵⁵   **kɤ²¹-xɯ⁵⁵**   kʰui⁵⁵   ji²¹   kʷɔ²¹
          eave   foot   sit-DUR   dog   one   CLF
          'There's a dog sitting under the eave.'
          屋檐下坐着一条狗。

Furthermore, *-xɯ⁵⁵* is also commonly used to denote manner in a serial verb construction, marking the V₁. In such a construction, i.e. [V₁-xɯ⁵⁵(O₁)V₂(O₂)], the two actions V₁ and V₂ take place simultaneously. The action V₁ accompanies the action V₂, while the action V₂ is performed in the manner of the action V₁ (cf. Zhu Dexi 1982: 164–165 for the case in Standard Mandarin). The following two examples illustrate this usage of *-xɯ⁵⁵*. In (10.117), the action of 'beating on the door' is accompanied by 'surrounding the house'. In (10.118), 'leaving home' occurs simultaneously with 'taking the kid along'.

(10.117) kʰɿŋ⁵⁵   pɤ²¹   mia²¹   tɯ²¹   ɣɯ²¹   tɤ⁵⁵-xɯ⁵⁵   ŋuɛ²¹
          sky   NEG   brighten   then   come   block-DUR   my.family
          ɔ⁵⁵   na²¹   nɛ⁵⁵   [...]
          house   beat   PRT
          'It was still dark. They came and beat (on the door), while surrounding our house.'
          天不亮就来围着我家打呢……
          (*Exempt from military service*, texts)

(10.118) sa³³   ŋui³³   noŋ³³   tɯ³³   li²¹-xɯ⁵⁵   ŋo²⁴
          three   month   some.day   then   take.along-DUR   1PL
          ma²⁴   mɔ²¹   ŋa⁵⁵   ni³³   ta⁵⁵   ŋo²¹
          there   that   child   CLF   with   1SG
          ji²¹hɔ⁵⁵   tɯ²¹   tsʰe⁵⁵   ma²¹kʰa⁵⁵.
          together   then   go.out   door
          'Some day in March, we left (our place) taking along a kid from our place together with me.'
          三月间就带着我们那儿那个小孩跟我一起出门了。
          (*The Cultural Revolution*, texts)

Finally, -xɯ⁵⁵ serves to mark the background continuous as well. The background continuous marks a predicate which is also part of a larger complex of sentences which involve two actions, i.e. background action and foreground action. The foreground action takes place at any time during the process of the background action. The verb designating the background action should be the bare form marked by -xɯ⁵⁵, and the marked form must be reduplicated, which can be schematized as [V₁-xɯ⁵⁵V₁-xɯ⁵⁵, VP₂]. This is the only situation that can involve change. In (10.119), children keep disappearing during the time the zombie wife is living back at home.

(10.119) ɛ,   tɯ²¹-xɯ⁵⁵   tɯ²¹-xɯ⁵⁵   nɛ⁵⁵,   tɯ⁵⁵   je³³
          INTJ   live-DUR   live-DUR   PRT   then   3SG
          mɔ²¹   tshɿ³³   mo³³   sɿ²¹   ŋa⁵⁵   tɯ⁵⁵
          that   village   inside   MOD   child then
          tɕie⁵⁵-ya³³,   ti²¹   tɕie⁵⁵-ya³³.
          do-fall   can   do-fall
          'During the time that (his zombie wife) was living (back at home), the children of his village would disappear.'
          住着住着呢，他村里的孩子就会不见。
          (*The zombie wife*, texts)

Another example is given in (10.120). The example in (10.119) above is a marginal case for determining if change is involved due to meaning, since the continuous action of living is stative, yet 'living' also implies one's daily activities. However, the following case is definitely a case involving change, because the continuous action of walking involves movement.

(10.120) ŋo³³   **ɣa²¹-xɯ⁵⁵**   **ɣa²¹-xɯ⁵⁵**   tɯ⁵⁵   ɣa²¹-tshɣ⁵⁵   hɔ⁵⁵   o.
          1SG   walk-DUR   walk-DUR   then   walk-be.wrong   road   CRS
          'I got lost when I was walking.'
          我走着走着就迷路了。

10.2.11 Frequentative [khã⁵⁵ VP]

The "frequentative includes habitual meaning – that a situation is characteristic of a period of time – but additionally specifies that it be frequent during that period of time" (Bybee et al. 1994: 127). It codes actions that occur frequently by means of a single morpheme.

Caijia adopts the preverbal auxiliary *kʰã⁵⁵*, derived from the verb 'be willing to', to code the frequentative. In Caijia, the verb *kʰã⁵⁵* either takes a VP as its object or functions intransitively. Its lexical uses are exemplified below. See also Chapter 11.

(10.121) a. je³³ tsʰɛ²¹ pɣ²¹ **kʰã⁵⁵** kɛ²¹ sɿ⁵⁵ je³³.
3SG thus NEG be.willing.to marry to 3SG
'She, thus, isn't willing to marry him.'
(就是因为这些,) 她才不肯嫁给他。

b. ŋo²¹ ɕiaŋ⁵⁵ tsa⁵⁵ mɔ²¹ ɣoŋ²¹ tɕi²¹ mi⁵⁵.
1SG want borrow that plough use a.little
je³³ pɣ²¹ **kʰã⁵⁵**.
3SG NEG be.willing.to
'I'd wanted to borrow that plough to use. (But) he didn't agree.'
我想借那个犁用一下。他不肯/同意。

Marking the frequentative, *kʰã⁵⁵* is not syntactically differentiated from its verbal form, but it is semantically different. The frequentative meaning of the sentence in (10.122) is the primary interpretation. If an appropriate context can be found, *kʰã⁵⁵* can still be interpreted as 'be willing to'. This is because the subject in (10.122) is human.

(10.122) ŋo³³ mɔ²¹ nioŋ²¹sɿ⁵⁵ ni²¹ **kʰã⁵⁵** lui⁵⁵ a⁵⁵ sʷɔ²¹kʷɔ⁵⁵.
1SG that granddaughter CLF FREQ chase duck play
'My granddaughter often chases ducks for fun.'
'My granddaughter likes to chase ducks for fun.'
我孙女常追鸭子玩。
我孙女喜欢追鸭子玩。

However, the meaning of *kʰã⁵⁵* has already shifted from 'be willing to' to 'frequently', 'often', or 'usually' in (10.123), since meteorological phenomena do not involve any meaning of willingness or desire and cannot be regarded as instigators.

(10.123) ŋo⁵⁵ mɔ²¹ sɿ⁵⁵lɛ²¹mo³³ kʷɔ²¹ xiŋ⁵⁵, pi⁵⁵ pi²¹ tsʰɿ⁵⁵ ka²¹.
1PL that place high very than low place cold
toŋ⁵⁵kʰɯŋ⁵⁵ la²¹ **kʰã⁵⁵** ɣɯ²¹ sɣ⁵⁵.
winter even FREQ come snow
'Our place is at a high altitude and is colder than those at a low altitude. It often snows in winter.'
我们这个地方高得很，比低处冷。冬天经常下雪。

By looking at the definition, it can be observed that the frequentative is semantically close to the habitual. It is true that contexts possessing both frequentative and habitual interpretations do exist in Caijia. In particular, when $k^h\tilde{a}^{55}$ is associated with the past tense it can be analyzed as 'used to', whereas the Caijia habitual is not overtly marked. Example (10.124) illustrates precisely one such ambiguous context. It describes a frequent or habitual act, i.e. drinking, in the past, but this habit has declined at the moment of speech.

(10.124) mɔ²¹ kʰɯ³³ nen²¹, ŋo²¹ kʰã⁵⁵ ã²¹ tso⁵⁵ sɿ²¹.
that several year 1SG FREQ drink alcohol CONT
ɔ²¹kɯ²¹ ã²¹ po³³ to³³ o.
now drink NEG can CRS
'I often drank during those years. Now I can't drink anymore.'
'I used to drink during those years. Now I can't drink anymore.'
我那几年常喝酒。现在喝不了了。

However, $k^h\tilde{a}^{55}$ cannot be used to mark predicates depicting one's daily routine, proving that $k^h\tilde{a}^{55}$ is a frequentative marker rather than a habitual marker. This is not difficult to explain, because 'daily' and 'frequently' cannot co-occur. Moreover, one's daily routine should be regarded as a prototypical habitual scenario. The example in (10.125a) describes the daily routine of males in the olden days. The expression tsa^{21} $tɕin^{21}$ 'go to the front' is metaphorically used to express 'go working'. In fact, $k^h\tilde{a}^{55}$ is barely compatible with this context. An adverb or intensifier, such as $tɯ^{33}$ 'then, even' and la^{21} 'also, all, even', must be used along with $k^h\tilde{a}^{55}$ to make the sentence more natural, but the meaning of the sentence will be entirely changed, i.e. the habitual meaning will shift to 'be willing to drive the cow to do farming', as shown in (10.125b).

(10.125) a. tɕie⁵⁵ ja²¹pa²¹ nɛ⁵⁵, ɔ²¹kɔ²¹ pa³³tso³³
do crops PRT INTJ man
tsɔ²¹ nɛ⁵⁵, tɔ²¹kʰɯ⁵⁵ kʰɯ⁵⁵-ɣɯ²¹
a.type.(of people) PRT morning rise-come
nɛ⁵⁵, lui⁵⁵-xɯ⁵⁵ ŋo²¹ ta⁵⁵-xɯ⁵⁵ ɣoŋ²¹
PRT drive-DUR cow carry-DUR plough
nɛ⁵⁵, tsa³³ tɕin²¹.
PRT go.up front
'As for farming, eh, men got up in the morning and then went to work driving the cow and carrying the plough.'
做农活呢，这个，男人呢，早上起来呢，赶着牛，抬着犁就去干活。
(*The fight on the hill*, texts)

b. tɔ²¹kʰɯ⁵⁵   kʰɯ⁵⁵-ɣɯ²¹   nɛ⁵⁵   tɯ²¹   kʰã⁵⁵
   morning   rise-come   PRT   even   be.willing.to
   lui⁵⁵-xɯ⁵⁵   ŋu²¹   tsa³³   tɕiŋ²¹.
   drive-DUR   cow   go.up   front
   'They got up in the morning and even volunteered to drive the cow to do farming'
   早上起来呢，就肯赶着牛去干活。

Similarly, in (10.126b), co-occurrence with *koŋ⁵⁵koŋ⁵⁵* 'every day' means that it is only possible to interpret *kʰã⁵⁵* as 'be willing to', while the adverb *la²¹* 'all', an intensifier, should be used to produce a natural utterance.

(10.126) a. koŋ⁵⁵koŋ⁵⁵   je³³   piɔ³³   tɯ²¹   mɔ²¹   je³³   mɔ²¹   kʰui⁵⁵
            every.day   3SG   run   to   that   3SG   that   dog
            hm̥⁵⁵   kã²¹   tv̩³³   kuɛ³³   jɔ²¹   [...]
            POSS   grave   upside   PURP   shake
            'He ran to the grave of his dog's to shake (those three bamboos) every day [...]'
            天天他跑到他那狗的坟头上去摇（那三棵竹子）......
            (*The ploughing dog*, texts)

        b. koŋ⁵⁵koŋ⁵⁵   je³³   la²¹   kʰã⁵⁵   piɔ³³   tɯ²¹   je³³
           every.day   3SG   all   be.willing.to run   to   3SG
           mɔ²¹   kʰui⁵⁵   hm̥⁵⁵   kã²¹   tv̩³³   kuɛ³³   jɔ²¹
           that   dog   POSS   grave   upside PURP   shake
           mɔ²¹   tsɔ³³   sa³³   tɔ³³.
           that   bamboo   three   CLF
           'He was always willing to run to the grave of his dog's to shake those three bamboos every day.'
           天天他都愿意跑到他那狗的坟头上去摇那三棵竹子。

10.3 Conclusion

This chapter has given a general description of the aspectual system in Caijia, illustrating eleven aspectual types identified in this language. As is typical of Sinitic languages, Caijia is also an aspect prominent language. As in Sinitic, verbs are important sources of aspectual markers in Caijia. Many Caijia aspectual markers show similarity with Sinitic languages from the perspective of their semantic fields. For example, the completive marker is derived from the verb 'finish'. The inchoative developed out of 'rise up', the durative marker is from 'rise', and the experiential is from 'experience'. Nevertheless, unlike Sinitic the Caijia aspectual markers are not commonly manifested in the form of suffixes. Instead, most of them are free morphemes. Unlike most of the Sinitic languages, Caijia does not overtly code the perfective, but reflects it via negation. Furthermore, Caijia uses a very special marker to code the continuous, i.e. the cleft and affirmative construction *(s1^{33})* . . . *s1^{21}*. Even though not yet treated as a type, we have also identified the manner continuous as an aspectual type.

Chapter 11
Modal system

11.1 Introduction

Modality is a cross-linguistically identified category of grammar related to possibility and necessity (Palmer 1986, 2001, Bybee et al. 1994, Bybee and Fleischman 1995, von Fintel 2006). It covers a broad range of semantic nuances including the jussive, desiderative, intentive, hypothetical, potential, obligative, dubitative, hortative, and exclamative, and can be expressed morphologically, lexically, syntactically, or via intonation. These modes are not mutually exclusive (Bybee and Fleischman 1995: 2).

In the realm of modality, scholars traditionally adopt a three-way distinction – dynamic, deontic, epistemic. These three terms all possess Greek origins. **Dynamic** is from Greek *dynamis* 'strength, power' referring to ability (both mental and physical one); **deontic** modality is "concerned with the necessity or possibility of acts performed by morally responsible agents" (Lyons 1977: 823) such as permission and obligation, and is from *deon* 'duty'; and **epistemic**, derived from Greek *episteme* 'knowledge', is "concerned with the nature and source of knowledge" (Lyons 1977: 793), and is thus about "an evaluation of the truth of a proposition" (Bybee and Fleischman 1995: 4). Nevertheless, this three-way distinction cannot cover all modal nuances. For example, 'One can take bus 95 or bus 39 to get to rue de Lille'; an instance treated as circumstantial modality by Kratzer (1991), and as non-deontic by van der Auwera and Plungian (1998). For the latter, this is a case of participant-external possibility.

Accordingly, different frameworks and terms are proposed when studying modality. Coates (1983) adopts a root modality which encompasses the dynamic and deontic. Bybee et al. (1994) propose dividing modality into four types: agent-oriented, speaker-oriented, epistemic, and subordinating. Van der Auwera and Plungian (1998: 82) propose a bipartition of modality, i.e. epistemic and non-epistemic or situational (van der Auwera and Ammann 2013), as summarized by (Chappell and Peyraube 2016a: 300) in Table 11.1.

As illustrated in the table below, situational modality is subdivided into participant-external and participant-internal modalities. Participant external modality "refers to circumstances that are external to the participant, if any, engaged in the state of affairs and that make this state of affairs either possible or necessary" (van der Auwera and Plungian 1998: 80). For example, 'One may be calmer after taking deep breaths'. On the contrary, participant-internal modality refers to "a kind of possibility or necessity internal to a participant engaged in

Table 11.1: Semantic nuances of Modality.

Epistemic	Situational (non-epistemic)	
	Participant-external	Participant-internal
possibility	possibility	
	permission	ability
probability	obligation	willingness
certainty	requirement	volition, intention
necessity	necessity	

the state of affairs" (van der Auwera and Plungian 1998: 80), i.e. a participant's ability or capacity (e.g. 'I can speak French') and a participant's internal need (e.g. 'You need to have a rest').

Languages do not always code these semantic nuances of modality differently. For example, the English modal auxiliary verb 'should' can not only be used to express deontic obligation as in 'You should leave' but can also be used to express epistemic possibility as in 'This should help'. The specific meaning of 'should' depends, to a large extent, on the context in which it is used. This is exactly what can be observed in Caijia as well. In Caijia, modality can be expressed in several different ways, including with the use of modal auxiliaries (AUX), lexical verbs (LEX. V), a cleft construction, a potential (POT) construction formed by the complementizer lu^{55}, experiential markers (EXP), post-VP 'can' modals, adverbs, as well as a final particle (F. PRT). See Table 11.2.

Table 11.2: Modal elements in Caijia.

	INTENTION	NECESSITY	CERTAINTY	ABILITY	POSSIBILITY	PERMISSION
AUX	$kʰã^{55}$ 'be willing to' ɕiaŋ^{55} 'want' niɔ^{33} 'want, need'	tɕʰiɔ^{21} 'be necessary' niɔ^{33}dv^{33} 'need'			ti^{33} 'know'	
LEX. V					tsʰŋ^{33} 'fear' dzɔ^{33} 'resemble'	
POST-VP					do^{33} 'achieve' tv^{33} VP do^{33} 'obtain...achieve' tv^{33} 'obtain'	
POT			tv^{33} 'obtain'		V lɯ^{55} VP	

Table 11.2 (continued)

	INTENTION	NECESSITY	CERTAINTY	ABILITY	POSSIBILITY	PERMISSION
ADV					kʰuɔ³³neŋ²¹ 'probably' niɔ³³sɿ³³ 'probably'	
CLEFT			sɿ³³…sɿ²¹			
EXP			gua³³ ja²¹			
F. PRT					ɔ pa	

11.2 Modal auxiliaries [AUX VP]

Modal auxiliaries may be the most common way to express modality in Sinitic languages (q.v. Chappell and Peyraube 2016a). Six auxiliary verbs are used to code modality in Caijia, as listed in Table 11.3. The auxiliary verbs $kʰ\tilde{a}^{55}$ 'be willing to', $\varepsilon iaŋ^{55}$ 'want', and $niɔ^{33}$ 'want, need' are used to express intention and volition; $niɔ^{33}$ 'want, need', $tɕʰiɔ^{21}$ 'be necessary', and $niɔ^{33}\text{-}dy^{33}$ 'want-need' are used to denote necessity; and ti^{33} 'know' is used to denote ability and possibility. See Table 11.3 for a synthesis of Caijia auxiliaries.

Table 11.3: Modal auxiliaries in Caijia.

kʰã⁵⁵	'be willing to'	WILLINGNESS, INTENTION, VOLITION, POSSIBILITY
ɕiaŋ⁵⁵	'want'	INTENTION, VOLITION, DESIRE
niɔ³³	'want, need'	INTENTION, VOLITION, NECESSITY, OBLIGATION
niɔ³³-dy³³	'want-need'	NECESSITY, OBLIGATION
tɕʰiɔ²¹	'need'	NECESSITY
ti³³	'know'	ABILITY, POSSIBILITY

The elements listed above are identified as auxiliary verbs on the basis of several features. See Chapter 4 §4.2.1.1 for the distributional features of ordinary verbs.
i. Unlike ordinary verbs, auxiliary verbs take VPs instead of NPs as objects or complements.
ii. They do not take resultative complements or are not modified by aspectual markers.

iii. However, they still possess some verbal features, such as, they can be negated by the general negator *pγ³³* 'not' and transformed into polar questions in the form of [AUX NEG AUX].
iv. They can be used as free elements especially when answering polar questions or in contexts of zero anaphora.

These features of auxiliaries in Caijia are also attested in Sinitic languages. Zhu Dexi (1982: 61) points out that the auxiliary verbs of Standard Mandarin cannot be reduplicated as ordinary verbs are. However, this feature cannot be a diagnostic criterion for Caijia auxiliaries, since ordinary verbs cannot be reduplicated in Caijia.

The following two examples show the uses of the auxiliary *kʰã⁵⁵* 'be willing to'. In (11.1i), the verb *tsʰaŋ⁵⁵* 'concede' is the object of *kʰã⁵⁵* 'be willing to'. The sentence in (11.1ii) is a case of zero anaphora with the negated *kʰã⁵⁵* as the predicate, since the object or the complement *tsʰaŋ⁵⁵* 'concede' has already been mentioned in the preceding sentence. Example (11.2) illustrates how the auxiliary *kʰã⁵⁵* 'be willing to' can be used to form a polar question.

(11.1) ji³³ ni²¹ tsʰaŋ⁵⁵ mi⁵⁵ tɯ³³ xa³³-kʰua²¹ to³³ o ma.
one 3 concede a.little then say-be.good can CRS PRT
i) tɯ³³sɿ³³ tɯ²¹ ha⁵⁵ o, lɔ²⁴ni³³ la²¹ pγ²¹
even be.at here CRS who all NEG
kʰã⁵⁵ tsʰaŋ⁵⁵.
be.willing.to concede
ii) ji³³ ni³³ la³³ pγ²¹ **kʰã⁵⁵.**
one 3 also NEG be.willing.to
'(If) each of them concedes a little bit, (the problem) can be solved. At this point, no one is willing to concede. Neither of them is willing to.'
一人退一步就能谈好了嘛。到如今了，谁都不肯妥协。一个都不肯。

(11.2) sɿ⁵⁵ je²¹ kuɛ²¹ na²¹koŋ³³.
let 3SG go work
je²¹ **kʰã⁵⁵** (lɔ²¹) pγ²¹ **kʰã⁵⁵**?
3SG be.willing.to or NEG be.willing.to
'(I'd like) him to get a job. Is he willing to (do it)?'
让他去打工。他肯不肯？

All of the modal auxiliaries in Caijia listed in Table 11.3 possess these features except the compound *niɔ³³tγ³³* 'need', which will be discussed further below.

One should also note that the main verbal uses for some of the modal auxiliaries co-exist with the modal uses. More details are given in the following sections.

11.2.1 $k^h\tilde{a}^{55}$ 'be willing to'

The auxiliary $k^h\tilde{a}^{55}$ 'be willing to' is probably cognate with Chinese *kěn* 肯 [kʰən²¹⁴] 'be willing to'. Examples (11.1) and (11.2) have already shown the primary meaning of $k^h\tilde{a}^{55}$, that is, a person shows willingness to do something. The negated $k^h\tilde{a}^{55}$ in (11.1) denotes the unwillingness of each person to concede, while the one in (11.2) denotes being in accordance with another's willingness, for which the participant *je³³* 'he' is the subject and can be interpreted as 'agree'. One more example is given below.

(11.3) nɯ³³ xa²¹ lɯ⁵⁵ tsʰɿ²¹pʰe²¹pʰe²⁴ o. niɔ³³ je²¹
        2SG say VCOMP light CRS need 3SG
        kʰã⁵⁵ ɣɯ²¹ sun³³ ŋo³³ lɛ²¹tsʰɛ²¹ kʰua²¹.
        be.willing.to come help 1SG only.then be.good
        'It's easy for you to say. It will be good only if he's willing to help me.'
        你说得轻巧。要他肯来帮我才好。

Apart from 'willingness', $k^h\tilde{a}^{55}$ also extends to express situational possibility, i.e. that the possibility exists in a given situation (van der Auwera and Ammann 2013), and so it denotes 'be more possible to'. In both (11.4) and (11.5), $k^h\tilde{a}^{55}$ cannot be interpreted as 'be willing to' any more, since neither of the subjects, i.e. *sɔ⁵⁵* 'tree' and *to²⁴* 'bean', are animate and cannot possess the property of willingness. Spring is the condition enabling trees to bud, while the condition for obtaining soft beans is to soak them (before cooking).

(11.4) tsʰun⁵⁵kʰɩŋ⁵⁵ sɿ²¹ sɔ⁵⁵ lɛ²¹tsʰe²¹ **kʰã⁵⁵** tɣ⁵⁵.
        spring MOD tree only.then be.willing.to grow
        'Trees can only bud in spring.'
        春天的树才肯长。

(11.5) mɔ²¹ to²⁴-sui⁵⁵ a³³ tso³³-kua³³
        that bean-PL DCR put.into.water-pass
        tsʰɛ²¹ **kʰã⁵⁵** niu²¹.
        only.then be.willing.to be.soft
        'Those beans can become soft only after soaking them (for quite a while).'
        那些豆子泡过才能软。

The semantic extensions, illustrated in (11.4) and (11.5), can be regarded as the result of metaphorization (Claudi and Heine 1986). To be more precise, inanimate objects are conceptualized metaphorically as human beings. When a person shows willingness or a desire to perform an action, it suggests that this action has a greater possibility or likelihood of being carried out. It is, thus, not difficult to understand the semantic extension of $k^h\tilde{a}^{55}$ from 'be willing to' to 'be more possible to'.

The auxiliary $k^h\tilde{a}^{55}$ has further undergone the process of demodalization, which refers to a modal word developing into a non-modal word (van der Auwera and Plungian 1998). It is used to mark the frequentative aspect. The example below is ambiguous. The word $k^h\tilde{a}^{55}$ can either denote 'be willing to' or 'often'.

(11.6) je²¹ kʰã⁵⁵ ɣɯ²¹ sɿ²¹.
3SG be.willing.to come AFF/CONT
'He's willing to come.'
'He often comes.'
他肯来。
他常来的。

See Chapter 10 on aspect for more examples of $k^h\tilde{a}^{55}$ as the frequentative marker.

11.2.2 ɕiaŋ⁵⁵ 'want'

Cognate with the (modal) verb *xiǎng* 想 [ɕiaŋ²¹⁴] 'want, think, miss' in Standard Mandarin, Caijia *ɕiaŋ⁵⁵* 'want, would like' is mainly used to denote intention and desire, i.e. an agent intends to carry out an action or shows a desire of wanting to perform or fulfill an action. Note that the verb *xiǎng* in Standard Mandarin possesses both lexical and modal uses. However, Caijia *ɕiaŋ⁵⁵* can only be used as a modal auxiliary verb. See the examples below.

(11.7) nɯ²¹ **ɕiaŋ⁵⁵** zɣ²¹ xɯ⁵⁵tsɿ⁵⁵ lɔ²¹ zɣ²¹ lɔ²¹po⁵⁵?
2SG want eat pear or eat peach
'Would you like to eat a pear or a peach?'
你想吃梨还是桃儿?

(11.8) ŋo³³ pɣ²¹ ɕiaŋ⁵⁵ ta⁵⁵ je²¹ kʰua²¹ o.
1SG NEG want with 3SG be.good CRS
'I don't want to be friends with her.'
我不想跟她好了。

11.2.3 nio^{33} 'want, need'

Derived from its lexical form 'want, need', the auxiliary nio^{33} can denotes intention, and desire, as well as necessity. Unlike $k^h\tilde{a}^{55}$ 'be willing to' and $\varcia\eta^{55}$ 'want', lexical and modal uses of nio^{33} co-exist. Example (11.9) illustrates its lexical use. It can be observed that nio^{33} takes a classifier phrase as its object, denoting 'want'.

(11.9) ŋo³³ **nio³³** [mɔ²¹ la²¹ sɿ²¹ ji²¹ pɔ⁵⁵].
1SG want that big MOD one CLF
'I want that big one.'
我要那个大的。

In fact, the **intention** and **desire** meanings of nio^{33} are backgrounded when compared with its other meanings, such as, necessity 'need', 'must', and the prospective 'will'. When denoting intention and desire, nio^{33} can be replaced by $\varcia\eta^{55}$. In (11.10), the context is one in which the speaker's hen is caught by a hawk. Before this happens, he sees the hawk flying around above his house. The speaker suddenly realizes why the hawk has been flying around and infers the intention of the hawk. The auxiliary nio^{33} in this example denotes 'want'. Neither the prospective meaning 'will' or the meaning of necessity 'need, must' is appropriate in this context.

(11.10) ŋo³³ xa²¹lɛ⁵⁵ mɔ²¹ li²⁴u³³pa²¹ tsɿ⁵⁵ tɯ²¹ ua²⁴
1SG wonder that hawk CLF at here
pa²¹pa²¹tɪŋ⁵⁵tɪŋ⁵⁵ lɛ²¹ py²¹. ɕia³³ti³³ɣɯ²¹ sɿ³³
hang.around ADV fly it.turns.out COP
nio³³/ɕiaŋ⁵⁵ ka³³ ŋo³³ mɔ²¹ kɪ²¹tɕie⁵⁵ tsɿ⁵⁵.
want catch 1SG that hen CLF
'No wonder the hawk was flying around. It turned out it wanted to catch my hen.'
我说那只鹰（怎么）在这儿转来转去地飞。原来是想/要抓我那只母鸡。

In example (11.11), the copula $sɿ^{33}$ links two clauses, EVENT₁ and EVENT₂. EVENT₂ is the purpose of EVENT₁. The purpose of buying a house in town is to make it easier for the children of the person to attend school. Before the action of buying a house is realized, we can deduce that there is an 'intentional' stage. The auxiliary nio^{33} can only be interpreted as 'want' in this sentence. Similarly, nio^{33} can also be replaced by $\varcia\eta^{55}$ 'want' without any change of meaning.

(11.11) EVENT1[je³³   ti²¹   ɔ⁵⁵   tɯ²¹   loŋ³³   mo³³]   sๅ³³
                3SG   move   house   to   city   inside   COP
        EVENT2[**niɔ²¹/ɕiaŋ⁵⁵** sๅ⁵⁵   ŋa⁵⁵-sui⁵⁵   kʰua²¹   kʷɔ³³   sy³³].
                want   let   child-PL   well   learn   book
        'She moved to the city. It is to facilitate the children attending school.'
        他把家搬到城里，是要让孩子们方便读书。

The prospective meaning of *niɔ³³* is closely connected with the meaning of 'want, desire'. In fact, verbs of wanting and desiring are a common source for the future tense (Bybee et al. 1994: 254–255, Kuteva et al. 2019: 453–456), such as *niɔ³³* in (11.12) below, which we analyze as the prospective type in Caijia. In the example below, the impersonal construction concerns a meteorological phenomenon that cannot involve any desire or intention. See Chapter 10 for more details.

(11.12) **niɔ³³**   ɣɯ²¹   zๅ⁵⁵   o.
        PROSP   come   rain   CRS
        'It's going to rain.'
        要下雨了。

Apart from intention and desire, the modal auxiliary *niɔ³³* 'want, need' is also used to express deontic **obligation** and **necessity**, i.e. what an engaged participant should or must do according to certain norms, or a speaker's expectation or desire. It can be used to denote either strong or weak obligation. Example (11.13) shows a case in which social norms oblige the participant to engage in the state of affairs, i.e. all people must respect the law.

(11.13) hu³³ni³³   la²¹   **niɔ³³**   səɯ³³   fa²¹.
        all.person   all   need   respect   law
        'All people must respect the law.'
        所有人都要守法。

Example (11.14) below illustrates what people should do according to funeral customs in the culture of Caijia. Compared to the case of (11.13), the obligation expressed by *niɔ³³* in (11.14) is less strong, since the consequence of violating an ethnic custom is much less severe than a violation of the law.

(11.14) ŋo⁵⁵ la²¹to⁵⁵ u²¹tsʰo²¹ pɣ³³ tɯ²¹ ha⁵⁵ nɛ⁵⁵ [. . .],
1PL old person NEG live COMPL PRT

i) **niɔ³³** ŋɯ²¹ tã³³, ŋɯ²¹ kɣ⁵⁵ tã²¹
 need light.up lamp light.up foot lamp
 pie⁵⁵ ti⁵⁵mi²¹ tso²¹ je³³.
 to ground light.up 3SG

ii) nɛ⁵⁵ je³³ kıŋ²¹ hɔ⁵⁵ ɣa²¹. tsə³³kə³³ti³³,
 INTJ 3SG see road walk INTJ

iii) sɿ⁵⁵nã²¹nioŋ³³ nɛ⁵⁵ **niɔ³³** tɯ²¹ mo²¹
 offspring PRT need at inside
 tɣ⁵⁵. [. . .]
 hold.vigil

iv) **niɔ³³** a³³ tsʰɔ³³tsʰɔ³³ pʰɣ²¹ tʰa⁵⁵
 need OM grass lay bed
 pi³³, pʰɣ²¹ pie⁵⁵ tʰɣ³³ tɣ³³
 beside lay to floor upside
 dzɿ²¹ e.
 sleep PRT

'When an old person passes away (in our place), [. . .], one **needs** to light up a lamp, to light up a (kind of) lamp (called) 'lamp for feet' on the ground in order to light (his/her way) so that the dead person can see his/her way (to leave the world). Eh. . . His/her offspring **should/must** come to hold vigil (for the dead person). (They) **should/must** lay some hay next to the bed. (They) lay the hay on the floor to sleep on.'

我们（这儿）老人不在了呢，[. . . . . .]，要点灯，点脚灯（给）他照（路）。他（就可以）看清路离开了。嗯，(他的) 子子孙孙呢， 要在家里守夜。[. . . . . .]。要把干草铺在床边，铺到地上睡。

(*Funeral customs*, texts)

The example below shows that a traditional healer is supposed to check the children's ears when performing vaccinations. In the past, people went to traditional healers to vaccinate their children in order to prevent cowpox or chicken pox. Vaccinations performed under such unsanitary conditions were very risky with the possibility of death. Traditional healers believed that whether a child can be vaccinated or not is something that can be seen from the shape of a child's ears. To avoid risks, traditional healers must check the ears of the child to decide if the vaccination can be performed. Therefore, checking the ears of children can be treated as a common practice in this specific field.

11.2 Modal auxiliaries [AUX VP]

(11.15) pʰɣ²¹ to²¹ ɕyn⁵⁵ ŋa⁵⁵ **niɔ³³** tsaŋ²¹ je³³ ni³³kʰa³³.
cover vaccine select child need look 3SG ear
'When selecting children to be vaccinated, one **should/must** check their ears.'
种痘选孩子，要看他耳朵。

Example (11.16) shows a case of a speaker's expectation expressed by *niɔ³³*.

(11.16) nɯ³³ niɔ³³ ã²¹ tsɣ⁵⁵. kʰua²¹kʰua²⁴ ã³³, nɯ³³
2SG need drink medicine well drink 2SG
ɔ²¹ soŋ²¹ lɛ²¹tsʰɛ²¹ kʰɯ³³-kʰua²¹ to³³. niɔ³³ ã²¹!
this sickness only.then treat-be.good can need drink
'You must take medicine. Take it properly. Only in this way can your disease be cured. You must take it.'
你要喝药。好好喝，你这病才能治好。要喝！

Certainly, *niɔ³³* 'want, need' can also be used to express non-deontic necessity or non-deontic obligation. Each of the sentences (i-v) in (11.17) contains an auxiliary *niɔ³³*, expressing necessities in the farming routine which are also necessities for living.

(11.17) i) ji³³ neŋ³³ nɛ³³ **niɔ³³** tsoŋ²¹ ma³³
one year PRT need plant crops
ji³³ tɕi²¹.
one season
ii) ji³³ tɕiu³³ ni²¹ sa³³ ŋoŋ³³ noŋ³³ nɛ³³,
once arrive two three month middle PRT
niɔ³³ pɣ³³ tsʰa³³, na³³ lɛ²¹,
need carry manure beat land
ʑi²¹ lɛ²¹, ɔ²⁴-sui⁵⁵ nɛ⁵⁵. [...]
plough land this-PL PRT
iii) kɣ⁵⁵ xa³³, tsoŋ²¹ xa³³, kʰɿŋ²⁴pa²¹mi²¹ a,
grain PRT wheat PRT corn PRT
tsʰɿ⁵⁵po⁵⁵ la³³ niɔ³³ tsoŋ³³. [...]
potato all need plant
iv) tɔ²¹kʰɯ⁵⁵ **niɔ³³** tɕɿŋ²¹tɕɿŋ²⁴ lɛ²¹ kʰɯ⁵⁵.
morning need early ADV rise
v) ja²¹kʰa³³pa²¹sa³³ tɕiu²¹ ɔ⁵⁵ ʑi²¹, xa²¹
middle.of.night arrive house inside still
niɔ³³ ɣɯ²¹ tɕie⁵⁵ zɣ²¹ tɕie⁵⁵ tsʰɯ²¹ [...]
need come do meal do dish

'We **need** to plant a season of crops every year. By the period of February or March, we **need** to carry some manure to the fields, loosen the soil and plow the fields, etc. [. . .] Millets, wheats, corns, and potatoes all **need** to be planted. [. . .] We **need to** get up early in the morning. When we get home late in the evening, we still **need** to cook.'
一年呢，要种一季庄稼。一到二三月间呢，要背粪、松土、犁地这些。[......]谷子啊，麦子啊，玉米啊，土豆，都要种。[......]早晨要早早地起。夜半三更回来，还要做饭做菜。
(*The life of farming*, texts)

In the example below, *niɔ³³* in (11.18i) should be interpreted as epistemic necessity, and is based on the speaker's own knowledge. By contrast, the necessity expressed in (11.18ii) is determined by the presence of a situation where someone is stuck in a bog.

(11.18) i) nɯ⁵⁵ tʰaŋ⁵⁵-ya²¹ ni²¹ta²¹ mo³³ kuɛ³³ nɛ³³
2SG sink-fall bog inside go PRT
niɔ³³ piɔ²⁴ jɔ²¹. [. . .]
need NEG.IMP move
ii) **niɔ³³** γã³³ u²¹tsʰo²¹ yɯ²¹ kʰɪŋ⁵⁵ nɯ³³
need there.be person come pull 2SG
lɛ²¹tsʰɛ²¹ tsʰe⁵⁵-yɯ²¹ to³³.
only.then be.out-come can

'If you get stuck in a bog, you **mustn't** move. [. . .] There **needs** to be someone coming to give you a tug so that you can get out of it.'
你陷到泥塘里呢要别动。[......]要有人来拉你才能出来。

Not surprisingly, the negated form of *niɔ³³* is used to express lack of necessity or prohibition. Examples (11.19) and (11.20) show two cases of lack of necessity expressed by the negated *niɔ³³*. See also §11.2.5.

(11.19) pγ³³ sɿ³³ sɿ²¹mɔ⁵⁵ la²¹ soŋ²¹. (ŋo³³) **pγ³³ niɔ³³**
NEG COP what big sickness 1SG NEG need
tsa²¹ ji³³jyɛn²⁴ lɛ³³.
go.up hospital PRT

'It's not a serious illness. (I) **don't need** to go to the hospital.'
不是什么大病。（我）不用去医院。

(11.20) kʰɪŋ⁵⁵neŋ²¹   sɿ²¹   ko²¹   **pɣ³³ niɔ³³**   tsa²¹   la²¹.
this.year   MOD   tax   NEG need   pay   PRT
'It's not necessary to pay the taxes this year.'
今年的税不用上了。

There exists a fused form of *pɣ³³ niɔ³³*, *piɔ²⁴* used as the imperative negator. When expressing prohibition, one can either use the non-fused form *pɣ³³ niɔ³³* or the fused form *piɔ²⁴*. *piɔ²⁴* is much more common. Several examples are given below in which both forms can be used, including (11.22) and (11.23). Note that *piɔ²⁴* is not, however, used to denote lack of necessity.

(11.21) ɕie²¹   ŋa⁵⁵   tsɔ²¹   **[pɣ³³   niɔ³³]/   [piɔ²⁴]**
small   child a.type.of.person   NEG   need   NEG.IMP
xa²¹ pia³³ŋoŋ³³.
say   lie
'Children mustn't tell lies.'
小孩子别说假话。

(11.22) nɯ³³   **piɔ²⁴**   tɕyn³³   je³³.
2SG   NEG.IMP   scold   3SG
'Don't scold him.'
你别骂他。

(11.23) nɯ³³   **piɔ²⁴**   tʰaŋ⁵⁵   ɔ²¹   tsoŋ⁵⁵   tɔ²¹   sɿ⁵⁵.
2SG   NEG.IMP   wade   this   type   muddy water
'Don't get involved in such troubles (LIT: don't wade into such muddy water)!'
你别淌这趟浑水。

It also should be mentioned that the fused form *piɔ²⁴* only possesses a modal use, i.e. as an imperative negator, while the lexical use of *pɣ³³ niɔ³³* still persists, denoting 'not want, not need'. In the following example, *niɔ³³* is a lexical verb forming a pivot construction, denoting 'want'. In this case, using the fused form *piɔ²⁴* would be ungrammatical. See also §11.4.2 for more discussion on emphatic prohibition.

(11.24) je³³   **[pɣ³³   niɔ³³]/   *[piɔ²⁴]**   ŋo³³   ɣɯ²¹   o.
3SG   NEG   need   NEG.IMP   1SG   come   PRT
'He doesn't want me to come.'
他不要我来了。

In conclusion, even though the auxiliary *niɔ³³* is mainly used to code intention and desire, i.e. participant-internal modality, it is more commonly used to express necessity and obligation which belong to participant-external modality. As can be observed from the examples in this section, whether *niɔ³³* denotes epistemic or situational necessity is entirely determined by its usage context.

11.2.4 *niɔ³³dɣ̩³³* 'need'

Expressing strong necessity or obligation, 'must, have to', the auxiliary *niɔ³³dɣ̩³³* 'need, must' is composed of two morphemes, *niɔ³³* 'want, need' and *dɣ̩³³* 'suffer, need, be worth, hit the target', both of which belong to the same semantic field. The lexical values of *niɔ³³dɣ̩³³* 'need' are illustrated in the two examples below. In both examples, *niɔ³³dɣ̩³³* 'need' can be replaced either by *niɔ³³* or *dɣ̩³³* without causing any semantic change. See Chapter 7 on passive constructions for more examples concerning the lexical uses of *dɣ̩³³*.

(11.25) ɣa²¹   hɔ⁵⁵   tɯ²¹   loŋ³³   mo³³   **[niɔ³³tɣ³³]/[niɔ³³]/[tɣ³³]**
        walk   road   to   city   inside   need
        ni²⁴   kʰua²¹tie⁵⁵?
        time   how.much
        'How much time is needed to walk to the town?'
        走路到城里要多长时间？

(11.26) A- ɔ²¹   ã²¹ã⁵⁵   po⁵⁵   **[niɔ³³tɣ³³]/[niɔ³³]/[tɣ³³]**
          this   jar   CLF   need
          tɕiŋ²¹   kʰua²¹tie⁵⁵.
          money   how.much
          'How much money is needed for this jar?'
          这个罐子要多少钱？

       B- **[niɔ³³tɣ³³]/[niɔ³³]/[tɣ³³]**   tɕiŋ²¹   tsaŋ³³   pʰe³³.
          need   money   ten   UNIT.FOR.MONEY
          'It's ten yuan.'
          要10块钱。

Unlike the other modal auxiliary verbs listed in Table 11.3, *niɔ³³dɣ̩³³* cannot be negated and can neither be used alone nor transformed into the form of [V NEG V], as the modal auxiliary *kʰã⁵⁵* 'be willing to' can in (11.1) and (11.2). Given that *niɔ³³dɣ̩³³* can always be replaced by *niɔ³³* 'want, need', which is identified as a

11.2 Modal auxiliaries [AUX VP]

typical auxiliary verb, we can thus identify *niɔ³³dʏ³³* 'need' as an auxiliary verb by analogy.

Let us see some examples of the modal uses of *niɔ³³dʏ³³* 'need', which is often used in a prospective context. The three examples below show epistemic inevitability. In (11.27), *ɔ²¹ hɔ⁵⁵ ta⁵⁵* 'this road' is metaphorically used to express 'death'. The modal auxiliary *niɔ³³tʏ³³* 'need' is used to express that every person has to face death, which is the law of nature.

(11.27) ɔ²¹   hɔ⁵⁵   ta⁵⁵   hu³³ni³³   la²¹   **niɔ³³tʏ³³**   ɣa²¹,
this   road   CLF   all.people   all   need   walk
lɔ²⁴ni³³   la³³   tsʏ²¹   pʏ³³   tʰʏ³³   sʅ²¹.
who   all   hide   NEG   be.off   AFF
'Everyone will die (LIT: everyone has to take this road). No one can escape from it.'
这条路人人都得走。谁都逃不脱的。

In both (11.28) and (11.29), the inevitability of the two events, i.e. 'the beans will rot away' and 'it will be sunny', are based on the speakers' own life experiences. Both events are believed to inevitably take place at some point.

(11.28) ɔ³³   kʰɯ²¹   koŋ⁵⁵   niɔ³³   piɔ²⁴   ɣɯ²¹   zʅ⁵⁵   lɛ²¹
this   several day   need   NEG.IMP   come   rain   PRT
jo³³.   ɣɯ²¹   zʅ⁵⁵   nɛ⁵⁵   ŋo³³   ɔ²¹   to²⁴   tɯ²¹
PRT   come   rain   PRT   1SG   this   bean   then
ka⁵⁵   pʏ²¹   ka⁵⁵   o.   **niɔ³³tʏ³³**   tsʰʅ²¹   kʷɔ²¹   lɛ²¹.
dry   NEG   be.dry CRS   need   rot   go.CRS   PRT
'It mustn't rain during these days. If it rains, my beans won't be dried and they'll rot away.'
这几天不能下雨。下雨的话，我的豆子晒不干了。得烂掉了。

(11.29) ɣɯ²¹   ɔ²¹   zʅ⁵⁵   ji³³   pʰo²¹   ha⁵⁵   kua³³,
come   this   rain   one   time   COMPL   EXP
niɔ³³tʏ³³   ta²¹   o.
need   be.sunny   CRS
'After this rainfall, it will be sunny.'
下过这一场雨，要晴了。

The wording in (11.30) is very similar to that in (11.29) above. Both of these examples concern the topic of rain. However, *niɔ³³tʏ³³* in the case of (11.30) is used to express the speaker's strong expectation that good weather must last longer, even though the speaker has no way of knowing whether or not it will actually be sunny when producing the sentence.

(11.30) ɣɯ²¹ ɔ²¹sɿ²¹ tie⁵⁵ ni²⁴ sɿ²¹ zɿ⁵⁵, **niɔ³³tɣ³³** ta³³ tɣ²¹ko³³
come this many day MOD rain need be.sunny be.long
o. pɣ³³ sɿ³³ nɛ³³ nɯ²¹ lɯ⁵⁵ pɣ³³sɿ³³ o.
CRS NEG COP PRT humid VCOMP very CRS
'It has been raining for quite a few days. The sunny weather needs to last longer. Otherwise, it will be so humid.'
下这么多天的雨，得晴久些。不然的话，潮得不行。

The following example illustrates a situational necessity expressed by *niɔ³³dɣ³³* 'need', which is determined by the situation at the reference time, i.e. the strong necessity to pry the wheels out.

(11.31) hɔ⁵⁵ naŋ²¹ xɪŋ⁵⁵ o. tɣ²¹ sɿ⁵⁵
road be.muddy very CRS PASS water
tso³³-niu²¹ kʷɔ²¹ o. tsʰɛ⁵⁵ la³³
soak-be.soft go.CRS CRS car all
tʰaŋ⁵⁵-tɕie²¹kuɛ²¹ o. ŋo²⁴ niɔ³³tɣ³³ a³³
sink-be.down.go CRS 1PL need with
ŋɔ²⁴ kʰɯ²¹ to³³ a³³ len²¹ tsʰaŋ⁵⁵-tsʰe⁵⁵ɣɯ²¹.
crowbar several CLF OM wheel pry-be.out.come
'The road is very muddy. It is all soaked and the car was stuck in the mud. We must pry the wheels out with several crowbars.'
路太泥了。被水泡软了。车都陷进去了。我们得拿几根撬棍把轮子撬出来。

We have to point out that, according to our fieldwork and sample of data, the use of *niɔ³³dɣ³³* 'need' is on the decline. There is a strong tendency for *niɔ³³* to entirely replace *niɔ³³dɣ³³*.

11.2.5 *tɕʰiɔ²¹* 'be necessary'

The auxiliary *tɕʰiɔ²¹* 'be necessary' is only used in negative contexts. Its negated form *pɣ³³ tɕʰiɔ²¹* is adopted to express lack of necessity, 'not necessary to do'. Examples (11.32) and (11.33) show that societal circumstances creating lack of necessity.

(11.32) pɣ³³ ɣã²¹ sa³³ tsʰʐ²¹ ta⁵⁵ sʐ²¹ ŋa⁵⁵
NEG have three foot two MOD child
pɣ³³ tɕʰiɔ²¹ mã²¹ pʰiɔ²⁴
NEG be.necessary buy ticket
'Children under 1.2 meters high don't need to buy a ticket.'
没有1米2高的孩子不用买票。

(11.33) kʰɪŋ⁵⁵koŋ⁵⁵ sʐ²¹ ɕɪŋ³³tɕʰi³³. **pɣ³³ tɕʰiɔ²¹**
today COP Sunday NEG be.necessary
kuɛ³³ kʷɔ³³ sɣ³³ o mɛ̃.
go learn book CRS PRT
'It's Sunday today. No need to go to school.'
今天是星期天。不用去上学。

Example (11.34) shows that the lack of necessity of 'closing the door' is speaker B's desire.

(11.34) A- ma²¹kʰa³³ niɔ³³ a³³ ta²¹-xɯ⁵⁵ pɣ³³ ta³³?
door need DCR close-up NEG close
'Shall I close the door'
门要不要关。

B- **pɣ³³ tɕʰiɔ²¹** la²¹!
NEG be.necessary PRT
'No, leave it open (LIT: not necessary).'
不用了。

In the example below, the lack of necessity of 'looking for you' is determined by the situation that 'you've arrived'.

(11.35) nɯ³³ la³³ ɣɯ²¹ ha⁵⁵ nɛ⁵⁵,
2SG all come COMPL PRT
ŋo³³ **pɣ³³ tɕʰiɔ²¹** kuɛ³³ ko²¹ nɯ³³ o mɛ̃.
1SG NEG be.necessary go look.for 2SG CRS PRT
'Now that you've arrived, I don't' need to look for you (in particular).'
你都来了,我就不用(专门)去找你了。

11.2.6 ti^{33} 'know'

Derived from the lexical form 'know clearly', the auxiliary ti^{33} is used to express participant-internal possibility, including mental ability and learned skill, as well as participant-external possibility. Verbs of knowing are attested as a lexical source for participant-internal possibility in many languages in the world (Bybee et al. 1994: 190, Kuteva et al. 2019: 249–250). In fact, the lexical use of ti^{33} 'know clearly' is much less frequent than its modal uses. Examples with ti^{33} taking NPs as its objects are not observed. In the example below, ti^{33} is used in the expression . . . $pγ^{33} ti^{33}$ 'who knows. . .', which is often used to emphasize 'not knowing', as shown in (11.36) and (11.37). The following examples show the lexical use of ti^{33} in Caijia. We treat ti^{33} as a lexical verb is on the basis of its meaning in these contexts. In both cases, even though ti^{33} does not take any nominal object it still denotes 'know'.

(11.36) tiu³³ la²¹ je³³ sı³³ lɔ²⁴ni³³ pγ³³ **ti³³** o.
know also 3SG COP who NEG know CRS
'I don't even know who he is.'
谁知道他是谁啊！

(11.37) tsʰɿ³³ tsɿ²¹ to³³ la³³ pγ³³ **ti³³**.
fear accomplish can even NEG know
'Who knows if it can be accomplished or not.'
谁知道能成不。

By contrast, when ti^{33} is used as a modal verb it denotes 'can'. First, ti^{33} 'know' is often used to express learned skills, which can be interpreted as **'know how to do'**. This modal use always involves animate participants as subjects and it is predictably followed by a second verb, such as xa^{33} 'speak, say'. Example (11.38a) illustrates that the participant je^{33} 'he' masters the Lolo language. When expressing the same situation of mastering a language, the verb $tiu^{33}u^{33}$ 'know' can also be used, taking a NP as its direct object, as shown in (11.38b). Therefore, in this case, $tiu^{33}u^{33}$ 'know' is clearly a lexical verb but not a modal verb.[14]

---

[14] In the Weining variety of Caijai, tiu^{33} can serve both as a lexical verb denoting 'know' and a modal verb denoting 'can'.

(11.38) a. je³³ **ti³³** xa³³ mia²¹ ŋoŋ³³.
3SG know say Lolo speech
'He can speak Lolo.'
他会说彝语。

b. je³³ **tiu³³u³³** mia²¹ ŋoŋ³³.
3SG know Lolo speech
'He can speak Lolo.'
他会彝语。

In example (11.39), the human participant can play a musical instrument. The sentence can be interpreted as 'my uncle knows how to play the Chinese spike fiddle'.

(11.39) ŋo²⁴ la²¹to⁵⁵ u²¹tsʰo²⁴-sui⁵⁵ ŋuɛ²¹ ko²¹ko²⁴ mɔ²⁴-sui⁵⁵
1PL old person-PL my.family uncle that-PL
a **ti²¹** kʰɪŋ⁵⁵ la²¹toŋ²¹toŋ²⁴.
INTJ know pull Chinese.spike.fiddle
'Our elders, such as my uncle, can play the Chinese spike fiddle.'
我们家老人们，我舅舅那些啊，会拉二胡。
(*Learning to play the Chinese spike fiddle*, texts)

In (11.40), the modal verb *ti³³* 'know' is used to express the ability of flying for birds. Flying may be regarded as an intrinsic ability of birds. However, no birds are born with this ability. Rather, they need to practice it. Similarly, 'birds can fly' can be understood as 'birds know how to fly'.

(11.40) tsɿ²¹tsɿ²⁴ **ti³³** pɣ²¹.
bird know fly
'Birds can fly.'
鸟会飞。

Second, *ti³³* 'know' can express possibilities related to participants' inner properties. If the lexical meaning of 'know' persists when *ti³³* is used to express mental abilities and learned skills, this meaning is entirely bleached when it is used to express possibilities related to inner properties. Examples (11.41)-(11.45) all involve inner properties of different types of participants, both animate and inanimate. Unlike the examples of learned skills illustrated above, neither of them can be interpreted as 'know how to do'. In (11.41), fatigue and death belong to the law of nature.

(11.41) lɔ²⁴ni³³ ti³³ kʰui²¹, hu³³ni³³ la²¹ **ti²¹** niaŋ⁵⁵.
who know be.tired all.people all know die
'Anyone can be tired; all people can die.'
谁都会累；所有人都会死。

The example below shows the possibility of snakes shedding their skin within their life cycle.

(11.42) la²¹fe⁵⁵ **ti²¹** tʰɣ⁵⁵ po²¹.
snake can slough skin
'Snakes can slough skin.'
蛇会蜕皮。

Examples (11.41) and (11.42) present animate participants, while examples (11.43) and (11.44) contain two sentences with inanimate participants. Apparently, no inanimate entities can master mental abilities. In (11.43), the possibilities for stones sinking and leaves floating in water are determined by the inner properties of stones and leaves, i.e. weight, as well as the buoyancy of water.

(11.43) tsa³³to²¹ **ti³³** tseŋ²¹ tɯ²¹ sɿ⁵⁵tie⁵⁵,
stone know sink to water.bottom
mo²¹se⁵⁵ **ti³³** po³³ tɯ²¹ sɿ⁵⁵pi²¹ tɣ³³.
leaf know float at water.surface upside
'Stones can sink to the bottom; leaves can float on water.'
石头会沉到水底，叶子会浮在水面。

The example below illustrates the negated form of *ti³³* 'know', denoting that when a corpse does not decay it may become mummified.

(11.44) je³³ mɔ²¹ tsʰɣ³³pa³³ pɣ³³ **ti³³** tsʰɿ²¹
3SG that corpse NEG know rot
tɯ⁵⁵ pi⁵⁵ ka³³sɿ³³ o.
then become dried.corpse CRS
'If his corpse can't decay, his body will become mummified.'
他那尸体不会烂（的话）就变干尸了。

Third, the modal verb *ti³³* 'know' extends to participant-external and epistemic possibilities. Examples (11.45a)-(11.48) illustrate participant-external possibilities which are all enabled by external states of affairs. Each example actually involves two events, with one of them being the enabling condition for the other.

Compare (11.45a) with (11.45b), the latter of which is a case of learned ability. In both examples, the modal verb *ti³³* 'know' takes the verb *ɣa²¹* 'walk' as its complement. It can be observed that the same clause *tɯ³³ ti³³ ɣa²¹ o* '(he) then can walk' is used to express different meanings. In (11.45a), the participant *je³³* 'he/she' can find his or her way under the condition that 'you show him the direction', while in (11.45b), it denotes that the participant has mastered the ability to walk.

(11.45) a. EVENT1[nɯ²¹   ta⁵⁵   je³³   tsɿ²¹   hɔ⁵⁵   mi⁵⁵],
              2SG   for   3SG   show   road   a.little
       EVENT2[je³³   **tɯ³³**   **ti³³**   **ɣa²¹**   o].
              3SG   then   know   walk   CRS
       'You show him the direction, and then he can find the way.'
       你给他指下路，他就会走了.

   b. je³³   pɣ³³-tɣ³³   ma³³   ji³³   neŋ²¹   tʰɔ²⁴
      3SG   NEG-PFV   be.full   one   year   moment
      [**tɯ³³**   **ti³³**   **ɣa²¹**   o].
       then   know   walk   CRS
      'He could even walk when he wasn't yet one.'
      他不满一岁的时候就会走了。

In (11.46), the possibility of getting lost is a result of the fact that the forest is very thick.

(11.46) ɔ²¹   sɔ⁵⁵ɣa²¹   saŋ²¹   xiŋ⁵⁵,   **ti³³**   ɣa²¹-tsʰɣ̍⁵⁵   hɔ⁵⁵   se.
        this   forest   be.deep   very   know   walk-be.wrong   road   AFF.PRT
        'This is a deep forest and one can get lost.'
        这树林很深，会走错路。

Two examples with negated *ti³³* 'know' are given below denoting 'impossibility'. Both of the two impossible situations are enabled by external conditions or circumstances. In (11.47), the impossibility of the town collapsing due to mudslides caused by heavy rains is guaranteed by the area's extensive forests.

(11.47) tsʰɛ²¹sɿ³³   mɔ²¹   ɕiŋ⁵⁵fa²¹tsʰaŋ²⁴   hu⁵⁵kʰa³³
        only   that   Xingfa_PLACENAME   everywhere
        la²¹   sɿ²¹   sɔ⁵⁵ɣa²¹   pɣ³³   **ti²¹**   tʰoŋ²¹.
        all   COP   forest   NEG   know   collapse
        'It is only in Xingfa that forests are everywhere. (Therefore, Xingfa) can't be washed away (in heavy rain).'
        只有那兴发，到处都是森林，不会塌。

In (11.48) immunity from chicken pox is a result of catching it, but has nothing to do with an inner property of the participant.

(11.48) ŋo²¹   tsʰe⁵⁵   ja²¹to²¹   ja²¹.
        1SG   come.out.(in a rash) chicken.pox   EXP
        tsʰe⁵⁵ ha⁵⁵   u³³   tɯ³³   **pɣ³³** **ti²¹**   tsʰe⁵⁵   o.
        vent   COMPL   back   then   NEG   know   vent   CRS
        'I've had chicken pox. After having had it, I can't have it (again).'
        我出过水痘。出过以后就不会出了。

Apart from participant-external possibility, the modal verb *ti³³* 'know' can also be observed in the expression of epistemic possibility, which is irrelevant to the arguments in the clause but related to the speaker's knowledge or presumptions. Examples (11.49)-(11.51) are possibilities based on each of the speakers' own life experiences or knowledge. Example (11.49) describes the possibility that one's mouth will burn and become numb after eating peppery milk-cap mushrooms. This may be either the speaker's own experience or acquired knowledge from others' experience.

(11.49) ɣã²¹.   ji²¹   tsoŋ⁵⁵   sɿ³³   tsa³³sɯ²¹   saŋ⁵⁵.
        there.be   one   type   COP   lime   mushroom
        zɣ²¹   pɣ³³   tɣ³³   se²¹.   zɣ²¹   ha⁵⁵
        eat   NEG   can   AFF.PRT eat   COMPL
        pi²¹   **ti²¹**   pe⁵⁵   ti³³   pi²¹.
        mouth know   burn   know   be.numb
        'There's a kind called 'lime mushroom' (peppery milk-cap mushroom). (They) aren't edible. After eating some, the mouth may burn and feel numb.'
        有一种是石灰菌。吃不得。吃了以后嘴会辣会麻。

Having lived in Xingfa for his whole, the speaker makes the following assertion in (11.50), based on his own experience.

(11.50) ŋo²⁴   ɕiŋ⁵⁵fa²¹   sɿ³³   kʰua²¹   sɿ⁵⁵lɛ²¹   kʷɔ²¹.   sɿ⁵⁵   la²¹
        1PL   Xingfa_PLACENAME   COP   good   place   CLF   water   also
        pɣ²¹   ti²¹   ã⁵⁵,   ka³³   la³³   ka³³-pɣ²¹-tɣ³³   je³³.
        NEG   know   flood   dry   also   be.dry-NEG-obtain   3SG
        'Our Xingfa is a blessed place. It can neither be flooded nor be struck by droughts.'
        我们兴发是个好地方。水也不会淹，旱也旱不到。

11.2 Modal auxiliaries [AUX VP]

Even though the saying 'playing with fire can make children wet the bed' lacks legs, it is what parents often say to their children across generations in order to prevent them from playing with fire. In other words, this possibility is based on the speaker's acquired knowledge.

(11.51) ŋo³³   ɕie²¹   tʰɔ⁵⁵   ŋo³³   ʑi²¹   koŋ⁵⁵koŋ⁵⁵
          1SG   small   moment   1SG   mother   every.day
          ta⁵⁵   ŋo²¹   xa²¹,   sɔ²¹kʷɔ⁵⁵ fɛ³³   **ti³³**
          with   1SG   say   play   fire   know
          sɿ³³   niɔ²¹   pie⁵⁵   tʰa⁵⁵   tʏ³³   sɿ²¹.
          pee   urine   to   bed   upside   AFF
          'When I was young, my mother always told me that, after playing with fire (children) can wet the bed.'
          我小时候我妈天天跟我说，玩火会尿床。

By contrast, the three examples below involve the speakers' assumption and presumption. The speaker of example (11.52) cannot believe that the subject, a person who was skilled at swimming, has drowned, and assumes that this drowned person was held under by a water ghost. The expression *pʏ³³ tsʰɿ³³ka³³ sɿ²¹* 'something dirty' is metaphorically used to refer to ghosts.

(11.52) ɣã²¹   ji²¹   koŋ⁵⁵   je³³   kuɛ²¹   po²¹sɿ⁵⁵   sɿ³³.
          there.be   one   day   3SG   go   swim   PRT
          ti³³   poŋ²¹-tʏ³³   pʏ³³   tsʰɿ³³ka³³   sɿ²¹.   tɯ³³
          know   meet-obtain   NEG   be.clean   NMLZ   then
          a³³   je²¹   kʰɪŋ⁵⁵-tɕie²¹   sɿ⁵⁵   kuɛ²¹   o.
          OM   3SG   pull-go.down   water   go   CRS
          'There was one day. He went to swim. (He) might have run into some dirty stuff. It pulled him down to the bottom.'
          有一天，他去游泳。可能碰到了不干净的东西。把他拉下去了。

In (11.53), the speaker makes the assumption that his father should have been on his way back home when checking the time.

(11.53) ɔ²¹kɯ²⁴   je³³   **ti³³**   tɕiu²¹   hɔ⁵⁵   mo³³   ɣɯ²¹   ɔ   pa.
          this.moment 3SG   know   arrive   road   inside   come   PRT   PRT
          'He may be probably on his way back now.'
          现在他该在路上了吧。

In the example below, it is by judging the subject's behaviors that the speaker is able to assert a possible outcome.

(11.54) (je³³) xa²¹ ua²⁴ xa²¹ ma²⁴ lɛ⁵⁵. ŋoŋ²¹ tie⁵⁵ xɪŋ⁵⁵
3SG say here say there CONT speech be.many very
kuɛ²¹, **ti²¹** ta⁵⁵ ni²¹ kʰɪŋ⁵⁵ pi²¹ pi²⁴ se²¹.
go know with 3 pull mouth nose AFF.PRT
'He gossips and talks a lot. It's certain that (he) may have spats with people.'
他这儿说那儿说地。话多得很，会跟人起口角的。

In sum, compared with the frequency of other modal strategies or forms and particles, auxiliary verbs are the most common way to code modality in Caijia. Six modal auxiliary verbs have been presented in this section: *kʰã⁵⁵* 'be willing to', *ɕiaŋ⁵⁵* 'want', *niɔ³³* 'want', *tɕʰiɔ²¹* 'be necessary', *niɔ³³-dʑ³³* 'want-need', and *ti³³* 'know'. The first five are mainly used to denote volition, necessity, or desire, while the last one, *ti³³* 'know', is used to denote ability and possibility. Their modal uses are, to a certain extent, related with their lexical meanings. All of them are polysemous, and context plays an important role in interpreting them correctly.

11.3 Lexical epistemic possibility: *tsʰʅ³³* 'fear' and *dzɔ³³* 'resemble'

Caijia also adopts a lexical strategy to code epistemic possibility. Two verbs are observed: *tsʰʅ³³* 'fear, be afraid, worry' and *dzɔ³³* 'resemble'. They are both used to denote speakers' presumptions, based on their own knowledge, experience, and judgement. Detailed descriptions are given below.

11.3.1 *tsʰʅ³³* 'fear'

When *tsʰʅ³³* denotes 'fear, be afraid, worry', it can serve either as an intransitive verb or a transitive verb taking an NP or a complement clause as its object, which can be schematized as [(NP) tsʰʅ³³] or [(NP) tsʰʅ³³ NP/[(NP) VP]]. Example (11.55) demonstrates the verb *tsʰʅ³³* denoting 'fear, be afraid, worry'. The one in (11.55i) serves as an intransitive verb expressing 'be scared'; while the one in (11.55ii) is the main verb with a complement clause as its object denoting 'be afraid, worry'.

11.3 Lexical epistemic possibility: *tsʰɿ³³* 'fear' and *dzɔ³³* 'resemble' — 377

(11.55) i) "ε⁵⁵ja²¹   jɔ²¹   ja²⁴   ta³³   piɔ³³   ŋo³³   **tsʰɿ²¹**   xıŋ⁵⁵
            INTJ   Hmong   woman   carry   hoe   1SG   fear   very
            a…" […] "tsγ̍³³   tɯ²¹   nɯ²¹   kγ̍⁵⁵   nε⁵⁵,
                     PRT   hide   to   2SG   foot   PRT
      ii)   **tsʰɿ⁵⁵**   ŋo²¹   tsʰɿ²¹-kuε²¹   mɔ²¹   kɯ²⁴
            fear   1SG   rot-go   that   moment
            tsʰɔ²¹-tγ̍³³   nɯ³³   e!"
            stink-obtain   2SG   PRT

"'Alas, the old Hmong woman is coming with her hoe and I'm very afraid…" (said the grass). "If I hide at your foot (= the foot of the corn plant), I'm afraid that when I rot away and stink, you'll smell it." (said the grass to the corn)'
"哎呀！苗婆扛锄头来了我怕得很……"（小草说）。
(*The grass and the corn*, texts)

Example (11.56) illustrates the transitive use with a nominal object, denoting 'be scared of'.

(11.56) je³³   **tsʰɿ²¹**   sγ̍⁵⁵.
        3SG   fear   mouse
        'He's scared of mice.'
        他害怕老鼠。

When expressing epistemic possibility, *tsʰɿ³³* is used impersonally in the form of [tsʰɿ³³ [(NP) VP]] 'it is probable that…', always occupying the position of matrix verb. Context aside, there is always a measure of ambiguity as to whether *tsʰɿ³³* either denotes the modal meaning 'it is probable that…' or denotes the meaning 'fear, be afraid, worry' always exists. This is the major reason the modal *tsʰɿ³³* is still treated as a verb. See the example below in (11.57). An important piece of information for determining whether or not this example is ambiguous is that Caijia is a language with extensive use of pro-drop. Therefore, this sentence can either be analyzed as an impersonal construction or a construction with the subject omitted. When *tsʰɿ³³* denotes 'be afraid, worry', the action of its clausal object is usually opposite to the wishes of the subject or the speaker or against his or her expectations. Therefore, if the clausal object 'the priest won't come' is against the speaker's expectation, *tsʰɿ³³* tends to be interpreted as 'be afraid, worry'. This use of *tsʰɿ³³* 'fear, be afraid' is similar to the counterpart morpheme, *kǒngpà* 'fear, be afraid, probably', in Standard Mandarin, which will be discussed further below.

(11.57) **tsʰɿ³³** [mɔ²¹ xɯ³³pa³³ pɣ³³ ɣɯ²¹ o].
fear that Taoism.priest NEG come CRS
'The priest probably won't come.'
'(I)'m afraid the priest won't come.'
那道士恐怕不来了。
(我) 恐怕那道士不来了。

By contrast, once there is an overt subject *tsʰɿ³³* is always interpreted as 'be afraid, worry', as shown below. Compare (11.57) with (11.58).

(11.58) ŋuɛ²¹ pa⁵⁵ **tsʰɿ³³** mɔ²¹ xɯ³³pa³³ pɣ³³ ɣɯ²¹ o.
my.family father fear that Taoism.priest NEG come PRT
'My father is worrying that the priest won't come.'
我爸担心那个道士不来了。

In the following two examples, the modal meaning of *tsʰɿ³³*, i.e. 'it is possible that. . .' is foregrounded. They can be used to answer the questions 'what is he?' and 'where is the key?', respectively.

(11.59) A- je³³ sɿ²¹ tɕie⁵⁵ sɿ²¹mɔ⁵⁵ sɿ²¹?
3SG COP do what NMLZ
'What is he?'
他是做什么的?

B- **tsʰɿ³³** mɔ²¹ u²¹tsʰo²⁴ ni³³ sɿ³³ kʷɔ³³sɣ³³pa³³ ɔ pa.
fear that person CLF COP teacher PRT PRT
'That person is probably a teacher.'
那个人可能是个老师吧。

(11.60) A- sɔ⁵⁵nioŋ³³ tɯ²¹ la²⁴?
key be.at where
'Where's the key?'
钥匙在哪?

B- **tsʰɿ⁵⁵** sɔ⁵⁵nioŋ³³ tɯ²¹ kʰa²⁴ mo³³ sɿ²¹.
fear key be.at drawer inside CONT
'The key is probably in the drawer.'
钥匙可能在抽屉里。

11.3 Lexical epistemic possibility: *tsʰɿ³³* 'fear' and *dzɔ³³* 'resemble' — **379**

Admittedly, in certain contexts such as those of (11.59B) and (11.60B), *tsʰɿ³³* can still be interpreted as its source meaning 'fear, be afraid, worry', as shown in (11.61B). Compare it with (11.59B).

(11.61) A- je³³   tsʰɿ³³   sɿ²¹mɔ⁵⁵   sɿ²¹?
           3SG   fear   what   CONT
           'What's he worrying about?'
           他在怕什么？

      B- (je³³)   **tsʰɿ³³**   mɔ²¹   u²¹tsʰo²⁴   ni³³
           3SG   fear   that   person   CLF
           sɿ³³   kʷɔ³³sɣ³³pa³³   ɔ   pa.
           COP   teacher   PRT   PRT
           '(He's) probably worrying that that person is a teacher.'
           (他) 可能在担心那个人是个老师吧。

Two more examples with the meaning of 'fear, be afraid, worry' backgrounded are given below. In (11.62), the speaker's expectation is that his goal can be achieved. The clausal object of the bolded *tsʰɿ³³*, *tsɿ²¹ to³³* 'can achieve' placed in brackets, is expected. The meaning 'fear, be afraid, worry' is not compatible with this expectation. Instead, *tsʰɿ³³* in this sentence can only denote 'it is possible that. . .', i.e. the speaker's presumption of the possibility. Note that the negated VP *pɣ³³ ti²¹* is used as a tag, increasing the uncertainty of the speaker's assumption.

(11.62) tiu³³   la²¹   tsɿ²¹   pɣ³³   tsɿ²¹   xa²¹tsɛ³³   pɣ³³   tiu³³u³³.
         know   also   achieve   NEG   achieve   still   NEG   know
         tsʰɿ³³   [tsɿ²¹   to³³]   la³³   pɣ³³   ti²¹   o.
         fear   achieve   can   all   NEG   know   CRS
         '(I) still don't know whether this will work out or not. It probably can, (but) who knows.'
         谁知道能不能成。应该能成吧，也说不准。

By witnessing the joy of the participant *je³³* 'she', the speaker presumes that it might be the case that the girl has been admitted to the university and so feels happy for her. This is not a context in which the speaker has any anxiety. On the contrary, the speaker has simply made an inference.

(11.63) je²¹   tɕʰi³³kʰa³³   lɯ³³   mɔ³³sๅ³³,   **tsʰๅ³³**   je²¹
         3SG   be.happy   VCOMP   very   fear   3SG
         kʰɔ²¹-tγ̞³³   o.   ŋo³³   la²¹
         take.exam-hit.(the.target)   CRS   1SG   also
         tɕʰi³³kʰa²¹-xɯ⁵⁵ɣɯ²¹   o.
         be.happy-INC   CRS
         'She is very happy as she has probably been admitted (to the university).
         It has also cheered me up.'
         她高兴得不行，应该是考上了。我也高兴起来了。

The verb 'fear, be afraid' is a rarely reported source for an epistemic marker in the languages of the world. However, it is attested at least in two Sinitic languages: Standard Mandarin and Cantonese (Yap et al. 2012). Standard Mandarin uses *kǒngpà* 恐怕 [kʰoŋ²¹⁴pʰa⁵¹] 'fear, be afraid, worry' to code epistemic possibility, while Cantonese uses *taipaa* 睇怕 'watch-fear'. See the Standard Mandarin example below. Note that *kǒngpà* in Standard Mandarin is no longer used as the lexical verb 'fear'. The sentence in (11.64) does not denote that the participant *tā* 'he' is afraid of coming, i.e. *tā* 'he' is not the agent of *kǒngpà*. It is the speaker who worries or assumes that the participant 'he' is not coming and *kǒngpà* thus shows the speaker's stance.

(11.64) 他恐怕不来。
         tā   **kǒngpà**   bù   lái.
         3SG   probably   NEG   come
         'He probably won't come.'

Yap et al. (2012) treat *kǒngpà* in Standard Mandarin as an adverbial, but *tsʰๅ³³* 'fear, be afraid, worry' in Caijia is a different case. First, we have shown that ambiguity always exists for *tsʰๅ³³*. Second, due to the fact that it denotes 'it is possible that. . .', *tsʰๅ³³* can never appear in the same position as *kǒngpà* does in (11.64) and it must precede a full clause, i.e. in the position of the matrix verb. If it is in the position of *kǒngpà*, it can only denote 'fear, be afraid, worry'. These properties mean that *tsʰๅ³³* 'fear, be afraid, worry' in Caijia is in the process of grammaticalization. The new meaning, 'it is possible that. . .', has already been reanalyzed from its source meaning 'fear, be afraid, worry'. However, its syntactic behavior, i.e. always occupying the position of matrix verb, suggests that a change of category has not yet taken place. Note that the modal use of *tsʰๅ³³* still differs from its source use, since it only forms impersonal constructions.

11.3.2 *dzɔ³³* 'resemble'

Apart from the verb *tsʰɿ³³* 'fear, be afraid, worry', the verb *dzɔ³³* 'resemble' is also used to express epistemic possibility. Denoting 'resemble', *dzɔ³³* only takes the phrase [NP + sɿ²¹] as its object with the morpheme *sɿ²¹* denoting 'manner, way'. The verb phrase *dzɔ³³* NP *sɿ²¹* can be interpreted as 'resemble the manner of NP'. It is also observed that the borrowed word *jaŋ²⁴* 'manner', i.e. *jaŋ²¹³* 样 'manner' in the local dialect of Southwestern Mandarin, is used after *sɿ²¹*, *dzɔ³³* NP *sɿ²¹ jaŋ²⁴*, expressing exactly the same meaning. Note that the absence of *jaŋ²⁴* 'manner' is more common in our sample of data. See the following example for the source meaning of *dzɔ³³*. See also Chapter 9 §9.3.2.2 for more examples and a description of *dzɔ³³*.

(11.65) mɔ²¹   nioŋ²⁴   ni³³   [**tsɔ³³**   [je²¹   ʑi⁵⁵   **sɿ²¹**   (**jaŋ²⁴**)]].
        that   girl   CLF   resemble   3SG   mother   way   way
        'The girl looks like her mother'
        那个女孩儿像她妈。

The verb *dzɔ³³* 'resemble' is used to express epistemic possibility via the fossilized construction [dzɔ³³ mɔ²¹ . . . sɿ²¹ (jaŋ²⁴)] 'seem in the way of . . ./it seems that. . .' in which the distal demonstrative *mɔ²¹* 'that' cannot be replaced by the proximal demonstrative *ɔ²¹* 'this'. Two configurations are observed:

i. Common: (NP) dzɔ³³ mɔ²¹ VP sɿ²¹ (jaŋ²⁴)
ii. Impersonal: dzɔ³³ mɔ²¹ (NP) VP sɿ²¹ (jaŋ²⁴)

In a common configuration, *dzɔ³³* 'resemble, seem' occupies the common position of a verb, while, in an impersonal configuration, *dzɔ³³* occupies the position of the matrix verb. These two configurations are syntactically different but they do not make a semantic contrast when expressing epistemic possibility. Examples for both the common and impersonal configurations are given below.

Examples (11.66a) and (11.67A) illustrate the common configuration (i). Both of them can be transformed into the impersonal configuration (ii) formed by *dzɔ³³* 'resemble', as shown in (11.66b). In (11.66), the inference that 'you don't seem to like him very much' can be made by the speaker on the basis of verbal and non-verbal behavior of the participant *nɯ³³* 'you'.

(11.66) **[NP dzɔ³³ mɔ²¹ VP sɿ²¹]**
    a. nɯ³³   **tsɔ³³**   mɔ²¹   pɣ²¹   taŋ²⁴   tɕʰi³³kʰa³³   je³³   **sɿ²¹**.
        2SG   resemble   that   NEG   so   like   3SG   way
        'You don't seem to like him very much.'
        你好像不太喜欢他。

[dzɔ³³ mɔ²¹ NP VP sɿ²¹]
b. **tsɔ³³** mɔ²¹ nɯ³³ pɣ²¹ taŋ²⁴ tɕʰi³³kʰa³³ je³³ **sɿ²¹**.
resemble that 2SG NEG so like 3SG way
'It seems that you don't like him very much.'
好像你不太喜欢他。

In (11.67), looking at the level of the liquor, the speaker of speech turn A compares the current quantity with what he recalls and makes the deduction that 'the liquor has probably been consumed'.

(11.67) **[NP dzɔ³³ mɔ²¹ VP sɿ²¹ jaŋ²⁴]**
A- ɔ²¹ tso⁵⁵ **tsɔ²¹** mɔ²¹ ɣã²¹mi⁵⁵
this liquor resemble that a.little
sɔ⁵⁵ **sɿ²¹ jaŋ²⁴** mẽ.
be.little way way PRT
'It seems that the liquor has been consumed.'
这酒好像有点少。

B- tɣ³³ ŋo³³ ã³³-kua²¹ mi⁵⁵ o.
PASS 1SG drink-pass a.little CRS
'(I')ve drunk some.'
让我喝了一点。

The following two examples show the impersonal configuration (ii). According to what is remembered about the elder brother of the Wang family, the speaker of speech turn B in (11.68) makes an assumption.

(11.68) A- mɔ²¹ sɿ²¹ sɿ⁵⁵pie²¹ hɛ⁵⁵
that COP Wang_NAME family
la²¹tso⁵⁵ pɣ³³ sɿ³³?
big.brother NEG COP
'Is that the elder brother of the Wang family?'
那是不是王家大哥?

[dzɔ³³ mɔ²¹ VP sɿ²¹ (jaŋ²⁴)]
B- tɯ³³ sɿ³³ ɔ pa. ɣã²¹mi⁵⁵ taŋ²¹.
indeed COP PRT PRT a.little be.similar
tsɔ³³ mɔ²¹ sɿ³³ je³³ **sɿ²¹** (**jaŋ²⁴**).
resemble that COP 3SG way way
'That probably is. (That person) looks a little like (him). It seems to be him.'
就是吧。有点像。好像是他。

The example below demonstrates how the speaker makes a judgement about the weather on seeing the clouds in the sky.

(11.69) tɪŋ⁵⁵ pʰɣ²¹-xɯ⁵⁵ o. **tsɔ³³** mɔ²¹ niɔ³³ ɣɯ²¹ zı⁵⁵ **sı²¹**.
cloud cover-INC CRS resemble that PROSP come rain way
'There are clouds now. It looks like it's going to rain.'
云铺起来了。好像要下雨。

See also (11.66b) above for another impersonal example.

11.4 Post-VP 'can' modals

Two post-VP modal elements are observed to code different types of possibilities in Caijia: *do³³* and *tɣ³³*, both of which can be interpreted as 'can' in English. They are labelled as 'post-VP' modals because they follow the object when there is one in a sentence, which can be schematized as [V (O) do³³/tɣ³³]. The modal element *do³³* is probably derived from its source form 'achieve, to', while *tɣ³³* is derived from its lexical form 'obtain, acquire', which is a common source for modal words in East and Southeast Asian languages (Enfield 2003).

In a nutshell, *do³³* can be used to express one's mental and physical abilities, i.e. it is dynamic, whereas *tɣ³³* can be used to denote deontic permission and possibility. The contrast between deontic and dynamic for these two modals is clear-cut. It should be mentioned that *do³³* is used along with the preverbal *tɣ³³* in a special structure to express ability and possibility for controllable events in the form of [tɣ³³ VP do³³]. Both *do³³* and *tɣ⁵⁵* are extended to non-deontic and epistemic possibilities. In such cases, both overlap and contrast for these two elements are observed in different contexts within the same type of modal category of possibility. In brief, in a non-deontic context, when *do³³* is used it is often related to a participant's inner or intrinsic capacity, while when *tɣ³³* is used a participant's inner or intrinsic capacity is usually not involved. Detailed discussions will be provided in the following sections. See Table 11.4 for a summary of the semantic nuances of *do³³* and *tɣ³³*.

Table 11.4: Post-VP 'can' modals in Caijia.

do³³	'achieve'	[VP do³³]	ABILITY, POSSIBILITY
		[tɣ³³ VP do³³]	ABILITY, POSSIBILITY
tɣ³³	'obtain'	[VP tɣ³³]	WEAK NECESSITY, PERMISSION, POSSIBILITY

As for their syntactic behaviors, despite their special post-verbal position, both *do³³* and *tɣ³³* can be negated, [VP po³³ do³³] and [VP pɣ³³ tɣ³³], which is one of the defining features for verbs. The negater *po³³* is probably a variant of the general negator *pɣ³³* 'not' and it only collocates with the modal *do³³* (see also Chapter 12). This means that these two modal elements are not highly grammaticalized, but they do form a fixed modal structure. When a sentence is formed with *do³³* or *tɣ³³*, the sentence final particle *mo³³* is commonly used to form a polar question, while [V NEG V] is the common strategy to negate an irrealis sentence without *do³³* or *tɣ³³*. Examples can be found in the following descriptions.

However, it is difficult to find any lexical use of the modal *do³³* in Caijia. We can only make deductions for tracing its lexical source. The following two examples show the prepositional use of *do³³* denoting 'to'. Note that this use of *do³³* is not productive at all and is only used in a very limited number of fossilized expressions, such as *do³³ to²¹* 'to the end (LIT: to head)' in (11.70b) and (11.71). In most of our data, it is *dʑiu⁵⁵* (< 'arrive') that is used to denote the equivalent meaning of *do³³* 'to'. For example, *dʑiu⁵⁵* can also be used in (11.70a). By analogy, we can assume that the lexical meaning of *do³³* 'to' is probably related to the meaning 'achieve, arrive'.

(11.70) a. ji²¹ koŋ⁵⁵ **do³³/dʑiu⁵⁵** mi²¹
　　　　　　 one day   to   dark
　　　　　　 'all day (LIT: one day to night)'
　　　　　　 一天到晚

　　　　　b. ji³³ neŋ²¹ **do³³** to²¹
　　　　　　 one year   to   end
　　　　　　 'all year (LIT: one year to end)'
　　　　　　 一年到头

(11.71) ɔ³³   ŋoŋ³³ xa²¹ **to³³** to²¹ kuɛ³³ sɿ³³,
　　　　　 this speech say to   end   go   PRT
　　　　　 pe⁵⁵ pɣ³³ yɯ²¹ sɿ²¹ le³³.
　　　　　 return NEG come AFF PRT
　　　　　 'Words that are so extreme, can't be taken back.'
　　　　　 这话说到头，回不来了。

By contrast, *tɣ³³* is still a lexical verb in Caijia, denoting 'obtain, acquire'.

(11.72) ŋo³³ **tɣ³³** soŋ²¹ o.
　　　　　 1SG   obtain illness CRS
　　　　　 'I got sick.'
　　　　　 我得病了。

In the following sections, the modal uses of both *do³³* (including the construction [tʏ³³ VP do³³]) and *tʏ³³* will be discussed in detail.

11.4.1 *do³³* 'can' [VP do³³] and *tʏ³³* ... *do³³* 'can' [tʏ³³ VP do³³]

Both the modal *do³³* and the construction [tʏ³³ VP do³³] are often used to express a certain possibility that a participant can realize an action or enter into a state, interpretations that are usually determined by the participant's inner abilities, capacity, or intrinsic properties. This means that there must be a participant, overt or covert, that can initiate an action or a state, encoded by *do³³* or [tʏ³³ VP do³³]. The construction [tʏ³³ VP do³³] is exclusively used to code possibilities of controllable events, whereas the modal *do³³* covers a wider range. It can be observed in our data and from our fieldwork that the use of [tʏ³³ VP do³³] is declining, with the modal *do³³* replacing its function. In other words, the modal construction [tʏ³³ VP do³³] can always be reduced to [VP do³³]. Let us examine these two modal elements respectively.

11.4.1.1 *do³³* 'can' [VP do³³]
Examples (11.73) and (11.74) are two cases of mental ability expressed by *do³³*: ability to recognize one's voice in (11.73) and ability to memorize things well and fast in (11.74).

(11.73) xa³³ ŋoŋ³³ sɿ²¹ sɿ³³ ŋo³³ tsa²¹tsa²⁴.
say speech NMLZ COP 1SG uncle
je³³ tshɿ²¹po⁵⁵ ŋo²¹ thi⁵⁵-tshe⁵⁵ɣɯ²¹ **to³³**.
3SG sound 1SG listen-be.out.come can
'The person who's speaking is my uncle. I can recognize his voice.'
说话的是我叔叔。他的声音我能听出来。

(11.74) mɔ²¹ u²¹tsho²⁴ ni³³ neŋ²¹saŋ³³ khua²¹ xɪŋ⁵⁵.
that person CLF memory good very
tsaŋ²¹ ji³³ ni³³tsɿ³³ je³³ tɯ³³ neŋ²¹-tʏ³³.
look one eye 3SG then remember-obtain
tie²¹sɔ⁵⁵ ni²⁴ je³³ la³³
how.many time 3SG even

nen²¹-tɣ³³　　　　　　**to³³**.
remember-obtain　　　　can

'That person has a very good memory. He can remember things from a glance and can remember them for a long time.'

那个人记性好得很。看一眼他就记住了。多长时间他都能记住。

One more example of mental ability is given below. Unlike the two examples above, example (11.75) is a case of non-deontic possibility, since having a rest is a prerequisite for the brain to work again.

(11.75)　sɯ⁵⁵　mi⁵⁵　nɔ²¹ka⁵⁵　tsʰɛ²¹　ʈɪŋ⁵⁵　**to³³**.
　　　　 rest　a.little　brain　only.then　spin　can

'Only after having a rest can my brain work (again).'

休息一下脑子才能转。

The following three examples concern physical abilities. Examples (11.76) and (11.77) have overt agent-participants. Example (11.77) is a case with *to³³* following the object *sa³³ la²¹ u³³* 'three big bowls (of rice)'.

(11.76)　ŋo³³　tɔ²¹　ni²⁴　tɯ³³　a³³　je²¹　kʰɪŋ⁵⁵-tsʰe⁵⁵ɣɯ²¹　**to³³**.
　　　　 1SG　alone　3　then　OM　3SG　pull-be.out.come　can

'I can pull it out all by myself.'

我一个人就能把它拔出来。

(11.77)　(je³³)　ji³³　ti²¹　zɣ²¹　sa³³　la²¹　u³³　**to³³**.
　　　　 3SG　one　CLF　eat　three　big　bowl　can

'(He) can eat three big bowls (of rice) in one go.'

（他）一顿能吃三大碗。

Whereas, example (11.78) is a negated context with a covert agent-participant. The NP *ɣa³³ loŋ³³ mo³³ kuɛ³³ sɿ²¹ tsʰɛ³³* 'the cars to the town' in the sentence-initial position is actually the topicalized object of the verb *kʰɯ³³* 'drive'. The agent-participant of this sentence is absent. This is an example of non-deontic possibility, but it is still related to the inferred participant's ability. It is the external circumstance of thick fog that prevents one's ability to drive.

(11.78) pʰɔ³³moŋ²⁴ la²¹ xɪŋ⁵⁵. ti²¹mĩ²¹ sɿ²¹ ɔ⁵⁵ la²¹
fog   be.big very   opposite MOD house even
tsaŋ²¹ pɤ²¹ kɪŋ²¹ o. ɣa³³ loŋ³³ mo³³ kuɛ³³
look   NEG see   CRS walk city inside go
sɿ²¹ tsʰɛ³³ la²¹ kʰɯ³³ kuɛ²¹ po³³ **to³³** o.
MOD car   even drive go   NEG can   CRS
'The fog is so thick. The houses across the street can't be seen. People can't drive to the city either.'
雾大得很。对面的房子也看不见。去城里的车也开不过去。

Examples (11.79) and (11.80) involve two inanimate participants with the notion of possibility related to the participant's capacity or intrinsic properties. In (11.79), the fact that three persons can sleep on the bed is determined by the capacity or the size of the bed, the subject noun. Example (11.79) contains a special type of construction used to express the capacity of an entity within which a normally intransitive verb is used to denote 'accommodate, provide space for'. This construction reflects how an object exists or is placed (the posture of) within this entity. In (11.79), the verb *dzɿ³³* 'sleep' is used. Unlike its canonical use, the agent of *dzɿ³³* 'sleep', 'three persons' is the object in this sentence, while the subject is the location, the bed. In addition, other verbs can also be used like this, such as *kɤ³³* 'sit' or *ɖaŋ³³* 'stand', since one can sit or stand on a bed.

(11.79) ɔ²¹ tʰa⁵⁵ ko²¹ **tsɿ²¹** u²¹tsʰo²¹ sa³³ ni³³ **to³³**.
this bed CLF sleep person three CLF can
'The bed can allow three persons to sleep on (it) together.'
这三张床能睡三个人。

The sentence in (11.80) combines both epistemic and non-deontic possibilities. The statement that peaches can only turn red after being exposed to the sun is based on the speaker's knowledge. The possibility for peaches turning red is conditioned by the sunlight, which means it belongs to the non-deontic and participant-external type. One should note that even though this possibility must be realized under the specific conditions given, it still remains an inner property of peaches.

(11.80) mɔ²¹ lɔ²¹po⁵⁵ niɔ³³ tɤ²¹ ɪŋ⁵⁵soŋ²¹ tsa⁵⁵-tɤ³³
that peach need PASS sun shine-obtain
lɛ²¹tsʰɛ²¹ tsʰɿ⁵⁵ **to³³**.
only.then be.red can
'Peaches can only turn read after being shone on by the sun.'
那桃子要被太阳晒到才能红。

We have mentioned above that when *do³³* is used, in most cases an action or a state is either enabled by a participant's inner ability or stimulated by a participant's intrinsic property. Compare example (11.81) with (11.80). With the same predicate *tsʰɿ⁵⁵ to³³* 'can be red', the sentence in (11.81) is ungrammatical since turning red is not an inner property of a roll of cloth.

(11.81) *mɔ²¹   pɣ²¹   ji³³   hɔ⁵⁵   tsʰɿ⁵⁵   **to³³**.
that   cloth   one   CLF   red   can
(Attempted: 'That roll of cloth can be red.')
*那匹布能红。

One more pair of contrastive examples is given in (11.82) to illustrate the conditions for the use of *do³³*. The context for (11.82a) is that a group of villagers went up the hill in order to find the nearest water source so that they could channel the water toward their village. After a few attempts, they gained some experience in judging as to where there might be possible water sources on a given hill. Upon observing the environment on the hill, the prediction in (11.82a) is made. The existence of a water source is very much related to the topography of a specific location, that is, the location's inner properties. By contrast, a bed is certainly not a place where a water source normally exists, so the sentence formed by *do³³* in (11.82b) is ungrammatical. To express the meaning 'there may be some water on the bed', it is the verb *tsʰɿ³³* 'fear, be afraid, worry' is used.

(11.82) a.   ma²⁴   ɣã²¹   sɿ⁵⁵   to³³.
there   have   water   can
'It may be a source of water over there.'
那儿可能有水。

b.   *tʰa⁵⁵   tɣ³³   ɣã²¹   sɿ⁵⁵   to³³.
bed   upside   have   water   can
'There may be some water on the bed.'
床上可能有水。

In our data, we have also observed that *do³³* extends in use to some possibilities that are weakly connected with participants' inner abilities or properties. The following two examples are both found in epistemic contexts. The phrase *kʰɯ⁵⁵ seŋ²¹* 'LIT: rise body' denotes 'set out, start off'.

(11.83)　ɔ²¹　　kɯ²⁴　　je²¹　　ta⁵⁵　　ɔ⁵⁵　　ʑi²¹
　　　　　this　　moment　3SG　　from　　house　inside
　　　　　kʰɯ⁵⁵　seŋ²¹　**to³³**　ɔ　　pa.
　　　　　rise　　body　　can　　PRT　PRT
　　　　　'Now, he may probably set out from home.'
　　　　　现在，他应该从家出发了。

(11.84)　je³³　　ɣã²¹　　tsɿ²¹tɕʰi⁵⁵　neŋ²¹　**to³³**　o.
　　　　　3SG　　have　　seventeen　　year　　can　　CRS
　　　　　'He may have attained 17 years old.'
　　　　　他能有17了。

It is necessary to recall that the modal *do³³* is often used in contexts with a certain degree of agentivity, no matter whether their agents are overt or covert. Take the verb *tɯ²¹* 'live, exist, be at', which is usually stative and takes a less agentive subject NP, as an example. In (11.85), *to³³* is used after the VP *tɯ²¹ ɔ⁵⁵ ʑi²¹* 'be at home' denoting that the human participant *je³³* 'he' may be at home. Even though *tɯ²¹* 'live, exist, be at' is a stative verb, it turns out that it involves a dynamic scenario when used with the post-VP modal *do³³*. As illustrated in (11.85), the speaker's assumption about whether 'he can be at home' or not, is produced under the context that he was aware that the participant left his house in the morning. Entering into the state of being at home after returning from the participant's working place is initiated, and movement is therefore involved. It is thus more appropriate to interpret the VP *tɯ²¹ ɔ⁵⁵ ʑi²¹ to³³* as 'may arrive home'.

(11.85)　kʰɿŋ⁵⁵　　tɔ²¹kʰɯ⁵⁵　ŋo³³　　tsaŋ³³-kɿŋ³³　je³³　　　　tsa²¹　ti²¹
　　　　　today　　　morning　　1SG　　look-see　　　3SG　　　　go.up　hill
　　　　　tɕie⁵⁵　ja²¹pa²¹　kuɛ²¹　o.　　tiu³³　　la²¹　je³³
　　　　　do　　　crops　　　go　　　CRS　know　　also　3SG
　　　　　tɯ²¹　　ɔ⁵⁵　　ʑi²¹　　**to³³**　pɣ³³　ti³³　　o.
　　　　　be.at　house　inside　can　　NEG　know　CRS
　　　　　'I saw him go up the hill to do farming this morning. I don't know if he may (have managed to) be at home by now.'
　　　　　今天早上我看见他上山干活去了。不知道他（现在）能不能在家。

By contrast, it is ungrammatical to use *to³³* after the VP *tɯ²¹ kʰa²⁴ mo³³* 'be in the drawer' with an inanimate participant *sɔ⁵⁵nioŋ³³* 'key', in (11.86), which is a pure stative context. Given that the participant *sɔ⁵⁵nioŋ³³* 'key' is inanimate and cannot initiate an action nor enter into a self-agentive state or cause an event, the verb *tɯ²¹* 'be at' possesses less agentivity here than it does in (11.85).

(11.86) *mɔ²¹ sɔ⁵⁵nioŋ³³ ka²¹ tɯ²¹ kʰa²⁴ mo³³ **to³³**.
that key CLF be.at drawer inside can
(Attempted: 'The key may be in the drawer.')
钥匙可能在抽屉里。

Another pair of contrastive examples of agentivity is given below. The copula is undeniably non-agentive. The modal *do³³* 'can' normally cannot be used after a copular predicate, as shown in (11.87a). To express the meaning 'he can be a good teacher', one must use the verb *tɕie⁵⁵* 'do', as in (11.87b). This sentence combines both epistemic assumption and the participant's ability, denoting the participant can or is able to be a good teacher. Note that 'he's probably a teacher' cannot be expressed by *do³³*, but is expressed by the verb *tsʰʅ³³* 'fear' as in (11.59).

(11.87) a. je³³ sʅ²¹kʰɯ⁵⁵ la²¹, *****sʅ⁵⁵** kʰua²¹ kʷɔ³³sɤ³³pa³³ ni³³ **to³³**.
3SG knowledge big COP good teacher CLF can
'He's very learned and can be a good teacher.'
? 他学问大，能是一名好老师。

b. je³³ sʅ²¹kʰɯ⁵⁵ la²¹, **tɕie⁵⁵** kʰua²¹ kʷɔ³³sɤ³³pa³³ ni³³ **to³³**.
3SG knowledge big do good teacher CLF can
'He's very learned and can be a good teacher.'
他学问大，能做一名好老师。

Examples (11.85) and (11.86) have shown that the agentivity of a verb varies in different contexts. In some contexts, especially those of strong emotion, the copula can also be used along with the modal *do³³* 'can'. For example, in (11.88), the speaker cannot believe that the participant *je³³* 'he' is a teacher and this fact is entirely beyond the speaker's expectation.

(11.88) ŋoŋ³³ la²¹ xa³³ pɤ³³ ti³³, je²¹ tɕiɔ⁵⁵mɔ⁵⁵ (ti³³)
speech even say NEG be.clear 3SG how know
sʅ³³ kʷɔ³³sɤ³³pa³³ ni³³ **to³³**.
COP teacher CLF can
'He can't even articulate clearly. How come he can be a teacher!'
话都说不清，他怎么能是个老师！

On the contrary, in (11.89), the participant's inappropriate behavior, i.e. dropping the pear kernels on the floor, is not a surprise at all to the speaker, though he is disgusted by this behavior. The combination of the copula *sʅ³³* and the modal *to³³* in (11.89iii) is used to express the speaker's certainty about his assumption in a rhetorical way.

(11.89) i) ɔ⁵⁵ ʑi²¹ tsʰɛ²¹ɣã²¹ je²¹ kʰã⁵⁵
house inside only 3SG be.willing.to
zɣ²¹ xɯ⁵⁵tsɿ⁵⁵.
eat pear
ii) ji²¹ tʰɣ⁵⁵ tɣ³³ la²¹ sɿ²¹ xɯ⁵⁵tsɿ⁵⁵ zɿ²¹po⁵⁵.
one ground upside all COP pear kernel
iii) pɣ³³ sɿ³³ je³³ xa²¹ **sɿ³³** lɔ²⁴ni³³ **to³³**!
NEG COP 3SG still COP who can

'At home, there's only him who likes eating pears. The pear kernels are littered all over the ground. If it was not him, who it could be!'
家里只有他喜欢吃梨。一地都是梨核。不是他还能是谁！

Like (11.88), the sentence in (11.90) is also a case which is contrary to the speaker's expectation, involving the stative verb $tɯ^{21}$ 'be at' and an inanimate subject. In (11.90) the speaker expresses disbelief at finding the key in a bowl. Compare this example with (11.86).

(11.90) sɔ⁵⁵nioŋ³³ tɕie⁵⁵me⁵⁵ **tɯ²¹** u³³ mo³³ **to³³**!
key how be.at bowl inside can
'How come the key can be got into the bowl!'
钥匙怎么会在碗里？

Next, we will present the modal construction [tɣ³³ VP do³³].

11.4.1.2 $tɣ^{33}$...do^{33} 'can' [$tɣ^{33}$ VP do^{33}]

In the modal construction $tɣ^{33}$...do^{33}, the VP is sandwiched between the elements $tɣ^{33}$ and do^{33}. Derived from its lexical form, $tɣ^{33}$ 'acquire, obtain', $tɣ^{33}$ functions like an auxiliary. This construction shows a great tendency for reduction from $tɣ^{33}$...do^{33} to do^{33}. We can observe that this merging is in process and is approaching its final stage, because $tɣ^{33}$ 'acquire, obtain' is not observed elsewhere in other constructions functioning as an auxiliary. This suggests that $tɣ^{33}$...do^{33} overlaps with do^{33} in the realm of modality. The three examples below respectively show the construction $tɣ^{33}$...do^{33} used to express mental ability, and epistemic possibility combined with physical ability and non-deontic possibility.

(11.91) je³³ **(tɣ³³)** xa³³ men²¹ni³³ŋoŋ³³ **to³³**.
3SG obtain say Caijia can
'He can speak Caijia.'
他会说蔡家话。

(11.92) je³³ ɣã³³ mɔ²¹ tsoŋ⁵⁵ po⁵⁵po⁵⁵ tɯ²¹ ma²⁴ mɛ̃!
3SG have that type height be.at there PRT
je³³ **(tɣ³³)** tɕiɔ²¹ lɯ⁵⁵ kʷɔ³³ **to³³**.
3SG obtain jump VCOMP be.high can
'He has great height! He can jump high.'
他有那种个子在那儿嘛！他能跳得高。

(11.93) zɿ⁵⁵ ɣɯ²¹ la²¹ xɪŋ⁵⁵ o.
rain come big very CRS
ŋo³³ **(tɣ³³)** kuɛ³³ me²¹ tsʰɿ⁵⁵po⁵⁵ po³³ **to³³** o.
1SG obtain go dig potato NEG can CRS
'It's raining heavily. I can't go to dig potatoes.'
雨下得大得很了。我不能去挖土豆了。

As mentioned earlier above, the construction *tɣ³³ . . . do³³* is restricted to events that can be controlled by the participants. Since only animate participants are able to control certain events, this means that the subject NP of a *tɣ³³ . . . do³³* construction is animate. Let us see some contrastive examples in (11.94) and (11.95) which illustrate very well the contrast between *tɣ³³ . . . do³³* and *do³³*. The same verb *ɣɯ²¹* 'come' is used in both examples. The pre-VP *tɣ³³* can only be used in (11.94) but cannot be used in (11.95). The action of coming in (11.94) can be controlled by the participant *sɿ⁵⁵pie²¹ hɛ⁵⁵ la²¹ tso⁵⁵* 'the elder brother of the Wang family', while the action of raining is not controllable. It bears mentioning that the question particle *mo³³* is exclusively used with the modals *do³³* and *tɣ³³*.

(11.94) sɿ⁵⁵pie²¹ hɛ⁵⁵ la²¹ tso⁵⁵ **tɣ³³** ɣɯ²¹ **to³³** mo³³?
Wang_NAME family big brother obtain come can Q
'Can the elder brother of the Wang family come?'
王家大哥能来吗？

(11.95) nɯ³³ tsaŋ²¹ kʰɪŋ⁵⁵koŋ⁵⁵ ɔ²¹ zɿ⁵⁵ **(*tɣ³³)** ɣɯ²¹ **to³³** mo³³.
2SG look today this rain obtain come can Q
'Is it possible that it will rain today, according to you?'
你看今天这雨能下么？

A further refinement is that even with animate agent-participants, the construction *tɣ³³ . . . do³³* may not be compatible with certain verbs. The verbs *tɯ²¹* 'attract, provoke' and *tɣ²¹* 'hit the target' are two such verbs. The expression *tɯ²¹ ni³³ tɣ²¹* in (11.96) denotes 'appeal to (LIT: attract others to love)'. It is one's unintentional behaviors that make oneself loved by others. Whether one is loved or not cannot be determined by one's own self. In (11.97), denoting 'to be to his liking (LIT: hit one's heart)', the subject of the phrase $tɣ^{21}$ je^{33} $saŋ^{33}$ cannot be the determining factor either, i.e. the subject cannot control the action of 'being to his liking'. Therefore, using the pre-VP $tɣ^{33}$ in either of these two examples would be ungrammatical.

(11.96) je³³   sɿ³³   tɔ²¹lɔ²⁴sɿ⁵⁵   sɿ²¹   u²¹tsʰo²⁴   ni³³   lɔ²¹?   xa²¹   **(*tɣ³³)**
        3SG   COP   how   MOD   person   CLF   PRT   still   obtain
        tɯ²¹   ni³³   tɣ²¹   **to³³**   mo³³   lɔ²¹?
        attract   3   like   can   Q   PRT
        'What kind of person is he? Could he be attractive?'
        他是什么样的人？会招人喜欢吗？

(11.97) mɔ²¹   u²¹tsʰo²⁴   ni³³   ɕyẽ⁵⁵   xiŋ⁵⁵.   lɔ²⁴ni⁵⁵   la²¹   **(*tɣ³³)**
        that   person   CLF   be.picky   very   what   even   obtain
        tɣ²¹   je³³   saŋ³³   po³³   **to³³**.
        hit.(the.target)   3SG   heart   NEG   can
        'That person is very picky. No one can satisfy him.'
        那个人挑剔得很。没人能中他的意。

In sum, compared with the post-VP modal do^{33}, the construction $tɣ^{33}$ ... do^{33} is very similar to the post-VP modal do^{33} when used to express ability or possibility, but is used with a more restricted range of predicates. In the next section, the post-VP modal $tɣ^{33}$ will be introduced.

11.4.2 $tɣ^{33}$ 'can' [VP $tɣ^{33}$]

Derived from the lexical verb 'obtain', $tɣ^{33}$ is another post-VP modal used to code modality in Caijia, including deontic permission and weak desire, as well as non-deontic possibility. We have indicated in Table 11.2 that $tɣ^{33}$ can also be used to express the notion of ability, but this use is extremely limited. Unlike the post-VP modal do^{33}, the post-VP $tɣ^{33}$ does not require agentive participants when denoting non-deontic possibility. Detailed descriptions are given below.

Deontic permission indicates a participant's action is performed under the condition that social norms, moral principles, or else the speaker, grant permission to the participant. The example (11.98) about the legal marriage age in China demonstrates an excellent contrast between the non-deontic possibility expressed by do^{33} and the deontic permission expressed by $tɣ^{33}$. There were no age restrictions for marriage until 1950 in China. The Chinese government raised the minimum ages from 20 to 23 for men and from 18 to 20 for women in 1980. Before 1950 one could get married when conditions were appropriate, by way of agreement from parents, physical maturity, or possibility of independence, etc. Therefore, the possibility of *tsɿ²¹ ɔ⁵⁵* 'get married (LIT: accomplish house)' is realized by *do³³* in (11.98i). On the contrary, nowadays the legal marriage age is around 20 in China. It is the law that gives permission to people to get married at a certain age. Therefore, *tɣ³³* is used in (11.98ii) to denote this permission.

(11.98) i) mɔ³³ to²¹ kʰɯ⁵⁵ nen²¹, tsɿ²¹ ŋoŋ⁵⁵ fɣ⁵⁵ nen²⁴
that head several year ten five six year
sɿ²¹ ŋa⁵⁵ la²¹ tsɿ²¹ ɔ⁵⁵ **to²¹** o.
MOD children all accomplish house can CRS

ii) ɔ²¹ kɯ²⁴ niɔ³³ nĩ²¹tɕi⁵⁵ kʰɯ⁵⁵ nen²¹
this moment need twenty several year
lɛ²¹tsʰɛ²¹ niu²¹ su⁵⁵po⁵⁵ **tɣ³³** o.
only.then marry wife can CRS

'Several years ago, children of about 15 years of age could get married. Nowadays, one may get married only at about 20.'
头几年，十五六的孩子就能成家了。现在要二十几岁才能娶老婆。

Example (11.99) shows how off-work time is set by rules and regulations in some unregulated working environments. However, it also belongs to an ambiguous context, since it can be interpreted as the speaker's permission.

(11.99) ŋoŋ⁵⁵ kɯ²¹ o. nɯ³³ ɣa²¹ **tɣ³³** o.
five hour CRS 2SG walk can CRS
'It's five o'clock. You can leave now.'
五点了。你可以走了。

The example below illustrates a case of a request for permission.

(11.100) "ʑi³³, ŋo³³ kuɛ³³ li²¹ xɯ⁵⁵tsɿ⁵⁵ po⁵⁵ **tɣ³³** mo³³?"
mother 1SG go pick pear CLF can Q
' "Mom, can I go to pick a pear?" '
"妈，我可以去摘个梨吗？"

Examples (11.101)-(11.103) demonstrate weak deontic obligation involving speakers' desires to the effect that *tɣ³³* in these cases ought to be interpreted as 'should'. The same VP *tsɿ²¹ ɔ⁵⁵* 'get married (LIT: accomplish house)' in (11.98i) is also used in (11.101iii). However, the VP *tsɿ²¹ ɔ⁵⁵ tɣ³³* in (11.101iii) does not express that it is possible for the participant to marry due to the fact that he is of a marriageable age or possesses a certain economic base. To the contrary, it denotes that the speaker thinks that the participant 'he' should get married, because he is not getting any younger.

(11.101) i) je^{33} nian^{21}tɕi^{55} la^{33} la^{21} o.
             3SG   age   also   big   CRS
         ii) sa^{33} tsʅ^{21} kʰɯ^{55} neŋ^{21} o.
             three   ten   several   year   CRS
         iii) la^{21} tsʅ^{21} ɔ^{55} **tɣ^{33}**   o.
              also   accomplish   house   can   CRS
         'He's not getting any younger and is more than 30. He should get married.'
         他年纪也大了。三十几岁了。该成家了。

In (11.102), the speaker thinks that an irrigation channel should be built in the field, while in (11.103) the speaker expects and hopes for rain.

(11.102) tɯ^{21} leŋ^{21} mo^{33} kʰɯ^{33} tɕi^{33}kʰa^{21} ta^{55} **tɣ^{33}**   o.
         at   field   inside   open   canal   CLF   can   CRS
         kʰua^{21} pɣ^{21} sʅ^{55}.
         well   put   water
         'A canal should be dug in the field so that it'll be easy to water it.'
         应该在田里开条渠。好放水。

(11.103) ka^{55} ɔ^{21}sʅ^{55} tie^{55} sʅ^{21} ni^{24} ɣɯ^{21} zʅ^{55} **tɣ^{33}**   o.
         be.dry   this   many   MOD   time   come   rain   can   CRS
         'It has been dry for such a long time. It should rain.'
         旱了这么久，该下雨了。

The negated form of *tɣ^{33}*, *pɣ^{33} tɣ^{33}*, is used to express sanctions against something, such as permissions or social norms. As shown in (11.104), sleeping on a bed is forbidden for people who attend a vigil for a dead person; part of the funerary customs of Caijia people. Example (11.105) is also a case that an old social norm forbidding an action, i.e. a daughter-in-law was not permitted to speak to her father-in-law. In (11.106), the action of going out to play is against the speaker's mother's will.

(11.104) tʰa⁵⁵   tɤ³³   tsɿ²¹   **pɤ³³** **tɤ³³**.
          bed   upside sleep   NEG   can
          'One cannot sleep on a bed.'
          床上不能睡。
          (*Funeral customs*, texts)

(11.105) to²¹pʰa³³   la²¹to⁵⁵   u²¹tsʰo²⁴-sui⁵⁵   nĩ²¹tɕi³³
          before   old   person-PL   rule
          tie²¹   xɯn⁵⁵.   tsɿ⁵⁵so⁵⁵po²¹   ta⁵⁵
          be.many   very   daughter-in-law   with
          pa⁵⁵   xa²¹   ŋoŋ³³   **pɤ³³**   **tɤ³³**.
          father   say   speech   NEG   can
          'There were many rules before. A daughter-in-law may not speak with her father-in-law'
          以前，老人们的规矩多得很。儿媳不能和公公说话。

(11.106) ŋo²¹   tsʰe⁵⁵-kuɛ²¹   ta⁵⁵   nɯ²⁴   sɔ²¹kʷɔ⁵⁵   **pɤ³³** **tɤ³³**.
          1SG   be.out-go   with   2PL   play   NEG   can
          ŋuɛ²¹   ʑi³³   pɤ²¹   sɿ⁵⁵   ŋo³³   kuɛ²¹.
          my.family mother   NEG   let   1SG   go
          'I can't go out to play with you. My mother doesn't allow me to go.'
          我不能出去跟你们玩儿。我妈不让我去。

When something is not strongly recommended, the negated *tɤ³³* is used along with *piɔ²⁴* 'not need, don't...', which can be schematized as [piɔ²⁴ VP pɤ³³ tɤ³³]. Even though the combination of *piɔ²⁴* and *pɤ³³ tɤ³³* forms a double negative, it does not denote a positive meaning. Instead, it emphasizes the meaning of prohibition expressed by *pɤ³³ tɤ³³*. Compare the double negation in (11.107) and the emphatic prohibition *piɔ²⁴ ... pɤ³³ tɤ³³* in (11.108). The sentence *pɤ³³ a³³ pɤ³³ tɤ³³* 'not paying (taxes) is not possible' can be interpreted as 'paying taxes is the only choice'. On the contrary, *piɔ²⁴ a³³ fɛ³³tsʰɿ³³ suɛ³³ pɤ³³ tɤ³³* can only denote '(children) mustn't toss lit kindling (for fun)'.

(11.107) neŋ²¹neŋ³³   la²¹   niɔ³³   tsa²¹   ko²¹.   [. . .].
          every.year   all   need   pay   tax
          pɤ³³   a³³   pɤ³³   tɤ³³.
          NEG   take   NEG   can
          'Every year, (people) had to pay poll taxes. Not paying (taxes) was not possible.'
          年年要上税。[……]不拿（钱上交）不行。
          (*Paying taxes*, texts)

11.4 Post-VP 'can' modals — 397

(11.108) ɕie²¹   ŋa⁵⁵   tsɔ²¹   **piɔ²⁴**   a³³   fɛ³³tsʰɿ³³
          little   children a.kind.of.person NEG.need   take   lit.kindling
          suɛ³³   **pɣ³³**   **tɣ³³**.
          toss   NEG   can
          'Children mustn't toss lit kindling (for fun).'
          小孩子不能甩火枝子（玩）。

Two more examples are given below.

(11.109) tɕie⁵⁵   pa⁵⁵ʑi³³   sɿ²¹   niɔ³³   saŋ³³tɣ²¹   mi⁵⁵,
          do   parent   NMLZ   need   be.patient   a.little
          piɔ²⁴   neŋ²¹na³³   na²¹   ŋa⁵⁵-sui⁵⁵   **pɣ³³**   **tɣ³³**.
          NEG.need   at.will   beat   child-PL   NEG   can
          'Those that are parents should be patient and mustn't beat (their) children at will.'
          做家长的要耐心些，不能随便打孩子。

(11.110) mɔ³³   ɕie²¹   ŋa⁵⁵   tsɔ²¹   **piɔ²⁴**   neŋ²¹na³³
          that   little   children a.kind.of.person NEG.need   at.will
          ta⁵⁵   **pɣ³³** sɿ³³   sɿ²¹   u²¹tsʰo²¹   ɣa²¹   **pɣ³³**   **tɣ³³**.
          with   NEG   recognize   REL   person   walk   NEG   can
          'Children mustn't go with any strangers as they like.'
          小孩子不能随便跟不认识的人走。

The post-VP *tɣ³³* can also be used to express the notion of possibility. It is mentioned above in §11.4.1 that a context for *do³³* requires an agent-participant which can either be overt or covert. The kind of possibility encoded by *do³³* denotes that the agent is capable of performing a certain action or entering into a certain state. By contrast, a possibility expressed by *tɣ³³* concerns the realizability of a certain event, which can be illustrated by the schema in (11.111). Whether or not the agent of the event is able to realize it is unimportant.

(11.111) [[(S) VP]   tɣ³³]
             EVENT   can
          INTERPRETATION: The EVENT is doable.

Let us consider some examples.

Both examples (11.112) and (11.113) show that an event can only be carried out under the condition that a preceding event is accomplished. Example (11.112) concerns procedures for cultivation. Planting can only be done after scarifying the soil. In (11.113), the condition for doing farming is a proper recuperation.

(11.112) nɣ²¹ tʰy⁵⁵ ha⁵⁵ kua³³ nɛ³³ tɯ³³ tsoŋ²¹ **tɣ³³** o.
loosen soil COMPL pass PRT then plant can CRS
'After scarifying the soil, (we) can plant (crops).'
松过土呢，就能种了。

(11.113) nɯ³³ niɔ³³ li²¹li²⁴ lɛ⁵⁵ niaŋ³³ soŋ²¹.
2SG need slowly ADV recover sickness
piɔ²⁴ tsʰo⁵⁵ tɕie⁵⁵ ja²¹pa²¹. soŋ²¹
NEG.IMP be.hurry do crops sickness
kʰɯ⁵⁵-kʰua²¹ ha⁵⁵ lɛ²¹tsʰɛ²¹ tɕie⁵⁵ **tɣ³³**.
cure-be.good COMPL only.then do can
'You should take your time to recuperate. Don't rush yourself to go back to farming. You can do it only after your sickness is cured.'
你要慢慢养病。别急着干活。病治好以后才能干。

Unlike (11.100), the question in (11.114A) is not asking for permission to spray water on the half-cooked rice. Instead, it serves to ask whether the rice is ready to have water sprayed on it. The negated *tɣ³³* which follows in (11.114B) does not denote, therefore, a prohibition but denotes that the rice is not yet ready to be sprayed with water.

(11.114) A- zɣ³³ pʰaŋ³³ **tɣ³³** ɔ²¹sɛ³³?
rice spray.(water.on.half-cooked.rice) can Q.PFV
'Is the rice ready for spraying water on it?'
饭可以馈了吗？

B- xa²¹tsɛ²¹ pʰaŋ³³ **pɣ³³ tɣ³³**.
still spray.(water.on.half-cooked.rice) NEG can
sɿ⁵⁵ je²¹ tsɣ²¹ ji²¹ tʰŋ²⁴ lɛ³³.
let 3SG steam one instant PRT
'It's not ready for it yet. Let it be steamed for a little longer.'
还不能馈。让它再蒸一会儿。

The example below involves two feasible events encoded by the modal *tɣ³³*. Both are related to an inner property of roadweeds (or broadleaf plantain), i.e. its medical value. The sentence in (11.115i) introduces the fact that roadweeds can be turned into medicine, while the one in (11.115iii) introduces in which situation they can be used.

(11.115) i)　　ɔ²⁴　　tsoŋ⁵⁵　　sɿ²¹　　ti³³　　a²¹　　tɕie⁵⁵　　tsɣ̩⁵⁵　　tɣ³³.
　　　　　　this　　kind　　　COP　　know　take　do　　　medicine　can
　　　　　　　　　　　　　　　　　　　　　　　　　　EVENT₁

ii)　　ɔ²¹　　ŋa⁵⁵　　pe²¹　　ɔ²⁴-sui⁵⁵　　sɿ³³,
　　　this　child　　burn　　this-PL　　　PRT

iii)　　a³³　　ɣɯ²¹　　zɿ⁵⁵　　sɿ⁵⁵　　ŋa⁵⁵　　ã³³　　tɣ̩³³　　sɿ²¹.
　　　take　PURP　　heat　give/to　child　drink　can　　　AFF
　　　　　　　　　　　　　　EVENT₂

'This type (= roadweed or broadleaf plantain) can be used to make medicine. When children get sick, such as get a fever, one can boil (some water with some roadweeds) and give it to them to drink.'
这种（=蛤蟆草/宽叶车前草）是可以用来做药。孩子发烧这些，可以拿来热给孩子喝。
(*Roadweed*, texts)

Two more examples are given below.

(11.116)　tsaŋ²¹　　mo³³　　ɣɯ²¹　　kʰɯ⁵⁵sɛ²¹　　xɪŋ⁵⁵　o.　　ta⁵⁵　**tɣ²¹**　o.
　　　　　rice.steamer　inside　come　steam　　　　　very　CRS　lift　can　CRS
'The steam has filled up a the steamer. (The steamer) can be lifted.'
甑子里上气了。能抬了。

(11.117)　mɔ²¹　　sɿ⁵⁵　　niɔ²¹　　sɿ⁵⁵　　je²¹　　piɔ²¹-kʰɯ²¹　　ha⁵⁵
　　　　　that　　water　　need　　let　　　3SG　　boil-be.open　　COMPL
　　　　　lɛ²¹tsʰɛ²¹　　ã³³　　**tɣ³³**.
　　　　　only.then　drink　can
'Only after being boiled, can the water be drinkable.'
那水要沸过以后才能喝。

The modal *tɣ³³* extends to express the concept of ability, that is participant-internal possibility, in contexts in which *tɣ³³* follows certain bare verbs of action, usually monosyllabic without any object, such as *zɣ²¹* 'eat', *tɕie⁵⁵* 'do', *ã³³* 'drink', *ɣa²¹* 'walk' etc. In these cases *tɣ³³* denotes 'be skilled at, be good at, or be capable of'. As shown in (11.118), *tɣ³³* is used respectively after the monosyllabic action verbs *zɣ²¹* 'eat' and *tɕie⁵⁵* 'do', denoting that the subject *je³³* 'he' possesses an ability as an articulate speaker and is also a capable person. Note that the modal in (11.118) can be replaced by the modal *do³³*.

(11.118)   je³³   xa²¹   **tɣ³³**   tɕie⁵⁵   **tɣ³³**.
           3SG   say   can   do   can
           'He's smart-talking and hardworking.'
           他能说能干。

This is the only context in which *tɣ³³* is used to express participant-internal possibility. As mentioned above, *tɣ³³* must follow bare action verbs. Compare the following example in which *tɣ³³* follows the object of the verb *xa³³* 'say, speak' with (11.118). In this context, the interpretation of ability is impossible. The sentence can only denote 'He can speak Lolo (because he can be understood)' or 'He is permitted to speak Lolo'.

(11.119)   je³³   xa³³   mia²¹ŋoŋ³³   **tɣ³³**.
           3SG   say   Lolo   can
           Situational: 'He can speak Lolo (because he can be understood).'
           Deontic: 'He (is permitted to) speak Lolo.'
           他可以说彝语（因为其他人能听懂）。
           他（被允许）说彝语。

One more example is given below. As in (11.118), *tɣ²¹* can also be replaced by *do³³* in (11.120).

(11.120)   je³³   zɣ²¹   **tɣ²¹**   xiŋ⁵⁵.
           3SG   eat   can   very
           'He's capable of eating a lot.'
           他很能吃。

11.4.3 Conclusion

In this section, we have presented the two post-VP 'can' modals in Caijia: *do³³* 'can' (< 'arrive, achieve') and *tɣ³³* 'can' (< 'acquire, obtain'). The modal *do³³* is used to express ability, capacity, and possibility, while *tɣ³³* is mainly used to code participant-external modality denoting permission, and weak obligation, as well as possibility. We have also shown that *tɣ³³* can code ability when it follows bare action verbs. The modal uses of *tɣ³³* contribute a piece of evidence to the hypothesis proposed by van der Auwera, Kehayov, and Vittrant (2009) that an ACQUIRE verb can first reach participant-external modality then it may continue into participant-internal possibility. The core use of the Caijia modal *tɣ³³* remains in the domain of participant-external modality with the use of denoting extremely limited ability (see also Vittrant and van der Auwera 2010 for similar uses of the ACQUIRE morpheme *ya¹* in Burmese). By way of contrast, the modal *do³³* is never used to denote permission and weak obligation. When denoting possibility, *do³³* is used to express situations that can be realized by agents, while *tɣ³³* is used to express that certain events are feasible.

Two pairs of examples that show the contrast between *tɣ³³* and *do³³* are given below. The verb *ã³³* 'drink' is used in both sentences in (11.121), both of which belong to the realm of non-deontic possibility. In (11.121a), the water is too hot to drink, which is not related to one's physical ability to drink, but only concerns the fact that the temperature of the water prevents the action of drinking. Therefore, using *to³³*, the voiceless form of *do³³*, is ungrammatical. By contrast, in (11.121b), there is so much water that one is not able to finish drinking it, which means the feasibility expressed in this sentence is related to one's physical ability and, thus, using *tɣ³³* would be ungrammatical in this context.

(11.121) a. tʰɣ²¹   xɪŋ⁵⁵,   ã³³   pɣ³³   **tɣ³³/*to³³**.
         be.hot   very   drink NEG   can
         '(The water) is very hot and is not drinkable.'
         太烫了，不能喝。

   b. tie²¹   xɪŋ⁵⁵   o,   ã³³   po³³   **to³³/*tɣ³³**   o.
      be.many very   CRS drink NEG   can   CRS
      '(This is) too much. I can't drink it all.'
      太多了，喝不了。

In (11.122), the same VP *tɕie³³ li²¹* 'feed pigs' is used in the two sentences of non-deontic possibility. The sentence in (11.122a) denotes that feeding pigs is possible after having dinner, while the one in (11.122b) means that the agent-participant *je³³* 'he' is old enough to have attained the physical ability to feed pigs.

(11.122) a. zɣ²¹   zɣ²¹   ha⁵⁵   tɯ³³   tɕie³³ li²¹   **tɣ³³/*to³³**   ɔ   mẽ.
            eat   meal   COMPL   then   feed   pig   can   PRT PRT
            '(We) can feed the pigs after dinner.'
            吃完饭就能喂猪了。

   b. je³³   tie²¹sɔ⁵⁵   la²¹   o.   tɕie³³ li²¹   **to³³/*tɣ³³**   ɔ   mẽ.
      3SG   quite   be.big   CRS   feed   pig   can   PRT PRT
      'He's old enough and can feed pigs.'
      他很大了。能喂猪了。

Undoubtedly, ambiguous contexts in which both of these two 'can' modals can be used also exist, as illustrated in the following two examples. In (11.123), when *tɣ³³* is used the sentence simply denotes that making cord mosses into medicine is feasible. When *to³³* is used, we obtain the contrasting interpretation that making medicine out of cord mosses, while possible, is a certain skill or a kind of ability that is not commonly mastered by just any person. Note that *do³³* can also be used in (11.115i) above for the same reason.

(11.123) to³³nie²¹tsʰɔ⁵⁵ a²¹   tɕie⁵⁵ tsɣ⁵⁵   **tɣ³³/to³³**.
          cord.moss   take   do   medicine can
          'Cord mosses can be made into medicine.'
          'Cord mosses, one can make them into medicine.'
          葫芦藓可以做药。

Similarly, example (11.124) is also found in an ambiguous context. Given that people's tastes vary, it is the speaker himself that is not able to bear the salty dish when *to³³* is used in (11.124a). By contrast, in (11.124b), the use of *tɣ³³* emphasizes that the very action of eating this salty dish is not possible.

(11.124) nɯ³³   ŋʷɔ²¹   ɔ²¹   tsʰɯ²¹sɿ⁵⁵ san²¹   tɣ³³   nɯ³³
          2SG   cook   this   dish   salt   PASS   2SG
          pɣ³³   tseŋ²¹   xɪŋ⁵⁵ o.
          put   be.salty very   CRS
          a. tseŋ²¹   lɯ⁵⁵   zɣ²¹   **po³³**   **to³³**.
             be.salty VCOMP   eat   NEG   can
          b. tseŋ²¹   lɯ⁵⁵   zɣ²¹   **pɣ³³**   **tɣ³³**.
             be.salty VCOMP   eat   NEG   can
          'You put too much salt into this dish.
          a. (I'm) not able to eat it.'
          b. It's too salty to be eatable.'
          这道菜被你把盐放多了。
          a. 咸得吃不了。
          b. 咸得吃不得。

As exemplified above, one can observe that the semantic difference between *do³³* and *tɣ³³* is very subtle in ambiguous contexts and the contrast between them is often vague. In our data, it is very common that *do³³* and *tɣ³³* are used alternatively in similar contexts when used to denote possibility, as shown in (11.124). By contrast, when *do³³* is used to denote ability and *tɣ³³* is used to denote permission and weak obligation, their difference is clear-cut.

11.5 Potential construction [V lɯ⁵⁵ VP]

Potential constructions expressing possibility are widely attested in Sinitic as well as many Southeast Asian languages (Enfield 2003: 250–288). Such constructions also exist in Caijia in the form of [V lɯ⁵⁵ VP]. These are labeled as 'extent/manner complementation' in this grammar. See Chapter 4 §4.2.4. When denoting possibility, a potential construction possesses the same semantic value as the modal *do³³*, as shown in the two examples below. In the context that the ditch is not very wide, the sentence formed by *to³³* 'I can jump over it' in (11.125b) can replace the one formed by *lɯ⁵⁵* in (11.125a) without any change of meaning.

(11.125) ɔ²¹ tɕʰi³³kʰa²¹ ta⁵⁵ pɣ³³ ɣã²¹ kʰua²¹ kʰua³³.
this ditch CLF NEG have good wide

a. ŋo³³ tɕiɔ²¹ lɯ⁵⁵ tɣ²¹-kuɛ²¹.
1SG jump VCOMP pass-go

b. ŋo³³ tɕiɔ²¹-tɣ²¹kuɛ²¹ to³³.
1SG jump-pass.go can

'The ditch isn't very wide. I can jump over it'
那条沟没有多宽，
a. 我跳得过去。
b. 我能跳过去。

Similarly, the response formed by *lɯ⁵⁵* given in (11.126B-a) and the one formed by *to³³* in (11.126B-b) denote the same meaning of '(The meal) can be ready'. Both (11.126B-a) and (11.26B-b) are able to serve as the answer to the question 'can the meal be ready before grandpa comes back?' in (11.126A).

(11.126) A- pa²¹ pe⁵⁵-ɣɯ²¹ tɕɪŋ²¹ tʰɔ⁵⁵ zɣ²¹
grandfather return-come front moment meal
tɕie⁵⁵-kʰua²¹ to³³ mo³³?
do-be.good can Q
'Can the meal be ready before grandpa comes back?'
爷爷回来前饭能做好吗？

B- a. tɕie⁵⁵ lɯ⁵⁵ kʰua²¹ sɿ²¹.
do VCOMP be.good AFF
'Yes, it can be ready then.'
做得好的。

b. tɕie⁵⁵-kʰua²¹   to³³.
   do-be.good   can
   'Yes, it can be ready then.'
   能做好。

The following two pairs of examples illustrate the negated form of the potential constructionl with *lɯ⁵⁵* – [V pɣ³³ VP] 'no be able to VP', which is semantically equivalent to the negated *do³³*, i.e. [VP po³³ do³³] 'not be able to, cannot VP'. It should be mentioned that a negated potential construction is possible in the form of [V NEG VP]. As it turns out, this is the same construction as the negated resultative complement construction (see Chapter 4 §4.2.4). Let us examine some examples.

(11.127) a. tsʰɿ⁵⁵pa²¹   nɯ²¹   ma²⁴   tɣ³³   pɣ³³   kʰua²¹   o.
            be.afraid   2SG   there   grow   NEG   be.good   CRS
            'I'm afraid your (wound) won't heal flawlessly (without leaving a scar).'
            你那儿长不好了。

       b. tsʰɿ⁵⁵pa²¹   nɯ²¹   ma²⁴   tɣ³³-kʰua²¹   po³³   to³³   o.
            be.afraid   2SG   there   grow-be.good   NEG   can   CRS
            'I'm afraid your (wound) won't heal flawlessly (without leaving a scar).'
            你那儿长不好了。

(11.128) a. ŋo²¹   kɣ⁵⁵   ʑi⁵⁵-tɣ²¹   piɔ³³   pɣ³³   tɕiu²¹.
            1SG   foot   twist-obtain   run   NEG   fast
            'My foot is twisted and I'm not able to run fast.'
            我的脚扭了，跑不快。

       b. ŋo²¹   kɣ⁵⁵   ʑi⁵⁵-tɣ²¹   piɔ³³-tɕiu²¹   po³³   to³³.
            1SG   foot   twist-obtain   run-fast   NEG   can
            'My foot is twisted and I'm not able to run fast.'
            我的脚扭了，跑不快。

The construction [V lɯ⁵⁵ VP] is often ambiguous if the context in which it appears is not taken into consideration. As shown in (11.129), the sentence *je³³ tɕiɔ²¹ lɯ⁵⁵ kʷɔ³³* possesses two interpretations, the non-modal reading 'he jumps high', and the modal reading 'he can jump high'.

(11.129) je³³ tɕiɔ²¹ lɯ⁵⁵ kʷɔ³³.
3SG jump VCOMPL be.tall
a. He jumps high.
b. He can jump high.
他跳得高。

Therefore, one has to rely on context to determine if the construction [V lɯ⁵⁵ VP] denotes modal or non-modal meanings. Yet, there are methods for avoiding ambiguity. By adding the degree marker xɪŋ⁵⁵ 'very' to the sentence (11.129), only the non-modal meaning can be interpreted, as shown in (11.130). By using the modal to³³ after the VP tɕiɔ²¹ lɯ⁵⁵ kʷɔ³³ 'jump high', the sentence denotes the modal meaning, i.e. the participant's physical ability, as in illustrated (11.131).

(11.130) je³³ tɕiɔ²¹ lɯ⁵⁵ kʷɔ²¹ **xɪŋ⁵⁵**.
3SG jump VCOMP be.tall very
'He jumps very high.'
他跳得很高。

(11.131) je³³ tɕiɔ²¹ lɯ⁵⁵ kʷɔ³³ **to³³**.
3SG jump VCOMP be.tall can
'He can jump high.'
他能跳得高。

Finally, to express possibility, the post-VP 'can' modal *do³³* is more commonly used in Caijia, than the potential construction [V lɯ⁵⁵ VP].

11.6 Modal adverbs

Two adverbs are observed to code epistemic possibility in Caijia: *niɔ³³sʅ³³* and *kʰuɔ³³neŋ²¹*. Both denote 'probably'. The adverb *niɔ³³sʅ³³* is composed of the verb/auxiliary *niɔ³³* 'want, need' and the copula *sʅ³³*. It is a multifunctional morpheme, for example, it can be used to mark a conditional clause denoting 'if', and it forms the correlative *niɔ³³sʅ³³ . . . niɔ³³sʅ³³* denoting 'either . . . or'. The adverb *kʰuɔ³³neŋ²¹* is borrowed from the local Southwestern Mandarin, for which the corresponding form in Standard Mandarin is *kěnéng* 可能 [kʰə²¹⁴nəŋ¹⁵] 'probably'. When denoting 'probably', these two adverbs are interchangeable.

(11.132) ɔ²¹   kɯ²⁴   tsʰɛ²¹   yã²¹   noŋ⁵⁵   kɯ²¹.
         this   moment   only   have   five   hour
         je³³   **[niɔ³³sɿ³³]/[kʰuɔ³³neŋ²¹]**   xa²¹   pɣ³³-tɣ³³   zɣ³³   zɣ³³.
         3SG   probably   still   NEG-PFV   eat   meal
         'Now it's only five o'clock. He probably hasn't had his meal yet.'
         现在才五点。他可能还没吃饭。

(11.133) ti⁵⁵m²¹   kɯ²⁴   ŋo³³   tsaŋ²¹   iŋ⁵⁵soŋ²¹   mi³³.
         just.now   moment   1SG   look   sun   a.little
         [niɔ³³sɿ³³]/[kʰuɔ³³neŋ²¹]   noŋ⁵⁵   kɯ²¹   o.
         probably   five   hour   CRS
         'I checked the sun just now. It's probably five o'clock.'
         刚才我看了下太阳。可能五点了。

(11.134) **[niɔ³³sɿ³³]/[kʰuɔ³³neŋ²¹]**   niɔ³³   ɣɯ²¹   zɿ⁵⁵   o.
         probably   PROSP   come   rain   CRS
         'It's probably going to rain.'
         可能要下雨了。

11.7 Epistemic final particle: ɔ pa [S VP ɔ pa]

The sentence-final particle ɔ pa, source unclear, is an overt marker of epistemic possibility, and the use of this particle serves to signify a speaker's own judgement of lack of certainty without requiring any additional situational context. The sentence-final particle can also be used along with other modal elements to express or reinforce the speaker's uncertainty about what he or she has said. See the following examples.

(11.135) lɛ²¹   mo³³   pɣ³³   naŋ²¹   o.   tɕi³³   tɣ³³   ɔ   **pa**.
         field   inside   NEG   be.muddy   CRS   plough   can   PRT   PRT
         'The field isn't muddy anymore. It probably can be ploughed (in my opinion).'
         地里不稀。能犁了吧。

(11.136) meŋ²¹ni³³ŋo³³,   tsɔ²¹   mɔ²¹   je³³   xa²¹   to³³   ɔ   **pa**.
         Caijia   resemble   that   3SG   say   can   PRT   PRT
         'As for Caijia, it seems that he probably can speak it.'
         蔡家话，他好像说得了吧。

(11.137) tsʰɿ⁵⁵ je³³ tɕʰi³³kʰa³³ to³³ ɔ **pa.**
fear 3SG like can PRT PRT
'He may probably like (it).'
他应该能喜欢吧。

(11.138) mɔ²¹ tʰɤ⁵⁵po²¹ tɤ²¹ tsʰɯ⁵⁵-xɯ⁵⁵ ɔ pa.
that stove PASS block-up PRT PRT
'The stove is probably blocked.'
炉子被堵住了吧。

11.8 Epistemic certainty: [S (sɿ³³) VP sɿ²¹]

Epistemic certainty is rarely described in the literature. The concept refers to a speaker's certainty of his or her own assertions. It indicates the speaker's certitude about what s/he says on the basis of the speaker's belief, knowledge, information, experience, or physical evidence and is highly subjective.

In Caijia, epistemic certainty or affirmation is expressed with the affirmative construction [(sɿ³³) VP sɿ²¹] '(I am) sure that…/It is certain that…', also known as a cleft construction, in which sɿ³³ is the copula and sɿ²¹ is the nominalizer or the modifier linker. This construction overarches the VP and is often reduced to just [VP sɿ²¹]. The term 'affirmative' is used by Yue-Hashimoto to describe one of the aspectual functions of the verb 'have, there be' in some Sinitic languages, such as Wu and Southern Min, as being to "affirm[ing] happening in the past and or existence in the present" (1993: 71). This definition seems suitable to some extent for the epistemic affirmation found in Caijia, except that Yu-Hashimoto considers it as an aspectual phenomenon. However, it is true that the Caijia affirmative construction also serves as an aspectual marker marking continuous aspect (see Chapter 10 §10.2.8). Another reason to adopt the term 'affirmative' is that the construction [(sɿ³³) VP sɿ²¹] is used to produce a positive, that is, an affirmative answer to a polar question, as shown below as well as above in (11.126B-a).

(11.139) A- tʰɪŋ²¹koŋ⁵⁵ nɯ³³ ɣɯ²¹ (lɔ⁵⁵) pɤ³³ ɣɯ²¹?
tomorrow 2SG come or NEG come
'Do you come tomorrow?'
明天你来不来？

B- i. **(sɿ³³)** ɣɯ²¹ **sɛ²¹**.
    AFF come AFF
    'Yes, I will.'
    来。
ii. pɣ³³ ɣɯ²¹.
    NEG come
    'No, I won't.'
    不来。

The affirmative construction is used to express a speaker's commitment to the truth of his or her own proposition. In other words, a proposition or an assertion is believed to be true by the speaker. Example (11.140) illustrate a case of affirming a happening in the past. The speaker believes that the event 'he came to see you' took place. This might be based on the speaker's own judgement or information garnered from other people. However, the affirmative construction in this sentence does not mean that the subject participant je^{33} 'he' is certain about his action.

(11.140) je³³ **(sɿ³³)** ɣɯ²¹ tsaŋ²¹ nɯ³³ **sɿ²¹**.
         3SG AFF come see 2SG AFF
         'It's certain that he came to see you.'
         他来看你的。

One should note that an assertion marked by the affirmative construction $sɿ^{33}$ ... $sɿ^{21}$ is not necessarily true. As shown in (11.141), the speaker's own opinion that 'he lied to you' turned out to be false. This nicely illustrates the subjectivity involved with the affirmative construction. It should be recalled that the morpheme $sɛ^{21}$ in this example is a fused form with $sɿ^{21}$ and the final particle e.

(11.141) ni²¹ ta⁵⁵ ŋo³³ xa²¹: "je³³ xɯ³³ nɯ³³ **sɛ²¹**.
         3 with 1SG say 3SG lie 2SG AFF.PRT
         nɯ³³ piɔ²⁴ niu³³ la²¹." ŋo³³ pɣ³³ sa²¹.
         2SG NEG.IMP wait PRT 1SG NEG believe
         u²¹so⁵⁵ je³³ tsɛ²¹tsɛ²⁴ ɣɯ²¹ o.
         afterward 3SG really come CRS
         'Someone told me: "He lied to you so don't wait for him (anymore)", but I didn't believe it. Afterward he really came.'
         人家跟我说："他骗你的。你别等啦。"我不信。后来他真的来了。

Example (11.142) shows a case of affirming existence in the presence.

(11.142) A- ŋo³³ meŋ²¹xa³³ ua²⁴ ɣã²¹ xɯ³³pa³³ ni³³ xa²¹.
1SG hear.say here there.be priest.of.Taoism CLF REP
'I heard that there's a priest of Taoism here.'
我听说这儿有一个道士。

B- **sɿ³³** ɣã²¹ ji³³ ni³³ **sɿ²¹**.
AFF there.be one CLF AFF
'It's certain that there's one.'
是有一个。

The affirmative construction can be used in many situations and can also be used along with other modal elements. The two examples below show a combination of the reduced affirmative construction with the modal auxiliary *ti³³* 'know'. The possible situations of 'everybody can encounter such kind of things' in (11.143) and 'he can take care of you' in (11.144) belong to the realm of epistemic possibility. Using the affirmative construction does not turn these two possibilities into certainties. Instead, it denotes that the two speakers are certain about what they assume. It should be pointed out that the expression *a⁵⁵ ni³³tsɿ³³ pʰɪŋ²¹ tsaŋ²¹* 'see with one eye' in (11.144) is metaphorically used to denote 'take care of, keep an eye on'. Note that *tɣ³³* in (11.143) is not a modal word but a resultative complement.

(11.143) ɔ²⁴ tsoŋ⁵⁵ nɛ⁵⁵ lɔ²⁴ni³³ la³³ **sɿ³³**
this kind PRT who all AFF
ti³³ poŋ³³-tɣ³³ **se²¹**.
know encounter-obtain AFF.PRT
'It's certain that everybody can encounter such kind of things.'
这种呢，谁都会碰到的。

(11.144) je³³ **ti²¹** a⁵⁵ ni³³tsɿ³³ pʰɪŋ²¹ tsaŋ²¹ nɯ³³ **se²¹**.
3SG know with eye CLF see 2SG AFF.PRT
'It's certain that he will take care of you.'
他会照顾你的。

The following two cases show the affirmative construction *sɿ³³* . . . *sɿ²¹* used with the post-VP modals *do³³* and *tɣ³³*.

(11.145) ta⁵⁵   nɯ²¹   tʰɣ⁵⁵   po²⁴   po³³   to³³   **se²¹**.
         with   2SG   take.off   bundle   NEG   can   AFF.PRT
         'It's certain that you can't get away from this.'
         跟你脱不了干系的。

(11.146) A- ŋo³³   tsaŋ²¹   ɔ²¹   kʷɔ²⁴   ko²¹   niɔ³³   tʰa²¹
            1SG   see   this   bridge   CLF   PROSP   be.broken
            sɿ²¹   jaŋ²⁴   o.   tsʰɿ²¹   xɪŋ⁵⁵   o.   ɣa²¹   pɣ³³
            way   way   CRS   rot   very   CRS   walk   NEG
            tɣ³³   o.   ŋo²⁴   pa²¹   hɔ⁵⁵   tɣ²¹-kuɛ²¹   niɔ³³
            can   CRS   1PL   detour   road   pass-go   want
            pɣ²¹saŋ⁵⁵   mi⁵⁵.
            be.eased   a.little
            'It seems to me that this bridge's going to collapse. It's pretty rotted. Walking over it isn't possible. Let's make a detour to be more assured.'
            我看这座桥好像要塌了。烂得很了。不能过。咱们绕过过去要放心些。

         B- nɯ³³   pɣ²¹saŋ⁵⁵   e.   ɣa²¹   tɣ³³   **se²¹**.
            2SG   be.eased   PRT   walk   can   AFF
            ŋo⁵⁵   koŋ⁵⁵koŋ⁵⁵ ta⁵⁵   tɣ³³   kua²¹,
            1PL   every.day   from   upside pass
            pɣ³³   kɪŋ²¹   sɿ⁵⁵mɔ⁵⁵   e.
            NEG   see   what   PRT
            'Don't worry. It's certain that walking over it is OK. We do it every day and nothing has happened.'
            你放心。能走。我们天天从上面过，也没见什么。

11.9 Reportative/quotative: *xa³³* < 'say' [(S) VP xa³³]

Languages may possess means of specifying the source of information, a type of evidentiality. Aikhenvald (2004) points out that about 25% of the world's languages possess some type of grammatical evidentiality. Belonging to an evidentiality system, the reportative is a grammatical strategy used to encode second-hand information, that is, information which is reported to the speaker by another person. In contrast, the quotative encodes first-hand information, i.e. direct quotation, and is not open to this interpretation. Evidentiality is often treated as a subtype of epistemic modality (Palmer 1986), while Aikhenvald (2004) considers

11.9 Reportative/quotative: xa^{33} < 'say' [(S) VP xa^{33}] — **411**

it a distinct category. Evidentiality systems are quite common and well developed in Tibeto-Burman languages (LaPolla 2003), while this is not the case in Sinitic languages, most of which nonetheless do morphologically mark some of the subtypes of evidentiality.

Even though Caijia is not a language possessing a developed system of evidentiality, as many Tibeto-Burman languages do, it does adopt grammatical means to code reported and quoted information by using the marker xa^{33}, derived from the verb 'say', in the form of [(S) VP xa^{33}]. The reportative/quotative marking appears to be, semantically, quite different from other modal elements introduced in this chapter, since it has nothing to do with certainty or possibility. This is also the reason why the reportative/quotative marker xa^{33} is not included in Table 11.2.

The example below shows both the lexical and grammatical uses of xa^{33} 'say'. In (11.147i), the narrator narrates what he was told or heard and xa^{33} is used to mark reported information in the sentence final position. In (11.147ii), it is the lexical use of xa^{33}, denoting 'say, speak' which is seen. Example in (11.147iii) is ambiguous, since the bracketed speech can be analyzed either as an direct one or indirect. If treated as indicating indirect speech, the verb xa^{33} that follows it is a reportative marker, while it is a quotative marker if the speech is considered direct. In (11.147iv), xa^{33} functions as the reportative marker marking the reported information 'he, the one from your place, of the family of Li, would wait there to kill me'.

(11.147) i) tɕiŋ²¹tʰɔ⁵⁵   nɛ⁵⁵   sɿ³³   a³³   tɔ²¹   sɿ⁵⁵
front.moment   PRT   COP   OM   marry   to
je²¹   me²¹tsɿ⁵⁵   hɛ²¹   **xa³³**.
3SG   Li$_{NAME}$ family   REP

ii) [...]   je³³   ma²¹ka³³   hɛ²¹   nɛ⁵⁵,   **xa²¹**
3SG   Zhang$_{NAME}$ family   PRT   say
[je³³,   je³³   sɿ³³   niɔ³³   tɯ²¹   mɔ³³
3SG   3SG   COP   PROSP   at   that
tsʰui⁵⁵tɕia⁵⁵   ja²¹kʰəu²¹   ma²⁴   pɔ²¹-xɯ⁵⁵   e,
Cuijia$_{PLACENAME}$ pass   there   squat-DUR   PRT

iii) niɔ²¹   ɕi⁵⁵   u²¹tsʰo²¹]   **xa³³**. [...]
PROSP   kill   person   REP

iv) "nɯ²⁴   ma⁵⁵   mɔ²⁴   ni³³,   me²¹tsɿ⁵⁵   hɛ²¹
2PL   there   that   CLF   Li$_{NAME}$ family
sɿ³³,   niɔ³³   pɔ³³   tɯ²¹
MOD   PROSP   squat   at
ma²⁴   ɕi⁵⁵   ŋo³³   **xa³³**. [...]"
there   kill   1SG   REP

'**It's said** that he (of the family of Zhang) would marry (his daughter) to the family of Li. [...] The (person from the) family of Zhang **said** that (they had heard) he, he (from the family of Li) was going to squat in the pass of Cuijia (to wait for the person from the family of Zhang) to kill him. [...] "**It is said** that the one from your place, of the family of Li, would wait there to kill me. [...]"'
开始说是把（女儿）许给李家。[......] 他张家呢说他，他是要在那个崔家垭口蹲着，要杀人。[......]"你们那儿那个，李家的，说是要在蹲在那儿（等着）杀我。[......]"
(*Two families*, texts)

One more example of *xa³³* serving as a quotative marker is given below. This is an example extracted from a narrative. The speaker repeats what he said to his late wife. As can be seen, the second person pronoun is used in this sentence, which nicely illustrates the quotative function of *xa³³*.

(11.148) "nɯ³³   pɣ³³   kɛ²¹   kʰɪŋ⁵⁵mi²¹sa³³   tsʰɛ²¹
         2SG   NEG   should   evening   only
         soŋ³³-ɣɯ²¹   mɛ̃!   nɯ³³   ɔ²¹   kɯ²⁴
         send-come   PRT   2SG   this   moment
         soŋ³³-ɣɯ²¹   tɕiɔ⁵⁵   mɔ⁵⁵!"   **xa³³**   nɛ³³.
         sent-come   do   what   QUOT   PRT
         ' "Why don't you bring (the meal) even later, like in the evening! Why'd you even bother to bring it now!" **(I) said**.'
         "你怎么不晚上再送（饭）来！现在送来干嘛！"
         (*The fight on the hill*, texts)

11.10 Inferential certainty: Experiential *ja²¹* and *gua³³* [(S) VP ja²¹/gua³³]

Inferential certainty also concerns a speaker's commitment to the truth of his or her own proposition or assertion about perfective events, but it involves the speaker's process of inference, which is often based on physical evidence or results. It is different from the affirmative construction *sɿ³³ . . . sɿ²¹*. The inferential is commonly recognized as a subtype of evidentiality as well (Aikhenvald 2004).

As in many Sinitic languages, in which experiential markers are often used to encode inferential certainty (Chappell 2001c), Caijia uses the two experiential markers, *ja³³* '< experience' and *gua³³* '< experience, pass, cross', to express this category and notion (see Chapter 10 §10.2.5 for their aspectual uses). There is no difference between these two markers and one can use either for this purpose.

The deduction that 'someone has come' is made in (11.149) on the basis of footprints left on the ground. In (11.150), having seen the puddles on the road, the speaker deduces that it must have rained the night before.

(11.149) ɣã²¹   u²¹tsʰo²¹   ɣɯ²¹   **ja²¹/kua³³**.
          there.be   person   come   EXP
          tʰɣ̣⁵⁵   tɣ³³   ɣã²¹   kɣ⁵⁵tsɿ²¹.
          ground   upside   there.be footprint
          'There must be someone who has come. There're footprints on the floor.'
          有人来过了。地上有脚印。

(11.150) me²¹sa³³   ɣɯ²¹   zɿ⁵⁵   **ja²¹/kua³³**.
          yesterday.evening   come   rain   EXP
          hɔ⁵⁵   mo³³   la²¹   kʰɯ⁵⁵   sɿ⁵⁵ta²¹-sui⁵⁵   o.
          road   inside   all   rise   water.pool-PL   CRS
          'It must have rained last night. There're some puddles on the road.'
          昨天晚上下过雨了。路上起水洼了。

A combination of modal forms is present in (11.151). The speaker makes the judgement that there used to be a river upon seeing the dried-up river bed. With this example, one can also verify that the affirmative construction sɿ³³ . . . sɿ²¹ is used along with *ja²¹/kua³³* to reinforce the certainty.

(11.151) ma²⁴   ɣã²¹   sɿ⁵⁵   ta⁵⁵   **ja²¹/kua³³**   sɿ²¹.
          there   there.be   river   CLF   EXP   AFF
          'It's certain that there must have been a river over there.'
          那有过一条河的。

11.11 Conclusion

In this chapter, we have presented the modal system of Caijia. As is introduced, Caijia adopts various strategies to express modality, such as modal auxiliaries, lexical verbs, post-VP 'can' modals, the potential construction, the affirmative construction, two experiential markers, two adverbs, a sentence final particle, and a clause-final reportative marker.

The lexical verbs *tsʰɿ³³* 'fear, it is probable that. . .' and *dzɔ³³* 'resemble', the adverbs *kʰuɔ³³neŋ²¹* 'probably' and *niɔ³³sɿ³³* 'probably', the affirmative construction $sı^{33}$ ... $sı^{21}$ 'it is certain that...', and the sentence final particle $ɔ$ pa are all exclusively used to express different epistemic modalities. The elements $tsʰı^{33}$ 'fear, it is probable that...', $dzɔ^{33}$ 'resemble', $kʰuɔ^{33}neŋ^{21}$ 'probably', $niɔ^{33}sı^{33}$ 'probably', and $ɔ$ pa are used to express possibility. Both the construction $sı^{33}$ ... $sı^{21}$ and the experiential markers ja^{21} and gua^{33} are used to express certainty. However, the markers ja^{21} and gua^{33} are used on the basis of either a speaker's own personal stance or some kind of inferred evidence, while the construction $sı^{33}$ ... $sı^{21}$ only focuses on the speaker's subjective certainty without considering the source of information. Derived from the verb 'say', xa^{33} is used to encode reported and quoted information. As for other modal elements, it is the context that determines which type of modality is denoted.

Of all the parts of speech, modal auxiliaries are the most common elements used for expressing modality in Caijia. Six auxiliary verbs are identified, including $kʰã^{55}$ 'be willing to', $ɕiaŋ^{55}$ 'want', $niɔ^{33}$ 'want, need', $tɕʰiɔ^{21}$ 'be necessary', $niɔ^{33}$-$dγ^{33}$ 'want-need', and ti^{33} 'know'. Only ti^{33} 'know' is used to denote ability and possibility, while the rest are related to necessity, willingness, and volition.

The two post-VP 'can' modals do^{33} '< arrive, to' and $tγ^{33}$ '< obtain' are not readily distinguishable. The modal do^{33} is used to express ability, capacity and possibility, while $tγ^{33}$ can be used to denote permission and weak obligation, as well as possibility. Conversely, the modal do^{33} is never used to denote permission and weak obligation, whereas the modal $tγ^{33}$ is rarely used to express ability. The modal do^{33} is used to express possibilities that are realizable by certain agents, while $tγ^{33}$ is used to express that given events are feasible. When denoting possibility, there are contexts in which both of them can be used interchangeably. When combined, these two elements together form the construction [$tγ^{33}$ VP do^{33}] to denote ability and possibility, which possesses the same semantic value as do^{33}, while being restricted to controllable events.

The potential construction [V $lɯ^{55}$ VP] also possesses the same semantic value as the modal do^{33}. However, it is often ambiguous and can denote both modal and non-modal meanings.

Chapter 12
Negation

12.1 Introduction

Negation has been well studied from cross-linguistic perspective, with general typological surveys beginning with Dahl (1979) and Payne (1985). "Standard negation", which refers to the type of negation having "as one function the negation of the most minimal and basic sentences" (Payne 1985), can be subsequently classified into three types: (i) morphological (or affixal) negation, (ii) negative particles, and (iii) negative verbs by several scholars (Dahl 1979, Payne 1985, Creissels 2006b Chapitre 29, Dryer 2013e). This classification is mainly based on the formal status of negators. See also Givón (2001: Chapter 8) for an analyses from semantic and pragmatic perspectives.

Croft (1991) identifies three types of languages on the basis of diachronic evolution of negation and correlation between verbal negators and negative existential forms. In Type A languages, the verbal negator is used to negate the existential predicate. In Type B languages, there is a special existential negator distinct from the verbal negator. In Type C languages, there is a special existential negator which is also used as the verbal negator. The special existential negator is "usually but not always a contraction or fusion of the verbal negator and the positive existential form" (Croft 1991: 7).

As for Sinitic languages, two phonetic forms of negators have been reconstructed with distinct initials. Hashimoto (= 桥本万太郎 1985 [1978]: 76–79) observes that the southern Sinitic languages (Yue, Min and Hakka) use *m-type negators, e.g. m̀h 'not' in Cantonese (Matthews and Yip 1994: 250–252), while *p-initial negators are used in the northern dialects, e.g. bù '不' [pu^{51}] in Standard Mandarin. He also points out that the m-initial negators are used to negate existential predicates in most of the Sinitic languages, e.g. méi 'not' 没 [mei^{15}] in Standard Mandarin.

Furthermore, Sinitic languages are characterized by a large set of semantically distinct negators and negative existential verbs are attested in most of the Sinitic languages. Chappell and Peyraube (2016b) thus propose a semantic typology of negation for Sinitic based on Chappell (2001a). This typology is comprised of three syntactic types of negation:
i. negative existential and possessive verb,
ii. standard negation, and
iii. prohibitive,

which can be classified into eight semantic types, including general or volitional, perfective, imminent, irrealis, prohibitive, injunctive negation, and negation of lack of necessity. Certainly, not every Sinitic language codes all of these eight types of negation. Southern Min possesses all of these eight types, whereas Standard Mandarin only has two main types of negation (Chappell and Peyraube 2016b). Here we select Southern Min as a representative language to illustrate these eight types of negation and give an overview regarding the specific Sinitic typology for negation. Southern Min data is presented alongside the types of negation found in Caijia in Table 12.1.

Table 12.1: Semantic typology of negation in Sinitic.

Semantic Typology of Negation in Sinitic			Southern Min	Caijia
Verbal	Negative $V_{EX/POSS}$		bo²⁴ 'not have'	
Adverbial	Standard Negation	General and Volitional	m²² 'not' mmai²¹ 'not want' boai²¹ 'not want'	pɣ³³ 'not'
		Perfective	bo²⁴ 'not have'	pɣ³³-tɣ³³ 'not obtain'
		Imminent	be²² 'not yet'	
		Irrealis	bue²²~be²² 'will not'	pɣ³³/po³³ 'not'
	Prohibitive	General prohibitive	mai²¹ 'don't'	pɣ³³niɔ³³>piɔ²⁴ 'not want>don't'
		Lack of necessity	bien⁵³ 'no need to'	pɣ³³tɕʰiɔ²¹ 'no need to'
		Injunctive	mo⁵³ 'better not to'	

12.2 Negation in Caijia

The general features of negation in Caijia can be outlined as follows:
i. Caijia uses the same adverbial negator *pɣ³³* to negate both non-existential and existential predicates.
ii. The negator *pɣ³³* is obviously cognate with the negator *bù* 不 [pu⁵¹] in Standard Mandarin or other similar forms in other Sinitic languages, i.e. with **p-*initial negators.
iii. The negator *pɣ³³* belongs to the grammatical category of adverbs as negators in Sinitic languages (Chappell and Peyraube 2016b). Its syntactic position, in a main clause, can be schematized as [NEG + (AUX) + (PREPP) + V]. For example,

(12.1) je³³ tɯ³³sɿ³³ pɣ²¹ kʰã⁵⁵ ta⁵⁵ ŋo²¹ xa³³ ŋoŋ³³.
3SG indeed NEG be.willing.to with 1SG speak speech
'He indeed doesn't want to speak with me.'
他就是不肯跟我说话。

iv. However, distinct from most of the Sinitic languages, there is no *m-initial negator or negative existential verb (this is certainly the case for our fieldwork site of Xingfa Caijia).
v. All types of negation are realized via the negator *pɣ³³* (its bare form, a variant, or other compound or fused forms [see Table 12.1 as well]).

Modeled on the semantic typology of negation in Sinitic languages, this chapter provides an elaborated description of the negation system in Caijia concerning the negative existential and possessive verb in one of the variants of Caijia, the standard negation, and the negative imperatives.

12.2.1 Negative existential and possessive verb

It is mentioned above that in Xingfa Caijia, the target language, there is no negative existential and possessive verb. However, it is attested in one of the variants of Caijia spoken in Fuchu, a township in Hezhang bordering Weining County. The verb is *paŋ³³* 'not have', which is the fused form of the negator *pɣ³³* and the verb *ɣaŋ³³* 'have' and it can take NPs as its direct objects. Compare the examples below from Xingfa Caijia and Fuchu Caijia.

Existential
(12.2) Xingfa Caijia
 a. ã²¹ mo³³ **pɣ³³** ɣã²¹ sɿ⁵⁵.
  jar inside NEG have water
  'There isn't any water in the jar.'
  缸里没水。

 Fuchu Caijia
 b. aŋ²¹ mo³³ **paŋ²¹** sɿ⁵⁵.
  jar inside not.have water
  'There isn't any water in the jar.'
  缸里没水。

Possession

(12.3) Xingfa Caijia
    a. ŋo³³ **pɣ³³** ɣã²¹ tɕɪŋ²¹.
       1SG NEG have money
       'I don't have money.'
       我没钱。

    Fuchu Caijia
    b. ŋo³³ **paŋ³³** tɕɪŋ²¹.
       1SG not.have money
       'I don't have money.'
       我没钱。

Moreover, the negative existential verb *paŋ³³* 'not have' in Fuchu Caijia can be used in any case where the negated 'have' is needed, for example, to express a comparison of inferiority.

(12.4) Xingfa Caijia
    a. ŋo³³ **pɣ³³** ɣã²¹ ŋuɛ²¹ tɕi⁵⁵ kʷɔ³³.
       1SG NEG have my.family eleder.sister tall
       'I'm not as tall as my elder sister.'
       我没有我姐姐高。

    Fuchu Caijia
    b. ŋo³³ **paŋ³³** ŋo²¹ tɕi⁵⁵ kʷɔ³³.
       1SG not.have 1SG elder.sister tall
       'I'm not as tall as my elder sister.'
       我没有我姐姐高。

Note that this fused form, *paŋ³³* 'not have', is not accepted in Xingfa Caijia.

12.2.2 Standard negation

12.2.2.1 General and volitional negation: *pɣ³³* 'not'

The negator *pɣ³³* in Caijia is functionally and semantically similar to the negator *bù* in Standard Mandarin when used in imperfective situations. It "refers to the type of sentence unmarked overtly by modal/aspects" (Yue-Hashimoto 1993: 90), namely the "present, future, habitual, and irrealis contexts" (Chappell and Peyraube 2016b: 502). Examples (12.5)-(12.7) illustrate respectively the negated copula *sɿ³³*, adjectival verb *kʰua²¹* 'good', and the stative verb *tɯ²¹* 'live, be at' in the context of future. Example (12.8) shows the negated action verb *ã³³* 'drink', is negated denoting a habitual event, and (12.9) illustrates a case with the auxiliary of possibility *ti³³* 'know'. As mentioned previously, the negator always precedes the auxiliary.

Copula
(12.5) ŋo³³ **pɣ³³** sı³³ kɔ³³sʏ²¹ŋa⁵⁵.
       1SG NEG COP student
       'I'm not a student.'
       我不是学生。

Adjectival verb
(12.6) mɔ²¹ u²¹tsʰo²⁴ ni³³ **pɣ³³** kʰua²¹.
       that person CLF NEG good
       'That person is not good.'
       那个人不好。

Stative verb in future
(12.7) tʰɪŋ²¹koŋ⁵⁵ ŋo³³ niɔ³³ kuɛ²¹ sun³³ je³³,
       tomorrow 1SG PROSP go help 3SG
       pɣ³³ tɯ²¹ ɔ⁵⁵ ʑi²¹.
       NEG be.at house inside
       'I'll go to help him tomorrow and won't be at home.'
       明天我要去帮他，不在家。

Habitual
(12.8) ŋo³³ **pɣ³³** ã²¹ tso⁵⁵. ã²¹ ha⁵⁵ nɛ⁵⁵
       1SG NEG drink alcohol drink COMPL PRT
       seŋ²¹tʰoŋ⁵⁵ zɣ²¹ xɪŋ⁵⁵.
       body itch very
       'I don't drink alcohol. My body itches after drinking.'
       我不喝酒。喝了呢身上很痒。

Irrealis
(12.9) ŋo³³ **pɣ³³** ti³³ xa³³ men²¹ni³³ŋoŋ³³.
       1SG NEG know speak Caijia
       'I can't speak Caijia.'
       我不会讲蔡家话。

Zhu Dexi (1982: 200) points out that the negator *bù* in Standard Mandarin often produces a meaning of unwillingness, i.e. volitional negation (see aslo Li and

Thompson 1981: 421–422, Chappell and Peyraube 2016b: 502), specifically when it is used to negate verbs of action or activity. This interpretation of unwillingness can also be produced when *pɣ^{33}* negates the same type of verbs in Caijia in certain appropriate contexts. As already demonstrated in (12.5)-(12.7) and (12.9), none of these negated predicates denote unwillingness, since the verbs in these examples are neither verbs of action nor verbs of activity. We reproduce as an example the action verb *ã^{33}* 'drink', whose negated form denotes a habitual event in (12.8). In example (12.10), by way of contrast, *pɣ^{33} ã^{33}* 'not drink (alcohol)' in speech turn B₁ denotes that the speaker refuses to drink (on a particular occasion), instead of habitually. Unwillingness is the only interpretation in this case.

(12.10) A₁- nɯ^{33} ã^{21} tso^{55} lɔ^{21} **pɣ^{33}** ã^{33}?
　　　　　 2SG drink alcohol or NEG drink
　　　　　 ŋo^{21} ta^{55} nɯ^{21} tʰɔ^{55} mi^{55} ã^{33}.
　　　　　 1SG for 2SG pour little drink
　　　　　 'Would you like to drink some alcohol? I'll pour you some.'
　　　　　 你喝酒不喝？我给你倒些喝。

　　　　 B₁- ŋo^{33} **pɣ^{21}** ã^{21} o.
　　　　　 1SG NEG drink CRS
　　　　　 ti^{55}ɪn^{21} kɯ^{24} tɯ^{21} ɔ^{55} ʑi^{21}
　　　　　 just now moment at house inside
　　　　　 ã^{33} ji^{21} la^{21} u^{55} ha^{55}.
　　　　　 drink one big bowl COMPL
　　　　　 pɣ^{21} ɕiaŋ^{55} ã^{33} o.
　　　　　 NEG want drink CRS
　　　　　 'No, I won't. (LIT: I don't (want to) drink). Just now I've had a big bowl (of alcohol), so I don't want to drink.'
　　　　　 我不喝。刚才在家喝了一大碗了。不想喝了。

The negated verbs of action or activity are often ambiguous if they are not considered in context. Example (12.11) has possible readings of both lack of willingness or negation of a presupposition, depending on the context.

(12.11)　tʰɪn^{21}koŋ^{55} ŋo^{33} **pɣ^{33}** ɣɯ^{21}.
　　　　　tomorrow 1SG NEG come
　　　　　'I don't want to come tomorrow.'
　　　　　'I won't come tomorrow (for it's my day off).'
　　　　　明天我不来。

12.2.2.2 Perfective negation: $pɣ^{33}$-$tɣ^{33}$ 'not-obtain'

Perfective negation in Caijia is realized by $pɣ^{33}tɣ^{33}$, a negator in the form of a compound and composed of the negator $pɣ^{33}$ and the verb $tɣ^{33}$ 'obtain'. It is mainly used in completive and experiential contexts as well as those concerning change of state. In completive and change-of-state contexts, the completive marker ha^{55} (< 'finish') and the marker of currently relevant state o (source unclear) are no longer used in the negative, which means completive negation and perfective negation are not morphologically contrastive. See also Chapter 10 §10.2.1.

Examples (12.12) and (12.13) demonstrate respectively the completive and change-of-state contexts. One can readily observe that there is no difference between completive and change-of-state negation.

Completive

(12.12) a. je³³ ɣɯ²¹ ha²¹ o.
3SG come COMPL CRS
'He came. (Here he is).'
他来了。

b. je³³ (a²¹) **pɣ³³-tɣ³³** ɣɯ²¹.
3SG still NEG-PFV come
'He hasn't come (yet).'
他(还)没来。

Change of state

(12.13) a. je³³ ɣɯ²¹ o.
3SG come CRS
'He came. (Here he is).'
他来了。

b. je³³ (a²¹) **pɣ³³-tɣ³³** ɣɯ²¹.
3SG still NEG-PFV come
'He hasn't come (yet).'
他(还)没来。

However, unlike the completive and change-of-state contexts, the experiential marker ja^{21} is retained in its corresponding negated sentence, as shown in the following example. This is also the case in Sinitic languages, such as Standard Mandarin, Hakka, and Gan etc. (see Zhang Shuangqing 1996).

Experiential

(12.14) a. mɔ²¹ tsoŋ⁵⁵ saŋ⁵⁵ ŋo³³ zɣ³³ ja²¹.
that kind mushroom 1SG eat EXP
'I've eaten that kind of mushroom.'
那种蘑菇我吃过。

b. mɔ²¹ tsoŋ⁵⁵ saŋ⁵⁵ ŋo³³ pɣ³³-tɣ³³ zɣ³³ ja²¹.
that kind mushroom 1SG NEG.PFV eat EXP
'I haven't eaten that kind of mushroom.'
那种蘑菇我没吃过。

Imminent negation is not specifically coded in Caijia. It can only be expressed in an analytic way via using the adverb a^{21}/xa^{21} 'still' before the negator $pɣ^{33}tɣ^{33}$ to express 'not yet'. See example (12.15).

(12.15) nɯ³³ tɕiu²¹ xɪŋ⁵⁵ a mẽ. ŋo³³ a²¹ pɣ³³-tɣ³³
2SG fast very PRT PRT 1SG still NEG-PFV
tɕie⁵⁵-kʰua²¹, nɯ³³ tɯ³³ pe⁵⁵-ɣɯ²¹ o.
do-be.good 2SG even return-come CRS
'You're so fast. I haven't got (the meal) ready yet. You've already come back.'
你快得很啊。我还没做好你就回来了。

Though the form [NEG + obtain] used as a perfective negator is not rare in Sinitic languages especially in Southwestern Mandarin, the negator $pɣ^{33}tɣ^{33}$ in Caijia shows other special features.

First, in Sinitic languages, it is common that the perfective negator is derived from the existential and possessive negator corresponding to 'there is not' and 'not have', as observed in Standard Mandarin, Southern Min (Taiwanese), Hong Kong Cantonese, and New Xiang by Chappell and Peyraube (2016b). Furthermore, this phenomenon is also observed in Waxiang (Wu 2006), the Ningbo (Tianluoshan) dialect of Wu (Ruan Guijun 2009), Meixian Hakka (Huang Xuezhen 1995: 66), Taiyuan Jin (Shen Ming 1994: 270), Nanchang Gan (Xiong Zhenghui 1994: 107), and Nanning Pinghua (Qin et al. 1997: 62–65), as well as in the local dialect of Southwestern Mandarin in Hezhang. By contrast, one can see from the examples above that the perfective negator is distinct from the existential and possessive negator in Caijia. Furthermore, $pɣ^{33}ɣã^{21}$ 'not have' in Caijia cannot be used as the perfective negator.

Second, in Sinitic languages, the form [NEG + obtain] can often be treated as a negative existential and possessive verb, whose positive counterpart is YOU 有 'have, there be' instead of DE 得 'obtain'. This phenomenon is detected in many dialects of Southwestern Mandarin, for example, the Hezhang dialect ($me^{13}te^{21}$ 'not obtain'), the Chengdu dialect ($mei^{55}te^{21}$ 'not obtain') (Liang and Huang 1998: 183), the Qiandongnan dialect ($mei^{35}tɛ^{21}$ 'not obtain') (Xiao Yali 2008: 29–30), the Guiyang dialect ($pu^{31}te^{31}/mei^{55}te^{31}$ 'not obtain') (Wang Ping 1994: 142), the Wuhan dialect ($mau^{35}tɤ^{213}$ 'not obtain') (Zhu Jiansong 1995: 180) and the Zigong dialect (Yin Runlin 2005: 52). All of these examples can be used as perfective negators except those in the Wuhan and Zigong dialects. Nevertheless, $pɤ^{33}tɤ^{33}$ in Caijia does not denote 'not have'. It is only used as a perfective negator.

12.2.2.3 Post-VP negative possibility and negative potential

Caijia uses several modal elements to code possibility, such as the auxiliary ti^{33} 'know' and two post-VP elements $tɤ^{33}$ 'can' (< 'obtain')'and do^{33} 'can' (< 'arrive, to') (see Chapter 11). Negation of these elements leads to the expression 'not able, not possible'. Unlike the irrealis negative in the Min group, this type of negation in Caijia does not form a semantic category. Sinitic languages often use auxiliaries to code possibility (Chappell and Peyraube 2016a). In Caijia, when coding possibility the auxiliary ti^{33} is less frequently used than the two post-VP elements $tɤ^{33}$ and do^{33}. We single these post-VP elements out here along with the negative potential construction because (i) the syntactic position of the negator is different from the one in standard negation and (ii) an allomorph of the negator $pɤ^{33}$, i.e. po^{33}, has been identified for negating do^{33}.

The meaning of impossibility denoted by ti^{33} belongs to the main type of general standard negation. See the following example and refer also to (12.9) above.

(12.16)　mɔ²¹　tsɿ²¹tsɿ²⁴　kɔ²¹　ɕie²¹　xɩŋ⁵⁵，a²¹　**pɤ³³**　ti³³　pɤ²¹.
　　　　that　bird　　　　CLF　small　very　still　NEG　know　fly
　　'That bird is so little and can't fly.'
　　那只鸟太小了，还不会飞。

In contrast to the situation with ti^{33}, it is the post-VP element $tɤ^{33}$ or do^{33} that has to be negated and not the main predicate verb in order to express the meaning of 'not able, not possible'. As mentioned above, instead of the negator $pɤ^{33}$, the allomorph po^{33} is used to negate do^{33}. This allomorph is not observed in any other Caijia construction.

(12.17)　tshɿ⁵⁵po⁵⁵　xa³³　nie²⁴　o.　zɤ²¹　**pɤ³³　tɤ³³**　o.
　　　　potato　　　grow　sprout　CRS　eat　NEG　can　CRS
　　The potatoes have sprouted. (They) aren't edible any more.
　　土豆发芽了。吃不得了。

(12.18) mɔ²¹ tʰɣ⁵⁵po²¹ po⁵⁵ xa²¹tsɛ³³ tʰa³³ sɿ²¹.
that stove CLF still be.broken CONT
ŋo³³ xa²¹ tɕie⁵⁵ zɣ²¹ **po³³** **to³³**.
1SG still do meal NEG can
'The stove is still broken. I still can't cook.'
炉子还坏着。我还做不了饭。

In addition, the negative potential construction can also denote 'not able, not possible' (see also Chapter 11 §11.5). It is the resultative complement of the main verb that is negated. Compare the positive resultative construction *tɕiɔ²¹-tɣ²¹kuɛ²¹* 'jump over' and its negative in example (12.19).

(12.19) a. mɔ²¹ tɕʰi³³kʰa²¹ ta⁵⁵ pɣ³³ ɣã²¹ kʰua²¹ kʰua²⁴ mi⁵⁵.
that ditch CLF NEG have how wide a.little
ji³³ tɕiɔ²¹ tɯ³³ **tɕiɔ²¹-tɣ²¹kuɛ²¹** o.
one jump then jump-pass.go CRS
'That ditch isn't wide. You can just jump over it.'
那条水沟没有多宽。一跳就跳过去了。

b. mɔ²¹ tɕʰi³³kʰa²¹ ta⁵⁵ kʰua²¹ xɪŋ⁵⁵ **tɕiɔ²¹-pɣ³³-tɣ²¹kuɛ²¹**.
that ditch CLF wide very jump-NEG-pass.go
'That ditch is very wide. You can't jump it over.'
那条水沟宽得很。跳不过去。

12.2.2.4 Negators in negative imperatives

12.2.2.4.1 General prohibitive: *piɔ²⁴* < *pɣ³³ niɔ³³* 'not want'

The negator *piɔ²⁴* is used as a general imperative negator in Caijia. It is the fused form of the negator *pɣ³³* and the verb/auxiliary *niɔ³³* 'want, need'. In a negative imperative clause, both the fused form and the non-fused form can be used. In each case, they denote 'don't. . .'.

(12.20) zɿ⁵⁵ ɣɯ²¹ lɯ⁵⁵ mɔ⁵⁵sɿ⁵⁵.
rain come VCOMP very
nɯ³³ **[piɔ²⁴]/[pɣ³³niɔ³³]** tsa²¹ ti²¹ la²¹!
2SG NEG.IMP go.up hill PRT
'It's raining heavily. Don't go up the hill.'
雨下得大得很。你别上山了。

It is certainly the case that BUYAO 不要 'not want' or its fused form BIAO 覅 and its cognates in Sinitc, used as an imperative negator, is very well attested in Sinitic languages, particularly in the Mandarin groups and Jin. To name a few examples, the *búyào* in Standard Mandarin, *pə^{22}iau^{45}* in the Taiyuan dialect of Jin (Shen Ming 1994: 268), *pu^{31}iau^{24}* in the Guiyang dialect of Southwestern Mandarin (Wang Ping 1994: 38), *pu^{23}iɔ^{21}* in the Jinan dialect of Jilu Mandarin (Qian Zengyi 1997: 45), *piau^{213}* in the Chengdu dialect of Southwestern Mandarin (Liang and Huang 1998: 223), *pɔ^{31}* in the Luoyang dialect of Central Plains Mandarin (He Wei 1996: 133), *pau^{21}* in the Xi'an dialect of Central Plains Mandarin (Wang Junhu 1996: 144), *piɔ^{53}* in the Xinzhou dialect of Jin (Wen and Zhang 1995: 139), and *pa^{13}* in the Yinchuan dialect of Northwestern Mandarin (Li and Zhang 1996: 71)

12.2.2.4.2 Lack of necessity: *pɣ^{33}tɕʰiɔ^{21}* 'not necessary'

As just explained, the negators *piɔ^{24}* and *pɣ^{33}niɔ^{33}* can be used to express lack of necessity when forming negative imperative clauses. This is probably because the verb *niɔ^{33}* itself possesses the meaning of 'need' in its basic lexical sense, as shown below.

(12.21) ŋo^{33} **niɔ^{21}** sɯ^{55} kʰɯ^{21} koŋ^{55} lɛ^{21}tsʰɛ^{21} tɕie^{55} ja^{21}pa^{21} to^{33}.
        1SG   need   rest   several   day   so that   do   crops   can
'I need to rest for several days so that I can do farming (again).'
我要休息几天才能干活。

In addition to *piɔ^{24}* and *pɣ^{33}niɔ^{33}*, *pɣ^{33} tɕʰiɔ^{21}* 'no need to, not necessary' is used exclusively to express lack of necessity. See Chapter 11 §11.2.5.

(12.22) ŋo^{33} pia^{33} je^{33} ja^{21} o.
        1SG   ask   3SG   EXP   CRS
        (nɯ^{33}) **[piɔ^{24}]/[pɣ^{33}niɔ^{33}]/[pɣ^{33}tɕʰiɔ^{21}]** pia^{33} la^{21}!
        2SG   NEG.IMP/not.want/not.need   ask   PRT
'I've already asked him. You don't need to ask.'
我问过他了。你别/不用/不消问了。

The source of *tɕʰiɔ^{21}* remains unclear. However, we find that there is a similar morpheme in Hezhang (Xingfa) Southwestern Mandarin, *ɕiɔ^{21}*, which is also used in its negative form *pu^{21}ɕiɔ^{21}* to express lack of necessity. The source of *ɕiɔ^{21}* in Hezhang Southwestern Mandarin is probably *xiāo* 消 [ɕiau^{55}] whose meaning of 'need' can be traced back to late Medieval Chinese (Wang et al. 2000: 589). See also Wang Ping (1994: 38) for the use of a similar morpheme in the Guiyang dialect.

12.3 Conclusion

Compared with the negatives in Sinitic languages, the representative forms for marking negation in Caijia are not characterized by any great diversity. As can be observed, Caijia has a quite straightforward system, as there is just one basic negator $pγ^{33}$ used to realize imperfective standard negation. This negator serves as both verbal negator and existential and possessive negator. This means that Caijia uses the *p-initial negator to express both existential and possessive predicates, whereas Sinitic languages often use the *m-initial negators. Caijia (the Xingfa variant) does not possess a negative existential and possessive verb as most of the Sinitic languages do. Given that $pγ^{33}$ in Caijia is cognate with *bù* 不 in Standard Mandarin, which has been used as a simple verbal negator in Chinese since the pre-archaic period (14th–11th BC) (Chappell and Peyraube 2016b), Caijia fits the category of a Type A language – one in which a verbal negator is used to negate the existential predicate – under Croft's (1991) framework. Most of the Sinitic languages, on the other hand, are Type B languages in which the verbal negator and existential and possessive negator are two distinct forms.[15]

Apart from the basic negator $pγ^{33}$, there are three types of negators in Caijia, all of which are formed with $pγ^{33}$. They are the perfective negator $pγ^{33}tγ^{33}$ 'not obtain', the general prohibitive negator $piɔ^{24}$ or $pγ^{33}niɔ^{33}$ 'not want ~ don't' and the lack of necessity negator $pγ^{33}tɕʰiɔ^{21}$ 'no need to, not necessary'. The negator $piɔ^{24}$ is the fused form of $pγ^{33}$ 'not' and $niɔ^{33}$ 'want, need', which is a very common phenomenon attested in Sinitic languages.

Sinitic languages show some correlations between existential and possessive negators and perfective negators, i.e. existential and possessive negator or verb > perfective negator, which means that the existential and possessive verb is used as a perfective negator or, if not, that existential and possessive negation and perfective negation share the same negator. However, perfective negation in Caijia does not follow this pattern. The negator $pγ^{33}tγ^{33}$ serves exclusively as a perfective negator. It cannot negate the existential and possessive verb nor serve as a negative existential and possessive verb.

---

[15] Certain Sinitic languages are Type C languages in Croft's typology (1991), or languages in which the existential negator is used as the verbal negator. The Qiandongnan variety of Southwestern Mandarin, a variety spoken in Guizhou Province, is of this type. The existential negator mei^{35}, an *m-initial negator, is used to form standard negation (Xiao Yali 2008: Chapter 3).

Chapter 13
Interrogatives

13.1 Introduction

Interrogatives, or questions, are one of the three prototypical speech-acts, i.e. declarative, interrogative, and imperative (see Givón 2001, Dixon 2012). In the literature, polar questions and content questions are the two most well-known interrogative constructions. Polar questions are also known as *Yes-No* questions. In other words, in asking a polar question, one expects an answer of *Yes* or *No*, as shown in (13.1a). Content questions, also known as *WH*-questions, ask for specific answers, as illustrated in (13.1b). Ultan's (1969) cross-linguistic survey on 79 languages identifies five strategies of coding interrogatives: intonation, inversion (change of word order), tags, interrogative particles, and interrogative words. The English polar question shown in (13.1a) uses both the intonation and the inversion strategies (with the auxiliary 'do' occupying the initial position), while the content question shown in (13.1b) uses an interrogative word and the inversion strategies.

(13.1) Polar question
  a. Do you like rock music?
     Yes, I do/No, I don't.

  Content question
  b. Who's that man?
     He's my uncle.

Admittedly, English questions are not limited to these two types. For example, alternative questions (e.g. 'Are you coming with us or staying at home?') are similar to polar questions but cannot be answered by yes or no; while rhetorical questions do not need to be answered. However, as Dixon observes (2012: 390), true questions expect answers.

Zhu Dexi (1982: 202, 1985) points out that three types of questions can be observed in Sinitic languages: content questions, polar particle questions, and alternative questions, i.e. "VP-neg-VP questions" (q.v. Yue-Hashimoto 1993: 41), also known as A-not-A questions (Li and Thompson 1981: 535, Matthews and Yip 1994: 311). In his typological survey, Zhang Min (1990: Chapter 5) reports a fourth type of polar question strategy in Sinitic: verb reduplication (see also Zhu Dexi 1990: 216 and Huang Borong 1996: 695, Luo 2016: Chapter 6).

On the basis of previous work on Sinitic questions (Zhu Dexi 1982, 1985, 1990, 1991, Li and Thompson 1984, Zhang Min 1990, Yue-Hashimoto 1993), we have summarized the Sinitic questions here in Table 13.1. Zhu Dexi (1982: 203) points out that the alternative polar questions in Table 13.1 are subtypes of alternative questions. Diachronically, the alternative questions may be the source constructions for the Sinitic yes-no questions in the literature (Zhu Dexi 1990). See Lin Su'e (2017) for a typological survey on polar questions in the form of [Q VP] in Sinitic languages, in which Q stands for a question marker.

Table 13.1: Typology of Sinitic question forms.

Types		Strategies
I	Alternative questions	i. Juxtaposition ∅: [VP₁ VP₂]
		ii. Juxtaposition by disjunction: [VP₁ DISJ VP₂]
II	i. Alternative polar questions	a. Juxtaposition ∅: [VPᵢ NEG VPᵢ]
		b. Juxtaposition by disjunction: [VPᵢ DISJ NEG VPᵢ]
		c. Condensed: [VP NEG]
		d. Preverbal question marker: [Q VP]
	ii. Particle polar questions	Question final particle: [VP Q]
	iii. Verb-reduplication polar questions	Verb-reduplication: [V-VP]
III	Content questions	In-situ question words

This chapter will introduce three types of questions in Caijia: (i) alternative questions, (ii) polar questions (alternative and particle) and (iii) content questions. In general, Caijia interrogatives mirror the Sinitic ones which use similar strategies. Alternative questions can be schematized as [VP₁ or VP₂]. VP-NEG-VP is the major strategy used for forming Caijia polar questions, and one which is very much related to alternative questions since an alternative with a disjunction can always be found, i.e. [VP-(DISJ)-NEG-VP]. The particle polar question strategy can also be observed to form polar questions, but is restricted to several specific types (see §13.3.2). Content questions are formed via in-situ question words. See Table 13.2 below.

13.2 Alternative questions and the disjunction *lɔ²¹* 'or'

When posing an alternative question, the questioner expects one of the options offered to be chosen. Alternative questions usually involve a binary choice in Caijia with two VPs connected by the alternative disjunction *lɔ²¹* 'or' or *xa²¹sɿ³³/*

Table 13.2: Caijia interrogatives.

Types		Strategies
I	Alternative questions	Juxtaposition by disjunction: [VP$_{1\ \text{DISJ}}$VP$_2$]
II	i. Alternative polar questions	a. Juxtaposition: [VP (DISJ) NEG V]
		b. Reduced: [VP (DISJ) NEG]
	ii. Particle polar questions	Question final particle: [VP Q]
III	Content questions	In-situ question words

$a^{21}s\mathsf{1}^{33}$ 'or'. The latter, cognate with the Chinese alternative disjunction *háishì* 还是 [xai²⁴ş̩⁵¹] 'or', is less frequently used than the former. Alternative questions can be roughly schematized as [NP VP$_1$ lɔ²¹ VP$_2$] or [NP VP$_1$ (x)a²¹sɿ³³ VP$_2$]. In speech turn (13.2Q), the alternative disjunction *lɔ²¹* or *(x)a²¹sɿ³³* 'or' connects two VPs which share the same subject *nɯ³³* 'you'. Speech turn (13.2A$_1$) provides a possible answer to (13.2Q), with the respondent choosing one of the options presented in the question. However, it should be noted that the respondent need not choose between one of the two offered options. Therefore, the answer to an alternative question varies due to the answerer's actual situation and may lie beyond the options offered, as shown in (13.2A$_2$).

(13.2) Q- nɯ³³ tɯ²¹ ɔ⁵⁵ ʑi²¹ **lɔ²¹/(x)a²¹sɿ³³** kuɛ²¹ ka²¹kʰɯ³³?
2SG be.at house inside or go go.to.the.fair
'Are you going to be at home or go to the market?'
你在家还是去赶集？

    A$_1$- ŋo³³ tɯ²¹ ɔ⁵⁵ ʑi²¹.
1SG be.at house inside
'I'll be at home.'
我在家。

    A$_2$- ŋo³³ niɔ³³ kuɛ²¹ pɤ²¹ tsʰa⁵⁵.
1SG PROSP go put dung
'I'll go to spread fertilizer (on the fields).'
我要去放肥。

The disjunction *lɔ²¹* 'or' connects two independent clauses in (13.3).

(13.3) nɯ²¹ ta⁵⁵ ŋo²¹ ʑa²¹ loŋ³³ mo³³ kuɛ²¹ lɔ²¹
2SG with 1SG walk town inside go or
je²¹ ta⁵⁵ ŋo²¹ ʑa²¹?
3SG with 1SG walk
'Will you go to the town with me, or will he?'
你跟我去城里还是他跟我去？

In (13.4), one can observe that *lɔ²¹* 'or' connects the VP *zɣ²¹ xɯ⁵⁵tsʅ⁵⁵* 'eat pears' and the noun *kʰɪŋ²⁴pa³³mi³³* 'corn'. This is because VP₁ and VP₂, connected by *lɔ²¹* in this alternative question, share the same verb *zɣ²¹* 'eat'. An absent verb *zɣ²¹* can always be restored to VP₂.

(13.4) nɯ³³ zɣ²¹ xɯ⁵⁵tsʅ⁵⁵ **lɔ²¹** (zɣ²¹) kʰɪŋ²⁴pa³³mi³³?
2SG eat pear or eat corn
'Do you eat a pear or eat a corncob?'
你吃梨还是（吃）玉米？

One should note that all the sentences above cannot be interpreted as declarative sentences. The alternative disjunction *lɔ²¹* 'or' is only used to form interrogatives. The disjunction used in declarative sentences is distinct, *xuɔ²¹tsɛ⁵⁵* 'or', a loan from the local Southwestern Mandarin corresponding to *huòzhě* 或者 [xuɔ⁵¹tʂə²¹⁴] 'or' in Standard Mandarin. As shown in (13.5), to express the meaning 'that kind (of person) is called teacher or teacher of healing', it is *xuɔ²¹tsɛ⁵⁵* 'or' that should be used. Using *lɔ²¹* 'or' will change the meaning of the sentence, transforming it into an alternative question, even though the sentence with *xuɔ²¹tsɛ⁵⁵* and the one with *lɔ²¹* share the same syntactic structure.

(13.5) ɣã²¹ ji²¹sui⁵⁵ ti³³ pʰɣ³³ to²¹.
there.be some know lay pox
mɔ²⁴ tsoŋ⁵⁵ sʅ³³ xaŋ²¹-tɕie⁵⁵
that type COP call-do
kɔ³³sɣ³³pa³³ **xuɔ²¹tsɛ⁵⁵/*lɔ²¹** kʰɯ⁵⁵ soŋ²¹ kɔ³³sɣ³³pa³³.
teacher or cure illness teacher
'There're some that can practice vaccination. That kind (of person) is called teacher or teacher of healing.'
有一些会种痘。那种（人）叫做老师或者治病老师。

Nevertheless, *lɔ²¹* 'or' can be observed in a limited number of non-interrogative cases. For example, alternative interrogatives can serve as subjects or as complement clauses. The bracketed alternative clause functions as the subject in (13.6a), while the one in (13.6b) serves as the object of the verb *pʰa³³me²¹* 'forget'.

(13.6) a. [niɔ²¹ tsʰe⁵⁵ ma²¹kʰa³³ ko²¹ tɕɪŋ²¹ lɔ²¹ tɯ²¹
 want be.out door find money or at
 ɔ⁵⁵ ʑi²¹ kʷɔ³³ sɤ³³] la²¹ tsɛ²¹
 house inside learn book all be.up.to
 nɯ³³ mɛ̃! nɯ³³ tsɿ²¹tɕia⁵⁵ tɯ²¹-kʰua²¹.
 2SG PRT 2SG oneself think-good
 'That you go out to work (LIT: find money) or stay at home to attend school (LIT: learn book) is all up to you. You consider it well.'
 要出门找钱还事在家读书都在你嘛！你自己想好。

b. ŋo³³ pʰa³³me²¹ [je³³ sa²¹ kɪ⁵⁵saŋ²¹
 1SG forget 3SG be.surnamed NAME
 lɔ²¹ loŋ³³tɤ³³].
 or NAME
 'I forgot whether his family name is kɪŋ⁵⁵saŋ²¹ or loŋ³³tɤ³³.'
 我忘记他姓吕还是姓陈。

13.3 Polar questions

"Polar questions are ones to which the expected answer is the equivalent of 'yes' or 'no' (and which are thus sometimes called *yes-no* questions)" (Dryer 2013f). We adopt the term 'polar question' instead of 'yes-no question' here since literal 'yes' and 'no' equivalents do not exist in Caijia. Caijia polar questions are divided into alternative and particle polar questions on the basis of their formation strategies (see Table 13.2). According to Dryer (2013c), the particle strategy is the most common strategy for forming the polar questions among the languages of the world (585/955 ≈ 61.3%). However, the major strategy for forming polar questions in Caijia is the V-NEG-V strategy.

13.3.1 Alternative polar questions

As illustrated earlier in Table 13.2, alternative polar questions can be further divided into two forms: the juxtaposition [VP (DISJ) NEG VP] and the reduced [VP (DISJ) NEG]. The former is used to form all non-perfective questions, while the latter is exclusively used to form perfective questions. The alternative disjunction *lɔ²¹* 'or' can be optionally used in both forms.

13.3.1.1 Juxtaposition [VP (DISJ) NEG VP]

The juxtaposition strategy is commonly used to transform irrealis declaratives into interrogatives. A polar question formed by this strategy can also be treated as an alternative question, especially when the disjunction *lɔ²¹* 'or' is used. In such an alternative question, VP_1 is in the positive form, while VP_2 is in the negative form; moreover, VP_1 and VP_2 will also share the same main verb. The difference between an alternative question and an alternative polar question is the difference in answer required. As illustrated in (13.2), the answer to an alternative question is not limited to the given options. By comparison, the answer to an alternative polar question has to be either positive or negative. Compare (13.7) and (13.2). Treating predicates formed with a single verb first, it can be observed from (13.7), that the simplest positive answer is formed by the verb *ɣɯ²¹* 'come' alone, and the simplest negative answer is formed by the verb's negated form alone.

(13.7) Q- tʰɪŋ²¹koŋ⁵⁵ nɯ³³ ɣɯ²¹ (lɔ²¹) pɣ³³ ɣɯ²¹?
           tomorrow 2SG come or NEG come
           'Will you come tomorrow or not?'
           明天你来（还是）不来？

      A_i- (ŋo³³) ɣɯ²¹ (se²¹).
           1SG come AFF.PRT
           'Yes, (I)'ll come.'
           （我）来（的）。

      A_{ii}- (ŋo³³) pɣ³³ ɣɯ²¹.
           1SG NEG come
           'No, (I) won't come.'
           （我）不来。

Turning to a more complex situation, Zhu Dexi (1990, 1991) identifies three different orders when objects are involved in Sinitic V-NEG-V polar questions:

Type i: [VO NEG V]
Type ii: [V NEG VO]
Type iii: [VO NEG VO].

As pointed out by Zhu Dexi (1990: 211, 213), the [VO NEG V] pattern is mainly attested in northern Mandarin in the provinces of Hebei, Shanxi, Henan, Shaanxi, Gansu, and Qinghai, while the [V NEG VO] pattern is widely attested in Southwestern Mandarin, Yue, Min, and Hakka. Regardless of being situated in an area of Southwestern Mandarin, Caijia belongs to the Type (i) languages of [VO NEG V], as shown in the following example with a VO predicate.

(13.8) Q- nɯ^{33} ɣã^{21} tɕɪŋ^{21} (lɔ^{55}) pɣ^{33} ɣã^{21}? tsa^{21} ŋo^{21}
          [v   o   NEG v]   lend 1SG
          2SG have money or   NEG have
          mi^{55}. ŋo^{21} pe^{55}-ɣɯ^{21} tɯ^{33} tsɣ^{21} nɯ^{33}.
          a.little 1SG return-come then return 2SG
          'Do you have some money or not? Lend me some. I'll pay you back when I get back.'
          你有钱没有？借我点。我回去就还你。

      A- ɣã^{21} sɿ^{21} e. nɯ^{33} niɔ^{33} kʰua^{21} tie^{55}?
          have AFF PRT 2SG want how much
          'Yes, I have (some). How much do you want?'
          有的。你要多少？

When an auxiliary is used in an alternative polar question, it is the auxiliary that should be repeated and negated, as shown in the following example.

(13.9) nɯ^{33} ti^{33} xa^{33} men^{21}ni^{33}ŋoŋ^{33} (lɔ^{21}) pɣ^{33} ti^{33}?
       2SG know speak Caijia   or NEG know
       'Can you speak Caijia or not?'
       你会说蔡家话不会？

It should be mentioned that the auxiliary *niɔ^{33}* 'want' can also be used as a prospective marker. However, when it is used to form an alternative polar question and is thereby repeated and negated, it denotes 'want' instead of the prospective, as shown in (13.10). The prospective in Caijia is usually not marked in interrogatives, as shown in the future context of (13.7).

(13.10) je^{33} niɔ^{33} ɣɯ^{21} (lɔ^{21}) pɣ^{33} niɔ^{33}?
        3SG want come or NEG want
        'Does he want to come or not?'
        他要不要来？

As for turning sentences of extent or manner complementation into questions, two contrastive orders are observed. In Caijia, a verbal complement construction with a complementizer such as $lɯ^{55}$ usually possesses two interpretations: stative and potential modal, as illustrated in (13.11a). This is true even though the modal meaning of the verbal complement constructions is often expressed by the post-modal element do^{33} 'can' (see also Chapter 11). One must use different strategies to obtain corresponding interrogatives. To obtain the stative, it is the negated verbal complement that is juxtaposed, optionally via the disjunction, with the declarative sentence, i.e. [V_{MATRIX} VCOMP [VP_i (DISJ) NEG VP_i]], as shown in (13.11b). To obtain the potential modal, one should juxtapose the whole negated VP with the main verb, schematized as [[V_{MATRIX} VCOMP VP_i] (DISJ) [V_{MATRIX} NEG VP_i]], as shown in (13.11c).

(13.11) a. mɔ²¹ pɣ²¹ ka²¹ ja²¹ lɯ⁵⁵ tsʰʅ³³ka³³.
that cloth CLF wash VCOMP clean
Stative: 'That cloth has been washed clean.'
Potential: 'That cloth can be washed clean.'
那块布洗得干净。

Stative: [V_{MATRIX} lɯ⁵⁵ [VP_i (DISJ) NEG VP_i]]
b. mɔ²¹ pɣ²¹ ka²¹ [ja²¹]$_{MATRIX}$ lɯ⁵⁵ [tsʰʅ³³ka³³
that cloth CLF wash VCOMP clean
(lɔ²¹) pɣ³³ tsʰʅ³³ka³³]?
or NEG clean
'Has that cloth been washed clean or not?'
那块布洗得干净不干净？

Potential: [[V_i lɯ⁵⁵ VP_{ii}] (DISJ) [V_i NEG VP_{ii}]]
c. mɔ²¹ pɣ²¹ ka²¹ [[ja²¹]$_{MATRIX}$ lɯ⁵⁵ tsʰʅ³³ka³³]
that cloth CLF wash VCOMP clean
(lɔ²¹) [[ja²¹]$_{MATRIX}$ pɣ³³ tsʰʅ³³ka³³]?
or wash NEG clean
'Can that cloth be washed clean?'
那块布洗得干净洗不干净？

13.3.1.2 Reduced [VP (DISJ) NEG]

Unlike the alternative polar questions formed via the juxtaposition strategy, the reduced form is limited to perfective questions. An alternative polar question of this form is realized by simply adding the perfective negator $pɣ^{33}tɣ^{33}$ (< 'not obtain') after the VP. The VP and the negator are optionally linked by the alternative disjunction $lɔ^{21}$, without which the negator $pγ^{33}tγ^{33}$ seemingly functions as a question particle due to it sentence-final position, as illustrated in (13.12) and (13.13). Though optional, the use of the alternative disjunction is the major reason the reduced form is not treated as one of the particle polar questions, since the disjunction may be easily re-added. The formation strategies for responses to such kinds of questions are similar to those for juxtapositions, as shown in (13.12A$_i$) and (13.12A$_{ii}$).

(13.12) Q- nɯ^{33} ã^{21} tsγ^{55} (ha^{55}) (lɔ^{21}) pγ^{33}tγ^{33}?
2SG drink medicine COMPL or NEG.PFV
'Have you drunk the medicine or not?'
你喝药了没？

A$_i$- ã^{21} ha^{55} o.
drink COMPL CRS
'Yes, I have.'
喝了。

A$_{ii}$- a^{21} pγ^{33}tγ^{33} ã^{33}.
still NEG.PFV drink
'No, I haven't yet.'
还没喝。

(13.13) γɯ^{21} zן^{55} kʰɯ^{55}yɯ^{21} (lɔ^{21}) pγ^{33}tγ^{33}?
come rain INC:rise.come or NEG.PFV
'Has it begun raining or not?'
开始下雨了没？

Furthermore, reduced alternative questions do not permit negated VPs, as they do in the particle questions with la^{21}, as shown in (13.14).

(13.14) *je^{33} a^{21} pγ^{33}tγ^{33} tsa^{21} ti^{21} pe^{55}-yɯ^{21} (lɔ^{21}) pγ^{33}tγ^{33}?
3SG still NEG.PFV go.up hill return-come or NEG.PFV
(Attempted: 'Hasn't he come back from the hill?')
他还没上山回来吗？

The phenomenon whereby clause-final negators develop into question particles is not only common in contemporary Sinitic languages (Zhu Dexi 1990, 1991, Zhang Min 1990) but also common in different periods throughout the evolution of Chinese languages. The Standard Mandarin question particle *mā* 吗 [ma^{55}] is historically derived from the negator *wú* 无, present from the time of Archaic

Chinese (see Aldridge 2011 and Wang Li 1958[1980: 452] for more discussion). From a synchronic perspective, the Standard Mandarin negators *bù* 不 [pu^{51}] and *méi* 没 [mei^{24}] can both be used to form polar questions. Moreover, this phenomenon is also attested in many Southeast Asian languages including Lao, Khmer (Clark 1985 1989), Thai (Fernandez-Vest et al. 2017: 437–438), and Vietnamese (Nguyên 1994), as well as in other languages of the world such as Old Written Estonian (Metslang et al. 2017: 494). Given that the alternative disjunction lo^{21} is optional, the Caijia perfective negator $py^{33}ty^{33}$ similarly possesses the right conditions and syntactic context needed to further develop into a question final particle.

13.3.2 Particle polar questions [VP Q]

As already foreshadowed above, the particle strategy is relatively limited. In final position, three question particles la^{21}, $ɔ^{21}sɛ^{55}$, and mo^{33} are used to form questions with presupposed answers (true or false), perfective questions, and questions containing the two post-verbal 'can' modals do^{33} and ty^{33}, respectively. Their sources are unclear.

13.3.2.1 Particle *la²¹* [VP la²¹]

When la^{21} is used to form a polar question, the questioner usually already has a certain presupposition about the answer. The question serves to check the validity of the questioner's assumption, which is usually based on known information (regardless of sources). Example (13.15) shows that the speaker has posed a question on the basis of his or her own deduction, after seeing that a light is on. There are three ways to produce a positive response to a polar question formed by la^{21}:
i. one can use the verb itself, as the positive answer to the alternative polar question,
ii. or use the copula to affirm the questioner's assumption,
iii. or simply use the interjection *o*, as shown in (13.15A_i).

For a negative response, one can:
i. negate the verb,
ii. use the negated copula to produce a negative answer denoting 'it's not like this', which cannot be used to answer an alternative polar question,
iii. or utter reality directly, as illustrated in (13.15A_ii).

Repeating the verb in the original question to produce the answer affirms or negates the action, while using the copula affirms or negates, instead, the speaker's assumption.

(13.15) Q- meŋ²¹sa³³ nɯ³³ tsaŋ²¹ sɣ³³ **la²¹?** ŋo³³ tsaŋ³³-kɪŋ³³
last.night 2SG look book Q 1SG look-see
nɯ³³ mɔ²¹ tã³³ sɿ³³ tso²¹-xɯ⁵⁵ sɿ²¹.
2SG that light CONT be.bright-DUR CONT
'Did you read last night? I saw your light was on.'
昨晚你看书了吗？我看见你那灯亮着的。

Positive responses:

A$_i$- (tsaŋ²¹) o.
look CRS
'Yes, I did.'
看了。

A$_{ii}$- (sɿ²¹) o.
COP PRT
'Yes, it's like this.'
是啊！

Negative responses:

A$_{iii}$- (pɣ³³ se³³!) ŋo³³ pʰa³³me²¹ ta³³ tã³³ o.
NEG COP.PRT 1SG forget close light CRS
'No, it's not so. I forgot to turn off the light.'
不是。/我没看。我忘记关灯了。

A$_{iv}$- ŋo³³ pɣ³³tɣ³³ tsaŋ²¹. ŋo³³ pʰa³³me²¹ ta³³ tã³³ o.
NEG NEG.PFV look 1SG forget close light CRS
'No, I didn't read. I forgot to turn off the light.'
不是。/我没看。我忘记关灯了。

The example below shows a context in which the speaker has understood that the respondent would go to his uncle's home. Seeing that the person in question was still at home, a situation at odds with the speaker's expectation, a question is posed containing the assumption that the respondent has already come back home. Note that the negated VP *pɣ³³tɣ³³ pe⁵⁵-ɣɯ²¹* 'haven't come back' cannot be used in reply to the question in (13.16Q). This is because the resultative complement *-ɣɯ²¹* 'come' indicates the action *pe⁵⁵* 'return' happens towards the direction of the speaker. If the respondent gives the answer *pɣ³³tɣ³³ pe⁵⁵-ɣɯ²¹* 'haven't come back', this would imply that the person is not at all in the same place as the questioner. Given that this is a face-to-ace conversation, and thus happening in the same place, the negated form $pý^{33}tý^{33}$ pe^{55}-$yɯ^{21}$ 'not return-come' would be unsuitable. This explains why the VP $k^hɯ^{55}$ $seŋ^{33}$ 'rise body' is found in the response to the question, denoting 'set out'. This shows that how a speaker gives a negative answer also depends on the context in which the question is asked. Negating the verb of the question is not always suitable. Example (13.16) is one such case.

(13.16) Q- nɯ²¹ ta⁵⁵ nɛ²¹ tsa²¹ mo²¹
  2SG from your.family uncle inside
  pe⁵⁵-yɯ²¹ (ha²¹) la²¹?
  return-come COMPL Q
  'You came back from your uncle's?'
  你从你叔家回来了吗?

  A- (pý³³ sɿ³³.) ŋo³³ a²¹ pý³³tý³³ kʰɯ⁵⁵ seŋ³³.
  NEG COP 1SG still NEG.PFV rise body
  '(No, it's not so.) I haven't set out yet.'
  我还没动身。

Negated declaratives can also be transformed into interrogatives by using la^{21} in the form of [NEG VP la²¹], as in (13.17). To affirm the validity of (13.17Q), one could use the negated VP as in (13.17 A_i) or the copula, or the interjection *o* as in (13.17A_{ii}). To negate the validity, one could use the VP or the negated copula, as in (13.17A_{iii}) and (13.17A_{iv}). Regardless of whether or not the VP is in its negated form in a particle polar question formed by la^{21}, if the assumption is true, the copula $sɿ^{33}$ can be used in isolation to answer the question; if the assumption is false, the negated copula $pý^{33}$ $sɿ^{33}$ can be used.

(13.17) Q- nɯ³³ pý³³tý³³ ã²¹ tsý⁵⁵ la²¹?
  2SG NEG.PFV drink medicine Q
  'You haven't taken your medicine?'
  你没吃药吗?

  A_i- xa²¹tsɛ⁵⁵ pý³³tý³³ ã³³.
  still NEG.PFV drink
  'I haven't taken it yet.'
  还没吃。

A$_{ii}$- (sɿ²¹) o.
COP PRT
'Yes, that's so.'
（是）啊。

A$_{iii}$- pɣ³³ se³³.
NEG COP.PRT
'Yes, I have.'
（不是的。）吃了。

A$_{iv}$- ã²¹ ha²¹ o.
drink COMPL CRS
'Yes, I have.'
吃了。

However, this rule does not apply to copular interrogatives. As illustrated in (13.18), the negated copula is used to affirm an assumption, while the copula alone is used to negate it.

(13.18) Q- nɯ³³ pɣ³³ sɿ³³ je²¹ hɛ⁵⁵ la²¹?
2SG NEG COP 3SG younger.brother Q
'You aren't his younger brother?'
你不是他弟吗？

A$_{i}$- pɣ³³ se³³.
NEG COP.PRT
'No, I'm not.'
不是的。

A$_{ii}$- sɿ²¹ e.
COP PRT
'Yes, I am.'
是的。

The particle polar question format can also be used to form rhetorical questions. Example (13.19) was produced in a context where someone has already been burnt by the stove and the speaker has commented on it using the polar question 'Can you touch it?' formed using *la²¹* to express 'You can't touch it' without expecting an answer from the person who has suffered the burn.

(13.19) mɔ²¹ tʰɣ⁵⁵po²¹ po⁵⁵ tʰɣ⁵⁵ xɪŋ⁵⁵. nɯ³³ mɣ²¹ tɣ³³ la²¹?
that stove CLF hot very 2SG touch can Q
That stove is very hot. (How) can you touch it?'
那炉子烫得很。你能摸吗？

13.3.2.2 Particle ɔ²¹sɛ⁵⁵ [VP ɔ²¹sɛ⁵⁵]

The disyllabic particle ɔ²¹sɛ⁵⁵ presents an alternative strategy for forming perfective polar questions. Unlike pɣ³³tɣ³³ polar questions, the alternative disjunction lɔ²¹ cannot be used to link the VP and ɔ²¹sɛ⁵⁵ in interrogatives. Semantically, ɔ²¹sɛ⁵⁵ questions do not differ from the pɣ³³tɣ³³ ones, but morphologically ɔ²¹sɛ⁵⁵ is a case of a fully-fledged particle. The following example shows both how an ɔ²¹sɛ⁵⁵ question is formed and how to respond.

(13.20) Q- mɔ²¹ to²⁴ po⁵⁵ nɯ²¹ tɕie⁵⁵-kʰua²¹ ɔ²¹sɛ⁵⁵?
that cupboard CLF 2SG do-good Q.PFV
'Have you completed the cupboard?'
那个柜子你做好了吗？

A₁- tɕie⁵⁵-kʰua²¹ o.
do-good CRS
'Yes, I have.'
做好了。

A₂- a²¹ pɣ³³tɣ³³ tɕie⁵⁵-kʰua²¹.
still NEG.PFV do-good
'No, I haven't.'
还没做好。

One should also be aware that ɔ²¹sɛ⁵⁵ cannot form questions with a negated VP as the particle la²¹ does.

13.3.2.3 Particle mo³³ [VP do³³/tɣ³³ mo³³]

The question particle mo³³ is used to transform declarative sentences formed with either of the two post-VP 'can' modals do³³ or tɣ³³ into polar questions. It cannot be used with negated VPs. The form [VP do³³/tɣ³³] is used to produce positive answers, while the form [VP NEG do³³/tɣ³³] is used to produce negative answers. See the examples in (13.21) and (13.22).

(13.21) Declarative
　　a.　meŋ²¹ni³³ŋoŋ³³　je³³　xa²¹　**to³³**.
　　　　Caijia　　　　　3SG　speak　can
　　　　'He can speak Caijia.'
　　　　蔡家话他会说。

　　Polar question
　　b.　Q-　meŋ²¹ni³³ŋoŋ³³　je³³　xa²¹　**to³³**　**mo³³**?
　　　　　　Caijia　　　　　3SG　speak　can　Q
　　　　　'Can he speak Caijia?'
　　　　　蔡家话他会说吗？

　　　Aᵢ-　xa²¹　to³³.
　　　　　speak　can
　　　　　'Yes, he can.'
　　　　　会说。

　　　Aᵢᵢ-　xa²¹　po³³　to³³.
　　　　　speak　NEG　can
　　　　　'No, he can't.'
　　　　　说不了。

(13.22) Declarative
　　a.　mɔ²⁴　tsoŋ⁵⁵　saŋ⁵⁵　zy̠²¹　**ty̠³³**.
　　　　that　kind　mushroom　eat　can
　　　　'That kind of mushroom is edible.'
　　　　那种蘑菇能吃。

　　Polar question
　　b.　Q-　mɔ²⁴　tsoŋ⁵⁵　saŋ⁵⁵　zy̠²¹　**ty̠³³**　**mo³³**?
　　　　　　that　kind　mushroom　eat　can　Q
　　　　　'Is that kind of mushroom edible?'
　　　　　那种蘑菇能吃吗？

　　　Aᵢ-　zy̠²¹　ty̠³³.
　　　　　eat　can
　　　　　'Yes, it is.'
　　　　　能吃。

　　　Aᵢᵢ-　zy̠²¹　py̠³³　ty̠³³.
　　　　　eat　NEG　can
　　　　　'No, it isn't.'
　　　　　不能吃。

13.4 Content questions

Content questions, or *wh*-questions, are used to make a request for specific missing information within the scope of the knowledge shared by the questioner and the respondent. The missing information may concern a person, thing, place, time, manner, selection from a range of objects, or reason.

> Content questions differ from polar questions [...] in that they elicit a specific answer other than 'yes' or 'no', and in containing interrogative phrases. All languages have a set of interrogative words that are characteristic of content questions, though in many languages they are identical in form to indefinite words (like *someone* in English) [...]. (Dryer 2013c)

On the basis of 68 languages from 38 families, Cysouw (2004) proposes four major interrogative categories: PERSON (who), THING (what), SELECTION (which) and PLACE (where).

Forming wh- *in situ* questions as most of the languages in Dryer's sample do (615/902 ≈ 61.2% [Dryer 2013c]), Caijia distinguishes nine main categories of interrogative pronouns, as shown in Table 13.3. Moreover, they also function as indefinite words (see Chapter 3 §3.4.4). These compound Caijia interrogative words show a tendency to formal regularity and all of them are analyzable, which

Table 13.3: Caijia interrogative words.

I	Which	bɔ²⁴+CLF	'which+CLF'
II	Who	bɔ²⁴ni⁵⁵	'which CLF$_{PERSON}$/person'
III	Whose	bɔ²⁴ni⁵⁵ hm̩⁵⁵	'which CLF$_{PERSON}$ POSS'
IV	What	bɔ²⁴tsoŋ⁵⁵	'which type'
		sɿ²¹mɔ⁵⁵	'what'
V	Where	bɔ²⁴kʰa³³	'which place'
		la²⁴	'where'
VI	When	bɔ²¹kɯ²⁴	'which moment'
VII	How (manner)	tɔ²¹bɔ²⁴sɿ⁵⁵	'be like which way'
		ɕie⁵⁵me⁵⁵(ɕie⁵⁵)	'do what do'
		ɕie⁵⁵mɔ⁵⁵(ɕie⁵⁵)	'do what do'
		ɕiɔ⁵⁵mɔ⁵⁵	'do-what'
VIII	Why	ɕie⁵⁵me⁵⁵ ~ ɕie⁵⁵mɔ⁵⁵	'do what'
		ɕiɔ⁵⁵mɔ⁵⁵	'do what'
		ɕie⁵⁵me⁵⁵ɕie⁵⁵	'how do'
IX	How many	kʰɯ³³	'several'
		kʰua²¹	'good'
		kʰua²¹tie⁵⁵	'good-many'
		tie²¹sɔ⁵⁵	'many-few'

provides counter evidence of Cysouw's claim that "[t]he categories PERSON and THING are almost never analysable" (see more discussion below). One can observe that most of the Caijia interrogative words, except for 'why' and 'how many/ much', are indeed formed by compounding the question morpheme $lɔ^{21}$ 'which' with a set of other morphemes such as nouns and classifiers. The interrogative morpheme used to code SELECTION is, thus, the major source for forming Caijia interrogative words. This is the morpheme $lɔ^{21}$ which shows both phonetic and semantic (i.e. selection) similarities with the alternative disjunction $lɔ^{21}$ 'or', but whether or not they are derived from the same source needs further exploration.

In the following sections, the nine types of interrogatives listed in the table above will be introduced.

13.4.1 'Which' questions

As mentioned and illustrated above, selection questions may be the source of other $lɔ^{21}$-questions. The morpheme $lɔ^{21}$ 'which' cannot stand alone as an interrogative pronoun but it does show adnominal or attributive features. It functions like a determiner, occupying the same syntactic position as demonstratives do (see also example [13.25]). Nonetheless, it cannot modify nouns directly, unlike English 'which' in 'which book', as in (13.23a). This is due to the fact that $lɔ^{21}$ 'which' should be used with a classifier. The phrase 'which book' should be expressed as illustrated in (13.23b): [N $lɔ^{24}$-CLF].

(13.23) a. *$lɔ^{24}$ $sɣ^{33}$
which book
(Attempted: 'which book')
哪本书

b. $sɣ^{33}$ $lɔ^{24}$ $peŋ^{21}$
book which CLF
'which book'
哪本书

Generally, the interrogative phrases used to form 'which' questions can be schematized as [$lɔ^{21}$ CLF]. The CLFs vary according to the semantic category of their referents. Given that one classifier often classifies a group of nouns, this means that the interrogative phrase formed by $lɔ^{21}$ and the same classifier can refer to many things. For example, bo^{55} is a frequently used classifier, and thus there are many possibilities for the referent of $lɔ^{24} bo^{55}$ without any context. It may be used to classify a well, a city, a potato or even a star. Due to this feature, the selection range of a 'which' question should somehow be mentioned or specified before a question is posed, for example, as a dangling topic. The phrase 'the white dog and the spotted dog' in (13.24aQ), both of which are referents of lɔ^{24} k^{w}ɔ^{21}, is situated outside of the 'which' question. Certainly, exceptions also exist. Example (13.24b) shows a case in which a copular sentence is transformed into a 'which' question. This sentence would not cause any confusion about the referent of the lɔ^{24} phrase, even if it were posed without any context. This is because, first, a copular construction is to express identity or equation between the copular subject and the copular complement; and second, in the particular case of (13.24b), the target referent sɔ^{55}nioŋ^{21} 'key', classified by ka^{21}, appears in the complement position.

(13.24) a. Q- pia^{21} k^{h}ui^{55} ta^{55} kua^{21} k^{h}ui^{55},
             white   dog   and   spotted   dog
             nɯ^{33} tɕ^{h}i^{33}k^{h}a^{33} lɔ^{24} k^{w}ɔ^{21}?
             2SG   like   which   CLF
             'The white dog and the spotted dog, which one do you like?'
             白狗和花狗，你喜欢哪只？

       A- ŋo^{33} tɕ^{h}i^{33}k^{h}a^{33} kua^{33} sɿ^{21} mɔ^{21} k^{w}ɔ^{21}.
          1SG   like   spotted   MOD   that   CLF
          'I like the spotted one.'
          我喜欢花的那只。

    b. lɔ^{21} ka^{21} sɿ^{21} k^{h}ɯ^{55} mɔ^{21} to^{24}
       which   CLF   COP   open   that   cupboard
       po^{55} sɿ^{21} sɔ^{55}nioŋ^{21}?
       CLF   MOD   key
       'Which one is the key to open the cupboard.'
       哪把是开那个柜子的钥匙？

The 'which' phrases, [lɔ^{21} CLF], are usually singular. When a question concerning selection concerns plurality, two strategies can be used. One can either compound lɔ^{24} with the pronoun or plural marker sui^{55} 'some', i.e. lɔ^{24} sui^{55}, or use the phrase [lɔ^{24} k^{h}ɯ^{33} CLF] 'which several CLF'. The latter is usually associated with the meaning of a small quantity and also offers major justification for not treating lɔ^{21} as a prefix. The phrase lɔ^{24} sui^{55} can refer to anything in the plural, while the classifier in the phrase [lɔ^{24} k^{h}ɯ^{33} CLF] narrows the plural meaning to a certain group of things. Therefore, the whichever of the referents lɔ^{24} sui^{55} and [lɔ^{24} k^{h}ɯ^{33} CLF] are coded need to be shared knowledge between the people involved in the conversation.

(13.25) Q- tɣ²¹   tɣ³³   sɿ²¹   sɣ²¹-sui⁵⁵
          table upside   MOD   book-PL
          [lɔ²⁴   sui⁵⁵]/ [lɔ²⁴   kʰɯ³³   pen²¹]   sɿ³³   nɯ²¹-hm̩⁵⁵?
          which   PL   which   several   CLF   COP   2SG-POSS
          'The books on the the table, which ones are yours?'
          桌子上的书，哪些/哪几本是你的？

     A-   [ɔ²¹   sui⁵⁵]/ [ɔ²¹   kʰɯ³³   pen²¹]   sɿ³³   ŋo²¹-hm̩⁵⁵.
          this   some/   this   several   CLF   COP   1SG-POSS
          'These are mine.'
          这些/这几本是我的。

Moreover, *lɔ²¹* can be used to modify time words, such as *koŋ⁵⁵* 'day', *ŋui⁵⁵* 'month', and *neŋ²¹* 'year', so as to make requests for specific time. In general, time words cannot be modified by classifiers, since they themselves are a kind of measure word (see Chapter 3 §3.5.2 on classifiers).

(13.26) Q- je³³   lɔ²⁴   koŋ⁵⁵   tɕiu⁵⁵?
          3SG   which   day   arrive
          'On which day will he arrive?'
          他哪天到？

     A-   tsaŋ²¹koŋ⁵⁵   tɕiu⁵⁵.
          the.day.after.tomorrow   arrive
          '(He) will arrive the day after tomorrow.'
          后天到。

13.4.2 'Who' questions

The word for 'who' in Caijia, *lɔ²⁴ni⁵⁵*, is formed with *lɔ²⁴* 'which' and the classifier *ni³³* which is exclusively used for humans. *ni³³* can also be used as a pronoun denoting 'one, other' and is probably cognate with *rén* 人 [ɻən¹⁵] 'person, other' in Standard Mandarin (< Middle Chinese *nyin* [Baxter and Sagart 2014: 157]). See the following example for the classifier *ni³³*.

(13.27) Classifier
     a. nioŋ²⁴   ta⁵⁵   ni³³
         girl   two   CLF
         'two girls'
         两个女孩

                            Pronoun
    b. […] ni^{24} a^{55} ã^{21}ã^{55} ɣɯ^{21} lɯ^{21} mi^{55}. […]
                3   take jar   come barter rice
       'One took a jar to exchange for some rice.'
       人家拿罐子来换米。
       (*Exchanging products*, texts)

Analyzable forms for 'who', such as 'which CLF/person' or 'what CLF/person', are very common in Sinitic languages (Lü Shuxiang 1985, Wang Jian 2016). The Caijia compound formation of 'who', [which + CLF], is widely attested in Xiang, Gan, Hakka, Yue, Jianghuai, and Southwestern Mandarin (Wang Jian 2016).

    It is true that 'who' can usually replace 'which person/one' in English, but not vice versa. Though they are not easy to distinguish as they share the same form, in Caijia there are contexts illustrating some contrasts between the 'who' *lɔ^{24}ni^{55}* and the selection *lɔ^{24}ni^{55}*. The 'who' *lɔ^{24}ni^{55}* is more semantically generalized. In the context of (13.28), the first speaker initiated a conversation by asking 'Who is outside?' without specifying or even being aware of any range of selection. The answer from the second speaker further confirms that this is not a selection context. Therefore, interpreting *lɔ^{24}ni^{55}* in (13.28Q) as 'which one' would be inappropriate. *lɔ^{24}ni^{55}* can also be used alone when answering the door in order to ask for the knocker's identity. This represents a context even more inappropriate for interpreting *lɔ^{24}ni^{55}* as 'which one'.

(13.28) Q- lɔ^{24}-ni^{55} tɯ^{21} ua^{33}lɛ^{21}?
                which-CLF be.at outside
                'Who is outside?'
                谁在外面？

          A- pɣ^{33} tiu^{33}u^{33} e.   sɿ^{55} ŋo^{21} tsʰe^{55}-kuɛ^{21}
                NEG know   PRT let 1SG go.out-go
                tsaŋ^{21} mi^{55} lɛ^{21}.
                look   a.little PRT
                'I don't know. Let me go out to check.'
                不知道啊。让我出去看下。

As mentioned above, the form [which CLF] codes the property of singularity. Specifically, the use of this form presupposes the response to be in the singular when a selection question is posed. However, *lɔ^{24}ni^{55}* as 'who' is not restricted to singularity. As shown in the following sentence, a quarrel is an event involving at least two participants. In such a context, the presupposition behind the use of *lɔ^{24}ni^{55}*

is that it refers to a plural entity. Semantically, the interrogative pronoun lɔ²⁴ni⁵⁵ for selection appears to require more specific reference in terms of its formative morphemes. Despite this, both examples (13.28) and (13.29) clearly demonstrate its semantic extension or generalization.

(13.29) lɔ²⁴-ni⁵⁵   tɯ²¹   ua³³lɛ²¹   ma²¹sa²¹tɔ²⁴   sɿ²¹?
        which-CLF   at   outside   quarrel   CONT
        'Who are quarrelling outside?'
        谁在外面吵架？

13.4.3 'Whose' questions

The question word lɔ²⁴ni⁵⁵ hm̩⁵⁵ 'whose' in Cajia is composed of 'who/which one' and the possessive marker hm̩⁵⁵ (source unclear), serving as either a determiner or a pronoun.

(13.30) a. ɔ²¹   sɿ³³   lɔ²⁴-ni⁵⁵   hm̩⁵⁵   sɣ³³?
           this   COP   which-CLF   POSS   book
           'Whose book is this?'
           这是谁的书？

        b. ɔ²¹   sɣ³³   peŋ²¹   sɿ³³   lɔ²⁴-ni⁵⁵   hm̩⁵⁵?
           this   book   CLF   COP   which-CLF   POSS
           'Whose is this book?'
           这本书是谁的？

Since this interrogative pronoun refers to persons as possessors, only the form with the classifier for humans, ni³³, is used with hm̩⁵⁵.

13.4.4 'What' questions

Caijia uses either sɿ²¹mɔ⁵⁵ or lɔ²⁴tsoŋ⁵⁵ to form 'what' questions. The pronoun sɿ²¹mɔ⁵⁵ might be cognate with shénme 什么 [ʂən²⁴mə] 'what' in Standard Mandarin, for which one of the earlier reconstructions in Late Medieval Chinese is shìwù 是物 'what' (Lü Shuxiang 1985: 123). Phonetically close to Caijia sɿ²¹mɔ⁵⁵, shìwù is composed of the copula shì 是 and wù 物 'object' (< Middle Chinese mjut [Baxter and Sagart 2014: 366]), as is the Caijia copula is sɿ³³. The pronoun lɔ²⁴tsoŋ⁵⁵ is composed of the 'which' interrogative lɔ²¹ and the morpheme tsoŋ⁵⁵

(< 'seed') serving both as a noun, 'kind, type', and a classifier for the noun 'thing', as shown below.

(13.31) a. ɣã²¹   ji²¹   **tsoŋ⁵⁵**   sɿ³³   tsa²¹sɯ⁵⁵   saŋ⁵⁵.
there.be one kind COP lime mushroom
'There's a kind of mushroom called lime mushroom (peppery milk-cap mushroom).'
有一种是石灰菌。

b. sɿ⁵⁵   ji²¹   **tsoŋ⁵⁵**
thing one CLF
'one thing'
一件事

The two 'what' words are basically exchangeable when serving as pronouns or arguments. See the following question asking about for one's profession.

(13.32) nɯ³³   sɿ²¹   tɕie⁵⁵   **[lɔ²⁴-tsoŋ⁵⁵]/ [sɿ²¹mɔ⁵⁵]**   sɿ²¹?
2SG COP do which-type/ what NMLZ
'What are you?'
你是做什么的？

It should be mentioned that *sɿ²¹mɔ⁵⁵* can be reduced as *mɔ⁵⁵* as in (13.33a). However, this reduced form is not entirely equivalent to the full form *sɿ²¹mɔ⁵⁵*. It can only be the object of the verb 'do' and cannot function autonomously elsewhere. Compare (13.33a) and (13.33b). Using *mɔ⁵⁵* as the object of the verb *kʷɔ³³* 'teach' is ungrammatical. Moreover, *mɔ⁵⁵* cannot function as an indefinite pronoun as *sɿ²¹mɔ⁵⁵* and *lɔ²⁴tsoŋ⁵⁵* do, as shown in (13.33c).

(13.33) a. nɯ³³   tɯ²¹   ʑi³³mo²¹   tɕie⁵⁵
2SG at inside do
[(sɿ²¹)mɔ⁵⁵]/[lɔ²⁴-tsoŋ⁵⁵]   sɿ²¹?   tɕiu²⁴   tsʰe⁵⁵-ɣɯ²¹   la²¹!
what/which-type CONT quickly be.out-come PRT
'What're you doing inside? Quickly come out!'
你在里面干嘛？快出来！

b. je³³   kʷɔ³³   nɯ³³   [*(sɿ²¹)mɔ⁵⁵]/[lɔ²⁴-tsoŋ⁵⁵]?
3SG teach 2SG what/which-type
'What does he teach you?'
他教你什么？

c. je³³ *(sɿ²¹)mɔ⁵⁵/lɔ²⁴-tsoŋ⁵⁵ la²¹ pγ²¹ tɕie⁵⁵.
   3SG what/which-type   all NEG do
   'He doesn't do anything.'
   他什么都不做。

One can observe that *lɔ²⁴tsoŋ⁵⁵* can also be used in all the sentences in (13.32) and (13.33). Nonetheless, it cannot be interpreted as 'which type' in any of the cases above. Undoubtedly, contexts in which *lɔ²⁴ tsoŋ⁵⁵* denotes 'which type' also exist, as shown below.

(13.34) je²¹   sɿ⁵⁵ nɯ²¹ mã²¹ lɔ²⁴   tsoŋ⁵⁵ pγ²¹?
        3SG let 2SG buy which   type   cloth
        'What kind of cloth does he want you to buy?'
        他让你买哪种布？

13.4.5 'Where' questions

The 'where' word *lɔ²⁴kʰa⁵⁵* is composed of morphemes for 'which' and 'place'. Its more frequently used fused form is *la²⁴*. One can use either form to request any information about places and locations. In (13.35), *la²⁴/lɔ²⁴kʰa²⁴* serves as the object of the displacement verb 'walk', while it serves as the prepositional object of the ablative preposition *ta⁵⁵* 'from' in (13.36).

(13.35) meŋ²¹koŋ⁵⁵ nɯ³³ ɣa²¹ la²⁴/lɔ²⁴-kʰa⁵⁵   kuɛ²¹ o?
        yesterday   2SG walk where/which-place   go   CRS
        'Where did you go yesterday?'
        你昨天到哪儿去了？

(13.36) je³³ sɿ²¹ ta⁵⁵ la²⁴/lɔ²⁴-kʰa⁵⁵   lɯŋ²¹-tɕie²¹kuɛ²¹ sɿ²¹?
        3SG AFF from where/which-place   roll-go.down   AFF
        'Where did he roll down?'
        他是从哪滚下来的？

In terms of the development of the fused form, the word *kʰa⁵⁵* 'place' probably first weakens to *xa⁵⁵* and then *lɔ²⁴* and *xa⁵⁵* before further fusing to *la²⁴*. There are some traces supporting this hypothesis. The deictic pronouns *ua²⁴* 'here' and *ma²⁴* 'there' are actually fused forms for the phrases *ɔ²¹ xa⁵⁵* 'this place' and *mɔ²¹ xa⁵⁵* 'that place'. The lenition phenomenon whereby [kʰ] weakens to [x] is also found on the word $k^hɯ^{55}$ 'rise', which weakens as $xɯ^{55}$ when serving as a resultative complement or a durative marker. Moreover, our consultants also explicitly claim that xa^{55} is a variant of k^ha^{55}.

13.4.6 'When' questions

The 'when' word $lɔ^{21}kɯ^{24}$ is formed with $lɔ^{21}$ 'which' and $kɯ^{24}$ 'moment'. The latter usually functions as an adverbial phrase of time in complex sentences, as shown in (13.37).

(13.37) je²¹ tsʰe⁵⁵-kuɛ²¹ tɕie⁵⁵ ja²¹pa²¹ **kɯ²⁴**,
 3SG be.out-go do crops moment
 nɯ³³ a²¹ py³³-ty³³ kʰɯ⁵⁵-yɯ²¹.
 2SG still NEG-PFV rise-come
 'The moment he went out to do farming, you hadn't gotten up yet.'
 他出去干活的时候，你还没起来。

Unlike time words, which either occupy sentence initial positions or precede VPs, as in (13.38a) and (13.38b), $lɔ^{21}kɯ^{24}$ can only be found in the pre-VP position, as in (13.38c). Compare (13.38c) with (13.38a) and (13.38b).

(13.38) a. **tʰɪŋ²¹koŋ⁵⁵** je²¹ tɕiu⁵⁵ la²¹sɿ⁵⁵ to³³ o.
  tomorrow 3SG arrive Guiyang_PLACENAME can CRS
  'Tomorrow, he can arrive in Guiyang.'
  明天他能到贵阳了。

 b. je³³ **tʰɪŋ²¹koŋ⁵⁵** tɕiu⁵⁵ la²¹sɿ⁵⁵ to³³ o.
  3SG tomorrow arrive Guiyang_PLACENAME can CRS
  'He can arrive in Guiyang tomorrow.'
  他明天能到贵阳了。

 c. je³³ **lɔ²¹-kɯ²⁴** tɕiu⁵⁵ la²¹sɿ⁵⁵ to³³?
  3SG which-moment arrive Guiyang_PLACENAME can
  'When can he arrive in Guiyang?'
  他什么时候到贵阳？

13.4.7 'How (manner)' and 'why' questions

Three 'how' words for manner can be observed in Caijia: *tɕie⁵⁵mɔ⁵⁵* 'do what', *tɕie⁵⁵me⁵⁵tɕie⁵⁵* 'how to do' and *tɔ²¹lɔ²⁴sɿ⁵⁵* 'be like which way'. Examples are given in (13.39).

(13.39) Q- mɔ²¹kuɯ²⁴ hɔ⁵⁵ la²¹ pɣ³³-tɣ³³ ɕiu²¹-kʰua²¹, nuɯ²⁴
before road all NEG-PFV pave-good 2PL
[tɔ²¹-lɔ²⁴-sɿ⁵⁵]/[tɕie⁵⁵-mɔ⁵⁵]/[tɕie⁵⁵me⁵⁵-tɕie⁵⁵]
be.like-which-way/do-what/how-do
ɣa²¹ tɕiu⁵⁵ti²¹ kuɛ⁵⁵?
walk Mount.Chive. go
'The road was not paved before, so how did you go to the Mount Chive?'
以前，路都没有修好，你们怎么去韭菜坪？

A- tuɯ³³sɿ³³ kuɯ²¹ mɛ³³ tsa²¹-kuɛ²¹ ɔ mẽ.
just ride horse go.up-go PRT PRT
'(We) just rode horses to go.'
就是骑马去了嘛。

(13.40) niɔ²¹ **tɕie⁵⁵me⁵⁵** ji²¹hɔ⁵⁵ kuɛ²¹ ji²¹hɔ⁵⁵ ɣuɯ²¹ nɛ⁵⁵?
need how together go together come PRT
'How shall (we) depart together and also return together?'
要怎么一起去一起回呢？
(*Three daughters-in-law*, texts)

All of the three 'how' words have verbal origins. Example (13.33a) illustrates the verbal use of *tɕie⁵⁵mɔ⁵⁵* denoting 'do what'. Allomorphs of *tɕie⁵⁵mɔ⁵⁵* also exist, i.e. *tɕie⁵⁵me⁵⁵* and *tɕiɔ⁵⁵mɔ⁵⁵*, both of which can be used in (13.39) and (13.40) to express 'how'. However, neither of these can be used as a VP. Furthermore, neither *me⁵⁵* nor *mɔ⁵⁵* is autonomous.

The 'how' word *tɕie⁵⁵me⁵⁵ tɕie⁵⁵* is derived from the VP 'how to do', as shown in (13.41).

(13.41) ŋo³³ niɔ³³ tsaŋ²¹ nuɯ²¹ **tɕie⁵⁵me⁵⁵ tɕie⁵⁵**.
1SG want see 2SG how do
'I want to see how you do (it).'
我要看你怎么做。

Example (13.42) shows the verbal use of *tɔ²¹lɔ²⁴sɿ⁵⁵* 'be like which way'.

(13.42) nɯ²¹ ta⁵⁵ nɛ²¹ tɕi⁵⁵ tɕɪŋ²¹ kɯ²⁴
2SG and your.family elder.sister front moment
kʰɪŋ⁵⁵pi²¹pi²⁴ mi⁵⁵. ɔ²¹kɯ²⁴ nɯ²⁴ ta⁵⁵
quarrel a.little now 2PL two
lɛ²¹ **tɔ²¹ lɔ²⁴ sɿ⁵⁵** o?
CLF be.like which way CRS
'You and your elder sister quarreled before. How are you now?'
你和你姐之前吵嘴。现在你们姊妹俩怎么样了？

With the exception of *tɔ²¹lɔ²⁴sɿ⁵⁵*, which is restricted to the meaning 'in which way', Caijia 'how' words, can also be used to form 'why' or 'how come' questions. The following example shows *tɕie⁵⁵me⁵⁵* being used to form two 'why' questions. Note *tɕie⁵⁵mɔ⁵⁵* and *tɕie⁵⁵me⁵⁵tɕie⁵⁵* can be used interchangeably.

(13.43) nɯ²¹ **tɕie⁵⁵me⁵⁵** pe⁵⁵-ɣɯ²¹ o?
2SG why return-come CRS
tɕie⁵⁵me⁵⁵ tɕɪŋ²¹kɯ²⁴ pɣ³³-tɣ³³ ta⁵⁵ ŋo²¹ xa²¹?
why earlier.before NEG-PFV with 1SG say
'Why have you come back? Why didn't (you) tell me earlier before?'
你怎么回来了？怎么之前没告诉我？

In spite of the fact that 'how' and 'why' share a form, misunderstandings rarely occur. This is because 'how' and 'why' possess different distributional features. Syntactic contexts can help one to identify the correct meaning. For example, 'why' can be used with negated predicates, as shown in (13.43) above, while 'how' cannot. 'How' usually follows auxiliaries or verbs taking verbal objects, while 'why' precedes them, as illustrated in (13.44).

(13.44) a. nɯ³³ tɕʰj³³kʰa²¹ **tɕie⁵⁵me⁵⁵** zɣ²¹ xa²¹zɣ²¹kuɛ²⁴?
2SG like how eat cucumber
a³³ ɣɯ²¹ ŋʷɔ²¹ lɔ²¹ tɕie⁵⁵-tsɿ²¹ sa³³tsʰɯ²¹.
take come stir-fry or do-become pickle
'How do you like to eat cucumbers? Stir-fried or make into pickled?'
你喜欢怎么吃黄瓜？拿来炒还是做成酸菜？

b. nɯ²¹ **tɕie⁵⁵me⁵⁵** tɕʰi³³kʰa³³ zɣ²¹ xa²¹zɣ²¹kuɛ²⁴ xɪŋ⁵⁵?
2SG why like eat cucumber very
'Why do you like eating cucumbers so much?'
你为什么很喜欢吃黄瓜？

Compare (13.40) and (13.45) as well. In (13.40) *tɕie⁵⁵me⁵⁵* follows the auxiliary *niɔ³³* 'need', while it precedes *niɔ³³* in (13.45). These differing syntactic contexts allow for correspondingly different interpretations of 'how' and 'why'.

(13.45) tɕie⁵⁵me⁵⁵ niɔ³³ ji²¹hɔ⁵⁵ kuɛ²¹ ji²¹hɔ⁵⁵ ɣɯ²¹ nɛ⁵⁵?
why need together go together come PRT
'Why shall (we) depart together and also return together?'
为什么要一起去一起回呢？

Perfective 'how' questions are formed with the affirmative or cleft construction (*sɿ³³*) ... *sɿ²¹*, while perfective 'why' constructions are formed with the sentence final particle *o*. See the minimal pairs in (13.46) and (13.43) above. One can readily see the difference between the two questions from their respective answers.

(13.46) How
a. Q- ɔ²¹sɿ⁵⁵ la²¹ sɿ²¹ sɣ⁵⁵
this big MOD snow
nɯ²¹ tɕie⁵⁵me⁵⁵ ɣɯ²¹ sɿ²¹?
2SG how come AFF
'How did you get here in such a big snowfall?'
这么大的雪你怎么来的？

A- pɣ³³ ɣã²¹ tsʰɛ⁵⁵ o.
NEG there.be car CRS
ŋo³³ ɣa²¹ hɔ⁵⁵ ɣɯ²¹ sɿ²¹.
1SG walk road come AFF
'There're no cars, so I walked.'
没车了。我走路来的。

Why
b. Q- ɔ²¹sɿ⁵⁵ la²¹ sɿ²¹ sɣ⁵⁵
this big MOD snow
nɯ³³ tɕie⁵⁵me⁵⁵ ɣɯ²¹ o?
2SG why come CRS
'Why did you come in such a big snowfall?'
这么大的雪你怎么来了？

A- ŋo³³ meŋ²¹xa³³ nɯ³³ soŋ²¹ o.
   1SG hear   2SG   be.ill PRT
   yɯ²¹ tsaŋ²¹ nɯ²¹ mi⁵⁵.
   come look   2SG a.little
   'I heard that you fell ill and came to pay a visit.'
   我听说你病了。来看你一下。

Admittedly, contexts of ambiguity exist, especially when a change of state is involved. In such contexts, it can be understood that manner equals reason, i.e. how a current state is caused is also the reason for its being so. Similarly, the answer to such a question can also be interpreted both in terms of manner and reason. In (13.47), the answer 'He borrowed (the money) from someone' explains both how and why the person in question suddenly has so much money.

(13.47) Q- je²¹ **tɕie⁵⁵me⁵⁵** ji²¹tʰȵ²⁴ yã²¹ ɔ²¹sɿ⁵⁵ tie⁵⁵ sɿ²¹ tɕiŋ²¹?
        3SG how/why   suddenly have this   many MOD money
        'How/Why does he suddenly have so much money?'
        他怎么/为什么一下子有这么多钱？

    A- je²¹ ta⁵⁵ ni²¹ tsa³³ sɿ²¹.
        3SG with other borrow AFF
        'He borrowed from someone.'
        他跟人借的。

In (13.48), being shone on by the sun explains how and why that peach turned red. Note that due to the nature of *tsʰȵ⁵⁵* 'be red', the sentence final particle *o* in (13.48Q) marks change of state instead of perfectiveness, as it does in (13.46b).

(13.48) Q- mɔ²¹ lɔ²¹po⁵⁵ po⁵⁵ tɕie³³me³³ tsʰȵ⁵⁵ o?
        that peach   CLF   how/why   be.red CRS
        tɕiŋ²¹ kʰɯ²¹ koŋ⁵⁵ a²¹tsɛ⁵⁵ pɣ³³-tɣ³³ tsʰȵ⁵⁵.
        front several day   still   NEG-PFV be.red
        'How come/Why did that peach turn red? It wasn't red several days ago.'
        那个桃儿怎么红了？前几天还没红。

    A- tɣ²¹ ŋ⁵⁵soŋ²¹ tsa⁵⁵-tɣ³³
        PASS sun   bake-hit.(the.target)
        tɯ²¹ tsʰȵ⁵⁵ o.
        then be.red   CRS
        'It turned red in the sunshine (LIT: after being shone on by the sun).'
        被太阳晒到就红了。

13.4.8 'How many/much' questions

Questions concerning quantity are realized by k^hua^{21} 'how (< good)', $k^hua^{21}tie^{55}$ 'how many/much (< good-many/much)', $tie^{21}sɔ^{55}$ 'how many/much (< many/much-few/little)' and $k^hɯ^{33}$ 'several'.

Derived from 'be good', as illustrated in (13.49), k^hua^{21} 'how' is used as an adverb, to form questions of degree. It is equivalent to English 'how + adjective' construction, as shown in (13.50). In the local dialect of Southwestern Mandarin, the morpheme 'good' is also the source of its 'how' words (cf. Ming Shengrong [2007] for the Bijie dialect).

(13.49) mɔ²¹   nioŋ²⁴   ni³³   **kʰua²¹**   xɪŋ⁵⁵.
        that   girl   CLF   good   very
        'That girl is very good.'
        那个女孩很好。

(13.50) ɔ²¹   hɔ⁵⁵   ta⁵⁵   γã²¹   **kʰua²¹**   tγ²¹?
        this   road   CLF   have   how   long
        'How long is this road?'
        这条路有多长？

(13.51) nɛ²¹   pa⁵⁵   γã²¹   **kʰua²¹**   la²¹?
        your.family   father   have   how   big
        'How old is your father?'
        你爸多大？

The question words $k^hua^{21}tie^{55}$ 'how many, how much', $tie^{21}sɔ^{55}$ 'how many, how much' and $k^hɯ^{33}$ 'several' are used to modify nouns. While $k^hua^{21}tie^{55}$ can be used as a pronoun, $k^hɯ^{33}$ cannot. In (13.52Q), $k^hua^{21}tie^{55}$ functions as a modifier, while it functions as a pronoun in (13.52A).

(13.52) Q-   ɔ²¹   lɔ²¹po⁵⁵   niɔ⁵⁵   tɕɪŋ²¹   **kʰua²¹tie⁵⁵**   ji²¹   je²¹?
        this   peach   need   money   how   one   half.a.kilo
        'How much per half a kilo are these peaches?'
        这桃子要多少钱一斤？

A- (tɕiŋ²¹) ta⁵⁵ pʰe⁵⁵ ji²¹ je²¹.
money two CURRENCY.UNIT one half.a.kilo
nɯ³³ niɔ³³ **kʰua²¹tie⁵⁵**?
2SG want how.many
'Two yuan per half a kilo. How many do you want?'
两块钱一斤。你要多少？

In (13.53), the phrase 'how much time' functions as an adverbial forming a question of frequency.

(13.53) nɯ³³ **kʰua²¹tie⁵⁵** ni²⁴ tsa²¹ ti²¹?
2SG how.much time go.up hill
'How often do you go up the hill?'
你多久上次山？

It should be mentioned that *tie²¹sɔ⁵⁵* is less frequently used than *kʰua²¹tie⁵⁵* in our database. There are only several cases in which *tie²¹sɔ⁵⁵* modifies time words forming questions, as shown below.

(13.54) ta⁵⁵ ua²⁴ tɕiu⁵⁵ loŋ³³ mo³³ niɔ³³ **tie²¹sɔ⁵⁵** kɯ²¹?
from here to city inside need how.many hour
'How long does it take to arrive in the city from here?'
从这到城要里多久？

Derived from 'several', as can be seen in (13.55), *kʰɯ³³* is restricted to questions about small quantities. Examples (13.55) and (13.56) are two contrastive examples. The phrase *kʰua²¹ la²¹* 'how big' in (13.55) can be used to ask for anyone's age, while *kʰɯ³³ neŋ²¹* 'several years' can only apply to questions about the ages of young people.

(13.55) ŋo³³ ɣã²¹ la²¹tɣ²¹ **kʰɯ²¹** kʰo⁵⁵ tɯ²¹ ɔ⁵⁵ ʑi²¹.
1SG have hoe several CLF be.at house inside
sɿ²¹ tʰɔ⁵⁵ se²¹. nɯ³³ a³³ ji²¹ kʰo⁵⁵
CONT idle CONT.PRT 2SG take one CLF
kuɛ²¹ tɕi⁵⁵ mẽ!
go use PRT
'I have several hoes at home lying idle. Take one to use.'
我有几把锄头在家，闲着没用。你拿一把去用嘛！

(13.56) nɛ²¹   nioŋ²¹hɛ⁵⁵   ɣã²¹   kʰɯ³³   neŋ²¹?
         your.family   younger.sister   have   several year
         'How old is your younger sister?'
         你妹妹几岁了？

13.5 Conclusion

This chapter introduced three basic types of questions in Caijia: (i) alternative questions, (ii) polar questions, and (iii) content questions. The interrogative patterns found in Caijia are similar to the general ones in Sinitic. Alternative questions are probably the source of one type of polar question, i.e. alternative polar questions. Being in situ, almost all the interrogative words used to form content questions in Caijia are analyzable. They show a tendency towards formal regularity, which is also common in Sinitic languages. 'How' of manner and 'why' are derived from verb phrases. 'How' of degree is derived from the morpheme 'good', a situation also attested in the local Southwestern Mandarin. A synthesis of the Caijia interrogatives is given below in Table 13.4.

Table 13.4: Caijia interrogatives (reproduced).

Types		Strategies	
I	Alternative questions	Juxtaposition by disjunction: [VP₁ DISJ VP2]	
II	i. Alternative polar questions	a. Juxtaposition: [V (DISJ) NEG VP]	
		b. Condensed: [VP (DISJ) NEG]	
	ii. Particle polar questions	Question final particle: [VP Q]	
III	Content questions	In-situ question words	
	i. Which	lɔ²⁴+CLF	'which+CLF'
	ii. Who	lɔ²⁴ni⁵⁵	'which CLF$_{PERSON}$'
	iii. Whose	lɔ²⁴ni⁵⁵ hm̩⁵⁵	'which CLF$_{PERSON}$ POSS'
	iv. What	lɔ²⁴tsoŋ⁵⁵	'which type'
		sɿ²¹mɔ⁵⁵	'what'
	v. Where	lɔ²⁴kʰa³³/la²⁴	'which place'
	vi. When	lɔ²¹kɯ²⁴	'which moment'
	vii. How (manner)	tɔ²¹lɔ²⁴sɿ⁵⁵'	'be like which way
		tɕie⁵⁵me⁵⁵/mɔ⁵⁵(tɕie⁵⁵)	'do what do'
		tɕiɔ⁵⁵mɔ⁵⁵	'do-what'

Table 13.4 (continued)

Types		Strategies	
	viii. Why	tɕie⁵⁵me⁵⁵	'do what'
		tɕiɔ⁵⁵mɔ⁵⁵	'do what'
		tɕie⁵⁵me⁵⁵tɕie⁵⁵	'how do'
	ix. How many/much	kʰɯ³³	'several'
		kʰua²¹	'good'
		kʰua²¹tie⁵⁵	'good-many'
		tie²¹sɔ⁵⁵	'many-few'

Chapter 14
Relative clauses

14.1 Definition and typology

Relative clauses and strategies of relativization have attracted much attention since Keenan and Comrie (1977) discussed in depth syntactic roles and strategies of relativization, proposing the famous implication for noun phrase accessibility, SU > DO > IO > OBL > GEN > OCOMP (1977: 66). Two of the common definitions of relative clauses can be found below.

> A relative clause (RC) is a subordinate clause which delimits the reference of an NP by specifying the role of the reference of that NP in the situation described by RC.
> (Andrews 2007: 206)

> A construction is considered a relative clause [. . .] if it is a clause which, either alone or in combination with a noun, denotes something and if the thing denoted has a semantic role within the relative clause. If there is a noun inside or outside the relative clause that denotes the thing also denoted by the clause, that noun will be referred to as the head of the relative clause.
> (Dryer 2013d)

By following the two definitions above, we can summarize that (i) a relative clause is a subordinate constituent or clause and (ii) the head noun or ∅ (i.e. the referent of a headless relative), plays a definable role in the relative clause.

The typology of relative clauses can be based on different perspectives (Comrie and Kuteva 2013a). From the point of view of linear order, relative clauses can be dichotomized into embedded relative clauses and adjoined relative clauses (Lehmann 1986, Andrews 2007), as listed in Table 14.1 below.

Table 14.1: Typology of relative clauses.

Embedded	headed	internal	
		external	prenominal
			postnominal
	headless (free)		
Adjoined	preposed		
	postposed		

An embedded relative clause is located within its matrix sentence wherein it plays an identifiable syntactic role together with its head noun (if there is one).

As shown in (14.1a), the *book* is the subject of the matrix sentence and is also the object of the relative clause. An adjoined relative clause is located outside of the matrix sentence (14.1b).

(14.1) a. *The book [I bought yesterday]* was a trade paperback
 b. *Somebody* lives nearby [who has a CD-burner]
  (cited from Andrews [2007: 206])

To form relative clauses, languages may adopt different syntactic or morphosyntactic strategies. On the basis of the current literature (Keenan and Comrie 1977, Keenan 1985, Andrews 2007, Comrie and Kuteva 2013b, 2013c, Arcodia 2017), six strategies for forming relative clauses are attested, as shown in Table 14.2.

Table 14.2: Strategies of relativization.

Relativized position	Gap
	Full NP
	Resumptive pronoun
Linking or verbal morphology	Relative pronoun (case-marking)
	Relativizer (invariant)
	∅

To code relativized positions, three strategies are observed in the current literature: these are the use of a GAP, a FULL NP (non-reduction [Comrie and Kuteva 2013c]), or a RESUMPTIVE PRONOUN. For the RESUMPTIVE strategy or 'pronoun-retention' (Comrie and Kuteva 2013c), both gap and resumptive strategies are adopted in Caijia and will be addressed in the following sections.

For linking morphology, relative pronouns, relativizers, or ∅ are used to link or introduce a relative clause and its head noun. We will use the term 'relative pronoun' to refer to a linking strategy that reflects the semantic and syntactic role of a relativized position, such as English 'whom', 'whose', and French *que* and *qui*, while we use the term 'relativizer' to refer to a linking strategy which does not code the case, number, or gender of a relativized position; for example, English 'which' and 'that' and *de* 的 [tə] 'REL' in Standard Mandarin, both of which are all invariant forms. 'Relativizer' can also be used in a broader sense. For example, the Korean relativizer/adnominal marker *-neun/-eun*, can be considered to show allomorphy in its verbal morphology, which is beyond our concerns in this chapter. The zero-marking strategy is not recorded in the classic literature on relative clauses, but it is attested in Sinitic languages (Arcodia 2017, Chen Weirong 2017, Li 2018).

In these languages, a relative clause immediately precedes its head noun without any linker.

Languages may use more than one strategy to form relative clauses. For example, French uses, at the same time, both the gap and the relative pronoun strategies to form a relative clause; and languages may shift strategies to relativize different positions. For example, Standard Mandarin uses the gap and the relativizer strategies to relativize subjects and direct objects, while the resumptive and the relativizer are used to relativize obliques.

Sinitic relative clauses show some consistent features, i.e. SVO languages with prenominal relative clauses and relativizers do not mark the syntactic/semantic roles of the relativized positions, i.e. they are invariant forms. The features of Caijia relative clauses are entirely in accordance with those of Sinitic relative clauses.

This chapter will present three types of Caijia relative clauses, four strategies of relativization and relativizable positions.

14.2 Relative clauses in Caijia

As in Sinitic languages, it is common that clauses can be used to modify nouns or NPs. However, not all clause modifiers can be treated as relative clauses. Following the two definitions for relative clauses presented above, we limit our scope to discussion of relative clauses for which the referents in the main clause possess corresponding coreferential positions inside the relative clauses. We do not target the so-called gapless relatives, which are not only a pan-Sinitic feature but are also attested in Japanese and Korean (Del Gobbo 2007). Unlike our target relative clauses, in a gapless relative, the coreferential position for the head noun does not exist, as shown in the examples below. The italicized clause modifier 'he stole money' in (14.2) can instead be treated as noun complementation, that is, 'he stole money' is the content of the head noun 'evidence'; while the one in (14.3) can be treated as the cause of the head noun. Consequently, both of these examples can be treated as instances of noun complementation (see Payne 2010 for more types of noun complementation in English). See also Comrie and Kuteva (2013b).

(14.2) *je^{33} tɔ^{21} ni^{33} tɕiŋ^{21}* sı^{21} [tie^{21}to^{21}]
3SG steal other money MOD evidence
'the evidence that he stole money'
他偷人钱的证据

(14.3) ŋo³³ kʰɤ³³-tɤ³³ ŋʷɔ²¹ tsʰɯ²¹sʅ⁵⁵ sʅ²¹
1SG smell-obtain stir.and.fry vegetable.water MOD
[kʰɯ³³sɛ²¹], mã²¹ xɪŋ⁵⁵.
smell savory very
'I smelt a smell of cooking. It smelt good.'
我闻到炒菜的味道。香得很。

However, it should be mentioned that such noun complementation is rarely used in Caijia, even though it is grammatical. Compare the two sentences below. The sentence in (14.4b) is preferred to the one in (14.4a).

(14.4) a. je³³ xa²¹ ŋoŋ³³ sʅ²¹ [tsʰʅ²¹po⁵⁵],
3SG say speech MOD sound
ŋo²¹ tʰi⁵⁵-tsʰe⁵⁵ɣɯ²¹ to³³.
1SG listen-come.out can
'I can recognize sound of his voice (LIT: the sound of his speaking).'
他说话的声音，我能听出来。

b. je²¹ hm̩⁵⁵ tsʰʅ²¹po⁵⁵ ŋo²¹ tʰi⁵⁵-tsʰe⁵⁵ɣɯ²¹ to³³.
3SG POSS sound 1SG listen-come out can
'I can recognize the sound of his voice.'
他的声音我能听出来。

The three types of relative clauses in Caijia can be summarized as follows:

Table 14.3: Relative clauses and strategies of relativization in Caijia.

	Type	Schema	LIK/NMLZ	Gap	Resumptive
Headed	I	VP-(REL)-DEM-NP	∅/REL	S, DO, GEN	IO, OBL, GEN
	II	(DEM)-VP-REL-NP	REL	S, DO, GEN	IO, OBL, GEN
Headless	III	(DEM)-VP-REL/NMLZ	REL/NMLZ	S, DO	

Both Types I and II are headed relative clauses. The use of a relativizer is optional for Type I relative clauses. When optional, Type I becomes a zero-marked relative clause. One can observe that the constituent orders are different in Types I and II. The demonstrative is obligatory and immediately precedes the head noun in a Type I relative clause, while the demonstrative is optional and precedes the VP in a Type II relative clause. The gap strategy is used to relativize subjects and direct objects, while the resumptive pronoun strategy is used to relativize indirect objects and obliques. Genitives can be relativized by both the gap and resumptive pronoun strategies. Headless relative clauses only involve the relativization of subjects and direct objects and the relativizer/nominalizer must be used.

We will now explore the three strategies of relativization and the three types of relative clauses by presenting different relativized positions.

14.2.1 Strategies of relativization in Caijia

As illustrated in Table 14.3, the strategies of relativization in Caijia are:
i. Gap
ii. Resumptive pronoun
iii. Relativizer

Gap refers to a relativized position which is an empty position coreferential with the head noun in a relative and is used to relativize subjects and direct objects in Caijia. This strategy is the most common one used to relativize subjects in languages around the world (Comrie and Kuteva 2013b). It should be mentioned that there may be more than one empty position in a Caijia relative, for Caijia is a pro-drop language. Only the empty relativized position can, however, be considered a gap. Examples can be found in §14.2.2.2.

The **resumptive pronoun** strategy, also known as the pronoun-retention strategy, codes the relativized position by using a resumptive pronoun coreferential with the head. This strategy is used to relativize indirect objects and obliques in Caijia, see §14.2.2.4.

The Caijia **relativizer** $sı^{21}$ does not code the case of a relativized position. Used to form headed relative clauses, it only serves as a ligature linking relative clauses and head nouns. It can be used to link various modifiers and the modified NP, except for genitive modifiers, as exemplified in (14.5) (see also [14.2]-[14.4a]).

(14.5) $ɔ^{21}sı^{55}$ $toŋ^{33}$ $sı^{21}$ $tsa^{33}to^{21}$
        this   heavy   MOD   stone
        'the stone (that is) heavy as this'
        这么重的石头

In addition to its function of ligature, it also serves as a nominalizer forming headless relative clauses, as will be discussed in §14.2.2.3. Lü (2019) argues that the relativizer $sı^{21}$ may share the same source as the copula $sı^{33}$ in Caijia, i.e. the demonstrative *SI, pointing out that this phenomenon of syncretism is rare in Sinitic languages. See Lü's discussion for more details.

14.2.2 Types I and II headed relative clauses

In Caijia, all the positions on the *accessibility hierarchy* (Keenan and Comrie 1977), i.e. SU > DO > IO > OBL > GEN > OCOMP, can be relativized, and they form headed relative clauses. In fact, Caijia does not distinguish objects of comparison from oblique arguments. On the basis of different strategies of relativization, the relativized positions in Caijia can be regrouped as <SUB, DO>, <GEN>, <IO, OBL>. The following sections will present the heads of headed relative clauses and these regrouped relativized positions.

14.2.2.1 Heads of headed relative clauses and orders of modifiers

Five types of minimal NP are observed as core elements of heads in headed relative clauses in Caijia. They are nouns, [DEM CLF], [NUM CLF], the plural generic pronouns *ji²¹sui⁵⁵* 'some', *ɔ²¹sui⁵⁵* 'these', *mɔ²¹sui⁵⁵* 'those', and location pronouns *ua²⁴* 'here' and *ma²⁴* 'there'. With these five types of minimal NP, different combinations of constituents of relative clauses can be observed. Next, we will exemplify Caijia relative clauses with the five types of heads listed above.

Among these types, nouns show the largest range of possibilities:

Head (I): Noun

Type I: Optional relativizer
   i.   [VP-(REL)-DEM-N]
   ii. [VP-(REL)-DEM-N-(NUM)-CLF]

Type II: Compulsory relativizer
   iii. [VP-REL-N]
   iv. [DEM-VP-REL-N]
   v.   [(DEM)-VP-REL-N-(NUM)-CLF]

As core elements of heads, nouns can be modified by other elements apart from relative clauses, such as classifiers and demonstratives. From all the possibilities listed above, we can summize that (i) it is the numeral 'one' that is often absent and that (ii) bare nouns themselves can function as heads. Let us see some examples of all of these possibilities.

(14.6)   [VP-(REL)-DEM-N-(NUM)-CLF]
   $_{RC}$[ti³³   xa³³   meŋ²¹ni³³ŋoŋ³³]   (sɿ²¹) $_{NP}$[[mɔ²¹ $_N$[u²¹tsʰo²⁴]]   [ta⁵⁵   ni³³]]
   know   say   Caijia   REL   that   people   two   CLF
   'those two people who can speak Caijia'
   会说蔡家话的那两个人

14.2 Relative clauses in Caijia

(14.7) [VP-REL-N]
ŋo³³   xa²¹sɿ³³   tɕʰi³³kʰa³³   zɤ²¹   [_RC[nɯ²¹   tɕie⁵⁵]   sɿ²¹   _N[zɤ²¹]].
1SG   all.the.same   like   eat   2SG   make   REL   meal
'(Compared with others), I like the meals that you cook.'
我还是喜欢吃你做的饭。

(14.8) [VP-REL-[N-CLF]]
_RC[jɯ²⁴   xa²¹   lɯ⁵⁵   kʰua²¹   jɯ²⁴   tɯ²¹   ni³³   tɤ²¹]   sɿ²¹
also   be.born   VCOMP   be.good   also   attract   3   like   REL
_NP[_N[nioŋ²⁴]   ni³³]
girl   CLF
'a girl that is beautiful and attractive'
又长得好又惹人喜欢的一个女孩

As in many Sinitic languages, classifier phrases in Caijia possess equivalent functions to nouns, pronouns, and pronominal phrases. Being a head and denoting the singular, [DEM CLF] can only form Type I relative clauses with an optional relativizer as an expansion of the head noun:

Head (II): [DEM CLF]]
Type I: Optional relativizer
         [VP-(REL)-[DEM-CLF]]

See an example of this type below.

(14.9) [VP-(REL)-[DEM-CLF]]
ti³³   xa²¹   ti²¹   tɕie⁵⁵   mɔ²⁴   ni³³
know   say   know   do   that   CLF
'the one who is articulate and capable'
能说能干那个

Another type of classifier phrase, [NUM CLF], can also serve as the core element of heads, forming both Type I and Type II relative clauses, as an expansion of the head noun.

Head (III): [NUM CLF]
Type I: Optional relativizer
         i. [VP-(REL)-DEM-[NUM CLF]]

Type II: Compulsory relativizer
    ii. [VP-REL-[NUM CLF]]
    iii. [DEM-VP-REL-[NUM CLF]]

(14.10) [VP-REL-[NUM CLF]]

mɔ²¹	kɯ²⁴	u²¹tsʰo²¹	sa³³	ni³³	kuɛ²¹	kʰɯ²¹xui²⁴.	ji³³
that	moment	people	three	CLF	go	attend.meeting	one

ni³³	nɛ³³	niɔ³³	ɣa²¹	kʰɯ³³loŋ²¹	kuɛ³³,	ta⁵⁵	ni³³	niɔ³³
CLF	PRT	PROSP	walk	Hezhang_PLACENAME	go	two	CLF	will

ɣa²¹	la²¹sʅ⁵⁵	kuɛ²¹.	[ɣa²¹	la²¹sʅ⁵⁵	kuɛ²¹]	sʅ²¹
go	Guiyang_PLACENAME	go	walk	Guiyang_PLACENAME	go	REL

[ta⁵⁵	ni²¹]	nɛ⁵⁵,	sʅ³³	ji³³	ni³³	pɣ³³	tɕʰi³³³kʰa³³	ji³³
two	CLF	PRT	CONT	one	CLF	NEG	like	one

ni³³	sʅ²¹.
CLF	CONT

'At that time, (there were) three people going to attend meetings. One would go to Hezhang, and two of them would go to Guiyang. Those two that were going to Guiyang had disliked each other.'
那时候，三个人去开会。一个呢，要去赫章。两个要去贵阳。去贵阳的两个呢，相互不喜欢。

In Standard Mandarin, personal pronouns can be observed in literary texts as heads of relative clauses. As shown below, the third person pronoun *tā* '3SG' is modified by a relative clause.

(14.11) 洗心革面的他决定离开这里。

ᴿᶜ[xǐxīngémiàn]	de	[tā]	juédìng	líkāi	zhèlǐ.
change.entirely	REL	3SG	decide	leave	here

'LIT: He that wants a fresh start has decided to leave here.'

However, as a colloquial language, Caijia does not uses its personal pronouns as the heads of relative clauses, but several plural generic pronominal phrases which can serve as heads of relatives, such as the non-specific quantifier phrase *ji²¹sui⁵⁵* 'some', and the specific phrases formed with demonstrative pronouns *ɔ²¹sui⁵⁵* 'these' and *mɔ²¹sui⁵⁵* 'those'. Due to its indefinite nature, the phrase *ji²¹sui⁵⁵* can only form Type II relatives, while *ɔ²¹sui⁵⁵* and *mɔ²¹sui⁵⁵* can only form Type I relatives.

Head (IV): ***ji²¹sui⁵⁵*** **'some';** ***ɔ²¹sui⁵⁵*** **'these',** ***mɔ²¹sui⁵⁵*** **'those'**
Type II: Compulsory relativizer
    [VP-REL-ji²¹sui⁵⁵]

Type I: Optional relativizer
[VP-ɔ²¹sui⁵⁵]
[VP-mɔ²¹sui⁵⁵]

See example (14.12) below.

(14.12) [VP-REL -ji²¹sui⁵⁵]

[pɣ³³	zɣ²¹	tsa²¹]	sɿ²¹	[ji²¹sui⁵⁵]	niɔ³³	ɣɯ²¹	nɛ⁵⁵,	nɯ³³
NEG	eat	meat	REL	some		will	come	PRT	2SG

tɯ³³	a³³	li²¹tsɿ²¹	ŋʷɔ²¹	tsʰɯ²¹sɿ⁵⁵	pɣ³³	tɣ³³.
then	with	lard	stir.and.fry	dish	NEG	can

'If those who don't eat meat come, you can't cook with lard.'
不吃肉的一些（人）要来呢，你就不能用猪油炒菜了。

The location pronouns *ua*²⁴ 'here' and *ma*²⁴ 'there' serve as heads of relatives as well. They can only form Type I relative clauses, because these two location pronouns are fused with demonstratives. See also §14.2.2.4.

Head (V): *ua*²⁴ [ɔ²¹ + ha⁵⁵] 'here [this + place]' and
*ma*²⁴ [mɔ²¹+ha⁵⁵] 'there [that+place]'
Type I: Optional relativizer
[VP-(REL)-ua²⁴/ma²⁴]

(14.13) [VP-(REL)-ua²⁴/ma²⁴]

nɛ²¹	ʑi²¹	tɕie⁵⁵	zɣ²¹	(sɿ²¹)	ma²⁴
your.family	mother	make	meal	REL	there

'the place where your mother cooks'
你妈做饭的那儿

14.2.2.2 Relativized subjects and direct objects

The gap strategy is mainly used to relativize subjects and direct objects in Caijia. Examples (14.14) and (14.15) are instances of relativized subjects, the empty relativized positions of which are indicated. The sentence in (14.14a) is a declarative simple sentence, on the basis of which the two relatives in (14.14b) and (14.14c) are formed. As mentioned above, a demonstrative is obligatory to form a zero-marked relative and must be situated immediately before the head noun, as in (14.14b). The presence of the relativizer is obligatory when the optional demonstrative precedes the relative clause in initial position, as in (14.14c).

(14.14) a. mɔ²¹ u²¹tsʰo²¹ fɛ⁵¹hɛ²¹ ta⁵⁵ suaŋ³³uɛ³³ ti³³-ɣɯ²¹.
that people family from Weining_PLACENAME move-come
'That family of people moved (here) from Weining.'
那家人从威宁搬来。

Relativized subject: Type I Optional relativizer
b. ᴿᶜ[Ø_i ta⁵⁵ suaŋ³³uɛ³³ ti³³-ɣɯ²¹]
 from Weining_PLACENAME move-come
(sʅ²¹) ᴴᴱᴬᴰ[mɔ²¹ u²¹tsʰo²¹ fɛ⁵¹hɛ²¹]_i
REL that people family
'that family of people which moved (here) from Weining'
从威宁搬来那家人

Relativized subject: Type II Compulsory relativizer
c. mɔ²¹ ᴿᶜ[Ø_i ta⁵⁵ suaŋ³³uɛ³³ ti³³-ɣɯ²¹] *(sʅ²¹)
that from Weining_PLACENAME move-come REL
ᴴᴱᴬᴰ[u²¹tsʰo²¹ fɛ²¹hɛ²¹]_i
people family
'that family which moved (here) from Weining'
那家从威宁搬来的人

(14.15) ᴿᶜ[Ø_i ɯ²¹ tsʰʅ³³ ɯ³³] ᴴᴱᴬᴰ[mɔ²¹ tsʅ⁵⁵ŋa⁵⁵ ni³³]_i kuɛ²¹
 wear blue clothes that boy CLF go
a³³ kʰa²⁴ po⁵⁵ ɣɯ²¹ kɔ²¹ ky⁵⁵.
take box CLF PURP prop.up foot
'The boy wearing a blue coat took a box to stand on.'
穿蓝衣服那男孩儿拿了个箱子来垫脚。

Examples (14.16) and (14.17a) demonstrate that the gap strategy can be used to relativize direct objects. In (14.17a) one can observe two empty positions in the relative clause. The empty position $\emptyset_s$ is the pro-drop for the subject ηo^{24} 'we', while $\emptyset_i$ is the relativized position of the object, $sʅ^{55}$ 'water'. The way to distinguish the pro-drop from the relativized position is that the pro-drop position can be filled, while the gapped position cannot. In (14.17a), the subject is omitted to avoid redundancy, since the locative phrase 'in our village' already implies the subject of the VP 'drink water' as 'we', making it unnecessary to state the subject 'we'. The locative phrase must not be used if one would like to produce a natural relative clause with an overt subject, as shown in (14.17b). By contrast, it would be ungrammatical to refill the gapped relativized position, as in (14.17c).

14.2 Relative clauses in Caijia

Relativized object: Type I Optional relativizer

(14.16) ŋo²¹ hɛ⁵⁵ pia³³ Ø_i (sɿ²¹) [mɔ²¹ so⁵⁵po³³]_i
1SG Y.brother marry REL that wife
sɿ³³ mia²¹ nioŋ²⁴.
COP Lolo girl
'The wife my younger brother married is a Lolo woman.'
我弟弟娶的老婆是彝族姑娘。

Relativized object: Type II Compulsory relativizer

(14.17) a. [ŋo²⁴ tsʰɿ⁵⁵ mo³³ Ø_S ã³³ Ø_i] sɿ²¹ [sɿ⁵⁵]_i la²¹
1PL village inside drink REL water all
sɿ²¹ ta⁵⁵ tɕiu⁵⁵ti²¹pɪŋ²⁴ u²¹ kʰɪŋ⁵⁵-ɣɯ²¹ sɿ³³.
AFF with Mount.Chive back pull-come AFF
'The water that (we) drink in our village is all drawn here from the back of Mount Chive.'
我们村里喝的水是从韭菜坪后面引过来的。

b. [ŋo²⁴ ã³³ Ø_i] sɿ²¹ [sɿ⁵⁵]_i
1PL drink REL water
'the water that we drink'
我们喝的水

c. *[ŋo²⁴ ã³³ je³³_i] sɿ²¹ [sɿ⁵⁵]_i
1PL drink 3SG REL water
(Attempted: '*the water that we drink it')
*我们喝它的水

14.2.2.3 Relativized genitives

Genitives or possessives can be relativized by both the gap and the resumptive pronoun strategies, as exemplified in (14.18) and (14.19). However, relativized genitives tend to form Type I relatives with the optional relativizer instead of Type II with the compulsory relativizer, even though Type II relatives with relativized genitives are grammatical. See Chapter 3 §3.4.2 for more on Caijia possessives.

Relativized genitive: Type I Optional relativizer

(14.18) je³³_i nioŋ²⁴ kʰɔ²¹-tɤ³³ ta²⁴ɕyɔ²¹ (sɿ²¹) [mɔ²¹ ni³³]_i
Ø_i
3SG girl take.exam-hit.the.target university REL that CLF
'the one whose daughter passed the university entrance examination'
（他）女儿考上大学那个

(14.19) je³³ᵢ mɛ³³ tγ²¹ kʰγ⁵⁵pa²¹ tɕʰɪŋ²¹-sɿ⁵⁵ [mɔ²¹ u²¹tsʰo²⁴ ni³³]ᵢ
∅ᵢ
3SG horse PASS tiger bite-die that people CLF
'the one whose horse was killed by a tiger'
（他）马被老虎咬死那个人

Between (14.20a) and (14.20b) the latter is preferred.

(14.20) Relativized genitive: Type II Compulsory relativizer
a. mɔ²¹ je³³ᵢ tɕɪŋ²¹ tγ³³ ni³³ tɔ²¹-kuɛ²¹
    ∅ᵢ
    that 3SG money PASS 3 steal-go
    sɿ²¹ [tsɿ⁵⁵ŋa⁵⁵ ni³³]ᵢ
    REL boy CLF
    'the boy whose money was stolen by someone'
    那个(他)钱被人偷走的男孩

Relativized genitive: Type I Optional relativizer
b. je³³ᵢ tɕɪŋ²¹ tγ³³ ni³³ tɔ²¹-kuɛ²¹ [mɔ²¹ tsɿ⁵⁵ŋa⁵⁵
    ∅ᵢ
    3SG money PASS other steal-go that boy
    ni³³]ᵢ tɯ²¹ ma²⁴ ɣɯ²¹ lɯ⁵⁵ pγ³³ sɯ³³.
    CLF at there cry VCOMP NEG rest
    'The boy whose money is stolen by someone can't stop crying.'
    (他)钱被偷那男孩在那儿不停地哭。

14.2.2.4 Relativized indirect objects and obliques

The resumptive pronoun strategy is adopted to relativize indirect objects and other types of obliques, just as the relativized genitives do. Examples (14.21) and (14.22) illustrate cases of relativized indirect objects. Each relativized position is occupied by the third person pronoun *je³³* 'she/he, her/him' coreferential with the head noun, i.e. 'that girl' in (14.21) and 'that beggar' in (14.22). One can observe that the relative clause in (14.21) is a dative construction and the indirect object is flagged by the dative preposition *sɿ⁵⁵* 'to', while the one in (14.22) is a double object construction in which the indirect object is zero marked. Flagged by prepositions or not, indirect objects cannot be relativized by the gap strategy.

14.2 Relative clauses in Caijia

Relativized indirect object: Type I Optional relativizer

(14.21) nuɯ³³ a³³ tɕɪŋ²¹ sɿ⁵⁵ je²¹ᵢ ja²¹ [mɔ²¹ pʰi⁵⁵hɔ⁵⁵ ni³³]ᵢ
　　　　　　　　　　　　　　*∅ᵢ
　　　　2SG take money to 3SG EXP that beggar CLF
　　　　jɯ²⁴ yɯ²¹ o.
　　　　again come PRT
　　　　'The beggar to whom you gave money is here again.'
　　　　你给过他钱的乞丐又来了。

Relativized indirect object: Type II Compulsory relativizer

(14.22) mɔ²¹ ŋo³³ kʷɔ³³ je³³ᵢ meŋ²¹ni³³ŋoŋ³³ sɿ²¹ [nioŋ²⁴ ni³³]ᵢ,
　　　　　　　　　　　　　　　　*∅ᵢ
　　　　that 1SG teach 3SG Caijia REL girl CLF
　　　　nuɯ³³ tsaŋ³³-kɪŋ²¹ je³³ lɔ²¹ pɣ³³-tɣ³³?
　　　　2SG look-see 3SG or NEG-PFV
　　　　'Have you seen the girl to whom I teach Caijia?'
　　　　那个我教她蔡家话的女孩，你看见了没？

The following examples illustrate the cases in which obliques are relativized. As mentioned above, being prepositional objects, "objects of comparison" (Keenan and Comrie 1977), i.e. comparative standards, do not differ from other obliques in Caijia when relativized. Compare (14.23) and (14.24).

(14.23) ŋo²¹ ta⁵⁵ je²¹ᵢ tɕie⁵⁵ ja²¹pa²¹ [mɔ²⁴ ni³³]ᵢ saŋ³³ kʰua²¹ xɪŋ⁵⁵.
　　　　　　　　　*∅ᵢ
　　　　1SG for 3SG do crop that CLF heart good very
　　　　'The person for whom I work is very kind.'
　　　　我给他干活那人心很好。

(14.24) Relativized comparative standard
　　　a. nuɯ²¹ pi⁵⁵ je³³ᵢ tɣ²¹ lɯ⁵⁵ kʷɔ³³ [mɔ²⁴ ni³³]ᵢ
　　　　　　　　　*∅ᵢ
　　　　　2SG than 3SG grow VCOMP tall that CLF
　　　　　'the person whom you're taller than'
　　　　　你比他高的那个人

　　　Relativized equative standard
　　　b. nɛ²¹ tɕi⁵⁵ ta⁵⁵ je²¹ᵢ
　　　　　　　　　　　　　*∅ᵢ
　　　　　your.family elder.sister with 3SG

ji²¹jaŋ²⁴ kʷɔ³³ [mɔ²¹ pa³³tsɔ³³ ni³³]ᵢ
equally tall that man CLF
'the man with whom your elder sister is equally tall'
你姐跟他一样高那男的

As illustrated by the examples above, it is the third personal pronoun *je³³* that is often observed as a resumptive pronoun. However, the resumptive pronoun used in a relative clause is not a fossilized form. It varies with its coreferential head noun. For example, if a head noun is plural, the corresponding plural pronoun should be used. In (14.25), the relativized oblique is plural, the third person plural pronoun *je²¹-xɯ⁵⁵* is thus used occupying the relativized position.

(14.25) nɯ²¹ peŋ⁵⁵ **je²¹-xɯ⁵⁵**ᵢ sɣ³³ [mɔ²¹ kʷɔ³³sɣ²¹ŋa⁵⁵ sui⁵⁵]ᵢ
2SG offer 3-PL book that student PL
nɛ⁵⁵, na²¹zɿ⁵⁵ nɯ²¹ xɪŋ⁵⁵.
PRT thank 2SG very
'The students to whom you offered books thank you very much.'
你送他们书的那些学生非常感谢你。

If an oblique of location is relativized, a corresponding locational pronoun, 'here' or 'there', should be used. In the following sentence, it is the distal place pronoun *ma²⁴* 'there', the fusion form of *mɔ²¹ ha⁵⁵* 'that place', that is used as the resumptive pronoun coreferential with the head *mɔ²¹ tsʰɿ³³kʰa³³* 'that place'.

(14.26) je²¹ ta⁵⁵ **ma²⁴**[mɔ²¹+ha⁵⁵]ᵢ lɪŋ²¹-tɕie²¹kuɛ²¹ [mɔ²¹ tsʰɿ³³kʰa³³]ᵢ
3SG from there[that+place] fall-down.go that place
ɣã²¹ la²¹ tsa³³to²¹ sui⁵⁵.
there.be big stone some
'There are many big stones at the place from which he fell down.'
他从那儿掉下去那地方有很多大石头。

However, it should be mentioned that locational prepositional phrases tend to be dropped when relativizing obliques of locations. This situation is different from that of other obliques. We may revisit (14.26) to illustrate this strategy. One can observe that the prepositional phrase *ta⁵⁵ ma²⁴* 'from there' is dropped in (14.27). Compared with (14.26), example (14.27) is preferred. Example (14.28) illustrates a case in which the post-verbal oblique of location, *ɔ²¹ kɔ²¹ kɣ⁵⁵* 'the bottom of this bridge', is relativized with the same strategy as the dropped locative oblique in (14.27).

(14.27) je³³ lɯ³³-tɕie²¹kuɛ²¹ mɔ²¹ tsʰɿ⁵⁵kʰa⁵⁵ ɣã²¹ la²¹ tsa³³to²¹ sui⁵⁵.
3SG fall-down.go that place there.be big stone some
'There are many big stones at the place from which he fell down.'
他掉下去那地方有很多大石头。

(14.28) a. je²¹-xɯ⁵⁵ pɣ³³ ɣã²¹ ɔ⁵⁵ tɯ²¹, tɔ²⁴ sa³³ ni³³
3-PL NEG have house live thief three CLF
tɯ³³ tsɣ³³ tɯ²¹ ɔ²¹ kɔ²¹ kɣ⁵⁵.
then hide at this bridge foot
'They didn't have a house to live in. The three thieves thus hid themselves under the bridge.'
他们没有房子住。三个贼就躲在桥下。

b. ɔ²¹ kɔ²¹ kɣ⁵⁵ tɯ³³ sɿ³³ je²¹-xɯ⁵⁵ tsɣ²¹ sɿ²¹ tsʰɿ³³kʰa³³.
this bridge foot indeed COP 3-PL hide REL place
'It is under the bridge that they hid themselves. (LIT: The foot of the bridge is where they hid).'
桥下就是他们躲的地方。

Obliques of time in Caijia often function as adverbials without any overt marking in the sentence initial position, as shown in (14.29a). The gap strategy is used to relativize temporal obliques but forms only Type I relative clauses, i.e. demonstratives must immediately precede the heads, as illustrated in (14.29b). Moreover, special classifiers for time words do not exist in Caijia, since these words themselves are a kind of measure word.

(14.29) a. tɕɯ²¹ɯ⁵⁵koŋ⁵⁵ je³³ ɣa²¹ loŋ³³ mo³³ kuɛ³³.
the.day.before.yesterday 3SG walk city inside go
mɔ²¹ zɿ⁵⁵ ɣɯ²¹ lɯ⁵⁵ la²¹ xɯ⁵⁵.
that rain come VCOMP big very
'The day before yesterday he went to the town. It rained heavily.'
前天他进城。那雨下得大得很。

Relativized temporal oblique: Type I Optional relativizer
b. je³³ ɣa²¹ loŋ³³ mo³³ kuɛ³³ (sɿ²¹) mɔ²¹ koŋ⁵⁵,
3SG walk city inside go REL that day
zɿ⁵⁵ ɣɯ²¹ lɯ⁵⁵ la²¹ xɯ⁵⁵.
rain come VCOMP big very
'It rained heavily the day he went to the town.'
他进城那天，雨下得大得很。

By way of contrast, when the time word $t^h ɔ^{55}$ 'moment' is the head of a relative clause, it can neither be modified by demonstratives nor be linked with the relative clause by the relativizer $sɿ^{21}$. The formula [VP $t^h ɔ^{55}$] is not included in Table 14.3. The time word $ti^{33}ɿn^{21}$ $kɯ^{24}$ 'just now' in (14.30a) is relativized with $t^h ɔ^{55}$ as its head, as illustrated in (14.30b). The noun phrase [$ŋo^{21}$ ta^{55} ni^{33} $na^{33}pia^{21}$ $t^h ɔ^{55}$] 'the moment I was chatting with someone' serves only as a time word.

(14.30) a. ti³³ɿn²¹kɯ²⁴ ŋo²¹ ta⁵⁵ ni³³ na³³pia³³ sɿ²¹. tɯ³³ tsaŋ³³-kɿŋ³³
just.now   1SG   with 3   chat   CONT   then look-see
je³³ pɔ²¹-xɯ⁵⁵ ŋa⁵⁵ tsʰe⁵⁵ ma²¹kʰa³³ kuɛ²¹ o.
3SG   hold-DUR child be.out door   go   CRS
'I was chatting with someone just now and saw that she went out with her child in her arms.'
刚才我在跟人聊天。就看到她抱着孩子出门了。

b. ŋo²¹ ta⁵⁵ ni³³ na³³pia²¹ **tʰɔ⁵⁵**, je³³ pɔ²¹-xɯ⁵⁵
1SG   with other chat   moment   3SG   hold-DUR
ŋa⁵⁵ tsʰe⁵⁵ ma²¹kʰa⁵⁵ kuɛ²¹ o.
child be.out door   go   CRS
'The moment when I was chatting with someone, she went out with her child in her arms.'
我跟人聊天的时候，她抱着孩子出门了。

Moreover, the time word $kɯ^{24}$ 'moment' is also observed as the head of a relative clause, even though it is less frequently used than $t^h ɔ^{55}$ 'moment'. Similar to $t^h ɔ^{55}$, the relativizer is rarely observed when $kɯ^{24}$ is the head noun, but unlike $t^h ɔ^{55}$ it can be modified by demonstratives. For example, in (14.31) two relative clauses follow one another but do not get linked by the relativizer with their own heads, while in (14.32) the distal demonstrative $mɔ^{21}$ 'that' modifies $kɯ^{24}$ 'moment'.

(14.31) je³³ pɣ³³ sɿ²¹ koŋ⁵⁵koŋ⁵⁵ la²¹ niɔ³³ ɣɯ²¹.
3SG   NEG COP   every.day   all   will   come
ɣã²¹ **[ɣɯ²¹]** kɯ²⁴, ɣã²¹ **[pɣ³³ ɣɯ²¹]** kɯ²⁴.
there.be come   moment there.be NEG come moment
'It is not every day that he comes. Sometimes he comes, sometimes he doesn't (LIT: There're moments he comes and moments he doesn't).'
他不是天天都要来。有来的时候，有不来的时候。

(14.32) je²¹ tsʰe⁵⁵-kuɛ²¹ mɔ²¹ kɯ²⁴
 3SG go.out-go that moment
 'the moment he went out'
 他出去那会儿

14.2.3 Type III headless relative clauses

Several features of the headless relative clauses in Caijia can be summarized: (i) only subjects and direct objects positions can be relativized as headless relative clauses; (ii) they are formed obligatorily by the relativizer/nominalizer $sɿ^{21}$ and the gap strategy; (iii) only those with relativized subjects can be modified by demonstratives. The schema can be illustrated as [(DEM) VP REL ∅]. See also Chapter 3 §3.7 on headless noun phrases.

In (14.33), it is the subject position that is relativized. Marked by $sɿ^{21}$, the bracketed relative clause serves as the subject of the copular construction referring to the gapped subject, $∅_1$. Furthermore, this headless relative clause can be optionally modified by demonstratives.

(14.34) (mɔ²¹) [∅₁ᵢ kʰɯ²¹ tsʰɛ²¹ sɿ²¹] ∅₂ᵢ sɿ³³ ŋo²¹ pa⁵⁵.
 that drive car NMLZ COP drive 1SG father
 'That one driving the car is my father.'
 开车的是我爸。

Example (14.34) illustrates a headless relative clause serving as the copular complement with a relativized object. The bracketed relative clause refers to the gapped object. Unlike the case of (14.33), demonstratives cannot be used to modify headless relatives with relativized objects. As shown in (14.34), using the demonstrative is ungrammatical. Moreover, the clause $sɿ^{33}$ $nɯ^{21}$ $tɕie^{55}$ $sɿ^{21}$ can be interpreted in two ways, if not in the context of (14.34): (i) 'It is you who made it' and (ii) 'It is what you made', as Caijia uses the construction $sɿ^{33}$...$sɿ^{21}$ to form cleft constructions (see Chapter 11 §11.8). The context 'I will totally like eating it' helps exclude the first interpretation, since the pro-drop position following the verb zy^{21} 'eat' is coreferential with the headless relative clause.

(14.34) tsʰɛ²¹niɔ³³ sɿ³³ (*mɔ²¹) [nɯ²¹ tɕie⁵⁵ ∅₁ᵢ sɿ²¹] ∅₂ᵢ,
 as.long.as COP that 2SG do NMLZ
 ŋo³³ la²¹ tɕʰi³³kʰa³³ zy²¹ ∅ᵢ.
 1SG all like eat
 'As long as it is what you made, I will entirely like eating it.'
 只要是你做的，我都喜欢吃。

It can be observed that a headless relative clause refers itself to the gapped position within it, i.e. a subject or direct object. One may be curious to find out why a headless relative clause formed by a bare transitive verb can either refer to the gapped subject or the gapped object. It is indeed rare in our database, but such cases do exist. As illustrated below, the relative clause *pɤ³³ tɕʰi³³kʰa³³ zɤ²¹ sɿ²¹* refers to the relativized subject in (14.35a), i.e. 'people who don't like to eat fish mint', while it refers to the relativized object in (14.35b), i.e. 'what (I) don't like to eat'. However, even so, ambiguity of the referent rarely arises, since context usually helps in figuring out referents. Take (14.35a) as an example. Given that 'fish mint' (a kind of edible herb) is the topic in (14.35a) and that the VP in the relative clause is 'like to eat', it is impossible to assign the referent of the relative clause (people) to the empty object position, $\emptyset_2$. Besides, the sentence 'can't even (bear to) smell it', which follows the relative clause, also determines that the referent has to be an agentive subject.

(14.35) a. mɔ²¹   tsʰɿ²¹ni³³kʰa³³tsʰɯ²¹   nɛ⁵⁵,   tɕʰi³³kʰa³³   zɤ²¹   sɿ²¹
that   fish.mint   PRT   like   eat   NMLZ
nɛ⁵⁵,   tɕʰi³³kʰa²¹   xɪŋ⁵⁵. $\emptyset_1$ **pɤ³³   tɕʰi³³kʰa³³   zɤ²¹**
PRT   like   very   NEG   like   eat
$\emptyset_2$ **sɿ²¹**   nɛ⁵⁵,   kʰɤ⁵⁵   la²¹   kʰɤ⁵⁵   po³³   to³³.
NMLZ   PRT   smell   even   smell   NEG   can
'As for the fish mint, those who like to eat it like it very much, while those who don't like to eat it, can't even (bear to) smell it.'
鱼腥草呢，喜欢吃的喜欢得很。不喜欢吃的，闻都闻不了。

b. tsaŋ²¹   kuɛ²¹   tsaŋ²¹   ɣɯ²¹   nɛ⁵⁵,   la²¹   sɿ³³
look   go   look   come   TOP   all   COP
$\emptyset_1$ **pɤ³³   tɕʰi³³kʰa³³   zɤ²¹** $\emptyset_2$ **sɿ²¹.**
NEG   like   eat   NMLZ
'(I) took a closer look and all the things are what I don't like to eat.'
看来看去，都是不喜欢吃的。

In comparison with the relativizer *sɿ²¹* in headed relative clauses, *sɿ²¹* functions more as a nominalizer rather than a linker in headless relative clauses, as already illustrated above. The optional use of *sɿ²¹* in Type I relative clauses illustrates well its role as a linker. Note that it cannot be treated as a linker in headless relatives. Rather, it nominalizes VPs, making them function as observed in (14.35). See examples (14.36) and (14.37). Compared with the headless relative clauses above, *tɕie⁵⁵ ja²¹pa²¹ sɿ²¹* 'those who do farming ~ peasant' in (14.36), *zɤ²¹ sɿ²¹* 'the things that can be eaten ~ food', *ã²¹ sɿ²¹* 'the things that can be drunk ~ drinks' in (14.37) all possess generic meanings rather than specific ones. It should be mentioned that the sentence *ŋo³³ sɿ²¹ tɕie⁵⁵ ja²¹pa²¹ sɿ²¹* can also be interpreted as 'I'm doing farming', if removed from the context of (14.36). This is because the construction *sɿ³³...sɿ²¹* serves also as an aspectual marker expressing continuousness (see also Chapter 10 §10.2.8).

(14.36) ŋo³³ sɿ²¹ **tɕie⁵⁵ ja²¹pa²¹ sɿ²¹**, pɣ³³ tsʰɿ³³ kʰɣ³³ sɿ²¹.
1SG COP do corps NMLZ NEG fear bitterness AFF
'I am a peasant. I'm definitely not afraid of hardship.'
我是做活计的，不怕苦的。

(14.37) **zɣ²¹ sɿ²¹, ã³³ sɿ²¹**, ji²¹ tsoŋ⁵⁵ la²¹ pɣ³³ ɣã²¹.
eat NMLZ drink NMLZ one kind even NEG have
'There is no food or drinks.'
吃的喝的什么都没有。

Uses of *sɿ²¹* go beyond that of nominalization. Used after nouns or NPs, it changes the semantic category of referents which are originally denoted by the nouns or NPs themselves. In (14.38), *sɿ²¹* is added after several place words, realizing changes of referents. These place words no longer denote specific places, but the people who come from these places in the context of (14.38). In (14.39), *sɿ²¹* is added after the NP 'white clothes' and forms a new NP designating the person who is wearing them. In such cases, it is hard to determine whether *sɿ²¹* is still a nominalizer.

(14.38) ŋo⁵⁵ tsʰɿ²¹ka⁵⁵ tɯ²¹ ha⁵⁵ e²¹, **ji²¹li²¹ se³³**,
1PL all be.at here PRT Yeli_PLACENAME NMLZ.PRT
ɕiŋ⁵⁵fa²¹ se³³, [...] **tʰie²¹tsɣ²⁴ se³³**,
Xingfa_PLACENAME NMLZ.PRT Tiezhu_PALCENAME NMLZ.PRT
ŋo²⁴ tɛ²¹tɕʰi²⁴ kʰɯ²¹ fɛ⁵¹ la²¹ tɯ²¹ ha⁵⁵ me³³.
1PL all several family all at here dig
'[...] We were all here. The one from Yeli, the one from Xingfa and the one from Tiezhu, all of us were here to dig (a pond). [...]'
我们全部都在这儿。野里的，兴发的，铁柱的，大家都在这儿挖（水塘）。
(*Building the reservoir*, texts)

(14.39) **pia³³ ɯ³³ sɿ²¹** tɯ³³ sɿ³³ mɔ²¹ tɔ²⁴ ni³³.
white clothes NMLZ indeed COP that thief CLF
'The one in white clothes is the thief.'
白衣服的就是那个贼。

14.2.4 Aspectual restrictions

Two aspectual restrictions are observed in relative clauses: (i) the continuous aspectual construction $sl^{33}\ldots sl^{21}$ and (ii) the currently relevant state marker *o* are not compatible with relative clauses. These two restrictions apply to both headed and headless relatives.

First, in Caijia, the continuous aspectual construction $sl^{33}\ldots sl^{21}$ and its reduced form sl^{21} cannot be used in relative clauses. A possible explanation for this is that the continuous sl^{21} and the relativizer/nominalizer sl^{21} are derived from the same source. Example (14.40a) shows how the construction $sl^{33}\ldots sl^{21}$ marks continuousness in a declarative sentence. If the subject 'he' is relativized, keeping this continuous marker in the relative clause will be ungrammatical, as shown in (14.40b).

(14.40) a. je^{33} (sl^{33}) po^{21}sl^{55} sl^{21}.
3SG CONT swim CONT
'He's swimming.'
他在游泳。

b. (*sl^{33}) po^{21}sl^{55} *sl^{21} sl^{21} mɔ^{21} u^{21}tsʰo^{24} ni^{33}
CONT swim CONT REL that people CLF
'the person who is swimming'
在游泳的那个人

Second, it is probably due to its syntactic and principal semantic features that the change-of-state marker *o* is incompatible with relative clauses in Caijia. Marking the change of state, *o* is a particle that only appears in the clause final position, as shown in (14.41a). The only grammatical way to relativize the subject in (14.41b) is to not use *o*, as shown in (14.41b) and (14.41c).

(14.41) a. pe^{55}sɔ^{21} tsʰɿ^{55} **o**. li^{21} tɣ^{33} **o**.
hot.pepper be.red CRS pick can CRS
'The hot peppers have all reddened. It's time to pick (them).'
辣椒都红了。可以摘了。

b. a^{21} tsʰɿ^{55} (*o) sl^{21} pe^{55}sɔ^{21} li^{21}-tɕie^{21}ɣɯ^{21}.
OM be.red CRS REL hot.pepper pick-descend.come
'Pick the ripened (red) hot peppers!'
把红了的辣椒摘下来。

c. li²¹   tɣ³³   (*o)   sı²¹   pe⁵⁵sɔ²¹
   pick   can   CRS   REL   hot.pepper
   'the peppers that are ready to pick'
   可以摘的辣椒

In most other possible cases, relativization does not reject aspectual marking inside relative clauses. Examples (14.42) and (14.43) illustrate relatives with the completive marker *ha⁵⁵* and the durative marker *-xɯ⁵⁵*, respectively.

(14.42) zɣ²¹   zɣ²¹   **ha⁵⁵**   sı²¹   ŋa⁵⁵-sui⁵⁵   nɛ⁵⁵
         eat   meal   COMPL   REL   child-PL   PRT
         tɯ³³   kuɛ²¹ sɔ²¹kʷɔ⁵⁵ tɣ³³   o.
         then   go   play   can   CRS
         'The children who have finished their meal can go play.'
         吃完饭的孩子们就可以去玩了。

(14.43) tɯ²¹   sɔ⁵⁵   kɣ⁵⁵   taŋ²¹-**xɯ⁵⁵**   mɔ²⁴   ni³³
         at   tree   foot   stand-DUR   that   CLF
         'the person that is standing under the tree'
         在树下站着那个

See the following example with the experiential marker *ja²¹* in a negated relative clause (see also [14.21]).

(14.44) lɔ²⁴kʰa³³   la²¹   pɣ³³-tɣ³³   kuɛ³³   **ja²¹**   mɔ²⁴-sui⁵⁵
         where   all   NEG-PFV   go   EXP   that-PL
         pɣ³³   tiu³³u³³   sı²¹mɔ⁵⁵.
         NEG   know   what
         'Those that have never been elsewhere don't know much (about the outside world).'
         哪儿都没去过的那些不知道什么。

14.3 Conclusion

This chapter has introduced the three strategies of relativization and the three types of relative clauses in Caijia. We also examined the patterns of syntactic behavior for head nouns and presented two aspectual restrictions found in relative clauses.

In Types I and II headed relative clauses, the relativizer $sɿ^{21}$ can function as a ligature linking the relative clauses and their heads, as does its counterpart *de* 的 in Standard Mandarin and many Sinitic languages. The relativizer is optional for Type I, but obligatory for Type II. This optionality may be related with the position of the demonstrative which directly precedes the head noun in Type I but not in Type II. The role of the demonstrative in forming relative clauses has been shown to be crucial by Matthews and Yip (1994: 111–112), Tang Zhengda (2007, 2008), and Chen Weirong (2017). By contrast, in headless relative clauses, i.e. Type III, $sɿ^{21}$ is rather like a nominalizer than a ligature.

In sum, Caijia uses preverbal relative clauses even though its basic order is SVO, whereas the harmonic combination would be with SOV. This combination, however, reflects a common Sinitic pattern. Compared with the case studies of several individual Sinitic languages, Yichun Gan (Li 2018: 241–253), Hui'an Southern Min (Chen Weirong 2017), and Yongshou Central Plains Mandarin (Tang Zhengda 2008), as well as Standard Mandarin, the Caijia patterns of relative clauses and the strategies of relativization can be seen to be similar to the general Sinitic patterns.

Chapter 15
Clause linking: Complementation, coordination and adverbial subordination

15.1 Introduction

In the literature, there are three basic ways that have been identified, via which two clauses can be linked to form a complex sentence. According to Dixon (2006) these are:
i.   complement clause constructions
ii. relative clause constructions
iii. coordinate and adverbial subordinate constructions.

English examples of each type are given below.

(15.1)　Complementation
　　　　I think [(that) he was right].

(15.2)　Relativization
　　　　This is the [book [I bought for him]].

(15.3)　a.　Coordination
　　　　　　[He came at three o'clock] but [left right away].

　　　　b.　Adverbial subordination
　　　　　　[If you don't go swimming], [I won't go either].

As can be observed from the English examples above, the first and the second types of clause linking are usually embedded constructions, while the third type is non-embedded or juxtaposes two clauses. The difference between a complement clause and a relative clause lies in their syntactic roles. A complement clause, as shown in (15.1) and (15.2), functions as an NP, while a relative clause functions as a modifier situated within an NP.

This chapter will present complement, coordinate, and non-embedded subordinate constructions in Caijia. See Chapter 14 for relative clauses in Caijia.

15.2 Complementation

Complementation typically refers to "the syntactic situation that arises when a notional sentence or predication is an argument of a predicate" (Noonan 1985: 42). A complement clause has two basic properties (Dixon 2006: 4):
i. It has the internal constituent structure of a clause.
ii. It functions as a core argument of a higher clause.

This means that a complement clause may function as a subject or object in a sentence. Languages may use different strategies to code complementation. The complement clause may be differentiated from its counterpart independent clause via certain kinds of marking (q.v. Dixon 2016). In English, independent clauses like that shown in example (15.1), infinitive clauses (*John wants Mary to* **finish the work**), and gerund clauses (e.g. **Making mistakes** *is normal*) can all serve as a complements. Different constructions select different complementizers to introduce the complement, such as the optional 'that' and the obligatory 'to' (Noonan 1985).

In the literature, Sinitic languages are commonly characterized by zero marked complementation, i.e. neither by verbal marking nor a complementizer. However, only recently has it been reported that certain Sinitic languages, such as Pekinese, Taiwanese Southern Min, and Taiwanese Mandarin, have developed complementizers from not only *say* verbs (Cheng 1991, Chappell 2008) but also from *see* verbs (Cheng 1991 on Taiwanese and Xu and Matthews 2007 on Chaozhou).

Caijia adopts two types of complementation: (i) the typical Sinitic zero marked type and (ii) the marked type with a complementizer. The zero marked type concerns core argument (subject or object) complementation, while the marked type involves non-argument complementation, i.e. extent and degree complementation. The latter challenges the traditional definition of complementation, yet is widely attested in languages of mainland East and Southeast Asia (Enfield 2003). As this type has already been presented in Chapter 4 §4.2.4, this section will introduce the zero marked type.

The core argument complementation in Caijia has the features below:
i. A complement clause can either function as the subject or as the object of a predicate:
    Subject complement: $[_{S\text{-}COMP}[(NP) \text{ VP}] \text{ VP}]$
    Object complement: $[(NP) \text{ V }_{O\text{-}COMP}[(NP) \text{ VP}]]$
ii. It can stand alone as an independent clause.
iii. No complementizer is needed to introduce a complement clause.

Example (15.4) illustrates three sentences, each of which contains a complement clause as the subject. None of these subject complements are introduced by a complementizer. By comparing (15.4a-i) and (15.4b), one can readily observe that the complement clause *tsɔ³³ mɔ²¹sʅ⁵⁵ tɕie⁵⁵* 'do like that' also functions as the independent imperative clause 'Do (it) like that'. It should be mentioned that the *say* verb *xa³³* in Caijia has not developed into a complementizer as it has in certain Sinitic languages, but it does develop into a clause-final reportative marker, as shown in (15.4a-iii) and discussed in Chapter 11 on modality in §11.9.

Subject complement [$_{\text{S-COMP}}$[(NP) VP] VP

(15.4) a. i) [tsɔ³³   mɔ²¹sʅ⁵⁵   tɕie⁵⁵]   niɔ²¹   pɣ³³   tɣ³³.
            resemble   that.way   do   want   NEG   obtain
            ―――――――――――――――――――――――――――――
                       SUBJECT

      ii) [niɔ²¹   tɛ²¹tɕʰi²⁴   lɛ²¹   kʰɯ⁵⁵-ɣɯ²¹],   ɔ,
           need   together   ADV   rise-come   INTJ
           ―――――――――――――――――――――――――――――
                            SUBJECT
          lɛ³³tsʰɛ²¹   kʰua³³.
          only   be.good

      iii) [tsʅ⁵⁵tsʅ⁵⁵   ji²¹sui⁵⁵   kʰɯ⁵⁵-ɣɯ²¹   nɛ⁵⁵]
           only   some   rise-come   PRT
           ―――――――――――――――――――――――――――――
                              SUBJECT
           pɣ³³   kʰua³³   xa³³   nɛ³³.
           NEG   be.good REP   PRT

      'Doing like that is not OK. It's only good when you have to rise up together (to fight). That only some of you rise up isn't good.'
      像这样做不行。要一起起来（反抗），哦，才好。只是一些起来（反抗）不好。
      (*The Cultural Revolution*, texts)

   b. (nɯ³³)   tsɔ³³   ɔ²¹sʅ⁵⁵.
      2SG   be.like   this.way
      'Do (it) like this.'
      (你)像这样做。

Given that Caijia is a language in which a series of VPs can be chained one after another without any linker, one may be curious about the difference between a subject complement construction and a serial verb construction. In fact, though the subject complement can be replaced by the question word *sʅ²¹mɔ⁵⁵* 'what' to form a What-question, this diagnostic test cannot operate on a serial verb construction. All three of the sentences in (15.4) can be transformed into What-questions with their underlined subject complements replaced by *sʅ²¹mɔ⁵⁵* 'what', as illustrated in (15.5) below.

(15.5) i) sɿ²¹mɔ⁵⁵ niɔ²¹ pɤ³³ tɤ³³?
　　　　 what　　 want　 NEG obtain

ii) sɿ²¹mɔ⁵⁵ lɛ³³tsʰɛ²¹ kʰua²¹?
　　 what　　 only　　　 be.good

iii) sɿ²¹mɔ⁵⁵ pɤ³³ kʰua²¹?
　　　 what　 NEG be.good

'What is not OK? What on earth is good? What's not good?'
什么不行？什么才好？什么不好？

By way of contrast, in the following sentence with several VPs chained together, the underlined part cannot be replaced by the 'what' word sɿ²¹mɔ⁵⁵. Instead, it is the NP je³³ ɔ²¹ so⁵⁵po³³ ni³³ 'his wife' that is the common subject for the three chained VPs.

(15.6) a. je³³　 ɔ²¹　 so⁵⁵po³³　 ni³³　 tɯ³³　 lɔ²⁴koŋ⁵⁵　 la²¹
　　　　 3SG　 this　 wife　　　 CLF　 then　 every.day　 all
　　　 <u>ᵥₚ₁[tɕie⁵⁵　 zɤ²¹　 mi⁵⁵]　 ᵥₚ₂[soŋ³³-ɣɯ²¹]　 ᵥₚ₃[sɿ⁵⁵　 je²¹　 zɤ²¹]</u>.
　　　　 do　　　 meal　 a.little　 send-come　　　 give　 3SG　 eat

'Every day his wife made meals and sent (the meals) to him to eat.'
他这个老婆就天天都做点饭送来给他吃。
(*The man and the stone*, texts)

b. *sɿ²¹mɔ⁵⁵　 soŋ³³-ɣɯ²¹　 sɿ⁵⁵　 je²¹　 zɤ²¹?
　　 what　　 send-come　　 give　 3SG　 eat

'What sent (the meals) to him to eat?'
*什么送来给他吃？

Examples (15.7)-(15.9) below show cases of object complementation with several different types of verbs. Like the subject complement illustrated above, the object complement can also stand alone as an independent clause. As shown in (15.7a), the How-question niɔ²¹ tɕie⁵⁵me⁵⁵tɕie⁵⁵ ta⁵⁵ je²¹ na²¹ 'how to fight for him' is the object complement of the speech act verb xa³³ 'say'; while it is an independent How-question in (15.7b). Note that the object complement itself is composed of a complement construction, i.e. tɕie⁵⁵me⁵⁵tɕie⁵⁵ ta⁵⁵ je²¹ na²¹ 'how to fight for him' is the complement of the auxiliary niɔ³³ 'should, need'. Similar to the subject complement cases presented above, the underlined object complement in (15.7) can also be replaced by the 'what' word to form a content question, as shown in (15.7c).

Object complement [$_S$(NP) V $_{O-COMP}$[(NP) VP]]

(15.7) a. ei⁵⁵, **xa²¹** [niɔ²¹ [tɕie⁵⁵me⁵⁵tɕie⁵⁵ ta⁵⁵ je²¹ na²¹]]
INTJ say need   how   for 3SG beat
                 <u>   OBJECT   </u>
'(He) said how (the people) should fight for him.'
说要怎么帮他打。
(*The family of Deng*, texts)

b. niɔ²¹ tɕie⁵⁵me⁵⁵tɕie⁵⁵ ta⁵⁵ je²¹ na²¹?
need how   for 3SG beat
'How (shall we) fight for him?'
要怎么帮他打？

c. xa³³ sɿ²¹mɔ⁵⁵?
say   what
'What (did he) say?'
（他）说什么？

In (15.8), two coordinate existential clauses with a zero coordinator form a complex object complement of the perception compound verb *tsaŋ³³-kɪŋ²¹* 'see'.

(15.8) **tsaŋ³³-kɪŋ²¹** [mɔ²¹ sɿ⁵⁵pin³³ ɣã²¹   mɔ²¹tɯ²⁴ po⁵⁵ ɣã²¹
look-see   that riverbank there.be hat   CLF there.be
                <u>   OBJECT   </u>
li²¹li²⁴ po⁵⁵ tɯ²¹ ma²⁴ kʰɔ²¹-xɯ⁵⁵].
bag   CLF at   there put-DUR
'I saw that there was a hat and a bag placed on the riverbank.'
看见那个河边有一个帽子，（还有）一个包在那儿放着。
(*Drowning persons*, texts)

In (15.9), the emotion verb *tsʰ1³³* 'fear' takes the clausal object: *je³³ xa²¹ pɣ³³-tɣ³³ tɕiu²¹ ɔ⁵⁵ ʑi²¹* 'he's not arrived at home yet' to express probability, that is, an irrealis situation.

(15.9) ɔ²¹kɯ²⁴ **tsʰ1³³** [je³³ xa²¹ pɣ³³-tɣ³³ tɕiu²¹ ɔ⁵⁵ ʑi²¹].
this.time afraid   3SG   still NEG-PFV   arrive house inside
                     <u>   OBJECT   </u>
'(I'm) afraid he probably hasn't arrived yet.'
现在恐怕他还没有到家。

Apart from nominal subject and object complements, the Caijia copula can also take clausal complements. As shown below, *ka⁵⁵ kuɯŋ³³* 'force people into the military service' is the complement of the copula *sɿ³³*.

Copular complement [(NP) COP _{COMP}[(NP) VP]]

(15.10) mɔ²¹kɯ²⁴,   kuɛ²¹min²¹taŋ²¹   so⁵⁵   mo³³   mɔ²¹kɯ²⁴ sɿ²¹
         that.time   Chinese.Nationalist.Party   hand   inside that.time COP
         [ka⁵⁵   kuɯŋ³³].
         grasp   soldier
         <u>COPULAR COMPLEMENT</u>
         'At that time, the time under the government of the Chinese Nationalist Party, they were pressing people into the military service.'
         那时候，国民党手里的时候，是抓兵。
         (*Exempt from the military service*, texts)

To conclude this section, in Caijia, both subject and object complementation are observed. Neither is marked by a complementizer. We have shown that it does not appear to be easy to distinguish a complementation construction from a serial verb construction, since they may share the same structure on the surface in certain contexts. However, since a complement either serves as the subject or the object in a sentence, it can be replaced by the 'what' word to form an *in-situ* content question, whereas this test cannot be performed on a serial verb construction. The complement clause serves as a core argument in a sentence, while chained VPs share a common argument in a sentence, which can either be a subject or a pivot.

15.3 Coordination

Coordination "refers to syntactic constructions in which two or more units of the same type are combined into a larger unit and still have the same semantic relations with other surrounding elements" (Haspelmath 2004: 34). Three major semantic types of coordination have been identified (Haspelmath 2004: 5):[16]

i.   conjunctive coordination (/conjunction), e.g. 'and';
ii. disjunctive coordination (disjunction), e.g. 'or'; and
iii. adversative coordination, e.g. 'but'.

---

16 Haspelmath (2007: 1–2) also mentions causal coordination as the fourth type of coordination but does not give any detailed discussion. In this chapter, the Caijia cause clauses will be discussed in §15.4 on adverbial subordination.

15.3.1 Conjunction

In Caijia, two types of conjunctions are observed: argument conjunctions and clause conjunctions. The conjunction equivalent to English *and*-coordination only applies to arguments. As for clause conjunction, several pairs of overt bisyndetic and correlative coordinators are used to form different semantic coordinands. More details are given in the following discussion.

15.3.1.1 Argument conjunction [CONJ ta⁵⁵ CONJ]

Argument conjunction is usually known as nominal conjunction in the literature, i.e. two nominal phrases, conjuncts, are joined by a coordinator. In Caijia it is realized by the coordinator *ta^{55}* (< comitative 'with' < lexical verb 'follow') in the form of [CONJ ta^{55} CONJ]. We propose to use the term 'argument conjunction' for one type of conjunction in Caijia, because the coordinator *ta^{55}* can join both nominal and verbal phrases under the condition that the coordinate phrase of [VP ta^{55} VP], or coordinand, serve as an argument in a sentence. However, *ta^{55}* cannot be used to link two clauses as English 'and' does, for example, 'He opened the door and left'.

Example (15.11) shows that the nominal conjunction ɔ^{21}m̥^{55}soŋ^{21}ta^{55}kʷɔ^{55}pe^{55}ja^{21} 'the sun and the moon' serves as the subject of the copula *s1^{33}*, while the nominal conjunction *meŋ^{21}ni^{33}ŋoŋ^{21} ta^{55} mia^{21}ŋoŋ^{33}* 'Caijia and Lolo' serves as the object of the verb *xa^{33}* 'say, speak' in (15.12).

(15.11) ŋo²¹   hm̥⁵⁵   pa²¹   ta⁵⁵   ŋo²¹   xa³³: "[$_{NP}$[ɔ²¹   m̥⁵⁵soŋ²¹]
         1SG   POSS   grandfather with   1SG   say   this   sun
         ta⁵⁵ $_{NP}$[kʷɔ⁵⁵pe⁵⁵ja²¹]]   s1²¹   ta⁵⁵   lɛ²⁴."   xa²¹.
         and   moon   COP   two   CLF   QUOT
         'My grandfather said to me: "The sun and the moon were brother and sister." '
         我爷爷跟我说："这太阳和月亮是两兄妹。"说。
         (*The sun and the moon*, texts)

(15.12) ŋo³³   ti³³   xa³³   [$_{NP}$[meŋ²¹ni³³ŋoŋ²¹]   **ta⁵⁵** $_{NP}$[mia²¹ŋoŋ³³]].
         1SG   know   speak   Caijia   and   Lolo.speech
         'I can speak Caijia and Lolo.'
         我会说蔡家话和彝话。

The following is two examples of verbal conjunction. The coordinand in (15.13) serves as the subject of the sentence, while that in (15.14) is the topicalized object situated in the sentence initial position.

(15.13) [$_{VP}$[ta⁵⁵ ua²⁴ tsa²¹ tɕiu⁵⁵ti²¹] **ta⁵⁵** $_{VP}$[ta⁵⁵ ma²⁴
from here go.up Mount.Chive and from there
tsa²¹-kuɛ²¹]] sı³³ ji²¹jaŋ²⁴ se²¹.
go.up-go AFF same AFF
'Climbing up Mount Chive from here and climbing up from there are all same.'
从这儿上韭菜坪和从那儿上去是一样的。

(15.14) [$_{VP}$[pɔ⁵⁵ ɔ⁵⁵] **ta⁵⁵** $_{VP}$[na²¹ kı³³]], ŋo³³ la²¹ tɕʰi³³kʰa²¹ xıŋ⁵⁵.
hug waist and beat chicken 1SG all like very
'I like wrestling and playing the game with a ball of chicken feather.'
摔跤和打鸡毛球，我都很喜欢。

The coordinator *ta⁵⁵* is a multifunctional word in Caijia. Apart from the coordinator function, it can serve as an ablative (as in [15.13]), a comitative (as in [15.11]), a benefactive, as well as a lative preposition (see also Chapter 4 §4.5 and Lü Shanshan 2021). Its lexical source is the verb *ta⁵⁵* denoting 'follow'. It is argued in Lü Shanshan (2021) that the coordinator function of *ta⁵⁵* is derived from its comitative function, a pattern widely attested in the languages of the world (Stassen 2000, Haspelmath 2004, Kuteva et al. 2019: 108–112).

In most of the cases, one can tell the two functions of coordinator and preposition apart by features of their functional distribution. For example, a prepositional phrase formed by *ta⁵⁵* is preverbal, while the position of the coordinand, *ta⁵⁵*, depends on its syntactic role, i.e. as subject, object or oblique. The prepositional object in a *ta⁵⁵* prepositional phrase can be relativized by the resumptive strategy, while neither of the conjuncts in a *ta⁵⁵* coordinand can be relativized (see Chapter 9 §9.3). The coordinator *ta⁵⁵* can link two VPs, as in (15.13) and (15.14), while the preposition *ta⁵⁵* can only mark NPs or pronouns. A *ta⁵⁵* coordinand denotes a plural meaning and can be thus replaced by a plural pronoun or NP. Hence, none of the examples above in (15.11)-(15.14) could be ambiguous. Example (15.11) is a copular construction which does not take any oblique argument, therefore analyzing *ta⁵⁵* as a preposition in the phrase ɔ²¹ ıŋ⁵⁵soŋ²¹ ta⁵⁵ kʷɔ⁵⁵pe⁵⁵ja²¹ 'the sun and the moon' is impossible.

However, as both derived from the comitative, it is not a coincidence that ambiguity exists between the coordinator and the comitative uses, i.e. when *ta⁵⁵* is preverbal. A diagnostic test can be done to show the ambiguity (see aslo Lü 2019 for more details). For example (15.15a), one can both relativize the NP ɔ²¹ kua²¹ kʰui⁵⁵ kɔ²¹ 'this spotted dog', as shown in (15.15b), and replace the phrase mɔ²¹ pia²¹ kʰui⁵⁵ kɔ²¹ **ta⁵⁵** ɔ²¹ kua²¹ kʰui⁵⁵ kɔ²¹ 'that white dog and this spotted dog' with a plural NP as in (15.15c).

(15.15) a. mɔ²¹ pia²¹ kʰui⁵⁵ kɔ²¹ **ta⁵⁵** ɔ²¹ kua²¹ kʰui⁵⁵
that white dog CLF and/with this spotted dog
kɔ²¹ ji²¹jaŋ²⁴ la²¹.
CLF equally big
LIT: 'That white dog and this spotted dog are equally big/That white dog is equally big with this spotted dog.'
那只白狗和这只花狗一样大。

Relativization
b. mɔ²¹ pia²¹ kʰui⁵⁵ kɔ²¹ ta⁵⁵ **je²¹** ji²¹jaŋ²⁴ la²¹
that white dog CLF with 3SG equally big
mɔ²¹ kʰui⁵⁵ kɔ²¹
that dog CLF
Lit: 'the dog with which that white dog is equally big'
那白狗跟它一样大的那只狗

Plural NP
c. **mɔ²¹ kʰui⁵⁵ ta⁵⁵** kɔ²¹ ji²¹jaŋ²⁴ la²¹.
that dog two CLF equally big
'Those two dogs are equally big.'
那两只狗一样大。

15.3.1.2 Clause conjunction

In Caijia, clause conjunction is not overtly marked, except when there is a specific semantic purpose. This means two clauses will simply be juxtaposed side by side without any coordinator, as shown below. See also example (15.6).

(15.16) niɔ³³ ɣã³³ u²¹tsʰo²¹ ta⁵⁵ ni²¹ tɯ²¹ ji³³ kʰa³³.
need there.be person two CLF be.at one place
nɯ³³ xa²¹ ŋo²¹ tʰi⁵⁵, ŋo³³ xa²¹ nɯ²¹ tʰi⁵⁵.
2SG say 1SG listen 1SG say 2SG listen
'There should be two persons together. We talk to each other (LIT: You speak to me to listen, I speak to you to listen).'
要有两个人在一起。你说给我听，我说给你听。
(*Chatting between Li and Chen*, conversation)

Three semantic types of clause conjunction which are observed in Caijia:
i. Emphatic conjunction: ALSO, NOT-SAY, EVEN-conjunction
ii. Correlative simultaneous
iii. Correlative comparative

All of these are formed with **bisyndetic** or **correlative coordinators**. We will present these in turn in the following sub-sections.

15.3.1.2.1 Emphatic conjunction

Emphatic conjunction refers to coordination possessing the equivalent meaning of 'both...and...' in English; a phenomenon is attested in many languages in the world (Haspelmath 2004, 2007). In Caijia, the emphatic conjunction only applies to clause conjunction but not to nominal conjunction. Four types of emphatic conjunction will be presented in this section:

A. ALSO₁-conjunction 'both...and...; in addition...'
B. ALSO₂-conjunction 'both...and...'
C. NOT-SAY-conjunction 'not only...but also...'
D. EVEN-conjunction '...even...'

Detailed descriptions are given below.

A. ALSO₁-conjunction [NP jɯ²⁴ VP₁, jɯ²⁴ VP₂]

Formed by the loanword *jɯ²⁴* 'again, also, still', which is cognate with *yòu* 又 [jəu⁵¹] 'again, also, still' in Standard Mandarin, the correlative coordinator *jɯ²⁴...jɯ²⁴...* 'also...also' is used for two conjunct clauses with a common subject, i.e. [NP jɯ²⁴ VP₁, jɯ²⁴ VP₂], which can be interpreted as **'in addition to VP₁, NP also VP₂'**. One should be aware that the common subject cannot be repeated or reprised by an anaphoric pronoun before the second *jɯ²⁴* conjunct. In example (15.17), each *jɯ²⁴* marks one of the qualities that the child possesses.

(15.17) mɔ²¹ ŋa⁵⁵ ni³³ **jɯ²⁴** xa²¹ lɯ⁵⁵ kʰua²¹
that child CLF also grow VCOMP good
jɯ²⁴ tɯ²¹ ni³³ tɣ²¹.
also attract 3 like
'That child is good-looking as well as lovely.'
LIT: 'That child is also good-looking, also attracts people to like him.'
那个孩子既长得好也惹人喜欢。

In (15.18), the morpheme *jɯ²⁴* marks two different language skills the subject has mastered in two separate conjuncts.

(15.18) je³³ **jɯ²⁴** ti³³ xa³³ men²¹ni³³ŋoŋ³³
3SG also know speak Caijia.speech
jɯ²⁴ ti³³ xa³³ mia²¹ŋoŋ³³.
also know say Lolo.speech
'He can speak Caijia as well as Lolo.'
LIT: 'He can also speak Caijia, can also speak Lolo.'
他既会说蔡家话也会说彝话。

In most cases the *jɯ²⁴*-conjunction is binary, though is not always the case. We do observe a series of *jɯ²⁴*-conjuncts juxtaposed, as shown below.

(15.19) mɔ²¹ ŋa⁵⁵ ni³³ saŋ³³ **jɯ²⁴** kʰua²¹, **jɯ²⁴**
that child CLF heart also good also
ɣã²¹ fɛ⁵⁵ka³³, je³³ **jɯ²⁴** sɿ³³ kʷɔ³³
have promise 3SG also AFF learn
la²¹ɕyɔ²¹ pe⁵⁵-ɣɯ²¹ sɿ³³, sɿ²¹kʰɯ⁵⁵ **jɯ²⁴** saŋ³³.
university return-come AFF knowledge also deep
'That child is kind-hearted and full of promise; he came back after accomplishing his university studies, and he is very knowledgeable as well.'
LIT: 'That child is also kind-hearted, also has promise, he also came back from accomplishing his study at university, his knowledge is also deep.'
那个孩子心又好，又有出息，他又是读大学回来的，学问又深。

From the three examples above, it can be observed that *jɯ²⁴* is not a linker but occupies the position of the adverb. In a non-coordinate sentence, *jɯ²⁴* is often used in reference to preceding context denoting 'in addition, also, still'. As shown in (15.20), it is used in the second sentence, (15.20ii), to express there were three thieves in addition to the two moons.

(15.20) i) mɔ²¹kɯ²⁴ a, tɔ²¹pa⁵⁵tɔ²¹pʰe³³,
that.time PRT once.upon.a.time
kʰɪŋ³³ tɣ³³ ɣã²¹ kɔ⁵⁵pe⁵⁵ja²¹ ta⁵⁵ po⁵⁵.
sky upside there.be moon two CLF
ii) mɔ²¹kɯ²⁴ **jɯ²⁴** ɣã³³ tɔ²⁴ sa³³ ni³³.
that.time also there.be thief three CLF
'At that time, once upon a time, there were two moons in the sky. There were also three thieves.'
那时候啊，很久以前，天上有两个月亮。那时候还有三个小偷。
(*Two moons*, texts)

The non-coordinator jw^{24} and the coordinator jw^{24} are semantically different, especially the first jw^{24} in the jw^{24}-conjunction, which cannot be interpreted as 'in addition'. The non-coordinator jw^{24} implies a preceding context, while the coordinator function does not possess such an implication.

B. ALSO$_2$-conjunction [NP$_1$ la^{33} VP$_1$, NP$_2$ la^{33} VP$_2$]
In contrast, the pair la^{33}... la^{33}... can be adopted for two conjunct clauses with the same subject, as shown in (15.21), and with different subjects, as in (15.22). It denotes that **two events share similarities.** In (15.21), this correlative is used to refer to the subject 'the girl and the boy' doing things together while in (15.22) it refers to both subjects being alone.

(15.21) mɔ³³   nioŋ²⁴   ni²¹   ta⁵⁵   mɔ²¹   tsɿ⁵⁵ŋa⁵⁵   ni³³   nɛ³³,   je⁵⁵
       that   girl   CLF   and   that   boy   CLF   PRT   3PL
       koŋ⁵⁵koŋ⁵⁵   tɕie⁵⁵   ja²¹pa²¹   **la²¹**   tɯ²¹   ji²¹   kʰa³³,
       every.day   do   crops   also   be.at   one   place
       ka²¹kʰɯ³³ka²¹ma²¹   **la²¹**   sɿ²¹   ji²¹hɔ⁵⁵.
       go.to.the.market   also   COP   together
       'That girl and that boy, every day they do farming together and go to the market together.'
       那个姑娘和和那个小伙子啊，他们天天干活也在一起，上街也在一起。
       (*The young couple*, texts)

(15.22) i) je³³   **la³³**   sɿ³³   je³³   tɔ²¹   ni²⁴   tɯ²¹   ɔ⁵⁵   ʑi²¹,
           3SG   also   COP   3SG   alone   CLF   be.at   house   inside
      ii) ŋo³³   **la³³**   sɿ³³   ŋo³³   tɔ²¹   ni²⁴.
          1SG   also   COP   1SG   alone   CLF
      'He was at home by himself and so was I.'
      LIT: 'He was also at home by himself, I was also at home by myself.'
      他也是一个人在家，我也是一个人。
      (*My friend and I*, texts)

Similar to jw^{24}, the coordinator la^{33} is not a linker and is semantically different from the non-coordinator la^{33}, an adverb which denotes 'all', 'even', or 'also'. Example (15.23) is a case in which la^{33} denotes 'also', since the speaker of this sentence wanted to do the same thing as the person je^{33} 'he' did. By way of contrast, example (15.22) uses the correlative la^{33}... la^{33}... to denote the similarity of the subjects 'I' and 'he', who were in their own respective homes alone. See also (15.24i) and (15.24iv) for the meaning 'all'.

(15.23) je³³ ɣa²¹ loŋ³³ mo³³ na²¹koŋ⁵⁵ kuɛ²¹ o.
3SG walk town inside work go CRS
ŋo³³ la²¹ ɕiaŋ⁵⁵ kuɛ²¹ na²¹koŋ⁵⁵ xɪŋ⁵⁵.
3SG also want go work very
'He went to the town to work. I also want to work very much.'
他去城里打工了。我也想去打工得很。

The coordinator *la³³* is not only restricted to binary coordination. The following example shows a case with several *la³³*-conjuncts chained together, i.e. the three conjuncts in (15.24ii)-(15.24iv). It should be mentioned that *la³³* in (15.24i), which gives the background information to a narrative, is an intensifier denoting 'all', as is the first *la²¹* in (15.24iv).

(15.24) i) mɔ²¹kɯ⁵⁵ a, tɯ²¹ mɔ²¹ kɣ²¹
that.time PRT be.at that old
kua³³ ni²¹ so⁵⁵ mo³³ tʰɔ²⁴
government.official CLF hand inside moment
nɛ⁵⁵, neŋ²¹neŋ³³ la²¹ niɔ³³ tsa²¹ ko²¹.
PRT EVERY.YEAR all must go.up tax
ii) fa³³tsɯ²¹ sฺɿ²¹ **la³³** niɔ³³ a³³, tie³³ a³³,
be.wealthy NMLZ also must take much take
iii) ɣã²¹ mi⁵⁵ sฺɿ²¹ **la³³** niɔ³³ a³³,
have little NMLZ also must take
iv) ji²¹ tsoŋ⁵⁵ la²¹ pɣ³³ ɣã²¹ mɔ²⁴sui⁵⁵
one type all NEG have those
la³³ niɔ³³ a³³.
also must take
'At that time, when the old government was in power, (people) had to pay taxes every year. The rich had to pay, pay more; those who had little had to pay; and those who had nothing had to also pay (taxes).'
以前啊，在旧官手里的时候，年年都要上税。有钱的也要上，多上，一般（家庭）的也要上，什么都没有的也要上。
(*Paying taxes*, texts)

Next, we discuss the coordination formed by NOT SAY denoting 'not only. . . but also. . .'.

C. NOT-SAY-conjunction

The NOT-SAY conjunction which codes the meaning 'not only. . .but also. . .' in Caijia can be formed in two ways with NOT-SAY found in two different positions in the first conjunct:

i. NOT-SAY₁: [piɔ²⁴xa²¹(lɛ⁵⁵) NP1 VP1, NP2 (x)a²¹ VP2], or
[piɔ²⁴xa²¹(lɛ⁵⁵) NP1 VP1, NP2 la³³ VP2];
ii. NOT-SAY₂: [NP1 VP1 pɣ³³xa³³, NP2 (x)a³³ VP2], or
[NP1 VP1 pɣ³³xa³³, NP2 la³³ VP2],

These can be alternatively recoded with the same meaning as:

[NP₁ VP₁, NP₂ (x)a³³ VP₂], or
[NP₁ VP₁, NP₂ la³³ VP₂]

In the coordinate construction of NOT-SAY₁, the first conjunct is marked by the clause-initial $piɔ^{24}xa^{21}(lɛ^{55})$, derived from 'don't say', while the second conjunct can either be marked by the adverb $(x)a^{21}$ 'still' or la^{21} 'all, also', as determined by context. In the coordinate construction of NOT-SAY₂, the first conjunct is marked by the clause-final $pɣ^{33}xa^{33}$ 'not say', and the second conjunct can be either marked by the adverb $(x)a^{21}$ 'still' or la^{33} 'all'. Compared with both the la^{33}- and the $jɯ^{24}$-conjunction, the NOT-SAY conjunction expresses a stronger rhetorical effect. Its meaning is rather equivalent to the English correlative coordinator 'not only... but also'. It is often presupposed by the speaker that the second conjunct in a NOT-SAY conjunction intensifies the event coded in the first conjunct.

In the coordinate construction NOT-SAY₁, the coordinator $piɔ^{24}xa^{21}lɛ^{55}$ still occupies the same position as it does when serving as the negated verb of an imperative clause. However, unlike an imperative clause, in which the subject can be optionally used (as in [15.4b]), coordinator $piɔ^{24}xa^{21}(lɛ^{55})$ cannot take a subject. Examples (15.25) and (15.26) illustrate conjunctions with the same subject and different subjects, respectively. The ellipsis of $ŋuɔ^{21}$ 'be evil', which is preferred, can be observed in (15.25). This makes it further possible to reanalyze $piɔ^{24}xa^{21}$ as 'let alone'. In addition, $piɔ^{24}xa^{21}(lɛ^{55})$ in both examples can be omitted.

NOT-SAY₁:
(15.25) **piɔ²⁴xa²¹lɛ⁵⁵** je³³ ti³³ xa³³ men²¹ni³³noŋ³³,
NEG.IMP.say 3SG know speak Caijia.speech
je³³ **a²¹** ti³³ xa³³ mia²¹noŋ³³.
3SG also know speak Lolo.speech
'He can speak Caijia as well as Lolo.'
LIT: Don't mention he can speak Caijia, he can also speak Lolo.
他既会说蔡家话也会说彝话。

(15.26) "a⁵⁵jou³³! ɔ²¹ sı⁵⁵lɛ²¹mo³³ ɣɯ²¹ pɣ³³ tɣ³³. **piɔ²⁴xa²¹**
INTJ this place come NEG can NEG.IMP.say
u³³tsʰo³³ (ŋuɔ²¹), tsʰɔ⁵⁵tsʰɔ⁵⁵ poŋ²¹ **la³³** sı³³ ŋuɔ²¹ xɪŋ⁵⁵."
person be.evil grass CLF all COP be.evil very
' "Oh my! This place is not where someone can pay an easy visit. Even the grass is evil, let alone the people." '
"哎呦！这个地方来不得。别说人（恶），一棵小草都恶得很。"
(*Joke: The evil place*, texts)

The following two examples show the conjunction with NOT-SAY₂, where it occurs in clause-final position. Similarly, *pɣ³³xa³³* can also be omitted in this clause-final position.

NOT-SAY₂:
(15.27) je³³ a³³ ni³³ tsʰɛ³³ tɔ²¹-kuɛ²¹ ha⁵⁵ la²¹ **pɣ³³xa³³**,
3SG OM 3 car steal-go COMPL even NEG.say
xa²¹ a³³ tsʰɛ³³ tɣ³³ sı²¹ ŋa⁵⁵ ɕi²¹-kuɛ²¹.
also OM car upside MOD child kill-go
'He not only stole that person's car but also killed the baby in the car.'
他偷了人家车不说，还杀了车上的孩子。

(15.28) mɔ²¹ sı⁵⁵pie²¹hɛ⁵⁵ la²¹ tso⁵⁵ a²¹ pɣ³³-tɣ³³
that Wang.family big elder.brother still NEG-PFV
pia³³-tɣ³³ so³³po²⁴ ni³³ **pɣ³³xa³³**, je³³ ɔ²¹
marry-obtain wife CLF NEG.say 3SG this
ʑi³³ ni³³ nɛ³³, ni³³tsı³³ **la³³** pɣ³³ kʰua²¹.
mother CLF PRT eye also NEG be.good
tsɔ⁵⁵ni²¹ xɪŋ⁵⁵.
be.miserable very
'Not only didn't the elder brother of the Wang family get married, his mother also had bad eyes. It's such a pity.'
那王大哥还没娶老婆不说，他妈妈眼睛也不好。太可怜了。

D. EVEN-conjunction [NP₁ VP₁, xuɔ³³ FOC la³³ VP₂]

The EVEN-conjunction in Caijia expresses a more emphatic meaning than the other three types of conjunctions presented above (A-C). Associating with the intensifier *la³³*, the coordinator *xuɔ³³* 'even', a loanword probably cognate with *hé* 和 [hə²⁴] 'with, and' in Standard Mandarin, is typically used to mark the last conjunct that is put into focus. *xuɔ³³* functions as a focus marker forming a kind of cleft construction. It must be followed by the word or phrase (NP, VP, or PrepP) that is put into focus, roughly schematized as [NP₁ VP₁, xuɔ³³ FOC la³³ VP₂]. Furthermore, the complexity of the EVEN-conjunction also resides in the fact that *xuɔ³³* does not form a semantically independent cleft construction and the *xuɔ³³* conjunct implies the presence of an obligatory context.

In (15.29), the focus phrase is the prepositional phrase *(ta⁵⁵) nɯ³³* 'for you', noting that the preposition *ta⁵⁵* can be dropped.

(15.29) ŋo²¹ ã⁵⁵sɿ²¹   je³³ pɤ³³ a³³ ɔ²¹ sɿ⁵⁵ xa²¹ sɿ⁵⁵ pʰa²¹sɿ²¹
         1SG   answer   3SG   NEG   OM this thing say   to   other
         lɔ²⁴ni⁵⁵ tʰi⁵⁵, **xuɔ²¹** (ta⁵⁵) nɯ³³ la³³ xa³³ pɤ³³ tɤ³³.
         who   listen even   with   2SG   also say   NEG   can
         'I promised her that I wouldn't tell this thing to anybody, and I can't even tell you either.'
         我答应她不把这件事讲给任何人听，连（跟）你也不能说。

One can observe in the following example that the marked focus *ŋoŋ³³* 'speech' is the object of the verb *xa³³* 'say'. However, it is situated before the bracketed VP instead of being in its canonical post-verbal position. This is the only possible word order when the object *ŋoŋ³³* is put into focus by *xuɔ³³*.

(15.30) mɔ²¹ ɕie²¹ ŋa⁵⁵   ni³³ tɪŋ²¹ xɪŋ⁵⁵, **xuɔ³³** ŋoŋ³³ la³³
         that   little child CLF   shy   very   even   speech also
         [pɤ²¹ kã⁵⁵   ta⁵⁵   ŋo³³ xa²¹] ji²¹   tɕie⁵⁵.
         NEG   dare   with   1SG   say   one   CLF
         'That little child is very shy and she doesn't even dare to say a word to me.'
         那个小孩儿害羞得很，连话都不敢跟我说一句。

Example (15.31) shows a sentence composed of three conjuncts marked by *la³³*. The marker *xuɔ³³* is used in the last clause, expressing the seriousness of the collapse by underlining that one cannot even walk through the affected area. It is the clause *u²¹tsʰo²¹ ɣa²¹ hɔ⁵⁵* 'people walk' that is put into focus.

(15.31) ma³³kɤ³³   ɔ²¹sui⁵⁵ la³³ tʰoŋ²¹   ha⁵¹   o.
         Magu_PLACENAME   these   all   collapse   COMPL CRS
         hɔ⁵⁵   la²¹ tɤ³³   je²¹   tɤ⁵⁵-xɯ⁵⁵ o,
         road   also PASS   3SG   block-up   CRS
         tsʰɛ³³ la³³ kʰɯ³³-kua²¹ po³³ tɔ³³, **xuɔ³³**
         car   also drive-pass   NEG   can   even

| u²¹tsʰo²¹ | ɣa²¹ | hɔ⁵⁵ | **la³³** | niɔ³³ | pa²¹ | hɔ⁵⁵ | o. |
| person | walk | road | also | must | detour | road | CRS |

'These places, such as Magu, have all collapsed. The roads are blocked (by the fallen rocks); one can't pass through by driving a car; even those who are walking must make a detour.'
妈姑那些（地方）都塌了。路也被堵住了，车也开不过去，连走路的人也要绕路。

In fact, $xuɔ^{33}$ can be absent in all of the three examples, (15.29)-(15.31). On the one hand, the emphatic meaning is lost when $xuɔ^{33}$ is not present. On the other hand, each conjunct can be treated as an independent clause if $xuɔ^{33}$ is not used in (15.29) and (15.30).

To conclude, this section has introduced four types of emphatic conjunctions in Caijia. Two pairs of correlative coordinators are used to realize the meaning 'both…and…': $juɯ^{24}…juɯ^{24}…$ and $la^{33}…la^{33}…$, denoting 'both X and Y' or 'X as well as Y'. Both $juɯ^{24}$ and la^{33} denote the meaning 'also'. These two pairs of correlative coordinators are used in different syntactic and semantic contexts, even though they are derived from the same semantic field. The $juɯ^{24}$-conjunction only applies to two conjuncts with the same subject, while there is no such restriction for the la^{33}-conjunction. The $juɯ^{24}$-conjunction denotes that the second conjunct is an addition to the first conjunct, whereas the la^{33}-conjunction denotes that two conjuncts share certain similarities. As pointed out by Haspelmath (2007: 16), it is common for correlative coordinators in emphatic coordination, to have the same form and to be identical to the single coordinator. Both the correlatives $juɯ^{24}…juɯ^{24}…$ and $la^{33}…la^{33}…$ are formed by two identical morphemes. However, neither $juɯ^{24}$ nor la^{33} can function like the coordinator ta^{55} 'and'. When they are used alone, $juɯ^{24}$ denotes 'again' and la^{33} denotes 'also'.

Two periphrastic strategies are observed to express the meaning 'not only…but also…': i.e. $piɔ^{24}xa^{21}(lɛ^{55})$ X $(x)a^{21}/la^{21}$ Y, and X $pγ^{33}xa^{33}$ Y $(x)a^{21}$. Both of them are related to 'not say'.

Forming the EVEN-conjunction along with the adverb la^{33} 'also, even', the coordinator $xuɔ^{33}$ 'even' is used with the last conjunct that is put into focus.

In the next two sections, simultaneous and comparative conjunctions will be introduced.

15.3.1.2.2 Correlative simultaneous construction [NP ʑi²¹hɔ⁵⁵ VP₁ ʑi²¹hɔ⁵⁵ VP₂]

Using the correlative coordinator $ʑi^{21}hɔ^{55}…ʑi^{21}hɔ^{55}…$ 'together…together', the simultaneous correlative construction is used to describe that two on-going actions or events are carried out by the same agent simultaneously. See the examples below.

(15.32) je^{33} **ji^{21}hɔ^{55}** ti^{55} pʰɪŋ^{21}pʰɪŋ^{24} **ji^{21}hɔ^{55}**
3SG together sew cloak together
jɔ^{21} mɔ^{21} ta^{55}ta^{55} kʷɔ^{21}.
shake that cradle CLF
'She was sewing the cloak while rocking the cradle.'
她一边缝斗篷一边摇摇篮。
(*The careless woman*, texts)

(15.33) mɔ^{21} ɕie^{21} mɔ^{24} ni^{33} nɛ^{33} **ji^{21}hɔ^{55}** ja^{21} nɛ^{55}
that little that CLF PRT together wash PRT
ji^{21}hɔ^{55} ma^{21} sɿ^{55}kʰa^{55} ɣɯ^{21} nian^{33} tɯ^{21} tɣ^{33}.
together fetch dirt PURP stick to upside
'That little one was fetching dirt to put it on (her feet) while washing.'
那个小的呢，一边洗呢，一边抓灰抹到（自己脚）上。
(*The nettle witch*, texts)

Composed of two morphemes, *ʑi^{33}* 'one' and *hɔ^{55}* 'road', the non-coordinator *ʑi^{21}hɔ^{55}* denotes 'together' and associates with a plural subject, for example, in a simple declarative clause. The example in (15.34) seemingly shares the same structure with the simultaneous *ʑi^{21}hɔ^{55}*-conjunction. However, it is simply a coordinate construction with zero coordinator, since one's departure and arrival cannot be realized at the same time. See also (15.21).

(15.34) "[...] nɯ^{24} sa^{21} lɛ^{33} niɔ^{33} **ji^{21}hɔ^{55}** kuɛ^{21} **ji^{21}hɔ^{55}** ɣɯ^{21}."
2PL three CLF must together go together come
'The three of you must depart and arrive on the same day'
你们三个要一起去一起回。
(*Three daughters-in-law*, texts)

One should be aware that *ʑi^{21}hɔ^{55}* does not denote 'one road', even if it is so composed. The meaning 'one road' is expressed in the following way.

(15.35) hɔ^{55} ji^{21} ta^{55}
road one CLF
'one road'
一条路

The lexical meaning of *ʑi^{21}hɔ^{55}* is 'a row of', while *hɔ^{55}* is used as a measure word or a classifier, as in the following examples.

(15.36) a. mɔ²¹ lɛ²⁴ **hɔ⁵⁵** mo³³ ɣã²¹ tsʰo²¹to²¹ **ji²¹** **hɔ⁵⁵**.
that field road inside there.be radish one road
'There's a row of radish in that patch of field.'
那块田里有一片萝卜。
(*Pulling up radishes*, texts)

b. ɣoŋ²¹ã²¹sɿ⁵⁵ **ji²¹** **hɔ⁵⁵**
rainbow one CLF
'a rainbow'
一道彩虹

However, there is not enough evidence to reconstruct how *ʑi²¹hɔ⁵⁵* has developed into an adverb meaning 'together' from a synchronic perspective. What is quite evident is that the meaning 'together' is very much related to the simultaneous correlative coordinator *ʑi²¹hɔ⁵⁵*...*ʑi²¹hɔ⁵⁵*....

15.3.1.2.3 Correlative comparative construction [NP₁ dzɔ³³ VP₁, NP₂ dzɔ³³ VP₂]

The comparative conjunction in Caijia is formed by the correlative coordinator *dzɔ³³*...*dzɔ³³*... 'the more...the more', i.e. [NP₁ dzɔ³³ VP₁, NP₂ dzɔ³³ VP₂], of which the lexical source is probably the verb *dzɔ³³* 'be like, resemble' (see [15.4] and [15.9]). In a construction with the comparative conjunction, the two conjuncts can share the same subject, as shown in (15.37), or each can have a different subject, as in (15.38).

(15.37) nɯ³³ a, nɯ³³ **tsɔ³³** la²¹to⁵⁵
2SG PRT 2SG the.more old
tsɔ³³ pɣ³³ xa²¹ me²¹tsɿ⁵⁵ o.
the.more NEG say reason CRS
'You! The older you become, the less reasonable you become.'
你越老越不讲道理了。
(*Three neighbors*, texts)

(15.38) ni²⁴ **tsɔ³³** tsaŋ³³-pɣ²¹-tsa²¹ je³³, je³³ tɯ³³ **tsɔ²¹**
3 the.more look-NEG-go.up 3SG 3SG then the.more
lɔ²¹sɿ⁵⁵ lɛ²¹ kuɛ²¹ peŋ³³.
hard ADV go strive
'The more others look down upon him, the more he works hard.'
人家越看不上他，他就越努力奋斗。

The correlative coordinator $dz\mathfrak{o}^{33}\ldots dz\mathfrak{o}^{33}\ldots$ further develops into a fossilized form with the verb $yɯ^{21}$ 'come' occupying the VP$_1$ position, i.e. $dz\mathfrak{o}^{33}yɯ^{21}dz\mathfrak{o}^{33}$. It serves as an adverb and modifies VPs of extent, denoting that the extent of the modified VP is continually increasing. It is equivalent to 'more and more' in English.

(15.39)   je^{33} ts$\mathfrak{o}^{33}$yɯ^{21}ts$\mathfrak{o}^{33}$ mia^{21} o.
         3SG   more.and.more   beautiful   CRS
         'She's more and more beautiful.'
         她越来越好看了。

15.3.1.3 Concluding remarks

This section has introduced argument conjunction and clause conjunction in Caijia.

Argument conjunction is realized by the coordinator ta^{55}, which is derived from a common source for coordinators, i.e. the comitative, but for which the lexical source 'follow' is only commonly attested with the Sinitic languages (Jin and Wu 2018, Kuteva et al. 2019: 181–182).

Clause conjunction is only overtly marked for particular semantic purposes. Three types of clause conjunction have been observed. They are the emphatic conjunction (including the four subtypes, (A) ALSO$_1$ (jɯ^{24})-conjunction, (B) ALSO$_2$ (la^{33})-conjunction, (C) NOT-SAY-conjunction (pi$\mathfrak{o}^{24}$xa^{21} 'don't say' and py^{33}xa^{21} 'not say'), and (D) EVEN (xu$\mathfrak{o}^{21}$)-conjunction), the correlative simultaneous construction, and the correlative comparative construction. All three are marked by correlative coordinators.

See the table below for a synthesis of the Caijia conjunctions.

Table 15.1: Conjunctions in Caijia.

	Type and Schema	Meaning	Source
I. Argument			
	NP$_1$/VP$_1$ ta^{55} NP$_2$/VP$_2$	'and'	ta^{55} < COM < 'follow'
II. Clause			
i	**Emphatic**		
	A. jɯ^{24}-conjunction:		
	NP jɯ^{24} VP$_1$, jɯ^{24} VP$_2$	'as well as'	jɯ^{24} < Mandarin 'also'
	B. la^{33}-conjunction:		
	NP$_1$ la^{33} VP$_1$, NP$_2$ la^{33} VP$_2$	'as well as'	la^{33} < 'also'

Table 15.1 (continued)

	TYPE AND SCHEMA	MEANING	SOURCE
	C. NOT-SAY-CONJUNCTION: (piɔ²⁴xa²¹(lɛ⁵⁵)) NP₁ VP₁, NP₂ (x)a²¹/la³³ VP₂	'not only…but also'	piɔ²⁴xa²¹lɛ⁵⁵ < 'don't say'
	NP₁ VP₁ (pɣ³³xa³³), NP₂ (x)a²¹/la³³ VP₂	'not only…but also'	pɣ³³xa³³ < 'not say'
	D. EVEN-CONJUNCTION [NP₁ VP₁, xuɔ⁵⁵ FOC la³³ VP₂]	'…even…'	xuɔ⁵⁵ < Mandarin 'with'
ii	CORRELATIVE SIMULTANEOUS NP ʑi²¹hɔ⁵⁵ VP₁ ʑi²¹hɔ⁵⁵ VP₂	'…while…'	ʑi²¹hɔ⁵⁵ < 'a row of'
iii	CORRELATIVE COMPARATIVE NP₁ dzɔ³³ VP₁, NP₂ dzɔ³³ VP₂	'the more…the more'	dzɔ³³ < 'be like, resemble'

15.3.2 Disjunction

The notion of disjunction refers to two counterparts, including words, phrases, or clauses, that are linked by a grammatical morpheme with the function of indicating a relation between alternatives, i.e. *or*-coordination in English and its semantic equivalents in other languages. Both conjunction and disjunction can be defined in terms of true value. Suppose *p* and *q* are two propositions that can form a coordination. A coordination type of conjunction is true, composed of *p* and *q*, if only either *p* is true or *q* is true (or both are true) (Lyons 1995: 162). Three types of disjunctions can be observed in Caijia:
i. Standard disjunction, i.e. 'or' in declaratives.
ii. Interrogative disjunction, i.e. 'or' in alternative questions.
iii. Emphatic disjunction, equivalent to English 'either…or'.

Note that Caijia does not contrast emphatic disjunction and emphatic negative disjunctions as English does, i.e. 'either…or' vs. 'neither…nor'. The negative disjunction is formed in the same way as the emphatic conjunction.
More details concerning the three types of disjunctions are given below.

15.3.2.1 Standard disjunction [[NP₁/VP₁] xuɔ²¹tsɛ⁵⁵ [NP₂/VP₂]]
Caijia is a language that contrasts standard disjunction and interrogative disjunction. This means that declaratives and interrogatives require different forms of 'or' to realize a disjunctive meaning. The loanword *xuɔ²¹tsɛ⁵⁵*, cognate with *huòzhě* 或者 [xuɔ⁵¹tʂə²¹⁴] 'or' in Standard Mandarin, is used to express alternatives, 'A or B',

in Caijia declarative constructions. The disjunctive *xuɔ²¹tsɛ⁵⁵* can link both NPs and VPs. In (15.40i), two VPs are linked by *xuɔ²¹tsɛ⁵⁵*, serving as the complement of the auxiliary *niɔ³³* 'must'. This disjunctive phrase provides two alternative ways to eat a meal during a funeral ceremony. In the following utterance, two NPs, two time words to be exact, are linked by *xuɔ²¹tsɛ⁵⁵*. This phrase serves as the subject of (15.40ii), denoting that the duration of the wake can be either seven days or three days.

(15.40) i) niɔ³³ pɔ²¹-xɯ⁵⁵ zɣ²¹ **xuɔ²¹tsɛ⁵⁵**
must squat-DUR eat or
kɣ²¹-xɯ⁵⁵ zɣ²¹ [. . .]
sit-DUR eat

ii) nɛ⁵⁵ ɔ²¹kʷo²¹ tɣ⁵⁵ nɛ⁵⁵, tɕʰi³³ koŋ³³
INTJ INTJ be.at.the.wake PRT seven day
xuɔ²¹tsɛ⁵⁵ sa³³ koŋ³³ la²¹ niɔ²¹tɣ³³.
or three day all be.all.right

'(One) must eat in the posture of squatting or sitting. [. . .] Eh, (you need) seven days to observe the wake, or (a wake of) three days is also all right.'
要蹲着吃或者坐着吃，[. . .]，嗯这个，守（丧）呢，（要）七天或者三天都可以。
(*Funeral customs*, texts)

In (15.41), *xuɔ²¹tsɛ⁵⁵* links two interrogative clauses from direct speech in brackets. The speaker provides two alternative options of what can be said while performing the chopstick-standing-on-end ceremony, a practice performed to expel evil spirits.

(15.41) tã³³ tɣ²¹ nɛ⁵⁵, tɯ⁵⁵ xaŋ³³ a mẽ,
stand chopstick PRT then yell PRT PRT
xaŋ³³ nɛ³³, əu a, ["nɯ³³ sɿ³³ la²¹to⁵⁵
yell PRT INTJ INTJ 2SG COP old
u²¹tsʰo²¹ lɔ²⁴ni⁵⁵?"] **xuɔ²¹tsɛ⁵⁵** ["nɯ³³ sɿ³³ tɕʰian³³
person who or 2SG AFF gun
na²¹-sɿ⁵⁵ se²¹?] [. . .]"
beat-die AFF.PRT

'(While) standing the chopsticks on end, (one must) say (something to the ghost). (One must) say (something to the ghost like) "which dead person are you?" or "did you die from gunshot [. . .]".'
立筷子呢，就（跟鬼魂）喊嘛，（跟鬼魂）喊呢，哦，"你是哪一位老人？"或者"你是枪打死的吗？"。
(*Standing chopsticks on end*, texts)

15.3.2.2 Interrogative disjunction [[NP₁/VP₁] lɔ²¹/(x)a²¹sʅ³³ [NP₂/VP₂]]

The interrogative disjunction in Caijia can be formed with either the coordinator *lɔ²¹* or the coordinator *(x)a²¹sʅ³³*, the latter being cognate with Standard Mandarin *háishì* 还是 [xai¹⁵ʂʅ⁵¹] 'or'. The disjunctive *lɔ²¹* is exclusively used for the interrogative disjunction, in the form of either embedded dependent or independent clauses, while *(x)a²¹sʅ³³* can also be used with the meaning of 'still'. See also Chapter 13 for more on *lɔ²¹*. In contrast to these two coordinators, *xuɔ²¹tsɛ⁵⁵* cannot be used in an interrogative context to express disjunction.

Examples (15.42) and (15.43) illustrate that *lɔ²¹/(x)a²¹sʅ³³* can link two pronouns as well as two embedded clauses.

(15.42) tsaŋ²¹koŋ⁵⁵ lɔ²⁴ni⁵⁵ kuɛ³³ kʰɯ²¹xui²⁴,
the.day.after.tomorrow who go attend.meeting
nɯ³³ **lɔ²¹/(x)a²¹sʅ³³** je³³?
2SG or 3SG
'Who will attend the meeting the day after tomorrow, you or him?'
后天谁去开会，你还是他？

(15.43) nɯ³³ xa²¹lɛ⁵⁵ kʰɯ³³loŋ²¹ la²¹
2SG say Hezhang_PLACENAME be.big
lɔ³³/(x)a²¹sʅ³³ suaŋ³³uɛ³³ la²¹?
or Weining_PLACENAME be.big
'Do you think Hezhang is bigger or Weining is bigger?'
你觉得赫章大还是威宁大？

Even though it is claimed by several consultants that *lɔ²¹* and *(x)a²¹sʅ³³* are interchangeable when forming an interrogative disjunction, it is always *lɔ³³* that is used in spontaneous data. Extracted from a narrative, the interrogative disjunction formed by *lɔ²¹* in (15.44) is the complement of the verb *tsaŋ³³* 'see', i.e. an alternative question embedded in a VP.

(15.44) tsaŋ²¹ sʅ³³ ɕin²¹ sʅ⁵⁵ toŋ³³ **lɔ³³** ko²¹ sʅ⁵⁵ toŋ³³.
see COP new water heavy or old water heavy
'To check whether it is the water of the New Year that is heavy or it is the water of the last year.'
看是新水重还是旧水重。
(*The water of the New Year*, texts)

15.3.2.3 Emphatic disjunction

Expressing an alternative in the same way as standard disjunction does, emphatic disjunction proves to be semantically more intense in its overall rhetorical effect. Three pairs of correlative coordinators are found to form the 'either. . .or' emphatic disjunction in Caijia: *xuɔ²¹tsɛ⁵⁵. . .xuɔ²¹tsɛ⁵⁵. . ., niɔ³³sɿ³³. . .niɔ³³sɿ³³. . .*, and *pɣ³³sɿ³³. . .tɯ³³(sɿ³³). . .*, which can be schematized as below.

xuɔ²¹tsɛ⁵⁵. . .xuɔ²¹tsɛ⁵⁵. . .
i. [(NP$_i$) xuɔ²¹tsɛ⁵⁵ VP$_1$, (NP$_i$) xuɔ²¹tsɛ⁵⁵ VP$_2$]
   [xuɔ²¹tsɛ⁵⁵ (NP$_1$) VP$_1$, xuɔ²¹tsɛ⁵⁵ (NP$_2$) VP$_2$]

niɔ³³sɿ³³. . .niɔ³³sɿ³³. . .
ii. [(NP$_i$) niɔ³³sɿ³³ VP$_1$, (NP$_i$) niɔ³³sɿ³³ VP$_2$]
    [niɔ³³sɿ³³ (NP$_1$) VP$_1$, niɔ³³sɿ³³ (NP$_2$) VP$_2$]

pɣ³³sɿ³³. . .tɯ³³(sɿ³³). . .
iii. [(NP$_i$) pɣ³³sɿ³³ VP$_1$, (NP$_i$) tɯ³³sɿ³³ VP$_2$]
     [pɣ³³sɿ³³ (NP$_1$) VP$_1$, tɯ³³sɿ³³ (NP$_2$) VP$_2$]

All of these can be interpreted as 'either. . .or. . .'. It has been mentioned earlier that the first, *xuɔ²¹tsɛ⁵⁵*, is a loanword denoting 'or'. Composed of the auxiliary *niɔ³³* 'must, need' and the copula *sɿ³³*, the second, *niɔ³³sɿ³³*, denotes 'if' or 'probably' when used alone (see §15.4.3.3.5 and Chapter 11 §11.6). The third, the correlative coordinator *pɣ³³sɿ³³. . .tɯ³³(sɿ³³). . ., pɣ³³sɿ³³*, is actually derived from the negated copula 'not be', while *tɯ³³sɿ³³* is an intensifier derived from the phrase *tɯ³³ sɿ³³* 'indeed be' when used alone, as in (15.57).

Examples below illustrate the usage of these three pairs of correlative coordinators. In each of them, two disjuncts share the same subject as the first schematicization. Moreover, all of the three correlative coordinators can be used in the contexts given for the following three examples, (15.45)-(15.47).

(15.45) ɔ²¹kɯ²⁴   ŋo²¹   ta⁵⁵   ni²¹   la²¹to⁵⁵   o.
         now   1PL   two   CLF   old   CRS
         la²¹   a²¹tsɛ⁵⁵   **xuɔ²¹tsɛ⁵⁵**   na²¹   mia²¹ŋoŋ³³   xa³³,
         all   still   or   with   Lolo   say
         xuɔ²¹tsɛ⁵⁵   na³³   meŋ²¹ni²¹ŋoŋ²¹   xa³³   nɛ³³.
         or   with   Caijia   say   PRT
         'Now, the two of us are old. (We) still either speak Lolo or Caijia (with each other).'
         现在我们两个老了。还是或者说彝话，或者说蔡家话。
         (*My friend and I*, texts)

15.3 Coordination — 505

(15.46) nɯ³³ **niɔ³³sɿ³³** nɛ³³ kʷɔ³³ sʏ̩³³, **niɔ³³sɿ³³** nɛ³³ na²¹koŋ⁵⁵.
2SG either PRT learn book or PRT work
piɔ²⁴ koŋ⁵⁵koŋ⁵⁵ tɯ²¹ ɔ⁵⁵ ʑi²¹ kʏ²¹-xɯ⁵⁵.
NEG.IMP every.day at house inside sit-DUR
'You either (continue) attending school or go to work. Don't stay at home'
你要么呢上学，要么呢打工。别在家坐着。

(15.47) lɔ²¹kɯ²¹ ŋo²¹ tɕiu⁵⁵ je³³ mo³³. je³³ **pʏ³³sɿ³³**
every.time 1SG arrive 3SG inside 3SG either
tsaŋ²¹ sʏ³³, **tɯ³³(sɿ²¹)** ta⁵⁵ je²¹ ʑi²¹ tɕie⁵⁵
look book or for 3SG mother do
ja²¹pa²¹. ka²¹ xɪŋ⁵⁵.
chore hardworking very
'Every time I went to his house, he was either reading or helping his mother out. He's very hardworking'
每次我去他家。他不是看书，就是帮他妈干活。勤快得很。

Within the second schematicization of two disjuncts possessing different subjects, the coordinator is in the initial position for each disjunct clause.

(15.48) niɔ³³ ji³³ ni³³ ɣa²¹ loŋ³³ mo³³ kuɛ³³ kʰɯ²¹
must one CLF walk city inside go attend
xui²⁴ xa³³. **xuɔ²¹tsɛ⁵⁵/niɔ³³sɿ³³/pʏ³³sɿ³³** nɯ³³ kuɛ³³
meeting REP or 2SG go
xuɔ²¹tsɛ⁵⁵/niɔ³³sɿ³³/tɯ³³sɿ³³ ŋo³³ kuɛ²¹.
or 1SG go
'It's said that one (of us) must go to the town to attend the meeting. Either you go, or I go.'
说是要一个人去城里开会。要么/不是你去，要么/就是我去。

Even though common contexts for all of the three coordinators exist, as in (15.45)-(15.47), there are still differences. The disjunction formed by *pʏ³³sɿ³³...tɯ³³(sɿ³³)*... semantically differs from the other two, whereas *niɔ³³sɿ³³...niɔ³³sɿ³³*... and *xuɔ²¹tsɛ⁵⁵...xuɔ²¹tsɛ⁵⁵*... appear to be interchangeable, as will be explained below.

Take (15.48) as an example. When *pʏ³³sɿ³³...tɯ³³(sɿ³³)*... is used, the speaker presupposes his or her proposition is true, i.e. the candidate attending the meeting must be either 'you' or 'I'. The use of *pʏ³³sɿ³³...tɯ³³(sɿ³³)*... may also imply that the disjunction it marks is not new information. On the contrary, other options can arise, when *niɔ³³sɿ³³...niɔ³³sɿ³³*... or *xuɔ²¹tsɛ⁵⁵...xuɔ²¹tsɛ⁵⁵*... are used, i.e. the possibility is not excluded that a third candidate may also attend the meeting. Furthermore, unlike the other two coordinators, *pɣ³³sɿ³³...tɯ³³(sɿ³³)...* is strictly used in the context of binary alternation, while *niɔ³³sɿ³³...niɔ³³sɿ³³...* and *xuɔ²¹tsɛ⁵⁵...xuɔ²¹tsɛ⁵⁵...* are not necessarily so restricted. In the context of (15.49), which comprises three disjunct clauses, *pɣ³³sɿ³³...tɯ³³(sɿ³³)...* cannot be used.

(15.49) ɕie²¹   ŋa⁵⁵-sui⁵⁵   tɯ²¹   ji²¹   kʰa³³   sɔ²¹kʷɔ⁵⁵   nɛ⁵⁵,
         little   child-PL   at   one   place   play   PRT
         niɔ³³sɿ³³/xuɔ²¹tsɛ⁵⁵   na²¹kɿ²¹,   **niɔ³³sɿ³³/xuɔ²¹tsɛ⁵⁵**
         or   play.ball.of.feather   or
         na²¹tɕʰiɯ²¹,   **niɔ³³sɿ³³/xuɔ²¹tsɛ⁵⁵**   nɛ³³   na²¹pʰe²¹.
         play.swing   or   PRT   play.dart
         'When children were playing together, they used to play the game with a ball of chicken feather, go on the swings or they played darts.'
         小孩子们在一起玩呢，要么打鸡毛球，要么荡秋千，要么呢打靶子。

15.3.2.4 Concluding remarks

Caijia contrasts standard disjunction and interrogative disjunction. The former is constructed with the loan disjunction *xuɔ²¹tsɛ⁵⁵*, while the latter is formed either by *lɔ²¹* or the loan, *(x)a²¹sɿ³³*. Three types of emphatic disjunction are observed: *xuɔ²¹tsɛ⁵⁵...xuɔ²¹tsɛ⁵⁵*, *niɔ³³sɿ³³...niɔ³³sɿ³³*, and *pɣ³³sɿ³³...tɯ³³sɿ³³*. All of these are semantically close to English 'either...or'. See Table 15.2 for a synthesis.

Table 15.2: Disjunctions in Caijia.

	Type and schema	Meaning	Source
I	Standard disjunction		
	[NP₁/VP₁ **xuɔ²¹tsɛ⁵⁵** NP₂/VP₂]	'or'	xuɔ²¹tsɛ⁵⁵ < Mandarin 'or'
II	Interrogative disjunction		
	[NP₁/VP₁ **lɔ²¹** NP₂/VP₂]	'or'	lɔ²¹ < ?
	[NP₁/VP₁ **(x)a²¹sɿ³³** NP₂/VP₂]		(x)a²¹sɿ³³ < Mandarin 'or'
III	Emphatic disjunction		
	i [(NPᵢ) **xuɔ²¹tsɛ⁵⁵** VP₁, (NPᵢ) **xuɔ²¹tsɛ⁵⁵** VP₂]	'either...or'	xuɔ²¹tsɛ⁵⁵ < Madarin 'or'
	[**xuɔ²¹tsɛ⁵⁵** (NP₁) VP₁, **xuɔ²¹tsɛ⁵⁵** (NP₂) VP₂]		
	ii [(NPᵢ) **niɔ³³sɿ³³** VP₁, (NPᵢ) **niɔ³³sɿ³³** VP₂]	'either...or'	niɔ³³ < 'want'
	[**niɔ³³sɿ³³** (NP₁) VP₁, **niɔ³³sɿ³³** (NP₂) VP₂]		sɿ³³ < copula
	iii [**pɣ³³sɿ³³** (NP₁) VP₁, **tɯ³³sɿ³³** (NP₂) VP₂]	'either...or'	pɣ³³sɿ³³ < 'not be'
	[(NPᵢ) **pɣ³³sɿ³³** VP₁, (NPᵢ) **tɯ³³sɿ³³** VP₂]		tɯ³³sɿ³³ < 'just be'

15.3.3 Contrastive coordination

Contrastive coordination is also a kind of clause linking in Caijia with two juxtaposed clauses in semantic opposition, i.e. the information conveyed by one clause contrasts with the other clause (q.v. Dixon 2009: 28). This type of coordination is identified as adversative coordination by Haspelmath (2007), e.g. the English *but*-coordination, as in 'John is very clever but not hardworking', or similar forms of coordination in other languages. In Caijia, two contrastive coordinators are observed to overtly link two clauses which semantically contrast with each other, i.e. *tɯ³³sɿ³³* and *ɕia³³ti³³ɣɯ²¹* in the form of:

[CLAUSE₁ tɯ³³sɿ³³ CLAUSE₂],
[CLAUSE₁ ɕia³³ti³³ɣɯ²¹ CLAUSE₂].

The term 'contrastive coordination' is used because the coordinators *tɯ³³sɿ³³* and *ɕia³³ti³³ɣɯ²¹* can express adversative as well as concessive meanings. While both concern 'contrast', they also denote that one admits or concedes what is conveyed by CLAUSE₁ despite the assertion made in CLAUSE₂. This is very similar to the contrastive coordinator *dànshì* 但是 [tan⁵¹ʂɿ⁵¹] 'but' in Standard Mandarin. Chao (1968: 115) treats it as a concessive marker. See also §15.4.4.

The examples (15.50)-(15.53) show the adversative uses of both *tɯ³³sɿ³³* and *ɕia³³ti³³ɣɯ²¹*. The examples containing 'being wealthy' and 'being unpopular' in (15.50), both linked by *tɯ³³sɿ³³*, form oppositions of a person's strengths and weaknesses. Example (15.51) provides a similar context.

(15.50) tɯ³³ xa²¹lɛ⁵⁵ ₍CLAUSE1₎[je³³ ɣã²¹ tɕiŋ²¹], **tɯ³³sɿ³³**
all say 3SG have money but
₍CLAUSE2₎[je³³ pɣ³³ tɯ²¹ ni³³ tɣ²¹].
3SG NEG attract 3 like
'Everyone says that he is rich, but people don't like him.'
都说他有钱，但是不招人喜欢。

(15.51) mɔ²¹ u²¹tsʰo²⁴ ni³³ ka²¹ xiŋ⁵⁵, **tɯ³³sɿ³³**
that person CLF hardworking very but
pɣ²¹ taŋ²⁴ ti³³ xa³³.
NEG so know speak
'That person is very hardworking, but not very talkative.'
那个人很勤快，但不是很健谈。

The two clauses 'he left' and 'I wasn't aware of (this)' in the example below are connected by ɕia³³ti³³ɣɯ²¹, since the fact that he left is supposed to be known by the speaker 'I' but is contrary to the actual situation.

(15.52) CLAUSE1[je³³ ɣa²¹-kuɛ³³ o], **ɕia³³ti³³ɣɯ²¹**
        3SG   walk-go   CRS   but
        CLAUSE2[ŋo³³ pɣ³³ tiu³³u³³].
        1SG   NEG   know
        'He left, but I wasn't aware of (this).'
        他走了，但我不知道。

Linked by ɕia³³ti³³ɣɯ²¹, the second clause 'she is beautiful' in (15.53) diverges from people's expectations.

(15.53) hu³³ni³³   la²¹   tɯ²¹-xɯ⁵⁵   mɔ²¹   ŋa⁵⁵   ni³³
         everyone   all   think-DUR   that   child   CLF
         xa³³fa²¹   kʰua²¹ tɕiu²¹   la²⁴   po³³   to³³,
         appearance be.good arrive   where   NEG   can
         ɕia³³ti³³ɣɯ²¹   xa²¹   lɯ⁵⁵   mia²¹kua³³kua²⁴   lɛ⁵⁵.
         but/it.turns.out   grow   VCOMP   beautiful   CONT
         'Everyone thought that the appearance of that child wouldn't be nice, but she is beautiful.'
         所有人都想着那孩子好看不到哪去，但（她）长得水灵灵的。

In contrast, the following examples illustrate the concessive uses of *tɯ³³sɿ³³* and *ɕia³³ti³³ɣɯ²¹*. In both (15.54) and (15.55), the fact conveyed by CLAUSE₁ is affirmed by the speaker via the copula *sɿ³³* and the repetition of the verb in the concessive form [VP sɿ³³ VP], against which the CLAUSE₂ assertion is made. Specifically, despite the admission that the person is good-looking in CLAUSE₁, the speaker still doesn't like her in (15.54); while in (15.55), the pear is not sweet, even though it is conceded to be big.

(15.54) CLAUSE1[je³³   kʰua²¹tsaŋ³³   sɿ³³   kʰua²¹tsaŋ³³],
        3SG   good-looking   indeed good-looking
        tɯ³³sɿ³³ CLAUSE2[ŋo³³ pɣ²¹ taŋ²⁴ tɕʰi³³kʰa³³].
        but   1SG   NEG   much   like
        'She may be good-looking, but I don't like (her) very much.'
        她好看是好看，但是我不太喜欢。

(15.55) CLAUSE1[mɔ²¹ xɯ⁵⁵tsʅ⁵⁵ po⁵⁵ la²¹ **sʅ³³** la²¹],
that   pear   CLF big COP big
ɕia³³ti³³ɣɯ²¹ CLAUSE2[pɣ³³ tɕian²¹].
but   NEG   sweet
'That pear is indeed big to be sure, but it isn't sweet.'
那个梨大是大，但是不甜。

The meaning of concession can be overtly expressed. As shown in both of the two examples above, a speaker's admission of the fact is overtly expressed by the repetition of the VP via the copula conveying a concession with the contrast overtly expressed by either tɯ³³sʅ³³ 'but' or ɕia³³ti³³ɣɯ²¹ 'but'. Nonetheless, the concessive meaning can also be simply expressed by the adversative coordinator tɯ³³sʅ³³ 'but' or ɕia³³ti³³ɣɯ²¹ 'but'. Example (15.56) is one such case, in which CLAUSE₁ is a common declarative clause. Both tɯ³³sʅ³³ 'but' and ɕia³³ti³³ɣɯ²¹ 'but' can be used in this example.

(15.56) CLAUSE1[mɔ²¹ xɯ⁵⁵tsʅ⁵⁵ po⁵⁵ la²¹ xɪŋ⁵⁵],
that   pear   CLF big very
ɕia³³ti³³ɣɯ²¹/tɯ³³sʅ³³ CLAUSE2[pɣ³³ tɕian²¹].
but   NEG   sweet
'That pear is very big, but it isn't sweet.'
那个梨很大，但是不甜。

It should be mentioned that the coordinator ɕia³³ti³³ɣɯ²¹ can often replace tɯ³³sʅ³³ but not vice versa. In a coordinate construction formed by tɯ³³sʅ³³, [CLAUSE₁ tɯ³³sʅ³³ CLAUSE₂], CLAUSE₂ always conveys a negative point of view or attitude. For example, the CLAUSE₂ in (15.51), pɣ²¹ taŋ²⁴ ti³³ xa³³ 'not skilled at talking ~ not talkative', conveys that the speaker thinks having poor speaking skills is a bad quality. Therefore, tɯ³³sʅ³³ can replace ɕia³³ti³³ɣɯ²¹ in (15.55), but cannot be used in (15.52) and (15.53).

The coordinator tɯ³³sʅ³³ is exactly the same word as in the correlative disjunction pɣ³³sʅ³³. . .tɯ³³sʅ³³. . .. It is probably derived from the phrase tɯ³³ sʅ³³ 'indeed be, just be', i.e. the copula sʅ³³ modified by the intensifier tɯ³³. As shown in (15.57), when modifying the copula, tɯ³³ is used in order to underline the speaker's certainty about his or her statement.

(15.57) tɔ²⁴ **tɯ³³** **sʅ³³** je³³.
thief indeed COP 3SG
'The thief is definitely him.'
小偷就是他。

As for the adversative coordinator ɕia³³ti³³yɯ²¹, the source meaning of each syllable can no longer be traced. However, it can also be used to denote 'it turns out that. . .'. It marks the truth value of new information and implies that the previous old information is false. See (15.58) for an example.

(15.58) ŋo³³   xa²¹lɛ⁵⁵   ɔ²¹   kɪ²¹tɕie⁵⁵ tsɿ⁵⁵   tɕiɔ⁵⁵mɔ⁵⁵   pɣ²¹
         1SG   say   this   hen   CLF   why   NEG
         ti³³   kuɯŋ²¹   pia²¹kʰɔ⁵⁵ o.   **ɕia³³ti³³yɯ²¹**   nɛ⁵⁵
         know   lay   egg   CRS   it.turns.out   PRT
         je³³   sɿ³³   kuɯŋ²¹   pie⁵⁵   pʰa²¹   fɛ⁵¹hɛ²¹   kɪ³³to³³
         3SG   COP   lay   to   other   family   chicken.cage
         mo³³   kuɛ²¹   o.
         inside   go   CRS
         'I was wondering how come the hen couldn't lay eggs anymore. It turns out that it laid them in another family's cage.'
         我说这母鸡怎么不会下蛋了。原来是下到别人家鸡笼里去了。

Actually, it is not difficult to establish a semantic connection between the meanings 'but' and 'it turns out that. . .'. It is mentioned above that ɕia³³ti³³yɯ²¹ often marks new information a person received which corrects earlier information they had. Contrast thus exists between the old information with its now false value and the new information which is true and marked by ɕia³³ti³³yɯ²¹. Therefore, the meaning 'but' can be furthered reanalyzed out of appropriate contexts. Example (15.53) of a child growing up to be pretty is such a case of ambiguity. ɕia³³ti³³yɯ²¹ can be interpreted both as 'it turns out that. . .' and as 'but'. However, tɯ³³sɿ³³ cannot be used to replace ɕia³³ti³³yɯ²¹ in (15.53), since the conjunction ɕia³³ti³³yɯ²¹ 'it turns out that. . .' links two clauses, with the first clause bearing an absolute false value and the second a value of truth. By contrast, when ɕia³³ti³³yɯ²¹ denotes 'but', the first clause is not necessarily false, so it serves to introduce the updated truth value in most of the cases. Just as in (15.55), the proposition in the first clause 'the pear is indeed big' is definitely true, and so ɕia³³ti³³yɯ²¹ can only be interpreted as 'but' and not as 'it turns out that. . .'.

In conclusion, complex sentences involving contrastive conjunctions can be formed either by tɯ³³sɿ³³ or ɕia³³ti³³yɯ²¹. Both of them can denote adversative as well as concessive meaning but are used in different semantic contexts. The coordinator tɯ³³sɿ³³ is derived from 'just be', while ɕia³³ti³³yɯ²¹ is derived from 'it turns out that. . .'. See Table 15.3 for a summary.

Table 15.3: Contrastive conjunctions in Caijia.

Type and schema	Meaning	Source
I. [CLAUSE₁ tɯ³³sɿ³³ CLAUSE₂]	'but'	tɯ³³sɿ³³ < 'just be'
II. [CLAUSE₁ ɕia³³ti³³ɣɯ²¹ CLAUSE₂]	'but'	ɕia³³ti³³ɣɯ²¹ < 'it turns out that'

15.4 Adverbial subordination

Adverbial subordination refers to dependent clauses functioning as adverbials (q.v. Thompson et al. 2007), i.e. clausal adverbials. For example, in 'He left in the morning' and 'He left when I arrived home', both the prepositional phrase 'in the morning' and the clause 'when I arrived home' serve as temporal adverbials. Adverbial clauses are syntactically non-embedded, as opposed to embedded structures like complement and relative clauses. Adverbial clauses function as a type of clause linker with respect to the main clause. They relate to the main clause as a whole (Thompson et al. 2007: 238), while complement and relative clauses are located within the main clause.

Five major types of adverbial clauses can be identified in Caijia:
i. Time
ii. Consequence and cause
iii. Conditional
iv. Concession
v. Substitutive (/preferred option)

Each type contains several subtypes and may be realized by different strategies. This section will present these five types of adverbial clauses in detail.

15.4.1 Time clauses

In Caijia, five types of time clauses are observed:
i. temporal sequence or then clauses: [CLAUSE₁ [THEN CLAUSE₂]];
ii. BEFORE clauses: [[CLAUSE₁ BEFORE], CLAUSE₂];
iii. AFTER clauses: [[CLAUSE₁ AFTER], CLAUSE₂];
iv. SINCE clauses: [SINCE CLAUSE₁, CLAUSE₂];
v. WHEN clauses: [[CLAUSE₁ WHEN], CLAUSE₂].

Note that the clause order is rigid in each type. Detailed schemata will be given in each section.

The THEN clauses are realized by adverbs. Both the BEFORE and AFTER clauses map spatial expressions. Even though the formation of the marker SINCE seems to calque the Mandarin pattern, it is also related to a spatial concept. Finally, the WHEN clauses are formed by relativization. We will now examine the five types of time clauses one by one.

15.4.1.1 Temporal sequence

Clauses of sequence can be simply explained as those in which a succession of events is signaled (Thompson and Longacre 1985: 180). In Caijia, three semantic types of sequence clauses are observed: (i) common sequence, (ii) compact sequence and (iii) emphatic sequence, which will be defined below, respectively. In each type, clauses are arranged according to their chronological order, i.e. the event conveyed in the first clause is understood to occur before the one in the second clause.

(i) In a sentence of the **common sequence type** there are two events. The first event is zero marked, while the second event, which follows the first, is marked by $tɯ^{33}$ 'just, then, indeed':

[(NP$_1$) VP$_1$, (NP$_2$) tɯ^{33} VP$_2$].

The marker $tɯ^{33}$ can thus be interpreted as 'then' in English.

In example (15.59), 'the ghost began to howl', marked by $tɯ^{33}$, follows '(we) walked to the side of the cave'.

(15.59) CLAUSE1[ɣa^{21} tɕiu^{55} kʰa^{33} pɪŋ^{33}],
        walk   to   cave   side
        ─────────────────────────────────
                    EVENT$_1$
        CLAUSE2[kui^{55} **tɯ^{33}** tɯ^{21} ma^{24} xã^{21}-xɯ^{55}ɣɯ^{24}].
        ghost   then   at   there   yell-INC
        ─────────────────────────────────
                    EVENT$_2$
'(We) walked to the side of the cave, and then the ghost began to howl.'
走到洞边，鬼就在那儿叫起来了。
(*Encountering the ghost*, texts)

In (15.60), the clause 'the illness is still on the opposite hill' precedes the one 'they have their beds prepared and wait for (it)' which is marked by $tɯ^{33}$. This sentence is metaphorically used by the speaker to express how some persons psychologically deal with illness.

(15.60) ɣã²¹ ji²¹sui⁵⁵ nɛ⁵⁵, soŋ²¹ xa²¹tsɛ⁵⁵ tɯ²¹
there.be some PRT illness still be.at
ti³³mi²¹ ti²¹, je⁵⁵ **tɯ³³** tɯ²¹ ha⁵⁵
opposite hill 3PL then at here
pʰɣ²¹ tʰa⁵⁵ niu²¹-xɯ⁵⁵ o.
prepare bed wait-DUR CRS
'For some people, even though they aren't attacked by any illness as yet, they've already entered into the state of being ill.'
LIT: 'There are some people. Their illness is still on the opposite hill, but they already have their beds prepared and wait for (it) then.'
有一些（人）呢，病还在对面山上，他们就在这儿铺好床等着了。

(ii) A sentence of the **compact sequence type** underlines immediate succession, semantically corresponding to 'as soon as' and 'once' in English. In a complex sentence of common sequence, the second clause is marked, as illustrated above. In contrast, in a sentence belonging to the compact sequence type, it is the first clause that is obligatorily marked by ʑi³³, derived from the numeral 'one', in a sentence of compact sequence. The second clause is optionally marked by the intensifier tɯ³³ 'indeed, then, just'. This can be schematized as:

[$_{EVENT1}$[(NP$_1$) ʑi³³ VP$_1$], $_{EVENT2}$[(NP$_2$) (tɯ³³) VP$_2$]],

denoting 'as soon as. . .'. The use of *tɯ³³* does not influence the meaning. Both of the strategies denote there is no temporal interval between two events, i.e. EVENT$_2$ immediately follows EVENT$_1$.

Examples (15.61) and (15.62) are examples with *ji³³* marking their first clauses, as shown in (15.61i) and (15.62i), while their second clauses remain unmarked, as in (15.61ii) and (15.62ii).

(15.61) kʰɯ²¹ koŋ⁵⁵ pɣ³³ kɪŋ²¹ tʰoŋ²¹tʰoŋ⁵⁵ o.
several day NEG see NAME CRS
i) $_{CLAUSE1}$[je³³ ji³³ tsaŋ²¹-kɪŋ²¹ ŋo³³],
3SG once look-see 1SG
EVENT$_1$
ii) $_{CLAUSE2}$[sɔ²¹ lɯ³³ mɔ³³sɿ³³].
laugh VCOMP very
EVENT$_2$

'I hadn't seen Tongtong for several days. As soon as she saw me, she began to laugh happily.'
几天没见童童了。她一见我就笑得不行。

(15.62) i) **ji²¹** tʰi⁵⁵-tγ²¹ u²¹tsʰɔ²¹ xaŋ³³ kγ²¹ mia³³,
once listen-obtain person yell save life
ii) je³³ ʑi²¹ la³³ pγ³³-tγ³³ ɯ³³ lɛ³³
3SG shoe all NEG-PFV wear ADV
piɔ²¹ tsʰe⁵⁵-ɣɯ²¹ o.
run come.out-come CRS
'As soon as (he) heard someone yelling for help, he ran out without even putting on his shoes.'
一听见有人喊救命，他鞋都没穿就跑出去了。

Below are two examples of *ʑi³³. . .tɯ³³. . .* In both cases, the clauses marked by *tɯ³³* occur with pro-dropped subjects. Once there is an overt subject, it should precede *tɯ³³*.

(15.63) CLAUSE1[kʰɪŋ⁵⁵ **ji³³** mia²¹], CLAUSE2[**tɯ³³** niɔ³³ ya³³
sky once brighten then PROSP walk
ŋã²¹kʰa³³ mo³³ kuɛ³³].
cliff.cave inside go
'As soon as the sky brightened, we would go to the cliff cave.'
天一亮就要到崖洞里去。
(*Childhood*, texts)

(15.64) i) **ji²¹** tɪŋ⁵⁵ seŋ²¹
once turn body
ii) **tɯ²¹** a³³ tsɔ³³ tsaŋ²¹ hu³³ mɔ²¹
then OM hold needle thread that
kʰa²⁴ na²¹pʰe³³ kuɔ²¹.
box beat-overturn go.CRS
'As soon as (she) turned, (she) overturned the sewing box (LIT: that box holding needles and threads).'
（她）一转身就把装针线那盒子打翻了。
(*The careless woman*, texts)

(iii) The third type, that of **emphatic sequence**, can be roughly paraphrased as 'only by the time EVENT₁ takes place, does EVENT₂ take place'. It can be either realized by *tsʰɛ²¹* 'just, only, only then' or *lɛ²¹tsʰɛ²¹* 'just, not until, only then' in the form of:

[(NP₁) VP₁, (NP₂) (lɛ²¹)tsʰɛ²¹ VP₂].

15.4 Adverbial subordination — 515

Below, the sequence marking function of *(lɛ²¹)tsʰɛ²¹* is exemplified. As mentioned above, the *(lɛ²¹)tsʰɛ²¹*-sequence and the common *tɯ³³*-sequence are semantically different. Example (15.65) does not simply mean EVENT₂ 'go to wash the face' follows EVENT₁ 'run a few laps'. Instead, it underlines the fact that washing the face occurs only after running a few laps.

(15.65) yã²¹   ji³³   tɔ²¹kʰɯ⁵⁵   ŋo³³   tɕiŋ²¹tɕiŋ²⁴   lɛ²¹   kʰɯ⁵⁵   kuɛ²¹
        there.be one   morning   1SG   early   ADV   rise   PURP
   i) CLAUSE1[piɔ³³   kʰɯ²¹   tɪŋ⁵⁵   ha⁵⁵]
        run   several circle   COMPL
                     EVENT₁
   ii) (lɛ²¹)tsʰɛ²¹   CLAUSE2[kuɛ³³   ja³³   mĩ²¹kʰɔ⁵⁵   sɿ³³].
        only.then   go   wash   face   PRT
                          EVENT₂
'One morning, I got up very early. Only after running a few laps, did I go to wash my face.'
有天早上我早早地起来，跑几圈以后才去洗脸。
(*Drowning persons*, texts)

Example (15.66) shows a very common case in which *(lɛ²¹)tsʰɛ²¹* is frequently used, namely, procedural discourse, including production processes and methods of fabrication like making a dish, cooking rice, or building a house. Each process can only proceed on the basis of the completion of a previous process. Therefore, the *(lɛ²¹)tsʰɛ²¹*-sequence usually interacts with the completive marker marking a previous process, i.e. EVENT₁. As exemplified below, only treated garlic can be used to fill scented sachets. Hence, garlic must be treated before filling a sachet.

(15.66) tso²¹   ha⁵⁵   nɛ⁵⁵   **(lɛ²¹)tsʰɛ²¹**   a³³   ɣɯ²¹   tsʰɯ³³.
        soak   COMPL   PRT   only.then   take   PURP   knit
'Only after (the garlic bulbs) are well soaked (in realgar wine), are they then used to make (scented sachets).'
（大蒜）泡完了呢，才拿来织（香包）。
(*The Dragon Boat Festival*, texts)

In fact, a conditional meaning can also be garnered from such kinds of contexts, since a previous process is the condition to proceed to a next step. This will be discussed later in this chapter.

The source of *lɛ²¹* remains unclear, while *tsʰɛ²¹* is both phonetically and functionally similar to *cái* 才 [tsʰai²⁴] 'just, not until, only then' in Standard Mandarin.

The following two examples show the uses of both $tsʰɛ^{21}$ and $lɛ^{21}tsʰɛ^{21}$ as intensifiers in non-sequential contexts. For example, $tsʰɛ^{21}$ denotes 'only, just' in (15.67). In (15. 68), apart from the meaning 'only, just', $lɛ^{21}tsʰɛ^{21}$ also implies that the result will turn out to be different from what is presupposed before the bet (see also [15.4ii]).

(15.67) ni³³ xa²¹ **tsʰɛ²¹** niɔ²¹ pa³³ seŋ³³ a,
3   say only want half UNIT PRT
je³³ a²¹ pe⁵⁵ seŋ²¹ sɿ⁵⁵ ni³³.
3SG take eight UNIT to   3
'He said he just wanted half a kilo (of rice), but she gave him eight kilos.'
人说才要半升（米），她给人八升。
(*Exchange of product*, texts)

(15.68) tɤ⁵⁵ pi²¹ xa²¹ lɔ²⁴ni³³ **lɛ²¹tsʰɛ²¹** xiŋ⁵⁵.
bet mouth say who   just   powerful
'(The tiger and the buffalo) made a bet (to see) who was really more powerful.'
(老虎和水牛)打赌说谁才厉害。
(*The tiger and the buffalo*, texts)

15.4.1.2 Before and after

BEFORE and AFTER clauses in Caijia share some similarities. Both are related with spatial concepts. BEFORE clauses are formed by the localizer $tɕiŋ^{21}$ 'front', while AFTER clauses are realized by the localizer u^{33} 'back'. Both $tɕiŋ^{21}$ and u^{33} are postposed at the end of the first clause:

BEFORE: [CLAUSE₁ $tɕiŋ^{21}$, CLAUSE₂];
AFTER: [CLAUSE₁ u^{33}, CLAUSE₂].

Examples (15.69) and (15.70) below are two complex sentences with BEFORE clauses. In Caijia, BEFORE clauses and negation interact optionally without any semantic change. As shown in (15.70), the verb yu^{21} 'come' is negated by the perfective negator $pɤ^{33}tɤ^{33}$, without which the meaning of the BEFORE clause does not change. This phenomenon is also attested in Standard Mandarin, as shown in (15.71), and can be noted in the use of the subjunctive mood in unrelated languages such as French: *avant qu'il **n'**arrive* 'before he (doesn't) arrive'. Compare (15.69) and (15.70).

15.4 Adverbial subordination — 517

(15.69) [pa³³ pe³³-ɣɯ²¹ **tɕɪŋ²¹**] zʏ̩²¹ tɕie⁵⁵kʰua²¹ to³³ mo³³?
grandfather return-come before meal make-be.good can Q
'Can the meal be ready before the grandpa comes back?'
爷爷回来前，饭能做好吗？

(15.70) [tseŋ²¹kʰa²¹-sui⁵⁵ **(pɣ³³-tɣ³³)** ɣɯ²¹ **tɕɪŋ²¹**] je³³ niɔ³³
relative-PL NEG-PFV come before 3SG need
a³³ zʏ̩²¹ tɕie⁵⁵-kʰua²¹.
OM meal make-good
'She needs to have the meal prepared, before the relatives arrive.'
亲戚（没）来之前她要把饭做好。

(15.71) Standard Mandarin
亲戚们（没）来之前，她要把饭做好。
qīnqi-men (méi) lái qián, tā yào
relative-PL NEG.PFV come before 3SG need
bǎ fàn zuò-hǎo.
OM meal make-be.good
'She needs to have the meal prepared, before the relatives arrive.'

It is often observed that *tɕɪŋ²¹* associates with the locative preposition *tɯ²¹* 'at' in the form of [tɯ²¹ CLAUSE₁ tɕɪŋ²¹] in BEFORE clauses. In this form, the BEFORE clause is actually realized by a prepositional phrase.

(15.72) ŋo³³ pa³³ pɣ³³ tɯ²¹ kuɛ³³ kʰɯ³³ neŋ²¹
1SG grandfather NEG exist go several year
ɔ ma. **tɯ²¹** ŋo²¹ tsʰe⁵⁵sŋ²¹ **tɕɪŋ²¹** tɯ³³
PRT PRT at 1SG be.born front then
pɣ³³ tɯ²¹ kuɛ³³ o.
NEG exist go CRS
'My grandfather has been dead for many years. Before I was born, (he) had passed away.'
我爷爷不在几年了。在我出世前就不在了。

When denoting 'before', the prepositional phrase [tɯ²¹ CLAUSE₁ tɕɪŋ²¹] can be situated within CLAUSE₂, i.e. in the pre-VP position in CLAUSE₂. This is a common position in general for a prepositional phrase, as shown in (15.73a). In this pre-VP position, the preposition *tɯ²¹* 'at' is obligatory. In contrast, if the *tɯ²¹* phrase is in the sentence initial position, as in (15.73b), it is optional.

(15.73) a. je³³ [*(tɯ²¹) ŋo²¹ tsʰe⁵⁵sɿ²¹ tɕɪŋ²¹] tɯ³³
  3SG at   1SG be.born   front   then
  pɣ³³ tɯ²¹ kuɛ³³ o.
  NEG exist go   CRS
  'Before I was born, he had passed away.'
  他在我出世前就不在了。

b. (tɯ²¹) ŋo²¹ tsʰe⁵⁵sɿ²¹ tɕɪŋ²¹
  at   1SG be.born   front
  je³³ tɯ³³ pɣ³³ tɯ²¹ kuɛ³³ o.
  3SG then NEG exist go   CRS
  'Before I was born, he had passed away.'
  （在）我出世前，他就不在了。

This expression syntactically maps the locative phrase 'in front of', formed by the locative verb/preposition *tɯ²¹* '(be) at', and the localizer *tɕɪŋ²¹* 'front', in which [NP tɕɪŋ²¹] forms a complex NP (Lü 2018) equivalent to a place word. As can be observed, the BEFORE clause in (15.72) and the locative phrase in (15.74) share the same syntactic structure. Example (15.72) denotes a temporal relation, while (15.74) denotes a spatial one.

Localizer 'front'
(15.74) tɯ²¹   nɯ³³ tɕɪŋ²¹ nɛ³³ sɔ²¹sɿ³³sɿ²⁴ lɛ³³ ta⁵⁵ nɯ³³ kʰua²¹.
  (be).at 2SG   front PRT smiley   ADV with 2SG be.good
  'In front of you, (he) is kind to you with smiles.'
  在你面前呢，笑嘻嘻地跟你好。

Examples (15.75) and (15.76) demonstrate two AFTER clauses.

(15.75) ŋo²¹ tsʰe⁵⁵   ja²¹to²¹   ja²¹. [tsʰe⁵⁵   ha⁵⁵   u³³],
  1SG come.out chickenpox EXP   come.out COMPL back
  tɯ³³ pɣ³³ ti²¹ tsʰe⁵⁵ o.
  then NEG can come.out CRS
  'I've had chickenpox. After (one) has it, (one'll never) have it again.'
  我出过水痘。出完以后就不会（再）出了。

(15.76) [nɯ³³   ja³³   ɣɯ²¹   ha⁵⁵   **u³³**]
        2SG   grandmother   come   COMPL   back
        nɯ³³   niɔ³³   tsɛ²⁴kʰã²¹   mi⁵⁵.
        2SG   need   be.well-behaved   little
        'After your grandmother arrives, you need to be (more) well-behaved.'
        你奶奶来了以后，你要乖一点。

The AFTER clause [CLAUSE₁ u³³] is also mapped onto the locational phrase [NP u³³]. Compare the two AFTER clauses above with the place phrase ŋo³³ u³³ 'my back' in (15.77). Unlike the BEFORE clauses exemplified in (15.72) and (15.73), in our data we rarely find that u³³ associates with the locative verb/preposition tɯ²¹ when forming AFTER clauses.

Localizer 'back'
(15.77) je³³   tɯ²¹   ŋo³³   **u³³**.
        3SG   be.at   1SG   back
        'He's behind me.'
        他在我后面。

Apart from clauses and VPs like those in (15.70)-(15.72), in (15.75) and (15.76) both tɕiŋ²¹ 'front' and u³³ 'back' can also follow time words, denoting 'ago' and 'later', respectively.

(15.78) sa³³   nen²¹   **tɕɪŋ²¹/u³³**
        three   year   front/back
        'three years ago' 三年前
        'three years later' 三年后

15.4.1.3 SINCE

SINCE clauses in Caijia are overtly marked by the compound marker tɕie²¹ta⁵⁵ 'since', preceding the clause it marks, as schematized below:

  [tɕie²¹ta⁵⁵ CLAUSE₁, CLAUSE₂].

This marker probably calques *zìcóng* 自从 [tsɿ⁵¹tsʰoŋ²⁴] 'since' in Standard Mandarin. In Standard Mandarin, both *zì* and *cóng* (< 'follow') denote 'from' and are closely related to the meaning 'since'. ta⁵⁵ in Caijia also denotes 'from' (< 'follow'), but the source of tɕie²¹ remains unclear. It is worth mentioning that tɕie²¹ can be used alone to denote 'since' in the Weining variety of Caijia, but this use is not attested in Hezhang Caijia, our target language. See the following two examples for the use of *tɕie²¹ta⁵⁵*.

(15.79) [**tɕie²¹ta⁵⁵** je³³ taŋ²¹ tsʰen³³tsaŋ²¹ ha⁵⁵ nɛ⁵⁵], tsʰɿ³³ mo³³
since 3SG 3SG village.chief COMPL PRT village inside
sɿ²¹ ni²⁴ ji²¹ koŋ⁵⁵ pi⁵⁵ ji²¹ koŋ⁵⁵ kʰua²¹.
MOD life one day CM one day good
'Since he began to serve as the village chief, life in the village is better and better day by day.'
自从他当了村长，村里的生活一天比一天好。

(15.80) **tɕie²¹ta⁵⁵** mɔ²¹ nioŋ²⁴ ni³³ kɛ³³ ɣa³³ ŋuɛ²¹
since that girl CLF marry to my.family
mo³³ ɣɯ²¹ ha⁵⁵ nɛ⁵⁵, ŋuɛ³³
inside come COMPL PRT my.family
pɣ³³-tɣ³³ tɕʰiŋ²¹tɕiŋ²¹ ja²¹.
NEG-PFV be.peaceful EXP
'Since that girl married into our family, we've never been peaceful.'
自从那个女孩嫁到我家，我家就没太平过。

In addition to its clause marking function, *tɕie²¹ta⁵⁵* can also mark NPs. In (15.81), it is the NP *mɔ²¹ mo³³* 'that time' that is marked by *tɕie²¹ta⁵⁵*. The morpheme *mo³³* in this sentence illustrates the extended meaning of the localizer 'inside', denoting 'a time, an occasion'.

(15.81) **tɕie²¹ta⁵⁵** mɔ²¹ mo³³, ŋo²⁴ ta⁵⁵ ni²¹ la²¹
since that inside 1PL two CLF even
pɣ³³-tɣ³³ kɯŋ³³ ja²¹.
NEG-PFV see EXP
'The two of us haven't seen each other since then.'
自从那次，我们两个就没有见过。

15.4.1.4 When

A WHEN clause can be formed either by the time word *tʰɔ²⁴* or the time word *kɯ²¹* in the form of:

[CLAUSE₁ tʰɔ²⁴, CLAUSE₂] or

[CLAUSE₁ kɯ²¹, CLAUSE₂].

Both denote 'moment' and like 'after' and 'before' above, occur in the final position of the first clause. In the copular construction of the equation in (15.82) both $t^h\mathrm{o}^{24}$ and ku^{21} can be used.

(15.82) ɔ²¹kɯ²⁴ sı²¹ zɣ²¹ saŋ³³ **tʰɔ²⁴/kɯ²¹** o.
now   COP eat mushroom moment   CRS
'Now it's the season to eat mushrooms.'
现在是吃菌子的时候了。

The way of forming a WHEN clause in Caijia is very similar to that of a relative clause with a time word as its head, namely [[CLAUSE] tʰɔ²⁴/kɯ²¹] (see Chapter 14). A VP or a clause can immediately precede tʰɔ²⁴ or kɯ²¹ without any linker, which is reflected in examples (15.83) and (15.84) as well as in (15.82). Note also that tʰɔ²⁴ can surface with a different tone value as tʰɔ⁵⁵, while kɯ²¹ can surface as kɯ²⁴. In the two examples below, both tʰɔ²⁴ and kɯ²¹ can be used in WHEN clauses. However, it is always tʰɔ²⁴ that is the first choice of our consultants. Furthermore, tʰɔ²⁴ is overwhelmingly observed in our spontaneous data.

(15.83) kʰıŋ⁵⁵ ka²¹ **tʰɔ⁵⁵/kɯ²⁴**, tɯ²¹ ti²¹ tɣ³³
sky   be.dry moment   be.at hill upside
niɔ³³ ɕie²¹saŋ²⁴ fɛ⁵⁵.
need be.careful fire
'Be careful with fire, when it's dry.'
天气干燥的时候，在山上要小心火。

(15.84) ɔ²¹   li²⁴ kʷɔ²¹ ŋo³³ tsʰɛ²¹ tɕie⁵⁵ pa³³ neŋ²¹,
this pig CLF   1SG only   feed   half year
ɕia³³ti³³yɯ²¹ tɕiu⁵⁵ kua³³ neŋ²¹ **tʰɔ²⁴/kɯ²⁴**,
but   arrive pass   year moment
tɯ³³ ɕi³³ zɣ²¹ tɣ³³ o.
then kill eat can CRS
'This pig, I've been feeding it for only half a year, but it will be ready to be killed and eaten when celebrating the New Year.'
这头猪我才养了半年，不过到过年的时候就能杀了吃了。

In Caijia, the WHEN clauses can also denote 'while' or 'as', i.e. what is labelled as "simultaneous clauses" by Thompson et al. (2007: 254), as illustrated in the following example. We recall that the continuous marker cannot be used in WHEN clauses or relative clauses. This is evident in (15.85), as the WHEN clause 'while he was cooking' is not marked by the continuous marker $(s\gamma^{33})\ldots s\gamma^{21}$, while the main clause 'I was reading' is marked by $s\gamma^{21}$ alone.

(15.85) je²¹ tɕie⁵⁵ zɣ²¹ **tʰɔ²⁴**, ŋo³³ tsaŋ²¹ sɣ³³ se²¹.
3SG do meal moment 1SG look book CONT.PRT
'While he was cooking, I was reading.'
他做饭的时候，我在看书。

It also deserves to be mentioned that $t^{h}ɔ^{24}$ cannot be modified by demonstratives as $kɯ^{21}$ can. In the following case, $kɯ^{24}$ is modified by the distal demonstrative $mɔ^{21}$ 'that', but using $mɔ^{21}$ to modify $t^{h}ɔ^{24}$ is ungrammatical.

(15.86) tsʰe⁵⁵ sɣ²¹ neŋ²¹ mɔ²¹ **kɯ²⁴/*tʰɔ²⁴**, pɣ³³ ɣã³³ ma²¹sɿ⁵⁵.
be.out poor year that moment NEG there.be grain
'When the years of famine came, there was no grain.'
出荒年的时候，没有粮食。

This contrast might be related to the source use and the meaning of $t^{h}ɔ^{24}$. The morpheme $t^{h}ɔ^{24}$ can follow measure expressions, such as those of height, weight, length, and width, indicating rough approximation, as in (15.87). This semantically contradicts the function of demonstratives, since demonstratives usually code definiteness and specificity.

(15.87) ŋo³³ ɣã²¹ ji²¹pia⁵⁵ je²¹ toŋ³³ **tʰɔ²⁴**.
1SG have one.hundred UNIT heavy or.so
'I weigh 50 kg or so.'
我100斤左右重。

The semantic expansion from 'or so, approximation' to 'moment' is also logical. When $t^{h}ɔ^{24}$ is used after a clause expressing an event, it can be interpreted as 'around the moment X takes place'. For example, kua^{33} $neŋ^{21}$ $t^{h}ɔ^{24}$ 'when celebrating the New Year' can be understood as 'around the New Year', since celebrating the New Year usually refers to a period of several or even more than several days in China, and not just one specific day. Under such contexts, it is reasonable to argue that $t^{h}ɔ^{24}$ can be further reanalyzed as 'moment'.

By contrast, 'moment' is probably the inherent meaning of $kɯ^{21}$, while it can also denote 'hour' and 'o'clock'. Furthermore, modified by different demonstratives, it can denote 'now', i.e. $ɔ^{21}kɯ^{24}$, with the proximal demonstrative, or 'in the past', $mɔ^{21}kɯ^{24}$, with the distal demonstrative.

To summarize, Caijia time clauses can be divided into five semantic types. They are: (i) temporal sequences including the common sequence, compact sequence, and emphatic sequence; (ii) BEFORE and (iii) AFTER clauses; (iv) SINCE clauses; and finally (v) WHEN clauses. The BEFORE, AFTER, and SINCE clauses are all related to the spatial concepts from which their forms are derived. In fact, it is a very common phenomenon for spatial and temporal expressions to share the same or similar structures and markers (Thompson et al. 2007). Table 15.4 lists the schema for each type and the potential sources of their respective markers.

Table 15.4: Time clauses in Caijia.

	TYPE AND SCHEMA	MEANING	SOURCE
I	Temporal sequence (THEN)	then	tɯ³³ < 'then, just, indeed'
	Common sequence		
	[(NP₁) VP₁, (NP₂) tɯ³³ VP₂]		
	Compact sequence	once; as soon as	ʑi³³ < 'one';
	[(NP₁) ʑi³³ VP₁, (NP₂) (tɯ³³) VP₂]		tɯ³³ < 'then, just, indeed'
	Emphatic sequence	only then; not until	lɛ²¹ < ?;
	[(NP₁) VP₁, (NP₂) (lɛ²¹)tsʰɛ²¹ VP₂]		tsʰɛ²¹ < Mandarin 'only, not until'
II	BEFORE	before	tɕiŋ²¹ < 'front'
	[CLAUSE₁ tɕiŋ²¹, CLAUSE₂]		
III	AFTER	after	u³³ < 'back'
	[CLAUSE₁ u³³, CLAUSE₂]		
IV	SINCE	since	tɕie²¹ < ?; ta⁵⁵ < 'from' < 'follow'
	[tɕie²¹ta⁵⁵ CLAUSE₁, CLAUSE₂]		
V	WHEN	when	tʰɔ²⁴ < 'or so, approximation'
	[CLAUSE₁ tʰɔ²⁴/kɯ²¹, CLAUSE₂]		kɯ²¹ < 'moment, hour'

15.4.2 Consequence and cause

Consequence and cause often pair together forming a complex sentence. In this section, these two types of clauses will be discussed separately. This is because two types of marking strategies are observed. One involves marking on the consequence clause and the other marking on the cause clause. Marking on the consequence clause is related to the sequence marking, or the common sequence type, while the marking on the cause clause is related to emphasis marking, or the emphatic sequence type. See §15.4.1.1 above.

15.4.2.1 Consequence

According to what can be observed in our data, consequence in Caijia can be coded in two ways: (i) by *tɯ³³* 'then, just, indeed' or (ii) by *(lɛ²¹)tsʰɛ²¹* 'not until, only then'. Both are also used as sequence markers. (See §15.5.1 as well as §15.5.3). In both *tɯ³³*-consequence and *lɛ²¹tsʰɛ²¹*-consequence, the overtly marked consequence clause follows the non-marked cause clause.

It is reported that WHEN and CAUSE clauses may share the same marker or structure, since two temporally adjacent events can be inferred to be causally related (Thompson and Longacre 1985: 181). For example, *When he reads, he doesn't even feel hunger* can be reinterpreted as 'reading' is the cause of 'his not feeling hunger'. In a similar fashion, the sequence markers *tɯ³³* 'then, just, indeed' and *(lɛ²¹)tsʰɛ²¹* 'not until, only then' can also be used to express the causal meaning of two events in Caijia. Unlike the WHEN cause in English, in which 'when' can be interpreted as marking on the cause clause, *tɯ³³* 'then' and *(lɛ²¹)tsʰɛ²¹* 'not until, only then', contrast in that they mark the consequence clause, denoting 'thus'.

We will now look into their syntactic and semantic features.

15.4.2.1.1 *tɯ³³*-consequence

Like the sequence structure, *tɯ³³* precedes the VP in a consequence clause:

[$_{CAUSE}$[(NP$_1$) VP$_1$], $_{CONSEQUENCE}$[(NP$_2$) tɯ³³ VP$_2$]].

As mentioned right above, a causal relation can be reanalyzed out of two sequential events. Example (15.88) is a case in which the *tɯ³³*-clause can be interpreted both as the sequence clause and as the consequence clause. The tiger first saw the turtledoves and then it wanted to catch them. In other words, seeing the turtledoves caused the tiger to want to catch them. It should be mentioned that the first *tɯ³³* in italics in (15.88i) does not literally denote 'then' or 'thus', since this sentence is neither the sequence nor the consequence of its preceding sentence. The morpheme *tɯ³³* in (15.88i) is rather like an episode marker and denotes that the clause or sentence it marks has a connection of some sort with its preceding clause, which allows a certain pragmatic inference. The verb *kuɛ³³* 'go' in the angle brackets is a slip of tongue, which the speaker quickly corrected. It should thus not be considered as one of the constituents in the sentence.

(15.88) i) ɔ²¹   kʰγ⁵⁵pa³³   tɯ³³   tsaŋ³³-kɪŋ²¹   mɔ²¹
         this   tiger   then   look-see   that
         kʰɪ²¹kʰo²⁴   ji³³   tsʰo²¹,
         turtledove   one   nest

ii) **tɯ³³** <kuɛ³³> ɕiaŋ⁵⁵ kuɛ²¹ ma³³ mɔ²¹ kʰɪ²¹kʰo²⁴ zɣ̩²¹.
   then go   want   go   fetch that turtledove   eat

'The tiger saw a nest of turtledoves, and it then wanted to catch those turtledoves to eat.'

这老虎就看见一窝斑鸠，就想抓那斑鸠吃。

(*The man and the tiger*, texts)

By contrast, the following two examples can only be interpreted as consequences. In each example, the sequential relation between the two clauses is very weak and contrived. The marker *tɯ³³* only denotes 'thus' in these two cases. The context of (15.89) is that the speaker was caught in the rain and got soaked. Having no clothes to change into leads to the consequence that he decided to crawl into to the haystack to cover himself. Certainly, this consequence is not necessary or predictable, but only one of a set of possibilities.

(15.89) lɯ²¹   sɿ²¹   la²¹   pɣ³³   ɣã²⁴,   **tɯ³³** tsɔ²¹   mɔ²¹
        change   NMLZ   even   NEG   there.be/have thus   be.like that
        sɿ⁵⁵   tʰo⁵⁵   tsoŋ²¹tsʰɔ⁵⁵ɣ²¹   o.
        way   get.into haystack   CRS

'There were no clothes for changing and (I), thus, crawled into the haystack like that.'

换的（衣服）也没有，就像那样钻进麦草垛子里去了。

(*Haystack*, texts)

Similarly, the sentence below should be interpreted as 'that person is lawless and unscrupulous, because he relies on his power and influence'.

(15.90) mɔ²¹   u²¹tsʰo²⁴   ni³³   tã²¹-tɣ̩³³   je³³   ɣã³³   tɕʰyɛ̃²¹
        that   person   CLF   rely.on-obtain   3SG   have   power
        ɣã³³   sɿ²⁴,   je³³   **tɯ³³**   tã³³kʰɪŋ³³tã²¹tʰɣ⁵⁵   lɛ³³,
        have   influence   3SG   thus   lawless   CONT
        tã²¹   xɪŋ⁵⁵.
        unscrupulous very

'Relying on his power and influence, that person is thus lawless and unscrupulous.'

那个人仗着他有权有势，就无法无天，嚣张得很。

15.4.2.1.2 *(lɛ²¹)tsʰɛ²¹*-consequence

Using *lɛ²¹tsʰɛ²¹* or *tsʰɛ²¹*, in the form of

$$[_{\text{CAUSE}}[(NP_1)\ VP_1],\ _{\text{CONSEQUENCE}}[(NP_2)\ (lɛ^{21})tsʰɛ^{21}\ VP_2]],$$

is another strategy for forming consequence clauses in Caijia and another piece of evidence to show the close relation between sequence and consequence, the notion of sequence with *(lɛ²¹)tsʰɛ²¹* having been already discussed in §15.4.1.1 above. This use of *(lɛ²¹)tsʰɛ²¹*, is very similar to the use of Standard Mandarin *cái* 'only then, not until', which denotes that its previous clause is its condition, cause, or purpose (Lü Shuxiang 1999: 107).

Examples (15.91)-(15.93) illustrate two cases of *tsʰɛ²¹* and two cases of *lɛ²¹tsʰɛ²¹*. The cause clauses in these three examples are all in their emphatic forms. However, one should be aware that the emphatic meaning is not a necessary condition for forming a consequence clause via *(lɛ²¹)tsʰɛ²¹*, even though it is very common. In (15.91), the copula *sɿ³³* is used to denote emphasis, but its absence does not make the whole sentence ungrammatical in any way.

(15.91) sɿ³³ ŋo³³ kʷɔ³³sɣ³³pa²¹ sɿ⁵⁵ ŋo³³ kʷɔ³³sɣ³³,
COP 1SG teacher let 1SG attend.school
ŋo³³ **tsʰɛ²¹** yã²¹ kʰɪŋ⁵⁵koŋ⁵⁵.
1SG thus have today
'It is my teacher that encouraged me to attend school, and thus I have what I've achieved.'
是我老师让我读书，我才有今天。

Example (15.92) shows a sentence with very complicated structure. The first clause, (15.92i), is combined with a *lɛ²¹tsʰɛ²¹*-consequence clause as well as a cleft emphatic construction. The first pair of CAUSE₁-CONSEQUENCE₁ clauses, marked by the cleft/affirmative construction *sɿ³³...sɿ²¹*, i.e. 'he behaved in this way', is the cause of 'went away' with the subject 'his ex-wife' situated on the left of the cleft construction. The second clause, (15.92ii), is the consequence of the first clause (15.92i), forming the second pair of CAUSE₂-CONSEQUENCE₂ clauses in which the consequence is marked by *tsʰɛ²¹*. Furthermore, three participants are involved in this sentence: the ex-wife of the man, the man, and the woman. In (15.92ii), the first instance of the third person singular pronoun refers to the woman, while the second one refers to the man.

(15.92) i) $_{\text{CAUSE2}}$[je^{33}$_i$ la^{21}so^{55}po^{21} tɯ^{33} [sʅ^{33}
         3SG$_i$ ex-wife   just   AFF
         $_{\text{CAUSE1}}$[je^{33}$_i$ tsɔ^{21} ɔ^{21} sʅ^{55}] $_{\text{CONSEQUENCE1}}$[lɛ^{21}tsʰɛ^{21}
         3SG$_i$ be.like   this   way   thus
         ɣa^{21}-kuɛ^{33} se^{21}]]],
         walk-go   AFF.PRT
   ii) $_{\text{CONSEQUENCE2}}$[je^{33}$_{ii}$ **tsʰɛ^{21}**   py^{21} kʰã^{55} kɛ^{21} sʅ^{55} je^{33}$_i$].
         3SG$_{ii}$ thus   NEG   be.willing.to   marry   to   3SG$_i$

'The reason why his ex-wife ran away is that he'd been behaving that way, so she doesn't want to marry him.'

他大老婆就是他总这样才走掉的，她才不肯嫁给他。

As for (15.93), the construction *mɔ^{21} sʅ^{33}*. . ., equivalent to its counterpart 'it is that. . .' in English, can be understood as one of the various means of emphasis in combination with *(lɛ^{21})tsʰɛ^{21}*.

(15.93)   mɔ^{21} sʅ^{33} je^{33} nioŋ^{33} py^{33} a^{33} tǫ^{21} sʅ^{55} ŋuɛ^{21}
          that   COP   3SG   daughter   NEG   DCR   marry   to   my.family
          xa^{33}nɛ^{33},   la^{21}pia^{33} **lɛ^{21}tsʰɛ^{21}**   neŋ^{21}na^{33} lɛ^{21}
          REP.PRT   1SAP   thus   indiscreetly   ADV
          xa^{21} je^{33} kʰɯ^{21} tɕie^{55} se^{21}.
          say   3SG   several   CLF   AFF.PRT

'That's because (he) didn't marry her daughter into my family (as promised), and so I (**thus**) swore at him indiscreetly.'

那是他女儿不嫁给我家呢，老子才胡乱地说他几句。

(*Two families*, texts)

In Caijia, consequence clauses can be either marked by *tɯ^{33}* or by *(lɛ^{21})tsʰɛ^{21}*, both of which can be used to mark temporal sequence clauses. However, the markers *(lɛ^{21})tsʰɛ^{21}* and *tɯ^{33}* are used in different semantic contexts. The marker *(lɛ^{21}) tsʰɛ^{21}* emphasizes the fact that the cause conveyed in CLAUSE$_1$ is the only reason leading to the consequence conveyed in CLAUSE$_2$. In contrast, in a complex sentence with a *tɯ^{33}*-consequence clause, CLAUSE$_1$ is not necessarily the only cause of the consequence conveyed in CLAUSE$_2$.

15.4.2.2 Cause

In Caijia, cause clauses are less commonly marked than consequence clauses. In all the CAUSE-CONSEQUENCE sentences illustrated above in §15.4.2.1, the cause clauses are only optionally marked by different emphasis markers to satisfy certain semantic requirements, whereas it is always the consequence clauses that are overtly marked. Nonetheless, overtly marked cause clauses do exist. Compared with those of overtly marked consequence, such sentences adopt an inverse order for cause and consequence, i.e. CONSEQUENCE-CAUSE, with the consequence unmarked but the cause emphatically marked using the copula. Emphasis marking on the cause in a CONSEQUENCE-CAUSE sentence is obligatory. Without this marking, the consequence and the cause, simply juxtaposed, cannot be treated as one sentence, since the logical binding would be lost.

Example (15.94) shows a case in which the cause is marked by the copula $sı^{33}$, which can be used in the function of an emphatic marker as well for forming an affirmative proposition. The emphatic meaning is further reinforced by the intensifier $xa^{21}py^{33}sı^{33}$, derived from the VP 'still not be' but denoting 'definitely'.

(15.94) CONSEQUENCE[ɕi³³ tsɔ²¹ ɔ²¹ sı⁵⁵ nian³³, CAUSE[xa²¹py³³sı³³ sı³³
knife be.like this way sharp definitely COP
ŋo³³ mɔ³³ ji³³ tsʰa²¹kɯ²⁴ ma].
1SG sharpen one afternoon PRT
'The knife is as sharp as this, because it's me who has been sharpening it the whole afternoon.'
刀这么快，还不是是我磨了一下午。

In addition to this structure, the cause clause can be marked by the cleft/affirmative construction [sı³³ VP sı²¹] 'it is...that...', another form of emphasis marking derived from the copula.

(15.95) CONSEQUENCE[ŋo²⁴ tsʰı³³ mo³³ ty²¹ sı⁵⁵ ã³³],
1PL village inside obtain water drink
CAUSE[sı³³ je³³ tɯ²¹ mo³³ tɕi²¹ɯ⁵⁵ sı²¹ mẽ].
AFF 3SG at inside exert.strength AFF PRT
'We (finally) have water to drink in our village, because it is him that has been working so hard on this.'
我们村里有水喝，是他在这件事上使劲。

In conclusion, the consequence clause is more frequently found to be marked than the cause clause in Caijia. The consequence marking sentences and the cause marking sentences show different word orders, i.e. CAUSE-CONSEQUENCE with consequence marking, while CONSEQUENCE-CAUSE is used in cause marking sentences. Significantly, both of the consequence markers are also used as sequence markers, while the cause markers are copula-derived emphasis markers. See Table 15.5 for a synthesis.

Table 15.5: Consequence and cause clauses in Caijia.

Type and Schema	Meaning	Source
I Consequence	thus/so	tɯ³³ < 'then, just, indeed'
tɯ³³-consequence		
[(NP₁) VP₁, (NP₂) **tɯ³³** VP₂]		
(lɛ²¹)tsʰɛ²¹-consequence	thus	lɛ²¹ < ?;
[(NP₁) VP₁, (NP₂) **(lɛ²¹)tsʰɛ²¹** VP₂]		tsʰɛ²¹ < Mandarin 'only, not until'
II Cause	it is because	EMPH < COP sɿ³³
[Consequence, ₑₘₚₕ[Cause]]		

15.4.3 Conditional

A conditional sentence usually involves a possible condition and its effect and can be interpreted as 'if. . .then. . .' in English. It is comprised of two clauses, an *if*-clause (protasis) and a *then*-clause (apodosis) (see Bybee et al. 1994: 322, 323), with one being the condition to achieve the situation expressed in the other. A division of the binary distinction for conditionals into a binary distinction between reality and unreality has been proposed by Thompson and Longacre (1985). This distinction can be attested in many European languages, for example English and French, in which this contrast is mainly reflected by verbal morphology. For instance, the English example *If I knew her number, I could ring her up* is a present hypothetical conditional in which the verb 'know' and the auxiliary 'can' are in their past forms.

However, this binary typology does not suit Caijia, since such a contrast is not coded by any grammatical means. Therefore, this section will only focus on different strategies used to form conditional sentences in Caijia. The terms CONDITION clause and EFFECT clause will be used for convenience.

In Caijia, the conditional meaning can be realized in nine different ways. Eight of these strategies can be considered to be within the sentence; these can be grouped into EFFECT marking, CONDITION marking, and double marking. The ninth, formed by *pγ³³ sɿ³³* 'not be', is beyond the clause-level and needs to be considered along with its previous context. It is similar to 'otherwise' in English. EFFECT marking can be realized by the sequence markers *tɯ³³* 'then' and *(lɛ²¹) tsʰɛ²¹* 'only then'. CONDITION marking can be realized by the topic particle *nɛ⁵⁵* and several *if*-words, including $kʰã^{55}$ 'if', $tsʰɛ^{21}niɔ^{33}$ 'as long as', $niɔ^{33}sɿ^{33}$ 'if', $niɔ^{33}pγ^{33}sɿ^{33}$ 'if not', and $tɯ^{33}sa^{21}$ 'even if'. Double marking combines EFFECT markers with different CONDITION marking strategies. In the following sections, the Caijia conditionals will be discussed in terms of these different markers.

15.4.3.1 Sequence/effect: *tɯ³³* and *(lɛ²¹)tsʰɛ²¹*

As mentioned above in §15.5.1 and §15.5.2, both the sequence markers $tɯ^{33}$ 'then' and $(lɛ^{21})tsʰɛ^{21}$ 'not until, only then' also serve to form conditional sentences. The relation between a sequence of events and its effect is just like the relation between a sequence and its consequence. In the context of two sequential events, EVENT₁ and EVENT₂, if EVENT₂ only happens under the condition that EVENT₁ is achieved, the sequence can be considered to possess a conditional meaning. Consider a sentence in a context where dinner is ready: *We're waiting for your father to come back, and then we'll begin to have dinner*. On the one hand, having dinner follows the father's return. On the other hand, having dinner is only possible under the condition that the father comes back. Such an implication between time and condition can be observed in other languages as well (Thompson et al. 2007: 257–258). It is thus logical that Caijia might have developed a similar form to express conditional sentences.

Just as in sequence and consequence clauses, conditional sentences can be formed by either $tɯ^{33}$ 'then' or $(lɛ^{21})tsʰɛ^{21}$ 'not until, only then', marking only the effect clauses in the form of [(NP₁) VP₁, (NP₂) $tɯ^{33}$/$(lɛ^{21})tsʰɛ^{21}$ VP₂]. Moreover, the effect follows the condition clause.

15.4.3.1.1 *tɯ³³*-effect

Below are two examples of $tɯ^{33}$ forming conditional sentences. Just as for the cause and consequence sentences, it is the effect clauses that are marked in both cases. However, the $tɯ^{33}$-effect clauses can interact with other condition markers, forming double marked conditional sentences (See further discussion below).

(15.96) CONDITION[soŋ³³ kʰua²¹ ha⁵¹ o], EFFECT[nɯ³³ **tɯ³³**
       sickness be.good COMPL CRS 2SG then
       tsʰe⁵⁵-kuɛ²¹ ta⁵⁵ tso³³hɛ³³-sui³³ sɔ²¹kʷɔ³³ o ma].
       be.out-go with brother-PL play CRS PRT
       'You can go out to play with your brothers if/when you recover.'
       病好了，你就（能）出去跟你哥哥弟弟们出去玩了嘛。

(15.97) u²¹pe⁵⁵ nɯ³³ xa²¹tsɛ⁵⁵ niɔ³³ tsɔ²¹ ɔ²¹ sɿ⁵⁵ tɕie⁵⁵
afterwards 2SG still PROS be.like this way do
ŋo³³ **tɯ³³** na²¹-sɿ⁵⁵ nɯ³³.
1SG then beat-die 2SG
'Afterwards, if you (keep) behaving like this, I'll beat the living daylight out of you.'
以后你还要这样做，我就打死你。

15.4.3.1.2 *(lɛ²¹)tsʰɛ²¹*-effect

In a conditional sentence formed by *(lɛ²¹)tsʰɛ²¹*, the first clause is also the condition, while the second clause codes the effect. This marker is special: it syntactically marks the EFFECT clause, but it semantically highlights the CONDITION clause, i.e. the **only** condition which can give rise to the effect. It differs semantically from the *tɯ³³*-conditional in terms of this specific feature. In (15.98), which is extracted from a narrative text, the CONDITION₂-EFFECT₂ pair formed by *(lɛ²¹)tsʰɛ²¹* denotes 'he hadn't told the truth until I persuaded him' or 'only when I persuaded him, did he tell the truth'. The CONDITION₁-EFFECT₁ pair is embedded in a sequence of direct speech and formed with a different strategy discussed further below. It should also be mentioned that the speaker used *lɛ²¹tsʰɛ²¹* in the original text, but he confirmed that *tsʰɛ²¹* is also acceptable.

(15.98) CONDITION2[ŋo³³ xa²¹lɛ⁵⁵: "CONDITION1[nen²¹na³³ xa³³ sɿ²¹ nɛ⁵⁵],
1SG say discreetly say AFF PRT
EFFECT1[nɯ³³ tɯ³³ niɔ³³ tsɿ²¹tɕia⁵⁵ pɣ²¹ o⁵⁵]]!"
2SG then need oneself carry PRT
EFFECT2[je³³ **(lɛ²¹)tsʰɛ²¹** xa²¹-tsʰe⁵⁵ɣɯ²¹].
3SG only.then say-be.out.come
'Only after I told (him): "… (and) if you (keep) talking crazy, you'll take full responsibility", did he spill out the truth.'
我说："……乱说的话，你就要自己负责啊！"，他才说出来。
(*Two families*, texts)

Similarly, in (15.99), the only condition to carry water easily with a carrying-pole is to keep the two ends equally balanced.

(15.99) ta⁵⁵ka²¹   ta²¹   sɿ⁵⁵   niɔ³³   ta⁵⁵   mĩ²¹
         carrying-pole   carry.on.the.shoulder water   need   two   end
         ji²¹jaŋ²⁴ toŋ³³ **(lɛ²¹)tsʰɛ²¹** kʰua²¹ ta³³.
         equally   heavy only.then   good   carry.on.the.shoulder
         'Carrying water on the shoulder with a carrying-pole, only when two sides of the pole carry are equally heavy weights, does it become easy to carry.'
         扁担担水要两面一样重才好担。

We have shown that *lɛ²¹tsʰɛ²¹* commonly precedes the VP in a sentence but is preceded by the subject if and when an overt subject is present, as in (15.98). However, we also observe that *lɛ²¹tsʰɛ²¹* can precede the whole effect clause, functioning rather like a linker, linking the condition and the effect clauses:

[CONDITION[(NP₁) VP₁], **lɛ²¹tsʰɛ²¹** EFFECT[NP₂ VP₂]].

As exemplified below, *lɛ²¹tsʰɛ²¹* precedes the whole effect clause of 'the fiddle can be loud' in (15.100). Compare it with (15.98), in which it follows the subject, an adverb. Note that the modal auxiliary verb *kʰã⁵⁵* does not denote its original meaning 'be willing to'. Rather, it denotes 'more possible'.

(15.100) ŋo⁵⁵   kʰɪŋ³³   toŋ²¹toŋ²⁴,   CONDITION[niɔ³³
          1PL   pull   two-stringed.fiddle   need
          a³³   mɔ²¹   tsoŋ²¹sɔ⁵⁵tsɿ⁵⁵   ɣɯ²¹   tɕʰi²¹   pie⁵⁵
          take   that   resin   PURP   wipe   to
          mɔ²¹   tɕioŋ³³tɕioŋ³³   tɤ³³,   nɛ⁵⁵],   **lɛ²¹tsʰɛ²¹**
          that   bow   upside   PRT/INTJ   only.then
          EFFECT[ɔ²¹   toŋ²¹toŋ²⁴   kʰã⁵⁵   mia²¹].
          this   spike.fiddle   be.willing.to   be.loud
          '(When) we play the Chinese spike fiddle, (we) need to apply some resin to the bow and only by this means can the fiddle be loud.'
          我拉二胡，要拿松香来抹到那二胡弓上，这二胡才容易响。
          (*Learning to play the Chinese spike fiddle*, texts)

15.4.3.2 *nɛ⁵⁵/Ø*-condition

The third strategy to form conditional sentences in Caijia is to use the topic marker *nɛ⁵⁵* (< ?) to mark CONDITION, a cross-linguistically attested phenomenon (Haiman 1978). In (15.101), the phrase *ŋo⁵⁵ ɔ²¹ tã³³ tɤ²¹* 'our (practice of) standing chopsticks on end' is marked by *nɛ⁵⁵* and serves as the dangling topic, denoting that the description which follows is related to this activity. See also (15.27).

(15.101) ₜₒₚɪc[ŋo⁵⁵ ɔ²¹ tã³³ tʏ²¹ **nɛ⁵⁵**],
    1PL this stand chopstick PRT
    niɔ³³ pa²¹ sɿ⁵⁵ pie⁵⁵ u³³ mo³³.
    need ladle.out water to bowl Inside
    'To stand chopsticks, (one) needs to put some water into a bowl.'
    我们这立筷子呢，要往碗里舀水。
    (*Standing chopsticks on end*, texts)

The particle *nɛ⁵⁵* marks conditionals in the form of

  [ᴄᴏɴᴅɪᴛɪᴏɴ[NP₁ VP₁] nɛ⁵⁵, ᴇꜰꜰᴇᴄᴛ[NP₂ VP₂]].

In certain cases, the use of *nɛ⁵⁵* is obligatory, and without it the conditional meaning cannot be realized, as shown in (15.102)-(15.104). In (15.102), if *nɛ⁵⁵* is omitted the semantic binding between the two clauses disappears and they can be treated as two independent sentences, denoting 'It's raining. Don't come' instead of denoting 'If it's raining, don't come'.

(15.102) ᴄᴏɴᴅɪᴛɪᴏɴ[ɣɯ²¹ zɿ⁵⁵ sɿ²¹ **nɛ⁵⁵**] ᴇꜰꜰᴇᴄᴛ[nɯ³³ piɔ²⁴ ɣɯ²¹ o].
    come rain CONT PRT 2SG NEG.IMP come CRS
    'If it's raining, don't come then.'
    在下雨的话，就别来了。

In (15.103), the activity of swinging together is conditioned by the fact that someone needs to first arrive. Similar to (15.102), the omission of *nɛ⁵⁵* in (15.103) will also turn this complex sentence into two independent sentences denoting 'He will come. We'll go on the swings together'.

(15.103) je³³ ɣɯ²¹ **nɛ⁵⁵**, ŋo²⁴ ji²¹hɔ⁵⁵ na²¹tɕʰiɯ²¹ sɔ²¹kʷɔ⁵⁵.
    3SG come PRT 1PL together play.swing play
    'If he comes, we'll go on the swings together.'
    他来的话，我们一起荡秋千玩。

One more example is given in (15. 104).

(15.104) ho³³lo³³to³³, je³³   xaŋ³³ **nɛ³³**,
          owl   3SG   yell   PRT
          je³³ sɿ³³ niɔ³³   ɣɯ²¹ ka⁵⁵   sv⁵⁵   sɿ²¹ ma.
          3SG   AFF   PROSP   come   catch mouse AFF   PRT
          'If an owl hoots, (it means that) it's definitely about to catch mice.'
          猫头鹰，如果它叫呢，（表示）它是要来抓老鼠。
          (*My friend and I*, texts)

In contrast, there are contexts in which marking conditionals with *nɛ⁵⁵* is optional. In these contexts, conditional meaning is coded by other means, while conditional clauses themselves usually cannot stand alone as independent sentences. In (15.105), the effect clause is marked by *tɯ³³*. Therefore, the marker *nɛ⁵⁵* in the condition clause is optional. One should be aware that if the effect clause is not marked by *tɯ³³*, *nɛ⁵⁵* is obligatory.

(15.105) nɯ³³   pɣ²¹   tʰɣ⁵⁵   nɯ²¹   po²⁴   **nɛ⁵⁵**,   e⁵⁵,
          2SG   NEG   take.off   2SG   bundle   PRT   INTJ
          u²¹koŋ⁵⁵   **tɯ³³**   sɿ³³   nɯ³³   pɣ²¹   sɿ³³   le³³.
          next.day   just   AFF   2SG   carry AFF   PRT
          'If you don't clear yourself, it will be you who will take (the responsibility) later.'
          你不洗清你自己呢，诶，以后就是你来承担（责任）。
          (*Two families*, texts)

Example (15.106) is a case with *nɛ⁵⁵* and *lɛ²¹tsʰɛ²¹* used together. The morpheme *nɛ⁵⁵* is optional in this case.

(15.106) je³³   tsɛ²¹tsɛ²⁴   pɣ³³   ɣã²¹   koʔ¹hɔ⁵⁵   (**nɛ⁵⁵**)
          3SG   really   NEG   have   option   PRT
          lɛ²¹tsʰɛ²¹   ko³³   ŋo³³.
          only.then   look.for   1SG
          'He comes to me (for help), only if he doesn't have any options.'
          他真的没办法才找我。

In the following two examples, neither of the condition clauses can stand alone as independent sentences and the effect clauses are not overtly marked. In each of the following examples, a conditional meaning is realized by logical connections between the two clauses and the word order. Hence, in this case, the CONDITION clause must precede the EFFECT clause.

(15.107) pɣ²⁴   ã²¹   tsɣ⁵⁵   Ø,   soŋ²¹   tɕie³³me³³   ti³³   kʰua²¹?
          NEG   drink   medicine   sickness how   know   be.good
          'If (you) don't take medicine, how can your sickness be cured?'
          不喝药，病怎么会好。

(15.108) tɯ²¹   ni³³   xɪŋ⁵⁵   xɪŋ⁵⁵   kuɛ³³   Ø,   niɔ³³   zɛ²¹xuɔ²¹   se²¹.
          attract CLF   hate   very   go   PROS   get.in.trouble AFF.PRT
          'If you're much-hated, you'll definitely get in trouble.'
          太惹人恨了要惹祸的。

15.4.3.3 *kʰã⁵⁵*-condition

Interacting with the EFFECT marker *tɯ³³*, the morpheme *kʰã⁵⁵* marks the CONDITION by taking the clause initial position in a conditional sentence, denoting 'if…then…':

[kʰã⁵⁵ (NP₁) VP₁, (NP₂) tɯ³³ VP₂].

This means that in the conditional sentences formed by *kʰã⁵⁵* in (15.109), the pair of pants would fit if they were only longer. The sentence in (15.110) denotes 'I'm not afraid under the condition that you accompany me'.

(15.109) ɔ²¹   kʰɣ²⁴   ɣa³³   tsʰo²¹   mi⁵⁵   o.
          this   pants   CLF   be.short   little   CRS
          CONDITION[kʰã⁵⁵   (je²¹)   kʷɔ²¹   mi⁵⁵]   EFFECT[tɯ³³   xu²¹   seŋ³³   o].
          if   3SG   be.tall   a.little   then   fit   body   CRS
          'This pair of pants is a little short. If they were longer, they would fit.'
          这条裤子有点短了。要是（它）长点，就合身了。

(15.110) kʰã⁵⁵   nɯ²¹   ta⁵⁵   ŋo²¹   tɕie⁵⁵   ɛ²¹,
          if   you   with   1SG   do   companion
          ŋo³³   tɯ³³   pɣ³³   tsʰɿ³³   o.
          1SG   then   NEG   fear   CRS
          'If you can come to accompany me, I won't be afraid.'
          如果你跟我作伴，我就不怕了。

The morpheme *kʰã⁵⁵* is probably derived from the modal verb 'be willing to', as shown in (15.111).

(15.111) nɯ³³ pɣ²¹ **kʰã̠⁵⁵** kɛ²¹ je³³ nɛ⁵⁵
2SG NEG be.willing.to marry 3SG PRT
tɯ³³ pɣ³³ kɛ²¹ o ma.
then NEG marry CRS PRT
'If you aren't willing to marry him, just don't do that.'
你不肯嫁他的话，就不嫁了嘛。

It is quite possible that *kʰã̠⁵⁵* is cognate with *kěn* 肯 [kʰən²¹⁴] 'be willing to' in Standard Mandarin, except that *kěn* has not developed into 'if'. Even though 'be willing to' is rarely reported among the languages of the world as the source of 'if' words, it is not entirely implausible. This is because the verb *niɔ³³* 'want' is from the same semantic field as *kʰã̠⁵⁵* and is also used to form the Caijia compound 'if' word, i.e. *niɔ³³sɿ³³*, which will be discussed in the next section. In addition, there are a handful of examples in which *kʰã̠⁵⁵* can be interpreted as both 'be willing to' and 'if', as exemplified in (15.112). According to the consultant, the clause in (15.112) can be used to replace the condition clause in (15.110) and *kʰã̠⁵⁵* in this sentence can be replaced by *niɔ³³sɿ³³* 'if' as well, without a change in meaning.

(15.112) nɯ²¹ **kʰã̠⁵⁵/niɔ³³sɿ³³** ta⁵⁵ ŋo²¹ tɕie⁵⁵ ɛ²¹ . . .
2SG be.willing.to/if with 1SG do companion
'If you accompany me (LIT: with me do companion) . . .'
'You're willing to accompany me (LIT: with me do companion) . . .'
如果你跟我作伴……
你愿意跟我作伴……

It is plausible that the meaning 'if' is derived from the meaning of possibility denoted by *kʰã̠⁵⁵*, since a conditional clause also express one's supposition or assumption. In the context of the following example, *kʰã̠⁵⁵* does not denote 'be willing to' as an inanimate subject such as 'words' cannot possess the quality of willingness. In such a context, the meaning 'if' can be more easily reanalyzed. Similar to (15.112), *niɔ³³sɿ³³* can also replace *kʰã̠⁵⁵* in (15.113) without causing any semantic changes.

(15.113) ɔ²¹ kʰɯ⁵⁵-sui⁵⁵ **kʰã̠⁵⁵/niɔ³³sɿ³³** la²¹ mi⁵⁵
this word-PL be.willing.to/if be.big a.little
ŋo³³ tɯ³³ tsaŋ³³-ti²¹ to³³ o.
1SG then look-be.clear can CRS
'If the words can be larger, I can see them.'
这些字要是大点，我就能看清了。

Synchronic data are probably not sufficient to explain why a displacement is involved when the modal auxiliary 'be willing to' shifts to the condition marker 'if', namely from the pre-VP position to a clause-initial position. As can be observed in (15.113), even though the meaning 'if' can be inferred, $k^h\tilde{a}^{55}$ still occupies the pre-VP position but not the clause-initial position, as in a true $k^h\tilde{a}^{55}$-condition sentence [$k^h\tilde{a}^{55}$ (NP₁) VP₁, (NP₂) tɯ³³ VP₂]. Change of syntactic position might be related to the heavy use of pro-drop, as seen in (15.109), and reinforced by the position of the marking in impersonal constructions, as in (15.114).

(15.114) tʰɪŋ²¹koŋ⁵⁵ **kʰã⁵⁵/niɔ³³sɿ³³** ɣɯ²¹ zɿ⁵⁵ tɯ³³ kʰua²¹ o.
tomorrow if come rain then be.good CRS
'It would be good, if it rains tomorrow.'
明天下雨就好了。

It can also be observed that $k^h\tilde{a}^{55}sɿ^{33}$ 'if' is formed by analogy with $niɔ^{33}sɿ^{33}$ 'if', even if it is $k^h\tilde{a}^{55}$ that is more common, as shown below.

(15.115) **kʰã⁵⁵(sɿ³³)** ŋo³³ tsa²¹ tɯ²¹ ha⁵⁵ tɯ³³ kʰua²¹ o.
if 1SG uncle be.at here then be.good CRS
je³³ ti³³ kʰɯ⁵⁵ son²¹ se²¹.
3SG know treat sickness AFF.PRT
'It would be good if my uncle were here. He can treat diseases.'
要是我叔叔在这儿就好了。他会看病。

15.4.3.4 tsʰɛ²¹niɔ³³-condition

Denoting 'as soon as.../provided that...', the marker tsʰɛ²¹niɔ³³, a compound of tsʰɛ²¹ 'only' and niɔ³³ 'want', marks the CONDITION by occupying the clause initial position in a conditional sentence, while EFFECT is marked by different intensifiers in different contexts:

[tsʰɛ²¹niɔ³³ (NP₁) VP₁, (NP₂) ₑₘₚₕ[VP₂]].

In (15.116)-(15.118), the effect clauses are marked by different emphatic markers, i.e. tɯ³³ 'then, just, indeed' in (15.116), the cleft/affirmative construction sɿ³³ ... sɿ²¹ 'it is...that...' in (15.117) and la³³ 'also, all, even' in (15.118).

(15.116) CONDITION[tsʰɛ²¹niɔ³³ nɯ³³   py³³   tsʰɿ³³   kʰɣ³³], EFFECT[ŋo³³
         as.long.as   2SG   NEG   fear   bitter   1SG
         tɯ³³   li²¹   nɯ²¹   ta⁵⁵   ŋo²¹   kuɛ²¹   na²¹koŋ²¹].
         then   take.along 2SG   with   1SG   go   work
         'As long as you're not afraid of hardship, I'll take you to work.'
         只要你不怕苦，我就带你去打工。

(15.117) tsʰɛ²¹niɔ³³   nɯ²⁴   nian²¹tɕi⁵⁵   tsʰɿ⁵⁵   sɿ²¹
         as.long.as   2PL   age   be.light NMLZ
         tɕʰi³³tɕʰi³³kʰa³³kʰa³³ lɛ³³,   kʰua²¹   nɛ⁵⁵,
         happy   CONT   be.good PRT
         ŋo³³   sɿ³³   tɕʰi³³kʰa³³   se²¹.
         1SG   AFF   be.happy   AFF.PRT
         'As long as you young people are happy and (live) well, I'm definitely happy.'
         只要你们年轻人高高兴兴的，（过得）好呢，我就高兴。
         (New Year's visit, texts)

(15.118) tsʰɛ²¹niɔ³³   je²¹   kʰã⁵⁵   kʰua²¹kʰua²⁴   kwɔ³³sɣ³³,
         as.long.as   3SG   be.willing.to well   learn.book
         ŋo²¹   tɕie⁵⁵me⁵⁵   tɕie⁵⁵   la²¹   niɔ³³   a³³
         1SG   how   do   even   PROSP   OM
         je³³   fɣ²¹tsɿ²¹-tsʰe⁵⁵yɯ²¹.
         3SG   support-come.out
         'As long as he's willing to study hard, I'll do my utmost to support him.'
         只要他肯好好学习，我无论如何都要把他培养出来。

15.4.3.5 *niɔ³³sɿ³³*-condition

Formed by the verb *niɔ³³* 'want' and the copula *sɿ³³*, *niɔ³³sɿ³³* mirrors exactly one of the 'if' words in Standard Mandarin (as well as in many Sinitic languages), *yàoshì* 要是 [jau⁵¹ʂ̩⁵¹] 'if' < 'want-be'. Marking the CONDITION, *niɔ³³sɿ³³* can either occur in the pre-VP position or in the clause-initial position:

[niɔ³³sɿ³³ (NP₁) VP₁, (NP₂) VP₂] or

[(NP₁) niɔ³³sɿ³³ VP₁, (NP₂) VP₂].

The 'if' word *niɔ³³sɿ³³* can interact with the effect marker *tɯ³³* as well. Example (15.119) demonstrates a CONDITION clause with a pro-drop subject marked by *niɔ³³sɿ³³*. Its following EFFECT clause is marked by *tɯ³³*.

(15.119) me²¹koŋ⁵⁵ kʰua²¹-tɤ³³ ŋɔ³³ pɤ³³ kuɛ³³ ka²¹kʰɯ³³.
yesterday be.good-obtain 1SG NEG go go.to.fair
CONDITION[**niɔ³³sɿ³³** kuɛ³³] EFFECT[**tɯ³³** tɤ²¹ zɿ⁵⁵ lã²¹ lɯ⁵⁵
if go then PASS rain pour VCOMP
tsɔ²¹ ɤa²¹ sɿ⁵⁵ kɿ²⁴ tsɿ⁵⁵ sɿ²¹ o].
be.like fall water chicken CLF way CRS
'Fortunately, I didn't go to the fair yesterday. If I had gone, I would have got caught in the rain like a drenched chicken.'
昨天幸亏我没去赶场。要是去就被雨淋成落汤鸡了。

The following two examples show *niɔ³³sɿ³³* in the clause-initial and pre-VP positions, respectively. Neither of the EFFECT clauses are overtly marked.

(15.120) **niɔ³³sɿ²¹** ŋa⁵⁵ pɤ³³ tɯ²¹ pɿŋ³³, tsɿ²¹tɕia⁵⁵ kuɛ³³ xã³³.
if child NEG be.at side oneself go call
'If the child is not at home, (she needs) to call (her parents-in-law to have a meal) herself.'
要是孩子不在旁边，自己去喊（公婆吃饭）。

(15.121) nɯ³³ **niɔ³³sɿ³³** tsʰɿ³³ ŋɔ²¹ ta⁵⁵ nɯ³³ tɤ³³-kuɛ³³.
2SG if fear 1SG with 2SG go.over-go
'If you're afraid, I'll go with you.'
你要是害怕，我跟你过去。

15.4.3.6 *niɔ³³pɤ³³sɿ³³*-condition

The marker *niɔ³³pɤ³³sɿ³³* 'if not', the negated form of *niɔ³³sɿ³³*, is the only overt way to form counterfactual conditional sentences in Caijia, i.e. a supposition or hypothesis contrary to fact. This type of conditional is labelled as "imaginative conditional" by Thompson et al. (2007: 259). In a complex sentence, the Caijia counterfactual 'if' word *niɔ³³pɤ³³sɿ³³* commonly marks the CONDITION clause in the clause-initial position along with the EFFECT clause marked by *la²¹* 'even', i.e.

[niɔ³³pɤ³³sɿ³³ (NP₁) VP₁, (NP₂) la²¹ VP₂].

To be specific, *niɔ³³pɤ³³sɿ³³* marks a CONDITION which has truth value, while *la²¹* marks an EFFECT with the false value. One uses *niɔ³³pɤ³³sɿ³³* to hypothesize what could have happened (effect clause), if the condition clause were not true. The imaginative conditional counterpart in Standard Mandarin is formed by the same strategy, i.e. *yàobúshì* 要不是 [jau⁵¹pu²⁴ʂɿ⁵¹] 'want-not-be'. Let us see some examples.

In (15.122), two CONDITION clauses are chained together. CONDITION₁ is marked by *niɔ³³pɣ³³sɿ³³* 'if not', to signal that the speaker imagines, and wants the addressee to imagine too, what might have taken place in the case that the other person had not helped him dig potatoes. The EFFECT clause deals with the counterfactual result: not being able to come back home after nightfall.

(15.122) CONDITION1[**niɔ³³pɣ³³sɿ³³** je²¹ ta⁵⁵ ŋo²¹ me²¹ tsʰɿ⁵⁵po⁵⁵ nɛ⁵⁵],
    if.not   3SG with 1SG dig potato PRT
CONDITION2[sɿ⁵⁵ ŋo²¹ me³³ nɛ³³], EFFECT[me²¹ tɕiu⁵⁵ kʰɿŋ⁵⁵
let   1SG dig PRT   dig   to sky
mi²¹ la²¹ pe⁵⁵-ɪn²¹kuɛ²¹ po³³ to³³].
darken even return-back.go NEG can
'If he hadn't dug potatoes with me and let me dig (alone), I would have dug until the night fell and still couldn't have come back (home).'
要不是他帮我挖土豆呢，让我（一个人）挖呢，挖到天黑也回不来。

Counter to the EFFECT that 'I went to work', the fact is that 'I haven't been working at all', as illustrated in (15.123).

(15.123) **niɔ³³pɣ³³sɿ²¹** ŋa⁵⁵-sui⁵⁵ lɛ²¹-xɯ⁵⁵ ŋo²¹ kɣ⁵⁵ nɛ⁵⁵,
    if.not   child-PL   drag-DUR 1SG foot PRT
ŋo²¹ ta⁵⁵ tɕɪŋ²¹ **la²¹** tsʰe⁵⁵ ma²¹kʰa³³ ko²¹ tɕɪŋ²¹ o.
1SG from front even be.out door   find money CRS
'If the children hadn't been dragging me down, I would have gone to work much longer ago.'
要不是孩子们拖累我，我早就出去打工了。

The 'if' word *niɔ³³pɣ³³sɿ³³* interacts with negation in (15.124). Similarly, the EFFECT 'I wouldn't come with him' is contrary to the facts.

(15.124) **niɔ³³pɣ³³sɿ³³** je³³ pɣ³³ ti³³ xa³³ mia²¹ ŋoŋ³³,
    if.not   3SG NEG know say Lolo speech
ŋo³³ la²¹ pɣ³³ ti²¹ ta⁵⁵ je²¹ ɣɯ²¹.
1SG even NEG know with 3SG come
'If he could speak Lolo, I wouldn't have come with him.'
要不是他不会说彝话，我不会和他来。

15.4.3.7 *tɯ³³sa²¹*-concessive condition

Calquing *jiùsuàn* 就算 [tɕiu⁵¹suɛn⁵¹] 'even if' (< 'even + calculate') in Standard Mandarin, as well as in many Sinitic languages, *tɯ³³sa²¹* is a compound of the two equivalent words in Caijia: *tɯ³³* 'then, indeed' and *sa²¹* 'calculate'. Conditional sentences formed by *tɯ³³sa²¹* can be schematized as:

[tɯ³³sa²¹ (NP₁) VP₁, (NP₂) la²¹ VP₂].

Apart from the conditional meaning, *tɯ³³sa²¹* also denotes a concessive meaning 'even if', as does *jiùsuàn* in Standard Mandarin. See the examples below.

(15.125) pɣ³³   xa²¹   ji²¹pia⁵⁵   o,   **tɯ³³sa²¹**   nɯ³³   a³³
          NEG   say   one.hundred   CRS   even.if   2SG   take
          ŋoŋ²¹pia⁵⁵   la²¹   ŋo³³   pɣ³³   mã²¹   sɿ⁵⁵   nɯ³³.
          five.hundred   even   1SG   NEG   sell   to   2SG
          'Even if you give 500 yuan, I won't sell (it) to you, let alone 100.'
          不说一百了，就算你给五百我也不卖给你。

(15.126) **tɯ³³sa²¹**   nɯ³³   ko²¹   je²¹   ta⁵⁵   ŋo²¹   xa³³
          even.if   2SG   find   3SG   with   1SG   say
          la²¹   nɯ³³   tʰɣ³³   po²⁴   po³³   to³³
          even   2SG   take.off   bundle   NEG   can
          'Even if you find him to intercede (for you) with me, you won't escape from taking responsibility.
          就算你找他跟我说情，你也脱不了干系。

15.4.3.8 *pɣ³³sɿ³³*-condition

A compound of the negator *pɣ³³* and the copula *sɿ³³*, the *pɣ³³sɿ³³*-condition in Caijia is unlike the other types of conditionals presented above. Syntactically, *pɣ³³sɿ³³* must co-occur with the clause final particle *nɛ⁵⁵*. Its functions already lie beyond the bounds of clause linking, since sentences formed with *pɣ³³sɿ³³* can stand alone but still involve conditional meaning. The configuration of a sentence with *pɣ³³sɿ³³* can be schematized as:

[pɣ³³sɿ³³ nɛ³³, (NP) VP].

Semantically, *pɣ³³sɿ³³* is closely related to previous context and it can be understood as a negated anaphoric element, simply interpreted as 'otherwise, not so, if not' in English. As such, it serves to connect the utterances in question and ensure discourse cohesion. Moreover, *pɣ³³sɿ³³* is semantically similar to *niɔ³³pɣ³³sɿ³³* 'if not'. If *niɔ³³pɣ³³sɿ³³* is considered counterfactual, *pɣ³³sɿ³³* is used to express what is contrary to the event denoted in the prior context.

Let us examine (15.127) so as to better understand how *pɣ³³sɿ³³* is involved with expressing a condition. In (15.127ii), the speaker expresses his desire for longer sunny days after a long rainy period. The *pɣ³³sɿ³³*-sentence in (15.127iii) denotes 'If not, it will be very damp', namely if the speaker's expectation is not fulfilled. In other words, the possibility of dampness arises under the condition that the speaker's expectation, that the period of sunny days should last longer, is not realized. To be specific, *pɣ³³sɿ³³ nɛ⁵⁵*, should be interpreted as 'if it is not like **this**' or 'if it is not **so**', where '**this**' or '**so**' refers back to the condition expressed earlier in the context of the sentence, i.e. 'it needs to be sunny longer' in the case of (15.127). This is the reason it is claimed above that *pɣ³³sɿ³³* possesses anaphoric semantic features. Lü (2019) argues that *sɿ³³* is cognate with the copula *shì* in Standard Mandarin, which is used to be the demonstrative/anaphoric pronoun 'this' in Archaic Chinese and this use of *sɿ³³* might turn out to be a retention of the demonstrative/anaphoric pronoun. The form *pɣ³³sɿ³³* always implies a previous condition.

(15.127) i) ɣɯ²¹   ɔ²¹sɿ³³   tie³³   ni²⁴   sɿ²¹   zɿ⁵⁵,
             come   this.way   many   day   MOD   rain
        ii) niɔ³³tɣ³³   ta³³   tɣ²¹ko⁵⁵   o.
             must   be.sunny long   CRS
        iii) **pɣ³³   sɿ³³   nɛ³³**, EFFECT[nɯ²¹   lɯ⁵⁵   pɣ³³   sɿ³³   o].
             NEG   COP   PRT   damp   VCOMP   NEG   COP   CRS
        'It was raining for such a long time and it should be sunny for a longer time. **Otherwise**, it will be very damp.'
        下了这么久的雨，必须晴久一点。不然，潮得不行。

Similarly, *pɣ³³sɿ³³* in (15.128) refers to if 'I don't repay him', which will lead to the effect that '(I feel) I'm unworthy of his kindness'.

(15.128) je²¹   tɕie⁵⁵   kʰua²¹   tɯ²¹   ŋo³³   tɣ³³   ja²¹,
         3SG   do   goodness   at   1SG   upside   EXP
         [...] niɔ³³   kuɛ²¹   tsɣ²¹   ni³³   tɕiaŋ²¹tsɯ²¹   mi⁵⁵.
                need   go   return   3   favor   a.little
         pɣ³³   sɿ³³   nɛ³³, ti²¹-pɣ³³-tɣ³³   ni³³.
         NEG   COP   PRT   face-NEG-obtain   3
         'He helped me before. . . . I must return him the favor. **Otherwise**, I'll be unworthy of his kindness.'
         他对我有过恩，……（我）要去还他人情。不然的话，对不住人家。

One more example is given below.

(15.129) ŋo³³ niɔ³³ tsʰeŋ³³   ɣã²¹   ɪŋ⁵⁵soŋ²¹ tʰɔ²⁴
          1SG need take.advantage.of there.be sun   moment
          a³³ to²⁴ tsaŋ²¹-li²¹ ɣɯ²¹   ka⁵⁵-ka³³.
          OM   bean pick.up-pick PURP   dry.in.the.sun-be.dry
          pɣ³³ sɿ³³ nɛ³³, kua³³ kʰɯ²¹ koŋ⁵⁵ ha⁵⁵,
          NEG   COP   PRT   pass   several day   COMPL
          tsʰɿ³³ ɣɯ²¹ zɿ⁵⁵ ɣɯ²¹, ɣɯ²¹ tɕiu⁵⁵ lɔ²⁴kɯ²¹
          fear   come rain INC   come   to   when
          la²¹   pɣ³³ tiu³³u³³].
          event NEG   know

'I need to take advantage of the moment when there is the sunshine to pick the beans and let them dry in the sun. **Otherwise**, several days later it will begin to rain and who knows until when it (will continue) raining.'
我要趁有太阳的时候把豆角摘了晒干。不然，过几天下起雨来，下到什么时候也不知道。

It is extremely difficult to judge the nature of *pɣ³³sɿ³³* in conditional sentences, since there are no efficient diagnostic tests that can be adopted to do this. On the one hand, *pɣ³³ sɿ³³* itself is a VP, and *pɣ³³sɿ³³ nɛ³³* can be thus treated as a dependent clause, i.e. *pɣ³³sɿ³³ nɛ³³* is a CONDITION clause. On the other hand, *pɣ³³sɿ³³* can be treated as a fossilized form, as shown in examples (15.127)-(15.129), due to its specific environment of use, namely an adversative context implying 'what would happen if something were not done', and the fact that it has an unchangeable form.

15.4.3.9 Summary

Caijia uses various methods to express conditional meanings. In a nutshell, 'if' words are the most common way to code conditions. The contrast between reality and unreality does not play an important role in forming most conditional sentences in Caijia. The only overt way to code a counterfactual EFFECT is to use the negated 'if' word *niɔ³³pɣ³³sɿ³³* to mark its CONDITION. In addition, despite the fact that the *pɣ³³sɿ³³*-condition transcends the function of clause-level linking, it shares some semantic similarities with *niɔ³³pɣ³³sɿ³³* with respect to counterfactuality, namely it conveys what kind of event would have resulted in an imagined situation contrary to the event to which it anaphorically refers. There are EFFECT markers in addition to CONDITION markers. Caijia is a solid case that shows the correlation between time and condition. The two EFFECT markers are derived from the sequence markers *tɯ³³* 'then' and *lɛ²¹tsʰɛ²¹* 'only then'. Modal auxiliaries

$kʰã^{55}$ 'be willing to' and $niɔ^{33}$ 'want, need', as well as the copula $sɿ^{33}$, are important sources of 'if' words. See Table 15.6 below for a synthesis.

Table 15.6: Conditionals in Caijia.

	Type and Schema	Meaning	Source
I	$tɯ^{33}$-sequence/effect [(NP$_1$) VP$_1$, (NP$_2$) **$tɯ^{33}$** VP$_2$]	'then'	$tɯ^{33}$ < 'then, just, indeed'
II	$(lɛ^{21})tsʰɛ^{21}$-sequence/effect [(NP$_1$) VP$_1$, (NP$_2$) **$(lɛ^{21})tsʰɛ^{21}$** VP$_2$] [(NP$_1$) VP$_1$, **$lɛ^{21}tsʰɛ^{21}$** (NP$_2$) VP$_2$]	'only then'	$lɛ^{21}$ < ?; $tsʰɛ^{21}$ < Mandarin 'only, not until'
III	$nɛ^{55}/\emptyset$-condition [(NP$_1$) VP$_1$ **$nɛ^{55}$**, (NP$_2$) VP$_2$] [(NP$_1$) VP$_1$ **$\emptyset$**, (NP$_2$) VP$_2$]	'if'	$nɛ^{55}$ < TOP
IV	$kʰã^{55}$-condition [**$kʰã^{55}$** (NP$_1$) VP$_1$, (NP$_2$) **$tɯ^{33}$** VP$_2$]	'if'	$kʰã^{55}$ < Mandarin 'be willing to'
V	$tsʰɛ^{21}niɔ^{33}$-condition [**$tsʰɛ^{21}niɔ^{33}$** (NP$_1$) VP$_1$, (NP$_2$) $_{EMPH}$[VP$_2$]]	'as long as'	$tsʰɛ^{21}$ < Mandarin 'only, not until' $niɔ^{33}$ < 'want'
VI	$niɔ^{33}sɿ^{33}$-condition [(NP$_1$) **$niɔ^{33}sɿ^{33}$** VP$_1$, (NP$_2$) VP$_2$] [**$niɔ^{33}sɿ^{33}$** (NP$_1$) VP$_1$, (NP$_2$) VP$_2$]	'if'	$niɔ^{33}$ < 'want' $sɿ^{33}$ < copula
VII	$niɔ^{33}pɣ^{33}sɿ^{33}$-condition (counterfactual) [**$niɔ^{33}pɣ^{33}sɿ^{33}$** (NP$_1$) VP$_1$, (NP$_2$) **la^{33}** VP$_2$]	'if'	$niɔ^{33}$ < 'want'; $pɣ^{33}$ < negator $sɿ^{33}$ < copula
VIII	$tɯ^{33}sa^{21}$-concessive condition [**$tɯ^{33}sa^{21}$** (NP$_1$) VP$_1$, (NP$_2$) VP$_2$]	'even if'	$tɯ^{33}$ < 'then, just, indeed' sa^{21} < 'calculate'
IX	$pɣ^{33}sɿ^{33}$-condition [**$pɣ^{33}sɿ^{33}$** $nɛ^{55}$, (NP) VP]	'if not'	$pɣ^{33}$ < negator $sɿ^{33}$ < copula

15.4.4 Concession

A concessive sentence includes two contrasting clauses. It is used to concede or admit the fact expressed in the dependent clause, regardless of what is asserted in the main clause. In English, it is marked by the conjunctions 'although' or 'though', for instance, *Although Kim is extraordinarily talented, she is too arrogant*. Concessive clauses can be divided into definite and indefinite clauses (Thompson et al. 2007: 262). Definite concessive clauses refer to those expressing semantic definiteness marked by a marker like 'though' or 'although' in English, which can usually be paraphrased as 'despite the fact that. . .'. Indefinite concessive clauses refer to those containing unspecified elements, such as indefinite or interrogative pronouns, and equivalent to the clauses marked by 'no matter. . .' in English (Thompson et al. 2007: 262, 263). In Caijia, two major strategies are used to form concessive sentences: *pɤ²¹kuɪŋ⁵⁵* and *tɯ³³*. The marker *pɤ²¹kuɪŋ⁵⁵* can form both indefinite and definite concessive clauses, whereas *tɯ³³* only forms definite clauses. We will now examine how these two markers form concessive sentences.

15.4.4.1 *pɤ²¹kuɪŋ⁵⁵*-concessive

The marker *pɤ²¹kuɪŋ⁵⁵* is actually formed by the negator *pɤ³³* and the verb *kuɪŋ⁵⁵* 'be in charge, discipline, be concerned/regarded', which mirrors or is cognate with the indefinite concessive marker *bùguǎn* 不管 [pu⁵¹kuɛn²¹⁴] 'no matter' (< 'not be in charge') in Standard Mandarin. The lexical use of *kuɪŋ⁵⁵* is exemplified below.

(15.130) ŋuɛ²¹   ŋa⁵⁵   ni³³   tɯ³³sɿ³³   pɤ³³   tsʰɿ³³ ŋo³³   [. . .]
          my.family child   CLF   just   NEG   fear   1SG
          niɔ³³   je²¹   pa⁵⁵   tsʰɛ²¹   **kuɪŋ⁵⁵**   to³³.
          need   3SG   father only   be.in.charge   can
          'My child does not obey me. . . . Only his father can discipline him.'
          我家孩子不怕我，……要他爸才能管得了。

(15.131) [. . .]   a³³   je²¹   pie⁵⁵-xɯ⁵⁵   **pɤ²¹**   **kuɪŋ⁵⁵**   [. . .]
                    OM   3SG   throw-down   NEG   be.in.charge
          '(His parents) walked away on him.'
          （他父母）把他丢下不管。

The concessive marker *pɤ²¹kuɪŋ⁵⁵* is used to form both indefinite and definite types of concessive clauses. However, these do not fully share the same structure. When *pɤ²¹kuɪŋ⁵⁵* precedes the concessive clause, it is used along with interrogative *in situ* pronouns, denoting the absolute indefinite, 'no matter/Q-ever. . .'. When *pɤ²¹kuɪŋ⁵⁵* follows the concessive clause, it can either be indefinite or definite, denoting 'no matter/Q-ever. . .' or 'although/though. . .', as schematized below.

    Indefinite: [**pɤ²¹kuɪŋ⁵⁵** (NP₁) VP₁, (NP₂) VP₂]

    Definite/Indefinite: [(NP₁) VP₁ **pɤ²¹kuɪŋ⁵⁵**, (NP₂) VP₂]

Note that Standard Mandarin *bùguǎn* can only be used to form the indefinite type of concessive clauses.

The semantic connection between the concessive *pɤ²¹kuɪŋ⁵⁵* 'no matter/although' and its lexical source *pɤ²¹ kuɪŋ⁵⁵* 'not be in charge' is quite transparent.

The VP *pɣ²¹kuɪŋ⁵⁵* 'not be concerned/disregarded' can be interpreted as 'regardless of. . .' or 'not concerning. . .'. In English, the concessive clause in *Although we disagree with each other sometimes, we're still friends* can be interpreted as 'regardless of' or 'not concerning the fact that we sometimes disagree with each other'.

15.4.4.1.1 No matter (Indefinite)

Indefinite concessive clauses signal a meaning equivalent to 'no matter' and typically interact with indefinite pronouns or question words. In Caijia, when associating with question words, the clause-initial *pɣ²¹kuɪŋ⁵⁵* immediately signals indefiniteness. On the other hand, whether or not the clause-final *pɣ²¹kuɪŋ⁵⁵* denotes 'no matter' depends on the context in which it is used. In both of the following examples, *pɣ²¹kuɪŋ⁵⁵* is used along with 'what'. In both cases, *pɣ²¹kuɪŋ⁵⁵* can be moved to the clause-final position without giving rise to any semantic change. As shown in (15.132), the concessive clause with the clause-initial *pɣ²¹kuɪŋ⁵⁵* in (15.132a) can be replaced by the one with the clause-final *pɣ²¹kuɪŋ⁵⁵* in (15.132b). One more indefinite concessive sentence with clause-initial *pɣ²¹kuɪŋ⁵⁵* is given in (5.133).

(15.132) a. **pɣ²¹kuɪŋ⁵⁵** nɯ²¹ tɕie⁵⁵ mɔ⁵⁵, kʰɪŋ⁵⁵koŋ⁵⁵ ŋɔ³³
no.matter 2SG do what today 1SG
tɯ³³sɿ³³ niɔ³³ ɣa²¹ kʰɯ⁵⁵loŋ²¹ kuɛ³³.
indeed need walk Hezhang_PLACENAME go
'Whatever you do, I must go to Hezhang today.'
不管你干什么，今天我就是要去赫章。

b. nɯ²¹ tɕie⁵⁵ mɔ⁵⁵ **pɣ²¹kuɪŋ⁵⁵**, [. . .]
2SG do what no.matter
'Whatever you do, . . .'
不管你干什么，……．

(15.133) ŋɔ³³ pa³³ ti²¹ ta⁵⁵ tsɣ²¹zɣ⁵⁵ kʰɯ⁵⁵ soŋ²¹.
1SG grandfather know for domestic.animal treat sickness
pɣ²¹kuɪŋ⁵⁵ sɿ²¹mɔ⁵⁵ tsɣ²¹zɣ⁵⁵ soŋ³³,
no.matter what domestic.animal be.sick
ŋɔ³³ la³³ tie²¹sɔ⁵⁵ tiu³³u²¹ mi⁵⁵.
1SG also somewhat know a.little
'My grandfather knows how to treat domestic animals. (Due to his influence,) no matter what kind of domestic animals get sick, I can, to some extent, treat them.'
我爷爷会给牲口看病，不管什么牲口生病，我也多少知道一点。

15.4.4.1.2 Although

By contrast, the semantic definiteness of concessive clauses can be paraphrased as 'in spite of the fact that. . .', as proposed by Thompson et al. (2007: 262). In Caijia, if the clause-final *pɣ²¹kuɪŋ⁵⁵* does not interact with an interrogative pronoun it codes a definite concessive clause. Furthermore, placing *pɣ²¹kuɪŋ⁵⁵* in the clause-initial position in a definite clause is ungrammatical. Compare the two sentences in (15.134). First, note that the concessive clause in (15.134a) can indeed be paraphrased as 'in spite of the fact that the child is suffering that illness'. Second, note that using the clause-initial *pɣ²¹kuɪŋ⁵⁵* to mark the clause is entirely unacceptable, in (15.134b).

(15.134) a. mɔ²¹ ŋa⁵⁵ ni²¹ tɣ³³ mɔ²⁴ tsoŋ⁵⁵ soŋ²¹
         that child CLF suffer that type illness
      pɣ²¹kuɪŋ⁵⁵ nɛ⁵⁵, lɔ²¹kɯ²⁴ la²¹ tsaŋ²¹-xɯ⁵⁵
      although PRT when all look-up
      je³³ ŋa²¹tʰɻ³³tʰɻ²⁴ lɛ⁵⁵.
      3SG tough CONT
      'Although that child is suffering from that (severe) illness, he looks very tough.'
      尽管那孩子得了那种病，但什么时候都看着他精精神神的。

    b. *__pɣ²¹kuɪŋ⁵⁵__ mɔ²¹ ŋa⁵⁵ ni²¹ tɣ³³
      although that child CLF suffer
      mɔ²⁴ tsoŋ⁵⁵ soŋ²¹ [. . .]
      that type illness
      'Although that child is suffering from that (severe) illness, . . .'
      尽管那孩子得了那种病，……

Two more examples are given below. In the same fashion, the clause-initial marking is ungrammatical in both cases.

(15.135) nɯ²¹ ta⁵⁵ ŋo²¹ tsɣ³³me²¹tsɿ⁵⁵ ha⁵⁵ pɣ²¹kuɪŋ⁵⁵ nɛ⁵⁵,
      2SG for 1SG apologize COMPL although PRT
      ŋo³³ la²¹ pɣ³³ ti²¹ ta⁵⁵ nɯ²¹ tɕie⁵⁵ ɛ³³tɯ²¹.
      1SG also NEG know with 2SG do friend
      'Although you apologized to me, I won't be friends with you.'
      尽管你跟我道了歉呢，我也不跟你做朋友。

(15.136) mɔ²¹ ŋa⁵⁵ ni³³ ɕiɔ²⁴tɔ²⁴ kʰua²¹ xıŋ⁵⁵.
that child CLF filial.ethnics be.good very
sı³³ je³³ u³³ʑi³³ la²¹ pɣ²¹kuɪŋ⁵⁵,
COP 3SG step-mother all although
je³³ a³³ tsɔ³³ je³³ ʑi³³ sı²¹ tsı²¹.
3SG DCR be.like 3SG mother way raise
'That child is a person of great filial piety. Even though (she) is his stepmother, he supports her as if (she's) his biological mother.'
那个孩子孝道好得很。尽管是他后妈，他也把（她）像亲妈一样养着。

15.4.4.2 *tɯ³³*-concessive

The other strategy for forming concessive clauses in Caijia is to use the intensifier *tɯ³³* 'just, then, indeed'; placing it in a position preceding the VP in a clause:

[(NP₁) **tɯ³³** VP₁, (NP₂) VP₂].

Semantically, *tɯ³³* can only form definite concessive clauses. Marked by *tɯ³³*, concessive clauses cannot stand alone as independent sentences. Similarly, the *tɯ³³*-concessive can also be paraphrased as 'in spite of the fact that. . .'. We have shown that the marker *tɯ³³* can be used to mark sequence and consequence, as well as effect clauses. Only the function of the *tɯ³³*-concessive appears in CLAUSE₁, while *tɯ³³* marks CLAUSE₂ for the other three types of dependent clauses.

The clause in (15.137) illustrated below can be used to replace the *pɣ²¹kuɪŋ⁵⁵* concessive clause in (15.136) without changing the meaning.

(15.137) **tɯ³³** sı³³ je³³ u³³ʑi³³, [. . .]
just COP 3SG step-mother
'Although (she) is his step-mother, . . .'
尽管是他后妈，……

The following examples are two complete sentences, each of which contains a *tɯ³³*-concessive which semantically contrasts with the main clause. In (15.138), the fact that 'he is old', combined with his lack of travel experience, creates a semantic contrast, since one probably expects a person of old age to have a lot of travel experience. The concessive clause and the main clause share the same subject.

(15.138) je³³ niã²¹tɕi⁵⁵ **tɯ³³** la²¹, je³³
          3SG   age   just   big   3SG
          pɣ³³-tɣ³³ ɣa²¹   la²⁴ kuɛ³³ ja²¹.
          NEG-PFV   walk   where go   EXP
          'Although he's indeed old, but he never went anywhere.'
          他年纪虽大，但没去过什么地方。

The example below shows two clauses with different subjects.

(15.139) tsɣ⁵⁵ **tɯ²¹** kʰɣ³³, kʰua²¹tɯ³³ nɯ³³ la³³ niɔ³³ ã²¹   mi⁵⁵.
          medicine just   bitter anyhow   2SG   all   need   drink a.little
          'Although the medicine is bitter, you need, anyhow, to drink a little.'
          药虽苦，好歹你都要喝点。

Moreover, in certain contexts, *tɯ³³* can also be interpreted as 'even though', which is more emphatic than 'although'. This must be related with the source meaning of *tɯ³³*, i.e. as an intensifier. See example (15.140) below.

(15.140) ŋo⁵⁵   ɕyɔ²¹ɕiɔ²⁴ mo³³   kʷɔ³³sɣ³³pa³³ tɯ³³
          1PL   school   inside teacher   just
          sɿ³³   ŋo³³   tɔ²¹ ni²⁴. [...] tsɔ²¹   ɔ²¹   sɿ⁵⁵
          COP   1SG   lone CLF   resemble this way
          tɯ³³   soŋ²¹   la²¹ pɣ³³ ɣɯ²¹   pɣ³³ tɣ³³.
          although be.sick even NEG   come   NEG   can
          'In our school, I'm the only teacher. . . . Therefore, even though I'm sick, I must come (to work).'
          我们学校里，老师就是我一个。……所以，即便生病也都要来。

In conclusion, Caijia concessive clauses are formed using the two markers *pɣ²¹kuŋ⁵⁵* and *tɯ³³*. Derived from the negated VP 'not be concerned, be disregarded', *pɣ²¹kuŋ⁵⁵* is related to the Mandarin *bùguǎn*. Different interpretations can occur due to the position of *pɣ²¹kuŋ⁵⁵* in a clause. When it is clause-initial, *pɣ²¹kuŋ⁵⁵* forms an indefinite concessive, as *bùguǎn* does in Standard Mandarin. However, when *pɣ²¹kuŋ⁵⁵* is clause-final, the clause can be either indefinite or definite. As for the marker *tɯ³³*, it is probably derived from the meaning 'just, indeed' and not the sequence meaning 'then' of the same word. We propose this source because the emphatic meaning still persists in certain contexts, as in (15.140). Unlike *pɣ²¹kuŋ⁵⁵*, the *tɯ³³*-concessive clauses are all definite. See Table 15.7.

Table 15.7: Concessive clauses in Caijia.

Type and Schema	Meaning	Source
I pɣ²¹kuɪŋ⁵⁵-concessive		
Indefinite	'no matter'	pɣ²¹ < negator
[pɣ²¹kuɪŋ⁵⁵ (NP₁) VP₁, (NP₂) VP₂]		kuɪŋ⁵⁵ < Mandarin 'be concerned'
(In)definite	'no matter/although'	
[(NP₁) VP₁ **pɣ²¹kuɪŋ⁵⁵**, (NP₂) VP₂]		
II **tɯ³³**-concessive	'although'	tɯ³³ < 'just, indeed, then'
[(NP₁) **tɯ³³** VP₁, (NP₂) VP₂]		

15.4.5 Substitutive clauses (preferred option)

Substitutive clauses refer to those that are formed by 'instead of' or 'rather than' (Thompson et al. 2007: 263). For example, *I returned what I ordered on Amazon rather than keep it*. Caijia possesses a similar type of clause, which is used in irrealis contexts and should be more specifically interpreted as 'would rather...than', for instance, *I'd rather return it than keep it*. This kind of clause is usually classified as *xuǎnzé fùjù* 选择复句 'complex sentence of presenting a preferable alternative' in the tradition of Chinese linguistics, since a 'rather...than' substitutive sentence comprises two options with one preferred over the other. In Caijia, substitutive clauses can be formed in two ways:

i. [(NPi) ɣã³³tɕʰi²¹ VP1, (NPi) pɣ³³lɛ²¹/neŋ²¹kɯ²⁴ VP2];
    [ɣã³³tɕʰi²¹ (NP1) VP1, pɣ³³lɛ²¹/neŋ²¹kɯ²⁴ (NP2) VP2];

ii. [(NPi) neŋ²¹kɯ²⁴ VP1, (NPi) NEG[VP2]].

First, one can use *ɣã³³tɕʰi²¹...pɣ³³ lɛ²¹/neŋ²¹kɯ²⁴...* with the first conjunction, *ɣã³³tɕʰi²¹*, marking the non-preferred option, and the second conjunction, *pɣ³³ lɛ²¹* or *neŋ²¹kɯ²⁴*, marking the preferred option. The sources of *ɣã³³tɕʰi²¹* and *neŋ²¹kɯ²⁴* are unclear, while *pɣ³³ lɛ²¹* is formed by the negator and the verb *lɛ²¹* 'reach' denoting 'be inferior to', which is also the strategy used to form comparisons of inferiority (see Chapter 9). When compared with *pɣ³³ lɛ²¹*, *neŋ²¹kɯ²⁴* is semantically more emphatic, as shown below.

(15.141) nɯ³³   **ɣã²¹tɕʰi²⁴**   kɣ³³   tseŋ²¹   nɛ⁵⁵,   **pɣ³³**   **lɛ²¹**   kɯ²¹   mɛ³³.
         2SG   rather.than   sit   boat   PRT   NEG   reach   ride   horse
         'You'd be better off riding a horse rather than taking a boat.'
         你与其坐船，不如骑马。

(15.142) **ɣã³³tɕʰi²¹** tsɔ²¹ ɔ²¹sɿ⁵⁵ jaŋ²⁴
rather.than be.like this.way manner
nen²¹kɯ²⁴ kuɛ²¹ li²¹xun³³ la.
rather go divorce PRT
'You'd be better off having a divorce, rather than being like this.'
与其像这样，宁可去离婚。

Examples (15.141) and (15.142) show cases where the preferred and the non-preferred clauses share the same subject. When dealing with two clauses with different subjects, both *ɣã³³tɕʰi²¹* and *pɣ³³lɛ²¹/nen²¹kɯ²⁴* precede the clauses they mark, as schematized above. See the example below.

(15.143) **ɣã³³tɕʰi²¹** nɯ³³ kuɛ²¹ [**pɣ³³ lɛ²¹**]/[**nen²¹kɯ²⁴**] ŋo³³ kuɛ²¹.
rather.than 2SG go NEG reach/rather 1SG go
'It's better that I go rather than you go.'
与其你去，不如我去。

Second, one can also use *nen²¹kɯ²⁴*… to mark the preferred option when the non-preferred option is in its negated form. In this construction, the preferred option precedes the non-preferred one. In (15.144), both (15.144a) and (15.144b) can interact with the preferred option 'we make a detour' marked by *nen²¹kɯ²⁴*, in the form of [(NP$_i$) nen²¹kɯ²⁴ VP$_1$, (NP$_i$) $_{NEG}$[VP$_2$]]. The clause in (15.144a) illustrates a case of imperative negation, while the one in (15.144b) is a case of post-VP modal negation.

(15.144) i) ŋo⁵⁵ **nen²¹kɯ²⁴** pa²¹ hɔ³³ mi⁵⁵ ɣa²¹,
1PL rather detour road a.little walk

a. **piɔ²⁴** to³³ ni²¹ hm̩⁵⁵ ma²¹sɿ⁵⁵.
NEG.IMP step 3 POSS crop

b. to³³ ni³³ ma²¹sɿ⁵⁵ **pɣ³³ tɣ³³**.
step 3 crop NEG can
'We'd better make a detour rather than (pass through by) trampling on other people's crops.'
我们宁可绕路走，也别/不能踩别人的庄稼。

The example below is a case of standard negation. One can observe that *la³³* 'all, also, even' is used here to highlight the non-preferred option. Using an intensifier to emphasize the non-preferred option in a substitutive sentence is commonly observed.

(15.145) je³³ xa³³ **neŋ²¹kɯ²⁴** sı⁵⁵, **la³³** **pɣ³³** kuɛ³³ kɛ³³
3SG say rather die even NEG go marry
mɔ²¹ u²¹tsʰo²⁴ ni³³.
that person CLF
'She said (she) would rather die than get married to that person.'
她说宁可死也不嫁给那个人。

In sum, a Caijia substitutive sentence is used to express the opposition of two options with one singled out as the preference of the speaker or the subject with respect to the other. These constructions are particularly used in irrealis contexts. See Table 15.8 for all the schemata.

Table 15.8: Substitutive clauses in Caijia.

	Type and Schema	Meaning	Source
I	[(NP$_i$) ɣā³³tɕʰi²¹ VP$_1$, (NP$_i$) pɣ³³lɛ²¹ VP$_2$]	'rather...than'	ɣā³³tɕʰi²¹ < ?
	[(NP$_i$) ɣā³³tɕʰi²¹ VP$_1$, (NP$_i$) **neŋ²¹kɯ²⁴** VP$_2$]		neŋ²¹kɯ²⁴ < ?
	[ɣā³³tɕʰi²¹ (NP$_1$) VP$_1$, **pɣ³³lɛ²¹** (NP$_2$) VP$_2$]		pɣ³³lɛ²¹ < 'not reach'
	[ɣā³³tɕʰi²¹ (NP$_1$) VP$_1$, **neŋ²¹kɯ²⁴** (NP$_2$) VP$_2$]		
II	[(NP$_i$) **neŋ²¹kɯ²⁴** VP$_1$, (NP$_i$) $_{NEG}$[VP$_2$]]	'rather...than'	

15.4.6 Tail-head linkage

Tail-head linkage is a device used for maintaining cohesion between successive paragraphs, "i.e. something mentioned in the last sentence of the preceding paragraph is referred to by means of back-reference in an adverbial clause in the following paragraph" (Thompson et al. 2007: 273). Here the term 'paragraph' refers to a coherent stretch of discourse larger than a sentence but smaller than the whole discourse (Thompson et al. 2007: 272). As opposed to the constructions that have been presented above in this chapter, this kind of linkage occurs above the sentence level.

This phenomenon is widely attested in Caijia narratives and procedural discourses. Let us see two excerpts, one from a narrative and one from a procedural discourse. Each excerpt contains four successive sentences and all the tail-head parts are highlighted in boldface. It is consistently the VP of the preceding sentence that is repeated to initiate the following sentence.

Narrative: *The man and the stone*

(15.146)

1 mɔ²¹   tsa³³to²¹   po⁵⁵   tɯ³³   ji³³tɕia²¹xuɔ⁵⁵
   that   stone   CLF   then   suddenly
   a³³   pi²¹   **mo⁵⁵-xɯ⁵⁵**   o.
   OM   mouth shut-up   CRS
   'The stone suddenly shut its mouth.'
   那石头就一下子把嘴闭上了。

2 **mo⁵⁵-xɯ⁵⁵**, je³³   ɔ²¹   so⁵⁵   kʰɪŋ⁵⁵-pɣ²¹-tsʰe⁵⁵ɣɯ²¹   o⁵⁵.
   shut-up   3SG   this   hand   pull-NEG-come.out   PRT
   'After the mouth shut, he couldn't pull his hand (from its mouth).'
   闭上（以后），他这手就抽出不来了。

3 kʰɪŋ³³-pɣ²¹-tsʰe⁵⁵ɣɯ²¹   sɿ⁵⁵,   koŋ⁵⁵koŋ⁵⁵   tɯ²¹   mɔ³³
   pull-NEG-come.out   PRT   every.day   then   that
   tsa³³tɔ²¹   pɪŋ³³   **tã²¹-xɯ⁵⁵**   o.
   stone   side   stand-DUR   CRS
   '(He) couldn't pull his hand out and (he) was standing beside the stone every day ever after.'
   抽不出来呢，每天就在那石头边站着。

4 ɛ   **tã²¹-xɯ⁵⁵**   nɛ⁵⁵,   je³³   ɔ²¹   so⁵⁵po²⁴   ni³³
   INTJ stand-DUR   PRT   3SG   this wife   CLF
   lɔ²⁴koŋ⁵⁵   la²¹   tɕie⁵⁵   zɣ²¹   mi⁵⁵
   every.day   all   do   meal   a.little
   soŋ³³-ɣɯ²¹   sɿ⁵⁵   je²¹   zɣ²¹.
   deliver-come   give/let   3SG   eat
   '(He) was standing (there), and his wife made a meal every day and brought him the meal to eat.'
   站着呢，他的老婆每天都做饭送来给他吃。
   …

Even though tail-head linkage is very common, it is not obligatory. As shown in (15.147-1) and (15.147-2), the VP *pa²¹ sɿ⁵⁵ pie⁵⁵ u³³ mo³³* 'ladle out some water to a bowl' is not repeated to initiate (15.147-2). The repetition only begins in (15.147-3).

Procedural discourse: *Standing chopsticks on end*
(15.147)
1 mɔ³³   tã³³   tɣ²¹,   nɛ⁵⁵, niɔ³³ pa²¹   sı⁵⁵   pie⁵⁵
   that   stand   chopstick INTJ   need   ladle.out water   to
   u³³   mo³³.
   bowl   inside
   'For standing chopsticks, (you) need to ladle out some water and put it into a bowl.'
   那立筷子啊，要舀水刀碗里。

2 nɯ³³   a³³   u³³   ti²¹-xɯ⁵⁵.
   2SG   OM   bowl   place-DUR
   'You set down the bowl firmly.'
   你把碗放着。

3 a⁵⁵   u²¹   ti²¹-xɯ⁵⁵   nɛ⁵⁵,   a³³   tɣ²¹   sa³³   pʰe³³
   OM   bowl   place-DUR   PRT   take   chopstick three   CLF
   ɣɯ²¹   tã³³   tɣ²¹   nɛ⁵⁵   tɯ³³   xã⁵⁵   o   mẽ.
   PURP   stand chopstick   PRT   then   yell   CRS   PRT
   'You position the bowl firmly, then you take three chopsticks to stand them (in the water) and then you talk (to the ghost).'
   把碗放着呢，拿三根筷子来立呢，就（跟鬼魂）喊嘛。

4 xã⁵⁵   nɛ⁵⁵, "əu   a,   nɯ³³   sı³³   la²¹to³³
   yell   PRT   INTJ   INTJ   2SG   COP   old
   u²¹tsʰo²¹   lɔ²¹ni⁵⁵?..."
   person   who
   '(You) talk (to the ghost): "Which dead person are you?"...'
   喊呢，哦，"你是哪位老人？"……
   …

15.5 Conclusion

This chapter has surveyed the strategies for complementation, coordination, and adverbial subordination in Caijia.

Canonical complementation is zero marked in Caijia.

Argument conjunction is realized by the coordinator/conjunction *ta⁵⁵* (< 'with' < 'follow'); a widely attested grammaticalization pathway in Sinitic. Clausal conjunction is only overtly marked, usually by correlative coordinators and for a specific semantic purpose, including the emphatic conjunction equivalent to

English 'not only...but also...' and the comparative correlative conjunction 'the more...the more'. Disjunctive coordination can be divided into standard disjunction 'or', interrogative disjunction 'or', and emphatic disjunction 'either...or'. These forms of disjunctive coordination are all coded in different ways. There are two contrastive coordinators: $tu^{33}sŋ^{33}$ (< 'indeed be') and $ɕia^{33}ti^{33}\gamma uɯ^{21}$ (< 'it turns out that...'). They can either denote adversative or concessive meanings.

We have presented five types of adverbial clauses in Caijia: (i) time, (ii) consequence and cause, (iii) conditional, (iv) concessive, and (v) substitutive. It is observed that time and space concepts often share the same coding in Caijia. Time and consequence, counterfactuality, as well as condition are all closely related in Caijia. The same markers are found to overlap in these three domains. It has also been ascertained that the morpheme tu^{33} 'just, indeed, then, although' plays a very important role in forming complex sentences. It is used in adversative coordination, sequence clauses, consequence and conditional effect clauses, as well as in concessive clauses. Finally, a large portion of the dependent clause markers found in Caijia are cognate with or mirror the general Sinitic ones.

Chapter 16
Conclusion

It has been almost four decades since the Caijia language was officially reported for the first time in 1982 by the Language Team of Bureau of Ethnic Identification in Bijie, yet this language has nevertheless remained under-described and understudied. The present work has provided the first detailed grammar of the Xingfa variety of Caijia, covering its sound system, word formation strategies, parts of speech, and syntax over fifteen chapters.

In addition to Bo Wenze's (2004) preliminary work on the Caijia consonant inventory, which represents a mixed version of the Xingfa and Songlin varieties, we found a previously unrecorded series of consonants, the retroflex plosives [ṭ, ṭʰ, ḍ], and the lateral retroflex [l͡ɖ]. We have also noted several syllabic consonants that were missing in the rime inventory in Bo Wenze (2004), including [ɣ̍], [m̥n̥] and [h̥m̥]. Another discovery is that voiced plosives and affricates are in the process of devocalization. They often surface as their voiceless counterparts, especially in connected speech. Both tone sandhi and tone change exist in Caijia. We have outlined several sandhi rules in Caijia, while both Bo Wenze and LTBEIB (1982) claim that tone sandhi is not attested in Caijia. Nonetheless, Caijia tone sandhi demands more research, since certain sandhi patterns remain a mystery. Notably, tone change is used to derive plural personal pronouns and to derive diminutive forms of nouns.

Throughout this grammar, we have shown that Caijia presents many common grammatical features attested in East and Southeast Asian languages (Matisoff 2019), for example, compounds, quadrisyllabic idiomatic expressions or elaborate expressions, lack of inflection, a classifier system, a strong relationship between nominalization and relativization, pro-drop or ellipsis, grammaticalization of verbs, and adversative passives. It has thus been argued that Caijia shares many similarities with Sinitic languages.

However, in addition to common areal features, Caijia also presents other special features. On the one hand, Caijia is an SVO language with prenominal modifiers, such as possessives, demonstratives, and relatives, but it also has postnominal classifier phrases [N NUM CLF]. While the general Sinitic order is prenominal modification, the verb-medial languages of [N NUM CLF] in the East and Southeast Asian area often possess postnominal demonstratives, such as Bai, Thai and Khmer.

As pointed out by Matisoff (2019: XII), reduplication is commonly attested in East and Southeast Asian languages. However, verbal and nominal reduplication are not at all systematic in Caijia.

Caijia is a language possessing an abundant set of numeral classifiers. Similar to many languages with numeral classifiers, classification in Caijia is based on animacy, physical properties, and functions, as well as the inherent nature of entities. It is worth mentioning that Caijia uses special classifiers to categorize human nouns on the basis of kinship.

The most frequently used classifier bo^{55}, derived from the noun bo^{55} 'fruit', has developed into a nominalizer. In this latter function, it follows emotion verbs or adjectives in the form of [V-bo^{55}] denoting 'the feeling of X'. When bo^{55} follows other types of verbs, such as action verbs, the form [V-bo^{55}] can be used as the object of the verb $\gamma\tilde{a}^{21}$ 'have, there be', along with the post-VP 'can' modal do^{33} in the form of [$\gamma\tilde{a}^{21}$ [V-bo^{55}] do^{33}] to express 'something is not worth being done' or 'there is no necessity to do something'.

Localizers are used in Caijia to code spatial relations. In Sinitic languages, monosyllabic localizers are not usually autonomous, while those in Caijia are nominal.

Caijia is a language in which the lexical verb $s1^{55}$ 'give' has already lost its lexical status. The typical ditransitive construction is formed by the verb a^{33} 'take' with the recipient argument marked by the dative preposition $s1^{55}$ (< 'give') in the form of [a^{33} THEME $s1^{55}$ RECIPIENT]. This form is the source from which the compound causative verb $a^{21}s1^{55}$ 'let' is derived. It has also developed into a passive agent marker.

The other passive agent marker, $d\gamma^{33}$, can be used to form both agentful and agentless passives, schematicized as [$d\gamma^{33}$ (NP$_A$) VP]. We have shown that the passive marker $d\gamma^{33}$ is probably cognate with ZHUO 着 'suffer, hit the target' in Middle Chinese.

There are three different object marking constructions in Caijia. One of these is the most common structural type attested in Sinitic languages, with the object marker a^{33} marking the direct object. The other two constructions, with the differential cross-reference marker a^{33} on the VP, are rarely reported in the literature on Chinese linguistics. Both the object marker and the cross-reference marker are derived from the verb a^{33} 'take', the most common lexical source for object markers in Sinitic languages. Despite having the same lexical source, we have argued that these two markers are derived from two different serial verb constructions.

It is a widespread phenomenon that locative verbs in East and Southeast Asian languages are used to mark progressive or continuous aspect. Despite this areal 'pressure', Caijia has developed another strategy to mark continuousness. The affirmative or cleft construction, which can denote epistemic certainty, is used to express an on-going action or state in the form of [$s1^{33}$ VP $s1^{21}$], which can be regarded as a language internal innovation.

The modal auxiliary $k^h\tilde{a}^{55}$ 'be willing to' is commonly used to express one's willingness. It extends to express situational possibility denoting 'more possible to'. It has undergone the process of demodalization, allowing it to code frequentative aspect. It has also developed into an *if*-word marking conditionals.

The lexical verb *tsʰı³³* 'fear' is used to express epistemic possibility.

The modal uses of ACQUIRE verbs are widely attested in East and Southeast Asian languages and both pre-VP and post-VP ACQUIRE can be used to express different types of possibility (Enfield 2003). In Caijia, the post-VP modal *ty³³* '< acquire, get' is mainly used to denote participant-external modalities, including deontic permission, a speaker's weak desire with respect to another participant (which is probably an extended meaning of deontic permission), and situational possibility. ACQUIRE verbs can also denote participant-internal possibility in some languages in East and Southeast Asia, such as, Xiang, Lahu, Lao, and Khmer (van der Auwera, Kehayov and Vittrant 2009: 292). By contrast, participant-internal possibility can be expressed by the other post-VP can modal *do³³* '< achieve, arrive'. The pre-VP *ty³³* only co-occurs with the post-VP *do³³* in the form of [ty³³ VP do³³], which is often reduced to [VP do³³], coding possibility for controllable events. Possibility expressed by [(ty³³) VP do³³] and [VP do³³] is often related to a participant's inner or intrinsic capacity. Only the latter, [VP do³³], can be used for uncontrollable events. In comparison, when the post-VP *ty³³* is used to denote possibility, the participant's inner or intrinsic capacity is usually not involved. It is not rare that ACQUIRE verbs develop into a complementizer introducing extent or manner complements in Sinitic languages (Enfield 2003), but the ACQUIRE verb *ty³³* has not developed such a function. Extent and manner complementation is realized via the complementizer *lɯ⁵⁵*, whose source is opaque.

As can be observed from what has been discussed above, grammaticalization and polysemy are fascinating domains for future exploration in Caijia.

Caijia is a dying language. The present grammar is not only the first global description of its grammatical system, but also a documentation, which we hope can be considered as the major contribution of this research work. Even though the inclusion of elicited data is inevitable, we have tried our utmost to illustrate the language with as many examples as possible extracted from spontaneous data in order to present the reality of Caijia. This work, thus, provides reliable linguistic data not only for further areal typological studies on East and Southeast Asian languages, but also provides valuable insight into the diversity of the languages of the area. While Caijia presents many common areal features, there are also a large number of features that are specific, if not unique, to this language.

Text 1

The man and the tiger

(1) mɔ²¹kɯ⁵⁵   ɣã²¹   u²¹tsʰo²⁴   fɛ⁵¹   sɿ³³.
    that.moment there.be person   family   CONT
    'There was once a family of persons.'
    以前，有家人。

(2) tsʰɛ²¹   sɿ³³   ta⁵⁵   tɕie⁵⁵   tɕie⁵⁵   ji²¹   ɔ⁵⁵.
    only   COP   two   CLF   do   one   house
    'It was only two members (that made up) this family.'
    只有两口人。

(3) nɛ⁵⁵,   je³³   ɔ²¹   ʑi³³   ni³³   nɛ⁵⁵,   ni³³tsɿ³³   pɣ³³   kʰua²¹.
    INTJ   3SG   this mother   CLF   TOP   eye   NEG   be.good
    'As for the mother, she was half-blind.'
    他这个妈妈呢，眼睛不好。

(4) je³³   ɔ²¹   tsɿ⁵⁵   ni³³   nɛ⁵⁵   koŋ⁵⁵koŋ⁵⁵   kuɛ²¹   tɔ⁵⁵   sɔ⁵⁵   mã²¹.
    INTJ   this son   CLF   TOP   every.day   go   chop   tree   sell
    'He went to chop wood to sell every day.'
    她这儿子呢，天天去砍柴卖。

(5) ai²¹!   ji²¹   koŋ⁵⁵   tɔ⁵⁵-ɣɯ²¹   ji²¹   koŋ⁵⁵   mã²¹   nɛ⁵⁵,
    INTJ   one   day   chop-come   one   day   sell   TOP
    tsʰɛ²¹   lʷɔ³³   je²¹   ta⁵⁵   tɕie⁵⁵   zɣ²¹.
    only   suffice   3SG   two   CLF   eat
    'One day for wood chopping and one day for wood selling. (He worked in this way and earned just) enough money for them to live on.'
    唉！一天砍回来，（再）一天卖，才够他们（母子）俩吃。

(6) ɣã²¹   ji²¹   koŋ⁵⁵,   je³³   kuɛ²¹   tɔ⁵⁵   sɔ⁵⁵   sɿ³³.
    there.be one   day   3SG   go   chop   tree   PRT
    'One day, he went to chop wood.'
    有一天，他去砍柴。

(7) ɔ²¹   kʰɣ⁵⁵pa³³ tɯ³³   tsaŋ³³-kɪŋ²¹ mɔ²¹ kʰɪ²¹kʰo²⁴   ji³³ tsʰo²¹,
    this   tiger   then   look-see   that turtledove   one   nest
    tɯ³³   <kuɛ³³>   ɕiaŋ⁵⁵ kuɛ²¹ ma³³ mɔ²¹ kʰɪ²¹kʰo²⁴   zɣ²¹.
    then   go   want   go   fetch that turtledove   eat
    'The tiger saw a nest of turtledoves, and it then wanted to catch those turtledoves to eat.'
    这老虎就看见一窝斑鸠，就想抓那斑鸠吃。

(8) nɛ⁵⁵   mɔ²¹   kʰɪ²¹kʰo²⁴   nɛ⁵⁵ tɯ²¹ mɔ²¹ sɔ⁵⁵ tsɣ²¹ tɣ³³.
    INTJ   that   turtledove   TOP   be.at that tree CLF   upside
    'The turtledove was up in the tree.'
    那斑鸠呢，在树上。

(9) mɔ²¹ sɔ⁵⁵tɕi²¹tɕi²⁴   nɛ⁵⁵   mɔ²¹   xɪŋ⁵⁵.
    that branch   TOP   be.thin very
    'The branch was very thin.'
    那树枝细得很。

(10) ɔ²¹   kʰɣ⁵⁵pa³³ ɕiaŋ⁵⁵ kuɛ²¹ ma²¹ nɛ⁵⁵, mɔ²¹ sɔ⁵⁵tɕi²⁴ ji²¹tɕia⁵⁵xʷɔ²⁴
     this   tiger   want   go   fetch PRT   that branch   suddenly
     tsɿ⁵⁵-kuɛ²¹ nɛ⁵⁵, je³³ tɯ³³   niɔ³³ <ɣa³³> lɪŋ³³-tɕie²¹ ŋã²¹ kuɛ³³.
     break-go   PRT   3SG   then   PROSP fall   roll-go.down cliff go
     'The tiger wanted to catch (the turtledoves), (but) if the branch suddenly broke, it would roll off the cliff.'
     这老虎想去抓，（可）那树枝一下子断了呢，它就要滚到山崖下去了。

(11) tɕɪŋ³³   tsaŋ³³.
     just   look
     '(The tiger) just watched.'
     只是看着。

(12) ta³³ to²¹to⁵⁵ tɕɪŋ³³ tsaŋ³³ mɔ²¹ kʰɪ²¹kʰo²⁴   ji³³ tsʰo²¹.
     lift head   just   watch   that turtledove   one   nest
     '(The tiger) raised its head and just watched the nest of turtledoves.'
     抬头光看着那窝斑鸠。

(13) so⁵⁵ nɛ⁵⁵ pa²¹-xɯ⁵⁵ mɔ²¹ sɔ⁵⁵ kɤ⁵⁵, tɯ⁵⁵ pɤ²¹
     hand PRT   cling.to-DUR that tree foot then NEG
     kã⁵⁵ tɤ²¹   so⁵⁵ tsa²¹ kuɛ²¹ ma³³ mɔ²¹ kʰɪ²¹kʰo²⁴.
     dare stretch.out hand go.up PURP catch that turtledove
     'The paws (of the tiger) were clinging to the tree trunk, but it didn't dare to stretch out to catch the turtledove.'
     （老虎的）手呢扒着那个树干，就是不敢伸手上去抓那斑鸠。

(14) tɔ⁵⁵ sɔ⁵⁵ ɔ²¹   la²¹ tso⁵⁵   ni³³ tɯ³³ tsaŋ³³-kɪŋ³³
     chop tree this big   elder.brother CLF   then look-see
     ɔ²¹   kʰɤ⁵⁵pa³³ tɯ²¹   ma²⁴.
     this tiger   be.at there
     'The big brother who was chopping wood saw the tiger.'
     砍柴这大哥就看见这只老虎在那儿。

(15) je³³ ɔ²¹ la²¹ tso⁵⁵   ni³³ sɿ³³ xã²¹-tɕie⁵⁵
     chop tree big   elder.brother CLF   then look-see
     sɿ⁵⁵pie²¹hɛ⁵⁵ la²¹ tso⁵⁵.
     Wang.family   big   elder.brother
     'This big brother is called the big brother of the Wang family.'
     这个大哥是叫王家大哥。

(16) nɛ⁵⁵, ɔ²¹   sɿ⁵⁵pie²¹   la²¹ tso⁵⁵   tɯ²¹ ta⁵⁵ mɔ²¹
     INTJ   this Wang.family big   elder.brother then with that
     kʰɤ⁵⁵pa³³ xa³³: "a³³jo³³ a,   mɔ²¹ tsʰɛ²¹ sɿ³³ ji²¹mi⁵⁵mi⁵⁵.
     tiger   say   INTJ   PRT that only   COP   little
     'This big brother of the Wang family then said to the tiger: "My! That's almost nothing.'
     这王大哥就跟那老虎说："哎呀！那才是一小点点。

(17) nɯ³³ kuɛ²¹ ma³³   je²¹ tɕie⁵⁵mɔ⁵⁵?   ai²¹, mɔ²¹ sɔ⁵⁵tɕi²¹tɕi²⁴
     2SG   go   catch 3SG   do.what   INTJ   that branch
     nɛ⁵⁵, mɔ²¹ lɯ⁵⁵   mɔ³³sɿ³³ e,   nɯ³³ tsa²¹-kuɛ²¹, tsɿ⁵⁵-kuɛ²¹
     PRT   thin VCOMP very   PRT 2SG   go.up-go   break-go
     mɔ²¹ kɯ²⁴   nɛ⁵⁵ nɯ³³ tɯ³³ ɣa³³-tɕie³³ ŋã²¹ kuɛ²¹ o.
     that moment PRT   2SG   then fall-go.down cliff go   CRS
     'What do you catch it for? The branch is so thin and if you climb up and the branch breaks, you will fall off the cliff.'
     你去抓它干嘛？哎，那树枝呢，细得不行，你上去，断了的话，你就摔到崖下面去了。

(18) <nɯ³³ a³³ je²¹> nɯ³³ pɣ²¹so⁵⁵ je³³ la³³.
    2SG   OM 3SG 2SG   let.go   3SG PRT
    'You leave it alone.'
    你放过它吧！

(19) ɣɯ²¹! ŋo³³ ta⁵⁵ nɯ³³ xa³³.
    come 1SG with 2SG say
    'Come here! Let me tell you (something).'
    来！我跟你说。

(20) nɛ⁵⁵, ŋo⁵⁵ ti³³mĩ²¹ mɔ²¹ pʰɪŋ²¹ mo³³ e, ɣã²¹
    INTJ 1PL opposite.side that flatland inside PRT there.be
    la²¹ li²⁴ kʷɔ²¹.
    big pig CLF
    'There's a big pig in the flatland opposite us.'
    我们对面那个坪子里，有头大猪。

(21) ei⁵¹ nɯ³³ kuɛ³³ a³³ mɔ²¹ la²¹ li²⁴ kʷɔ²¹ ka³³-kuɛ³³ nɛ⁵⁵, <nɯ³³>
    INTJ 2SG go OM that big pig CLF catch-go PRT 2SG
    lʷɔ³³ nɯ²¹ zɣ²¹ kʰɯ³³ koŋ⁵⁵ o. mɔ²⁴ tsoŋ⁵⁵ nɯ³³ pɣ³³ ti²¹
    suffice 2SG eat several day CRS that kind 2SG NEG know
    tɕie⁵⁵, nɯ³³ niɔ³³ tɕɪŋ³³ tɯ²¹ ha⁵⁵ a³³ ɔ²¹ ɕie²¹mi⁵⁵mi⁵⁵."
    do 2SG want just at place take this little.thing
    'If you snatch that pig, that will last you a few days. (Instead of) doing that, you're here to catch this little thing!"'
    诶！你去把那头大猪抓走，够你吃几天了。那种你不知道做，竟在这儿抓这小东西！"

(22) tsɔ²¹ ɔ²¹sɿ⁵⁵ ta⁵⁵ je³³ xa²¹ sɿ³³.
    resemble this.way with 3SG say PRT
    '(The big brother of the Wang family) said so to it.'
    像这样跟它说。

(23) je³³ tɯ³³ <kuɛ³³> tsɛ²¹tsɛ²⁴ kuɛ³³ a³³ mɔ²¹ la²¹ li²⁴ kʷɔ²¹
 3SG then go really go OM that big pig CLF
 ka²¹-xɯ⁵⁵ kuɛ²¹ o.
 catch-up go CRS
 'It then really went to snatch that big pig.'
 它就真的去把那头大猪抓走了。

(24) ka²¹-xɯ⁵⁵ kuɛ²¹, je³³ tɯ³³ a³³ mɔ²¹ la²¹ li²⁴ kʷɔ²¹ tɯ³³
 catch-up go 3SG then take that big pig CLF then
 kuɛ²¹ zɣ²¹ kʰɯ²¹ koŋ⁵⁵.
 PURP eat several day
 'It snatched (the big pig) and it ate the big pig for several days.'
 抓走了呢，它就拿那头大猪去吃了几天。

(25) zɣ²¹ kʰɯ²¹ koŋ⁵⁵ nɛ⁵⁵, je³³ sɿ³³ na²¹zɿ³³ ɔ³³kʷɔ³³ ai²¹,
 eat several day PRT 3SG COP appreciate INTJ INTJ
 sɿ⁵⁵pie²¹ la²¹ tso⁵⁵ xa⁵⁵nɛ⁵⁵, je³³ tɯ³³ ɔ³³ mɔ²¹
 Wang big elder.brother PRT 3SG then keep that
 li²¹to⁵⁵to⁵⁵ po⁵⁵.
 pig.head CLF
 '(The tiger) ate (the pig) for several days and it was to thank the big brother of the Wang family, it kept the pig head.'
 吃了几天呢，它是要谢谢，这个，王大哥，它就留下那个猪头。

(26) ɔ³³ li²¹to⁵⁵to⁵⁵ po⁵⁵ nɛ⁵⁵, soŋ²¹ sɿ⁵⁵ mɔ²¹ sɿ⁵⁵pie²¹ la²¹
 keep pig.head CLF PRT send to that Wang big
 tso⁵⁵ kuɛ²¹ zɣ²¹ xa²¹.
 elder.brother PURP eat PRT
 '(The tiger) kept the pig head and sent it to the big brother of the Wang family to eat.'
 留了猪头呢，送去给王大哥吃。

(27) ai⁵⁵ soŋ³³-kuɛ²¹ nɛ⁵⁵, tsaŋ³³-kɿŋ²¹ je²¹ ta⁵⁵ tɕie⁵⁵
 INTJ send-go PRT look-see 3SG two CLF
 nɛ⁵⁵ tsɔ³³nie²¹ xɿŋ⁵⁵.
 PRT be.pathetic very
 '(The tiger) brought (the pig head to him) and saw that he and his mother was living a very poor life.'
 唉，送去呢，看见他们母子俩可怜得很。

(28) je³³   mɔ²¹   ʑi³³   ni³³   la³³   ni³³tsɿ³³   pɣ³³   kʰua²¹   nɛ⁵⁵,
     3SG   that   mother   CLF   also   eye   NEG   be.good PRT
     je³³   tɯ³³   ta⁵⁵   je³³   xa³³: "ai³³ja³³,   nɛ⁵⁵   la²¹   tso⁵⁵
     3SG   then   with   3SG   say   INTJ   INTJ   big   elder.brother
     a,   nɯ³³   pɣ²¹   pia⁵⁵   so⁵⁵po²⁴   ni³³   la²¹?"
     PRT   2SG   NEG   marry   wife   CLF   Q
     'Seeing that his mother couldn't see well, it then said to him: "Big brother, (why) don't you get married?" '
     他妈妈眼睛也不好，它就跟他说："哎呀，大哥，你不讨个老婆吗？"

(29) "ai³³jəu³³!   ŋɔ²¹   ɔ⁵⁵ʑi²¹   tsɔ²¹   ɔ²¹sɿ⁵⁵.   ŋɔ²¹   ta⁵⁵
     INTJ   1SG   family   resemble   this.way   1SG   from
     la²⁴   yɯ²¹   pia⁵⁵   so⁵⁵po²¹?   lɔ²⁴ni³³   kʰã³³   kɛ²¹   ŋɔ³³?
     where   PURP   marry   wife   who   will   marry 1SG
     ' "My family is (poor) like this. Where can I find a wife? Who is willing to marry me?" '
     "哎呦！我家里像这样。我从哪去讨老婆呢？谁愿意嫁给我呢？"

(30) "ai²¹ja²¹!   ŋɔ²¹   ta⁵⁵   nɯ²¹   tsʰe⁵⁵   tsɣ²¹ji⁵⁵   ji³³   kʷɔ²¹   e.
     INTJ   1SG   for   2SG   come.out   idea   one   CLF   PRT
     ' "Hey! Let me give you an idea!'
     "哎呦！我给你出个主意！

(31) lɔ²⁴koŋ⁵⁵   ni³³   niu²¹   so⁵⁵po²¹   ta⁵⁵   ma²⁴   kua³³   nɛ⁵⁵,   nɯ³³   ɣa³³
     when   3   greet   wife   from   there pass   PRT   2sg   go
     tɕiŋ²¹mĩ³³   mo³³kʷɔ³³   ti²¹ka²⁴   mo³³   kuɛ³³   kɣ²¹-xɯ⁵⁵.   nɛ⁵⁵,   ŋɔ³³
     front   that   fork   inside go   sit-DUR   INTJ   1SG
     tɯ³³   kuɛ²¹   ta⁵⁵   nɯ²¹   ti²¹   ji³³   ni³³."
     then   go   for   2SG   rob   one   CLF
     'When someday someone greets his wife and passes by, you go to the fork (of the road) and wait there. I'll snatch a wife for you." '
     哪天人家迎亲从那儿过，你去前面，那个，垭口那儿坐着（等我），我去给你抢一个。"

(32) ei²¹,   ɣã²¹   ji²¹   koŋ⁵⁵   sɿ²¹,   tsɛ²¹tsɛ²⁴   ni³³   niu²¹   so⁵⁵po²¹
     INTJ   there.be   one   day   CONT   really   3   greet   wife
     ta⁵⁵   ma²⁴   kua³³   o.
     from   there pass   CRS
     'One day, someone really greeted his wife and passed by.'
     有一天呢，真的（有人）迎亲从那儿经过。

(33) niu²¹ so⁵⁵po²¹ ta⁵⁵ ma²⁴ kua²¹ sɿ²¹, je³³ tɯ³³ sɿ⁵⁵ mɔ²¹
     greet wife   from there pass CONT 3SG then let that
     la²¹ tso⁵⁵   ni³³ ɣa³³ tɕiŋ²¹mĩ³³ mɔ³³kʷɔ³³ ti²¹ka²⁴
     big elder.brother CLF walk front   that   fork
     tɣ³³   kuɛ³³ kɣ²¹-xɯ⁵⁵ sɿ²¹.
     upside go   sit-DUR   CONT
     'When (they) were passing by, it then asked the big brother to wait ahead at the fork of the road.'
     迎亲的从那儿过的时候，它就让那大哥在前面垭口那儿等着。

(34) je⁵⁵ mɔ²⁴-sui⁵⁵ niu²¹ so⁵⁵po²¹ tɕiu²¹ ma²⁴ je³³ tɯ³³
     3PL that-PL   greet wife   arrive there 3SG then
     tɕiɔ²¹-tsʰe⁵⁵ɣɯ²¹ tɯ³³ a³³ mɔ²¹ ɕiŋ²¹ so⁵⁵po²¹ ni³³ ji²¹tɕia⁵⁵xʷɔ³³
     jump-come.out   then OM that new wife   CLF suddenly
     tɯ³³ ta²¹-xɯ⁵⁵ tɯ³³ tsʰɔ²¹-tɣ³³ mɔ²¹ ai²¹ lian²⁴ tɣ³³,
     then lift-up   then face-obtain that INTJ slope upside
     tɯ³³ ɣa³³ mɔ²¹kʷɔ²¹ ti²¹ka²⁴ mɔ³³.
     then walk that   fork   inside
     'When those greeting the bride arrived there, it suddenly jumped out and then grasped the bride running toward the slope to go to the fork of the road.'
     他们那些迎亲的一到那儿，它就跳出来，就把新娘子一下子就抬走了，朝着梁子上（跑），就去垭口那里了。

(35) mɔ²¹ la²¹ tso⁵⁵   ni³³ tɯ³³ tɯ²¹ ma²⁴ a³³ je²¹ poŋ²¹
     that big elder.brother CLF then at   there with 3SG stick
     tɔ⁵⁵ na³³ na³³ na³³ na³³ na³³ na³³ na³³ na²¹ lɛ⁵⁵.
     CLF hit hit hit hit hit hit hit hit CONT
     'The big brother was there (pretending to) fight (the tiger) with his stick.'
     那个大哥就在那儿，用他的棍子打呀打呀打呀打地。

(36) <je³³ je³³> xun²¹na³³ je³³ na²¹ sɿ³³, je³³ tɯ³³ a³³ ɕiŋ²¹
     3SG 3SG   at.random 3SG hit CONT 3SG then OM new
     so⁵⁵po²⁴ ni³³ pɣ²¹ pie⁵⁵ <mɔ²¹ mɔ²¹ mɔ²¹> ei²¹ je³³ mɔ²¹
     wife   CLF put to   that that that INTJ 3SG that
     la²¹ tso⁵⁵   ni³³ tɕiŋ²¹ o.
     big elder.brother CLF front CRS
     '(While) he was fighting vaguely, it (= the tiger) put the bride down in front of the big brother.'
     他胡乱打的时候，老虎就把新娘子放到那大哥面前了。

(37) ai⁵⁵ mɔ²¹ la²¹ tso⁵⁵ ni³³ tɯ³³ a³³ li²¹-pe³³m²¹
INTJ that big elder.brother CLF then DCR bring-turn.home
kuɛ²¹ tɕie⁵⁵ so⁵⁵po²¹ o.
PURP do wife CRS
'The big brother then brought (the bride) back home and (she) became his wife.'
哎！那大哥就（把她）领回家做老婆了。

(38) ai²¹! u²¹so⁵⁵ ɔ²¹ fɛ⁵¹hɛ²¹ tɯ³³ pɣ²¹ kʰã⁵⁵ pɣ²¹so⁵⁵.
INTJ afterwards this family then NEG be.willing.to let.go
'Afterwards this family couldn't accept that (the bride became the wife of the brother of the Wang family).'
唉！后来，这家人就不肯撒手。

(39) ɔ²¹ niu²¹ so⁵⁵po²¹ ɔ²⁴ fɛ⁵⁵ tɯ³³ pɣ²¹ kʰã⁵⁵ pɣ²¹so⁵⁵
this greet wife this family then NEG be.willing.to let.go
sɿ³³, tɯ³³ kuɛ³³ ɣa³³ kua³³tɣ³³ kuɛ³³ lɛ³³ je³³.
CONT then go walk court go sue 3SG
'The family who greeted the bride (that day) wouldn't back down on (the lost bride) and went to the local court to sue him.'
娶亲这家就不愿意放手，就去官上告他。

(40) je³³ ti³³ je²¹ so⁵⁵po²¹ kuɛ²¹ xa³³.
3SG rob 3SG wife to say
'(They) said that he snatched his wife.'
说他抢了他老婆。

(41) ji³³ kuɛ³³ ji³³ xa³³, sɿ³³ tɕie⁵⁵me⁵⁵ kuɛ²¹ tɕie⁵⁵me⁵⁵ ɣɯ²¹ xa³³.
one go one say COP how go how come say
'(The big brother of Wang's) went to (the local court) to clarify what had happened.'
（王大哥）就去（官上）说（这件事），（说了到底）是怎么一回事。

(42) je³³ xa³³ sɿ³³, "ɔ²¹ sɿ³³ tɣ²¹ kʰɣ⁵⁵pa³³ ta³³ tɕiu²¹ ma²⁴ nɛ⁵⁵
3SG say CONT this COP PASS tiger lift at there PRT
ŋo³³ tɯ²¹ ma²⁴ pon³³-tɣ³³ ŋo³³ na²¹ nɛ⁵⁵, ei²¹ <je³³ lɛ²¹tsʰɛ²¹>
1SG at there meet-obtain 1SG hit PRT INTJ 3SG only.then
kɣ²¹-tɣ³³ je³³ ɔ²¹ <mia²¹ ji³³ kʷɔ²¹ nɛ⁵⁵> mia²¹ ji³³
save-obtain 3SG this life one CLF PRT life one

tsղ²¹ nɛ⁵⁵ je³³ lɛ²¹tsʰɛ²¹ kuɛ³³ kɛ²¹ ŋo³³ sղ²¹.
CLF PRT 3SG only.then go marry 1SG AFF
'He said: "(the fact is that she) was snatched by a tiger and I was there running into this (incident). I fought (the tiger) and saved her life. Then she was married to me." '
他说："这是被老虎抬到那儿，我在那儿碰到（这事儿），然后我打（老虎），救了她一命，她才嫁我的。"

(43) kua³³tɣ³³ xa²¹lɛ⁵⁵: "a²⁴! mɔ²¹ nɛ⁵⁵, je³³ sղ²¹ ta⁵⁵ kʰɣ⁵⁵pa²¹
     court   say   that   PRT 3SG AFF from tiger
     pi²¹ mo³³ kuɛ³³ ei³³ ti³³-ɣɯ²¹ sղ³³ a³³.
     mouth inside PURP INTJ snatch-come AFF PRT
'The judge said: "(It turns out that) that, it is from the tiger's mouth that he snatched (her life).'
官上说："（原来）那个呢，他是从老虎嘴里抢来的啊！

(44) nɯ³³ a²¹ ɣã²¹ sղ²¹mɔ⁵⁵ me²¹tsղ⁵⁵ ta⁵⁵ ni³³ xa³³?"
     2SG still have what   reason   with 3 say
'What kind of reason do you have to sue him?" '
你还有什么理跟人家说？"

Text 2

The zombie wife

(1) mɔ²¹kɯ²⁴   ɣã²¹   u²¹tsʰo²⁴ ji²¹   fɛ⁵¹hɛ²¹.
that.moment there.be person one family
'There was once a family of persons.'
以前，有家人。

(2) u²¹tsʰo²¹ ta⁵⁵ kʰo⁵⁵.
only   two   CLF
'A couple.'
（夫妻）二人。

(3) kʰua²¹   xiŋ⁵⁵.
be.good   very
'(They were) very close.'
好得很。

(4) nɛ⁵⁵, je³³ ɔ²¹ su⁵⁵po³³ ni³³ sɿ⁵⁵ kʷɔ²¹.
INTJ 3SG this wife   CLF   die   go.CRS
'His wife died.'
他这个妻子死了。

(5) sɿ⁵⁵ kuɛ³³ nɛ⁵⁵, tɯ⁵⁵   pi⁵⁵   ka³³sɿ³³.
die   3SG   PRT   then   turn.into   dried.corpse
'(The wife) died and (she) turned into a zombie.'
死了（以后）呢，就变干尸了。

(6) pi⁵⁵   ka³³sɿ³³   nɛ⁵⁵, koŋ⁵⁵koŋ⁵⁵   nɛ⁵⁵ pe⁵⁵-ɣɯ²¹.
turn.into dried.corpse PRT   every.day   PRT   return-come
'(The wife) turned into a zombie and (she) came back home every day.'
死了（以后）呢，就变干尸了。

(7) tɯ²¹ je²¹ ɔ⁵⁵ʑi²¹, ma³³   ɔ²⁴   tsoŋ⁵⁵ ma³³   mɔ²⁴ tsoŋ⁵⁵.
at   3SG   house   grasp this type   grasp that type
'(The wife) did the chores in his house.'
'LIT: (The wife) grabbed this and that in his house.'
在他家里，弄弄这弄弄那。

(8) ta⁵⁵ je²¹ ɔ⁵⁵ʑi²¹ ma³³.
    for 3SG house grasp
    '(The wife) did the (chores) for the family.'
    给他家弄（这弄那）。

(9) tɯ⁵⁵ tsɔ²¹ mɔ²¹ pɣ³³-tɣ³³ sɿ⁵⁵ sɿ²¹ jaŋ²⁴.
    then resemble that NEG-PFV die so way
    'It seemed that she had never died.'
    就像没死似的。

(10) je³³ ɔ²¹ mo³³ ni³³ pɣ³³ tiu³³u³³.
     3SG this husband CLF NEG know
     'The husband wasn't aware of this.'
     她这老公不知道。

(11) "ai⁵⁵ja³³ nɯ²¹ sɿ⁵⁵-ha⁵⁵ sɿ⁵⁵-ha⁵⁵, nɯ²¹ koŋ⁵⁵koŋ⁵⁵ pe⁵⁵-ɣɯ²¹."
     INTJ 2SG die-finish die-finish 2SG every.day return-come
     '"You died, (but how come) you come back every day?"'
     "哎呀，你死都死了，（怎么）你怎么天天回来？"

(12) "ŋo³³ pɣ³³-tɣ³³ sɿ⁵⁵ sɿ²¹ lo³³. e⁵⁵a, ŋo³³ sɿ³³
     1SG NEG-PFV die AFF/CONT PRT INTJ 1SG AFF
     tɯ²¹ sɿ³³ ma³³.
     be.alive AFF PRT
     '"I didn't die. I'm alive.'
     "我没有死。我是活着的。

(13) nɯ³³ piɔ²⁴ tsʰe³³.
     2SG NEG.IMP fear.PRT
     'Don't be afraid.'
     你别怕。

(14) ŋo²¹ koŋ⁵⁵koŋ⁵⁵ ɣɯ²¹ ta⁵⁵ nɯ²¹ tɕie⁵⁵ ɛ³³." xa³³ nɛ.
     1SG every.day come with 2SG do company say PRT
     'I'll come back every day to accompany you." (she) said.'
     我天天来跟你作伴。"说呢。

(15) ε, tɯ²¹-xɯ⁵⁵ tɯ²¹-xɯ⁵⁵ nɛ⁵⁵, tɯ⁵⁵ je³³ mɔ²¹ tsʰɿ³³ mo³³
INTJ live-DUR live-DUR PRT then 3SG that village inside
sɿ²¹ ŋa⁵⁵ tɯ⁵⁵ tɕie⁵⁵-ya³³, ti²¹ tɕie⁵⁵-ya³³.
MOD child then do-fall can do-fall
'During the time that (his zombie wife) was living (back at home), the children of his village would disappear.'
住着住着呢，他村里的孩子就会不见。

(16) ji²¹ tsɔ²⁴ ji²¹ tsɔ²⁴ nɛ⁵⁵ jɯ²⁴ tɕie⁵⁵-ya³³kuɛ³³ ji³³ ni³³.
one period one period PRT again do-fall.go one CLF
'Once a while, again, a child disappeared.'
一阵子，又不见一个孩子。

(17) ji²¹ tsɔ²⁴ ji²¹ tsɔ²⁴ jɯ²⁴ tɕie⁵⁵-ya³³kuɛ³³ ji³³ ni³³ nɛ⁵⁵, ni³³
one period one period again do-fall.go one CLF PRT 3
tɯ³³ tiu³³u³³ sɿ³³ je³³ ɔ²¹ so⁵⁵po³³ ni³³, e²¹ ka³³-kuɛ³³ sɿ²¹.
then know AFF 3SG this wife CLF INTJ grasp-go AFF
'A child disappeared once a while and people (began to) know that it was his wife who took away (the children).'
每隔一阵子不见一个孩子，人家就知道是他这个老婆抓走的。

(18) tɯ³³ ɣã²¹ kʷɔ³³sɣ³³pa³³ tɯ³³ ta⁵⁵ je³³ ɔ²¹ mo³³ ni³³
then there.be teacher then with 3SG this husband CLF
xa³³: "əu²⁴! nɯ³³ mɔ²¹ so⁵⁵po³³ ni³³ sɿ²¹ sɿ⁵⁵-ha⁵⁵ lɛ²¹tsʰɛ²¹
say INTJ 2SG that wife CLF AFF die-finish only.then
pi⁵⁵ ka³³sɿ³³ sɿ²¹ uo²⁴! ei²¹! nɯ²¹ koŋ⁵⁵koŋ⁵⁵ ta⁵⁵
turn.into dried.corpse AFF PRT INTJ 2SG every.day with
je³³ tɯ²¹ e, nɯ²¹ py³³ tsʰɿ³³ la²¹?"
3SG live PRT 2SG NEG fear Q
'There was a Taoist teacher (who) said to the husband: "Your wife is dead and she turned into a zombie. You live with her every day. Don't you fear?"'
就有道士就跟这个丈夫说："哎呦！你那个老婆是死了以后才变干尸的。你天天跟他住，你不怕吗？"

(19) "a³³ja²¹! tsʰɿ³³ sɔ²¹mɔ⁵⁵ lo²¹! je³³ sɿ³³ ŋo²¹ so⁵⁵po³³."
INTJ fear what PRT 3SG COP 1SG wife
' "I'm not afraid. She's my wife." '
"哎呀！怕什么啊！她是我老婆。"

(20) "jei²⁴! <ŋo³³> nɯ³³ pɤ³³ sa²¹ nɛ⁵⁵, ŋo³³ ʑe²¹, tsɯ³³kə²¹te³³,
INTJ 1SG 2SG NEG believe PRG 1SG write INTJ
sɿ⁵⁵ ji²¹ kʷɔ²¹ sɿ⁵⁵ nɯ³³ e. nɯ³³ a³³ tʰie²¹ pie⁵⁵ nɯ²¹
spell one CLF to 2SG PRT 2SG DCR stick to 2SG
ma²¹kʰa³³ tɤ³³. hu³³kʰa³³ tʰie²¹-xɯ⁵⁵.
door upside everywhere stick-INC
' "If you don't believe (me), I'll write you a spell. You stick (the spell) on your door. Stick (the spells) everywhere.'
"诶！你不信的话，我写个符给你。你把（符）贴到你家门上。到处都贴上。

(21) nɛ⁵⁵, je³³ kuɛ²¹ tʰɔ⁵⁵ nɛ⁵⁵, nɯ³³ tsuan²¹ tsɿ³³ni³³."
INTJ 3SG go moment PRT 2SG pretend sleep
'When she goes out, you pretend to be asleep."'
她出去的时候，你装睡。"

(22) nɛ⁵⁵, je³³ sɿ²¹ sa⁵⁵sa⁵⁵ lɛ²¹ sɿ⁵⁵ je³³ ɔ²¹ mo³³ ni³³
INTJ 3SG COP every.night ADV let 3SG this husband CLF
tsɿ³³tsɿ³³ni²¹ ha⁵⁵, a²¹ ŋa⁵⁵-sui⁵⁵ li²¹ tsɿ³³tsɿ³³ni²¹
sleep COMPL OM child-PL take.along sleep
ha⁵⁵ je³³ lɛ²¹tsʰɛ²¹ kʰɯ⁵⁵ seŋ³³ kuɛ²¹.
COMPL 3SG only.then rise body go
'Every night, she went out only after her husband and her children were asleep.'
她是每天晚上让她丈夫睡了以后，领孩子睡了以后，她才起身出去。

(23) ei²⁴! mɔ²⁴ sa⁵⁵ nɛ⁵⁵, je³³ ɔ²¹ mo³³ ni³³ tɯ⁵⁵ tʰi⁵⁵ mɔ²¹
INTJ that night PRT 3SG this husband CLF then listen that
kʷɔ³³sɤ³³pa³³ ni³³ ŋoŋ²¹ nɛ⁵⁵, tɯ³³ a³³ mɔ²¹-sui⁵⁵ ji³³
teacher CLF speech PRT then OM that-PL one
tʰie²¹-xɯ⁵⁵.
stick-INC
'That night, the husband listend to the Taoist teacher and he stuck those (spells everywhere).'
诶！那天晚上，这个老公就听了那个道士的话，就把那些（符）贴上了。

(24) tʰie²¹-xɯ⁵⁵ ha⁵⁵ nɛ⁵⁵, tɯ³³, tsɯ²¹kə²¹ti³³, li²¹
stick-INC COMPL PRT then INTJ take.along
ŋa⁵⁵ tsɿ²¹ nɛ⁵⁵, tɯ³³ tsuan²¹ tsɿ³³ni³³.
child sleep PRG then pretend sleep
'After he stuck (the spells) everywhere, (he) then accompanied the children to go to sleep. (He) then pretended to be asleep.'
贴了以后呢，就领孩子去睡了，就装睡。

(25) tsɿ³³ni²¹ xiŋ⁵⁵. ɣa²¹ lɯ⁵⁵ mɔ³³sɿ³³ nɛ²¹.
sleep very snore VCOMP very PRT
'(He pretended to) have a deep sleep and snored loudly.'
（假装）睡得很沉。呼噜打得震天响。

(26) ɔ²¹! je³³ ji²¹ pʰa⁵⁵ ji²¹ pʰa⁵⁵ lɛ⁵⁵ a³³ mɔ²¹ pʰe²⁴
INTJ 3SG one pat one pat ADV OM that quilt
pʰa²¹ pie⁵⁵ je³³ mo³³ ty³³ nɛ⁵⁵, kʰɯ³³ ma²¹kʰa³³
pat to 3SG husband upside PRT open door
nɛ⁵⁵ tɯ³³ kuɛ³³ kʷɔ²¹ o.
PRT then go go.CRS CRS
'Patting him, she tucked her husband in, opened the door and went out.'
她一拍一拍地把被子植物拍到她丈夫身上，（然后）开门就出去了。

(27) kuɛ³³ kuɛ²¹ nɛ⁵⁵, je³³ ɔ²¹ mo³³ ni³³ tɯ³³ …
go go PRT 3SG this husband CLF then
'(The wife) went out and her husband then…'
（老婆）出去了，她这丈夫就……

(28) <mɔ²¹ kʷɔ³³sɣ³³pa³³ ni³³ ta⁵⁵ je³³ xa²¹ sɿ³³.>
that teacher CLF with 3SG say CONT
'The Taoist teaher was speaking to him.'
那个老师在跟他说。

(29) "a²¹! ɔ²¹ pe⁵⁵ sɿ⁵⁵ ŋo³³ tɕiu²¹me³³me³³ lɛ²¹ a³³ ni³³tsɿ³³
INTJ this time let 1SG quiet ADV with eye
tsaŋ³³ nɯ³³." xa³³.
look 2SG say
' "This time, let me have a secret look at you!" he said.'
"啊！这次让我看看你！"说。

(30) je³³ tɯ³³ tɕiu²¹me³³me³³ lɛ⁵⁵ a³³ ni³³tsɿ³³ ji³³ tsaŋ³³,
3SG then quiet ADV with eye one look
sɿ³³ tɯ³³ pɔ²¹-xɯ⁵⁵ ŋa⁵⁵ to²¹to⁵⁵ po⁵⁵ ji²¹ hɔ⁵⁵ tɕʰɪŋ²¹ ji²¹
COP then hold-DUR child head CLF one road chew one
hɔ⁵⁵ lɛ⁵⁵ pe⁵⁵-ɣɯ²¹ o.
road ADV return-come CRS
'He then took a secret look at (his wife). It was that she was walking back (home) while chewing the head of a child.'
他就悄悄地一看，（就看见他老婆）抱着一个小孩儿头，一边啃一边往回走。

(31) je³³ ji²¹ hɔ⁵⁵ tɕʰɪŋ²¹ ji²¹ hɔ⁵⁵ pe⁵⁵-ɣɯ²¹ nɛ⁵⁵, tɯ³³
3SG one road chew one road return-come CRS then
tsaŋ³³-kɪŋ²¹ mɔ²¹ <tʰie²⁴-sui⁵⁵> tɯ²¹ mɔ²¹ ma²¹kʰa³³ mɔ²⁴-sui⁵⁵
look-see that stick-PL at that door that-PL
tʰie²¹-xɯ⁵⁵ sɿ²¹.
stick-DUR NMLZ
'She was walking back (home) while chewing the head of a child and then she saw those (spells) stuck on the door and other things.'
她一边啃一边往回走，就看见门上和其他东西上贴的那些。

(32) je³³ tɯ³³ pe⁵⁵-ɣɯ²¹ pɣ³³-tɣ³³. tɯ³³ a³³ ŋa⁵⁵ to²¹to⁵⁵ ji²¹
3SG then return-come NEG-PFV then OM child head one
fe⁵⁵-pie⁵⁵kuɛ²¹ tɯ²¹ tɕiɔ²¹-pe⁵⁵ɣɯ²¹ tɯ³³ pɔ²¹-xɯ⁵⁵ je³³ mo³³
throw-toss.go then jump-return.come then hold-DUR 3SG husband
sɿ³³, a³³ je³³ mo³³ tsʰa²¹pɣ²¹tɔ⁵⁵ kʰoŋ²¹-sɿ⁵⁵ kwɔ²¹.
PRT OM 3SG husband almost frighten-die go.CRS
'She then couldn't enter (into the house). Then (she) threw away the child's head jumped back and held her husband. Her husband was frightened almost to death.'
她就回不来了。就把小孩儿头一下子甩出去就跳回来抱住了她丈夫。差点把她丈夫吓死。

(33) nɛ⁵⁵, ta⁵⁵ u²¹sui³³ nɛ⁵⁵ tɯ³³, ai²¹, je³³ tɯ³³
INTJ from afterward PRT then INTJ 3SG then
pi⁵⁵ sɿ²¹mɔ⁵⁵ sɿ³³kʰa³³ ha²¹ ma!
turn.into what dust COMPL PRT
'After this, she turned into ashes.'
从此呢，她就化成灰了嘛！

Bibliography

Adams, Karen L. 1989. *Systems of numeral classification in the Mon-Khmer, Nicobares and Aslian subfamilies of Austroasiatic*. (Pacific Linuigstics, B-101). Canberra: Research School of Pacific Studies, Australian National University.

Adams, Karen L. and Nancy F. Conklin. 1973. Toward a Theory of Natural Classification. In Claudia Corum, T. Cedric Smith-Stark, and Ann Weiser (eds.), *Papers from the Ninth Regional Meeting Chicago Linguitic Society*, April 13–15, 1973. Chicago: Chicago Linguitic Society. 1–10.

Aikhenvald, Alexandra Y. 2000. *Classifiers: A typology of noun categorization devices*. Oxford: Oxford University Press.

Aikhenvald, Alexandra Y. 2004. *Evidentiality*. Oxford: Oxford University Press.

Aissen, Judith. 2003. Differential object marking: iconicity vs. economy. *Natural Language and Linguistic Theory* 21. 425–448.

Aldridge, Edith. 2011. Neg-to-Q: The historical origin and development of question particles in Chinese. *The Linguistic Review* 28(4). 411–447.

Allan, Keith. 1977. Classifiers. *Language* 53(2). 285–311.

Andrews, Avery D. 2007. Relative clauses. In Timothy Shopen (ed.), *Language Typology and Syntactic Description Volume II: Complex Constructions*. 2nd edition. 206–236.

Arcodia, Giorgio F., Bianca Baciano and Chiara Melloni. 2015. Areal perspectives on total reduplication of verbs in Sinitic. *Studies in language* Vol. 39.4. 836–872.

Arcodia, Giorgio Francesco. 2017. Towards a typology of relative clauses in Sinitic: headedness and relativization strategies. *Cahies de Linguistique Asie Orientale*, Vol. 46-1. 32–72.

Baxter, William. 1992. *A Handbook of Old Chinese Phonology*. Berlin: De Gruyter.

Baxter, William and Laurent Sagart. 2014. *Old Chinese A New Reconstruction*. Oxford: Oxford University Press.

Becker, Alton L. 1975. A linguistic image of nature: the Burmese numerative classifier system. *Linguistics* 16(5). 109–121.

Bei, Luobei 贝罗贝 (= Alain Peyraube). 1986. Shuangbinyu Jiegou – Cong Handai zhi Tangdai de Lishi Fazhan 双宾语结构——从汉代至唐代的历史发展 [On the diachronic evolution of the double object constructions from the Han Dynasty to the Tang Dynasty]. *Zhongguo Yuwen* 中国语文 [Languages in China] 5. 204–217.

Bei, Luobei 贝罗贝 (= Peyraube Alain). 1989. Zaoqi 'Ba' Zi Ju de Jige Wenti 早期"把"字句的几个问题 [Several issues on the earlier ba constructions]. *Yuwen Yanjiu* 1. 1–9.

Bisang, Walter. 1993. Classifiers, Quantifiers and Class Nouns in Hmong. *Studies in Language* 17.1. 1–51.

Bisang, Walter. 1996. Areal typology and grammaticalization: Processes of grammaticalization based on nouns and verbs in East and mainland South East Asian languages. *Studies in Language*, 20.3. 519–597.

Bisang, Walter. 1998. Adverbiality: The view from the Far East. In Johan van der Auwera and Dónall P. Ó Baoill (eds.), *Adverbial constructions in the languages of Europe*. Berlin: Mouton de Gruyter. 641–812.

Bisang, Walter. 1999. Classifiers in East and Southeast Asian languages Counting and beyond. In Jadranka Gvozdanović (ed.), *Numeral Types and Changes Worldwide*. Berlin: De Gruyter. 113–186.

Bisang, Walter. 2004. Grammaticalization without coevolution of form and meaning: The case of tense-aspect-modality in East and manland Southeast Asia. In Walter Bisang, Nikolaus

P. Himmelmann and Björn Wiemer (eds.), *What Makes Grammaticalization? A Look from its Fringes and its Components*. Berlin: Mouton de Gruyter. 109–138.

Bisang, Walter. 2006. South East Asia as a Linguistic Area. In Keith Brown (ed.), *Encyclopedia of Language and Linguistics*, Vol. 11. Boston: Elsevier. 587–595.

Bisang, Walter. 2012. Numeral classifiers with plural marking. A challenge to Greenberg. In Xu Dan (ed.), *Plurality and Classifiers across languages in China*. Berlin: de Gruyter. 23–42.

Bo, Wenze 薄文泽. 2004. Caijiahua Gaikuang 蔡家话概况 [A sketch of Caijia]. *Minzu Yuwen* 民族语文 [Minority languages in China] 2. 68–81.

Bossong, Georg. 1985. *Differentielle objektmarkierung in den Neuiranischen Sprachen*. Tübingen: Narr.

Bybee, Joan, Revere Perkins and William Pagliuca. 1994. *The Evolution of Grammar: Tense, Aspect, and Modality in the Languages of the World*. Chicago: The University of Chicago Press.

Bybee, Joan L. and Suzanne Fleischman. 1995. An introductory essay. In Joan L. Bybee and Suzanne Fleischman (eds.), *Modality in grammar and discourse*. Amsterdam/Philadelphia: John Benjamins Publishing Company. 1–14.

Cao, Zhiyun 曹志耘 et al. 2008. *Hanyu Fangyan Ditu Ji · Yufa Juan* 汉语方言地图集·语法卷 [The linguistic atlas of Chinese dialects (Grammar)]. Beijing: The Commercial Press.

Cao, Wei 曹炜. 1987. Ye Tan 'You' de Cixing 也谈"有"的词性 [On the nature of 'you']. *Hanyu Xuexi* 汉语学习 [Chinese Learning] 2. 21–22.

Chao, Yuen Ren. 1968. *A Grammar of Spoken Chinese*. Berkeley: University of California Press.

Chappell, Hilary. 1992. Towards A Typology of Aspect in Sinitic Languages. *Zhongguo Jingnei Yuyan ji Yuyanxue: Hanyu Fangyan* [Chinese Languages and Linguistics: Chinese dialects] 1.1. Taipei: Academia Sinica. 67–106.

Chappell, Hilary. 2001a. Language contact and areal diffusion in Sinitic languages: Problems for typology and genetic affiliation. In Alexandra Y. Aikhenvald and R. M. W. Dixon (eds.), *Areal diffusion and genetic inheritance: Problems in comparative linguistics*. Oxford: Oxford University Press. 328–357.

Chappell, Hilary. 2001b. Synchrony and diachrony of Sinitic languages: A brief history of Chinese dialects. In Hilary Chappell (ed.), *Sinitic Grammar: Synchronic and Diachronic Perspectives*. Oxford: Oxford University Press. 3–28.

Chappell, Hilary. 2001c. A typology of evidential markers in Sinitic languages. In Hilary Chappell (ed.), *Sinitic Grammar: Synchronic and Diachronic Perspectives*. Oxford: Oxford University Press. 56–84.

Chappell, Hilary. 2008. Variation in the grammaticalization of complementizers from *verba decendi* in Sinitic languages. *Linguistic Typology* 12. 45–98.

Chappell, Hilary. 2013. Pan-Sinitic Object Marking: Morphology and Syntax. In Cao Guangshun, Hilary Chappell, Redouane Djamouri and Thekla Wiebusch (eds.), *Breaking Down the Barriers: Interdisciplinary Studies in Chinese Linguistics and Beyond*. Taipei: Academia Sinica. 785–816.

Chappell, Hilary. 2015a. Reanalysis of analytic causative and passive constructions in Sinitic languages with source verbs of giving and waiting. Presentation given at the International Conference on Linguistic Typology (ICLT2), Nanchang University, Nanchang China. 16–20 October, 2015.

Chappell, Hilary. 2015b. Linguistic areas in China for differential object-marking, passive and comparative constructions. In Hilary Chappell (ed.), *Diversity in Sinitic Languages*. Oxford: Oxford University Press. 13–52.

Chappell, Hilary. 2017. Pan-Sinitic Equatives in Their Asian Context. Presentation given in Shanghai Jiao Tong University, Shanghai, China.
Chappell, Hilary and Shanshan Lü. 2022. A Semantic Typology of Location, Existence and Possession Verbs: Polysemy Sharing in Mainland East and Southeast Asia. *Linguistics* 60(1). 1–82.
Chappell, Hilary and Alain Peyraube. 2006. The Analytic Causatives of Early Modern Southern Min in Diachronic Perspective. In Dah-an Ho (ed.), *Linguistic Studies in Chinese and Neighboring Languages: Festschrift in Honor of Professor Pang-Hsin Ting on His 70th Birthday*. Taipei: Academia Sinica. 973–1011.
Chappell, Hilary and Alain Peyraube. 2007. Diachronic Syntax of Ditransitive Constructions: from Archaic Chinese to early Southern Min (Sinitic). Presentation for the Conference on Ditransitive Constructions, 23–25 November 2007, Max Planck Institute for Evolutionary Anthropology, Leipzig.
Chappell, Hilary and Alain Peyraube. 2008. Chinese localizers: Diachrony and some typological considerations. In Xu Dan (ed.), *Space in languages of China*. Berlin: Springer. 15–37.
Chappell, Hilary and Alain Peyraube. 2015. The comparative constructions in Sinitic languages: synchronic and diachronic variation. In Hilary Chappell (ed.), *Diversity in Sinitic Languages*. Oxford: Oxford University Press. 134–155.
Chappell, Hilary and Alain Peyraube. 2016a. Modality and Mood in Sinitic. In Jan Nuyts and Johan Van Der Auwera (eds.), *The Oxford Handbook of Modality and Mood*. Oxford: Oxford University Press. 296–329.
Chappell, Hilary and Alain Peyraube. 2016b. A Typological Study of Negation in Sinitic Languages: Synchronic and Diachronic Views. In Pang-hsin Ting et al. (eds.), *New Horizons in the Study of Chinese: Dialectology, Grammar, and Philology – Studies in Honor of Professor Anne Yue*. Hong Kong: The Chinese University Press. 483–534.
Chappell, Hilary, Li Ming and Alain Peyraube. 2007. Chinese linguistics and typology: the state of the art. *Linguistic Typology* 11.1: 187–211.
Chappell, Hilary, Alain Peyraube and Wu Yunji. 2011. A comitative source for object markers in Sinitic languages 跟 *kai*[55] in Waxiang and 共 *kaŋ*[7] in Southern Min. *Journal of East Asian Linguistics* 20. 291–338.
Chen, Hao 陈浩. 1760–1820. *Mán Miáo Tú Shuō* 蛮苗图说 [*A Picture Book of Hmong*]. http://www.wul.waseda.ac.jp/kotenseki/search.php
Chen, Houguang 谌厚光 and Xu Fengyu 徐丰玉. 1848. *Píngyuǎnzhōu Zhì* 平远州志·卷十六 [Gazetteer of Pingyuan, Vol. 16]. https://books.google.fr/books?id=xlosAAAAYAAJandprintsec=frontcoverandhl=zh-CNandsource=gbs_ge_summary_randcad=0#v=onepageandqandf=false
Chen, Shilin 陈士林, Bian Shiming 边仕明 and Li Xiuqing 李秀清. 1985. *Yiyu Jianzhi* 彝语简志 [A sketch grammar of Lolo]. Beijing: Minzu Publisher.
Chen, Yujie 陈玉洁. 2010. *Hanyu Zhishici de Leixinxue Yanjiu* 汉语指示词的类型学研究 [Demonstratives in Sinitic languages from a typological perspective]. Beijing: China Social Sciences Press.
Chen, Weirong 陈伟蓉. 2017. Fujian Hui'an Minnan Fangyan de Guanxi Congju Biaoji 福建惠安闽南方言的关系从句标记 [Relativizers in the Hui'an Southern Min dialect]. *Fangyan* 方言 [Dialects]. 352–359.
Cheng, Robert L. 鄭良偉. 1991. Taiyu yu Taiwan Huayu-li de ziju jiegou biaozhi 台語與台灣華語裏的句結構標誌 [The complementation markers kóng 'say' and k'uàn 'see' in Taiwanese and Taiwanese Mandarin]. In Di San-jie Shijie Huayu Wenjiaoxue Yantaohui 第三世界華

語文教學研討會 [The Third World Symposium on Chinese Culture and Education]. Taipei. (Reprinted in Cheng (ed.) 1997, vol. II: 105 – 132.)

Chin, Chi On. 2009. *The Verb GIVE and the Double-object Construction in Cantonese in Synchronic, Diachronic and Typological Perspectives*. Washington: University of Washington PhD thesis.

Chin, Andy C. 2011. Grammaticalization of the Cantonese Double Object Verb [pei³⁵] 畀 in Typological and Areal Perspectives. *Languages and Linguistics* 12.3. 529–563.

Chu, Chauncey C. 1973. The passive construction: Chinese and English. *Journal of Chinese Linguistics* 1. 437–470.

Claudi, Ulrike and Bernd Heine. 1986. On the metaphorical base of grammar. *Studies in Language* 10-2. 297–335

Clark, Eve. 1978. Locationals: Existential, locative, and possessive constructions. In Joseph H. Greenberg (ed.), *Universals of human language*, vol. IV: Syntax. Stanford, CA: Stanford University Press. 85–126.

Clark, Marybeth. 1974. Submissive Verbs as Adversatives in Some Asian Languages. In N. D. Liem (ed.), *South-east Asian Linguistic Studies* Vol. 1. Canberra: ANU Asia-Pacific Linguistics/Pacific Linguistics Press. 89–110.

Clark, Marybeth. 1985. Asking questions in Hmong and other South-East Asian languages. *Linguistics of the Tibeto-Burman Area* 8-2. 60–67.

Clark, Marybeth. 1989. Hmong and areal Southeast Asia. In David Bradley (ed.), *Papers in Southeast Asian Linguistics* 11: *Southeast Asian syntax*. Canberra: Pacific Linguistics. 175–230.

Coates, Jennifer. 1983. The Semantics of Modal Auxiliaries. London: Croom Helm.

Comrie, Bernard. 1976. *Aspect*. Cambridge: Cambridge University Press.

Comrie, Bernard. 1989. *Language Universals and Linguistic Typology* (2nd edition). Oxford: Blackwell.

Comrie, Bernard and Tania Kuteva. 2013a. Relativization Strategies. In Matthew S. Dryer and Martin Haspelmath (eds.), *The World Atlas of Language Structures Online*. Leipzig: Max Planck Institute for Evolutionary Anthropology. (Available online at http://wals.info/chapter/s8, Accessed on 2018-06-06.)

Comrie, Bernard and Tania Kuteva. 2013b. Relativization on Subjects. In Matthew S. Dryer and Martin Haspelmath (eds.), *The World Atlas of Language Structures Online*. Leipzig: Max Planck Institute for Evolutionary Anthropology. (Available online at http://wals.info/chapter/122, Accessed on 2018-06-06.)

Comrie, Bernard and Tania Kuteva. 2013c. Relativization on Obliques. In Matthew S. Dryer and Martin Haspelmath (eds.), *The World Atlas of Language Structures Online*. Leipzig: Max Planck Institute for Evolutionary Anthropology. (Available online at http://wals.info/chapter/123, Accessed on 2018-06-06.)

Creissels, Denis. 2006a. Syntaxe générale, une introduction typologique 1. Paris: Lavoisier.
Creissels, Denis. 2006b. Syntaxe générale, une introduction typologique 2. Paris: Lavoisier.
Creissels, Denis. 2014. Functive phrases in Typological and diachronicperspective. *Studies in Language* 38.3. 605–647.

Croft, William. 1991. The Evolution of Negation. *Journal of Linguistics*, Vol. 27, No.1. 1–27.
Croft, William. 1994. Semantic universals in classifier systems. *Word*, 45-2. 145–171.
Croft, William. 2012. *Verbs: Aspect and Causal Structure*. Oxford: Oxford University Press.

Cui, Rongchang 崔荣昌. 1985. Sichuan Fangyan de Xingcheng 四川方言的形成 [The emergence of the Sichuan dialects]. *Fangyan* 方言 [Dialects]. 1985-1.

Cysouw, Michael. 2004. Interrogative words: an exercise in lexical typology. Presentation at "Bantu Grammar: Description and Theory Workshops 3", ZAS Berlin, 13 February 2004.
Dahl, Östen. 1979. Typology of Sentence Negation. *Linguistics* 17. 79–106.
Dahl, Östen. 1985. *Tense and aspect systems*. New York: Basil Blackwell.
DCF. *Dictionnaire Chinois-Français de la Langue Mandarine Parlée dans l'Ouest de la Chine*. 1893. Hongkong: Imprimerie de la Société des Missions Etrangères.
de Sousa, Hilário. 2015. Language contact in Naning: Nanning Pinghua and Nanning Cantonese. In Hilary Chappell (ed.), *Diversity in Sinitic Languages*. Oxford: Oxford University Press. 157–189.
Del Gobbo, Francesca. 2007. A comparison between Japanese and Chinese relative clauses. *University of Venice Working Papers in Linguistics* 17. 177–197.
Dickey, Stephen. 2007. A prototype account of the development of delimitative po- in Russian. In Dagmar Divjak and Agata Kochańska (eds.), *Cognitive Paths into the Slavic Domain*. Berlin: Mouton de Gruyter. 329–373.
Diessel, Holger. 1999. *Demonstratives: form, function, and grammaticalization*. Amsterdam/Philadelphia: Benjamins.
Ding, Shengshu 丁声树. 1999. *Xiandan Hanyu Yufa Jianghua* 现代汉语语法讲话 [Modern Chinese Grammar]. Beijing: Beijing: The Commercial Press.
Dixon, R. M. W. 2000. A typology of causatives: Form, syntax and meaning. In R.M.W. Dixon and Alexandra Y. Aikhenvald (eds.), *Changing valency: Case studies in transitivity*. Cambridge: Cambridge University Press. 30–83.
Dixon, R. M. W. 2004. Adjective classes in typological perspective. In R. M. W. Dixon and Alexandra Y. Aikhenvald (eds.), *Adjective Classes: A cross-linguistic typology*. Oxford: Oxford University Press. 1–49.
Dixon, R. M. W. 2006. Complement Clauses and Complementation Strategies in Typelogical perspective. In R. M. W. Dixon and Alexandra Y. Aikhenvald (eds.), *Complementation*. Oxford: Oxford University Press. 1–48.
Dixon, R. M. W. 2009. The semantics of clause linking in typological perspective. In R. M. W. Dixon and Alexandra Y. Aikhenvald (eds.), *The semantics of clause linking: A cross-linguistic typology*. Oxford: Oxford University Press. 1–55.
Dixon, R. M. W. 2010. *Basic Linguistic Theories 2*. Oxford: Oxford University Press.
Dixon, R. M. W. 2012. *Basic Linguistic Theories 3*. Oxford: Oxford University Press.
Downer, G.B. 1959. Derivation by Tone-Change in Classical Chinese. *Bulletin of the School of Oriental and African Studies*, Vol.22-2. 258–290.
Dryer, Matthew S. 2007. Noun phrase structure. In Timothy Shopen (ed.), *Language Typology and Syntactic Description Volume II: Complex Constructions*. 2nd edition. Cambridge: Cambridge University Press. 151–236.
Dryer, Matthew S. 2013a. Position of Pronominal Possessive Affixes. In Matthew S. Dryer and Martin Haspelmath (eds.), The World Atlas of Language Structures Online. Leipzig: Max Planck Institute for Evolutionary Anthropology. (Available online at http://wals.info/chapter/57, Accessed on 2020-05-07.)
Dryer, Matthew S. 2013b. Order of Genitive and Noun. In Matthew S. Dryer and Martin Haspelmath (eds.), The World Atlas of Language Structures Online. Leipzig: Max Planck Institute for Evolutionary Anthropology. (Available online at http://wals.info/chapter/86, Accessed on 2019-08-24.)
Dryer, Matthew S. 2013c. Position of Interrogative Phrases in Content Questions. In Matthew S. Dryer and Martin Haspelmath (eds.), *The World Atlas of Language Structures Online*.

Leipzig: Max Planck Institute for Evolutionary Anthropology. (Available online at http://wals.info/chapter/93, Accessed on 2018-08-23.)

Dryer, Matthew S. 2013d. Relationship between the Order of Object and Verb and the Order of Relative Clause and Noun. In Matthew S. Dryer and Martin Haspelmath (eds.), *The World Atlas of Language Structures Online*. Leipzig: Max Planck Institute for Evolutionary Anthropology. (Available online at http://wals.info/chapter/96, Accessed on 2018-06-03.)

Dryer, Matthew S. 2013e. Negative Morphemes. In Matthew S. Dryer and Martin Haspelmath (eds.), The World Atlas of Language Structures Online. Leipzig: Max Planck Institute for Evolutionary Anthropology. (Available online at http://wals.info/chapter/112, Accessed on 2020-05-07.)

Dryer, Matthew S. 2013f. Polar Questions. In Matthew S. Dryer and Martin Haspelmath (eds.), *The World Atlas of Language Structures Online*. Leipzig: Max Planck Institute for Evolutionary Anthropology. (Available online at http://wals.info/chapter/116, Accessed on 2018-07-06.)

Enfield, N. J. 2003. *Linguistic Epidemiology: Semantics and grammar of language contact in mainland Southeast Asia*. London: Routledge Curzon.

Enfield, N. J. 2018. *Mainland Southeast Asian Languages: A concise typological introduction*. Cambridge: Cambridge University Press.

Evans, Nicholas and David Wilkins. 2000. In the mind's ear: the semantic extensions of perception verbs in Australian languages. *Language* 76. 546–592.

Feng Chuntian 冯春田. 1991. *Jindai hanyu yufa wenti yanjiu* 近代汉语语法问题研究 [Grammar of Chinese of the modern period]. Jinan: Shandong Educational Publishing House.

Fernandez-Vest, M. M. Jocelyne, Marri Amon, Karl-Erland Gadelii, Victor Junnan Pan, Jirasak Achariyayos and Danh-Thành Do-Hurinville. 2017. Information structuring of dialogic pairs from a cross-linguistic perspective: Evidence from some European and Asian languages. *STUF* Vol. 70 (3): 391–453.

Fuca, Fuheng 富察·傅恒 (ed.). 1751–1805. *Huángqīng Zhígòng Tú* 皇清职贡图 [Portraits of Periodical Offering of Qing]. https://archive.org/details/06046713.cn/page/n52

Gerner, Matthias. 2009. Instruments as verb classifiers in Kam (Dong). *Linguistics* 47(3). 697–742.

Gerner, Matthias. 2013. *A grammar of Nuosu*. Berlin: Mouton de Gruyter.

Gerner, Matthias. 2014. Verb classifiers in East Asia. *Functions of Language* Vol. 21:3. 267–296.

Gerner, Matthias and Walter Bisang. 2008. Inflectional speaker-role classifiers in Weining Ahmao. *Journal of Pragmatics* 40.4. 719–732.

Gil, David. 2013. Numeral Classifiers. In Matthew S. Dryer and Martin Haspelmath (eds.), The World Atlas of Language Structures Online. Leipzig: Max Planck Institute for Evolutionary Anthropology. (Available online at http://wals.info/chapter/55, Accessed on 2019-08-20.)

Givón, Talmy. 2001. *Syntax: An Introduction*, Vol. I. Amsterdam/Philadelphia: John Benjamins. (new edition of Syntax: A functional-typological introduction, 1984).

Greenberg, Joseph H. 1974. Numeral Classifiers and Substantival Numbers: Problems in the Genesis of a Linguistic Type. In Luigui Heilmann (ed.), *Proceedings of the 11th International Congress of Linguistics*. Bologna: Nulino. 17–37.

Grinevald, Colette. 2000. A morphosyntactic typology of classifiers. In J. Senft (ed.), *Systems of nominal classification*. Cambridge: Cambridge University Press. 50–92.

Grinevald, Colette. 2004. Classifiers. In Geert Booij, Christian Lehmann, and Joachim Mugdan in collaboration with Wolfgang Kesselheim and Stavros Skopeteas (eds.), *Morphology: A handbook on inflection and word-formation* 2. Berlin: De Gruyter. 1016–1032.

Haiman, John. 1978. Conditionals are topics. *Language*, Vol 54-3. 564–589.
Hashimoto, Mantaro. 1973. *The Hakka dialect: A linguistic study of its phonology, syntax and lexicon.* Cambridge: Cambridge University Press.
Hashimoto, Mantaro. 1976. Language diffusion on the Asian continent: Problems of typological diversity in Sino-Tibetan. *Computational Analyses of Asian and African Languages 3.* 49–65.
Hashimoto, Mantaro (=桥本万太郎). 1985. *Yuyan Dili Leixingxue* 语言地理类型学 [Linguistic Typology from Geographical Perspective] (Yu Zhihong 余志鸿 Trans. from Japanese to Chinese). Beijing: The Pekin University Press.
Hashimoto, Mantaro J. 1988. The structure and typology of the Chinese passive construction. In Masayoshi Shibatani (ed.), *Passive and Voice.* Amsterdam/Philadelphia: Benjamins. 329–354.
Haspelmath, Martin. 1990. The grammaticization of passive morphology. *Studies in Language* 14-1. 25–72.
Haspelmath, Martin. 2004. Coordinating constructions: An overview. In Martin Haspelmath (ed.), *Coordinating Constructions.* Amsterdam/Philadel phia: John Benjamins. 3–40.
Haspelmath, Martin. 2007. Coordination. In Timothy Shopen (ed.), *Language Typology and Syntactic Description Volume II: Complex Constructions.* 2nd edition. Cambridge: Cambridge University Press. 1–51.
Haspelmath, Martin and the Leipzig Equative Constructions Team. 2017. Equative constructions in world-wide perspective. In Yvonne Treis and Martine Vanhove (eds.), *Similative and Equative Constructions: A Cross-linguistic Perspective.* Amsterdam/Philadelphia: John Benjamins. 9–32.
Haspelmath, Martin and Oda Buchholz. 1998. Equative and similative constructions in the languages of Europe. In van der Auwera, Johan (ed.), *Adverbial constructions in the languages of Europe.* Berlin: Mouton de Gruyter. 277–334.
He, Wei 贺巍. 1996. *Luoyang Fangyan Zidian* 洛阳方言字典 [Dictionary of the Luoyang Dialect]. Nanjing: Jiangsu Education Publishing House.
Heine, Bernd. 1997. *Cognitive foundations of grammar.* New York/Oxford: Oxford University Press.
Heine, Bernd. 2002. On the Role of Context in Grammaticalization. In Ilse Wischer and Gabriele Diewald (eds.), *New Reflections on Grammaticalization.* Amsterdam/Philadelphia: John Benjamins. 83–101.
Heine, Bernd, Ulrike Claudi and Friederike Hünnemeyer. 1991. *Grammaticalization: A conceptual framework.* Chicago: The University of Chicago Press.
Heine, Bernd and Mechthild Reh. 1982. *Patterns of Grammaticalization in African Languages. AKUP 47* (Arbeiten des Kölner Universalien-Projekts). Cologne: Institut für Sprachwissenschaft, Universität zu Köln.
Heine, Bernd and Mechthild Reh. 1984. *Grammaticalization and Reanalysis in African Languages.* Hamburg: Buske.
Heine, Bernd and Tania Kuteva. 2002. *World Lexicon of Grammaticalization.* Cambridge: Cambridge University Press.
Henkelmann, Peter. 2006. Constructions of equative comparison. *STUF-Sprachtypologie und Universalienforschung* 59(4). 370–398.
Hopper, Paul J. 1991. On some principles of grammaticization. In Elizabeth C. Traugott and Bernd Heine (eds.), *Approaches to Grammaticaliztion,* Vol I. Amsterdam/Philadelphia: John Benjamins. 17–36.

Hopper, Paul J. and Elizabeth Closs Traugott. 1993. *Grammaticalization*. Cambridge: Cambridge University Press.

Hu, Hongyan 胡鸿雁. 2013. Caijiahua Daici Xitong Tanxi 蔡家话代词系统探析 [Pronominal system in Caiji]. *Minzu Yuwen* 民族语文 [Minority Languages in China] 6. 34–40.

Huang, Borong 黄伯荣 (ed.). 1996. *Hanyu fangyan yufa leibian* 汉语方言语法类编 [Grammatical sketch of Chinese dialects]. Qingdao: Qingdao Chubanshe.

Huang, Xuezhen 黄雪贞. 1995. *Meixian Fangyan Zidian* 梅县方言字典 [Dictionnary of the Meixian Dialect]. Nanjing: Jiangsu Education Publishing House.

Iemmolo, Giorgio. 2011. *Towards a typological study of differential object marking and differential object indexation*. Pavia: Università degli Studi di Pavia PhD thesis.

Jenny, Mathias. 2014. Modern Mon. In Paul Sidwell and Mathias Jenny (eds.), *The Handbook of Austroasiatic Languages*. Leiden: Brill. 553–600.

Jiang, Shaoyu 蒋绍愚. 2006. Hanyu Ciyi he Cihui Xitong de Lishi Yanbian Chutan – Yi 'Tou' Wei Li 汉语词义和词汇系统的历史演变初探——以"投"为例 [On the diachronic evolution of Chinese semantic and lexical system: the case of 'toss']. *Journal of Peking University (Philosophy and Social Sciences)* 43-4. 84–105.

Jiang, Lansheng 江蓝生 and Cao Guangshun 曹广顺. 1997. *Tang Wudai Yuyan Cidian* 唐五代语言词典 [A dictionary of the language spoken in the Tang and Five dynasties]. Shanghai: Shanghai Educational Publishing House.

Jing, Daomo 靖道谟 and Sirin Gioro·Ortai 西林觉罗·鄂尔泰. 1736–1795. *Guìzhōu Tōngzhì* 贵州通志·卷七 [Gazetteer of Guizhou Province, Vol. 7] https://iiif.lib.harvard.edu/manifests/view/drs:50913961$247i

Jin, Xiaodong 金小栋 and Wu Fuxiang 吴福祥. 2018. Hanyu Fangyan Duogongneng Yusu 'Gen' de Yuyi Yanbian 汉语方言多功能语素"跟"的语义演变 [On the semantic extension of the multi-functional word 'follow' in Chinese dialects]. *Yuyan Yanjiu* 语言研究 [Language Research] 3. 50–58.

Kam, Tak Him. 1977. Derivation by Tone Change in Cantonese: A preliminary survey. *Journal of Chinese Linguistics*, Vol. 5-2. 186–210.

Ke, Lisi 柯理思 (= Christine Lamarre). 2001. Cong Putonghua Li Gen 'De' Youguan de Ji Ge Geshi Qu Tantao Fangyan Leixingxue 从普通话里跟"得"有关的几个结构讨论探讨方言类型学 [On the complements of De in Standard Mandarin and several equivalent constructions in Chinese dialects]. *Yuyan Yanjiu* 语言研究 [Language Studies] 2001-2. 7–18.

Keenan, Edward L. 1985. Relative clauses. In Timoghty Shopen (ed.), *Language typology and syntactic description* Vol. 2. Cambridge: Cambridge University Press. 141–170.

Keenan, Edward L. and Bernard Comrie. 1977. Noun phrase accessibility and universal grammar. *Linguistic Inquiry*, Vol. 8, No. 1: 63–99.

Keenan, Edward L. and Matthew S. Dryer. 2007. Passive in the World's Languages. In Timothy Shopen (ed.), *Language Typology and Syntactic Description Vol. I: Clause Structure*. 2nd edition. Cambridge University Press. 325–361.

Killingley, Siew-Yue. 1983. *Cantonese classifiers: syntax and semantics*. Newcastle: Grevatt and Grevatt.

Kittilä, Seppo. 2005. Recipient-prominence vs. beneficiary-prominence. *Linguistic Typology* 9(2). 269–297.

König, Ekkehard. 2017. The deictic identification of similarity. In Yvonne Treis and Martine Vanhove (eds.), *Similative and Equative Construction: A Cross-linguistic Perspective*. Amsterdam/Philadelphia: John Benjanims. 143–164.

König, Ekkehard and Volker Gast. 2002. Reflexive pronouns and other uses of self-forms in English. *Zeitschrift fur Anglistik und Amerikanistik* 50.3. 1–14.

Kratzer, Angelika. 1991. Modality. In Arnim von Stechow and Dieter Wunderlich (eds.), *Semantics: An International Handbook of Contemporary Research*. Berlin: de Gruyter. 639–650.

Kuteva, Tania, Bern Heine, Bo Hong, Haiping Long, Heiko Narrog and Seongha Rhee. 2019. *World Lexicon of Grammaticalization* 2nd Edition. Cambridge: Cambridge University Press.

Kwok, Bit-Chee, Andy C. Chin and Benjamin K. Tsou. 2011. Poly-functionality of the preverbal "acquire" in the Nanning Yue dialect of Chinese: an areal perspective. *Bulletin of SOAS* 74.1. 119–137.

Lai, Huei-ling. 2015. Profiling Hakka *Bun*[1] Causative Constructions. *Language and Linguistics* 16(3). 369–395.

Lamarre, Christine. 2003. Hanyu kongjian weiyi Shijian de yuyan biaoda—jianlun shuqu shi de jige wenti 汉语空间位移时间的语言表达——兼论述趋式的几个问题 [The linguistic encoding of motion events in Chinese], *Xiandai Zhongguoyu Yanjiu* 现代中国语研究 [Studies on Comtemporary Chinese] 5. 1–18.

Langacker, Ronald W. 1987. Nouns and verbs. *Language* 63. 53–92.

LaPolla, Randy. 1998. Topicalization and the question of lexical passives in Chinese. Third Annual Conference on Chinese Linguistics, 13–14 May 1988, Columbus: Ohio University.

LaPolla, Randy. 2003. Overview of Sino-Tibentan Morphosyntax. In Graham Thurgood and Randy J. LaPolla (eds.), *The Sino-Tibetan Languages*. London: Routledge. 22–42.

Leclère, Christian. 1978. Sur une classe de verbes datifs. *Langue Française* 39. Paris: Larousse. 66–75.

Lehmann, Christian. 1986. On the typology of relative clauses. *Linguistics* 24 (4). 663–680.

Li, Charles N. and Sandra A. Thompson. 1981. Mandarin Chinese: A Functional Reference Grammar. Berkeley: The University of California Press.

Li, Lan 李蓝. 2006. 'Zhuo' Zi Shi Beidong Ju de Gongshi Fenbu yu Leixing Chayi "着"字式被动句的共时分布与类型差异 [Synchronic distribution and typological difference between the two kinds of passives with 'zhuo' in Chinese dialects]. *Zhongguo Fangyan Xuebao* 中国方言学报 [Journal of Chinese Dialects] 1. 194–205.

Li, Lan 李蓝 and Cao Xilei 曹茜蕾 (= Hilary Chappell). 2013a. Hanyu Fangyan Zhong de Chuzhishi he 'Ba' Zi Ju (Shang) 汉语方言的处置式和"把"字句（上）[On the disposal constructions and *Ba* constructions in Chinese dialects, Part I]. *Fangyan* 1. 11–30.

Li, Lan 李蓝 and Cao Xilei 曹茜蕾 (= Hilary Chappell). 2013b. Hanyu Fangyan Zhong de Chuzhishi he 'Ba' Zi Ju (Xia) 汉语方言的处置式和"把"字句（下）[On the disposa constructions and *Ba* constructions in Chinese dialects, Part II]. *Fangyan* 2. 97–110.

Li, Shuyan 李树俨 and Zhang Ansheng 张安生. 1996. *Yinchuan Fangyan Zidian* 银川方言字典 [A dictionary of the Yinchuan dialect]. Nanjing: Jiangsu Education Press.

Li, Wei 李炜 and Liu Yanan 刘亚男. 2015. Xinan Guanhua de 'Gen' 西南官话的"跟"——从《华西官话汉法字典》说起 [On the morpheme 'follow' in Southwestern Mandarin]. *Zhongguo Yuwen* [Languages in China] 2015-4. 358–363.

Li, Xian 李贤 and Peng Shi 彭时. 1461. *Dà Míng Yī Tǒng Zhì* 大明一统志·卷八十八 [Gazetteer of the Ming Dynasty, Vol. 88]. https://books.google.fr/books?id=xlosAAAAYAAJandprintsec=frontcoverandhl=zh-CNandsource=gbs_ge_summary_randcad=0#v=onepageandqandf=false

Li, Xuping and Walter Bisang. 2011. Classifiers in Sinitic languages: From individuation to definiteness-marking. *Lingua* 122(4). 335–355.

Li, Xuping. 2018. *A Grammar of Gan Chinese*. Berlin: De Gruyter.

Liang, Deman 梁德曼 and Huang Shangjun 黄尚军. 1998. *Chengdu Fangyan Zidian* 成都方言字典 [A dictionary of the Chengdu dialect]. Nanjing: Jiangsu Education Publishing House.
Lin, Su'e 林素娥. 2017. On construction of *ke*-VP interrogatives with *you* (in Chinese). *Journal of Chinese Linguistics*, vol. 45.2. 290–312.
Lin, Taian 林泰安. 1986. Zhe Ge 'You' Keyi Kanzuo Jieci 这个"有"可以看作介词 [This 'you' can be treated as a preposition]. *Hanyu Xuexi* 汉语学习 [Chinese Learning]. 1986–5. 33.
Lin, Taian 林泰安. 1993. Jieci 'You' San Tan 介词"有"三探 [Further issues on the preposition 'you']. *Yindu Xuekan* 殷都学刊 [Journal of Yindu]. 1993. 100–104.
Liu, Boyang. 2022. *A typological study of verbal classifiers in Sintic languages*. Paris: EHESS PhD thesis.
Liu, Cunhan 刘村汉. 1995. *Liuzhou Fangyan Zidian* 柳州方言字典 [A dictionary of the Liuzhou dialect]. Nanjing: Jiangsu Education Publishing House.
Liu, Feng-Hsi. 1997. An Aspectual Analysis of *Ba. Journal of East Asian Linguistics* 6. 51–99.
Long, Qian'an 龙潜庵. 1985. *Song Yuan Yuyan Cidian* 宋元语言词典 [A dictionary of the language in the Song and Yuan dynasties]. Shanghai: Shanghai Cishu Publishing House.
Lord, Carol. 1993. *Historical change in serial verb constructions*. Amsterdam/Philadelphia: John Benjamins.
Lord, Carol, Foong Ha Yap and Shoichi Iwasaki. 2002. Grammaticalization of 'give': African Asian perspectives. In Ilse Wischer and Gabriele Diewald (eds.), *New reflections on grammaticalization*. Amsterdam: John Benjamins. 217–235.
LTBEIB 毕节民族识别办公室语言组 [Language Team of Bureau of Ethnic Identification in Bijie], 1982. *Caijia de Yuyan* 蔡家的语言 [Language of the Caijia], unpublished manuscript.
Lü, Shanshan. 2016. From Affirmation to Continuousness: The Usual Case of Construction $s_1^{33}...s_1^{21}$ in Caijia, Presentation given at the Syntax of the World's Languages VII. National Autonomous University of Mexico, Mexico City, Mexico.
Lü, Shanshan 吕珊珊. 2017. Caijiahua Qizhong Youbiju de Leixingxue Kaocha 蔡家话七种优比句的类型学考察 [Seven Superior Comparatives in Caijia: A Typological Perspective]. *Fangyan* 方言 3. 341–351.
Lü, Shanshan. 2018. Two Locative Constructions in Caijia from the Typological Perspective of Asian Languages. *Studies in Language* Vol. 42(3). 600–640.
Lü, Shanshan. 2019. Equative and similative constructions in Caijia (Sino-Tibetan). *Faits de langues*. Vol.50-1. 203–225.
Lü, Shanshan 吕珊珊. 2021. Caijiahua 'Gen' Yi Dongci ta^{55} de Duogongnengxing Jiqi Yanhua Lujing 蔡家话"跟"义动词的多功能性及其演化路径 [On the multi-functionality of ta^{55} 'Follow' in Caijia]. *Changshu Ligong Xueyuan Bao* 常熟理工学院报 [Journal of Changshu Institute of Techonology] 4. 43–53.
Lü, Shuxiang 吕叔湘. 1948. Ba Zi Yongfa de Yanjiu "把"字用法的研究 [On the uses of the 'bǎ' construction] *Zhongguo Wenhua Yanjiu Huikan* 中国文化研究汇刊 [Bulletin of Chinese Studies] Vol. 8. 111–130.
Lü, Shuxiang 吕叔湘. 1985. *Jindai Hanyu Zhidaici* 近代汉语指代词 [Pronouns in Morden Chinese]. Beijing: Xuelin Press.
Lü, Shuxiang 吕叔湘. 1999. Xiandai Hanyu Babai Ci 现代汉语八百词 [800 grammatical words in Chinese]. Beijing: Commercial Press.
Luo, Raodian 罗绕典. 1847. *Qiánnán Zhígfāng Jǐluè* 黔南职方纪略 [A Sketch of the Local History in Qiannan] http://www.wul.waseda.ac.jp/kotenseki/html/ru05/ru05_03294/index.html
Luo, Tianhua. 2016. *Interrogative Strategies: An Areal Typology of the Languages of China*. Konstanz: Universität Konstanz PhD thesis.

Lyons, John. 1977. *Semantics*, Vol. 1. Cambridge: Cambridge University Press.
Lyons, John. 1995. *Linguistic Semantics: An Introduction*. Cambridge: Cambridge University Press.
Ma, Beijia 马贝佳. 2002. Jindai Hanyu Jieci 近代汉语介词 [Prepositions in Modern Chinese]. Beijing: Zhonghua Book Company.
Malchukov, Andrej, Martin Haspelmath, and Bernard Comrie. 2010. Ditransitive constructions: A typological overview. In Malchukov, Andrej, Martin Haspelmath, and Bernard Comrie (eds.), *Studies in Ditransitive Constructions: A comparative handbook*. Berlin: De Gruyter Mouton. 1–64.
Matisoff, James. 1991. Areal and universal dimensions of grammatization in Lahu. In Elizabeth C. Traugott and Bernd Heine (eds.), *Approaches to Grammaticalization* Vol. 2. 383–453.
Matisoff, James. 2019. *Preface*. In Alice Vittrant and Justin Watkins (eds.), *The Mainland Southeast Asia Linguistic Area*. Berlin: De Gruyter. VI-XVI.
Matthews, Stephen and Virginia Yip. 1994. Cantonese: A comprehensive grammar. Routledge: New York.
Mei, Zulin 梅祖麟. 1981. Xiandai Hanyu Wancheng Mao Jushi He Ciwei de Laiyuan现代汉语完成貌句式和词尾的来源 [On the origin of the perfective constructions and the perfective marker in Standard Mandarin]. *Yuyan Yanjiu* 语言研究 [Language Research] 0. 65–77.
Meillet, Antoine. 1923. Le développement du verbe 'avoir'. In *Antidoron: Festschrift Jacob Wackernagel zur Vollendung des 70. Lebensjahres am 11. Dezember 1923, gewidmet von Schülern, Freunden und Kollegen*. Göttingen: Vandenhoeck & Ruprecht. 9–13.
Metslang, Helle, Külli Habicht and Karl Pajusalu. 2017. Where do poloar question marker come from? *STUF* 70(3). 489–521.
Ming, Shengrong 明生荣. 2007. *Bijie Fanyan Yanjiu* 毕节方言研究 [A study on the Bijie dialect]. Beijing: China Social Sciences Press.
Mourelatos, Alexander P. D. 1978. Events, processes and states. *Linguistics and philosophy* 2. 415–423.
Nedjalkov, Vladimir P. and Sergej Je. Jaxontov. 1988. The typology of resultative constructions. In Vladimir P. Nedjalkov (ed.), *Typology of Resultative constructions*. Translated from the original Russian edition (1983). Translation edited by Bernard Comrie. 3–62.
Newman, John. 1996. *Give: a cognitive linguitic study*. Berlin: Mouton de Gruyter.
Niohuru, Aibida 钮祜禄·爱必达 and Zhang Fengsheng 张风笙. 1749. 黔南识略·卷一 [Local History and Gazetteer of Qiannan Area, Vol. 1] http://archive.wul.waseda.ac.jp/kosho/ru05/ru05_03150/ru05_03150_0001/ru05_03150_0001.pdf
Nguyen, Dang Liem. 1970. *Four-syllable idiomatic expressions in Vietnamese*. Canberra: Pacific Linguistics.
Nguyên, Phu Phong. 1994. Quelques aspects de la négation en vietnamien. *Cahiers de linguistique Asie orientale* 23(1):231–239.
Noonan, Michael. 1985. Complementation. In Timothy Shopen (ed.), *Language typology and syntactic description: Volume II Complex constructions*. Cambridge: Cambridge University Press. 42–140.
Norman, Jerry. 1988. *Chinese*. Cambridge: Cambridge University Press.
Palmer, Frank R. 1986. *Mood and Modality*. Cambridge: Cambridge University Press.
Palmer, Frank R. 2001. *Mood and Modality*. 2nd edition. Cambridge: Cambridge University Press.
Paris, Marie-Claude. 2013. Verbal reduplication and verbal classifiers in Chinese. In Guangshun Cao, Hilary Chappell, Redouane Djamouri, and Thekla Wiebusch (eds.), Breaking down

the barriers: interdisciplinary studies in chinese linguistics and beyond. Taipei: Academia Sinica. 257–278.

Payne, John R. 1985. Negation. In. Timothy Shopen. *Language typology and syntactic description. Vol. I: Clause structure*. Cambridge: Cambridge U.P. 197–242.

Payne, Thomas E. 2010. Noun Complements vs. Post-Nominal Modifiers. (Available online at http://pages.uoregon.edu/tpayne/UEG/UEG-additionalreading-ch9-nouncomplements.pdf , Accessed on 2018-06-03.)

Peyraube, Alain. 1980. *Les constructions locatives en chinois moderne*. Paris: Langages croisés.

Peyraube, Alain. 1985. Les forms en *ba* en chinois vernaculaire médiéval et moderne. *Cahiers de Linguistique Asie Orientale* XIV-2, 193–213.

Peyraube, Alain. 1988. *Syntaxe diachronique du chinois: Évolution des constructions datives du XIVe siècle av. J.-C. au XVIIIe siècle*. Paris: Collège de France.

Peyraube, Alain. 1989. History of the passive constructions in Chinese until the 10th century. *Journal of Chinese Linguistics*. 225–372.

Peyraube, Alain. 1996. Recent issues in Chinese historical syntax. In C.-T. James Huang and Y.-H. Audrey Li (eds.), *New Horizons in Chinese Linguistics* (Studies in Natural Language and Linguistic Theory 36). Dordrecht: Kluwer Academic Publishers. 161–213.

Peyraube, Alain and Thekla Wiebusch. 2020. New insights on the historical evolution of the differential object marking (DOM) in Chinese. In Janet Zhiqun Xing (ed.), *A Typological Approach to Grammaticalization and Lexicalization: East Meets West*. Berlin: De Gruyter. 101–130.

Qian, Zengyi 钱曾怡. 1997. *Jinan Fangyan Zidian* 济南方言字典 [Dictionary of the Jinan Dialect]. Nanjing: Jiangsu Education Publishing House.

Qin, Yuanxiong 覃远雄, Wei Shuguan 韦树关 and Bian Chenglin 卞成林. 1997. *Nanning Pinghua Zidian* 南宁平话字典 [Dictionary of the Nanning Pinghua]. Nanjing: Jiangsu Education Publishing House.

Ruan, Guijun 阮桂君. 2009. *Ningbo Fangyan Yufa Yanjiu* 宁波方言语法研究 [Studies on the Grammar of the Ningbo Dialect]. Wuhan: Huazhong Normal University Press.

Sagart, Laurent. 2011. Classifying Chinese dialects/Sinitic languages on shared innovations. Talk given at Centre de recherches linguistiques sur l'Asie orientale, Norgent sur Marne.

Schachter, Paul and Timothy Shopen. 2007. Parts-of-speech systems. In Timothy Shopen (ed.), *Language Typology and Syntactic Description Volume I: Clause Structure*. 2nd edition. Cambridge: Cambridge University Press. 1–60.

Shen, Ming 沈明. 1994. *Taiyuan Fangyan Zidian* 太原方言字典 [Dictionary of the Taiyuan Dialect]. Nanjing: Jiangsu Education Publishing House.

Sheng, Yimin 盛益民. 2014. *Wuyu Shaoxing Keqiaohua cankao yufa* 吴语绍兴柯桥话参考语法 [A reference grammar of Shaoxing Keqiao Wu]. PhD Thesis. Tianjin: Nankai University.

Sheng, Yimin 盛益民. 2014. *Wuyu Shaoxing Keqiaohua cankao yufa* 吴语绍兴柯桥话参考语法 [A reference grammar of Shaoxing Keqiao Wu]. Tianjin: Nankai University PhD Thesis.

Shi, Dingxu. 1997. Issues on Chinese Passive. *Journal of Chinese Linguistics* Vol. 25-1. 41–70.

Shibatani, Masayoshi. 1976. The grammar of causative constructions: A conspectus. In Masayoshi Shibatani (ed.), *The grammar of causative constructions*. New York: Academic Press. 1–42.

Siewierska, Anna. 2013. Passive Constructions. In Matthew S. Dryer and Martin Haspelmath (eds.), *The World Atlas of Language Structures Online*. Leipzig: Max Planck Institute for Evolutionary Anthropology. (Available online at http://wals.info/chapter/107, Accessed on 2018-05-03.)

Song, Jae Jung. 2001. *Linguistic typology: Morphology and syntax*. Harlow: Pearson Education.
Song, Jae Jung. 2013. Periphrastic Causative Constructions. In Matthew S. Dryer and Martin Haspelmath (eds.), The World Atlas of Language Structures Online. Leipzig: Max Planck Institute for Evolutionary Anthropology. (Available online at http://wals.info/chapter/110, Accessed on 2019-01-08.)
Song, Na 宋娜 and Bei Luobei (=Alain Peyraube) 贝罗贝. 2019. 保定方言时间前置介词"投"及其历时演变 [The temporal preposition *tou* in the Baoding dialect and its diachronic evolution: A comparative analysis with the postposition *zhiqian* in Standard Mandarin]. *Zhongguo Yuwen* 中国语文 [Languages in China] 2019-1. 102–110.
Song, Yuzhu 宋玉柱. 1987. Jieci 'you' yinggai kending 介词"有"应该肯定 [The prepositional use of 'you' should be confirmed], *Hanyu Xuexi* 汉语学习 [Chinese learning] 2. 20–21.
Smith, Carlota S. 1994. Aspectual viewpoint and situation type in Mandarin Chinese. *Journal of East Asian Linguistics*, Vol. 3-2. 107–146.
Stassen, Leon. 2000. And-languages and With-languages. *Linguistic Typology* 4 (2000). 1–51.
Stassen, Leon. 2013a. Predicative Possession. In Matthew S. Dryer and Martin Haspelmath (eds.), The World Atlas of Language Structures Online. Leipzig: Max Planck Institute for Evolutionary Anthropology. (Available online at http://wals.info/chapter/117, Accessed on 2020-05-07.)
Stassen, Leon. 2013b. Comparative Constructions. In Matthew S. Dryer and Martin Haspelmath (eds.), *The World Atlas of Language Structures Online*. Leipzig: Max Planck Institute for Evolutionary Anthropology. (Available online at http://wals.info/chapter/121, Accessed on 2020-02-18.)
Su, Ling 苏玲. 2013. *Sichuan Yibin Luorunxiang Fangyan Beidong Jushi he Shiyi Jushi Yanjiu* 四川宜宾落润乡被动句式和使役句式研究 [A study on the passive and causative constructions in the Yibin Luorun dialect in Sichuan]. Xi'an: Shaanxi Normal University MA thesis.
Sun, Chaofen. 1996. *Word-Order Change and Grammaticalization in the History of Chinese*. Stanford: Standord University Press.
Sun, Yan 孙艳. 2005. *Hanzangyu Siyige Yanjiu* 汉藏语四音格研究 [A study on the four-syllable expressions in Sino-Tibetan languages]. Beijing: Minzu University PhD thesis.
Tang, Sze-Wing. 2001. A complementation approach to Chinese passives and its consequences. *Linguistics* 39. 257–295.
Tang, Zhengda 唐正大. 2007. Guanxihua Duixiang yu Guanxi Congju de Weizhi 关系话对象与关系从句的位置 [Relativized positions and constituent order in relative clauses]. *Dangdai Yuyanxue* 当代语言学 [Comteporary Linguistics] 9-2. 139–150.
Tang, Zhengda 唐正大. 2008. Guanzhong Yongshouhua de Guanxi Congju Leixing 关中永寿话的关系从句类型 [A typologicaly of relative clauses in the Yongshou dialect]. *Fangyan* 方言 [Dialects] 3. 244–251.
Teng, Shou-Hsin. 1982. Disposal structures in Amoy. *Bulletin of the Institute of History and Philology Academia Sinica* 53.2. 331–352.
Thepkanjana, Kingkarn and Satoshi Uehara. 2008. The verb of giving in Thai and Mandarin Chinese as a case of polysemy: A comparative study. *Language Sciences* 30. 621–651.
Thompson, Sandra A. and Robert E. Longacre. 1985. Adverbial clauses. In Timothy Shopen (ed.), *Language Typology and Syntactic Description Volume II: Complex Constructions*. Cambridge: Cambridge University Press. 171–234.

Thompson, Sandra A., Robert E. Longacre, and Shin Ja J. Hwang. 2007. Adverbial clauses. In Timothy Shopen (ed.), *Language Typology and Syntactic Description Volume II: Complex Constructions*. 2nd edition. Cambridge: Cambridge University Press. 237–300.

Tian, Wen 田雯. 1760–1820. *Qián Shū* 黔书 [A Book of Guizhou]. http://www.wul.waseda.ac.jp/kotenseki/html/ru05/ru05_04017/index.html

Tian, Chunlai. 田春来. 2009. Jindai Hanyu 'Zhuo' Zi Beidongju 近代汉语"著"字被动句 [Passives with 'zhuo' in Morden Chinese]. 语言科学 [Linguistic Sciences] 2006-5. 517–524.

Tsao, Feng-fu. 2001. Semantics and sytax of verbal and adjectival reduplication in Mandarin and Taiwanese Southern Min. In Hilary Chappell (ed.), *Sinitic Grammar: Synchronic and Diachronic Perspectives*. Oxford: Oxford University Press. 285–308.

Ultan, Russell. 1969. Some general characteristics of interrogative system. *Working Papers in Language Universals 1*. 41–63.

Ultan, Russell. 1972. Some Features of Basic Comparative Constructions. *Working Papers on Language Universals* (Stanford) 9. 117–162.

van der Auwera, Johan and Vladimir Plungian. 1998. Modality's Semantic Map. *Linguistic Typology* 2. 79–124.

van der Auwera, Johan, Petar Kehayov and Alice Vittrant. 2009. Acquisitive modals. In Lotte Hogeweg, Helen de Hoop, and Andrej Malchukove (eds.), *Cross-linguistic Semantics of Tense, Aspect and Modality*. Amsterdam/Philadelphia: John Benjamins. 271–302.

van der Auwera, Johan and Andreas Ammann. 2013. Overlap between Situational and Epistemic Modal Marking. In Matthew S. Dryer and Martin Haspelmath (eds.), *The World Atlas of Language Structures Online*. Leipzig: Max Planck Institute for Evolutionary Anthropology. (Available online at http://wals.info/chapter/76, Accessed on 2018-07-04.)

von Fintel, Kai. 2006. Modality and language. In Donald M. Borchert (ed.), *Encyclopedia of philosophy* – 2nd edition, vol. 10. Detroit: MacMillan Reference USA. 20–27.

Vittrant, Alice and Johan van der Auwera. 2010. Epistemic modality or how to express likelihood in Burmese. *Cahiers de linguistiques – Asie orientale*, vol. 39.1. 41–80.

Vittrant, Alice and Justin Watkins. 2019. Introduction: Languages of the Mainland Southeast Asia linguistic area – Grammatical Sketches. In Alice Vittrant and Justin Watkins (eds.), *The Mainland Southeast Asia Linguistic Area*. Berlin: De Gruyter. 1–11.

Vittrant, Alice and Justin Watkins. 2019. Appendix. In Alice Vittrant and Justin Watkins (eds.), *The Mainland Southeast Asia Linguistic Area*. Berlin: De Gruyter. 653–710.

Wang, Jian. 2015. Bare classifier phrases in Sinitic languages: A typological perspective. In Hilary Chappell (ed.), *Diversity in Sinitic Languages*. Oxford: Oxford University Press. 110–133.

Wang, Jian. 2016. How to as 'who' without 'who': A typological study on interrogative words for 'person' in Sinitic languages. Invited lecture at CRLAO in Paris. Feb. 2016.

Wang, Junhu 王军虎. 1996. *Xi'an Fangyan Zidian* 西安方言字典 [Dictionary of the Xi'an Dialect]. Nanjing: Jiangsu Education Publishing House.

Wang, Li 王力. 1945. *Zhongguo Yufa Lilun* 中国语法理论 [Theories in Chinese grammar]. Reprinted in 1984 in *Wang Li Wenji* (Di Yi Juan) 王力文集（第一卷）[The collected works of Wang Li Vol. I]. Jinan: Shandong Education Press.

Wang, Li 王力. 1958. *Hanyu Shi Gao* 汉语史稿 [Writings on the history of Chinese]. Reprinted in 1980. Beijing: Zhonghua Book Company.

Wang, Li et al. 王力等. 2000. *Wang Li Gudai Hanyu Zidian* 王力古代汉语字典 [Dictionary of Classic Chinese Edited by Wang Li]. Beijing: Zhonghua Book Company.

Wang, Miao 王苗. 2015. Lun Jiegou Zhuci 'Jia' de Laiyuan he Yanbian 论结构助词"家"的来源和演变 [On the origin and the evolution of the morpheme 'jia']. *Guhanyu Yanjiu* 古汉语研究 [Studies in Historical Chinese] 3. 29–38.

Wang, Ping 汪平. 1994. *Guiyang Fangyan Zidian* 贵阳方言字典 [A dictionary of the Guiyang dialect]. Nanjing: Jiangsu Education Publishing House.

Wen, Duanzheng 温端政 and Zhang Guangming 张光明. 1995. *Xinzhou Fangyan Zidian* 忻州方言词典 [Dictionary of the Xinzhou Dialect]. Nanjing: Jiangsu Education Publishing House.

Wiedenhof, Jeroen. 2015. *A Grammar of Mandarin*. Amsterdam: John Benjamins.

Wu, Fuxiang 吴福祥 1997. Tang Song Chuzhishi Jiai Laiyuan 唐宋处置式及其来源 [The disposal constructions in Tang and Song Dynasties and their origins]. *Cahiers de Linguistique – Asie Orientale* 26(2). 201–220.

Wu, Fuxiang 吴福祥. 2001. Nanfang Fangyan Ji Ge Zhuangtai Buyu Biaoji de Laiyuan 南方方言几个状态补语标记的来源（一）[On the sources of markers of manner complement in several southern Chinese dialects (1)]. *Fangyan* 方言 [Dialects] 2001-4. 344–354.

Wu, Fuxiang 吴福祥. 2002. Nanfang Fangyan Ji Ge Zhuangtai Buyu Biaoji de Laiyuan 南方方言几个状态补语标记的来源（二）[On the sources of markers of manner complement in several southern Chinese dialects (2)]. *Fangyan* 方言 [Dialects] 2002-1. 24–34.

Wu, Yunji. 2006. The Evolution of the Negative Forms in the Hunan Waxiang Dialect. In Dah-an Ho Hongnian Zhang, Wuyun Pan and Fuxiang Wu (eds.), *Linguistic Studies in Chinese and Neighboring Languages: Festschrift in Honor of Professor Pang-Hsin Ting on His 70th Birthday*. Taipei: Academia Sinica. 1123–1142.

Wurm, Stephen, Rong Li, Theo Baumann, and Mei W. Lee (eds.). 1987. *Language Atlas of China/ Zhongguo Yuyan Dituji* 中国语言地图集. Hong Kong: Longman

Xiao, Yali 肖亚丽. 2008. *Qiandongnan Fangyan Yufa Yanjiu* 黔东南方言语法研究 [Studies on the Grammar of the Qiandongnan Dialect]. Shanghai: Shanghai Normal University MA thesis.

Xing, Zhiqun. 2003. Grammaticalization of verbs in Mandarin Chinese. *Journal of Chinese Linguistics Vol. 31*. 101–144.

Xiong, Zhenghui 熊正辉. 1995. *Nanchang Fangyan Zidian* 南昌方言字典 [A dictionary of the Nanchang dialect]. Nanjing: Jiangsu Education Publishing House.

Xu, Huiling and Stephen Matthews. 2007. Cong dongci dao ziju jiegou biaoji: Chaozhou fangyan he Taiwan Minnan hua dongci 'shuo' he 'kan' de xuhua guocheng 從動詞到子句標記: 潮州方言和台灣閩南話動詞'説'和'看'的虛化過程 [From verb to complementizer: the grammaticalization process for the verbs 'say' and 'see' in the Chaozhou dialect and Taiwanese Southern Min]. *Zhongguo Yuwen Yanjiu* 中國語文研究 [Studies in Chinese Linguistics] 23. 61–72.

Xu, Ying 徐英. 2016. Hanyu Fangyan 'Tuo' Zi Beidongju de Tezheng Ji Qi Shengcheng 汉语方言中"驮"字被动句的特征及其生成机制 [The passive constructions with 'Tuo' in Chinese dialects and their rise]. *Wuhan Ligong Dauxe Xubao* 武汉理工大学学报（社会科学版）[Journal of Wuhan University of Technology (Social Science Edition)] 2016-6. 1233–1237.

Yap, Foong Ha, and Shoichi Iwasaki. 2003. From causatives to passives: a passage in some East and Southeast Asian languages. In Eugene H. Casad and Gary B. Palmer (eds.), *Cognitive Linguistics and Non-Indo-European Languages*. Berlin and New York: Mouton de Gruyter. 419–445.

Yap, Foon Ha, Winnie Chor and Jiao Wang. 2012. On the development of epistemic 'fear' markers: an analysis of Mandarin Kongpa and Cantonese Taipaa. In W. Abraham and

E. Leiss (eds.), *Covert patterns of modality*. Newcastle upon Tyne: Cambridge Scholars Publishing. 412–432.

Yin, Runlin 殷润林. 2005. *Zigong Fangyan Yufa Yanjiu* 自贡方言语法研究 [Studies on the Grammar of the Zigong Dialect]. Kunming: Yunnan Normal University MA thesis.

Yuan, Haixia 袁海霞. 2010. 'Bi' Zi Ju Zai Minzu Yuyan Zhong de Kuosan. "比"字句在民族语文中的扩散 [The Proliferation of Sentence Bi(比) in Minority Languages]. *Yuyan Yanjiu* 语言研究 [Language Studies]. 2010-3. 84–89.

Yuan, Jiahua et al. 袁家骅等. 2001. *Hanyu Fangyan Gaiyao* 汉语方言概要 [An introduction to Chinese dialects], second edition. Beijing: Language and Culture Press.

Yue-Hashimoto, Anne. 1971. Mandarin syntactic structures. *Unicorn* 8. 1–149.

Yue-Hashimoto, Anne. 1993. *Comparative Chinese dialectal grammar: Handbook for investigators*. Paris: EHESS.

Yue-Hashimoto, Anne. 2001. The verb-complement construction in historical perspective with special reference to Cantonese. In Hilary Chappell (ed.), *Sintic Grammar: Synchronic and Diachronic Perspectives*. Oxford: Oxford University Press. 232–265.

Zhai, Huifeng 翟会锋. 2011. *Sanguanzhai Yiyu cankao yufa* 三官寨彝语参考语法 [A Reference Grammar of Yi (Sanguanzhai)]. Beijing: Minzu University of China PhD thesis.

Zhang, Cheng 张赪. 2000. 魏晋南北朝时期"著"字的用法 [On the uses of the word 'zhuo' in the period of the Wei, Jin and Northern and Southern dynasties]. *Zhongwen Xuekan* 中文学刊 [Journal of Chinese] 2000-2. 121–128.

Zhang, Cheng 张赪. 2010. *Hanyu Yuxu de Lishi Fazhan* 汉语语序的历史发展 [Evolution of word orders in Chinese]. Beijing: Beijing Language and Culture University Press.

Zhang, Min 张敏. 1990. *Hànyǔ Fāngyán Fǎnfù Wènjù de Lèixíngxué Yánjiū* 汉语方言反复问句的类型学研究：共时分布及其历时蕴含 [A typological study of yes-no questions in Chinese dialects in diachronic perspective]. Beijing: Peking University PhD thesis.

Zhang, Min 张敏. 1997. Cong leixingxue he renzhi yufa de jiaodu kan Hanyu chongdie xianxiang 从类型学和认知语法的角度看汉语重叠现象 [The phenomenon of reduplication in Chinese from a perspective of typology and cognitive grammar]. *Guowai Yuyanxue* 国外语言学 [Contemporary Linguistics] 2. 37–45.

Zhang, Min 張敏. 2002. Shanggu, Zhonggu Hanyu Ji Xiandai Nanfang Fangyan Limian de 'Fouding-Cunzai Yanhuaquan' 上古、中古漢語及現代南方言裡的"否定-存在演化圈"[The negative-existential cycle as manifested in Archaic Chinese, Middle Chinese and the Modern Southern dialects]. In Anne Yue (ed.), *International Symposium on the Historical Aspect of the Chinese Language: Commemorating the Centennial Birthday of the Late Professor Li Fang-Kue*. Vol. II. Seattle: University of Washington. 571–616.

Zhang, Min. 2009. How to Give in a Language Without 'Give': Towards a New Typology of Ditransitive Constructions in Sinitic Languages. Paper for the 17th Annual Conference of the International Association of Chinese Linguistics (IACL-17). 2–4 July 2009, Ecole des Hautes Etudes en Sciences Sociales, Paris.

Zhang, Shuangqing 張雙慶 (ed.). 1996. *Dongci de ti* 動詞的體 [Aspect]. Hongkong: T. T. Ng Chinese Language Research Centre-The Chinese University of Hong Kong.

Zhengzhang, Shangfang 郑张尚芳. 2010. Caijiahua Baiyu Guanxi Ji Cigen Bijiao 蔡家话白语关系及词根比较 [Comparison of Lexicon Between Caijia and Bai]. In Pan Wuyun 潘悟云 and Shen Zhongwei 沈钟伟 (eds.), *Yanjiu Zhi Le: Qingzhu Wang Shiyuan Xiansheng 75 Shouchen Xueshu Lunwen Ji* 研究之乐：庆祝王士元先生75寿辰学术论文集 [Joy of Research: Collection of essays for the 75th anniversary of Pr. William S.-Y Wang]. 389–400. Shanghai: Shanghai Educational Publishing House.

Zhu, Dexi 朱德熙. 1979. Yu Dongci 'Gei' Xiangguan de Yufa Wenti 与动词'给'相关的语法问题 [On the verb 'give']. *Fangyan* 方言 [Dialects] 2. 81–87.

Zhu, Dexi 朱德熙. 1982. *Yufa Jiangyi* 语法讲义 [Lectures on grammar]. Beijing: The Commercial Press.

Zhu, Dexi 朱德熙. 1985. Hanyu Fangyan Li de Liang Zhong Fanfu Yiwenju 汉语方言里的两种反复问句 [Two types of alternative questions in Chinese dialects]. *Zhongguo Yuwen* 中国语文 [Languages in China] 1.

Zhu, Dexi. 1990. A preliminary survey of the dialectal distribution of the interrogative sentence patterns V-NEG-VO and VO-NEG-V in Chinese. *Journal of Chinese Linguistics* Vol. 18, No.2. 209–230.

Zhu, Dexi 朱德熙. 1991. 'V-neg-VO' yu 'VO-neg-V' Liang Zhong Fanfu Yiwenju Zai Hanyu Fangyan Li de Fenbu "V-neg-VO"与"VO-neg-V"两种反复问句问句在汉语方言里的分布 [Distributions of the alternative questions 'V-neg-VO' and 'VO-neg-V' in Chinese dialects]. *Zhongguo Yuwen* 中国语文 [Languages in China] 5.

Zhu, Jiansong 朱建颂. 1995. *Wuhan Fangyan Zidian* 武汉方言字典 [Dictionary of the Wuhan Dialect]. Nanjing: Jiangsu Education Publishing House.

Zhu, Minche 祝敏彻. 1957. Lun Chuqi Chuzhishi 论初期处置式 [On the early disposal forms]. *Yuyanxue Luncong* 语言学论丛 [Anthology of Chinese Linguistics] 1. 17–33.

Index

ABILITY 355, 356, 383
ABLE TO 11
absolute causative contexts 211
accessibility hierarchy 464
ACQUIRE 11, 142, 223, 309–311, 383, 384, 391, 400, 401, 558
adposition 193
adverb 7, 40, 48, 49, 72–74, 104–106, 108, 109, 112, 116–119, 121–123, 138, 145, 151–160, 181, 182, 249, 258, 264, 265, 266, 285, 334, 339, 341, 351, 352, 355, 405, 413, 416, 422, 455, 491, 492, 494, 497, 499, 500, 512, 532
– adverb of time 151, 156
– degree adverb 40, 108, 118, 151, 154, 156, 160
– manner adverb 121, 151–153, 160, 181
– manner adverbial 7, 147, 148, 152–154, 160, 181, 341, 344
– scope adverb 73, 74, 159, 160, 182
adversative passive 556
affirmative 123, 278, 335, 353, 407–409, 412, 413, 453, 526, 528, 537, 557
affixation 7
– prefixation 53
– suffixation 53, 57, 61, 103, 303, 305
agentful passive 233–236, 240, 242
agentless passive 172, 219, 226, 233–234, 236, 240, 242, 557
ambiguity 10, 170, 211, 239, 256, 270, 272, 284, 334, 377, 380, 405, 454, 476, 488, 510
analytic causative construction 200, 201, 203, 218
– extent complement causative 204, 206, 218
– pivot-causee causative 207, 208
apposition 60
argument 9, 45, 48, 50, 51, 59, 68, 69, 120, 124, 125, 142, 160, 171, 183–187, 190, 191, 193–200, 204, 212, 234, 236, 270, 274, 276, 277, 374, 448, 464, 482, 486–488, 500, 554, 557
– A(gent) argument 183
– experiencer argument 234

– P(atient) argument 183, 185, 234, 236
– pivotal argument 234
– R(ecipient) argument 171, 183, 184, 186, 187, 193–196, 199, 557
– T(heme) argument 183, 185, 190, 191, 193–196, 199
aspect 7, 12, 105, 108, 112, 121, 127, 128, 138, 142, 146, 244, 302–305, 313, 323, 330, 331, 334, 338, 340, 341, 343, 344, 352, 359, 407, 418, 557, 558
– completive 121, 128, 132, 304, 305, 311–313, 352, 421, 479, 515
– continuous 112, 121, 127, 146, 302, 304, 305, 314, 331, 334–340, 345–347, 349, 353, 407, 478, 521, 522, 557
– continuous (manner) 304, 305, 340–345
– currently relevant state 105, 178, 304, 305, 313–315, 317, 325, 421, 478
– delimitative 127, 168, 304, 305, 330–334
– durative 126, 127, 138, 139, 172, 175, 247, 250, 253, 269, 302, 303, 305, 316, 331, 338, 340, 345, 346, 353, 450, 479
– experiential 304, 305, 308, 322–327, 353, 355, 412–414, 421, 422, 479
– frequentative 305, 349–351, 359, 558
– inchoative 105, 141, 227, 304, 305, 315, 317–321, 353
– perfective (negated) 108, 121, 129, 131, 136, 137, 304–307, 309, 311, 324, 416, 421–423, 426, 434, 436, 516
– prospective 105, 270, 304, 305, 315, 327–329, 360, 361, 367, 433
aspectual marker 105, 121, 128, 146, 172, 181, 269, 274, 304, 305, 314, 317, 352, 353, 407, 477
atelic 302, 304, 305, 331
ATTACH 164, 165
attributive adjective 109
auxiliary 104, 172, 219, 220, 222, 234, 236, 237, 265, 294, 298, 305, 328, 350, 355–361, 363, 366–368, 370, 376, 391, 405, 409, 414, 419, 423, 424, 427, 433, 453, 484, 502, 504, 529, 532, 537, 557

bă construction 243, 244, 252
bounded 302–306, 330–332, 338

causation 200, 201, 206–208
causative verb 68, 184, 188, 192, 193, 200, 201, 203–205, 207–211, 215, 217, 218, 220, 221, 233, 234, 237, 239, 240, 557
causative-passive contexts 211, 215, 217
CAUSE-clause 205, 216
causee 204, 205, 211, 234
CERTAINTY 355, 356
change of state 127, 222, 226, 243, 253, 304, 307, 314, 315, 317, 421, 454, 478
classifier 7, 10, 45, 50, 51, 55, 57, 59, 62, 73–76, 78–83, 85–87, 89–92, 98–101, 103–105, 107, 115, 120, 152, 153, 156, 160–171, 182, 244, 274, 296, 299, 324, 330, 331, 360, 443–445, 447, 448, 464, 465, 473, 498, 556, 557
– nominal classifier 160, 162, 556
– numeral classifier 10, 59, 76, 78, 80, 89, 103, 115, 169, 170, 557
– verbal classifier 104, 105, 107, 156, 160–171, 182, 274, 296, 299, 324, 330
  – double classifier 169
  – instrument verbal classifier 162, 164–166, 168, 169
  – mensural verbal classifier 162, 165–169, 171
clause-initial position 8, 537–539, 547
clause linking 12, 158, 160, 481, 507, 541
– adverbial subordination 481, 486, 511, 554
  – conditional 11, 130, 329, 405, 511, 515, 529–537, 539, 541, 543, 544, 555, 558
  – consequence and cause 511, 523, 529, 555
  – substitutive clause 550, 552
  – tail-head linkage 552, 553
  – concession 509, 511, 544
  – see time clause
– complementation 142–144, 147, 156, 181, 204, 266, 291, 403, 434, 461, 462, 481, 482, 484, 486, 554, 558
– coordination 56, 481, 486, 487, 490, 493, 497, 501, 507, 554, 555
– contrastive coordination 507

– see conjunction
– see disjunction
cleft construction 122, 355, 407, 453, 475, 496, 557
coda 14, 33, 35
cognate 4, 15, 55, 78, 82, 85, 89, 119, 126, 226, 233, 241, 299, 322, 358, 359, 416, 425, 426, 429, 445, 447, 490, 495, 501, 503, 536, 542, 545, 555, 557
complement 7, 38, 55, 72, 100, 104–107, 120, 121, 124, 127–129, 131–134, 136–145, 151, 172, 175, 181, 196, 201–204, 206, 207, 212, 218, 220, 222–224, 226, 230, 234, 241, 244, 250–253, 273, 274, 276, 282, 292, 293, 295, 299, 306, 311, 318, 319, 321–323, 325–327, 337, 338, 356, 357, 373, 376, 404, 409, 424, 434, 437, 444, 450, 475, 481–486, 502, 503, 511, 558
– copular complement 55, 72, 100, 120, 337, 444, 486
– directional complement 7, 127, 133, 134, 137, 139, 141, 181, 306, 319
– extent complement 7, 144, 145, 203, 204, 206, 218
– general achievement complement 127, 128
– manner complement 142, 144, 145, 151, 558
– resultative complement 7, 38, 105, 121, 127–129, 131–133, 138, 139, 142, 172, 181, 196, 201, 202, 212, 223, 226, 241, 250–252, 292, 293, 295, 338, 356, 404, 409, 424, 437, 450
complementary distribution 33, 34, 345
complementizer 7, 107, 142, 143, 145, 204, 216, 217, 223, 266, 283, 284, 355, 434, 482, 483, 486, 558
complex stative construction 142
component of comparative 263
– comparee 263, 269, 273, 280, 285, 287, 288, 290, 293, 296–298, 333
– degree marker 145, 249, 252, 263, 266–269, 273–277, 279, 282, 284, 285, 296, 300, 333, 405
– parameter 79, 81, 192, 200, 263–265, 269, 273, 274, 276, 279, 281, 285, 287, 288, 290, 292, 294, 295, 297, 299

- standard 263, 269, 273, 276, 277, 280, 282–285, 287, 288, 290, 293, 295–300, 471
- standard marker 263, 267, 269, 272–274, 284, 288, 290–293, 299, 300

compound 14, 37–41, 51, 53–56, 68, 127, 177, 193, 196, 209, 218, 225, 230, 237, 239, 240, 265, 293, 357, 417, 421, 442, 444, 446, 485, 536, 537, 541, 556, 557
- conjunct compound 54, 56
- head-modifier compound 54, 56
- modifier-head compound 54, 55
- (S)VO compound 54, 56

compound marker 177, 519
compounding 6, 40, 46, 53, 94, 127, 201, 223, 224, 226, 241, 306, 321, 338, 443
concessive 507–510, 541, 544–550, 555
conjunction 158, 160, 169, 174, 268, 269–271, 284, 300, 486, 487, 489–501, 510, 511, 544, 550, 554, 555
- argument conjunction 487, 500, 554
- clause conjunction 487, 489, 490, 500
  - correlative comparative construction 499, 500
  - correlative simultaneous construction 497, 500
  - emphatic conjunction 158, 160, 489, 490, 497, 501, 554

construction of comparison 12, 107, 263–265, 300, 333
- comparative construction of inequality 263
  - inferior comparative 263, 264, 285–288, 300, 301
  - superior comparative 263, 264, 285, 288–290, 300, 301
- equative construction 263, 264, 266, 267, 269, 273, 274, 280, 282, 284
- relative superlative construction 263

conventionalization 236
copula 119–124, 145, 289, 308, 335, 360, 390, 405, 407, 418, 419, 436–439, 447, 463, 486, 487, 504, 506, 508, 509, 526, 528, 538, 541, 542, 544
copular 46, 55, 63, 72, 100, 104, 119, 120, 124, 148, 337, 339, 390, 439, 444, 475, 486, 488, 521
co-referent 68

co-referential 9, 69, 100, 205, 215, 216, 234, 235, 254, 255
cross-reference maker 11, 193–195, 199, 246, 247, 252, 253, 256, 259, 557
cross-referencing 10, 12

deictic verb 133, 134, 137, 178, 250, 316
delexicalization 234
demonstrative 37, 41, 45–52, 59, 92, 96–98, 103, 152, 153, 155, 160, 181, 273, 275, 276, 279, 282–285, 381, 443, 462–464, 466, 467, 473–475, 480, 522, 542, 556
- basic demonstrative 46
- manner/degree demonstrative 46, 48
- place demonstrative 48
- time demonstrative 48

deontic 354, 355, 361, 383, 393, 394, 400, 558
derivational adverb 116, 118, 153, 160, 181, 182, 266
desemanticization 249
DESIRE 356
devocalization 17, 32, 33, 44, 115, 556
diminutive 7, 43, 89, 330, 556
disjunction 428–430, 432, 434–436, 440, 443, 457, 486, 501, 503–506, 509, 555
- emphatic disjunction 501, 504, 506, 555
- interrogative disjunction 501, 503, 506, 555
- standard disjunction 501, 504, 506, 555

disposal construction 243–246, 248, 250
distinctive feature 105, 108, 112, 116
distributional feature 45, 49, 50, 68, 103, 105, 109, 172, 181, 250, 356, 452
ditransitive construction 12, 171, 174, 177, 180, 183–185, 189–191, 193–199, 208, 214, 217, 237, 246, 557
- differential object marking construction 12, 184, 185, 193, 194, 198, 199, 202, 243, 259
- cross-reference marking construction 194, 246, 252, 253, 260
- double marked construction 195, 246, 262
- object marking construction 7, 9, 12, 51, 64, 135, 178, 184, 185, 190, 191, 193, 194, 198, 199, 202, 222, 224–226, 243–246, 248–254, 258–261, 315, 346, 557

– double object construction 184, 185, 187, 197, 199, 229, 470
– indirective construction 184, 185, 187, 188, 191, 193, 197, 198
– V-s₁⁵⁵ construction 196, 199
– comitative construction 184, 196, 199
dynamic 106, 112, 139, 178, 234, 302, 303, 307, 334, 338, 341, 342, 354, 383, 389

EFFECT-clause 216
ellipsis 494, 556
epistemic 354, 355, 364, 366, 367, 372, 374, 376, 377, 380, 381, 383, 387, 388, 390, 391, 405–407, 409, 410, 414, 557, 558
evidentiality 410–412
existential verb 104, 119, 125, 347, 415, 417, 418

free alternation 39, 40
free variant 24, 36, 319
functional contrast 68
functional distribution 488
functional feature 249
functional morpheme 258
functional similarity 226
functional word 10, 172, 247, 254
fusion 7, 209, 415, 472
fusional-affixing 11

genetic affiliation 3, 15
gerund 482
gradable property 263, 265, 282, 285, 287, 288, 294, 299
grammatical feature 3, 5, 13, 556
grammatical function 45, 142, 270
grammatical relation 6
grammaticalization 138, 181, 191, 217, 220, 234, 236, 239, 242, 249, 251, 254, 380, 554, 556, 558

haplology 234
HAVE TO/MUST 11
homophonic 132
homophonic noun 81
homophonic root 115
honorific 61

impersonal 125, 283, 361, 377, 380–383, 537
inceptive 318
infinitive 482
inflected case-marking 10, 11
ingressive 318
intensifier 157, 351, 352, 493, 495, 504, 509, 513, 516, 528, 537, 548, 549, 551
INTENTION 355, 356
interrogative 12, 71–73, 427–430, 432–434, 438–440, 442, 443, 447, 457, 501–503, 506, 545, 547, 555
– alternative question 427–430, 432, 435, 457, 501, 503
– content question 427–429, 442, 457, 484, 486
  – 'how (manner)' and 'why' question 451
  – 'how many/much' question 455
  – 'what' question 447
  – 'when' question 450
  – 'where' question 449
  – 'which' question 443, 444
  – 'who' question 445
  – 'whose' question 447
– polar question 105, 106, 120, 121, 274, 278, 357, 407, 427–429, 431–436, 438–442, 457
  – alternative polar question 428, 429, 431–434, 436, 457
  – particle polar question 428, 429, 431, 435, 436, 438, 439, 457
irrealis 158, 315, 325, 328, 384, 416, 418, 419, 423, 432, 485, 550, 552

lexical tone 11
loan 15, 147, 155, 430, 506
loan adverb 264
loan classifier 90
loan disjunction 506
loan marker 299
loan morpheme 58
loan suffix 61
loanword 77, 168, 269, 490, 495, 501, 504
localizer 92, 94–98, 103, 169, 175, 516, 518–520, 557
locative verb 103, 119, 123, 335, 518, 519, 557

MANAGE/GET TO 11
measure word 50, 51, 59, 76, 78, 90–92, 99, 163, 164, 169, 473, 498
metaphorical meaning 149
metaphorization 359
minimal pair 14, 15, 18, 31, 32, 453
modal 11, 12, 102, 105, 121, 145, 265, 294, 328, 329, 334, 354–361, 365–367, 370–374, 376–378, 380, 383–385, 389–393, 398–401, 403–406, 409, 411, 413, 414, 418, 423, 434, 436, 440, 532, 535, 537, 543, 551, 557, 558
– epistemic certainty 407, 557
– epistemic final particle 406
– inferential certainty 412
– modal adverb 405
– modal auxiliary 294, 355, 359, 361, 366, 367, 376, 409, 532, 537, 557
– lexical epistemic possibility 376
– post-VP 'can' modal 102, 105, 121, 145, 383, 400, 405, 413, 414, 440, 557
– potential construction 403–405, 413, 414, 423, 424
– reportative/quotative 410, 411, 413, 483
modality 121, 123, 145, 230, 335, 354–356, 366, 376, 391, 393, 400, 410, 413, 414, 483
modification 6, 103, 556
morphology 6, 14, 49, 151, 181, 219, 225, 460, 529
morphological process 7
multifunctional morpheme 405
multifunctional word 488
multifunctionality 173, 186

NECESSITY 355, 356, 383
negator 108, 121, 123, 126, 129–131, 136, 137, 145, 147, 151, 155, 306, 308, 309, 311, 324, 357, 365, 384, 415–419, 421–426, 434–436, 516, 541, 544, 545, 550
– existential negator 415, 426
– imperative negator 147, 365, 424, 425
– perfective negator 108, 121, 129, 131, 136, 137, 309, 311, 324, 422, 423, 426, 434, 436, 516
– possessive negator 422, 426

negation 12, 74, 108, 129, 131, 136, 137, 151, 306, 353, 396, 415–423, 426, 516, 540, 551
– negative existential and possessive verb 415, 417, 422, 426
– standard negation 415, 417, 418, 423, 426, 551
nominalizer 7, 57, 67, 100, 101, 335, 407, 463, 475–478, 480, 557
nominalization 45, 101–103, 477, 556
noun formation 53
noun phrase 12, 45, 65, 78, 100–103, 279, 459, 474, 475
– complex noun phrase 45
– headless noun phrase 45, 100–102, 475
– simple noun phrase 45
num. class. construction 11
numeral 10, 30, 45, 50, 59, 71, 76–80, 89, 91, 92, 97, 99, 103, 115, 160, 161, 166–170, 330, 464, 513, 557
– cardinal numeral 77, 78
– ordinal numeral 78

object-topicalized construction 7
obligation 354–356, 361, 363, 366, 394, 400–402, 414
omission 63, 171, 197, 340, 341, 533
on-going 334–336, 340, 341, 497, 557
onset 14, 15, 17, 33, 35, 36, 44, 226, 227
– affricate 14, 25, 26, 28, 29, 32–34, 44, 227, 556
  – alveolar affricate 25, 26, 34, 44
  – alveolo-palatal affricate 25, 28, 44
– fricative 14, 30–32
  – non-sibilant fricative 30, 31
– lateral approximant 31
– lateral fricative 31, 32
– lateral retroflex 31, 32, 556
– nasal 14, 24, 29, 33, 35
– plosive 14, 15–21, 24, 26, 29, 32–34, 44, 556
  – alveolar plosive 18
  – bilabial plosive 16, 19
  – retroflex plosive 20, 21, 34, 44, 556
  – velar plosive 24
operator 158

particle 121, 305, 313, 314–316, 335, 340, 355, 376, 384, 392, 406, 408, 413–415, 427–429, 431, 435, 436, 438–440, 453, 454, 457, 478, 529, 533, 541
passive agent marker 177, 193, 200, 211, 215–218, 220, 237–240, 242, 557
passive construction 12, 172, 177, 210, 216, 219, 220, 222, 223, 226, 234–236, 366
path verb 133, 134, 137
periphrasis 334, 340
PERMISSION 355, 356, 383
phonetic similarity 226
place word 52, 92–94, 96, 105, 123, 125, 149, 202, 477, 518
plural 7, 10, 37, 43, 46, 48, 50, 58–62, 64, 75, 82, 103, 270–272, 298, 444, 447, 464, 466, 472, 488, 489, 498, 556
polysemy 151, 169, 173, 227, 558
possession 66, 119, 125, 126, 214, 280, 418
possessive verb 119, 125, 126, 415, 417, 422, 426
possessor 64–66, 125, 447
possessum 63–67
POSSIBILITY 355, 356, 383
post-nominal 30, 331, 333, 334
post-verbal 8, 131, 134, 135, 142, 154, 155, 160, 180, 194, 195, 245, 255, 265, 314, 384, 436, 472, 496
pragmatic context 33, 94
pragmatic feature 243
pragmatic inference 524
pragmatic perspective 415
pragmatically inferred 9
pragmatically restricted 219
predicate 68, 104, 105, 107, 108, 112, 120, 122, 123, 125, 127, 144, 146, 147, 149–152, 156, 157, 160, 171, 172, 180, 181, 190, 192, 200, 201, 227, 237, 249, 250, 265, 269, 273, 288, 318, 320, 322, 334, 349, 351, 357, 388, 390, 393, 415, 416, 420, 423, 426, 432, 433, 452, 482
predicative adjective 109
preposition 6, 7, 9, 45, 48, 92, 93, 97, 98, 103, 104, 162, 163, 171–182, 184–189, 191, 194, 196, 197, 208, 234, 236, 247, 249, 250, 268–270, 274, 276, 278, 284, 290, 291, 294, 300, 449, 470, 488, 496, 517–519, 557

– ablative 171, 173, 186, 449, 488
– allative 9, 171, 172, 179, 181
– benefactive 11, 171, 173, 174, 184, 197–199, 278, 488
– comitative 171, 173, 174, 184, 196, 197, 199, 244, 267–272, 284, 300, 487, 488, 500
– dative 184, 187–189, 194, 196, 470, 557
– instrumental 171, 176, 247
– lative 171–175, 488
– locative 92, 93, 172, 517–519
– object marker 171, 176, 189, 194, 195, 235, 243–247, 250, 557
– passive agent 171, 172, 177, 193, 200, 211, 215–218, 220, 222, 237–240, 242, 557
– perlative 171
prepositional status 250
pronoun 7, 9, 37, 43, 45–46, 50, 58–66, 68–76, 79, 90, 92, 103, 160, 170, 181, 208, 216, 244–246, 270–272, 290, 331, 412, 442–449, 455, 460–467, 469, 470, 472, 488, 490, 503, 526, 542, 545–547, 556
– indefinite pronoun 71–75, 160, 448, 546
– personal pronoun 7, 43, 60, 65, 66, 68, 466, 472, 556
– possessive pronoun 50, 63, 64
  – adnominal possessive 62–64
  – pronominal possessive 62, 63
– reciprocal pronoun 70
– reflexive pronoun 68
  – anaphoric reflexive 68, 69
  – emphatic reflexive 68
pro-drop 9, 104, 128, 209, 325, 377, 463, 468, 475, 537, 538, 556
progressive 11, 302, 303, 334, 335, 341, 557
purposive 11, 180, 192, 193, 208, 237, 246, 248

quadrisyllabic descriptive phrase 145
quadrisyllabic idiomatic phrase 146–151
quantifier 50, 51, 161, 331, 333, 334, 466

realis 156, 158
reciprocal meaning 70
reduplication 7, 53, 83, 99, 105, 108, 112, 116, 118, 161, 162, 181, 182, 200, 330, 343, 427, 428, 556

relative clause 8, 45, 50, 93, 97, 98, 100, 142, 270, 336, 459–468, 470, 472–476, 478–481, 511, 521
– headed relative clause 462–464, 476, 480
– headless relative clause 100, 463, 475, 476, 480
relativization 12, 100, 270, 272, 459–464, 479–481, 489, 512, 556
rime 13, 14, 16, 18, 20, 24, 31, 33, 35, 36, 44, 556
– diphthong 33–35
– monophthong 33
– rime of nasal coda 35
– syllabic consonant 14, 33, 36, 44, 556

semantic difference 240, 280, 319, 402
semantic similarity 82, 90, 116, 164, 233, 241, 543
serial verb construction 10, 180, 192, 193, 197, 201, 207, 208, 211, 237, 238, 246, 248, 249, 251, 254, 257, 258, 262, 283, 325, 483, 486, 557
singular 10, 43, 46, 50, 61, 62, 64, 66, 70, 79, 88, 444, 446, 465, 526
sinitic language 7, 12, 13, 46, 54, 67, 79, 103, 105, 112, 119, 126, 127, 131, 145, 171, 173, 174, 176, 177, 180–182, 184, 188, 191, 193, 197, 200, 207, 211, 217, 218–220, 233, 234, 241, 244, 246, 264, 266, 267, 269, 275, 284, 285, 288, 300, 303, 305, 318, 322, 330, 332, 352, 353, 357, 380, 407, 412, 415–417, 421–423, 426, 427, 435, 446, 457, 460, 461, 463, 465, 480, 482, 483, 500, 538, 541, 556–558
source construction 207, 209, 212, 217, 233–236, 428
stative 106, 112, 139, 142, 143, 265, 290, 302, 303, 307, 308, 315, 320, 334, 335, 338, 340–342, 349, 389, 391, 418, 419, 434
stative verb 265, 290, 308, 320, 338, 340, 389, 391, 418, 419
strategy of relativization 459, 460, 462–464, 479, 480
– gap 270, 460–463, 467–470, 473, 475

– relativizer 45, 100, 103, 335, 336, 460–471, 473–476, 478, 480
– resumptive pronoun 244, 270–272, 460, 462, 463, 470, 472
structure of DE 142
SUFFER passive 233, 236

telic 127, 128, 244, 302, 304, 305, 330, 331
tentative 105, 304, 332
three-way contrast 15, 17, 18, 25, 32
time clause 97, 511, 512, 523
– AFTER clause 511, 512, 516, 518, 519, 523
– BEFORE clause 511, 516–519
– SINCE clause 511, 519, 523
– temporal sequence 511, 512, 523, 527
– WHEN clause 511, 512, 520, 521, 523
time word 92, 97–99, 107, 156, 167, 304, 317, 445, 450, 456, 473, 474, 502, 519–521
tonal language 6
tone 6, 11, 14, 17, 19, 22, 33, 36–44, 60, 64, 67, 103, 113, 145, 200, 269, 311, 324, 340, 521, 556
– high-level tone 17, 39, 43, 60
– high-rising 37, 43
– low-falling 39
– low-level tone 36, 37, 41
– mid-level tone 17, 22, 38, 39, 43
tone change 6, 37, 43, 44, 103, 200, 556
tone sandhi 14, 17, 37, 39, 40, 44, 145, 556
topicalizer 11
TRANSMIT 164, 165

unbounded 302–305, 331, 332, 338
universal 239
universal pattern of verb bleaching 11

verb of existence 93, 280
verb of giving 197, 218, 239
verb of movement 93, 202
verb of perception 140
verb of placement 253, 347
verb serialization 11
vivid adjectival form 108, 112, 113, 116, 117, 152

voice onset time (VOT) 17–19, 21–25
VOLITION 355, 356

WILLINGNESS 355, 356
word formation 6, 53, 55, 556

zero anaphora 9, 10, 135, 194, 253–256, 262, 357
zero coordinator 485, 498
zero marked complementation 482